Symbole und Abkürzungen:

- CD Verweis auf die Audio-CD hinten im Buch
- DVD Verweis auf die Lehrer-DVD, enthalten im Teacher's Manual
- *AE* American English
- *BE* British English
- *e.g.* exempli gratia (Latin) = for example
- *i.e.* id est (Latin) = that is
- *infml* informal
- *pl.* plural
- *sb* somebody
- *sth* something
- *vs.* versus

Materialien für Lehrkräfte:

- Teacher's Manual mit Lehrer-DVD (978-3-425-73645-7)
- Klausurvorschläge (978-3-425-73646-4)
- Materialien für Sprechprüfungen (978-3-425-73641-9)

Vorbereiten. Organisieren. Durchführen.
BiBox ist das umfassende Digitalpaket zu diesem Lehrwerk mit zahlreichen Materialien und dem digitalen Schulbuch. Für Lehrkräfte und für Schülerinnen und Schüler sind verschiedene Lizenzen verfügbar. Nähere Informationen unter **www.bibox.schule**

westermann GRUPPE

© 2019 Bildungshaus Schulbuchverlage Westermann Schroedel Diesterweg Schöningh Winklers GmbH
Braunschweig, www.westermann.de

Das Werk und seine Teile sind urheberrechtlich geschützt. Jede Nutzung in anderen als den gesetzlich zugelassenen bzw. vertraglich zugestandenen Fällen bedarf der vorherigen schriftlichen Einwilligung des Verlages. Nähere Informationen zur vertraglich gestatteten Anzahl von Kopien finden Sie auf www.schulbuchkopie.de.

Für Verweise (Links) auf Internet-Adressen gilt folgender Haftungshinweis: Trotz sorgfältiger inhaltlicher Kontrolle wird die Haftung für die Inhalte der externen Seiten ausgeschlossen. Für den Inhalt dieser externen Seiten sind ausschließlich deren Betreiber verantwortlich. Sollten Sie daher auf kostenpflichtige, illegale oder anstößige Inhalte treffen, so bedauern wir dies ausdrücklich und bitten Sie, uns umgehend per E-Mail davon in Kenntnis zu setzen, damit beim Nachdruck der Verweis gelöscht wird.

Druck A^2 / Jahr 2021
Alle Drucke der Serie A sind im Unterricht parallel verwendbar.

Redaktion: Thorsten Schimming, Dr. Philippa Söldenwagner-Koch (www.lektoratbilingual.de), Bettina Hammersen-Schiffner, Alina Kuck
Umschlaggestaltung: Gingco.Net Werbeagentur GmbH & Co. KG, Braunschweig
Layout: Visuelle Lebensfreude, Hannover
Druck und Bindung: Westermann Druck GmbH, Braunschweig

ISBN 978-3-425-**73642**-6

westermann

CAMDEN TOWN
Oberstufe

Qualifikationsphase

Erarbeitet von

Stephanie Claussen
Pamela Hanus
Christiane Dietz
Christoph Reuter
Mirja Schnoor
Christian Seydel
Sylvia Wauer

Fachliche Beratung

Hans Georg Henkel
Ilka Kratz
Florian Nuxoll
Ulrike Schuh-Fricke

Introduction to *Camden Town Oberstufe*

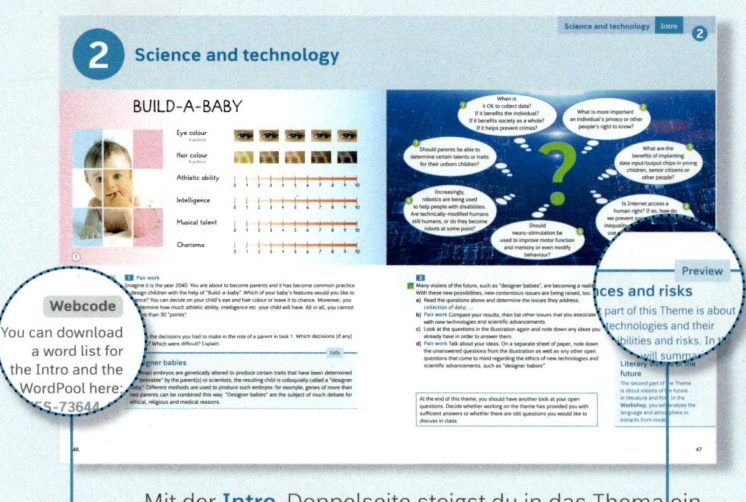

Der **WordPool** führt inhaltlich in das Kapitelthema ein. Außerdem kannst du dich hier schon einmal mit dem Wortschatz vertraut machen.

Dieses Symbol kennzeichnet Aufgaben zur Medienbildung.

Mit der **Intro**-Doppelseite steigst du in das Thema ein. Was dich erwartet, erfährst du in der **Preview-Box**.

Auf manchen Seiten findest du **Webcodes**, die dich zu zusätzlichen Materialien führen. Gib dazu einfach den Code auf www.westermann.de ins Suchfeld ein.

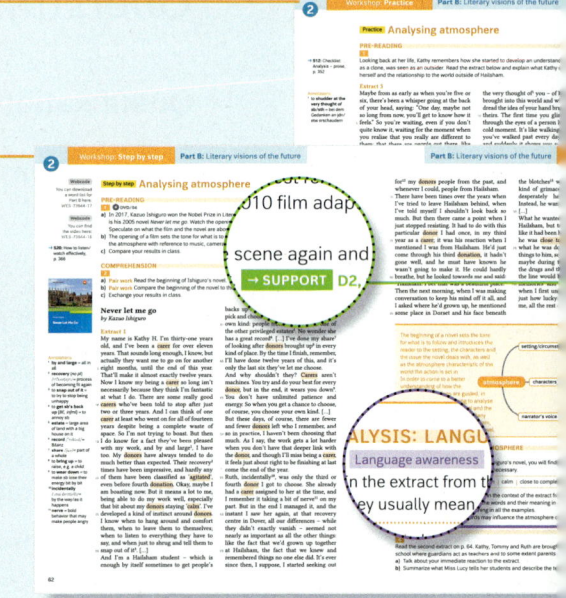

Im **Workshop** erlernst du den Umgang mit einer wichtigen Textsorte. Zunächst erarbeitest du dir im **Step by step**-Abschnitt notwendiges Handwerkszeug. Im **Practice**-Teil kannst du dann zeigen, dass du das Gelernte auch anwenden kannst.

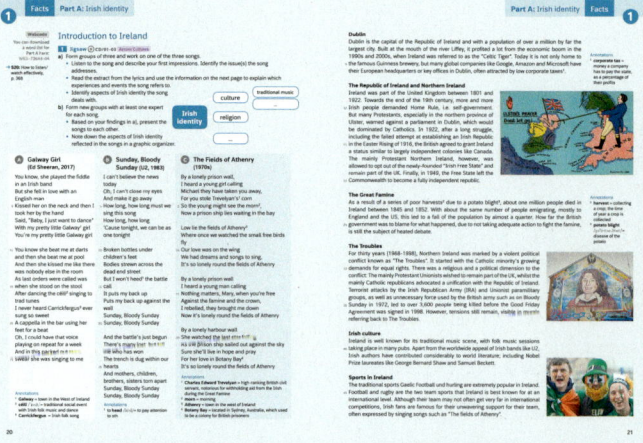

Auf den **Facts**-Seiten findest du Daten, Fakten und historische Hintergründe, die für das Verständnis der folgenden Materialien wichtig sind.

Introduction to *Camden Town Oberstufe*

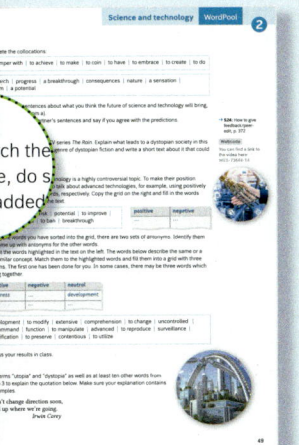

Die **Texts**-Seiten enthalten unterschiedliche Materialien und abwechslungsreiche Aufgaben aus allen Kompetenzbereichen.

Grüne Unterlegungen weisen dich auf Differenzierungsangebote hin. So gekennzeichnet sind etwas anspruchsvollere **CHALLENGE** -Aufgaben, zusätzliche **EXTRA** -Aufgaben und **CHOOSE** -Aufgaben, bei denen du aus mehreren Optionen auswählen kannst. Außerdem macht dich der Hinweis → **SUPPORT** auf Unterstützungsangebote in der **Diff section** aufmerksam.

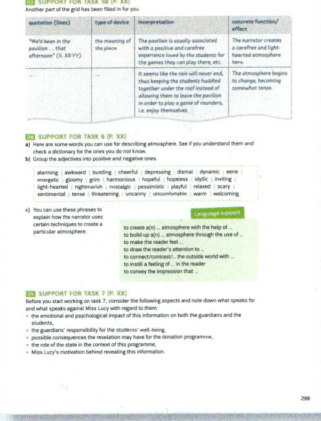

Die vielfältigen Aufgaben zur Sprachbewusstheit sind als **Language awareness** gekennzeichnet. Auch deine interkulturelle Kompetenz kannst du trainieren. Dazu dient das Sonderelement **Across cultures**.

Am Ende des Buches erwarten dich verschiedene Übungs- und Nachschlageanhänge zu wichtigen **skills**, zu **common mistakes** und zur **Facharbeit**, sowie ein **Glossar**.

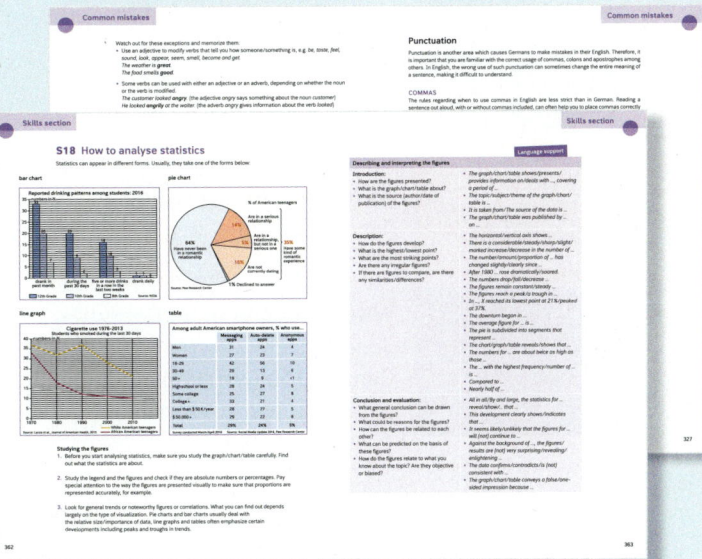

Die **Advanced texts**-Seiten enthalten anspruchsvollere Materialien, die sich besonders für Kurse auf erhöhtem Anforderungsniveau eignen.

3

Contents

Section		Texts	Central skills
Theme 1		**The individual and society**	
16	Intro	Cartoon maps, diagram Two speeches *by Justin Trudeau and Michael D. Higgins* (videos)	Speaking Viewing
18	WordPool	Informative text	Working on vocabulary
Part A		**Irish identity**	
20	Facts	**Introduction to Ireland** Three songs (lyrics and audios), informative text	Listening Speaking
22	Workshop: Analysing narrative perspective	Newspaper article, photo **The green road** *by Ann Enright* (novel extract) **Love my enemy** *by Kate MacLachlan* (novel extract)	Speaking Writing a comment Intercultural learning Writing a discussion Creative writing
28	Texts	**Irish clichés: All Guinness and leprechauns?** Two videos **Land of drunks, poets, friendly fans. How true are Irish cliches?** *by Darragh Murphy* (newspaper article)	Viewing Intercultural learning Creative writing
30		**Mediation: National identity in Germany** **Warum „Heimat" plötzlich wieder in ist** *by Gregor Tholl* (German online article)	Intercultural learning Mediation Writing a blog post
31	Advanced texts	**The individual and Irish society** **Leo Varadkar is Ireland's new prime minister. He's also openly gay and an immigrant's son.** *by Lindsay Maizland* (online article) **Abortion in Ireland: The fight for choice** *by Joel Gunter* (online article)	Reading Working on vocabulary Writing a discussion
Part B		**Canadian identity**	
34	Facts	**Introduction to Canada** Informative text	
35	Workshop: Rewriting from a different perspective	Radio report, two photos **As long as the rivers flow** *by James Bartleman* (novel extracts)	Listening Creative writing
40	Texts	**What it means to be Canadian** Song (video) **Canada 150: What does it mean to be Canadian today?** *by Gavin Hewitt* (online article)	Viewing Writing a comment Writing a discussion

Contents

	Section	Texts	Central skills
42	Advanced texts	**Gender identity** Video **For today I am a boy** by Kim Fu (two novel extracts)	Viewing Writing a summary **Intercultural learning** Writing a comment
44		**Language issues** Map, video **Referendum** by Sonnet L'Abbé (poem)	Viewing Writing a speech

Theme 2 Science and technology

	Section	Texts	Central skills
46	Intro	Ethical questions	Speaking
48	WordPool	Informative text	Working on vocabulary Viewing **Language awareness**

Part A Chances and risks

	Section	Texts	Central skills
50	Workshop: Understanding and summarizing texts	Radio programme, two poems, book front and back cover, review **Homo Deus** by Yuval Noah Harari (non-fiction text)	Listening Speaking Reading strategies Writing a summary
55	Texts	**Driverless cars – debating an ethical dilemma** **Why self-driving cars must be programmed to kill** (online article) Diagram	Speaking Having a debate
57	Advanced texts	**Artificial intelligence – friend or foe?** Quotation by I.J. Good, two diagrams **Life 3.0** by Max Tegmark (non-fiction text)	Speaking
60		**Cyborgs – merging humans and machines** Four photos **The age of cyborgs has arrived** by Vanessa Bates Ramirez (online article)	Working on vocabulary Writing a letter to the editor

Part B Literary visions of the future

	Section	Texts	Central skills
62	Workshop: Analysing atmosphere	**Never let me go** (film extract) **Never let me go** by Kazuo Ishiguro (novel extracts) News report (video), extract from a newspaper article	Viewing **Language awareness** Writing a summary Writing a discussion
68	Texts	**Life in the future – just a virtual reality?** **Ready player one** by Ernest Cline (novel extract)	Speaking Writing an article Writing a short speech **Language awareness** Creative writing

Contents

	Section	Texts	Central skills
70	Advanced texts	**What is the true meaning of equality?** **Harrison Bergeron** by Kurt Vonnegut, Jr. (short story)	Language awareness Speaking
73		**AI – the end of humanity?** Informative video **Ex Machina** (three film extracts)	Viewing Working on vocabulary

Theme 3 The media

	Section	Texts	Central skills
74	Intro	Photos, dictionary definition, diagram	Writing a definition Working on vocabulary
76	WordPool	Informative text, photos	Working on vocabulary

Part A Opinion-makers

	Section	Texts	Central skills
78	Texts	**Media literacy** **Factors influencing public opinion** (from the *Encyclopedia Britannica*) Information on media literacy	Speaking Writing a summary
80		**Working with statistics** Four statistics	Speaking
82	Advanced texts	**Filter bubbles and echo chambers** **The myth of the online echo chamber** by David Robson (online article)	Mediation Viewing Writing an article Writing a comment
84		**Fake news** Informative video **Why the invention of the fridge could be responsible for our love of fake news** by Ian Leslie (online article)	Viewing Writing a discussion

Part B Living in the digital age

	Section	Texts	Central skills
86	Workshop: Analysing a feature film	**Nerve** (film extracts) Four film stills, extract from a review	Viewing Writing a summary Writing a discussion Creative writing Writing a comment
90	Texts	**App crazes** **Teens Explain Their Obsession With Sarahah, Summer's Hottest Anonymous-Gossip App** by Madison Malone Kircher (online article)	Writing a discussion Language awareness
92		**Analysing a dystopian novel** **Cell 7** by Kerry Drewery (three novel extracts)	Language awareness Writing a comment Writing a discussion

Contents

	Section	Texts	Central skills
95	Advanced texts	**The future of news** Statistic **The future of news** *by James Harding* (online article)	Speaking

Part C   English as a global language

	Section	Texts	Central skills
98	Workshop: Mediation	**Lustig? Nicht auf Deutsch!** *by Klaus Ungerer* (German newspaper article) **Warum Englisch nicht als Weltsprache taugt** (German online article)	Mediation **Intercultural learning** Writing a speech
101	Texts	**The global language of the future** Statistic Talk *by David Crystal* (audio)	Listening Writing a discussion
102	Advanced texts	**The value of language learning apps** Map **Are Duolingo Users Actually Learning Anything Useful?** *by Mike Pearl* (online article)	**Intercultural learning** Creating a flyer
104		**The future of English** **Have we reached peak English in the world?** *by Nicholas Ostler* (newspaper article) **What will the English language be like in 100 years?** *by Simon Horobin* (online article)	Creating a timeline Writing a summary **Language awareness**

Theme 4   Globalization

	Section	Texts	Central skills
108	Intro	Photos, informative video	Viewing Working on vocabulary Writing an entry for a young people's encyclopedia
110	WordPool	Informative text, photos	Working on vocabulary

Part A   Global responsibility for the environment

	Section	Texts	Central skills
112	Workshop: Analysing a speech	Infographic, film trailer **Before the flood** (extract from a documentary) Speech *by Leonardo DiCaprio* (audio and transcript) Speech *by Barack Obama*	Viewing Listening **Language awareness** Writing a comment
118	Texts	**Plastic waste – a growing problem** **The oceans are drowning in plastic – and no one's paying attention** *by Dominique Mosbergen* (online article)	Designing a poster **Language awareness**
120	Advanced texts	**Preparing to leave planet Earth?** **The terranauts** *by T.C. Boyle* (two novel extracts) Informative video	**Language awareness** Creative writing Viewing Writing a comment

Contents

	Section	Texts	Central skills
	Part B	**Globalization and the economy**	
122	Texts	**Globalization and the fashion industry** Two infographics, film trailer **The Zara workers' protest shows why fast fashion should worry all of us** by Daisy Buchanan (newspaper article) **Wozu Mode kaufen, wenn man sie mieten kann?** by Anne Kohlick (German online article)	Conducting a class survey Viewing Writing a discussion **Language awareness** Mediation Writing a speech
126	Advanced texts	**Globalization defined – and re-defined** Quotation by Thomas L. Friedman **Thank you for being late** by Thomas L. Friedman (non-fiction text)	Writing a discussion
127		**Backlash – globalization and its discontents** Column: **Why there's a backlash against globalization and what needs to change** by John Rennie Short (online article)	Writing a discussion Writing a comment
	Part C	**Migration and the world of work**	
130	Workshop: Writing a comment	Informative video, comment (model text), German-language informative video **Transmission** by Hari Kunzru (novel extract) **The emperor of shoes** by Spencer Wise (two novel extracts)	**Intercultural learning** Viewing Writing a discussion **Language awareness** Writing a comment Mediation
136	Texts	**The future of work** Video **Homo Deus** by Yuval Noah Harari (non-fiction text)	Viewing Writing a comment **Language awareness** Designing a leaflet
138	Advanced texts	**Migration between India and the US: Listening** Radio programme	Listening
138		**Globalization and migration in an age of accelerations** **Thank you for being late** by Thomas L. Friedman (non-fiction text)	Writing a comment
	Part D	**Living in a globalized world**	
140	Workshop: Speaking	Video, three audios, photos	Viewing Giving a three-minute talk Listening **Language awareness** Speaking: Interview, Monologue, Dialogue

Contents

	Section	Texts	Central skills
146	Texts	**Globalization – the state of affairs** Speech *by Barack Obama* Two cartoons	**Language awareness** Writing a speech
148	Advanced texts	**Effects of globalization: Working with drama** **Bodies** *by Vivienne Franzmann* (drama extract)	Writing a discussion

Theme 5 Britishness

	Section	Texts	Central skills
150	Intro	Photos, comments on Britishness (audio, text)	Speaking Listening
152	WordPool	Informative text	Working on vocabulary

Part A British identity

	Section	Texts	Central skills
154	Workshop: Analysing a newspaper article	**Brexit is entrenching some dangerous myths about 'British' culture** by *Afua Hirsch* (newspaper article) Cartoon **The Observer view on Britain becoming mean and narrow-minded** (newspaper article)	Writing a very short story Speaking **Language awareness**
160	Texts	**Listening** Statements about Britishness (audio)	Listening
160		**Viewing** Video	Viewing Speaking Producing a video
160		**Mediation: Differences in humour** **Wir sollten Ernst und Humor häufiger mischen** (German-language interview)	Speaking Mediation Writing a blog post **Intercultural learning**
162	Advanced texts	**Englishness** **What It Means to Be English in 2017** *by Angus Harrison* (online article)	Writing a comment
165		**Listening: "Hybrid identities"** Radio programme	Listening **Intercultural learning**

Part B The monarchy and the political system

	Section	Texts	Central skills
166	Facts	**Introduction to the political system of the United Kingdom** Informative text	**Intercultural learning**
168	Workshop: Writing an opinion piece	**Should Britain abolish the monarchy?** (online article) Statistics, informative video	Viewing **Language awareness** Writing an opinion piece

Contents

	Section	Texts	Central skills
173	Texts	**Analysing a feature film:** *The Queen* Diagram ***The Queen*** (two film extracts)	Viewing Writing a discussion
175	Advanced texts	**Britain's constitution** **Britain's unwritten constitution** *by Robert Blackburn* (online article)	Writing a summary Writing a discussion Writing a comment

Part C The many faces of Britain

	Section	Texts	Central skills
176	Workshop: Analysing modern poetry	Two quotations **The British (serves 60 million)** *by Benjamin Zephaniah* (poem) **Listen Mr Oxford don** *by John Agard* (poem: video, text)	Writing a definition Reading strategies Language awareness Writing a poem Mediation Intercultural learning Viewing Writing a comment
181	Texts	**Scottishness** Statistic **The business of being Scottish: Are you one of 50 million?** *by Lennox Morrison* (online article)	Creative writing Intercultural learning Writing a discussion
183	Advanced texts	**Class** Class descriptions, two character profiles **Social class in the 21st century** (interview)	Intercultural learning Speaking
186		**The North-South divide** **From the Midlands** *by Toby Campion* (poem: video) **The North-South divide is getting worse – because London is sucking all opportunity from the rest of the UK** *by Juliette Bretan* (online article)	Intercultural learning Viewing Writing a summary Language awareness Writing a comment

Theme 6 The American experience

	Section	Texts	Central skills
188	Intro	Photos, quotation *by Bono*	Speaking Writing a comment
190	WordPool	Informative text	Working on vocabulary Language awareness

Part A The American Dream

	Section	Texts	Central skills
192	Facts	**The American Dream** Informative video, informative text	Viewing Creating a timeline Intercultural learning
193	Workshop: Analysing a cartoon	Cartoons	Giving a presentation

Contents

	Section	Texts	Central skills
196	Texts	**The American Dream in a political speech** Speech *by Michelle Obama*	Language awareness Intercultural learning
198	Advanced texts	**American nightmare? Working with newspaper articles** **Is the American Dream killing us?** *by Robert J. Samuelson* (newspaper article) **Trump is killing the American Dream** *by Kashana Cauley* (newspaper article)	Writing a comment
201		**Let America be America again – a poem** Let America Be America Again *by Langston Hughes* (poem)	Writing a comment

Part B Culture wars

	Section	Texts	Central skills
202	Facts	**Contested issues in a diverse country** Photos, informative text, four maps	Intercultural learning Creating a map
206	Workshop: Listening	Two radio programmes, photos	Listening Speaking Intercultural learning
209	Texts	**The two sides in the US culture wars** **Confederate flag is a symbol of America's culture wars** *by Matt K. Lewis* (newspaper article)	Intercultural learning Writing a letter to the editor
211	Advanced texts	**Mediation: Gun culture** Statistic **Ex-Schützenfunktionär: Waffenrecht in Deutschland und den USA vergleichbar** (German-language interview)	Intercultural learning Mediation
212		**US society today: Culture wars or class war?** **How America's culture wars have evolved into a class war** *by James Davison Hunter* (newspaper article)	Intercultural learning Writing a discussion

Part C African American experiences

	Section	Texts	Central skills
214	Facts	**African Americans and the struggle for equality** Informative text, three quotations **America** *by James M. Whitfield* (poem)	Writing a discussion Preparing a presentation
217	Texts	**Poems about the African American experience** **I, Too** *by Langston Hughes* (poem) **We Own the Night** *by Amiri Baraka* (poem) **Harlem** *by Langston Hughes* (poem) **Feeding the Lions** *by Norman Jordan* (poem) **Nikki-Rosa** *by Nikki Giovanni* (poem)	Language awareness Writing a comment Writing a poem Preparing a presentation
219		**Brothers: Working on a short story** **Sonny's Blues** *by James Baldwin* (short story extract)	Language awareness Writing a discussion

Contents

	Section	Texts	Central skills
220	Texts	**Being black in Germany: Mediation** **Das deutsche Krokodil** by Ijoma Mangold (German non-fiction text)	Mediation Intercultural learning Writing an article
222	Advanced texts	**The last day in the life of Martin Luther King: Working with a play** **The Mountaintop** by Katori Hall (two drama extracts)	Language awareness Writing a comment

Theme 7 Postcolonial experiences

	Section	Texts	Central skills
226	Intro	Two cartoons, map, quotations, informative video, definition	Viewing Speaking
228	WordPool	Informative text	Working on vocabulary

Part A India

	Section	Texts	Central skills
230	Workshop: Writing an interior monologue	Informative video **Death on Facebook** by Claude Forthomme (short story)	Viewing Creative writing Writing a discussion
235	Texts	**Women in India** **Full steam ahead: India's first women-run train station blazes a trail** by Annie Banerji (online article)	Intercultural learning Writing an interview
237	Advanced texts	**India's caste system today** **India's caste system is alive and kicking – and maiming and killing** by Mari Marcel Thekaekara (newspaper article)	Language awareness Writing a discussion
239		**Colonial India: Working with a feature film** **A passage to India** (three film extracts)	Viewing Writing a discussion

Part B Nigeria

	Section	Texts	Central skills
240	Facts	**Nigeria past and present** Two maps, photos, informative text	Intercultural learning Creating a timeline
242	Workshop: Analysing characters	**Americanah** by Chimamanda Ngozi Adichie (novel extracts)	Intercultural learning Writing a discussion Writing a summary Writing an article
247	Texts	**Nigerian poetry** **Let our voices ring** by Efe Paul Azino (poem: audio, text) **Becoming** by Titilope Sonuga (poem: audio, text)	Listening Language awareness Intercultural learning Creative writing
248		**The danger of a single story: Viewing** Talk by Chimamanda Ngozi Adichie (video)	Viewing

Contents

	Section	Texts	Central skills
249	Advanced texts	Oil production in the Niger Delta **Oil on water** by Helon Habila (two novel extracts)	Language awareness Writing a commentary
251		Nollywood – Nigeria's dream factory Three film trailers **Nollywood – the making of a film empire** by Emily Witt (non-fiction text)	Writing a discussion

Part C Multicultural Britain today

	Section	Texts	Central skills
254	Facts	Immigration to Britain Informative text, statistic	Intercultural learning
255	Workshop: Working with a screenplay	**My son the fanatic** (film extracts) **My son the fanatic** by Hanif Kureishi (extracts from a screenplay) Two film stills, film trailers	Viewing Writing a summary Language awareness Writing a discussion Writing a comment
262	Texts	Multicultural Britain: Working with cartoons Two cartoons	Speaking
262		Multicultural Britain: Working with a blog post Blog post by Jermain Jackman	Writing a comment
264		British intercultural experiences: Watching a video Poem, video	Viewing
265	Advanced texts	A Jamaican immigrant's story **Small Island** by Andrea Levy (novel extract)	Writing a summary Writing a letter Intercultural learning Writing a comment

Theme 8 Shakespeare

	Section	Texts	Central skills
268	Intro	Photos, quotations, humorous video	Writing a discussion Viewing
270	WordPool	Informative text	Working on vocabulary
272	Facts	Shakespeare and the world that made him Informative text	

Part A Shakespeare's sonnets

	Section	Texts	Central skills
274	Workshop: Analysing a Shakespearean sonnet	Sonnet 18 Sonnet 116 Sonnet 130	Listening Language awareness Writing a discussion Creative writing Speaking

Contents

	Section	Texts	Central skills
278	Texts	**Pop sonnets** **We Are Never Ever Getting Back Together** *by Taylor Swift* (song lyrics) Pop sonnet *by Erik Didriksen*	Writing a comment Creative writing
279	Advanced texts	**Relating Shakespeare's sonnets to the place you live** Videos	Creating a video
279		**Discussion of Sonnet 66** Sonnet 66	Writing a discussion
	Part B	**Shakespearean drama**	
280	Facts	**The theatre in Shakespeare's time** Informative text	
281	Workshop: Working with Shakespearean drama	**Romeo and Juliet** (drama extracts) **Romeo and Juliet** (video: film extract) **Romeo and Juliet** (video: theatre performance) Photo	Viewing Reading Dramatic reading Writing a letter Writing a discussion Language awareness Writing a comment
288	Texts	**Love at first sonnet** Photo, informative video **Romeo and Juliet** (drama extract)	Viewing
289	Advanced texts	**The seven ages of man** Video	Writing a comment Creative writing
289		**Listening: Could Shakespeare survive in Hollywood?** Radio programme	Listening
289		**Shakespeare retold: The Taming of the Shrew** **The Taming of the Shrew** (drama extract) **Vinegar girl** *by Anne Tyler* (novel extract) Plot summary **Shakespeare retold: The Taming of the Shrew** (film extract)	Speaking Writing a discussion Writing a comment Writing a speech Viewing
292		**Henry V: Shakespeare for managers** **Henry V** (drama extract) **Inspirational leadership** *by Richard Olivier* (non-fiction text)	Writing a comment Language awareness Writing a speech

Contents

Diff section

294	**Theme 1:** The individual and society	Support and additional tasks
298	**Theme 2:** Science and technology	Support and additional tasks
302	**Theme 3:** The media	Support and additional tasks
304	**Theme 4:** Globalization	Support and additional tasks
312	**Theme 5:** Britishness	Support and additional tasks
314	**Theme 6:** The American experience	Support and additional tasks
318	**Theme 7:** Postcolonial experiences	Support and additional tasks
322	**Theme 8:** Shakespeare	Support and additional tasks

325	**Common mistakes**

Skills section

Writing skills

330	**S1:** Checklist: Summary	338	**S6:** How to write a discussion/comment
331	**S2:** Checklist: Creative writing	340	**S7:** Writing a blog post
334	**S3:** Checklist: Formal letter	341	**S8:** How to improve your text
336	**S4:** Checklist: Letter to the editor	344	**S9:** How to structure a text
337	**S5:** Checklist: Writing a speech		

Analysis skills

347	**S10:** How to work with poetry	358	**S15:** How to describe pictures
350	**S11:** How to work with drama	359	**S16:** Checklist: Analysis of a film scene
352	**S12:** Checklist: Analysis – prose	361	**S17:** How to work with cartoons
354	**S13:** Checklist: Analysis – non-fictional texts	362	**S18:** How to analyse statistics
355	**S14:** How to analyse a speech		

Study skills

364	**S19:** How to improve your mediation skills	371	**S23:** How to quote
366	**S20:** How to listen/watch effectively	372	**S24:** How to give feedback/peer-edit
367	**S21:** How to succeed in oral exams	374	**S25:** How to work with a dictionary
370	**S22:** How to stage a debate		

376	**Practising scientific writing:** The *Facharbeit*
380	**Glossary:** Literary terms
388	**Standardized language for tasks** *(Operatoren)*
390	**Acknowledgements, solutions**

1 The individual and society

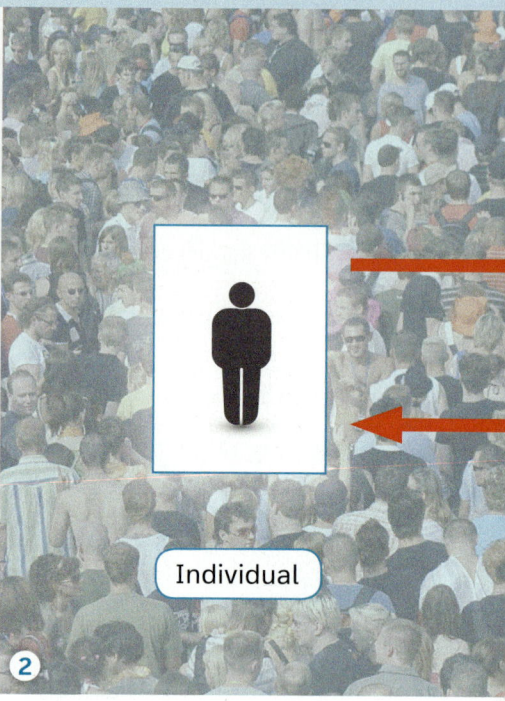

Individual

Webcode
You can download a word list for the Intro and the WordPool here:
WES-73644-001

1 Pair work
a) Talk about the relationship between an individual and society.
b) Look at diagram 2 above. How would you label the arrows?

2 Placemat Across cultures
a) In your section of the placemat, write down four aspects of the society you live in which have influenced or shaped your identity.
b) Turn the paper clockwise. Read your classmates' ideas and write down any comments you may have about them. Do not talk.
c) Repeat this until you have read and commented on all your classmates' ideas.
d) Discuss your ideas among the group and agree on the four most important aspects. Write them in the middle of the placemat.
e) Present your results to the class.

3 Across cultures
a) **Group work** Stay in your groups from task 2. Discuss to what extent national identity featured in your placemat discussion.
b) In class, discuss what it means to be German.

4
a) Look at the posters 1 and 3 above and state which countries they refer to.
b) Describe how the two countries are portrayed in the posters.
 • What aspects of each country are illustrated?
 • What similarities and differences are there?
c) Decide which poster you prefer and explain why.
d) **EXTRA** Across cultures Design a poster showing different aspects of Germany and explain it to the class.

→ **S15:** How to describe pictures, p. 358

The individual and society — Intro 1

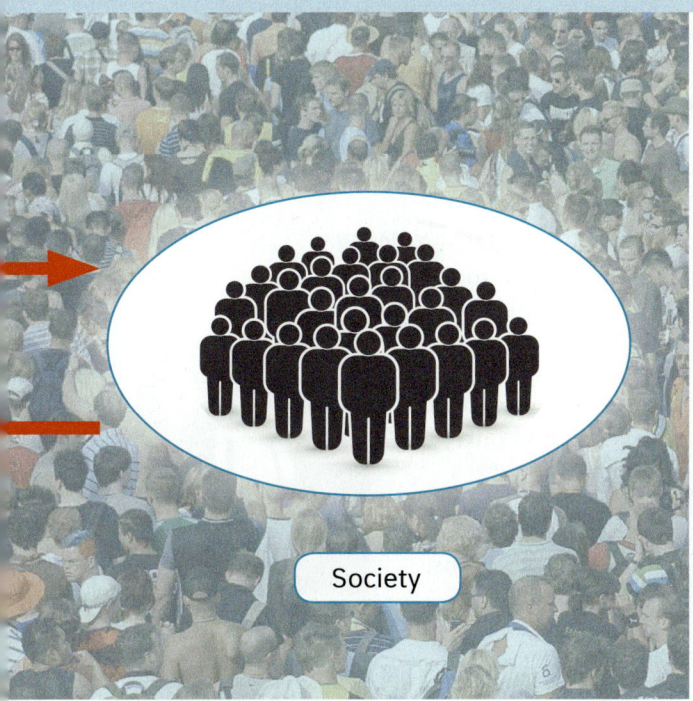

Society

③

5 ● DVD/01
a) You are going to watch a video of Canada's Prime Minister, Justin Trudeau, talking about his country. Before you start watching, read the annotations.
b) Watch the video and state which aspect of Canada Trudeau stresses in particular.
c) Watch again and note down his examples of Canadian diversity and their advantages.
d) Examine to what extent Canadian diversity is reflected in poster 1 above.

Webcode
You can find the video here:
WES-73644-002

→ **S20:** How to listen/watch effectively, p. 366

inclusion = the act of including sb or sth
indigenous /ɪnˈdɪdʒənəs/ = refers to people who have lived in a place before others arrived, like the Inuit in northern Canada

6 ● DVD/02
a) Watch and listen to Ireland's President Michael D. Higgins speak. State his main message.
b) Note down the aspects of diversity in Ireland that he mentions.
c) Compare Trudeau and Higgins's speeches taking into consideration how they deliver their speeches and their messages.
d) Explain what you find remarkable about the two speeches.

Webcode
You can find the video here:
WES-73644-003

Preview

Irish identity
The first part of this Theme is about different aspects of Irish identity. In the **Workshop**, you will analyse the narrative perspective in an extract from a novel.

Canadian identity
The second part of the Theme is about different aspects of Canadian identity. In the **Workshop**, you will rewrite a scene in a novel from another perspective.

7
You are taking part in a Model United Nations conference on the subject of diversity in German society. Prepare a short statement to present at that conference.
- Describe the situation in Germany.
- Refer to any problems that exist.
- Present your own point of view.

→ **S5:** Checklist: Writing a speech, p. 337

The individual and society

A MUTUALLY-DEPENDENT RELATIONSHIP

We humans are social creatures: we cannot survive in isolation from other humans. The communities we belong to, the customs we follow and other aspects of our way of life are influenced by society. At the same time, this is exactly what society is made up of: without individuals, there would be no societies – and vice versa.

But while almost all individuals rely to some extent on society, the extent to which we choose to conform to the norms and standards imposed by society varies from person to person. Many, whether intentionally or not, assimilate in every way possible. They wear the same clothes, speak the same language, believe the same things, and generally do their best to blend in. Others reject some of the norms of society or find it difficult to fit in.

PERSONAL IDENTITY

Every individual has their own perception of who they are. This is called personal identity. Society in general and the way we are brought up in particular, play a part in shaping our personal identities. Based on our interactions with other individuals in our communities and social circles, we develop an idea of our place in the world. As well as society, a person's nationality, ethnicity, religion, political views, age, gender and sexuality are all involved in the formation of a personal identity.

DIVERSITY WITHIN SOCIETY

Not all individuals in a given society necessarily share the same values, culture, faith, or language. In modern-day nations and metropolises the coexistence of numerous different ethnicities and their respective ways of life is quite an ordinary phenomenon.

Nowadays, most longstanding citizens of diverse societies, such as the USA, identify as nationals of their particular country of residence. That is to say that other defining characteristics such as ethnic descent, social status and religion are overlooked more often than not. There are also individuals who, in spite of many years of residence in a particular country, choose to hold on to the national identity associated with their own heritage or birth. In the case of many indigenous peoples, e.g. in North America, their own culture may be quite different from the mainstream culture of the country they live in. Over time, they have often been made to feel inferior and have in many cases been forced to adapt.

GENDER AND SEXUALITY

In progressive societies, previously controversial practices such as abortion and same-sex relationships are now widely accepted. Many conservative societies, however, maintain a negative attitude towards these issues. Because of this, many homosexual or transgender people across the world still conceal their true personal identity.

TENSIONS AND PRESSURES

Ideally, all mature, adult individuals should be able to make their own lifestyle choices and express themselves without being persecuted or made to feel ashamed. While many societies aim to celebrate the diversity of their members, tensions between different ethnic, religious, and political groups can easily arise. Perhaps it is simply an inherent part of human nature to be suspicious of individuals who wear different clothes, speak a different language, pray to a different God and have different points of view. Or perhaps the constraints and norms set by society are to blame for conflicts that may arise.

The individual and society — WordPool

1
Replace the underlined words with words or phrases from the text. Note: you may have to change the form, e.g. singular/plural, different tense.
1 How parents raise their children can have a significant impact on their identity.
2 Particularly in more traditional families, one's religious beliefs can influence their priorities in life.
3 For many migrants, their ethnic background can also be an important factor as certain traditions may be passed down between generations, including: language, culture and values.
4 As a consequence, it may be difficult to feel at home in a new environment, especially if cultural differences are not appreciated as a positive contribution to society.
5 In some countries like Canada, the US and Australia, it is not mostly the immigrant population who feel discriminated against, but actually the native population.
6 Discrimination against minority groups can make living together in society very difficult.

2
Find the opposites to the following words from the text. Use a dictionary for help if necessary.
1 inferior
2 ordinary
3 mature
4 necessary
5 intentional
6 controversial
7 negative
8 progressive

3
Find cover terms in the text for the following word fields.
1 race, customs, language, country of origin, traditions
2 clothes, behaviour, hairstyles, typical jobs, roles in the family
3 piety, worship, festivals, values
4 income, property, reputation, influence
5 traditions, ancestors, monuments, history

4
Find words in the text with the same or a similar meaning.
1 to hide
2 to come up
3 to completely adapt to sth
4 to connect
5 restrictions/limitations
6 to make sb/sth responsible for sth bad
7 to form
8 to consider oneself

5
Explain how the pictures on this double page reflect the relationship between an individual and society.

1 Facts — Part A: Irish identity

Introduction to Ireland

1 Jigsaw CD/01-03 Across cultures

a) Form groups of three and work on one of the three songs.
- Listen to the song and describe your first impressions. Identify the issue(s) each song addresses.
- Read the extract from the lyrics and use the information on the next page to explain which experiences and events the song refers to.
- Identify aspects of Irish identity the song deals with.

b) Form new groups with at least one expert for each song.
- Based on your findings in a), present the songs to each other.
- Note down the aspects of Irish identity reflected in the songs in a mind map.

Webcode
You can download a word list for Part A here:
WES-73644-004

→ **S20:** How to listen/watch effectively, p. 366

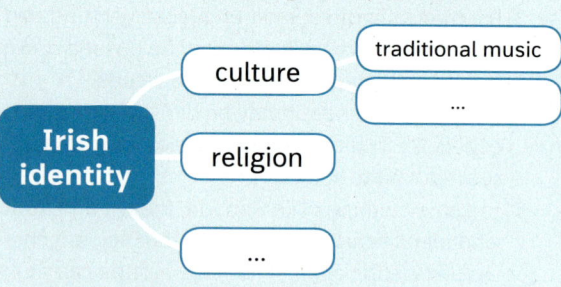

A Galway Girl (Ed Sheeran, 2017)

You know, she played the fiddle in an Irish band
But she fell in love with an English man
5 Kissed her on the neck and then I took her by the hand
Said, "Baby, I just want to dance"
With my pretty little Galway[1] girl
You're my pretty little Galway girl

10 You know she beat me at darts and then she beat me at pool
And then she kissed me like there was nobody else in the room
As last orders were called was
15 when she stood on the stool
After dancing the céilí[2] singing to trad tunes
I never heard Carrickfergus[3] ever sung so sweet
20 A cappella in the bar using her feet for a beat
Oh, I could have that voice playing on repeat for a week
And in this packed out room
25 swear she was singing to me

Annotations
[1] **Galway** = town in the West of Ireland
[2] **céilí** /ˈkeɪli/ = traditional social event with Irish folk music and dance
[3] **Carrickfergus** = Irish folk song

B Sunday, Bloody Sunday (U2, 1983)

I can't believe the news today
Oh, I can't close my eyes
And make it go away
5 How long, how long must we sing this song
How long, how long
'Cause tonight, we can be as one tonight

10 Broken bottles under children's feet
Bodies strewn across the dead end street
But I won't heed[1] the battle
15 call
It puts my back up
Puts my back up against the wall
Sunday, Bloody Sunday
20 Sunday, Bloody Sunday

And the battle's just begun
There's many lost, but tell me who has won
The trench is dug within our
25 hearts
And mothers, children, brothers, sisters torn apart
Sunday, Bloody Sunday
Sunday, Bloody Sunday

Annotations
[1] to **heed** /hiːd/ = to pay attention to sth

C The Fields of Athenry (1970s)

By a lonely prison wall,
I heard a young girl calling
Michael they have taken you away,
For you stole Trevelyan's[1] corn
5 So the young might see the morn[2],
Now a prison ship lies waiting in the bay

Low lie the fields of Athenry[3]
Where once we watched the small free birds fly
10 Our love was on the wing
We had dreams and songs to sing,
It's so lonely round the fields of Athenry

By a lonely prison wall
I heard a young man calling
15 Nothing matters, Mary, when you're free
Against the famine and the crown,
I rebelled, they brought me down
Now it's lonely round the fields of Athenry

By a lonely harbour wall
20 She watched the last star falling
As the prison ship sailed out against the sky
Sure she'll live in hope and pray
For her love in Botany Bay[4]
It's so lonely round the fields of Athenry

Annotations
[1] **Charles Edward Trevelyan** = high-ranking British civil servant, notorious for withholding aid from the Irish during the Great Famine
[2] **morn** = morning
[3] **Athenry** = town in the west of Ireland
[4] **Botany Bay** = located in Sydney, Australia, which used to be a colony for British prisoners

Dublin

Dublin is the capital of the Republic of Ireland and, with a population of over a million, is by far the largest city. Built at the mouth of the river Liffey, it profited a lot from the economic boom in the 1990s and 2000s, when Ireland was referred to as the "Celtic Tiger". Today it is not just home to the famous
5 Guinness brewery, but also the European headquarters of many other global companies like Google, Amazon and Microsoft. They are often attracted by low corporate taxes[1].

Annotations
[1] **corporate tax** = money a company has to pay the state, as a percentage of their profits

The Republic of Ireland and Northern Ireland

Ireland was part of the United Kingdom between 1801 and 1922. Towards the end of the 19th century, more and more
10 Irish people demanded Home Rule, i.e. self-governance. But many Protestants, especially in the northern province of Ulster, warned against a parliament in Dublin, which would be dominated by Catholics. In 1922, after a long struggle, including the failed attempt at establishing an Irish Republic
15 in the Easter Rising of 1916, the British agreed to grant Ireland a status similar to largely independent colonies like Canada. The mainly Protestant Northern Ireland, however, was allowed to opt out of the newly-founded "Irish Free State" and remain part of the UK. Finally, in 1949, the Free State left the
20 Commonwealth to become a fully independent republic.

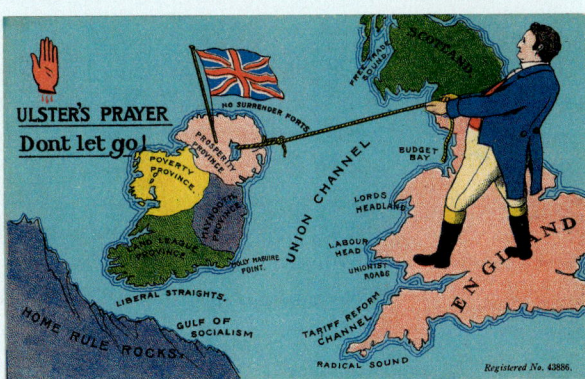

The Great Famine

As a result of a series of poor harvests[2] due to a potato blight[3], about one million people died in Ireland between 1845 and 1852. With about the same number of people emigrating, mostly to England and the US, this led to a fall of the population by almost a quarter. How far the British
25 government was to blame for what happened, due to not taking adequate action to fight the famine, is still the subject of heated debate.

Annotations
[2] **harvest** = collecting a crop; the time of year a crop is collected
[3] **potato blight** /pəˈteɪtəʊ ˌblaɪt/ = disease of the potato

The Troubles

For thirty years (1968-1998), Northern Ireland was marked by a period of violent political conflict known as "The Troubles". It started with the Catholic minority's
30 growing demands for equal rights. There was a religious and a political dimension to the conflict: the mainly Protestant Unionists wished to remain part of the UK, whilst the mainly Catholic republicans advocated a unification with the Republic of Ireland. Terrorist attacks by the Irish Republican Army (IRA) and Unionist paramilitary groups, as well as unnecessary force used by the British army such as
35 on Bloody Sunday in 1972, led to over 3,600 people being killed before the Good Friday Agreement was signed in 1998. However, tensions still remain, particularly visible in murals which refer back to "The Troubles".

Irish culture

Ireland is well known for its traditional music scene, with folk music sessions
40 taking place in many pubs. Apart from the worldwide appeal of Irish bands like U2, Irish authors have contributed considerably to world literature; including Nobel Prize laureates like George Bernard Shaw and Samuel Beckett.

Sports in Ireland

The traditional sports Gaelic Football und hurling are extremely popular in Ireland.
45 Football and rugby are the two team sports for which Ireland is best known at an international level. Although their team may not often progress deep into international competitions, Irish fans are famous for their unwavering support for their team, often expressed by singing songs such as "The fields of Athenry".

Workshop: Step by step — Part A: Irish identity

Step by step: Analysing narrative perspective

PRE-READING

1 Across cultures

a) **Think-pair-share** Talk about the role religion plays in your life and how important it is to the people around you.

b) Read the following extract from a newspaper article. Explain the relevance of the Catholic Church to the Irish and compare it to what you have said in a).

Annotations
1 **all-pervading** /ˌɔːl pə(r)ˈveɪdɪŋ/ = being part of everything
2 **devotional** = relating to religious practices
3 **parish** = a district within the Church; the people living in this district who are members of the Church
4 **rite of passage** = ceremony that marks an important stage in sb's life
5 **solace** /ˈsɒləs/ = act of comforting sb who is sad

Catholicism was once so all-pervading[1] in Irish life that it seemed a definition of Irishness: but now [...] the Irish are losing their faith quicker than most [...].
5 There was the effect of the 1960s. There was the effect of the pill, which, contrary to legend, was legal in Ireland. There was television. There was modernisation [...].
But there were a lot of concerned parents, 10 too, writing to the devotional[2] magazines saying that they were in despair because they just couldn't get their offspring to pray [...]. Gradually, you could see traditional Irish Catholicism unravelling. [...]
15 Yet I would distinguish between "religion" and "faith" in the Irish context. If the traditional structures of "religion" are weaker, there remains a strong deposit of "faith" among the people. Country 20 pilgrimages still thrive. When there is a local tragedy – fishermen drowned at sea, teenagers killed in a bad road collision – the parish[3] priest still speaks for the people, and organises the rites of passage[4]. And solace[5].

2
Based on the extract from the article and what you have learnt from the songs on p. 20, name factors that might have influenced the identity of someone growing up in Ireland in the 1980s.

COMPREHENSION

3
a) Read the extract from the beginning of Anne Enright's 2015 award-winning novel *The Green Road*, which is set in 1980. Note down the role the Catholic Church plays in the lives of the Madigans, especially of the younger family members Hanna, Emmet and Dan. Keep your notes for later use.

b) Complete a timeline of the events the narrator refers to.

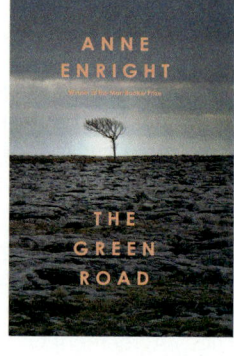

Annotations
1 **seminary** /ˈsemɪnəri/ = place where priests learn how to be a priest

The Green Road
by Anne Enright

Hanna's mother had taken to the bed. She had been there for two weeks, nearly. She had not dressed herself or done her hair since the Sunday before Easter, when Dan 5 told them all that he was going to be a priest. Dan was in his first year of college up in Galway. They would let him finish his degree, he said, but he would do it from the seminary[1]. So in two years he would be 10 finished in ordinary college and in seven years he would be a priest, and after that he would be off on the missions. It was all decided. He announced all this when he came home for the Easter holidays and their 15 mother went upstairs and did not come down. She said she had a pain in her elbow. Dan said he had little enough to pack and then he would be gone.

Part A: Irish identity — Workshop: Step by step

"Go up to the shops," said her father, to Hanna. But he didn't give her any money, and there was nothing she wanted to buy. Besides, she was afraid that something would happen if she left, there would be shouting. Dan would not be there when she got back. His name would never be mentioned again.

But Dan did not leave the house, not even to go for a walk. He hung around the place, sitting in one chair and then moving to another, avoiding the kitchen, accepting the offer of tea or turning it down. Hanna carried the cup to Dan's room, with something to eat tucked in on the saucer; a ham sandwich or a piece of cake. Sometimes he only took a bite of the food and Hanna finished it as she took it back to the kitchen, and the stale edge to the bread made her even more fond of her brother, in his confinement[2].

Dan was so unhappy. Hanna was only twelve and it was terrible for her to see her brother so pent up – all that belief, and the struggle to make sense of it. [...]

Hanna blamed the Pope. He came to Ireland just after Dan left for college and it was like he flew in specially, because Galway was where the big Youth Mass was held, out on the racecourse at Ballybrit. Hanna went to the Limerick Mass, which was just like standing in a field with your parents for six hours, but her brother Emmet was let go to Galway too, even though he was only fourteen and you were supposed to be sixteen for the Youth Mass. He left in a minibus from the local church. The priest brought a banjo and when Emmet came back he had learned how to smoke. He did not see Dan in the crowd. He saw two people having sex in a sleeping bag, he said, but that was the night before, when they all camped in a field somewhere – he could not tell his parents what was the place.

[...] On New Year's Day a priest called[3] to the house and Hanna saw him sitting in the front room with both her parents. The priest's hair had the mark of the comb in it, as though it was still wet, and his coat, hanging under the stairs, was very black and soft.

After this, Dan went back to Galway and nothing happened until the Easter break[4], when he said he wanted to be a priest. He made the big announcement at Sunday dinner, which the Madigans always did with a tablecloth and proper napkins, no matter what. On that Sunday, which was Palm Sunday, they had bacon and cabbage with white sauce and carrots - green, white and orange, like the Irish flag. There was a little glass of parsley sitting on the tablecloth, and the shadow of the water trembled in the sunshine. Their father folded his large hands and said grace, after which there was silence. Apart from the general sound of chewing, that is, and their father clearing his throat, as he tended to do, every minute or so.

"Hehm-hehmm."

The parents sat at either end of the table, the children along the sides. Girls facing the window, boys facing the room. Constance-and-Hanna, Emmet-and-Dan.

There was a fire in the grate and the sun also shone, now and then, so they were as warm as winter and warm as summer for five minutes at a time. They were twice as warm.

Dan said, "I have been speaking again with Father Fawl."

It was nearly April. A dappled kind of day. The clean light caught the drops on the windowpane in all their multiplicity while, outside, a thousand baby leaves unfurled against branches black with rain.

Inside, their mother had a tissue trapped in the palm of her hand. She lifted it against her forehead.

"Oh, no," she said, turning away, and her mouth sagged open so you could see the carrots.

"He says I must ask you to think again. That it is hard for a man who does not have his family behind him. It is a big decision I am making, and he says I must ask you – I must plead with you – not to spoil it, with your own feelings and concerns."

Dan spoke as though they were in private. Or he spoke as though they were in a great hall. But it was a family meal, which was not the same as either of these things. You could see their mother had an impulse to rise from the table but would not allow herself to flee.

"He says I am to ask your forgiveness, for the life you had hoped for me, and the grandchildren you will not have."

Annotations
[2] **confinement** = imprisonment
[3] to **call** = *here:* to visit sb
[4] **break** = *here:* the holidays

Workshop: Step by step — Part A: Irish identity

Preview

In this Workshop, you will analyse the narrative perspective in extracts from a novel. To do so, you will focus on the sequence of events, the voice adopted by the narrator and the modes of presentation.

ANALYSIS

4 → SUPPORT D1, p. 294

→ **S12:** Checklist: Analysis – prose, p. 352

a) Read a short passage from the extract of *The Green Road* that you already know, as well as the info box below and on p. 25 to identify the narrative perspective.
b) Explain which modes of presentation are used in the highlighted passages.
c) Compare your results in class.

"Go up to the shops," said her father, to Hanna. But he didn't give her any money, and there was nothing she wanted to buy. Besides, she was afraid that something would happen if
5 she left, there would be shouting. Dan would not be there when she got back. His name would never be mentioned again.
But Dan did not leave the house, not even to go for a walk. He hung around the place, sitting
10 in one chair and then moving to another, avoiding the kitchen, accepting the offer of tea or turning it down.

Info

Narrative perspective and mode of presentation

It is important to distinguish between the author – a real-life person – and the narrator, a kind of speaker through whom the author presents the development of the story. This difference becomes most obvious when the narrator is dramatized, i.e. a character in the story from whose point of view the story is told. In addition, the mode of presentation has an impact on what the reader thinks about the characters and the plot and how much the reader feels drawn into a situation in the story.

a) Narrative perspective

First-person narration	Third-person narration	
	a) omniscient narrator (unlimited point of view)	b) selective narrator (limited point of view)
• uses "I" and "me" • usually the novel's central character, sometimes a minor character who observes the action • reader can easily identify with the narrator • information not always reliable since narrator provides a very subjective view of events	• knows everything about characters – can look inside their minds • may comment on events or characters' behaviour • knows how the plot will develop • can switch between places and times (e.g. flashbacks, foreshadowing)	• only has insight into one character's thoughts and feelings • story's development seen and judged through this character's eyes only • easy for reader to identify with that character, but also be influenced by his/her interpretation of events.

Part A: Irish identity | **Workshop: Step by step**

b) Mode of presentation

telling (panoramic mode)	showing (scenic mode)	stream of consciousness
The narrator tells the reader what happens over a longer period of time, without going into detail. The reader feels a certain distance to the events and the characters.	The narrator describes in detail what happens in a scene, often using dialogue. The characters' feelings may also be related. This makes the reader feel close to the action and allows him or her to empathize with the characters in the scene.	The reader is introduced directly to a character's interior life as the character's experiences in a situation are mixed with ideas from both the past and present that come to the character's mind as well as random associations.

5
Read the complete extract from *The Green Road* again. Analyse why the narrator uses different modes of presentation, taking into account what effect they are meant to have on the reader.

→ **S12:** Checklist: Analysis – prose, p. 352

EXAMPLE:
As the narrator concentrates on what Hanna can observe, he/she sums up what happens to Dan, e.g. while he is at university (cf. ll. 69-70), using telling, and presents situations in which Hanna is involved in greater detail so that …

Language support

to provide an overview of a person's background/family relations/… | to focus on a scene that is exemplary of a character's behaviour/of how (dys)functional the family is/… | to shed light on a character's development in various places/over time/… | to allow the reader to witness a conflict as it unfolds/a character's development at a crucial moment in his/her life/…

6
Analyse the sequence of events. A narrator may choose to present the events chronologically. Alternatively, he/she may decide not to present events chronologically using his/her knowledge of what is to come. Explain what purpose a certain sequence of events may serve.

EXAMPLE:
The narrator refers to the mother's reaction to the news of Dan wanting to become a priest right at the start (cf. ll.1-5) before explaining which steps contributed to this development …

Language support

to build up tension gradually | to introduce the key issue right at the start | to puzzle the reader | to bring the passage full circle | to reveal the background to an event gradually | to let the reader experience the events alongside the characters

7 EXTRA
Imagine you are asked to rewrite the passage from a different point of view. Say which one you would choose and explain how it would influence the effect on the reader.

COMMENT

8
Comment on the impact religion can have on a family. Consider both the role the Catholic church plays in the Madigan family as well as what you know about the role of religion in families today. → **S6:** How to write a discussion/comment, p. 338

Workshop: Practice — Part A: Irish identity

Practice Analysing narrative perspective

PRE-READING

1

a) Although Northern Ireland has come a long way since the Good Friday Agreement of 1998, there are still signs of conflict. The mural on the left can be found in the Tiger's Bay area of Belfast, the capital of Northern Ireland, and is not the only one that still expresses the tensions between more militant members of the Catholic and Protestant communities. Describe the mural and your first reaction.

b) Find out more about the conflict the mural refers to. Divide the following key words among the members of your class. Research the terms and note down key information.

c) Exchange your findings in class.

→ **S15:** How to describe pictures, p. 358

> YCV (Young Citizen Volunteers) | PAF (Protestant Action Force) | Ulster | IRA | Ulster Unionist Party | Democratic Unionist Party | Sinn Fein | SDLP | The Troubles | Good Friday Agreement | Orange Order | Fenian | Loyalists | shamrock | Red Hand of Ulster

2

→ **S9:** How to structure a text, p. 344

a) Use the information from task 1 to explain the message of the mural above and the larger context it illustrates in a short essay.

b) Swap essays with your neighbours to find out about how your classmates interpret the mural.

c) **Across cultures** Discuss in class whether there are any similar expressions of political beliefs in your home area.

COMPREHENSION

3

Kate MacLachlan's novel *Love my enemy* is set in Belfast in the late 1990s. With peace starting to take hold, the 15-year-old Protestant girl Zee hopes for a better life alongside her new neighbour from England, Tasha. However, things start to take a turn for the worse when Conor, a Catholic boy, appears at a bonfire, organized by Protestants, to see Zee.
Describe the Protestants' reactions to Conor.

ANALYSIS

4 → **SUPPORT** D2, p. 294

→ **S12:** Checklist: Analysis – prose, p. 352

Analyse how the narrative perspective and the mode of presentation guide the reader's understanding of the relationship between Zee and Conor.

COMMENT/CREATIVE WRITING

5 **CHOOSE**

Choose one of the following tasks.
Discuss under what conditions Zee and Conor's relationship may have a future.
OR

→ **S2:** Checklist: Creative writing, p. 331

After Zee and Conor leave the bonfire, they discuss their situation. Write their dialogue. Consider the situation and their attitudes as shown in the extract.

Love my enemy
by Kate MacLachlan

"Hello, Zee," came a deep voice.
"Hello!" Zee glanced self-consciously around the crowd then back at the grinning face above her. "What are you doing here?"
"It's a free country," he said, "I thought it was you I heard laughing. Who's your friend?"
Zee introduced them as quietly as she could. Tasha looked confused.
"I thought you said," she began in her clear English voice, "that any name beginning with O is a Cathol –"
"Ssh!" hissed Zee and whispered in her ear. "Of course Con O'Keefe's a Catholic name. Heaven only knows what he's doing here but keep quiet – and don't use his first name either. Even that's a giveaway."
Tasha looked flustered.[1] Zee, remembering the peace protest earlier that day, stood on her tiptoes and said politely to him, "You're very welcome here, you know."
"Dunno if I'd go as far as to say that ... but it's good to see you, Zee."
There was something in his voice that reached right inside her and squeezed her stomach. His eyes held hers just a moment too long to be casual. They had lived in the same street for five years but she had never stood this close to him before. He had the most amazing melt-you-in-a-minute, drop-dead-dreamy-deep, coffee-coloured eyes. Zee almost fell over backwards looking up at them and her voice disappeared altogether. Fortunately she didn't have to speak because Conor started chatting to Tasha. Then the crowd crushed forwards, pressing her against him so hard that she could smell his soap.
"You okay?" he asked.
Before she could answer they saw the cause of the crush. A line of thugs[2], some with shaved heads, were trawling[3] the crowd like a net. "You won't be OK," Zee said nervously. "Better lose yourself[4] – quick!"
But it was too late. Two lads[5] marched straight up to them. One with golden curls[6] and biro-blue eyes planted himself right in front of Conor, hands on hips.
"Well, well," he called out loudly, "look what we have here, lads. A Fenian[7]!"
Anticipation shivered across the crowd. For a moment all that could be heard was the frenzied crackling of the fire. People began edging back, their faces reflecting wild, cavorting[8] flames. Zee could taste the smoke, the danger, even her own fear. She must overcome it, she had to speak out. She couldn't just stand by and see Conor get beaten up.
"Leave him alone!" she squealed, and then, finding more authority, she said, "D'you hear me, Gary? Just you leave Conor alone."
"Your Gary?" asked Tasha, her voice incredulous. "He's your brother?"
"Yes," Zee admitted and she felt shrunk somehow. Gary was standing close up to Conor, eyeballing him like a boxer.
"What are you doing here?" he demanded, but before Conor could answer, the other youth butted in.
"And you, Zee? What the hell are you doing with the likes of him?"
"Mind your own business, Des Gordon!"
Her voice sounded an awful lot braver than she felt, and she shuddered as Des's eyes roved up and down her body.
"I just came over to say hello to Zee," Con told them, "that's all."
"You stay away from her," snarled Des. "Stick to your own kind."
Tasha cleared her throat but if she was trying to catch their attention she failed completely.
Gary punched Conor's shoulder, none too lightly. "You should be at home, pillock[9]. This is our night."
Conor kept his balance, and looked Gary straight in the eye. "There's supposed to be peace, isn't there? I can go anywhere I want."
"In your dreams!" Gary hissed. "Peace? Too many scores to be settled for that."
"Not between us, Gary. It's not long since you and me were kids playing football in the street."
Des moved in, pushing his fist hard into Conor's chest, forcing him back a step. "You two were never mates, Fenian boy." [...] "You should watch the company you keep," he growled at Zee. "And Gary – you should make her. I would if she was my sister."
In the end Zee felt she had no choice but to leave [...].
"God, I can't wait to get out of this country!"
"Can't you?" Conor sounded surprised.
„No. Even if the peace works, it'll make no real difference – not deep down."

Annotations
[1] **flustered** = confused
[2] **thug** /θʌg/ = violent man
[3] to **trawl** = durchkämmen
[4] to **lose oneself** = *here*: to disappear
[5] **lad** = boy
[6] **curl** /kɜː(r)l/ = Locke
[7] **Fenian** = originally name for a member of an Irish secret society that wanted to establish an Irish republic; now used as an insulting term for sb Irish
[8] to **cavort** = to play, dance or jump around
[9] **pillock** (BE, *informal*) = idiot

1 Texts — Part A: Irish identity

Irish clichés: All Guinness and leprechauns?

1

a) `Across cultures` When you meet people from abroad, they often have expectations based on clichés that exist about Germans and Germany. Collect some examples in class that you have encountered.

b) Watch a group of young Irish people being confronted with clichés about their country and their people. Note down what the clichés are and which of them are true to an extent according to the young people's comments.

c) Create categories to label the clichés from the video. You can use this grid. Leave room for more categories and clichés as well as a third column.

category	cliché
outward appearance	…
free-time habits	…
…	…

Webcode
You can find a link to the video here: WES-73644-005

→ **S20:** How to listen/watch effectively, p. 366

2

a) Read extracts from a special report published in the *Irish Times*. Compare the points addressed in the article to your findings from task 1. Add any new categories and clichés to your overview.

b) Add a third column to your grid and fill in evidence to prove or disprove the clichés you have already noted down.

3 `CHOOSE`

Take the report from the *Irish Times* as a model for a similar text dealing with clichés about Germans.

- Starting out from what you have already mentioned in task 1a), collect further clichés you have come across or you can find online about Germany and the Germans. Take the categories you have come up with for Ireland to structure your ideas.
- Choose the clichés from your list that you feel you can write about.
- Create a list with humorous comments and truth ratings similar to the article from the *Irish Times*.
- Present your article in class and ask your classmates to comment on how appropriate your examples and truth ratings are.

→ **S8:** How to improve your text, p. 341

→ **S24:** How to give feedback/peer-edit, p. 372

OR

Watch a video advertising Ireland as a tourist destination.
- Analyse which aspects of Ireland the video concentrates on and how the clip tries to attract tourists. Consider both the content and any striking cinematic devices.
- Watch the clip for a second time and identify any clichés it plays with.
- Present the clip in class. Introduce the content of the clip first and explain your findings afterwards.

Webcode
You can find a link to the video here: WES-73644-006

DARRAGH MURPHY   The Irish Times, 29 October 2016

Land of drunks, poets, friendly fans. How true are Irish cliches? We separate the truths, half-truths and lies about Ireland

There are many shades of Irish identity: some clichéd and untrue; others pinpoint accurate. We take some of the most common labels attached to Ireland and put
5 them through the truth test. [...]

2. A bucolic[1] tourist paradise
Although around 60 per cent of us are urbanised, Ireland is the world's 143rd most densely populated country, behind
10 Ethiopia and Jordan. More than three million tourists visited between June and August, a record.
Truth rating: 8/10 [...]

Annotations
[1] **bucolic** /bjuːˈkɒlɪk/ = rural

Part A: Irish identity — Texts

4. The best small country in the world to do business

It's Enda Kenny's[2] most frequently articulated vision for Ireland – especially when he is overseas. Yet, despite the "leprechaun[3] economics" of Ireland's 26.3 per cent GDP growth in 2015, analysts say "underlying growth" was still 6 per cent in 2015, and Ireland is the seventh most competitive country in the world.
Truth rating: 7/10

5. A land of drunks and "junk"[4]

Ireland sober is Ireland stiff, wrote James Joyce in Finnegans Wake, and alcohol consumption trebled between 1960 and 2001. In 2014, the World Health Organisation found Ireland to have the second highest rate of binge-drinking[5] in the world and, in 2011, Ireland was found to have the highest heroin use in Europe.
Truth rating: 10/10 [...]

7. The best fans in the world

Fans of the two Irish teams at Euro 2016 in France serenaded[6] nuns, sang lullabies to babies, and fixed flat tyres. The mayor of Paris Anne Hidalgo even awarded the city's Grand Vermeil medal to Irish fan Jamie Monaghan, from Louth, who received it on behalf of Irish fans.
Truth rating: 9/10 [...]

12. "Priest-ridden"

There are 2,019 priests in active ministry in Ireland, a drop of 43 per cent since 1995.
Truth rating: 2/10

13. A Catholic country

In the 2011 census, 84.2 per cent of people in the State described themselves as Catholic. Yet, seven out of 10 Catholics did not attend weekly Mass, and one in eight Dubliners having no religion. With 96 per cent of national schools still run by religious orders, "sham[7] baptisms" to secure school places are on the rise.
Truth rating: 4/10

14. A well-travelled nation

According to a 2013 UN migration report

of 72 countries, more than three quarters of a million Irish-born people were living abroad. We have the highest number of native-born emigrants, in the OECD, living abroad.
Truth rating: 10/10 [...]

17. A gay-friendly land

In 2015, Ireland became the first country worldwide to vote by referendum to permit same-sex marriage. A Gallup poll of 129 states last year put Ireland as the ninth most gay-friendly country.
Truth rating: 8/10 [...]

24. A land of poets and scribes

Four Irish men have won a Nobel Prize in Literature – W.B. Yeats, George Bernard Shaw, Samuel Beckett, and Seamus Heaney – with James Joyce overlooked. John Millington Synge, Frank O'Connor, Flann O'Brien, Brian Friel and modern novelists such as Anne Enright, Colm Tóibín and Roddy Doyle confirm a sterling[8] reputation.
Truth rating: 9/10 [...]

27. Good Europeans

We've come a long way from rejecting the Nice and Lisbon Treaties[9]. As other countries weigh up the idea of leaving the EU, just one in five of us wants to leave.
Truth rating: 8/10 [...]

29. Home of violence and terrorism

Ireland is still dealing with the reverberations of the bombings, shootings and atrocities known as The Troubles, though the Belfast Agreement has been in force since 1998.
Truth rating: 7/10

Annotations
[2] **Enda Kenny** = Irish Prime Minister 2011-2017
[3] **leprechaun** /ˈleprəkɔːn/ = in Irish folklore, a small man with magic powers
[4] **junk** = here: drugs
[5] **binge drinking** /ˈbɪndʒ ˌdrɪŋkɪŋ/ = drinking lots of alcohol in a short period of time
[6] to **serenade** /ˌserəˈneɪd/ = to perform a song or piece of music for sb
[7] **sham** = fake, only simulated
[8] **sterling** /ˈstɜː(r)lɪŋ/ = of high quality
[9] **Nice and Lisbon Treaties** = two treaties aimed at a reform of the European Union and initially rejected by the Irish electorate in two referenda held in 2001 and 2008

Mediation: National identity in Germany

4 Across cultures

a) **Round Robin** Say what "Heimat" means to you.
b) Read the article and compare the different aspects of the term "Heimat" with your associations.
c) Your school is taking part in a project with schools from all over Europe on the issue of how people feel about their home countries. Your initial findings are collected in a blog on the project website. Use the information from the article below to write a blog post on how Germans feel about their home country and why. Also refer to the political consequences. Make sure that you explain anything that someone not familiar with German culture may not understand.

→ S19: How to improve your mediation skills, p. 364

Sehnsucht nach einem Gefühl
Warum „Heimat" plötzlich wieder in ist

Gregor Tholl, 08. Februar 2018

Laut „Duden" ist Heimat „ein Land, Landesteil oder Ort", in dem man geboren und aufgewachsen ist oder sich zu Hause fühlt. Es sei ein gefühlsbetonter „Ausdruck enger Verbundenheit" gegenüber einer
5 Gegend. Das Wort wirkte lange verpönt [...]. Zurzeit erlebt es ein Comeback.

Die zwei bevölkerungsreichsten Bundesländer haben bereits Ministerien mit der Bezeichnung Heimat: in Bayern seit 2014 unter Markus
10 Söder das „Staatsministerium der Finanzen, für Landesentwicklung und Heimat", in Nordrhein-Westfalen unter Ina Scharrenbach wird das Wort seit 2017 sogar als erstes im Titel geführt: „Ministerium für Heimat, Kommunales, Bau und
15 Gleichstellung".

Auch Bundespräsident Frank-Walter Steinmeier griff das Trendwort am Tag der Deutschen Einheit auf. „Ich bin überzeugt, wer sich nach Heimat sehnt, der ist nicht von gestern", sagte er. „Im
20 Gegenteil: Je schneller die Welt sich um uns dreht, desto größer wird die Sehnsucht nach Heimat." Das dürfe man nicht den Nationalisten und dem rechten Rand überlassen. Heimat sei ein Ort des „Wir", ein Ort, der verbinde. [...]
25 Kulturwissenschaftler sehen ganz grundsätzlich eine Suche nach Halt angesichts der Globalisierung, aber auch des Wandels der Geschlechterrollen oder des Generationenverhältnisses. Ein Gefühl des Kontrollverlusts führe zu einer Sehnsucht nach
30 Identität. [...]

[Der Publizist Christian] Schüle hat 2017 das Buch „Heimat – Ein Phantomschmerz" veröffentlicht und lehrt an der Berliner Universität der Künste im Fachbereich Kulturwissenschaft.

35 Seine These: „Über Heimat spricht man dann, wenn sie einem verloren geht. Und ich glaube, dass es in den vergangenen Jahren einige Heimatverluste gegeben hat." Die klare Bipolarität von Ost und West sei weg, durch die Computerisierung und
40 die Globalisierung verschwinde ein bisschen die deutsche Sprache durch immer mehr Englisch. „Und in den ländlichen Räumen, egal ob in Baden-Württemberg oder Mecklenburg-Vorpommern, gingen Gasthäuser verloren, Buslinien wurden
45 eingestellt, Clubhäuser, Vereinsräume: Dann entsteht so das Gefühl, selber weniger wert zu sein." Mit der Aufnahme der Flüchtlinge seien dann gefühlt auf einen Schlag viele Menschen gekommen, die aus Kulturkreisen stammten, die
50 aus Sicht der Kritiker mit dem unsrigen nichts zu tun haben, sagt Schüle. „Und dann fangen die Leute an zu sagen, das sei ungerecht, hier geht mir die Heimat verloren und die Politik tut nichts."

Das seien oft sozialpolitische Ängste, die weniger
55 mit dem Hass auf andere Menschen als vielmehr mit dem Gefühl des Verlusts des Eigenen zu tun hätten. Er sieht den Begriff Heimat so angesagt, weil Wörter wie Vaterland, Nation und Volk belastet seien aus der Nazi-Zeit. „Um all das zu
60 umgehen, aber trotzdem einen Begriff zu haben, der auf das gleiche Gefühl der Geborgenheit und Zugehörigkeit zielt, wird Heimat genommen."

Der ganze Trend habe auch mit der Fußball-WM 2006 in Deutschland zu tun, zumindest sei ein
65 gewisser Normalisierungsprozess in Sachen Nation damals verstärkt worden, auch wenn es nationalkonservative Sehnsüchte bis in die bürgerliche Mitte eigentlich immer gegeben habe. Jahrzehntelang seien sie aber nicht politisch
70 repräsentiert worden. Jetzt werde sich darum vielleicht umso mehr gekümmert.

Part A: Irish identity — Advanced texts

The individual and Irish society

COMPREHENSION

Read the article on this and the next page and choose the correct answers.

1. Ireland today is considered to be a country that is:
   a strictly Catholic.
   b highly traditional.
   c extremely conservative.
   d undergoing significant changes.

2. The legalization of same-sex marriage in Ireland is characteristic of a decidedly more liberal public opinion as:
   a it was achieved in a referendum.
   b it already came into effect in 1993.
   c it fell together with Varadkar's election.
   d Ireland was the first European country to grant this right.

3. The main focus of the public's perception towards Varadkar is on his:
   a coming out.
   b Indian roots.
   c political expertise.
   d sexual orientation.

4. Varadkar's political agenda concentrates on:
   a expanding gay rights.
   b achieving a multicultural society.
   c integrating Ireland even more into Europe.
   d protecting the economy from international competition.

5. Varadkar's start in office:
   a is viewed critically because of his young age.
   b is the beginning of a new conservative era.
   c comes at a time without any difficult issues to deal with.
   d is made easier by his political experience.

6. All in all, the author of the article:
   a is doubtful that Ireland has already overcome its conservatism despite Varadkar's election.
   b welcomes Varadkar's election as an important step in the transformation of Ireland into a more liberal country.
   c sees Varadkar's election as the latest step in a long history of the Irish combining Catholic conservatism and modernity.
   d criticizes that issues such as Varadkar's sexual orientation, ethnic background and age attract more attention than his qualifications.

Leo Varadkar is Ireland's new prime minister. He's also openly gay and an immigrant's son.
He leads Ireland's conservative center-right party.

Lindsay Maizland, 14 June 2017

Ireland just elected its youngest and first openly gay prime minister. Leo Varadkar, 38, who is also the son of an Indian immigrant and is the first Irish leader of Indian descent, was confirmed in a
5 parliamentary vote on Wednesday.
This is a big deal for the once staunchly Catholic Republic of Ireland. At one point, it was the most socially conservative country in Europe – for example, it only decriminalized homosexual activity
10 in 1993. But Varadkar's election is part of a broader transformative shift that has taken place in Ireland in recent decades – Ireland actually legalized same-sex marriage in 2015, the first country to do so by popular vote.

15 "If my election today shows anything, it is that prejudice has no hold in this Republic," said Varadkar in early June when he became the leader of Ireland's ruling center-right party, Fine Gael, reported Reuters.
20 Even though the center-right party tends to be more socially conservative, many of its top members supported Varadkar because of his personality, background, and political experience.
Outgoing Prime Minister Enda Kenny – who,
25 now age 66, was first elected to parliament before Varadkar had even been born – endorsed Varadkar, saying that he represents a younger generation. "He represents a modern, diverse and inclusive Ireland and speaks for them like no
30 other, an Ireland in which each person can fulfill their potential and live their dreams," said Kenny, according to the BBC.
The fact that local media in Ireland have barely mentioned Varadkar's identity, choosing to focus

on his political qualifications instead, also shows how far Ireland has come in becoming more socially liberal.

Varadkar himself has also downplayed his sexuality after coming out during a radio interview five months before Ireland voted "yes" on the 2015 same-sex marriage referendum in Ireland. "It doesn't define me," he said at the time.

Instead, his political platform[1] focuses on rejecting nationalism and protectionism and extolling[2] the benefits of global free trade and "fewer borders and barriers." He's given speeches about moving beyond left-wing or right-wing politics toward a new, pro-European centrist approach.

In his first speech as prime minister, he reiterated this platform:

"The government I lead will be one of the new European center as we seek to build a republic of opportunity. And that is a republic in which every citizen gets a fair go and has the opportunity to succeed."

Varadkar isn't new to Ireland's political scene, despite now being the youngest prime minister. He launched his political career when he was a teenager by joining the youth wing of Fine Gael[3], and was elected to parliament in 2007. After that, he worked as Fine Gael's minister for transport, tourism, and sport, and then as health minister. Most recently, he oversaw Ireland's welfare system.

As he moves forward as prime minister, he will face challenges including addressing Brexit, monitoring his country's relationship with Northern Ireland (which is part of the UK), and pushing government to run effectively. But his election is still an exciting step forward for the traditionally conservative country.

Annotations
[1] **(political) platform** = what a politician stands for
[2] to **extol** = to praise
[3] **Fine Gael** = conservative political party in Ireland

ANALYSIS

2
a) Read the article again and identify what qualifies Varadkar as a good Prime Minister.
b) Explain how Varadkar's appointment is representative of the modernization of Ireland.

→ **S13:** Checklist: Analysis – non-fictional texts, p. 354

3
Analyse how Lindsay Maizland tries to convince her readers of her view. Consider her choice of words, rhetorical strategies and stylistic devices.

Info

Abortion referenda

In a referendum held in 1983, 67 percent of Irish voters voted in favour of adding an amendment to the Irish constitution outlawing abortion completely. In another referendum held in 2018, 66 percent of voters voted in favour of legalizing abortion under certain circumstances.

PRE-READING

4
Ireland has seen two major referenda in recent years that dealt with very personal issues regulated by the state: same-sex marriage and abortion. Read the extract from a newspaper article below and explain how referenda on these issues are connected to the development of Irish national identity.

Ireland was long a bastion of Catholic conservatism, a place where pedestrians might tip their hats and hop off the footpath when a priest walked past. But economic and technological changes helped propel a shift in attitudes that accelerated with the unfolding of far-reaching abuse scandals in the Roman Catholic Church in the 1990s. Over a generation, Ireland transformed from a country where 67 percent of voters approved the constitutional abortion ban to one where, in 2015, 62 percent voted to legalize same-sex marriage.

COMPREHENSION

5
Read the article on the next page and collect arguments for and against the new abortion law.

WORDS

6
a) Match words you can use to express your opinion with their definitions.

Part A: Irish identity — Advanced texts

1	to wonder	A	to prove that something is not true
2	to claim	B	to support and argue for
3	to deny	C	to be in doubt about
4	to refute	D	to say in a strong way that something is wrong
5	to condemn	E	to say that something is not true
6	to advocate	F	to say that something is true when some people may say it isn't

b) Use five words from a) to refer to views presented in the article.

ANALYSIS

7 Explain whether the author of the article is biased or presents the topic objectively. Give evidence.

WRITING: DISCUSSION

8 `CHALLENGE`
Discuss to what extent the state has the right or even duty to decide about very intimate personal issues like same-sex relationships and abortion. → **S6:** How to write a discussion/comment, p. 338

Annotations
[1] **hierarchy** = *here:* a group of people controlling an organization
[2] **Abortion Support Network** = UK-based charity that supports women in Ireland who want to have an abortion

Abortion in Ireland: The fight for choice
Joel Gunter, 8 March 2017, BBC News

Sarah didn't know where to turn when she found out she was pregnant. It was May last year, she was 23, finishing her final year at university, and working in a cafe to save for a move from her small
5 Irish hometown to Dublin. Waiting for her in the city were her boyfriend and a traineeship. She wasn't ready to be a mother, but her birth control had failed. Sat in her bedroom at home, she started to panic.
10 "I felt so alone," she said tearfully, over tea in Dublin last week. "You want to take it a step at a time but I had no idea what the next step was." Downstairs at home were her parents, who would have forced her to have the baby, she said. When she tried to raise
15 the issue of abortion, hypothetically, they told her it was murder. "Murder, they said, and that was that." The Irish Republic has a near-total ban on abortion, including in cases of rape, incest or fatal foetal abnormalities, and a 14-year prison sentence
20 hangs over anyone who has one. In the early 1980s, fearing that it could be legalised via the courts, the country's Catholic hierarchy[1] pushed for an amendment to be added to the constitution. The Eighth Amendment passed in 1983 and granted a
25 foetus equal right to life as its mother, effectively outlawing abortion in all circumstances. [...]
More than 3,500 Irish women are estimated to travel abroad every year to terminate crisis pregnancies – an average of 12 per day. Mostly
30 they go to England, often in difficult, sometimes traumatic circumstances.
Women who can't afford the costs involved – up to £2,000 for travel, accommodation, and the procedure – or who can't take time away from
35 work, have two choices: take illegal abortion pills ordered online, or give birth. Of the estimated three women taking the pills every day, some will fear going to a doctor in the event of complications.
Sarah and her boyfriend combined their savings,
40 borrowed some more and came up with £200. The Abortion Support Network[2] pitched in the rest and put her in touch with a volunteer who would meet her at Liverpool airport. She took two days off work and on a cold, overcast day, boarded a budget
45 flight to meet a stranger in a different country.
"It's traumatising to have an abortion," she said. "To not be able to do that in your own country, to not be able to return to your own home or be near your friends …" she trailed off. "I'm not ashamed
50 I had an abortion, but to come home to a country that thought I was a criminal … I was devastated."
[...]
Early advocates of the Eighth Amendment hoped it would permanently protect Ireland from the
55 spectre of so-called abortion-on-demand. But the amendment didn't ensure Irish women wouldn't have abortions, it just pushed them out of sight, to clinics in London and Liverpool, and to rooms around the country where they criminalise
60 themselves by taking pills freely prescribed elsewhere.

Facts **Part B:** Canadian identity

Webcode
You can download a word list for Part B here: WES-73644-007

Introduction to Canada

Geography
Canada is the second-biggest country in the world with an area of almost 10,000 square kilometres, stretching from the Arctic in the north to the United States in the south. However, Canada is also one of the most sparsely populated countries with only about 35 million inhabitants. The capital and
5 seat of government is Ottowa, its fourth-largest city after Toronto, Montreal and Vancouver. It is in these cities and in the area close to the US border that the majority of people live. Canada is officially bilingual in English and French. The national symbols are the maple leaf and the beaver.

Economy
Canada is one of the most prosperous nations in the world. It is one
10 of the world's major exporters of agricultural products, although its economy is dominated by the service industry, which employs about 75% of the population. Other important industries include transport, timber, minerals, natural gas, fish products and chemicals. Canada is a member of the G7 and the OECD. The economy relies strongly on international
15 trade with the US being the largest trading partner.

Indigenous population
When the first explorers arrived in Canada, the country was populated by an estimated 500,000 indigenous First Nation and Inuit people. As a consequence of European colonization, their numbers declined rapidly.
20 Some First Nation and Inuit married European settlers. Their children are known as Métis.

In the beginning, the relations between the settlers and the indigenous peoples were relatively peaceful. However, in the 19th and early 20th centuries, attempts were made to force indigenous peoples to adapt to
25 mainstream Canadian culture. Some peoples had to relocate to reserves, where it was easier for the government to control them. The aim of these initiatives was to force the indigenous peoples of Canada to adapt to a European way of life. They focussed on Christianisation and promoted education and agriculture.
30 From 1847 to 1996, the Canadian government and the Catholic Church ran 130 residential schools for indigenous children, who were forcibly separated from their parents. It was not until 2008 that the Canadian government offered an apology for their treatment of these children.

Diversity
35 Canada is a very liberal country and proud of its diversity. It is also a nation of newcomers. After British and French colonization, immigration to Canada continued. During and after the two world wars, waves of immigration brought many new cultures and languages into the country. With this came the first laws to encourage diversity. In 1971 Canada became the first country to have an official policy of multiculturalism. Today immigrants represent 20% of the population.
40 However, not everyone is allowed to immigrate to Canada. The government employs a points system for immigration. It distinguishes between skilled workers and other kinds of immigrants and factors such as education, language proficiency, work experience, age, health and whether the applicant has an outstanding job offer play a decisive role in who is allowed to become a Canadian and whose application is rejected. People who are likely to be a burden on the health and welfare system will
45 most likely be refused.

Part B: Canadian identity | **Workshop: Step by step**

1

Step by step Rewriting from a different perspective

Webcode
You can find a link to the audio file here:
WES-73644-008

PRE-READING

1 CD/04 → **S20:** How to listen/watch effectively, p. 366

a) Kim Wheeler is First Nation Mohawk and Anishinaabe. Listen to her story and sum up what happened to her as a young child.

b) Listen again and answer these questions in a few words.
   1. What was the government policy known as the 'Sixties Scoop'?
   2. What was the government's aim regarding First Nation children?
   3. How did Kim's adoptive parents try to fulfil this aim? Name two things.
   4. Which event made Kim realize she was never going to be part of the family?
   5. When did Kim find out more about her heritage?
   6. How has Kim brought up her own children?
   7. What might cause Kim's culture to disappear?

c) Read the info box and find similarities and differences between Kim and the children described in it. Explain what has happened to their identity.

d) **CHALLENGE** Analyse the view of the residential school system as expressed in the info box.

> **Info**
>
> ### Residential school system
>
> Some First Nation children were not adopted but forced to attend residential schools for the greatest part of the year. These schools were usually run by churches and although the nominal aim was to educate the children, their explicit objective was to indoctrinate them into the Euro-Canadian and Christian way of life and to assimilate them into mainstream society.
> Children were forbidden to speak their own language or acknowledge their own culture and punished severely if they broke these rules. Their education was designed to train them for manual and domestic work and inferior to the general education received in state schools.
> Not until the 1990s did the government and the churches begin to acknowledge their responsibility for an education scheme designed to "kill the Indian in the child". Despite a government apology in Parliament on 11 June 2009, the effects still remain.

COMPREHENSION

2

You are going to read an excerpt from James Bartleman's novel *As long as the rivers flow* (2011). The novel tells the story of Martha, from the Cat Lake First Nation in Northern Ontario, from her birth in 1956 to her mid-fifties.

a) Read the extract and describe the similarities between her fate and that of Kim Wheeler.
b) State your first impressions of Martha's situation. Refer to what you have learned about the Canadian government's policy towards indigenous children.

As long as the rivers flow
by James Bartleman

Extract 1

Martha was only a little girl with big, bright, black-wet eyes, blue-black hair, dark brown chubby[1] cheeks and pudgy[2] hands. In height, she did not even reach the waist of
5 her mother.
What was school anyway? Apparently she had to go there but she only had a vague understanding from overhearing the conversations of the older kids about what
10 that meant. None of them liked it. Did that mean it was a place where kids were sent to be punished? If so, why her? She had been a good girl. Her mother had just told her so.
15 Trusting, affectionate[3] and with a ready smile, Martha looked up at her mother with inquisitive[4] eyes and remained silent. Surely the person who loved her more than anyone else in the whole wide world did not mean
20 it when she said she would be going away and not be home again for such a long time? But the next morning, Mary prepared her daughter to depart, dressing her in a new calico[5] dress, putting up her hair in braids,
25 helping her pull up the long stockings she wore each day to protect her legs from

Annotations
[1] **chubby** = slightly fat, like a healthy baby
[2] **pudgy** *(AE)* = somewhat fat
[3] **affectionate** = showing that you care for sb
[4] **inquisitive** /ɪnˈkwɪzətɪv/ = curious, asking lots of questions
[5] **calico** /ˈkælɪkəʊ/ = cotton clothing with a coloured printed pattern

Workshop: Step by step — Part B: Canadian identity

Annotations
[6] to **taxi** = a plane moving when not airborne
[7] **trader/Indian agent** = here: government official who overlooks education and trade
[8] **Spitfire** = British fighter plane used during the Second World War
[9] **RCAF** = Royal Canadian Air Force
[10] to **ferry** /ˈferi/= to take sb somewhere
[11] **Métis** /meɪˈtiːs/ = part First Nation and part white
[12] to **buckle** = anschnallen
[13] **uncomprehending** = not able to understand
[14] to **billow** = to fill with air
[15] **blade** /bleɪd/= here: Rotorblatt

mosquito and black fly bites, and slipping onto her feet a pair of moccasins she had made for the occasion and decorated with red and blue beads in the shape of flowers. After Isaac gave Martha a long and silent hug, Mary led her to the beach.

Soon a float plane appeared in the sky, circled the lake, came in for a landing and taxied[6] to the shore in front of the reserve. [...] The little girl did not want to go, and hid behind her mother. But to her surprise, her mother allowed the trader[7] to take her hand and lead her to the pilot.

Like the Indian agent, the pilot had served in the armed forces during the war. But he had joined the air force and not the army and had been sent overseas immediately after flight training to fly Spitfires[8] in the RCAF[9]. When the fighting ended, he had come north in search of a job, arriving just as the region was being opened up by bush pilots flying single-engine de Havilland Beaver airplanes on the lakes and rivers [...]

He was less enthusiastic about the work he obtained from the Canadian government ferrying[10] Native kids to and from residential schools, even if it paid well. He had married a Métis[11] woman soon after he arrived in the north and they had six children who attended a local school in a white community, and he couldn't imagine what it would be like if he wasn't surrounded at all times by his large and loving family. There was something fundamentally wrong with separating kids from their parents, but he had a living to make, a contract to do the work, and if he didn't do it, someone else would snap up the business. Thankfully, his dark aviator sunglasses would hide his uneasy eyes from those of the little girl.

The pilot carried Martha into the aircraft cabin and buckled[12] her into a back seat. "It's okay, little girl," he told the uncomprehending[13] child, "Nobody's gonna bite you. We're just going on a nice airplane ride. Once we're in the air, we'll fly higher than the birds and it's so clear you'll be able to see everything." [...]

The roar of the engine and the sight of the propeller slashing the air panicked the little girl and she began screaming for her mother. But her mother stood unknowing on the shore, squinting into the sun, with her calico dress billowing[14] out behind her from the back draft of the rotating blades[15] and with her hands on her head to keep her kerchief from flying away.

Preview

This Workshop will enable you to rewrite a scene from a different point of view, using the first person narration. In order to do so, you will need to look closely at the following aspects:
- plot
- narrative perspective
- characters

COMPREHENSION: PLOT

3

a) Read the text again and outline what happens in the form of a timeline. You can start like this:
  - *Martha finds out that she will be sent away to school.*
  - *Mary ...*

b) **Pair work** Compare your results, adding anything you might have missed.

Tip
Do not get lost in detail. Keep the central idea in mind.

ANALYSIS: NARRATIVE PERSPECTIVE

4

As you will be asked to change the narrative perspective in your piece of creative writing, you need to identify it first.

a) Examine the narrative perspective used by the author and its effect on the reader.
b) Analyse how this effect will change when the first person narration is used.
c) Explain what information the narrator cannot be aware of if the focus of narration changes to the first person.

Tip
For more information on narrative perspective, refer to the Workshop: Analysing narrative perspective, pp. 22 ff.

Part B: Canadian identity   Workshop: **Step by step**   **1**

ANALYSIS: CHARACTERS

5 Pair work → SUPPORT D3, p. 296

In order to rewrite the scene from the point of view of one of the characters, you will need to look carefully at the characters and their relationships to each other.

a) Copy the grid below. Identify the characters in this scene and write their names in the left-hand column. Note down what personal details the narrator reveals about them and where you can find the information in the text. In the right-hand column, note down what you can infer from this information.

b) Now note down what information the reader is given about the characters' personality. Also include what you learn about the characters' thoughts, actions and words and what this reveals about their personality (interpretation).

→ **S12:** Checklist: Analysis – prose, p. 352

Tip
Not every piece of information requires an interpretation.

name	category	information from the text/quote	interpretation
Martha	personal details	"Martha was only a little girl" (l. 1)	She does not fully understand what is going on.
	character	"Trusting, affectionate and with a ready smile" (ll. 15-16)	Martha is described as a happy child.
		...	...
...	...	...	...

6 EXTRA Group work

Using the information from the grid about the characters, consider their relationships to one another.
- Construct a freeze frame showing the relationships of the characters to one another in a specific scene.
- Ask another group to identify the characters.
- Take turns to step out of the frame and explain your feelings as a character in this particular situation.

Webcode
You can download the grid here:
WES-73644-009

CREATIVE WRITING: REWRITING A SCENE FROM ANOTHER PERSPECTIVE

7

a) CHOOSE Rewrite the scene in the first person, either from the point of view of Martha
   OR
   from the point of view of the pilot.
   → SUPPORT D4, p. 296

b) **Group work** Compare your scene with those written by others from the same point of view and choose the most convincing version in the group. Pay close attention to these criteria:
   - the register fits the narrator's character
   - the narrator's character traits are consistent with the original extract
   - the plot of the original version has not been changed

c) Read out two of the best versions (one for each point of view) to the class and talk about how the change of perspective changes your view of the characters.

→ **S2:** Checklist: Creative writing, p. 331

→ **S24:** How to give feedback/peer-edit, p. 372

Checklist
✓ Remember that you will only be able to write about things your narrator knows about.
   - e.g. Martha will have no idea about the pilot's feelings, family background etc.
✓ Think about the kind of language/register you should use. This will depend on the narrator you choose.
   - In this excerpt, Martha is a young, uneducated girl, but she will be writing about the events later, when she has already finished residential school at the age of 16.
   - The pilot is a white educated middle-aged man.

Practice: Rewriting from a different perspective

PRE-READING

1 Look at the photographs and describe what has happened to Thomas Moore.

→ **S15:** How to describe pictures, p. 358

Provincial Archives of Saskatchewan, R-A8223-1 Thomas Moore before admission to the Regina Indian Industrial School

Provincial Archives of Saskatchewan, R-A8223-2 Thomas Moore after admission to the Regina Indian Industrial School, ca. 1896

COMPREHENSION

2 Read another extract from the novel *As long as the rivers flow* and outline the plot.

Extract 2

When Martha returned home at the age of sixteen, the chubby six-year-old who had been taken away in a float plane so many years before had become a tall, attractive, physically mature young woman with fine, dark-brown facial features and angry black eyes. Much of this anger she reserved for her mother. For Martha had never forgotten what her mother had told her that summer after her first year at the residential school.

"Stop making up stories," she had said, squeezing¹ her arm and hurting her when her daughter tried to tell her Father Antoine was touching her where he shouldn't. "The government will cut off² our family allowance³ cheques," she had said, "if you don't go back to school."

From that moment Martha believed that her mother valued the money she received from the government over the well-being of her daughter.

Martha never mentioned Father Antoine to her mother again in the years she was away. After the death of her father, who had been the quiet but solid force keeping the peace in the family, a gulf⁴ opened between mother and daughter that grew more pronounced⁵ each time she returned home for the summers. When Martha entered the family cabin⁶ in late June 1972 carrying a bag filled with her possessions from the school, her mother sensed veiled⁷ hostility.

"So look who's finally made it home," she said, taking the initiative. "I guess we're going to have to find some way to get along. But I can't afford to feed you out of my welfare money and you better get down to the band office⁸ and apply for your own."

Annotations
¹ to **squeeze** /skwiːz/ = *drücken, quetschen*
² to **cut off** = *here: kürzen*
³ **allowance** = money sb receives regularly to pay for the things he/she needs
⁴ **gulf** /ɡʌlf/ = a gap between people that cannot be crossed easily
⁵ **pronounced** = clearly marked
⁶ **cabin** = small house
⁷ to **veil** /veɪl/ to hide sth
⁸ **band office** = administrative unit running the affairs of a First Nation people

Part B: Canadian identity | Workshop: **Practice**

When Martha responded in what she
40 remembered of her language, her mother laughed at her.

"You know even less Anishinaabemowin than you did last summer. You'd think you'd put a little effort into keeping your
45 language."

When Martha tried to help run the household, her mother was not impressed.

"What sort of person have you become, anyway! You come home spoiled by that
50 school, expecting to be fed the food of the white man. But people like me can't live without country food. You can't shoot a gun, set a net, light[9] a fire, chop[10] wood, clean[11] fish, cook bannock[12] or smoke[13] geese
55 – let alone make moosehide[14] moccasins and gloves. Why, when I was a girl, I could do these things before I was ten!"

Martha's mother was not alone in finding it hard to love a child from whom she had
60 become estranged after years of absence at residential school. Her remarks, however, confirmed her daughter's impression that she belonged neither among the whites nor among her own people.

65 As the months went by and her relations with her mother remained strained, Martha slipped into a depression. Lacking the energy to get out of bed in the mornings, she sat around doing nothing in the afternoons,
70 abandoned her efforts to learn how to fish and hunt, and no longer tried to help her mother with the cooking and cleaning. From time to time, for no obvious reason, she broke down in tears.

75 Her mother was appalled when her daughter turned to her for help.

"You're bringing shame on our family! You lie around all day letting your old mother do all the work and expect to be waited
80 on hand and foot[15]. In my day, Anishinabe people never got sick in the head. You're just lazy and spoiled. Pull yourself together and above all don't let the neighbours know what's wrong with you!"

85 But Martha's condition worsened and she was soon unable to sleep. Matters reached a crisis one night when she was, as usual, lying awake and rigid[16] in bed, her senses on high alert. A cold moonlight flooded in
90 through the open window, casting[17] sinister shadows against the walls, and the normal sounds of the northern community assumed a menacing[18] air[19]. Children running and playing behind her house were making
95 fun of her, the hoot[20] of an owl was a premonition[21] of death, and the distant howling of wolves was a direct threat. The dogs, responsible for protecting their human masters from wild animals, answered them
100 from backyards throughout the reserve with irresolute and fearful barking, as if to say, "If it's Martha you want, just come and get her. We won't stop you."

The wind in the black spruce[22] trees
105 whispered that she came from bad seed[23], from a flawed, inferior race, doomed to disappear and leave no mark[24] on history. It said the nuns had been right – she and her people were Stone Age accidents of
110 history who had been clothed in the skins of animals when the white man arrived, with no alphabet, no books, no music, no calendar, no domesticated animals[25], no cities and no monuments. It said the Native
115 gods were inferior to the white gods, had been vanquished[26] and would never return, leaving nature empty and forlorn[27]. It said she was weak, friendless and unwelcome in her mother's house, in her community
120 and in her country. It said she came from a place that no longer existed, was living a life that had no purpose, and ultimately, she and her people would disappear from history without a trace.

Annotations
[9] to **light** = to make sth burn
[10] to **chop** /tʃɒp/ = to cut into small pieces
[11] to **clean** = here: ausnehmen
[12] **bannock** = small, flat kind of bread
[13] to **smoke** = *räuchern*
[14] **moosehide** = skin of a moose (i.e. a large kind of deer)
[15] to **wait on sb hand and foot** = to do everything for sb so that they needn't do anything themselves
[16] **rigid** = stiff, unable to move
[17] to **cast** /kɑːst/ = to throw
[18] **menacing** = threatening
[19] **air** = here: feeling, attitude
[20] **hoot** = sound an owl makes
[21] **premonition** = feeling that sth bad is going to happen
[22] **spruce** = Fichte
[23] **seed** /siːd/ = what you put into the ground in order to grow a plant
[24] to **leave a mark** = to make a lasting impression
[25] **domesticated animal** = animal that is kept to serve a specific purpose, e.g. give milk
[26] to **vanquish** = to defeat
[27] **forlorn** /fə(r)ˈlɔː(r)n/ = seeming lonely and sad

ANALYSIS: CHARACTERS

3 → SUPPORT D5, p. 297

Explain how and why Martha has changed when she returns home at 16 and how this affects her relationship to her mother.

→ **S12:** Checklist: Analysis – prose, p. 352

CREATING WRITING: REWRITING A SCENE FROM ANOTHER PERSPECTIVE

4 → SUPPORT D6, p. 297

Rewrite the scene in the first person from the point of view of Mary, Martha's mother. Take into account her character, her relationship with Martha and the type of language she is likely to use.

→ **S2:** Checklist: Creative writing, p. 331

Part B: Canadian identity

What it means to be Canadian

Webcode
You can find a link to the video here: WES-73644-010

→ **S20:** How to listen/watch effectively, p. 366

→ **S6:** How to write a discussion/comment, p. 338

1 Pair work

a) Watch the performance of a song about Canada and talk about your first impressions.
b) Watch the video again and note down what constitutes Canadian identity. Compare your notes and add any information you missed.
c) Discuss the intention of the two performers. What elements of the video suggest that the message should not be taken too seriously?

2

a) Now read the following article which also deals with Canadian identity. Note down information to answer the question posed in the headline.
b) Comment on Gord Downie's view that Canada is not actually a nation.
c) Discuss the problems and challenges facing Canada in the future.

Canada 150: What does it mean to be Canadian today?

Gavin Hewitt, 30 June 2017, BBC news

This week will see many full-throated[1] renditions[2] of "O Canada!"
The "Happy Canada Day"
5 signs are already planted in front yards and the country is preparing to celebrate a birthday on Saturday, 150 years after British and former French
10 colonies bonded together at confederation[3] to form the Dominion of Canada.
Hanging over the ceremonies is the question of identity – the great driver of so much of today's politics.
15 Canada, like other countries, poses the question of who we are and how we define ourselves in a churning[4] global world. Some say it is insecurity, the changing face of communities, which has been a
20 recruiter for so much of the recent anti-establishment politics and that the call to take back control of countries and borders reflects a broader unease.

Fault line[5]
25 The Canadian anniversary is gathering attention because Canada is increasingly saluted by some as a champion of liberal democracy.
The Canadian Prime Minister Justin
30 Trudeau has become a standard bearer[6] for internationalism in stark[7] contrast to the economic nationalism of Donald Trump. Canada finds itself astride[8] one of the great fault lines of modern politics.
35 Canadians are immensely proud of what has been carved out[9] of wilderness and a harsh climate, but they wear their identity lightly.
When asked "What defines a Canadian?",
40 they often answer with symbols: ice hockey, Tim Hortons coffee, wilderness, a canoe and portage[10], an array[11] of singers – but the list usually comes with an ironic smile.
45 Canadians often define themselves by what they are not: their neighbour to the

---

Annotations
[1] **full-throated** = spoken/sung loudly and with conviction
[2] **rendition** /renˈdɪʃ(ə)n/ = a way of performing e.g. a song
[3] **Confederation** = name given to the day the Dominion of Canada was established (1 July 1867)
[4] **to churn** = to move around quickly
[5] **fault line** /ˈfɔːltˌlaɪn/ = area where many earthquakes happen
[6] **standard bearer** = sb who leads a group of people with similar ideas
[7] **stark** /stɑː(r)k/ = extreme, clearly marked
[8] **astride** /əˈstraɪd/ = sitting as if on a horse
[9] **to carve out** = to develop sth through hard work
[10] **portage** = the practice of carrying a canoe
[11] **array** /əˈreɪ/ = a large group

south. There is an appetite for a more positively-defined Canadian identity, but for most of the time, many Canadians seem happy for it to remain largely undefined. Mr Trudeau has offered his own take[12] on what Canada is and how it is defined. "This is something," he said, "we are able to do in this country, because we define a Canadian not by a skin colour or a language or a religion or a background, but by a set of values, aspirations, hopes and dreams that not just Canadians but people and the world share."

Difficult past

Canada is perhaps one of the few countries in the world where welcoming refugees is regarded as patriotic.

But as the anniversary approaches, the past intrudes.

The lead singer of *The Tragically Hip*, often referred to as "Canada's band", has spoken of a country incomplete.

Gord Downie asked: "What is it about this country that is not a country?"

Canada, in his view, could not be a country until it had reconciled itself to the First Nations, the indigenous people.

As we celebrate doughnuts and ice hockey, he said, we are not actually a nation, we're a country that hasn't embraced its history. The scars[13] of the recent past still wound[14]: the 150,000 Inuit and Metis children who were removed from their communities between 1840 and 1996, and sent to residential schools in order to assimilate them.

Some of the First Nations want to be part of modern Canada, but many grieve for land and culture that they believe was stolen from them.

In recent years Canada has undergone immense change. Toronto is now one of the most multicultural cities in the world, although economic power still largely rests[15] with older Canadian families.

The British connection

For much of the time, the world ignores this country and the immensity of its wilderness. I emigrated to Canada in the 1980s. What I saw then – and it remains

true – is that for many people in the world the flag is a symbol of tolerance, of refuge, and of a civilised country.

As the country looks to the future, there is the issue of the British connection and the role of head of state. On the prairies of Saskatchewan or in the increasingly diverse city of Vancouver, Britain seems far away, a distant relative.

There is speculation as to what will happen when Prince Charles inherits the throne. Will Canada welcome him as its head of state?

The younger Royals have been attentive to Canada, but polls suggest Canadians will eventually vote for change.

However, changing the head of state does not seem to be an immediate priority. Indeed, many Canadians are wary of opening up the issue of identity.

Defining how a Canadian head of state was chosen or elected would be hugely sensitive, not least to the French-speaking Quebecois, who held two referendums on independence in 1980 and 1995. The majority for staying in Canada in the latter[16] vote was wafer-thin[17].

Annotations

[12] **take** = *here:* attitude, opinion
[13] **scar** = a permanent mark on the skin after a wound has healed
[14] to **wound** /wuːnd/ = *here:* to hurt
[15] to **rest** = *here:* to remain
[16] **the latter** = the second one
[17] **wafer-thin** = very thin

1 Advanced texts | Part B: Canadian identity

Gender identity

Webcode
You can find a link to the video here:
WES-73644-011

→ **S20:** How to listen/watch effectively, p. 366

Annotations
1. **exalted** = having an important position
2. **shrewd** /ʃruːd/ = clever in practical terms
3. **bon vivant** = sb who enjoys eating well, drinking good wine etc.
4. to **simmer** /ˈsɪmə/ = to cook slowly
5. to **light out** = to leave in a hurry

→ **S1:** Checklist: Summary, p. 330

1
a) Watch the video clip of Canadian singer-songwriter k.d. lang, who has openly lived as a lesbian since 1992, receiving a music award. Identify what makes Canada special according to her.
b) Now read this introduction to Kim Fu's novel *For today I am a boy* and say how its theme relates to k.d. lang's speech.

At birth, Peter Huang is given the Chinese name Juan Chaun, "powerful king". To his parents, newly settled in small-town Ontario, he is the exalted[1] only son in a sea of daughters, the one who will finally fulfill his immigrant father's dreams of Western masculinity.
Peter and his sisters – elegant Adele, shrewd[2] Helen, and Bonnie the bon vivant[3] – grow up in an airless house of order and obligation, though secrets and half-truths simmer[4] beneath the surface. At the first opportunity, each of the girls lights out[5] on her own, scattering to Montreal, California, and Berlin. But for Peter, escape is not as simple as fleeing his parents' home. Though his father crowned him "powerful king", Peter knows otherwise. He knows he is really a girl.

2
a) Read the first extract from the novel and summarize what happens to Peter.
b) Analyse Peter's feelings about himself.

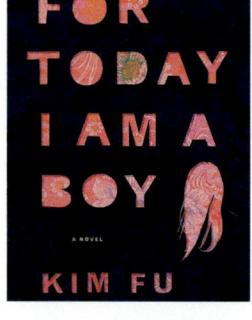

For today I am a boy
by Kim Fu

Extract 1

Annotations
1. **Village des Valeurs** = chain of second-hand clothing shops
2. **gown** = long dress for special occasions
3. to **clean out** = sold out
4. **bouffant** /ˈbuːfɒ̃/ = aufgebauscht
5. **bare-faced** = without make-up
6. **heels** = here: high heels
7. **constraint** = here: tightness
8. **sausage casing** = the outside of a sausage that contains the meat
9. **train** = long part at the back of a dress
10. **Audrey** = reference to actress Audrey Hepburn (1929–1993)
11. **drawn** = thin and tired-looking

The day of the party, Eileen led us through the Village des Valeurs[1]. She ran her hand along the dress rack without looking, seeking out satin by feel. She picked a violet
5 strapless gown[2] and a fake pearl necklace, four rows deep. We went to a costume store that was nearly cleaned out[3], but John found a brown wig in a high bouffant[4], a twenty-five-cent tiara to slip into it, opera gloves,
10 and a long-stemmed cigarette holder.
We got dressed at their apartment. They had to explain to me that Eileen was supposed to be Michael Jackson and John was supposed to be Justin Timberlake, as their costumes
15 were a lot less elaborate than mine. Eileen just had a white suit jacket and John dressed the way he always did, in a hoodie and his red skate shoes.
Eileen did my makeup first. She wouldn't
20 let me look in the mirror while she worked. "For effect," she said. I'd never seen her anything other than bare-faced[5]. She curled my eyelashes, filled in my eyebrows with a pencil, and applied mascara, blue-gray eye
25 shadow, and maroon lipstick. She zipped the dress as far as she could up my back, then closed the top with a series of safety pins. John arranged the wig and tiara on my head. I put on my gloves and necklace.
30 I borrowed some clunky, too-big shoes of Eileen's. I didn't tell them I already had my own collection of heels[6].
I almost didn't want to look. Nothing would be as good as how it felt: the sweet
35 constraint[7] around my hips from the dress, tight as a sausage casing[8], squeezing joy into my skull, making it swell. The satin on my hands, my spidery eyelashes, the weight of the hair and the jewelry. I loved the sound of
40 the gown's train[9] swishing behind me. It felt like something restored: a tail cut off and regrown.
They held each one of my arms and guided me to the full-length mirror in their bedroom.
45 There she stood, at last: the iconic Audrey[10], only with Adele's almond eyes, her sloping cheekbones. The face a little more drawn[11], a little harder, but undeniably her.
"Let's take this on the road," John said.
50 I panicked at the threshold, after Eileen had

42

Part B: Canadian identity — **Advanced texts**

already opened the door. "I can't go outside."
"Why not?" John said. Eileen went to the kitchen.
I thought about walking on the street, riding
55 the Métro. I shook my head.
"It's Halloween," John insisted. "Everybody's dressed up." I kept shaking my head. I was trembling, the outside world blowing in, so close I could trip and tumble into it.

60 Eileen reappeared with a water bottle of what looked like orange juice. She held my head and brought the bottle to my mouth as though coaxing a baby to drink. The alcohol stung my nostrils. "Drink," she said.
65 I pulled away. "I don't like –"
"This is exactly why God invented vodka," Eileen said.
I stared down into the bottle. "You look beautiful," John said.

Annotations
[12] to **trip** = to stumble, nearly fall
[13] to **tumble** /ˈtʌmb(ə)l/ = to fall to the ground
[14] to **coax** sb to do sth /ˌkəʊks ˌsʌmbədi tə ˈduː, ˌsʌmθɪŋ/ = to persuade sb to do sth
[15] to **sting** /stɪŋ/ = to bite like an insect
[16] **nostril** /ˈnɒstrəl/ = hole in your nose

3
Peter, John, Eileen and a few friends go to a Halloween party, Peter dressed as a woman for the first time in public. On their way to the party, they are insulted by two young men but their group of ten outnumbers them and Eileen courageously stands her ground. At first, Peter is afraid but at the party he feels at ease as a woman. The next day, John visits Peter in the restaurant, where he works as a cook, and shows him a newspaper article. A cross-dresser known as Dana, who was alone on the streets, was attacked and murdered. John asks Peter to come to a vigil he has organized for the murdered woman. Peter refuses.

a) Read the second extract and outline what happens.
b) Analyse Peter's motives for his change of heart.

→ **S12:** Checklist: Analysis – prose, p. 352

Extract 2
John continued to stand there, arms hanging down. The knife skidded so much I lost my grip and had to pick it up again. "It could've been you," he said finally.
5 "No," I said, chopping bluntly[1], breaking more than slicing the lettuce, "it couldn't. I've worked my whole life so that it couldn't be me." White flash of a face. Where did they go, these boys, after they left us behind?
10 "Last night," John began. He paused, still looking wounded. "You were so happy."
I gathered the lettuce into a bin and held it against my stomach like a barrier. "If it had been me, it would've been your fault."
15 John reeled[2] as though I'd struck[3] him. "You're a coward," he said. "You've worked your whole life because you're a coward."
"What do you know? What do you know about anything?" His family moved for him.
20 The hormones. The surgery he was allowed to accept or reject. I waved my arm around the kitchen, at the stunned cooks watching us. "Nobody has to know about you! You can blend in whenever you want!"
25 "You honestly believe that? You think my life's been easy?"
"Yes, I think it's been fucking easy!" I screamed. "They don't know! I didn't know! I wish I still didn't know!"

30 I tried to shove past him. He touched my back. I remembered Humphrey Bogart's hand[4], I remembered dancing, I remembered the gown twirling, I remembered the boy who complimented my ass, I remembered
35 being told I was beautiful. I remembered the woman staring back at me in the Métro windows, her wink.[5] I tried to pull away. John embraced me with my arms pinned to my sides, the lettuce bin between us, its raw,
40 wet smell pushed toward our faces.
In full view of the entire kitchen, he kissed me. A kiss that made me think of the woefully[6] few people I had kissed in my life. A kiss that reminded me I had never been
45 loved. A kiss that said I could not be John unless I risked being Dana.

My bedside clock rolled past eight. Somewhere, Dana on the cross[7]. I remembered
50 something Claire said, in a vulnerable moment, her blond hair against my mouth: "Even Jesus didn't want to be Jesus. He cried out at the last minute." I missed her, and Margie, and Chef, and Ollie, and Bonnie
55 and Adele and Helen – the comfort of being only partly understood. Eileen and John saw straight through me, past me, like a hole had been bored through my chest.

Annotations
[1] **bluntly** = without thinking
[2] to **reel** = to move backwards quickly
[3] to **strike** sb /straɪk/ = to hit sb
[4] **Humphrey Bogart's hand** = During the Halloween party, John danced with Peter, who was dressed up as Audrey Hepburn and imagined John to be actor Humphrey Bogart in a scene from the movie *Sabrina* (1954), in which Hepburn and Bogart starred.
[5] On the way to the party, Peter looks at himself in the subway window and winks so that his reflection winks back at him.
[6] **woeful** /ˈwəʊf(ə)l/ = sad, regretful
[7] **cross** /krɒs/ = Kreuz

Advanced texts — Part B: Canadian identity

Annotations
[8] **paralyzed** /ˈpærəlaɪzd/ = unable to move
[9] to **tuck** /tʌk/ = to put sth below/behind/into sth else
[10] **down** = feather used as a filling material to make warm clothes
[11] **riddled with punctures** = full of small holes
[12] to **rush** /rʌʃ/ = to move quickly
[13] **barren** /ˈbærən/ = dry and empty
[14] **plea for** /ˈpliː fɔː/ = a request
[15] **chill** /tʃɪl/ = cold, icy feeling

I tried to imagine eight people watching. Their shadows in the box lights of a deserted parking lot. Their impassive faces. Stepping back as I bled on the ground and reached for them.

I found the newspaper in my bag. John had stuffed it inside before I left. In the second picture, Dana was laughing, looking right into the camera. Who took this picture? Ten of them and one of her. Ten of us and two of them.

Teenage Daniel had dark circles under his eyes. He seemed caught by the camera, paralyzed[8] by worry. I folded the newspaper over, tucking[9] his picture underneath. Dana continued to laugh.

I dug through the kitchen drawer until I found the scissors. I cut both parts of the story out of the paper and sealed them into an envelope. Addressed it, stamped it, tucked it into the inner pocket of my winter coat, my down parka[10] riddled with punctures[11]. It left a trail of feathers. The empty fabric sagged but still kept out the wind.

The postcard would come weeks later, signed by both Bonnie and Adele. A vintage oil painting with GERMANY! across the top – a church on the far background, futuristic neon in the foreground, boxy cars rushing[12] in between. A phone number, an e-mail address, and these words: *Come to Berlin, sister*.

I watched them from far away, in a small crowd gathered across the street. A few police cars stood between us and the field of candles, under a barren[13], starless sky. Thin paper skirts between their fists and the dripping wax, their faces wrapped in hoods and scarves and lit from below. A prayer, a plea[14] for witnesses, a song. Silence. Silence settled in like a chill[15].

I waited as they blew out the lights, as the onlookers around me left and the shadows on the field spread out. Two of them walked toward me, stopped short.

"You came," John said.

4 Across cultures

Comment on k.d. lang's statement that "only in Canada could there be such a freak as k.d. lang receiving this award".

→ S6: How to write a discussion/comment, p. 338

Language issues

1
Look at the following map and explain it briefly.

Part B: Canadian identity — **Advanced texts**

2 DVD/03

a) Watch a video in which immigrant and Anglophone students explain what life is like under Quebec's Bill 101, which defines French, the language of the majority of the inhabitants, as the official language.
b) Watch the video again and note down the advantages and disadvantages of the Bill.

Webcode
You can find the video here:
WES-73644-012

→ **S20:** How to listen/ watch effectively, p. 366

3

a) Look at the title of this poem. Speculate on its theme.
b) Read the poem and say whether your speculations were correct.
c) Examine whose point of view it is written from.
d) Explain the message of the last two lines of the poem.

→ **S10:** How to work with poetry, p. 347

Referendum[1]

Of course, you want your country
to be one long season[2],
when snow hides the dark mud,
when nothing moves and nothing grows,
5 when the white sky and white land agree
to dissolve the horizon *à la lointaine*[3], and one
can judge no distances.
The treachery[4] of spring, when the land
changes colours, the leaves[5] are turncoats[6],
10 and the rippling[7] fields
are stripped of[8] their sheets
and wait to be stained with seed.
You are waiting for another winter,
when the *fleur-de-lys*[9] white petals
15 will cover the earth in a garden of snow,
the cold air will remain cloudless,
free of the visible breath of spoken h's[10],
and your swallowed aspirations
will take root[11] in your body and grow
20 out of your mouth, watered[12] by a clean tongue.
Ton pays est une frontière
ineffaceable, une cicatrice dans la terre,
dont la terre ne se gêne pas
parce qu'elle est portée
25 *sous un manteau de castor, sous une ceinture*
flechée[13].
Here, what have I proven? All depends
on where you're coming from.
My country is not your country of snow.
30 *Mon pays, ce n'est pas un pays, c'est ma peau*[14].

Sonnet L'Abbé

> **Info**
>
> **Sonnet L'Abbé,** born in 1973, is a Canadian poet and academic. She is of Franco-Canadian and Guyanese descent.

Annotations
[1] In 1995, the population of Quebec voted against independence from Canada in a referendum. However, it was a very close 50.6% opposed to against 49.4% in favour of independence. This was the second referendum on this issue after 1980.
[2] reference to the famous song Mon pays ("my country") by Quebecois poet and song-writer Gilles Vigneault, which starts like this:
Mon pays ce n'est pas un pays, c'est l'hiver
Mon jardin ce n'est pas un jardin, c'est la plaine
Mon chemin ce n'est pas un chemin, c'est la neige ("My country is not a country, it is the winter; my garden is not a garden, it is the plain; my road is not a road, it is the snow").
[3] **à la lointaine** = "in the distance"
[4] **treachery** /ˈtretʃəri/= *Verrat*
[5] **leaf** /liːf/= one of the green bits in a tree
[6] **turncoat** /ˈtɜː(r)n,kəʊt/= sb who changes sides in a conflict
[7] to **ripple** /ˈrɪp(ə)l/= to make a wave
[8] to **be stripped of** sth = to have sth taken away from you
[9] **fleur-de-lys** = the provincial flower of Quebec
[10] **spoken h's** = one mark of an anglophone
[11] to **take root** = *Wurzeln schlagen*
[12] to **water** = to give water to a plant
[13] **Ton pays est …** = "Your country is a border which cannot be obliterated, a scar on the earth which it is not ashamed of because it wears it beneath a beaver pelt and an arrowed belt."
[14] **Mon pays, …** = "My country, it is not a country, it is my skin."

4

Using the material in this section, write a speech you would give in a debate on the following motion: "In order to guarantee the dominance of the French language in Quebec, the Bill 101 must be enforced rigorously." Choose either to support or oppose the motion.
→ **S5:** Checklist: Writing a speech, p. 337

2 Science and technology

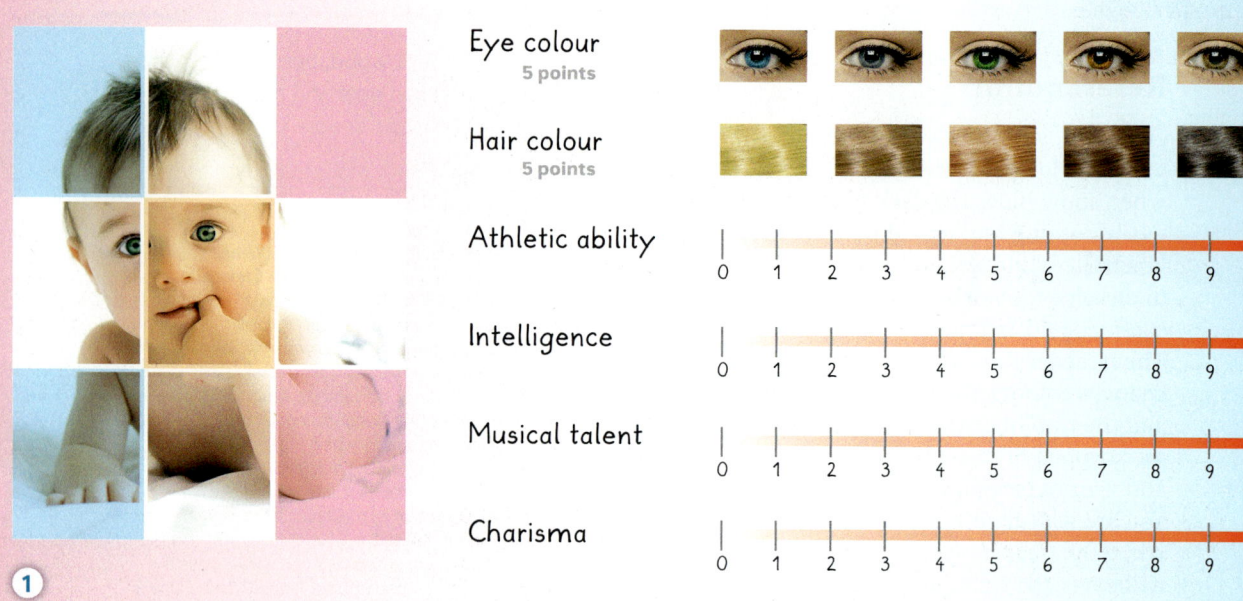

①

1 Pair work

Imagine it is the year 2040. You are about to become parents and it has become common practice to design children with the help of "Build-a-baby". Which of your baby's features would you like to influence? You can decide on your child's eye and hair colour or leave it to chance. Moreover, you can determine how much athletic ability, intelligence etc. your child will have. All in all, you cannot use more than 30 "points".

2

Reflect on the decisions you had to make in the role of a parent in task 1. Which decisions (if any) were easy? Which were difficult? Explain.

Webcode
You can download a word list for the Intro and the WordPool here: WES-73644-013

Info

Designer babies

If human embryos are genetically altered to produce certain traits that have been determined as "desirable" by the parent(s) or scientists, the resulting child is colloquially called a "designer baby". Different methods are used to produce such embryos: for example, genes of more than two parents can be combined this way. "Designer babies" are the subject of much debate for ethical, religious and medical reasons.

Science and technology — Intro 2

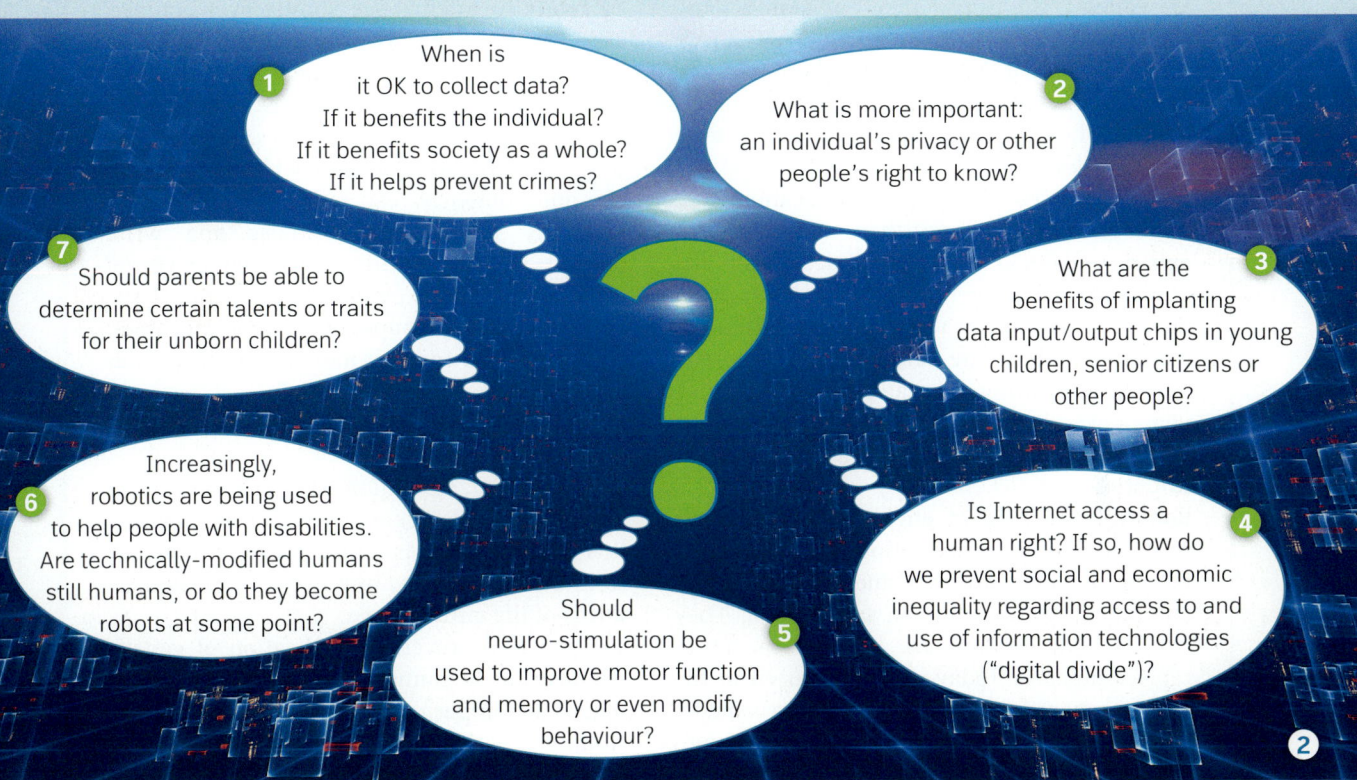

1. When is it OK to collect data? If it benefits the individual? If it benefits society as a whole? If it helps prevent crimes?
2. What is more important: an individual's privacy or other people's right to know?
3. What are the benefits of implanting data input/output chips in young children, senior citizens or other people?
4. Is Internet access a human right? If so, how do we prevent social and economic inequality regarding access to and use of information technologies ("digital divide")?
5. Should neuro-stimulation be used to improve motor function and memory or even modify behaviour?
6. Increasingly, robotics are being used to help people with disabilities. Are technically-modified humans still humans, or do they become robots at some point?
7. Should parents be able to determine certain talents or traits for their unborn children?

3

Many visions of the future, such as "designer babies", are becoming a reality. With these new possibilities, new contentious issues are being raised, too.
a) Read the questions above and determine the issues they address.
collection of data; …
b) **Pair work** Compare your results, then list other issues that you associate with new technologies and scientific advancements.
c) Look at the questions in the illustration again and note down any ideas you already have in order to answer them.
d) **Pair work** Talk about your ideas. On a separate sheet of paper, note down the unanswered questions from the illustration as well as any other open questions that come to mind regarding the ethics of new technologies and scientific advancements, such as "designer babies".

At the end of this Theme, you should have another look at your open questions. Decide whether working on the Theme has provided you with sufficient answers or whether there are still questions you would like to discuss in class.

Preview
Chances and risks
The first part of this Theme is about different technologies and their future possibilities and risks. In the **Workshop**, you will summarize complex texts and employ techniques to help you understand them better.

Literary visions of the future
The second part of the Theme is about visions of the future in literature and film. In the **Workshop**, you will analyse the language and atmosphere in extracts from a novel.

WordPool — Science and technology

VISIONS OF THE FUTURE

There are (and always have been) countless visions of what the future might bring. Simply put, if these predictions are positive, they are called UTOPIAS; if they envision a dark, threatening future, they are called DYSTOPIAS. The term "utopia" was coined by Thomas More in his 16th-century work of the same name, in which he depicts an ideal society. The term derives from the two Greek words for "not" and "place", thus describing a place that cannot (yet) be found in reality. Since then, many fictional and non-fictional works have dealt with the question of what the future may hold. In many fields, the technological progress made leads to discussions about the consequences this may have in the future. The categories below give you an overview of some of these debates.

Robotics

Robotics is a field of engineering that deals with designing, constructing and operating robots. Robots are machines that operate autonomously from human supervision. They can be built for any use and are meant to replace humans. Today robots are used in the main for manufacturing, by the military and by scientists. They can take on any form, though in fictional works, they often resemble humans. These kinds of robots are called "androids".

In 1942, author Isaac Asimov came up with three laws of robotics, which are still valid:
1. Robots must never harm human beings.
2. Robots must follow instructions from humans without violating rule 1.
3. Robots must protect themselves without violating the other rules.

Cyborgs

The term "cyborg" is short for "cybernetic organism" and describes a being with both natural, organic as well as mechanical body parts. It is not the same as a robot or android, as the term describes a being that has had their natural functions either restored or enhanced (or both) by some sort of technology or artificial body part. There is no universal agreement as to what makes a human a cyborg. Some argue that any artificial component, for example a hearing aid, is enough, while others believe that more visible and/or more extreme human-machine-combinations are necessary to constitute a cyborg.

Artificial Intelligence (AI)

AI refers to intelligence shown by machines, as opposed to natural intelligence found in humans and other beings. Many tasks originally thought to be beyond the abilities of AI have by now been completed by machines. For instance, they can play strategic games like chess, drive cars autonomously, read, talk and even simulate creativity (e.g. compose music and write poems). The use of AI is a highly controversial topic and many experts warn about the potential risks of super-intelligent machines. Others wish to conduct more research in order to fully embrace their potential.

Genetic engineering

The direct manipulation of genes within an organism is called genetic engineering. During this process, DNA is either added or removed from the organism to improve it or create new forms of life entirely.

The most controversial application of genetic engineering is human cloning, which critics regard as tampering with nature. Therapeutic cloning, i.e. the reproduction of human cells or tissue to use in transplants, however, is already widely recognized as a helpful technology. Reproductive cloning, meaning the reproduction of entire human beings, on the other hand, is currently banned in many countries. There are no (known) human clones, but a breakthrough has been achieved in the field in 2018 when the first primates were successfully cloned.

Virtual realities

Virtual reality (VR) is a form of experience or scenario generated by a computer. VRs can be experienced through devices like glasses, goggles or headphones, and can be fantastical or realistic in nature. The devices for today's VRs are designed to create images and sounds, haptic or other sensations in order to make a user believe they are in another environment. Users may look and move around in this "world" or even interact within the virtual scenario. In these cases, avatars (graphic representations) are often used as the users' virtual personalities.

Science and technology — WordPool

1

a) Complete the collocations:

> to achieve | to coin | to create | to do | to embrace | to have | to make | to tamper with

> research | progress | a breakthrough | consequences | nature | a sensation | a term | a potential

b) Write down five sentences about what you think the future of science and technology will bring, using collocations from a).

c) **Pair work** Read your partner's sentences and say if you agree with the predictions.

→ **S24:** How to give feedback/peer-edit, p. 372

2

Watch the trailer for dystopian TV series *The Rain*. Explain what leads to a dystopian society in this case, do some research into this genre of dystopian fiction and write a short text about it that could be added to the text on page 48.

Webcode
You can find a link to the video here:
WES-73644-014

3 Language awareness

a) The future of science and technology is a highly controversial topic. To make their position known, people may choose to use positively or negatively connotated words to talk about advanced technologies, for example. Copy the grid on the right and fill in the words below that are taken from the text.

> natural | artificial | risk | potential | to improve | to create | helpful | to ban | breakthrough

positive	negative
…	…

b) Among the words you have sorted into the grid, there are two sets of antonyms. Identify them and come up with antonyms for the other words.

c) Look at the words highlighted in the text on the left. The words below describe the same or a very similar concept. Match them to the highlighted words and fill them into a grid with three columns. The first one has been done for you. In some cases, there may be three words which belong together.

positive	negative	neutral
progress	…	development
…	…	…

> development | to modify | extensive | comprehension | to change | uncontrolled | to command | function | to manipulate | advanced | to reproduce | surveillance | modification | to preserve | contentious | to utilize

d) Discuss your results in class.

4

Use the terms "utopia" and "dystopia" as well as at least ten other words from tasks 1 to 3 to explain the quotation below. Make sure your explanation contains some examples.

> If we don't change direction soon,
> we'll end up where we're going.
> *Irwin Corey*

Workshop: Step by step   **Part A:** Chances and risks

Webcode
You can download a word list for Part A here:
WES-73644-015

Webcode
You can find a link to the audio file here:
WES-73644-016

→ **S20:** How to listen/watch effectively, p. 366

Step by step Understanding and summarizing texts

PRE-READING

1 ⊙ CD/05

Listen to a radio programme about computers that can write poetry.
a) Explain why, according to the scientist who is interviewed in the programme, people try to teach computers to write poetry.
b) Try to determine which poem (A or B) was created by a human being and which one was written by a computer. Examining the poems with the help of these categories might give you clues:
- theme(s)
- imagery
- rhyme
- metre
- rhythm
- message

c) **Pair work** Go to p. 392 to check whether you were correct. Then talk about what surprised and what impressed you about the two poems.

A
Create an endless voting paradox
until another day of constant leaving
becomes a tiny little music box[1]
and our ideas have become misleading.
5 The people know exactly where or whether.
Remember me without an honest word.
The very moment we belong together –
another simple story so absurd.
I take a message from a repetition
10 and never ever follow my regards
or not forget the secret definition
or come together like a house of cards.
And I consider you a friend of mine.
Think about the other equals sign.

B
Adjust my aperture[2] towards the deep sky.
Behold[3] the gems of heaven on this world.
Pray my gaze will not be sullied[4]
by the light from the strip and the street malls and
5 suburbs.
Discover in the glass the Pleiades[5], those sisters.
Seven sapphires in the dark glow pretty,
keen with visibility, the celestial[6] beings who guide
my heart.
10 But through the other micro lens
I see an eye for science,
an iris clear-blue,
more stirring than the Whirlpool Galaxy[7],
much brighter than the craters of the moon.
15 Which lens could I look through for a longer time,
observing each vast creation sublime.

Annotations
[1] **music box** = *Spieldose*
[2] **aperture** /ˈæpə(r)tʃə(r)/ = opening, especially at the front of a camera that lets light in
[3] to **behold** *(old-fashioned)* = to see
[4] to **sully** /ˈsʌli/ = to get sth dirty
[5] **Pleiades** = a number of stars in our galaxy that form a cluster
[6] **celestial** = referring to the sky
[7] **Whirlpool Galaxy** = a galaxy at a distance of probably 28 million light years from our galaxy

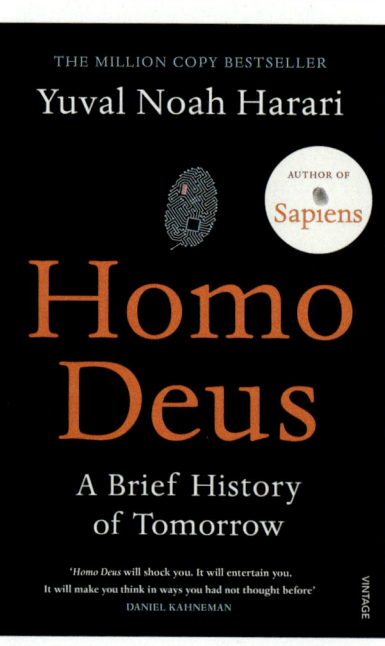

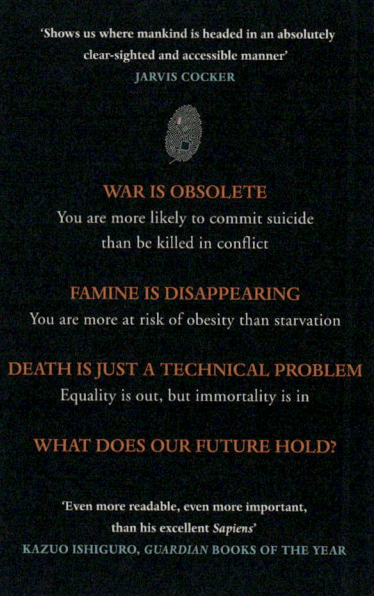

2

Israeli historian Yuval Noah Harari published the non-fiction book *Homo Deus* in 2015.
Look at the front and back covers of the English translation and speculate on the book's content.

Part A: Chances and risks — Workshop: Step by step 2

3
a) **Pair work** Read the extract from a review of Harari's book. Examine whether your speculations were correct and discuss your results with a partner.
b) Discuss Harari's visions in class.

In this gripping tour de force[1], Harari declares that we are no longer at the mercy of disease, famine and war. These ancient enemies of mankind have, if not disappeared, then at least become manageable – for the first time in history. The author points out that "more people die today from eating too much than from eating too little; more people die from old age
5 than from infectious diseases; and more people commit suicide than are killed by soldiers, terrorists and criminals combined." Instead of the age-old struggle to survive, mankind's new quest[2] will be to prolong human lifespan, enhance human cognition and upgrade human physical constitution well beyond biological norms.

At a first glance, this bodes well[3] for mankind. But Harari envisages something far more
10 troubling. As technology becomes more advanced, machines and algorithms will replace humans in the workforce. People left without work will seek refuge in various forms of escapism[4]. With these "useless masses" absorbed in specially designed virtual realities, the elite classes will direct the course of evolution in their own interests, most likely going so far as to altering their own DNA and mechanizing their bodies.
15 Harari even forecasts the eventual evolution of Homo sapiens into a very different organism, which he refers to as Homo deus. Comparing themselves to this new biological elite, the rest of mankind will be left feeling hopelessly outdated.

Annotations
[1] **tour de force** = an impressive achievement or display of skill
[2] **quest** = a difficult task or search
[3] to **bode well** = to look good
[4] **escapism** = sth pleasant that helps you forget about the real world

---

Preview

In this Workshop, you will focus on understanding and summarizing challenging non-fiction texts. You will employ different techniques to understand these texts better and learn how to sum up the content of a text.

READING STRATEGIES: UNDERSTANDING THE TEXT

When summarizing a text, you create a short version of the text intended to inform somebody of its essence. In order to prepare a summary of a rather complex text like the one below, it is important that you read and understand the text thoroughly. Tasks 4 and 5 will focus on strategies that can help you to understand the texts that you are reading better.

4 Asking questions
Read the first part of an extract from *Homo Deus* on the next page.
a) Form questions about the topic introduced in the extract. These questions should focus on
  1. what information you are given in the text,
  2. what additional information you need to know in order to fully understand the text.
  Copy the grid and find two more questions for each category.

What is the content?	What remains unclear?
Who possesses economic power today?	What exactly are algorithms?
…	…

b) **Pair work** Swap questions with a partner and try to answer all of his or her questions. If necessary, research the things that remain unclear.
c) **Pair work** Talk to your partner about his or her questions and your answers.

5 **Making a diagram**

Read the second part of the extract. Use diagrams to present the content visually. You can follow these examples for the development of the realization that art is not "safe" from AI (1) and for the controversy between David Cope and some classical music enthusiasts (2). Or you can make your own diagrams.

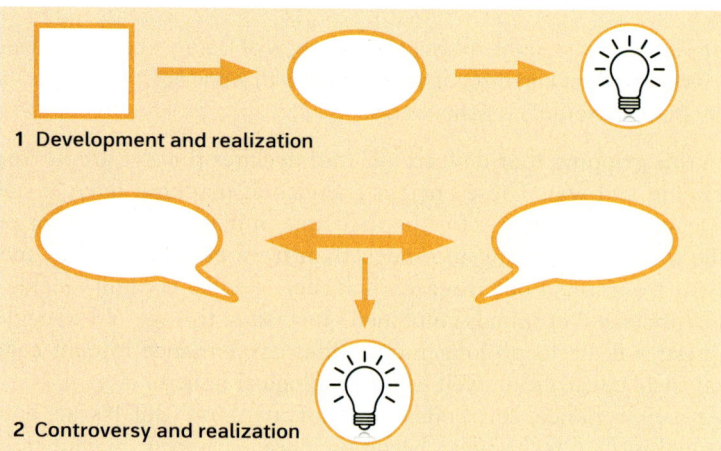

1 Development and realization

2 Controversy and realization

Homo Deus
by Yuval Noah Harari

1 As algorithms push humans out of the job market, wealth and power might become concentrated in the hands of the tiny elite that owns the all-powerful
5 algorithms, creating unprecedented social and political inequality. Today millions of taxi drivers, bus drivers and truck drivers have significant economic and political clout[1], each commanding a tiny share of
10 the transportation market. If their collective interests are threatened, they can unionise, go on strike, stage boycotts and create powerful voting blocks. However, once millions of human drivers are replaced by a
15 single algorithm, all that wealth and power will be cornered by the corporation that owns the algorithm, and by the handful of billionaires who own the corporation.

Alternatively, the algorithms might
20 themselves become the owners. Human law already recognizes intersubjective entities like corporations and nations as 'legal persons'. Though Toyota or Argentina has neither a body nor a mind, they are subject
25 to international law, they can own land and money, and they can sue and be sued in court. We might soon grant similar status to algorithms. An algorithm could then own a transportation empire or a venture-capital
30 fund[2] without having to obey the wishes of any human master.

If the algorithm makes the right decisions, it could accumulate a fortune, which it could then invest as it sees fit, perhaps buying
35 your house and becoming your landlord. If you infringe on the algorithm's legal rights – say, by not paying rent – the algorithm could hire lawyers and sue you in court. If such algorithms consistently outperform[3]
40 human capitalists, we might end up with an algorithmic upper class owning most of our planet. This may sound impossible, but before dismissing the idea, remember that most of our planet is already legally owned
45 by non-human intersubjective entities, namely nations and corporations. Indeed, 5,000 years ago much of Sumer was owned by imaginary gods such as Enki and Inanna. If gods can possess land and employ people,
50 why not algorithms?

2 So what will people do? Art is often said to provide us with our ultimate (and uniquely human) sanctuary[4]. In a world where computers have replaced doctors,
55 drivers, teachers and even landlords, would everyone become an artist? Yet it is hard to see why artistic creation would be safe from the algorithms. Why are we so confident that computers will never be able to outdo[3]
60 us in the composition of music? According to the life sciences, art is not the product of some enchanted[5] spirit or metaphysical soul, but rather of organic algorithms recognising mathematical patterns. If so, there is no
65 reason why non-organic algorithms couldn't master it.

David Cope is a musicology professor at the University of California in Santa Cruz. He is also one of the more controversial figures

---

Annotations
[1] **clout** /klaʊt/ = power
[2] **venture-capital fund** = *Wagniskapitalfonds*
[3] to **outperform/outdo** sb = to be better at sth than sb else
[4] **sanctuary** = a safe place
[5] **enchanted** = magical

| Part A: Chances and risks | Workshop: **Step by step** |

in the world of classical music. Cope has written computer programs that compose concertos, chorales, symphonies and operas. His first creation was named EMI (Experiments in Musical Intelligence), which specialised in imitating the style of Johann Sebastian Bach. It took seven years to create the program, but once the work was done EMI composed 5,000 chorales à la Bach in a single day. Cope arranged for a performance of a few select chorales at a music festival in Santa Cruz. Enthusiastic members of the audience praised the stirring performance, and explained excitedly how the music had touched their innermost being. They didn't know that it had been created by EMI rather than Bach, and when the truth was revealed some reacted with glum silence, while others shouted in anger.

EMI continued to improve and learned to imitate Beethoven, Chopin, Rachmaninov and Stravinsky. Cope got EMI a contract and its first album – Classical Music Composed by Computer – sold surprisingly well. Publicity brought increasing hostility from classical-music buffs[6]. Professor Steve Larson from the University of Oregon sent Cope a challenge for a musical showdown. Larson suggested that professional pianists play three pieces one after the other: one each by Bach, by EMI, and by Larson himself. The audience would then be asked to vote on who composed which piece. Larson was convinced that people would easily distinguish between soulful human compositions and the lifeless artefact of a machine. Cope accepted the challenge. On the appointed date hundreds of lecturers, students and music fans assembled in the University of Oregon's concert hall. At the end of the performance, a vote was taken. The result? The audience thought that EMI's piece was genuine Bach, that Bach's piece was composed by Larson, and that Larson's piece was composed by a computer.

Annotations
[6] **buff** = expert/fan

SUMMARIZING THE TEXT

6

Using your results from tasks 4 and 5, summarize the complete extract. Make sure your writing carefully considers the logic and structure of the text while also summarizing the content. Include all the important information that someone who has not actually read the text needs in order to understand the message of the text. → **SUPPORT** D1, p. 298

→ **S1:** Checklist: Summary, p. 330

Language support

Expressing sequence and adding points:
To introduce the topic, …
In this context, …
After this, the question whether …
To illustrate this point, …
As a result of / Due to / Because of / Since …
Consequently / Therefore / Thus …
Accordingly …
Following this / Subsequently / Finally …
Previously / Before this …
Simultaneously / Concurrently / Meanwhile …

Expressing contrast:
As a contrast, …
In contrast to this first point, …
Whereas / Although / Despite …
However / Nevertheless …

REFLECTION

7

Reflect on the strategies for reading and understanding texts that you used in tasks 4 and 5.
a) Explain which strategy or strategies you find helpful and why.
b) Name other strategies you know and use when dealing with complex texts.
c) **Group work** Talk about your ideas and create a list of useful reading techniques.

2 Workshop: Practice — Part A: Chances and risks

Practice Understanding and summarizing texts

Annotations
[1] **mammoth** = *here:* very big
[2] **Know thyself** = Know yourself (ancient Greek maxim)

1
a) Read a second extract from *Homo Deus*. Find a way to present its most important content visually. Focus on the contrast between the positive impact of massive databases such as Google and the potential dangers posed by such an extensive accumulation of data.

b) **Pair work** Compare your results and decide which version best captures the core problem the text deals with.

The Google Baseline Study is an even more ambitious project. Google intends to build a mammoth[1] database on human health, establishing the 'perfect health' profile.
5 Identifying even the smallest deviations from the baseline will hopefully make it possible to alert people to burgeoning health problems such as cancer when they can be nipped in the bud. The Baseline Study dovetails with an entire
10 line of products called Google Fit that will be incorporated into wearables such as clothes, bracelets, shoes and glasses, and will collect a never-ending stream of biometrical data. The idea is for Google Fit products to collect the
15 never-ending stream of biometrical data to feed the Baseline Study.
Yet companies such as Google want to go much deeper than wearables. The market for DNA testing is currently growing in leaps and bounds.
20 One of its leaders is 23andMe […] [P]ay 23andMe a mere $99, and they will send you a small package with a tube. You spit into the tube, seal it and mail it to Mountain View, California. There the DNA in your saliva is read, and you receive
25 the results online. You get a list of the potential health hazards you face, and your genetic predisposition to more than ninety traits and conditions ranging from baldness to blindness. 'Know thyself'[2] was never easier or cheaper.
30 Since it is all based on statistics, the size of the company's database is key to making accurate predictions. […]
If we connect all the dots, and if we give Google and its competitors free access to our biometric
35 devices, to our DNA scans and to our medical records, we will get an all-knowing medical health service that will not only fight epidemics, but will also shield us from cancer, heart attacks and Alzheimer's. Yet with such a database at its
40 disposal Google could do far more. Imagine a system that, in the words of the famous Police song, watches every breath you take, every move you make and every bond you break; a system that monitors your bank account and your heartbeat,
45 your sugar levels and your sexual escapades. […] Many of us would be happy to transfer much of our decision-making processes into the hands of such a system, or at least consult with it whenever we face important choices. Google will advise us
50 which movie to see, where to go on holiday, what to study in college, which job offer to accept, and even whom to date and marry. 'Listen, Google,' I will say, 'both John and Paul are courting me. I like both of them, but in different ways, and it's
55 so hard to make up my mind. Given everything you know, what do you advise me to do?'
And Google will answer: 'Well, I've known you from the day you were born. I have read all your emails, recorded all your phone calls, and know
60 your favourite films, your DNA and the entire biometric history of your heart. I have exact data about each date you went on […] And naturally, I know them as well as I know you. Based on all of this information, on my superb algorithms, and
65 on decades' worth of statistics about millions of relationships – I advise you to go with John, with an 87 per cent probability that you will be more satisfied with him in the long run.
'Indeed, I know you so well that I also know
70 you don't like this answer. Paul is much more handsome than John, and because you give external appearances too much weight, you secretly wanted me to say "Paul". […] My algorithms – which are based on the most up-
75 to-date studies and statistics – say that looks only have a 14 per cent impact on the long-term success of romantic relationships. So, even though I took Paul's looks into account, I still tell you that you would be better off with John.'
80 In exchange for such devoted counselling services, we will just have to give up the idea that humans are individuals, and that each human has a free will determining what's good, what's beautiful and what is the meaning of life.

2
Write a summary of the extract. Start with an introductory sentence that includes information on the core question or problem that the extract highlights.

→ **S1:** Checklist: Summary, p. 330

Driverless cars – debating an ethical dilemma

1
You are going to read an article titled "Why self-driving cars must be programmed to kill". Speculate on the problem(s) it might deal with.

2
Read the article below and outline the main problem in no more than 50 words.

3
In your own words, explain the illustration and the dilemma it illustrates.

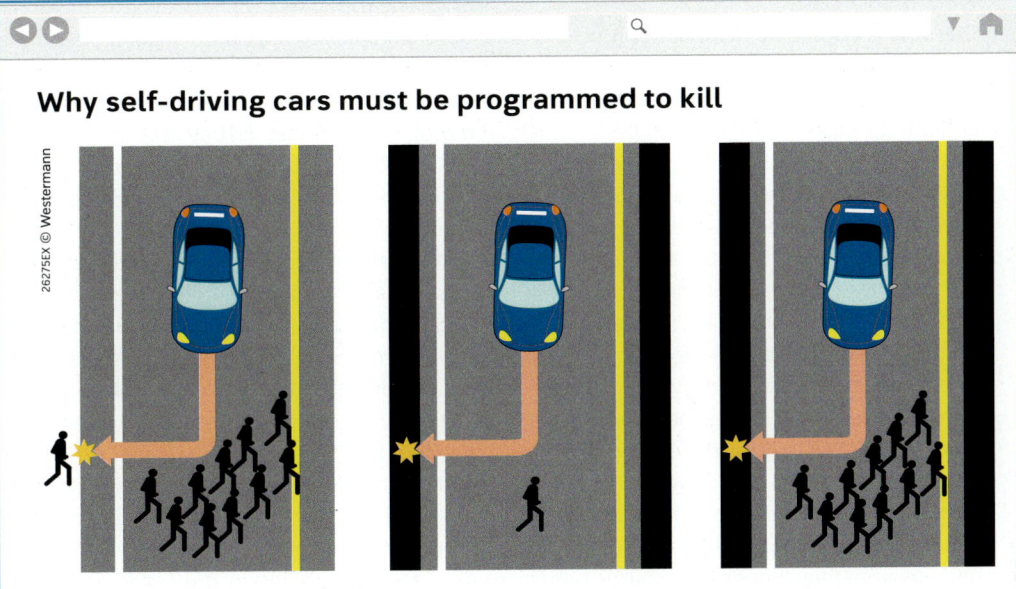

Why self-driving cars must be programmed to kill

22 October 2015

Self-driving cars are already cruising the streets. But before they can become widespread, carmakers must solve an impossible ethical dilemma of
5 **algorithmic morality.**

When it comes to automotive technology, self-driving cars are all the rage[1]. Standard features on many ordinary cars include intelligent cruise control[2], parallel parking
10 programs[3], and even automatic overtaking – features that allow you to sit back, albeit a little uneasily, and let a computer do the driving.
So it'll come as no surprise that many car
15 manufacturers are beginning to think about cars that take the driving out of your hands altogether. These cars will be safer, cleaner, and more fuel-efficient than their manual counterparts. And yet they can never be
20 perfectly safe.
And that raises some difficult issues.
How should the car be programmed to act in the event of an unavoidable accident? Should it minimize the loss of life, even
25 if it means sacrificing the occupants, or should it protect the occupants at all costs? Should it choose between these extremes at random?
The answers to these ethical questions
30 are important because they could have a big impact on the way self-driving cars are accepted in society. Who would buy a car programmed to sacrifice the owner?
So can science help? Today, we get an
35 answer of sorts thanks to the work of Jean-Francois Bonnefon at the Toulouse School of Economics in France and a couple of pals[4].
These guys say that even though there is no right or wrong answer to these questions,

Annotations
[1] **to be all the rage** = to be very fashionable
[2] **intelligent cruise control** = feature that maintains a speed and changes it if necessary
[3] **parallel parking program** = programme that parks a car automatically
[4] **pal** = friend

Part A: Chances and risks

public opinion will play a strong role in how, or even whether, self-driving cars become widely accepted. [...]

Here is the nature of the dilemma. Imagine that in the not-too-distant future, you own a self-driving car. One day, while you are driving along, an unfortunate set of events causes the car to head toward a crowd of 10 people crossing the road. It cannot stop in time but it can avoid killing 10 people by steering into a wall. However, this collision would kill you, the owner and occupant. What should it do?

One way to approach this kind of problem is to act in a way that minimizes the loss of life. By this way of thinking, killing one person is better than killing 10.

But that approach may have other consequences. If fewer people buy self-driving cars because they are programmed to sacrifice their owners, then more people are likely to die because ordinary cars are involved in so many more accidents. [...]

Bonnefon and co are seeking to find a way through this ethical dilemma by gauging public opinion. Their idea is that the public is much more likely to go along with a scenario that aligns with their own views.

So these guys posed these kinds of ethical dilemmas to several hundred workers [...] to find out what they thought. The participants were given scenarios in which one or more pedestrians could be saved if a car were to swerve[5] into a barrier, killing its occupant or a pedestrian.

At the same time, the researchers varied some of the details such as the actual number of pedestrians that could be saved, whether the driver or an on-board computer made the decision to swerve and whether the participants were asked to imagine themselves as the occupant or an anonymous person.

The results are interesting, if predictable. In general, people are comfortable with the idea that self-driving vehicles should be programmed to minimize the death toll. This utilitarian approach is certainly laudable but the participants were willing to go only so far. [...]

And therein lies the paradox. People are in favor of cars that sacrifice the occupant to save other lives – as long they don't have to drive one themselves.

Bonnefon and co are quick to point out that their work represents the first few steps into what is likely to be a fiendishly[6] complex moral maze. Other issues that will need to be factored into future thinking are the nature of uncertainty and the assignment of blame.

Bonnefon and co say these issues raise many important questions: "Is it acceptable for an autonomous vehicle to avoid a motorcycle by swerving into a wall, considering that the probability of survival is greater for the passenger of the car, than for the rider of the motorcycle? Should different decisions be made when children are on board, since they both have a longer time ahead of them than adults, and had less agency in being in the car in the first place? If a manufacturer offers different versions of its moral algorithm, and a buyer knowingly chose one of them, is the buyer to blame for the harmful consequences of the algorithm's decisions?"

These problems cannot be ignored, say the team: "As we are about to endow millions of vehicles with autonomy, taking algorithmic morality seriously has never been more urgent."

Annotations
[5] to **swerve** = to move out of the way
[6] **fiendishly** = extremely

→ **S22:** How to stage a debate, p. 370

4

Imagine you work at a company that, among other things, specializes in driverless, "intelligent" cars. You work as a programmer and your team has been trying to decide how to solve the dilemma of how driverless cars should react in a crisis, i.e. which algorithms to give them for a potentially fatal situation. Stage a debate on the motion: "Driverless cars should save their driver and passengers at all costs".

Part A: Chances and risks | Advanced texts

Artificial intelligence – friend or foe?

1

a) Read the quotation by British scientist I.J. Good and explain his reasoning in your own words.

> Let an ultraintelligent machine be defined as a machine that can far surpass all the intellectual activities of any man however clever. Since the design of the machines is one of these intellectual activities, an ultraintelligent machine could design even better machines; there would then unquestionably be an "intelligence explosion", and the intelligence of man would be left far behind. Thus the first ultraintelligent machine is the last invention that man need ever make, provided that the machine is docile enough to tell us how to keep it under control.

b) **Pair work** Talk to a partner to see whether you have come to the same conclusion about Good's warning.

c) Speculate whether the "last invention" Good mentions will be made during your lifetime.

2

Max Tegmark, a Swedish-born professor of physics at the *Massachusetts Institute of Technology* (MIT) and the president of the *Future of Life Institute*, published the non-fiction book *Life 3.0 – Being human in the age of Artificial Intelligence* in 2017. In the book, he explains likely and unlikely scenarios of a near future with AI, describes where different experts stand on the issue and raises the question of which kind of future we want and what we must do now to ensure it.
Read the following extract from Tegmark's book and outline the controversy about AI.

Life 3.0
by Max Tegmark

In summary, we can divide the development of life into three stages, distinguished by life's ability to design itself:
- Life 1.0 (biological stage):
5 evolves its hardware and software
- Life 2.0 (cultural stage): evolves its hardware, designs much of its software
- Life 3.0 (technological stage): designs its hardware and software

10 After 13.8 billion years of cosmic evolution, development has accelerated dramatically here on Earth: Life 1.0 arrived about 4 billion years ago, Life 2.0 (we humans) arrived about a hundred millennia ago, and many
15 AI researchers think that Life 3.0 may arrive during the coming century, perhaps even during our lifetime, spawned by progress in AI. What will happen, and what will this mean for us? [...]
20 This question is wonderfully controversial, with the world's leading AI researchers disagreeing passionately not only in their forecasts, but also in their emotional reactions, which range from confident
25 optimism to serious concern. They don't even have consensus on short-term questions about AI's economic, legal and military impact, and their disagreements grow when we expand the time horizon and
30 ask about artificial general intelligence (AGI) – especially about AGI reaching human level and beyond, enabling Life 3.0. General intelligence can accomplish virtually any goal, including learning, in contrast to, say,
35 the narrow intelligence of a chess-playing program.
Interestingly, the controversy about Life 3.0 centers around not one but two separate questions: when and what? When (if ever)
40 will it happen, and what will it mean for humanity? The way I see it, there are three distinct schools of thought that all need to be taken seriously, because they each include a number of world-leading experts.
45 As illustrated in figure 1.2, I think of them as digital utopians, techno-skeptics and members of the beneficial-AI movement, respectively. Please let me introduce you to some of their most eloquent champions.

Digital Utopians

[...] When I first met Larry Page at Google in 2008, he totally shattered these stereotypes. Casually dressed in jeans and a remarkably ordinary-looking shirt, he would have blended right in at an MIT picnic. [...] I struggled to remind myself that he might go down in history as the most influential human ever to have lived: my guess is that if superintelligent digital life engulfs our Universe in my lifetime, it will be because of Larry's decisions. [...] I view Larry as the most influential exponent of digital utopianism. He argued that if life is ever going to spread throughout our Galaxy and beyond, which he thought it should, then it would need to do so in digital form. His main concerns were that AI paranoia would delay the digital utopia and/or cause a military takeover of AI that would fall foul of[1] Google's "Don't be evil" slogan. [...]

Techno-skeptics

Another prominent group of thinkers aren't worried about AI either, but for a completely different reason: they think that building super-human AGI is so hard that it won't happen for hundreds of years, and therefore view it as silly to worry about it now. I think of this as the techno-skeptic position, eloquently articulated by Andrew Ng: "Fearing a rise of killer robots is like worrying about overpopulation on Mars." Andrew is the chief scientist at Baidu, China's Google, and he recently repeated this argument when I spoke with him at a conference in Boston. He also told me that he felt that worrying about AI risk was a potentially harmful distraction that could slow the progress of AI. [...] I find it interesting that although the digital utopians and the techno-skeptics agree that we shouldn't worry about AI, they agree on little else. Most of the utopians think human-level AGI might happen within the next twenty to a hundred years, which the techno-skeptics dismiss as uninformed pie-in-the-sky[2] dreaming, often deriding the prophesied singularity[3] as the "rapture of the geeks."[4] [...]

The Beneficial-AI Movement

In the spring of 2014, I'd founded a nonprofit organization called the Future of Life Institute (FLI; http://futureoflife.org) together with my wife, Meia, my physicist friend Anthony Aguirre, Harvard grad student Viktoriya Krakovna and Skype founder Jaan Tallinn. Our goal was simple: to help ensure that the future of life existed and would be as awesome as possible. Specifically, we felt that technology was giving life the power either to flourish like never before or to self-destruct, and we preferred the former. Our first meeting was a brainstorming session at our house on March 15, 2014, with about thirty students, professors and other thinkers from the Boston area. There was broad consensus that although we should pay attention to biotech, nuclear weapons and climate change, our first major goal should be to help make AI-safety research mainstream. [...] The next goal of our FLI beneficial-AI campaign was to bring the world's leading AI researchers to a conference where misunderstandings could be cleared up, consensus could be forged, and constructive plans could be made. [...]

The AI researchers were joined by top economists, legal scholars, tech leaders (including Elon Musk) and other thinkers [...]. The outcome surpassed even our most optimistic expectations. Perhaps it was a combination of the sunshine and the wine, or perhaps it was just that the time was right: despite the controversial topic, a remarkable consensus emerged, which we codified in an open letter that ended up getting signed by over eight thousand people, including a veritable who's who in AI. The gist of the letter was that the goal of AI should be redefined: the goal should be to create not undirected intelligence, but beneficial intelligence. The letter also mentioned a detailed list of research topics that the conference participants agreed would further this goal. The beneficial-AI movement had started going mainstream. We'll follow its subsequent progress later in the book.

Another important lesson from the conference was this: the questions raised by the success of AI aren't merely intellectually fascinating: they're also morally crucial, because our choices can potentially affect the

---

Annotations

[1] to **fall foul of** = to get into conflict with
[2] **pie-in-the-sky** = unrealistic
[3] **singularity** = *here*: reference to a theory which predicts the development of super-intelligent machines which can do anything humans can do
[4] **rapture of the geeks** = enthusiasm of the geeks; the Rapture as a biblical term also refers to the end of the world, so there is also the connotation that "singularity" will not happen before the world will end, i.e. never

entire future of life. The moral significance of humanity's past choices were sometimes great, but always limited: we've recovered even from the greatest plagues, and even the grandest empires eventually crumbled. Past generations knew that as surely as the Sun would rise tomorrow, so would tomorrow's humans, tackling perennial scourges[5] such as poverty, disease and war. But some of the Puerto Rico speakers argued that this time might be different: for the first time, they said, we might build technology powerful enough to permanently end these scourges – or to end humanity itself. We might create societies that flourish like never before, on Earth and perhaps beyond, or a Kafkaesque global surveillance state so powerful that it could never be toppled.

Annotations
[5] **scourge** /skɜː(r)dʒ/ = Geißel

3
Pair work Use your understanding of the debate around AI to explain one of the following figures to a partner. One of you should work on figure A, the other one on figure B. Use your own words.

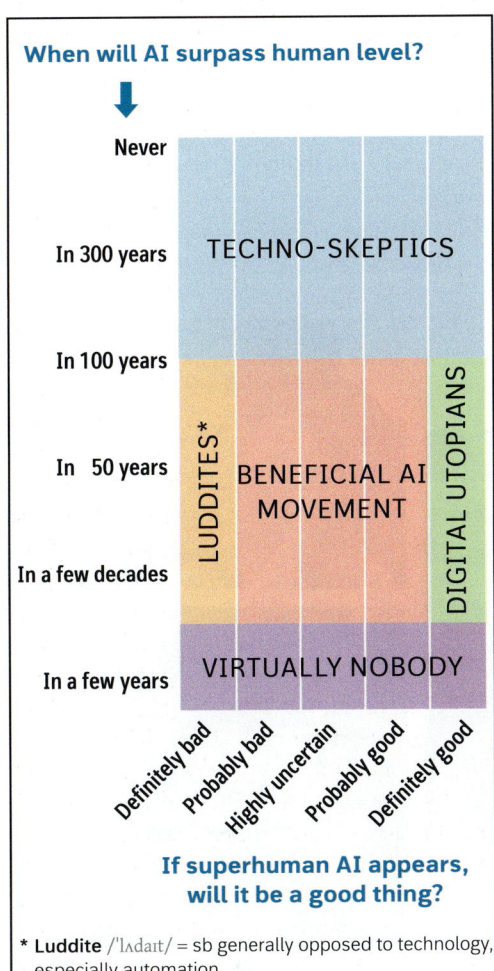

A

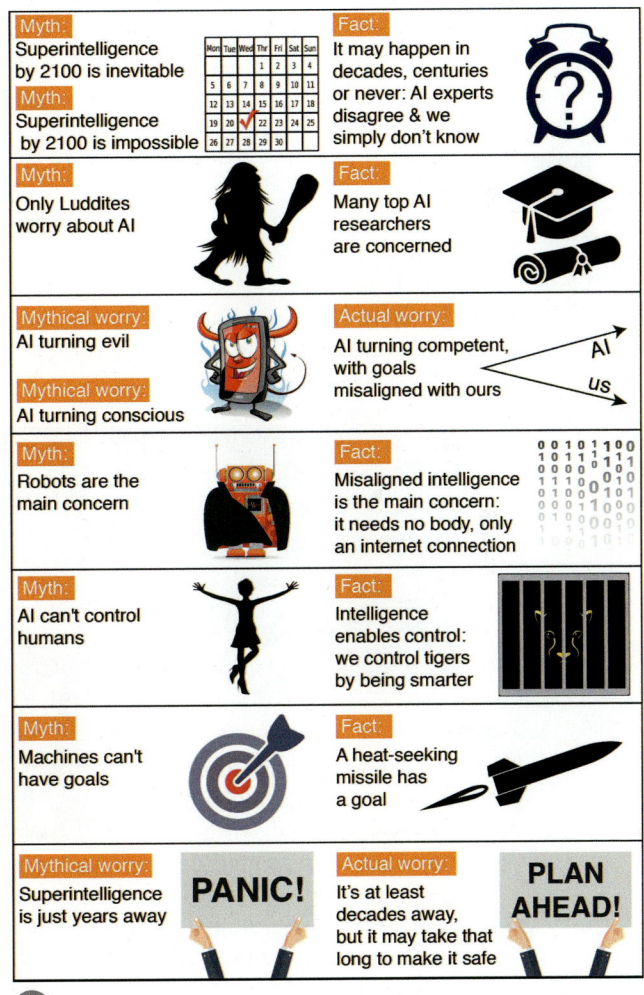

B

4
 Reconsider the groups outlined in figure A. Decide which group you would belong to.
 In class, justify why you share the views associated with that particular group.

Advanced texts — Part A: Chances and risks

Cyborgs – merging humans and machines

1

a) These two pages deal with "cyborgs". To be able to talk about this topic, you will need a specific kind of vocabulary. Look at the words and phrases below and match them with their definitions.

1. bionic
2. biohacking
3. body modification
4. (NFC) chip
5. augmentation
6. to enhance
7. application
8. sensory
9. miniaturization of technology
10. exoskeleton
11. prosthesis

A deliberate changes to the human body, e.g. tattoos, piercing, but also much more severe alterations
B to further improve
C process of creating technology that becomes smaller and smaller in size and is thus able to fit into veins, organs, etc.
D artificial body part, usually to replace a missing limb
E relating to the senses (smell, hearing, touch, sight, taste)
F (Near Field Communication) chip to enable transactions, e.g. payments, via chip technology that can be embedded in your credit card etc., but also inside the human body
G methods to change your own or other bodies with the help of technology or genetic modification
H having modified/electronic body parts
I a wearable, moveable machine, like a suit, that allows you to move with greater speed or strength
J putting something, especially scientific theories, to practical use
K process of increasing the value, size, amount, power etc. of something

→ **S15:** How to describe pictures, p. 358

b) Pair work Look at the pictures. Take turns to describe and explain the use of the devices you see. Use as many of the words from a) as possible.

2

a) Read the article on the next page and state how the author defines "cyborgs".

b) Pair work List advantages and disadvantages of "biohacking".

→ **S13:** Checklist: Analysis – non-fictional texts, p. 354

c) Examine the author's view – does she have a negative, positive or neutral view of "biohacking"? Give evidence from the article.

→ **S4:** Checklist: Letter to the editor, p. 336

d) CHOOSE Write a letter to the editor in which you
- express your concern regarding cyborgs and biohacking
  OR
- support a positive view of cyborgs and biohacking. Refer to arguments from the article, as well as putting forward your own views. You can also use the pictures from task 1 for inspiration.

Part A: Chances and risks — Advanced texts

The age of cyborgs has arrived

Vanessa Bates Ramirez, 04 August 2017

How many cyborgs did you see during your morning commute[1] today? I would guess at least five. Did they make you nervous? Probably not; you likely didn't even realize they were there.

In a presentation titled "Biohacking and the Connected Body" at Singularity University Global Summit, Hannes Sjoblad informed the audience that we're already living in the age of cyborgs. Sjoblad is co-founder of the Sweden-based biohacker network Bionyfiken. [...]

Sjoblad said the cyborgs we see today don't look like Hollywood prototypes; they're regular people who have integrated technology into their bodies to improve or monitor some aspect of their health. Sjoblad defined biohacking as applying hacker ethic to biological systems. Some biohackers experiment with their biology with the goal of taking the human body's experience beyond what nature intended.

Smart insulin monitoring systems, pacemakers[2], bionic eyes, and Cochlear implants[3] are all examples of biohacking, according to Sjoblad. He told the audience, "We live in a time where, thanks to technology, we can make the deaf hear, the blind see, and the lame walk." He is convinced that while biohacking could conceivably end up having *Brave New World*-like dystopian consequences, it can also be leveraged[4] to improve and enhance our quality of life in multiple ways.

The field where biohacking can make the most positive impact is health. In addition to pacemakers and insulin monitors, several new technologies are being developed with the goal of improving our health and simplifying access to information about our bodies.

Ingestibles are a type of smart pill that use wireless technology to monitor internal reactions to medications, helping doctors determine optimum dosage levels and tailor treatments to different people. Your body doesn't absorb or process medication exactly as your neighbor's does, so shouldn't you each have a treatment that works best with your unique system? Colonoscopies and endoscopies could one day be replaced by miniature pill-shaped video cameras that would collect and transmit images as they travel through the digestive tract[5]. [...]

Biohacking can also simplify everyday tasks. In an impressive example of walking the walk rather than just talking the talk[6], Sjoblad had an NFC chip implanted in his hand. The chip contains data from everything he used to have to carry around in his pockets: credit and bank card information, key cards to enter his office building and gym, business cards, and frequent shopper loyalty cards. When he's in line for a morning coffee or rushing to get to the office on time, he doesn't have to root around[7] in his pockets or bag to find the right card or key; he just waves his hand in front of a sensor and he's good to go[8].

Evolved from radio frequency identification (RFID) – an old and widely distributed technology – NFC chips are activated by another chip, and small amounts of data can be transferred back and forth. No wireless connection is necessary. Sjoblad sees his NFC implant as a personal key to the Internet of Things, a simple way for him to talk to the smart, connected devices around him. [...]

You can feel connected to our planet, too: North Sense makes a "standalone artificial sensory organ" that connects to your body and vibrates whenever you're facing north. It's a built-in compass; you'll never get lost again.

Biohacking applications are likely to proliferate in the coming years, some of them more useful than others. But there are serious ethical questions that can't be ignored during development and use of this technology. To what extent is it wise to tamper with nature, and who gets to decide? [...]

If it's frightening to think of criminals stealing our wallets, imagine them cutting a chunk of our skin out to have instant access to and control over our personal data. The physical invasiveness and potential for something to go wrong seems to far outweigh the benefits the average person could derive from this technology.

But that may not always be the case. It's worth noting the miniaturization of technology continues at a quick rate, and the smaller things get, the less invasive (and hopefully more useful) they'll be. Even today, there are people already sensibly benefiting from biohacking.

Annotations

[1] **commute** = journey to work
[2] **pacemaker** = Herzschrittmacher
[3] **Cochlear implant** = Hörprothese für Gehörlose, deren Hörnerv funktionsfähig ist
[4] to **leverage sth** /ˈliːvərɪdʒ/ = to put sth to use
[5] **digestive tract** = Verdauungstrakt
[6] to **walk the walk rather than just talk the talk** = to do sth instead of just talking about it
[7] to **root around for sth** = to search for sth
[8] to **be good to go** = to be ready

Workshop: Step by step — Part B: Literary visions of the future

Step by step **Analysing atmosphere**

PRE-READING

1 🔘 DVD/04

a) In 2017, Kazuo Ishiguro won the Nobel Prize in Literature. One of his most renowned works is his 2005 novel *Never let me go*. Watch the opening scene of the 2010 film adaptation. Speculate on what the film and the novel are about.

b) The opening of a film sets the tone for what is to follow. Watch the scene again and describe the atmosphere with reference to music, camera work and lighting. → SUPPORT D2, p. 298

c) Compare your results in class.

COMPREHENSION

2

a) **Pair work** Read the beginning of Ishiguro's novel. Tell your partner what the extract is about.

b) **Pair work** Compare the beginning of the novel to the film adaptation.

c) Exchange your results in class.

Webcode
You can download a word list for Part B here:
WES-73644-017

Webcode
You can find the video here:
WES-73644-018

→ **S20:** How to listen/watch effectively, p. 366

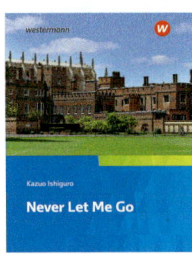

Never let me go
by Kazuo Ishiguro

Extract 1

My name is Kathy H. I'm thirty-one years old, and I've been a carer for over eleven years. That sounds long enough, I know, but actually they want me to go on for another
5 eight months, until the end of this year. That'll make it almost exactly twelve years. Now I know my being a carer so long isn't necessarily because they think I'm fantastic at what I do. There are some really good
10 carers who've been told to stop after just two or three years. And I can think of one carer at least who went on for all of fourteen years despite being a complete waste of space. So I'm not trying to boast. But then
15 I do know for a fact they've been pleased with my work, and by and large¹, I have too. My donors have always tended to do much better than expected. Their recovery² times have been impressive, and hardly any
20 of them have been classified as 'agitated', even before fourth donation. Okay, maybe I am boasting now. But it means a lot to me, being able to do my work well, especially that bit about my donors staying 'calm'. I've
25 developed a kind of instinct around donors. I know when to hang around and comfort them, when to leave them to themselves; when to listen to everything they have to say, and when just to shrug and tell them to
30 snap out of it³. [...]
And I'm a Hailsham student – which is enough by itself sometimes to get people's backs up⁴. Kathy H., they say, she gets to pick and choose, and she always chooses her
35 own kind: people from Hailsham, or one of the other privileged estates⁵. No wonder she has a great record⁶. [...] I've done my share⁷ of looking after donors brought up⁸ in every kind of place. By the time I finish, remember,
40 I'll have done twelve years of this, and it's only the last six they've let me choose.
And why shouldn't they? Carers aren't machines. You try and do your best for every donor, but in the end, it wears you down⁹.
45 You don't have unlimited patience and energy. So when you get a chance to choose, of course, you choose your own kind. [...]
But these days, of course, there are fewer and fewer donors left who I remember, and
50 so in practice, I haven't been choosing that much. As I say, the work gets a lot harder when you don't have that deeper link with the donor, and though I'll miss being a carer, it feels just about right to be finishing at last come the end of the year.
55 Ruth, incidentally¹⁰, was only the third or fourth donor I got to choose. She already had a carer assigned to her at the time, and I remember it taking a bit of nerve¹¹ on my part. But in the end I managed it, and the
60 instant I saw her again, at that recovery centre in Dover, all our differences – while they didn't exactly vanish – seemed not nearly as important as all the other things: like the fact that we'd grown up together
65 at Hailsham, the fact that we knew and remembered things no one else did. It's ever since then, I suppose, I started seeking out

Annotations
¹ **by and large** = all in all
² **recovery** (no pl) /rɪˈkʌv(ə)ri/ = process of becoming fit again
³ to **snap out of it** = to try to stop being unhappy
⁴ to **get sb's back up** (BE, infml) = to annoy sb
⁵ **estate** = large area of land with a big house on it
⁶ **record** /ˈrekɔːd/ = Bilanz
⁷ **share** /ʃeə/ = part of a whole
⁸ to **bring up** = to raise, e.g. a child
⁹ to **wear down** = to make sb lose their energy bit by bit
¹⁰ **incidentally** /ˌɪnsɪˈdent(ə)li/ = by the way/as it happens
¹¹ **nerve** = bold behavior that may make people angry

Part B: Literary visions of the future — Workshop: Step by step

for[12] my donors people from the past, and whenever I could, people from Hailsham. There have been times over the years when I've tried to leave Hailsham behind, when I've told myself I shouldn't look back so much. But then there came a point when I just stopped resisting. It had to do with this particular donor I had once, in my third year as a carer; it was his reaction when I mentioned I was from Hailsham. He'd just come through his third donation, it hadn't gone well, and he must have known he wasn't going to make it. He could hardly breathe, but he looked towards me and said: "Hailsham. I bet that was a beautiful place." Then the next morning, when I was making conversation to keep his mind off it all, and I asked where he'd grown up, he mentioned some place in Dorset and his face beneath the blotches[13] went into a completely new kind of grimace. And I realized then how desperately he didn't want reminded. Instead, he wanted to hear about Hailsham. [...]

What he wanted was not just to hear about Hailsham, but to remember Hailsham, just like it had been his own childhood. He knew he was close to completing and so that's what he was doing: getting me to describe things to him, so they'd really sink in, so that maybe during those sleepless nights, with the drugs and the pain and the exhaustion, the line would blur between what were my memories and what were his. That was when I first understood, really understood, just how lucky we'd been – Tommy, Ruth, me, all the rest of us.

Annotations
[12] to **seek out for** sb = to look for sb
[13] **blotch** = red mark on sb's skin

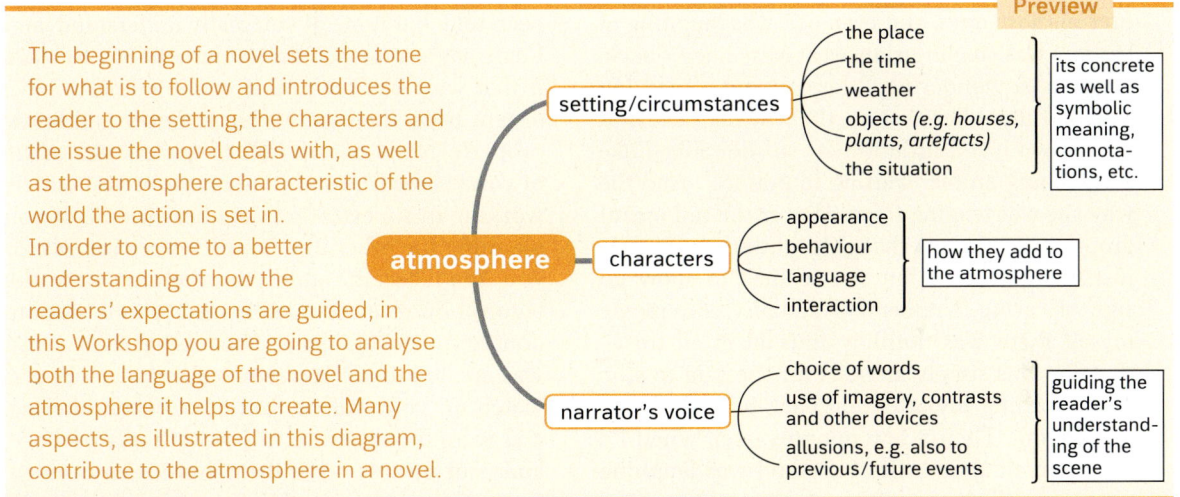

Preview

The beginning of a novel sets the tone for what is to follow and introduces the reader to the setting, the characters and the issue the novel deals with, as well as the atmosphere characteristic of the world the action is set in.
In order to come to a better understanding of how the readers' expectations are guided, in this Workshop you are going to analyse both the language of the novel and the atmosphere it helps to create. Many aspects, as illustrated in this diagram, contribute to the atmosphere in a novel.

ANALYSIS: LANGUAGE AND ATMOSPHERE

3 Language awareness

a) In the extract from the beginning of Ishiguro's novel, you will find the following words. Say what they usually mean. Use a dictionary if necessary.

> carer | donor | agitated | donation | calm | close to completing

b) Describe the meaning of the words in the context of the extract from *Never let me go*.
c) Compare the general meaning of the words and their meaning in the extract. Analyse whether there is a similar change in meaning in all the examples.
d) Explain how this choice of words may influence the atmosphere created by the narrator.

COMPREHENSION

4
Read the second extract on p. 64. Kathy, Tommy and Ruth are brought up in Hailsham, a boarding school where guardians act as teachers and to some extent parents. Miss Lucy is one of them.
a) Talk about your immediate reaction to the extract.
b) Summarize what Miss Lucy tells her students and describe the teenagers' reaction.

→ **S1:** Checklist: Summary, p. 330

Extract 2

We were fifteen by then, already into our last year at Hailsham. We'd been in the pavilion getting ready for a game of rounders[1]. The boys were going through a phase of 'enjoying' rounders in
5 order to flirt with us, so there were over thirty of us that afternoon. The downpour had started while we were changing, and we found ourselves gathering on the veranda – which was sheltered by the pavilion roof – while we waited for it
10 to stop. But the rain kept going, and when the last of us had emerged, the veranda was pretty crowded, with everyone milling around restlessly. I remember Laura was demonstrating to me an especially disgusting way of blowing your nose
15 for when you really wanted to put off[2] a boy.
Miss Lucy was the only guardian present. She was leaning over the rail at the front, peering into the rain like she was trying to see right across the playing field. I was watching her as carefully as
20 ever in those days, and even as I was laughing at Laura, I was stealing glances at Miss Lucy's back. I remember wondering if there wasn't something a bit odd about her posture, the way her head was bent down just a little too far so she looked like
25 a crouching animal waiting to pounce[3]. And the way she was leaning forward over the rail meant drops[4] from the overhanging gutter[5] were only just missing her – but she seemed to show no sign of caring. I remember actually convincing
30 myself there was nothing unusual in all this – that she was simply anxious for the rain to stop – and turning my attention back to what Laura was saying. Then a few minutes later, when I'd forgotten all about Miss Lucy and was laughing
35 my head off at something, I suddenly realized things had gone quiet around us, and that Miss Lucy was speaking.
She was standing at the same spot as before, but she'd turned to face us now, so her back was
40 against the rail, and the rainy sky behind her.
"No, no, I'm sorry, I'm going to have to interrupt you," she was saying, and I could see she was talking to two boys sitting on the benches immediately in front of her. Her voice wasn't
45 exactly strange, but she was speaking very loudly, in the sort of voice she'd use to announce something to the lot of us, and that was why we'd all gone quiet. "No, Peter, I'm going to have to stop you. I can't listen to you any more and
50 keep silent." [...]

"Peter, go on. Please tell the others what you were just saying."
Peter shrugged. "We were just talking about what it would feel like if we became actors. What sort
55 of life it would be."
"Yes," Miss Lucy said, "and you were saying to Gordon you'd have to go to America to stand the best chance."
Peter J. shrugged again and muttered quietly:
60 "Yes, Miss Lucy."
But Miss Lucy was now moving her gaze over the lot of us. "I know you don't mean any harm. But there's just too much talk like this. I hear it all the time, it's been allowed to go on, and it's
65 not right." I could see more drops coming off the gutter and landing on her shoulder, but she didn't seem to notice. "If no one else will talk to you," she continued, "then I will. The problem, as I see it, is that you've been told and not told. You've
70 been told, but none of you really understand, and I dare say[6], some people are quite happy to leave it that way. But I'm not. If you're going to have decent lives, then you've got to know and know properly. None of you will go to America, none
75 of you will be film stars. And none of you will be working in supermarkets as I heard some of you planning the other day. Your lives are set out for you. You'll become adults, then before you're old, before you're even middle-aged, you'll start to
80 donate your vital organs. That's what each of you was created to do. You're not like the actors you watch on your videos, you're not even like me. You were brought into this world for a purpose, and your futures, all of them, have been decided.
85 So you're not to talk that way any more. You'll be leaving Hailsham before long, and it's not so far off, the day you'll be preparing for your first donations. You need to remember that. If you're to have decent lives, you have to know who you
90 are and what lies ahead of you, every one of you." Then she went silent, but my impression was that she was continuing to say things inside her head, because for some time her gaze kept roving[7] over us, going from face to face just as if
95 she were still speaking to us. We were all pretty relieved when she turned to look out over the playing field again.
"It's not so bad now," she said, even though the rain was as steady as ever. "Let's just go out there.
100 Then maybe the sun will come out too."

Annotations

[1] **rounders** = a game similar to baseball
[2] to **put** (sb) **off** = to make sb not want to do sth
[3] to **pounce** = to jump
[4] **(rain)drops** = the bits of water rain consists of
[5] **gutter** = Regenrinne
[6] **I dare say** = I suppose/I assume
[7] to **rove** = to wander

Part B: Literary visions of the future — Workshop: Step by step

ANALYSIS: ATMOSPHERE

5

In a novel, the atmosphere is the general feeling the author creates by using certain elements such as imagery and setting to guide the reader's expectation of how the plot will develop. You have already analysed how euphemisms are used in extract 1 to present the society Kathy lives in. Some of the results above can also be applied to find out more about the atmosphere.

Checklist

Apart from the use of language, consider these other aspects when analysing atmosphere:

Setting/circumstances
- **setting:** the meaning of the setting for the students (e.g. neutral, positive, negative, certain associations/experiences connected with the place)
- **the description of objects:** a certain choice of words to describe something/someone (e.g. as a threat)

The narrator's voice
- **imagery:** the symbolic/metaphorical meaning of places, objects, circumstances (e.g. weather conditions)

- **allusions:** expressions, objects, etc. that may refer back to previous events (flashback) or to what is to happen later (foreshadowing)
- **contrasts:** contrasts (or the opposite: harmony) between characters, objects, setting

The characters
- **the characters' language:** addressing issues directly or indirectly, use of exaggeration or euphemisms
- **the way the characters look and behave:** characters may create tension by expressing their emotions in what they do and how they look

a) Look at the beginning of the extract and study the highlighted passages which illustrate:
- **the setting and circumstances:**
  – the meaning of the place (here: the pavilion) to the students at that time,
  – the symbolic meaning of the weather,
- **the narrator's voice:** the choice of words to describe the situation on the veranda
- **the characters:** the description of other characters in that situation

b) Explain what each of these passages reveals about the atmosphere. Start a grid to note down the main information. → SUPPORT D3, p. 299

→ **S12:** Checklist: Analysis – prose, p. 352

quotation	type of device	interpretation	concrete function/effect
"She was leaning over the rail at the front, peering into the rain like she was trying to see right across the playing field." (ll. 17-20)	the symbolic meaning of the weather	Miss Lucy appears to be absent-minded and focused on what she wants to tell the students, which is as unpleasant as the rain.	The narrator contrasts the weather and Miss Lucy's behaviour on the one hand with the students' carefree behaviour on the other. The reader feels that something important is about to happen.

6 → SUPPORT D4, p. 299

a) Read the rest of the extract. Continue your grid from task 5 and analyse what each example contributes to the atmosphere.
b) Compare your results in class and add any relevant points to your grid.
c) Use your grid to write an analysis of the atmosphere in extract 2.

COMMENT

7 → SUPPORT D5, p. 299

Miss Lucy is the first one to tell her students openly about their future. Discuss whether she does the right thing and whether she uses the right strategy to confront the students with their fate.

Webcode
You can download the grid here:
WES-73644-019

→ **S8:** How to improve your text, p. 341

→ **S6:** How to write a discussion/comment, p. 338

Workshop: Practice — Part B: Literary visions of the future

Practice: Analysing atmosphere

PRE-READING

1 Looking back at her life, Kathy remembers how she started to develop an understanding that she, as a clone, was seen as an outsider. Read the extract below and explain what Kathy realizes about herself and the relationship to the world outside of Hailsham.

→ **S12:** Checklist: Analysis – prose, p. 352

Annotations
[1] to **shudder at the very thought of** sb/sth = *bei dem Gedanken an jdn/etw erschaudern*

Extract 3

Maybe from as early as when you're five or six, there's been a whisper going at the back of your head, saying: "One day, maybe not so long from now, you'll get to know how it
5 feels." So you're waiting, even if you don't quite know it, waiting for the moment when you realise that you really are different to them; that there are people out there, like
10 Madame, who don't hate you or wish you any harm, but who nevertheless shudder at the very thought of[1] you – of how you were brought into this world and why – and who dread the idea of your hand brushing against
15 theirs. The first time you glimpse yourself through the eyes of a person like that, it's a cold moment. It's like walking past a mirror you've walked past every day of your life, and suddenly it shows you something else,
20 something troubling and strange.

COMPREHENSION

2 From a young age, the children at Hailsham are encouraged to be creative and produce art that is collected at least twice a year by a French-speaking woman they call Madame. The works chosen by her are supposed to go into "the Gallery" although the children cannot be sure that it really exists.
Read extract 4 and summarize what Kathy and Tommy assume about the significance of their artwork and "the Gallery".

→ **S1:** Checklist: Summary, p. 330

ANALYSIS

3 Language awareness
Analyse the atmosphere and use of language in this extract. → SUPPORT D6, p. 300

→ **S12:** Checklist: Analysis – prose, p. 352

COMMENT

4  DVD/05

a) In January 2018, Chinese scientists revealed that they had cloned macaque monkeys by using fetal tissue. Before you watch a video giving you more information on the issue, make sure you understand what the following terms refer to:

| primate | nucleus | fetus/fetal | genome | ethical |

b) Watch a video which provides you with background information on the wider implications of the cloning of macaque monkeys. Take notes on:
1. what this scientific achievement means for the possibility of human cloning,
2. which ethical concerns are raised by such research.

Webcode
You can find the video here: WES-73644-020

→ **S20:** How to listen/watch effectively, p. 366

5 In a *Guardian* newspaper article from 25 January 2018, author Philip Ball states:

> The cloning of macaque monkeys in China makes human reproductive cloning more conceivable. At the same time, it confirms how difficult it would be to clone a random adult – Adolf Hitler, say – from a piece of their tissue. And it changes nothing in the debate about whether such human cloning should ever happen.

Discuss the opportunities from and risks of cloning, bearing in mind the information from the video in task 4 and the plot of *Never let me go*.

Part B: Literary visions of the future — Workshop: Practice

Extract 4

As we came out of the shop, I was keen to regain the carefree, almost silly mood we'd been in before. But when I made a few little jokes, Tommy was lost in his thoughts and
5 didn't respond.

We began going up a steeply climbing path, and we could see – maybe a hundred yards farther[1] up – a kind of viewing area right
10 on the cliff edge with benches facing out to sea. It would have made a nice spot in the summer for an ordinary family to sit and eat a picnic. Now, despite the chilly wind, we found ourselves walking up towards it,
15 but when there was still some way left to go, Tommy slowed to a dawdle[2] and said to me: "Chrissie and Rodney, they're really obsessed with this idea. You know, the one about people having their donations
20 deferred if they're really in love. They're convinced we know all about it, but no one said anything like that at Hailsham. At least, I never heard anything like that, did you, Kath? No, it's just something going around
25 recently among the veterans[3]. And people like Ruth, they've been stoking it up[4]."

I looked at him carefully, but it was hard to tell if he'd just spoken with mischievous affection or else a kind of disgust. I could
30 see anyway there was something else on his mind, nothing to do with Ruth, so I didn't say anything and waited. [...]

"Actually, Kath," he said, "I've been thinking about it for a while. I'm sure we're right,
35 there was no talk like that when we were at Hailsham. But there were a lot of things that didn't make sense back then. And I've been thinking, if it's true, this rumour, then it could explain quite a lot. Stuff we used to
40 puzzle over."

"What do you mean? What sort of stuff?"

"The Gallery, for instance." Tommy had lowered his voice and I stepped in closer, just as though we were still at Hailsham, talking
45 in the dinner queue or beside the pond[5]. "We never got to the bottom of it, what the Gallery was for. Why Madame took away all the best work. But now I think I know. [...] Well, there was something Miss Emily said
50 then, something she let drop[6], and that's what's been making me think."

Two women were passing by with dogs on leads[7], and although it was completely stupid, we both stopped talking until they'd
55 gone further up the slope and out of earshot. Then I said: "What thing, Tommy? What thing did Miss Emily let drop?" [...]

"She told Roy that things like pictures, poetry, all that kind of stuff, she said they
60 revealed what you were like inside. She said they revealed your soul."

When he said this, I suddenly remember a drawing Laura had done once of her intestines[8] and laughed. But something was
65 coming back to[9] me.

"That's right," I said, "I remember. So what are you getting at[10]?"

"What I think," said Tommy slowly, "is this. Suppose it's true, what the veterans are
70 saying. Suppose some special arrangement has been made for Hailsham students. Suppose two people say they're truly in love, and they want extra time to be together. Then you see, Kath, there has to be a way
75 to judge if they're really telling the truth. That they aren't just saying they're in love, just to defer their donations. You see how difficult it could be to decide? Or a couple might really believe they're in love, but it's
80 just a sex thing. Or just a crush. You see what I mean, Kath? It'll be really hard to judge, and it's probably impossible to get it right every time. But the point is, whoever decides, Madame or whoever it is, they need
85 something to go on[11]."

I nodded slowly. "So that's why they took away our art …"

"It could be. Madame's got a gallery somewhere filled with stuff by students
90 from when they were tiny. Suppose two people come up and say they're in love. She can find the art they've done over the years and years. She can see if they go. If they match. Don't forget, Kath, what she's
95 got reveals our souls. She could decide for herself what's a good match and what's just a stupid crush."

I started to walk slowly again, hardly looking in front of me. Tommy fell in step,
100 waiting for my response.

"I'm not sure," I said in the end, "What you're saying could certainly explain Miss Emily, what she said to Roy. And I suppose it explains too why the guardians always
105 thought it was so important for us, to be able to paint and all of that."

Annotations

[1] **farther** = further
[2] **dawdle** /ˈdɔːd(ə)l/ = walking somewhere or doing sth very slowly
[3] **veterans** = the older students
[4] to **stoke up** = anfachen
[5] **pond** = small, usually artificial lake
[6] to **let** sth **drop** = hier: etw verraten
[7] **lead** = hier: Hundeleine
[8] **intestines** = Eingeweide
[9] to **come back to** = hier: to remember
[10] to **get at** sth = auf etw hinaus wollen
[11] to **have** sth **to go on** = to know sth that gives you an idea about sth else

2 Texts — Part B: Literary visions of the future

Life in the future – just a virtual reality?

PRE-READING

1

a) **Card survey** Imagine what life will be like in the year 2044. Write your ideas on cards (one idea per card) and put them on the wall/blackboard.
b) Cluster the cards and find categories for them.
c) Discuss whether your class has a more positive or negative outlook on the future and why.

COMPREHENSION

2

a) Read this extract from the novel *Ready player one* by Ernest Cline. Check whether any of your ideas about life in the year 2044 match the society presented in the novel.
b) The story is told from Wade Watts's point of view, a teenager living in Oklahoma City. Collect information on his character and the circumstances under which he lives.
c) **Double circle** Talk to your classmates about whether you would like to go to a school like the OASIS public school or not and why.

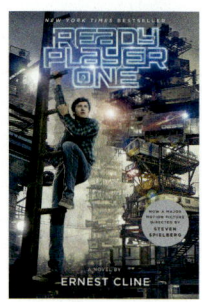

Ready player one
by Ernest Cline

I'd attended school in the real world up until the sixth grade. It hadn't been a very pleasant experience. I was a painfully¹ shy, awkward kid, with low self-esteem and almost no social skills – a side effect of spending most of childhood inside the OASIS². Online, I didn't have a problem talking to people or making friends. But in the real world, interacting with other people – especially kids my own age – made me a nervous wreck. I never knew how to act or what to say, and when I did work up the courage to speak, I always seemed to say the wrong thing.

My appearance was part of the problem. I was overweight, and had been for as long as I could remember. My bankrupt³ diet of government-subsidized sugar-and-starch-laden⁴ food was a contributing factor, but I was also an OASIS addict, so the only exercise I usually got back then was running away from bullies before and after school. […] Then, one glorious day, our principal⁵ announced that any student with a passing grade-point average⁶ could apply for a transfer to the new OASIS public school system. The real public school system, the one run by the government, had been an underfunded, overcrowded train wreck⁷ for decades. And now the conditions at many schools had gotten so terrible that every kid with half a brain was being encouraged to stay at home and attend school online. I nearly broke my neck sprinting to the school office to submit my application. It was accepted, and I transferred to OASIS Public School #1873 the following semester. […]. All of my teachers were pretty great. Unlike their real-world counterparts, most of the OASIS public school teachers seemed to genuinely enjoy their job, probably because they didn't have to spend half their time acting as babysitters and disciplinarians. The OASIS software took care of that, ensuring that students remained quiet and in their seats. All the teachers had to do was teach.

It was also a lot easier for online teachers to hold their students' attention, because here in the OASIS, the classrooms were like holodecks⁸. Teachers could take their students on a virtual field trip every day, without ever leaving the school grounds. During our World History lesson that morning, Mr Avenovich loaded up a stand-alone simulation so that our class could witness the discovery of King Tut's tomb by archaeologists in Egypt in AD 1922. (The day before, we'd visited the same spot in 1334 BC and had seen Tutankhamen's empire in all its glory.)

In my next class, Biology, we traveled through a human heart and watched it pumping from the inside […].

Logging into the OASIS was free, but

Annotations
¹ **painfully** = *here:* very
² **OASIS** = a virtual reality which is the home of a virtual society and also serves as an online gaming platform; it is used with the help of visors and special gloves
³ **bankrupt** = *here:* lacking in sth
⁴ **laden** = *here:* full of
⁵ **principal** (*AE*) = head teacher (*BE*)
⁶ **grade-point average** (*AE*) = Notendurchschnitt
⁷ **train wreck** (*AE, infml*) = total mess
⁸ **Holodeck** = plot device from *Star Trek*, a virtual reality environment

Part B: Literary visions of the future — Texts

traveling around inside it wasn't. Most of the time, I didn't have enough credits to teleport off-world and get back to Ludus[9]. When the last bell rang each day, the students who had things to do in the real world would log out of the OASIS and vanish. Everyone else would head off-world. A lot of kids owned their own interplanetary vehicles. School parking lots all over Ludus were filled with UFOs, TIE fighters, old NASA space shuttles, Vipers from Battlestar Galactica, and other spacecraft designs lifted from every sci-fi movie and TV show you can think of. Every afternoon I would stand on the school's front lawn and watch with envy as these ships filled the sky, zooming off to explore the simulation's endless possibilities. The kids who didn't own ships would either hitch a ride with a friend or stampede to the nearest transport terminal, headed for some offworld dance club, gaming arena, or rock concert. But not me. I wasn't going anywhere. I was stranded on Ludus, the most boring planet in the entire OASIS. […] I stopped hitching rides with Aech[10] at the end of the previous school year. […] If I didn't earn enough credits to pay for my fare back to Ludus, I'd wind up missing school because I was stuck on some other planet. This was not an acceptable excuse. I'd now racked up[11] so many unexcused absences that I was in danger of being expelled. If that happened, I would have to return my school-issued OASIS console and visor. Worse, I'd be transferred back to school in the real world to finish out my senior year there. I couldn't risk that. […]

In desperation, I'd tried to find a part-time after-school job, just to earn some walking-around money. I applied for dozens of tech support and programming jobs (mostly grunt construction work[12], coding parts of OASIS malls and office buildings), but it was completely hopeless. Millions of college-educated adults couldn't get one of those jobs. The Great Recession was now entering its third decade, and unemployment was still at a record high. Even the fast-food joints in my neighborhood had a two-year waiting list for job applicants.

So I remained stuck at school. I felt like a kid standing in the world's greatest video arcade without any quarters, unable to do anything but walk around and watch the other kids play.

Annotations
[9] **Ludus** = planet within the OASIS where all the schools are
[10] **Aech** = one of Wade's better-off fellow students at the OASIS public school
[11] to **rack up** = to get a lot of sth
[12] **grunt work** = unpopular work often given to the lower ranks of the workforce

COMMENT
3
Assess whether the society in the novel can be described as a utopia or dystopia.

WRITING
4
a) **CHOOSE** Choose one of the following tasks.
   You are a writer for a young people's online magazine. Write an article in which you write about what the school of the future should look like. The extract from *Ready player one* has inspired you to think about positive and negative developments in the use of modern technology in this context.
   OR
   You take part in a youth conference on the future of education and have been given the chance to deliver a statement on what schools of the future should look like . The extract from *Ready player one* has inspired you to think about positive and negative developments in the use of modern technology in this context. Write a short speech.
b) **Language awareness** Read out examples of texts in class that were written for the two different tasks in a). Identify similarities and differences between the texts and explain how the required text type influences your way of writing.

→ **S8:** How to improve your text, p. 341

→ **S5:** Checklist: Writing a speech, p. 337

5 **EXTRA**
Wade is afraid that he might have to go back to his old school. Online, he talks to one of his old classmates who he got along with. Write a chat dialogue between Wade and his former classmate Aaron about their school lives and how they feel about them.

→ **S2:** Checklist: Creative writing, p. 331

Advanced texts — Part B: Literary visions of the future

What is the true meaning of equality?

1

The short story you are going to read starts as follows:
"The year was 2081, and everybody was finally equal. They weren't only equal before God and the law. They were equal every which way."
Speculate on what this society could be like and if it should be classified as utopian or dystopian.

2

a) **Pair work** Read the short story *Harrison Bergeron* by Kurt Vonnegut, Jr. Talk about your first reaction to the story and to what extent it has matched your expectations from task 1.

b) Read the story again and describe the vision of society that the government would like to achieve and the measures that are taken to put this vision into effect.

Harrison Bergeron
by Kurt Vonnegut, Jr.

The year was 2081, and everybody was finally equal. They weren't only equal before God and the law. They were equal every which way. Nobody was smarter than anybody else. Nobody
5 was better looking than anybody else. Nobody was stronger or quicker than anybody else. All this equality was due to the 211th, 212th, and 213th Amendments to the Constitution, and to the unceasing vigilance of agents of the United
10 States Handicapper General.
   Some things about living still weren't quite right, though. April for instance, still drove people crazy by not being springtime. And it was in that clammy[1] month that the H-G men took
15 George and Hazel Bergeron's fourteen-year-old son, Harrison, away. It was tragic, all right, but George and Hazel couldn't think about it very hard. Hazel had a perfectly average intelligence, which meant she couldn't think about anything
20 except in short bursts. And George, while his intelligence was way above normal, had a little mental handicap radio in his ear. He was required by law to wear it at all times. It was tuned to a government transmitter. Every twenty seconds
25 or so, the transmitter would send out some sharp noise to keep people like George from taking unfair advantage of their brains.
   George and Hazel were watching television. There were tears on Hazel's cheeks, but she'd
30 forgotten for the moment what they were about.
   On the television screen were ballerinas. A buzzer sounded in George's head. His thoughts fled in panic, like bandits from a burglar alarm[2].

"That was a real pretty dance, that dance they
35 just did," said Hazel.
   "Huh" said George.
   "That dance – it was nice," said Hazel.
   "Yup," said George. He tried to think a little about the ballerinas. They weren't really very
40 good – no better than anybody else would have been, anyway. They were burdened with sashweights[3] and bags of birdshot[4], and their faces were masked, so that no one, seeing a free and graceful gesture or a pretty face, would
45 feel like something the cat drug in. George was toying with the vague notion that maybe dancers shouldn't be handicapped. But he didn't get very far with it before another noise in his ear radio scattered his thoughts.
50 George winced. So did two out of the eight ballerinas. Hazel saw him wince. Having no mental handicap herself, she had to ask George what the latest sound had been.
   "Sounded like somebody hitting a milk bottle
55 with a ball peen hammer[5]," said George.
   "I'd think it would be real interesting, hearing all the different sounds," said Hazel a little envious. "All the things they think up."
   "Um," said George.
60 "Only, if I was Handicapper General, you know what I would do?" said Hazel.
   Hazel, as a matter of fact, bore a strong resemblance to the Handicapper General, a woman named Diana Moon Glampers. "If I was
65 Diana Moon Glampers," said Hazel, "I'd have chimes[6] on Sunday – just chimes. Kind of in honor of religion."
   "I could think, if it was just chimes," said George.
   "Well – maybe make 'em real loud," said Hazel.

Annotations
[1] **clammy** = wet and cold
[2] **burglar alarm** = *Alarmanlage*
[3] **sashweight** = *Gegengewicht*
[4] **birdshot** = small metal balls
[5] **ball peen hammer** = special kind of hammer
[6] **chimes** = a set of bells

70

"I think I'd make a good Handicapper General."

"Good as anybody else," said George.

"Who knows better than I do what normal is?" said Hazel.

"Right," said George. He began to think glimmeringly[7] about his abnormal son who was now in jail, about Harrison, but a twenty-one-gun salute in his head stopped that.

"Boy!" said Hazel, "that was a doozy[8], wasn't it?"

It was such a doozy that George was white and trembling, and tears stood on the rims of his red eyes. Two of the eight ballerinas had collapsed to the studio floor, were holding their temples[9].

"All of a sudden you look so tired," said Hazel. "Why don't you stretch out on the sofa, so's you can rest your handicap bag on the pillows, honeybunch."

She was referring to the forty-seven pounds of birdshot in a canvas bag, which was padlocked[10] around George's neck. "Go on and rest the bag for a little while," she said. "I don't care if you're not equal to me for a while."

George weighed the bag with his hands. "I don't mind it," he said. "I don't notice it any more. It's just a part of me."

"You been so tired lately – kind of wore out," said Hazel. "If there was just some way we could make a little hole in the bottom of the bag, and just take out a few of them lead[11] balls. Just a few."

"Two years in prison and two thousand dollars fine for every ball I took out," said George. "I don't call that a bargain."

"If you could just take a few out when you came home from work," said Hazel.

"I mean – you don't compete with anybody around here. You just set around."

"If I tried to get away with it," said George, "then other people'd get away with it – and pretty soon we'd be right back to the dark ages again, with everybody competing against everybody else. You wouldn't like that, would you?"

"I'd hate it," said Hazel.

"There you are," said George. "The minute people start cheating on laws, what do you think happens to society?"

If Hazel hadn't been able to come up with an answer to this question, George couldn't have supplied one. A siren was going off in his head.

"Reckon it'd fall all apart," said Hazel.

"What would?" said George blankly.

"Society," said Hazel uncertainly. "Wasn't that what you just said?"

"Who knows?" said George.

The television program was suddenly interrupted for a news bulletin[12]. It wasn't clear at first as to what the bulletin was about, since the announcer, like all announcers, had a serious speech impediment. For about half a minute, and in a state of high excitement, the announcer tried to say, "Ladies and Gentlemen."

He finally gave up, handed the bulletin to a ballerina to read.

"That's all right –" Hazel said of the announcer, "he tried. That's the big thing. He tried to do the best he could with what God gave him. He should get a nice raise for trying so hard."

"Ladies and Gentlemen," said the ballerina, reading the bulletin. She must have been extraordinarily beautiful, because the mask she wore was hideous. And it was easy to see that she was the strongest and most graceful of all the dancers, for her handicap bags were as big as those worn by two-hundred pound men.

And she had to apologize at once for her voice, which was a very unfair voice for a woman to use. Her voice was a warm, luminous, timeless melody. "Excuse me –" she said, and she began again, making her voice absolutely uncompetitive. "Harrison Bergeron, age fourteen," she said in a grackle[13] squawk[14], "has just escaped from jail, where he was held on suspicion of plotting to overthrow the government. He is a genius and an athlete, is under-handicapped, and should be regarded as extremely dangerous."

A police photograph of Harrison Bergeron was flashed on the screen – upside down, then sideways, upside down again, then right side up. The picture showed the full length of Harrison against a background calibrated in feet and inches. He was exactly seven feet[15] tall. The rest of Harrison's appearance was Halloween and hardware. Nobody had ever born heavier handicaps. He had outgrown hindrances faster than the H-G men could think them up. Instead of a little ear radio for a mental handicap, he wore a tremendous pair of earphones, and spectacles with thick wavy lenses. The spectacles were intended to make him not only half blind, but to give him whanging[16] headaches besides. Scrap metal[17] was hung all over him. Ordinarily, there

---

Annotations

[7] **glimmering** = *schimmernd, flimmernd*
[8] **that was a doozy** (AE, infml) = *das war ja ein Hammer/heftig/krass*
[9] **temples** = *Schläfen*
[10] to **padlock** = *mit einem Vorhängeschloss befestigen*
[11] **lead** = *Blei*
[12] **bulletin** = news report
[13] **grackle** = a kind of bird
[14] **squawk** = sound a bird makes
[15] one **foot** equals about 30 centimetres
[16] to **whang** (infml) = to bang
[17] **scrap metal** = old metal that is not needed any longer

was a certain symmetry, a military neatness to the handicaps issued to strong people, but Harrison looked like a walking junkyard[18]. In the race of life, Harrison carried three hundred pounds.

And to offset his good looks, the H-G men required that he wear at all times a red rubber ball for a nose, keep his eyebrows shaved off, and cover his even white teeth with black caps at snaggle-tooth[19] random.

"If you see this boy," said the ballerina, "do not – I repeat, do not – try to reason with him."

There was the shriek of a door being torn from its hinges[20]. Screams and barking cries of consternation came from the television set. The photograph of Harrison Bergeron on the screen jumped again and again, as though dancing to the tune of an earthquake.

George Bergeron correctly identified the earthquake, and well he might have – for many was the time his own home had danced to the same crashing tune. "My God –" said George, "that must be Harrison!" The realization was blasted from his mind instantly by the sound of an automobile collision in his head.

When George could open his eyes again, the photograph of Harrison was gone. A living, breathing Harrison filled the screen. Clanking[21], clownish, and huge, Harrison stood – in the center of the studio. The knob of the uprooted studio door was still in his hand. Ballerinas, technicians, musicians, and announcers cowered on their knees before him, expecting to die.

"I am the Emperor[22]!" cried Harrison. "Do you hear? I am the Emperor! Everybody must do what I say at once!" He stamped his foot and the studio shook.

"Even as I stand here" he bellowed[23], "crippled, hobbled[24], sickened – I am a greater ruler than any man who ever lived! Now watch me become what I can become!"

Harrison tore the straps of his handicap harness[25] like wet tissue paper, tore straps guaranteed to support five thousand pounds. Harrison's scrap-iron handicaps crashed to the floor. Harrison thrust his thumbs under the bar of the padlock that secured his head harness. The bar snapped like celery. Harrison smashed his headphones and spectacles against the wall. He flung away[26] his rubber-ball nose, revealed a man that would have awed Thor, the god of thunder.

"I shall now select my Empress[27]!" he said, looking down on the cowering people. "Let the first woman who dares rise to her feet claim her mate[28] and her throne!" A moment passed, and then a ballerina arose, swaying like a willow[29]. Harrison plucked the mental handicap from her ear, snapped off her physical handicaps with marvelous delicacy. Last of all he removed her mask. She was blindingly beautiful.

"Now –" said Harrison, taking her hand, "shall we show the people the meaning of the word dance? Music!" he commanded. The musicians scrambled back into their chairs, and Harrison stripped them of their handicaps, too. "Play your best," he told them, "and I'll make you barons and dukes and earls."

The music began. It was normal at first – cheap, silly, false. But Harrison snatched two musicians from their chairs, waved them like batons[30] as he sang the music as he wanted it played. He slammed them back into their chairs. The music began again and was much improved.

Harrison and his Empress merely listened to the music for a while – listened gravely, as though synchronizing their heartbeats with it. They shifted their weights to their toes. Harrison placed his big hands on the girl's tiny waist, letting her sense the weightlessness that would soon be hers.

And then, in an explosion of joy and grace, into the air they sprang! Not only were the laws of the land abandoned, but the law of gravity and the laws of motion as well.

They reeled, whirled, swiveled, flounced, capered, gamboled, and spun[31]. They leaped like deer[32] on the moon. The studio ceiling was thirty feet high, but each leap brought the dancers nearer to it.

It became their obvious intention to kiss the ceiling. They kissed it. And then, neutraling gravity with love and pure will, they remained suspended in air inches below the ceiling, and they kissed each other for a long, long time.

It was then that Diana Moon Glampers, the Handicapper General, came into the studio with a double-barrelled ten-gauge shotgun[33]. She fired twice, and the Emperor and the Empress

---

Annotations

[18] **junkyard** = where you bring your waste
[19] **snaggle-tooth** = with uneven teeth
[20] **hinges** = Angeln, Scharniere
[21] to **clank** = make a loud sound like metal
[22] **Emperor** = man who rules an empire
[23] to **bellow** = to shout or scream loudly
[24] **hobbled** = unable to walk properly
[25] **harness** = Gurt, Pferdegeschirr
[26] to **fling** = to throw
[27] **Empress** = woman who rules an empire
[28] **mate** = here: (sexual) partner
[29] **willow** = Weide
[30] **baton** = Dirigentenstab
[31] to **reel**, to **whirl**, to **swivel**, to **flounce**, to **caper**, to **gambole**, to **spin** = to dance and turn around in different ways
[32] **deer** = Rotwild, Hirsch
[33] **double-barrelled ten-gauge shotgun** = zweiläufige Schrotflinte mit zehn Schuss

Part B: Literary visions of the future — Advanced texts

were dead before they hit the floor. Diana Moon Glampers loaded the gun again. She aimed it at the musicians and told them they had ten seconds to get their handicaps back on. It was then that the Bergerons' television tube burned out.

Hazel turned to comment about the blackout to George. But George had gone out into the kitchen for a can of beer. George came back in with the beer, paused while a handicap signal shook him up. And then he sat down again. "You been crying" he said to Hazel.

"Yup," she said.

"What about?" he said.

"I forget," she said. "Something real sad on television."

"What was it?" he said.

"It's all kind of mixed up in my mind," said Hazel.

"Forget sad things," said George.

"I always do," said Hazel.

"That's my girl," said George. He winced. There was the sound of a rivetting gun[34] in his head.

"Gee – I could tell that one was a doozy," said Hazel.

"You can say that again," said George.

"Gee –" said Hazel, "I could tell that one was a doozy."

Annotation
[34] **rivetting gun** = *Gerät zum Nieten setzen*

3

a) Explain how the system of complete equality in the short story affects the characters and their relationships.

b) `Language awareness` Analyse how the author's use of language as well as elements of the plot influence the reader's perception of the society presented in the story. → SUPPORT **D7, p. 301**

→ **S12:** Checklist: Analysis – prose, p. 352

4

a) `Card survey` In our society, steps are taken to improve equality and the equality of opportunities. Consider for example supportive measures to help people with a different ethnic background/disability/etc. Note down steps that are taken and cluster them on the board.

b) `Group work` Discuss which of the steps towards more equality you support and which you view more critically. Note down the three main results of your discussion.

c) Compare the outcome of your discussions in class.

AI – the end of humanity?

1

a) Define what is meant by Artificial Intelligence.

b) Watch an informative video about the Turing Test. Before you start watching the film, look at the list of words on the right and make sure that you know their meaning

c) Use some of the words to explain what the Turing Test is and how computers were able to pass.

d) Compare your definition of AI with the basic idea underlying the Turing Test.

Webcode
You can find the videos for tasks 1-4 here:
WES-73644-021

→ **S20:** How to listen/ watch effectively, p. 366

consciousness
to measure
to fool
judge
to mislead
to mimic
schizophrenic
to attribute to
approach
database
phenomenon
to baffle
underlying
knowledge

2 DVD/06

a) In the film *Ex Machina*, Caleb has won a coding competition and spends a week at the home of Internet entrepreneur Nathan to carry out a kind of Turing Test with Ava, Nathan's AI project. Watch a scene from Caleb and Ava's first meeting. Explain to what extent Ava appears human.

b) Watch the scene again and analyse what kind of atmosphere is created and how.

3 DVD/07

a) Watch another scene. Explain whether there is a change in the relationship of Ava and Caleb.

b) Watch the scene a second time. Analyse how cinematic devices are used to underline the atmosphere as well as changes in Ava's behaviour.

4 DVD/08

a) Watch a scene with Caleb and Nathan and explain the logic behind Caleb's stay at the house.

b) Assess to what extent the Turing Test proved successful.

3 The media

Webcode

You can download a word list for the Intro and the WordPool here:
WES-73644-022

1
In this Theme, you will deal with different types of media and the way people use them.
a) Write your own definition of "media".
b) **Group work** Compare your definitions. Which one is the most fitting? Give reasons.
c) Read the following definition of media from a dictionary. Compared to your definitions, which differences and similarities do you find?

> **media**
> Communication channels through which news, entertainment, education, data, or promotional messages are disseminated. Media includes every broadcasting and narrowcasting medium such as newspapers, magazines, TV, radio, billboards, direct mail, telephone, fax, and internet. Media is the plural of medium and can take a plural or singular verb, depending on the sense intended.

2

→ **S25:** How to work with a dictionary, p. 374

a) Think about what types of media you use. Use a dictionary to look up words, if necessary.
b) Make a grid with three columns. Label the columns "nouns", "verbs" and "adjectives". Put all the nouns you find into the first column of your grid.
c) Exchange your ideas with a partner.
d) Now add verbs and adjectives related to the topic of media to your grid.

nouns	verbs	adjectives
blog	follow	educational
newspaper	subscribe to	interesting
…	inform	…
	…	

The media   Intro   3

3 Pair work
Look at the photos on this double page and say
- what types of media you recognize,
- what function they serve.

4
a) **Pair work** Look at the diagram below and explain it to your partner.
b) Have a closer look at the overlapping areas. Find more examples to add to these areas.
c) Look at the three functions again. Do they cover all aspects of media use? Discuss which other functions could be added.

Three functions of media

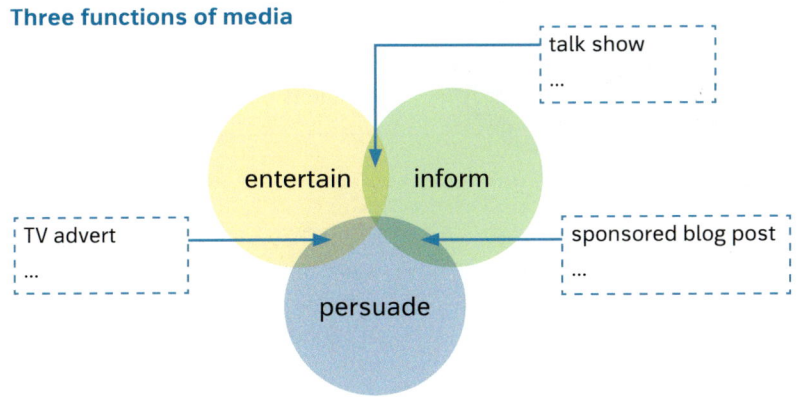

Preview

Opinion-makers
The first part of this Theme is about opinion-makers in society.

Living in the digital age
The second part of the Theme deals with our digital age. In the **Workshop**, you will analyse a feature film.

English as a global language
The third part of the Theme is about English as a global language. In the **Workshop**, you will practise mediation.

Webcode
You can download the diagram here:
WES-73644-023

WordPool — The media

OPINION-MAKERS

Media are essentially the means or institutions used to publish and broadcast information. Media can influence how people form opinions on matters such as politics, current affairs, science and technology, and the economy. With the advent of the digital age, media has become an all-pervasive part of everyday life. Media literacy is an essential skill, enabling individuals to judge for themselves whether or not a particular media source is reliable.

The term "mass media" refers to a range of diverse media technologies that reach their audience via mass communication. The press is an example of a mass media outlet. Journalists and editors who work for the press seek to document and present the latest information on various topics. Their articles are then published online or in newspapers and distributed widely.

SOCIAL MEDIA

Social media are digital platforms that enable users to connect and communicate with other individuals and groups online. One feature shared by many social media platforms is that they facilitate the propagation of other forms of digital media. A social media user can, for instance, easily share links to videos, images or news articles with his friends or followers.

Besides being used to publish information and advertise commercial products, media is often simply a source of entertainment. Television, film, music, video games and novels are common forms of entertainment media. Many users of social media subscribe to websites devoted to culture and entertainment, resulting in news feeds populated not only by articles on current affairs, but also by film trailers, clips from popular television series and the latest Internet memes.

FILTER BUBBLES AND FAKE NEWS

With so many people in possession of a handheld device with Internet access, it has never been easier for people to view the world from various political standpoints. However, rather than broadening our minds, we tend to seek out media content that consolidates our own worldview and to dismiss content that contradicts it. The phenomenon that ensues has been described as the filter bubble: unconscious of the fact that algorithms are personalizing their browsing experience, Internet users find their own views consolidated time and again online, leading to further political polarization in society.

Furthermore, the credibility of online media is increasingly questionable. False news stories and hoaxes, collectively referred to as fake news, proliferate unchecked on social media, leading to widespread disinformation.

ENGLISH: A GLOBAL LANGUAGE

Most modern-day media are to some extent reliant on language. Newspapers, weather forecasts, novels and documentaries are just some examples. The fact that most publishers or broadcasters seek to target as large an audience as possible encourages the use of a widely-spoken language.

Initially spread by the expansion of the British Empire, and more recently by influential US pop culture and media, English has come to be regarded as a kind of global *lingua franca*. Today, to be fluent in English is to be at an advantage when it comes to working, travelling and accessing media content. But will English retain its position as the global language in the future? Some predict that the power of the United States and Britain will decline in the future, but whether this will have any implications for the status of English as a global language is uncertain.

1
Find words/phrases with a similar meaning in the text above.

1. to make easier
2. not aware
3. at first
4. omnipresent
5. gadget
6. topical news items
7. significant
8. to foresee
9. dependent
10. to go down

The media — WordPool 3

2
a) Add more words to the grid.

printed media	audio media	audiovisual media	digital media
magazine	radio	...	...
...	...		

b) Write down at least eight sentences about which media you use/read/listen to/access/... and give examples of what you enjoy in particular.

c) Combine the verbs and the nouns.

> to publish / to broadcast / to release
>
> a music album / a film / a TV show / a radio report / a novel / an article

3
Label the photos. Which type of TV programme/film/Internet phenomenon etc. do they show?

1   2   3

"Go to the beach"
They said
"It will be fun"
They said

4   5   6

4
Write prepositions in the boxes where necessary.
1. Many streaming companies target ☐ a young audience.
2. These companies want many teenagers to subscribe ☐ their service.
3. If you are fluent ☐ English, you can watch programmes in many different languages with the help of English subtitles.
4. When you surf the net, you need to be conscious ☐ which websites you access.
5. Internet companies collect data about your online behaviour, which has implications for the links and advertisements suggested ☐ you.
6. Carelessness may result ☐ serious issues such as identity theft and phishing.

5
a) Make as many compound nouns as possible. Use a dictionary if necessary.

> media | news | film | Internet

b) Choose five words from a). Prepare quizzes with three clues for your partner like the one below.
1. Everybody uses them.
2. They reach a lot of people.
3. TV and the Internet are typical examples.
   (The answer is mass media.)

Read out the clues one by one. Your partner must guess the word.

Media literacy

1

a) In class, agree on a recent controversial issue. Here are some ideas: alternative energy, gun control, abortion.
b) Decide on your personal view regarding that issue. After that, think about how you came to that opinion. List all the sources that influenced your opinion.
c) Compare your sources (NOT your opinion!) with those of your classmates. Agree on the three biggest influences on how you formed your opinion.

2

a) Look at the information on public opinion from the *Encyclopedia Britannica* on p. 79.
Some keywords you will need in b) have been highlighted. If necessary, look up their meaning in a dictionary.
b) Read the article and, using all of the highlighted words, summarize the role of the mass media for the public opinion as defined in the article.

3

a) Look at the overview of "media literacy" below and sum up its most important message in no more than three sentences.
b) In many countries, "media literacy" is part of the compulsory curriculum in schools. Use the overview to explain why this subject is seen as so important by many school authorities today.

Media are constructions
- They don't simply reflect external reality.
- What goes into them is based on many conscious decisions (e.g. to inform, persuade, move to action, scare, stir up emotions, entertain, sell).

Media literacy: Key concepts

Audiences negotiate meaning
- Different audiences can take away different meanings from the same media.
- Factors such as age, gender, race, ethnicity, and social status can influence a person's interpretation of media.

Media have commercial implications
- It is a business and it must make money.
- Businesses and corporations influence content and distribution.

Media are social and political
- They convey values, power and authority.
- They can be non-inclusive and affect social norms regarding acceptance.
- They can drive political change.

Factors influencing public opinion

Environmental factors

Environmental factors play a critical part in the development of opinions and attitudes. Most pervasive is the influence of the social environment: family, friends, neighbourhood, place of work, church, or school. People usually adjust their attitudes to conform to those that are most prevalent in the social groups to which they belong. [...]

The mass media

Newspapers, radio, television, and the Internet – including e-mail and blogs – are usually less influential than the social environment, but they are still significant, especially in affirming attitudes and opinions that are already established. The news media focus the public's attention on certain personalities and issues, leading many people to form opinions about them. [...]

The mass media can also reinforce latent attitudes and "activate" them, prompting people to take action. Just before an election, for example, voters who earlier had only a mild preference for one party or candidate may be inspired by media coverage not only to take the trouble to vote but perhaps also to contribute money or to help a party organization in some other way.

The mass media play another important role by letting individuals know what other people think and by giving political leaders large audiences. [...] In areas where the mass media are thinly spread, as in developing countries or in countries where the media are strictly controlled, word of mouth can sometimes perform the same functions as the press and broadcasting, though on a more limited scale. In developing countries, it is common for those who are literate to read from newspapers to those who are not, or for large numbers of persons to gather around the village radio or a community television. Word of mouth in the marketplace or neighbourhood then carries the information farther. In countries where important news is suppressed by the government, a great deal of information is transmitted by rumour. Word of mouth (or other forms of person-to-person communication, such as text messaging) thus becomes the vehicle for underground public opinion in totalitarian countries, even though these processes are slower and usually involve fewer people than in countries where the media network is dense and uncontrolled.

Interest groups

Interest groups, nongovernmental organizations (NGOs), religious groups, and labour unions (trade unions) cultivate the formation and spread of public opinion on issues of concern to their constituencies. These groups may be concerned with political, economic, or ideological issues, and most work through the mass media as well as by word of mouth. [...]

Opinion leaders

Opinion leaders play a major role in defining popular issues and in influencing individual opinions regarding them. Political leaders in particular can turn a relatively unknown problem into a national issue if they decide to call attention to it in the media. [...]

Opinion leadership is not confined to prominent figures in public life. An opinion leader can be any person to whom others look for guidance on a certain subject. [...]

Complex influences

Because psychological makeup, personal circumstances, and external influences all play a role in the formation of each person's opinions, it is difficult to predict how public opinion on an issue will take shape. The same is true with regard to changes in public opinion. Some public opinions can be explained by specific events and circumstances, but in other cases the causes are more elusive. [...]

People presumably change their own attitudes when they no longer seem to correspond with prevailing circumstances and, hence, fail to serve as guides to action. Similarly, a specific event, such as a natural disaster or a human tragedy, can heighten awareness of underlying problems or concerns and trigger changes in public opinion. Public opinion about the environment, for instance, has been influenced by single events such as [...] the nuclear accident at Chernobyl, Ukraine, in 1986 [...]. It is nonetheless the case that whether a body of public opinion on a given issue is formed and sustained depends to a significant extent on the attention it receives in the mass media.

3 Texts — Part A: Opinion-makers

Working with statistics

→ **S18:** How to analyse statistics, p. 362

→ **S24:** How to give feedback/peer-edit, p. 372

1 Group work (4)

a) Each member of the group concentrates on one of the statistics (1-4).
b) Study your statistic and prepare a presentation. The checklist below can help you.
c) Present your statistics to each other. Use the checklist to give your partners feedback on their presentation.
d) In class, talk about what the statistics reveal about the issue of being well-informed by media.

Checklist

	Useful phrases
✓ Introduce what kind of statistic/diagram it is, what it is about and what data it is based on (e.g. country, year, survey).	This pie chart/bar chart/line graph/diagram deals with/is about/presents figures about … It includes data/figures/numbers/… for … It is taken from/The source of the data is …
✓ State the main idea (the heading/title may not always represent it adequately) in one sentence.	Generally speaking, the diagram reveals/shows/highlights that …
✓ Describe the information in detail and explain its implications. (Note: do not cover every single figure, concentrate on the most noteworthy ones.)	The first/second/third/… column shows … There is a considerable/steady/sharp/slight/marked increase/decrease in the number of … The most striking figure is … The numbers for … are about twice as high as those … Compared to … Nearly a third of …
✓ Conclude by summing up the overall message of the statistic.	All in all/By and large, the statistics for … reveal/show/ … that This development clearly shows/indicates that …

①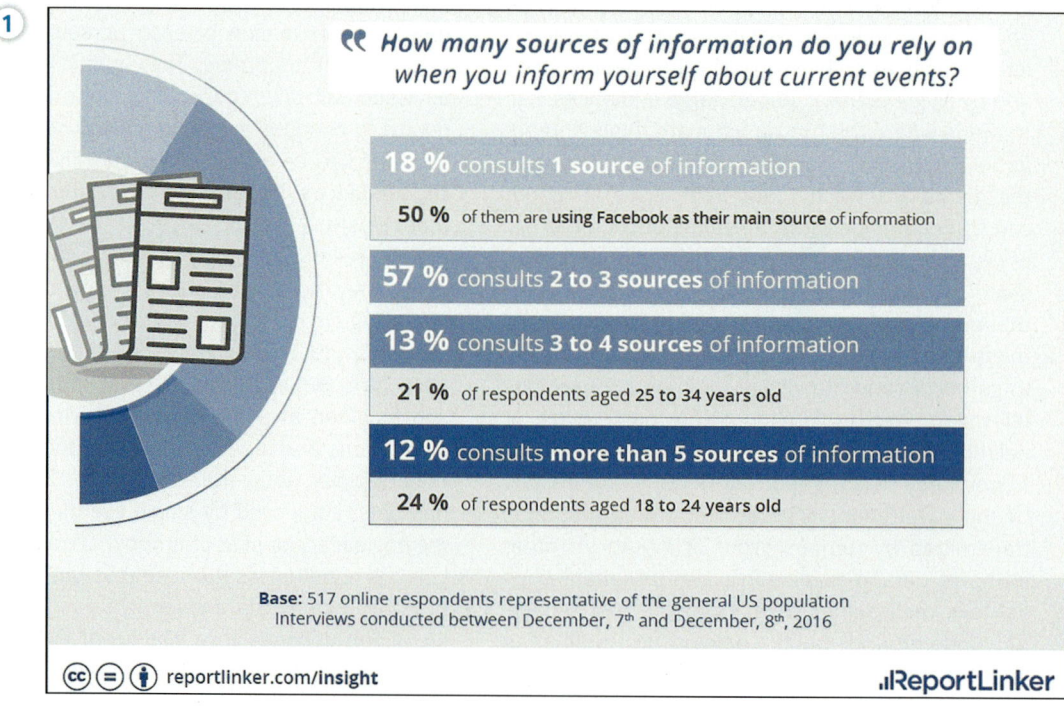

> **How many sources of information do you rely on when you inform yourself about current events?**

18 % consults **1 source** of information
50 % of them are **using Facebook as their main source** of information

57 % consults **2 to 3 sources** of information

13 % consults **3 to 4 sources** of information
21 % of respondents aged 25 to 34 years old

12 % consults **more than 5 sources** of information
24 % of respondents aged 18 to 24 years old

Base: 517 online respondents representative of the general US population
Interviews conducted between December, 7th and December, 8th, 2016

reportlinker.com/insight   ReportLinker

Part A: Opinion-makers — Texts 3

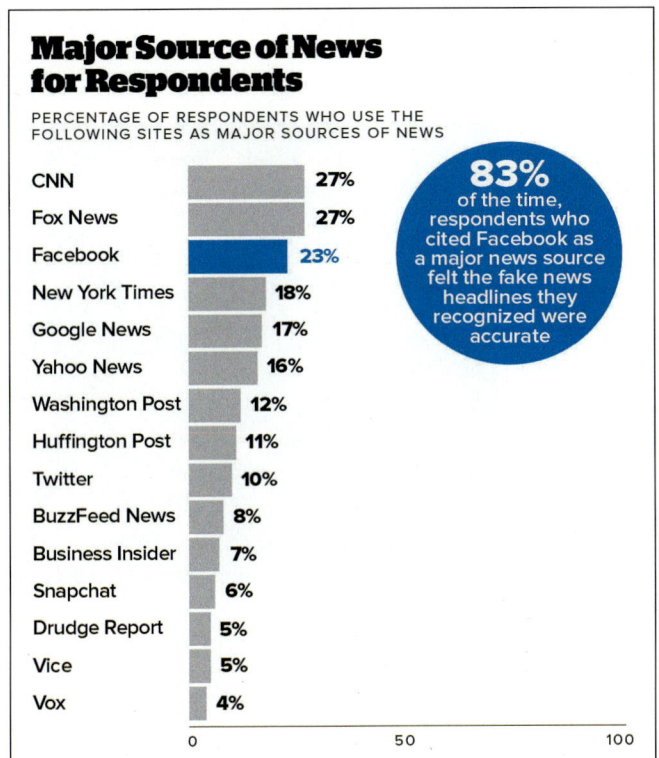

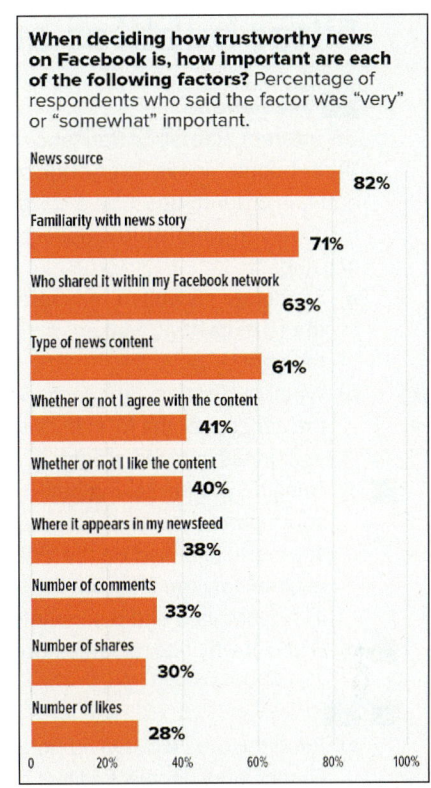

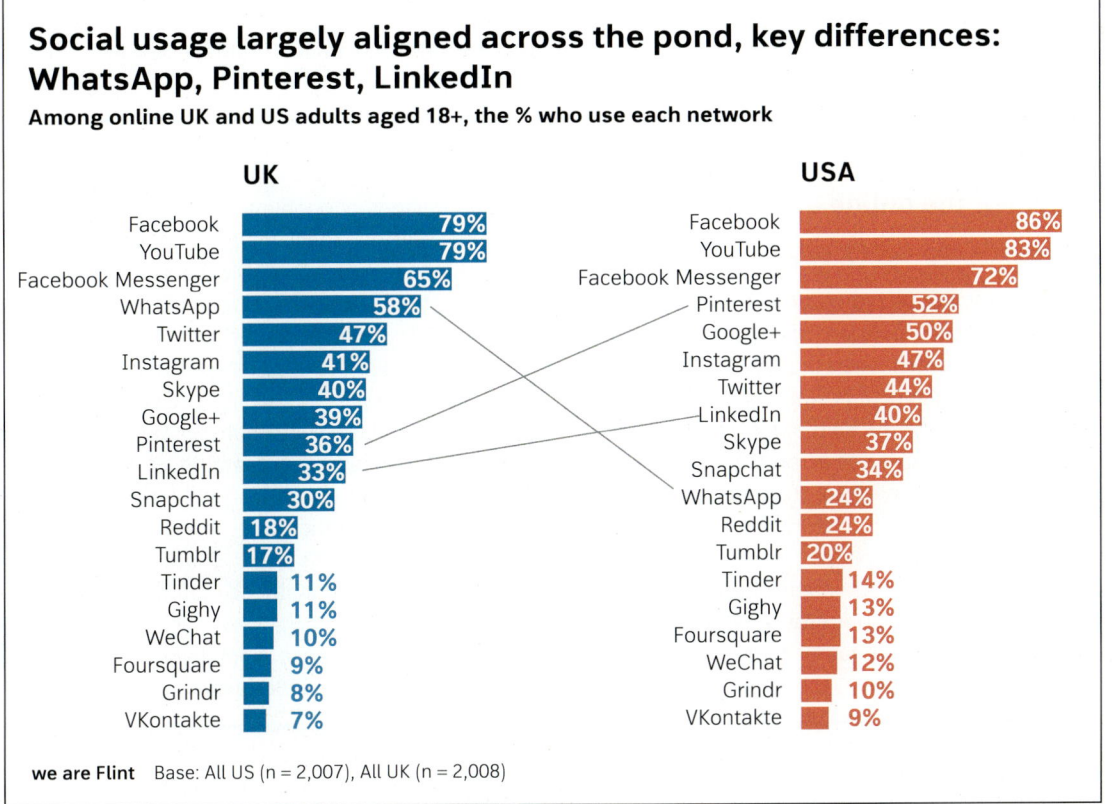

Filter bubbles and echo chambers

S19: How to improve your mediation skills, p. 364

1 Mediation

US Internet activist Eli Pariser coined the term "filter bubble" in his 2011 book of the same name in order to describe a certain phenomenon he observed when studying people's online activities.

a) Speculate on what it may refer to based on the term itself as well as its visualization on the right.

Webcode
You can find a link to the video here:
WES-73644-025

b) Watch a German-language video explaining the concept of the filter bubble to find out if your ideas in a) were right.

c) Imagine you are taking part in an Erasmus+ youth project on media awareness. Write a short article based on the video in which you explain how the filter bubble works and what its advantages and disadvantages are. → SUPPORT D1, p. 302

d) Discuss why filter bubbles can have a significant impact on people's views.

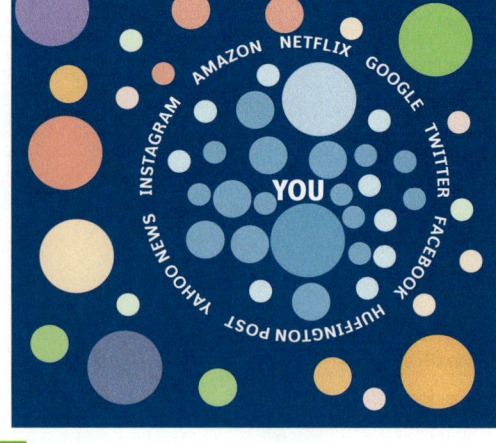

2

a) Read the article by David Robson on the concepts of filter bubbles and online echo chambers. Outline how people's online behaviour and their political views are related.

S13: Checklist: Analysis – non-fictional texts, p. 354

S6: How to write a discussion/comment, p. 338

b) Analyse how the role of filter bubbles and echo chambers is presented in the article.

c) Robson finishes his article saying that the "World Wide Web may be approaching its 30th birthday, but we still have a lot to learn about the best ways to navigate the online environment" (ll. 141-144).
Comment on the risks and pitfalls of the Internet as a forum of political opinion and the consequences that could be drawn from it.

The myth of the online echo chamber

David Robson, 17 April 2018, BBC

Back in the early 2000s many commentators were still marvelling at the freedom of the internet and its democratic potential when the US legal scholar Cass Sunstein offered a stark warning.
5 This virtual Wild West, he said, might allow us to overcome some of the social and geographical barriers between people, so that we establish a more balanced view of the world around us. But it was equally possible that we would simply
10 erect new fences, as like-minded people siphon[1] themselves into homogenous groups who all share the same viewpoints and gather their information from the same sources.

"Although millions of people are using the Internet
15 to expand their horizons, many people are doing the opposite, creating a Daily Me that is specifically tailored to their own interests and prejudices," he wrote. They would, in effect, live in 'echo chambers', leading to greater polarisation in a
20 country's politics. [...]

Today, the risks of the echo chamber and the "filter bubble" are considered something of a truism[2], explaining the bitter divides in public opinion that often appear to toe strict party lines[3]. Nearly 78%
25 of Hillary Clinton voters support the Black Lives Matter movement, for instance, compared to just 31% of Trump voters.
But does this really arise from blinkered[4] online behaviour? Or are more subtle dynamics at work?

Annotations
[1] to **siphon** = *here:* to separate
[2] **truism** = a general assumption shared by many
[3] to **toe the line** = to obey
[4] **blinkered** = narrow

Although there's little doubt that our reading habits shape our political opinions – and it's as-yet unclear the extent to which targeted advertising might sway[5] voter behaviour – some striking recent studies suggest that the influence of echo chambers and filter bubbles may have been overstated.

Consider a paper by Seth Flaxman and colleagues at Oxford University, which examined the browsing histories of 50,000 users based in the US. In line with the received wisdom[6], social media and search users tended to land upon more polarised news sources – Breitbart compared to Fox News, for instance – which might translate to a more extreme world view.

Crucially, however – and contrary to the concept of the online echo chamber and filter bubble – they were also more likely to visit sites expressing opposing viewpoints. Their media diet was more varied, overall. "It seems counterintuitive, but direct browsing often just consists of one or two sites that you regularly read – such as the BBC and CNN – while by its nature, social media will expose you to a number of other sources, increasing the diversity," says Flaxman, who is now based at Imperial College London.

Flaxman emphasises that the study is based on data from 2013, and times may have changed. But a Pew survey around the 2016 US Presidential Election broadly agrees with his findings, with the majority of people reporting a range of opinions in their social media feeds. And the University of Ottawa's [Elizabeth] Dubois has come to similar conclusions with her own studies.

Using a survey of 2,000 British adults, she found that the majority of people already reach outside their political comfort zone: they actively seek out additional sources that convey diverse views that do not match with their preconceptions. Indeed, just 8% of Dubois's participants scored so low on her measures of media diversity that they could be considered at risk of living [in] an echo chamber, visiting just one or two news services without other perspectives.

Dubois emphasises that even 8% of people living in an echo chamber is still a "worrying" number. But it is far less than most pundits[7] would have anticipated. [...]

Indeed, there is now evidence that well-meaning attempts to counter the echo chamber and filter bubble, by reading more diverse news sources, may actually backfire – leading to more, and not less, political polarisation.

Along these lines, a team led by Christopher Bail at Duke University measured a group of more than 1,600 Twitter users' political positions before paying them a small fee to follow a 'bot'[8] that would retweet influencers from across the political divide. About half of the participants took them up on the offer, but rather than developing a more moderate or nuanced stance on issues such as gay rights, most simply came to be more confident of their initial beliefs. [...]

Various psychological theories might explain these findings. One is "motivated reasoning". Countless studies have shown that we are so attached to our political identities that we will devote extra cognitive resources to dismissing any evidence that disagrees with our initial point of view, so that we end up even more sure of our convictions. [...]

But an alternative possible explanation comes from the psychology of 'self-licensing' – the unconscious belief that once we have shown our open-mindedness in one situation, we have somehow earned the credentials[9] to be more prejudiced later on. One study from 2008 found that people who had supported Barack Obama were subsequently more likely to express a potentially racist view, for instance. By reading a few dissenting voices on Facebook or Twitter, we may feel that we have already gained the right to be more dogmatic about our existing opinions. [...]

All of which suggests that the problems of political discourse online appear not to come from the range of voices that we hear – as the idea of the echo chamber would suggest – but our unconscious reactions to them. [...]

The anonymity of our interactions online seem to make it particularly easy to dismiss other's views, creating a more hostile environment for debate. [...] "[The influence of] echo chambers in social media has been highly over-estimated. But that doesn't mean that political polarisation isn't being driven by other factors," agrees Dubois.

Nor does any of this recent research deny the deliberate manipulation of social media and

---

Annotations

[5] to **sway** = to move from one side to the other
[6] **received wisdom** = a generally accepted assumption
[7] **pundit** = expert
[8] **bot** = a computer programme that is designed to perform repetitive tasks such as retweeting certain messages
[9] **credentials** (*pl.*) = quality

the influence that may have had on subsequent political events. A recent study in Science journal, for instance, confirmed that false news spreads much more rapidly than verified information from respectable sources. "It's very possible that most people are not at risk of being stuck in an echo chamber, but they are still being targeted with specific ads based on their behaviour, or they are still being targeted with misinformation," says Dubois.

Although there appears to be no easy solution to this online disharmony, experts such as Dubois hope that media literacy education at schools and university may help, teaching basic critical thinking skills and the ways to identify bias in an argument, allowing us to appraise news sources more thoughtfully. The World Wide Web may be approaching its 30th birthday, but we still have a lot to learn about the best ways to navigate the online environment.

Fake news

Webcode
You can find a link to the video here:
WES-73644-026

a) Watch a BBC video explaining what fake news is.
b) **Pair work** One of you writes down possible reasons why fake news is produced. The other writes down possible reasons why fake news is being read.
c) Discuss your notes for b) with your partner.

→ **S6:** How to write a discussion/ comment, p. 338

a) Read the article by Ian Leslie and outline why fake news has been popular among media consumers in recent years.
b) The scientist David Rand proposes that "history cycle[s] erratically through periods of rationality and forethought followed by conflict and chaos" (ll. 115–117). Following his hypothesis, discuss which period we are living in at the moment.

Why the invention of the fridge could be responsible for our love of fake news

The technology benefits everyone, which then erodes the advantage of controlled thinking – for instance, by the over-consumption of food.

Ian Leslie, 10 October 2018, New Statesman

A psychologist at the University of Cambridge has developed a vaccine against fake news. It comes in the form of an online game called *Bad News*, which aims to inoculate[1] its users against disinformation by giving them the opportunity to create some. You can make your own news site (mine reads "Honest Truth Online: what they don't want you to read!"), design memes attacking climate change science, and post alarming tweets from a fake presidential account. The game's designer, Sander van der Linden, hopes that by showing people how it's done, the game will generate "mental anti-bodies" in those who play it, which will then protect them against disinformation.

It's often assumed that if Twitter can delete all the Russian bots, or if Facebook can write algorithms that distinguish truth from lies, the fake news problem will be solved. But the uncomfortable truth is that, like drug addiction, fake news is a demand-side problem as much as a supply-side one. If we're ever going to fix it, we will need to fix our brains. Specifically, we will need to learn, or relearn, how to think.

The dominant explanation for why people believe fake news is that they want to. The theory of "motivated cognition" proposes that people are reasoning backwards: voters take a side and then believe anything that seems amenable[2] to their side, while

Annotations
[1] to **inoculate** = to immunize, to protect against a disease
[2] **amenable** = agreeable

dismissing any news that does not. That makes sense to me, but then maybe I want
35 it to. It sounds like something other people do.

David Rand, a professor at MIT, has a different theory, one that puts the emphasis on how we think, rather than what we want.
40 In a paper on fake news, co-authored with Gordon Pennycook, Rand argues that people who fall for online lies are "lazy, not biased". He suggests that the biggest factor distinguishing those who believe blatantly
45 inaccurate information from those who don't is not partisanship[3], but the care they take over reaching conclusions. Those who react intuitively and quickly to new information are more gullible[4] than those who exercise analytical reasoning, or what Rand calls
50 "cognitive control". In one of Rand and Pennycook's experiments, the same people who fell for fake news headlines were more likely to deem[5] Deepak Chopra[6] quotes profound.
55 Cognitive control is required to engage in reasoned argument, or make plans, or do maths. It is hard. Most of us, most of the time, avoid it. The psychologist Daniel Kahneman likens our capacity for analytical
60 reason to the ability of cats to swim. We can do it, but only with effort and discomfort, and we'd rather not unless we have to.

The internet makes us less likely to think about the news we see, simply because
65 it facilitates instantaneous reactions. Headlines, pictures and memes slide quickly across our visual field, spraying emotionally charged messages at us as they go. Technologists like to talk about
70 creating "frictionless" user experiences. In the context of news, frictionless means thoughtless.

There is an interesting irony here, out of which Rand has constructed a grand theory
75 of history. The internet itself is a product of cognitive control. It took many minds, applying effortful thinking over many years, to invent and implement the electronic infrastructure that now encourages us to
80 abandon all critical faculties. I'm reminded of a famous Reddit answer to the question of what would be the most difficult thing to explain to someone who arrived here from the 1950s: "I possess a device in my pocket
85 that is capable of accessing the entirety of information known to man. I use it to look at pictures of cats and get into arguments with strangers."

Cognitive control underpins humanity's
90 greatest achievements, from irrigation systems to railways, the separation of powers to the symphony. Given the riches it generates, says Rand, you might imagine that we would do more and more of it,
95 resulting in inexorable human progress – yet you do not need to be John Gray to see that this isn't so. Societies that invented sophisticated technologies have collapsed into decay and ruin, and they
100 often do so precisely because of what those technologies enable: the machine gun being an obvious example. [...]

Rand's hypothesis is that in an inhospitable, difficult world, controlled thinking has a high
105 reward, because you need to think carefully about how to survive – for instance, how to plan your food consumption when food is scarce. Controlled thinking then produces technologies to solve such problems, like
110 the fridge. These technologies benefit everyone, even those who do not act with control, which then erodes the advantage of controlled thinking – for instance by the overconsumption of food. Thus does
115 history cycle erratically through periods of rationality and forethought followed by conflict and chaos.

You can't help but wonder where we are in the cycle. After the Second World War, nations
120 built a complex system of international treaties and trading agreements that formed the basis of an unprecedented period of prosperity, allowing billions of us to live in relative comfort. It's hard, these
125 days, to imagine that war or mass chaos might return. Voters and politicians seem increasingly happy to be led by what they feel. A world built on the hard mental labour of cognitive control may be freeing us from
130 the need to think at all.

So what comes next?

Annotations
[3] **partisanship** = bias
[4] **gullible** = naive
[5] to **deem** = to consider
[6] a popular author of esoteric books

Workshop: Step by step — Part B: Living in the digital age

Webcode
You can download a word list for Part B here:
WES-73644-027

Step by step: Analysing a feature film

Preview

In this Workshop, you will learn how to analyse a feature film. You will pay special attention to cinematic devices and their functions in films.

Webcode
You can find the video here:
WES-73644-028

1 🔘 DVD/09

The 2016 feature film *Nerve* revolves around a game of the same name, which the protagonists get involved in. The game starts with the question whether you are "a watcher" or "a player".

a) Speculate on what this game could be about, what the distinction between watchers and players could mean and what the aim of the game may be.
b) Watch an extract from *Nerve*. Find out how the game Nerve works and compare it to your assumptions in a).
c) Talk about whether you would like to join the game and, if so, whether you would be a watcher or a player.

Webcode
You can find the video here:
WES-73644-029

2 🔘 DVD/10

a) Watch the beginning of *Nerve*. Note down what protagonist Vee, a high school student from New York City, does.
b) **EXTRA** Use your notes to write a summary of the extract.
The extract from the 2016 feature film "Nerve", directed by Henry Joost and Ariel Schulman, deals with …
c) Compare her media habits to yours and that of your peers.
d) Start character fact files for Vee and Sydney. Watch the extract again and note down what you find out about them. Add points as you watch more extracts from the film. → **SUPPORT** D 2, p. 302

Webcode
You can download the grid here:
WES-73644-030

3

a) In films, cinematic devices such as camera work, editing and lighting are used to convey a certain atmosphere and influence our understanding of the characters, their relationships and their problems.
Before you identify these, look at the film stills 1-4. Copy the grid below and describe how you perceive the emotional state of the respective persons and their relationships as well as the atmosphere.

picture	emotion(s)/relationship/ atmosphere conveyed	type of cinematic device	function/effect
1	romance between Vee and Ian, happy atmosphere	…	…
2	…	…	
3	…		
4	…		

Part B: Living in the digital age   **Workshop: Step by step**

3

4

b) Now read about different cinematic devices in the info box on pp. 87-88. Note down for each still which cinematic device(s) is/are used and enter them in your grid. Note that not all the definitions have a corresponding still. At the same time some stills may be labelled with more than one term.

c) Explain the effect the camera work is supposed to have on you with regard to the situation depicted in the still. → SUPPORT D 3, p. 303

Info

Cinematic devices

device	definition	function/effect
field size (distance between the camera and the object filmed)		
long shot	a view of characters or a setting from a distance	to provide an overview, often used as an introduction to a new scene or location
full shot	a view of the entire figure of a person	to show a person in action or to give an impression of how the characters/ the characters and their environment are related to each other
medium shot	a view of a person down to his/ her waist	to give a better impression of a person's looks and behaviour, often used to present two people in conversation
close-up	a full-screen shot of a person's face or other body part or object	to reveal a character's emotions by showing their facial expressions clearly; to draw attention to an object that is crucial to the plot or has symbolic value
camera angle		
high-angle shot	the camera looks down on a person or object	to make a person/object seem smaller, less important, inferior
low-angle shot	the camera looks up at the person or object	to make a person/object seem more powerful, more important, superior or even intimidating
eye level shot	the camera looks straight at a person or object	to provide a neutral view or to present two characters as equal and on the same level

87

Workshop: Step by step — Part B: Living in the digital age

point of view/camera position		
point of view shot	a scene is filmed as if looking through a character's eyes	to experience a situation as if part of the scene, possibly to identify/ sympathize with the character
over the shoulder shot	the camera looks at a character from behind another character's back	to show two people in conversation and draw attention to a character's reaction to what is being said
reverse-angle shot	a shot in a sequence of point of view shots in which the other character's perspective is shown	to allow the viewer to perceive how a conversation develops on both sides
establishing shot	a shot that provides an overview of a scene/setting	to introduce the viewer to a new location or situation
camera movement		
panning shot	the camera moves horizontally, e.g. from left to right	to follow an object or person, often used to speed up the action and make the viewer follow the plot development
tilting shot	the camera moves vertically, i.e. upwards or downwards	
tracking shot	the camera follows a person or object	
zooming in/out	the camera moves closer to or further away from a person or object	to draw attention to a detail or connect a detail to its environment
other cinematic techniques		
special effects	an unusual piece of action in a film for which technical equipment is used	often meant to make a scene more impressive or to include features that have not been invented or realized in our world and society today
overlay	the technique of putting a transparent image over another one to combine two images at the same time	to add information that the viewer needs in order to understand the scene better or to create a visual effect that reminds the viewer of a different context

Webcode
You can find the video here:
WES-73644-031

Webcode
You can download the example of a viewing log here:
WES-73644-032

4 DVD/11

At the local diner, Sydney dares Vee to open up to her crush, J.P., but Vee refuses to do so. Sydney then walks over to J.P. and reveals how Vee feels about him in front of a lot of fellow high school students. J.P. replies that Vee is not his type. Feeling humiliated, Vee leaves the diner.
In order to analyse the extract that follows this incident, work with a partner. A viewing log may help you structure your notes (see p. 89).
a) Watch the extract and note down what happens in the scenes.
b) Note down what cinematic devices are used and explain their function in the context of the scene. As you cannot document every single detail of the camera work, concentrate on devices that stand out and are meant to guide the viewer's understanding of the scene. Consider both the elements of camera work described in 3, but also other features (e.g. lighting, music, special effects) that may be relevant in this context.

Part B: Living in the digital age | **Workshop: Practice**

c) Add more points to your character sheet about Vee.
d) Analyse how cinematic devices help to bring out Vee's state of mind and change in behaviour. Use your notes from the viewing log.

→ **S16:** Checklist: Analysis of a film scene, p. 359

EXAMPLE OF A VIEWING LOG:

scene	action	cinematic devices	function/effect
Vee cycling home	…	…	…
Vee arriving at home	…	…	…
Vee in front of her PC	…	…	…
Vee leaving her home and going in Tommy's car	…	…	…

5 CHOOSE

Work on either of the tasks below.
Discuss what you think about Vee's decision to join Nerve as a player.
Consider:
- what you think of Nerve as a game
- how you see Vee's character and situation

OR

Imagine Vee's caring and protective mother finds out about Vee playing Nerve, especially considering the death of her brother two years before. Write a dialogue between them in which Vee has to explain herself. Consider what you have learnt about Vee and the nature of the game.

→ **S6:** How to write a discussion/comment, p. 338

→ **S2:** Checklist: Creative writing, p. 331

Practice Analysing a feature film

Unaware that her conversation is broadcast via the Nerve app and watched by Sydney and her friends at a party, Vee expresses her frustration to Ian about always being Sydney's sidekick and being treated as insecure.

1 DVD/12
Watch the excerpt that follows this conversation.
Summarize what Sydney does and how her friends and other watchers react.

Webcode
You can find the video here:
WES-73644-033

2
Analyse how cinematic devices emphasize Sydney's state of mind and the effect Nerve has on her.

→ **S16:** Checklist: Analysis of a film scene, p. 359

3
In a film review for the magazine *Variety*, Owen Gleiberman says about the dare in this scene:

"It works as the ultimate bad dream of peer pressure – the notion that *this* is how far someone will go to please her followers. In "Nerve," the rule of the Internet mob is all-powerful: You want something because everyone else wants it, and their will becomes yours, a dynamic that can leave your very identity hanging in the air."

Comment on this statement based on the scene you have analysed as well as what else you know about the film and its characters.

→ **S6:** How to write a discussion/comment, p. 338

3 Texts — Part B: Living in the digital age

App crazes

1

a) Name apps that are currently very popular among your peers and describe what they are used for. Collect the names of the most commonly used examples in class.

b) Discuss which of the apps may be problematic because of how they are used by teens.

c) Read the article from the *Select All* section of the *New York Magazine*, which refers to an app that was in fashion among US teenagers in 2017. Describe what *Sarahah* is used for and how teenagers and adults view the features of the app.

d) Language awareness Analyse the author's opinion on the use and popularity of *Sarahah* and similar apps. Consider:
- the choice of words
- the use of rhetorical devices
- the structure of the article

e) The author claims "Chances are good, by September, the teens will be all over some new anonymous-gossip app" (ll. 96-98). Discuss to what extent the author is right in believing that there is a constant flow of dubious apps with short-lived success among teenagers.

→ **S13:** Checklist: Analysis – non-fictional texts, p. 354

→ **S6:** How to write a discussion/comment, p. 338

Teens Explain Their Obsession With Sarahah, Summer's Hottest Anonymous-Gossip App

Madison Malone Kircher, 27 July 2017, Select All

If you're over the age of 18 and have recently browsed the "top downloads" chart on Apple's App Store, you might find yourself wondering what the hell "Sarahah" is, and
5 how it became the most popular app on the iPhone. The anonymous-commentary app launched in February; loosely translated, its name means "honesty" in Arabic. The app, theoretically, does what it says on the tin: It
10 allows users to submit honest comments, questions, and critiques to their peers. How do you know they're honest? Because the comments are submitted anonymously. You can guess where this is headed.

15 "People find their friends' profiles and leave comments and questions either with their profile or anonymously," Kenny, an 11th-grader from West Virginia told me about the app. "It seems like a way for teens to
20 continue the drama and say things about people without revealing their identity, which is a whole lot like the app Ask.fm from a while ago that everyone used to use for the exact same reason."

25 Sarahah's creator, Saudi Arabian developer Zain al-Abidin Tawfiq, said he initially built the app so people could give anonymous feedback in the workplace without fear of retribution from their bosses. The "lack of
30 fear of consequences" bit stuck, though the

app seems to have found its niche among high schoolers loafing around on summer vacation, rather than office workers looking for an outlet. [...]

To use Sarahah, or, rather, to use it like a teen, you also need to have a Snapchat account. After setting up a Sarahah account through Sarahah's website, you're given a custom link you can give to people who want to send you comments. This is where Snapchat comes in – it's a Sarahah distribution platform. Kids will embed their Sarahah link into a snap in their Snap Story – in layman's terms, they'll post the link where all their Snapchat followers can access it – where friends, or anybody if their account is public, can click it and anonymously comment. [...]

The next step, of course, is to screenshot all the complimentary comments you've received – or all the cruel ones – and upload those images to your Snap Story as a humble brag[1]. (Comments are only visible to the recipient unless they choose to share.) "A lot of people are screenshotting the anonymous messages and putting them on their Snapchat Story for everyone to see," said June, a 17-year-old from Ohio. "The messages are usually either really nice or really mean."

"Honestly, I've only gotten good messages," said Sam, a high-school student from North Carolina. "It seems that more girls are getting kinda[2] bullied because guys are commenting sexual stuff. [...]"

"I've used it a couple times to see what it's all about," June also told Select All, noting she'd received both positive and negative comments. "For me, the good outweighs the bad, but I know for other people, they are getting some pretty mean comments," she said. "I don't feel comfortable saying some of the stuff because the mean ones have vulgar language, and the nice ones are kinda personal."

Despite the potential for bullying, and the actual bullying happening, on the app, the teens who talked to Select All didn't seem too concerned. (Their parents, however, seem to feel markedly different. "My son signed up for an account, and within 24 hours someone posted a horrible racist comment on his page, including saying that he should be lynched," reads one review of the app. "The site is a breeding ground for hate.")

"[I've seen] a lot of inappropriate stuff," said Travis, 18, from Michigan. "Nobody has been too hurt over what has been said that I've seen so far." When asked why he thinks people flock to apps like Sarahah, his answer was simple. "My guess is they like the attention and drama." "Everyone's into drama and making people feel bad to make themselves feel better," Kenny said, echoing Travis. "It's what teens do. Not necessarily me, but teens in general." [...]

[M]ultiple teens told Select All they don't think Sarahah is long for this world. "I don't think it'll last very long," Sam said. "People will probably start to see it going negatively and getting old soon."

"It may be [a problem for school administrators and teachers]," Kenny explained. "School starts soon, so it [the app] may stay [popular]."

Though teachers likely needn't concern themselves with Sarahah. [...] Chances are good, by September, the teens will be all over some new anonymous-gossip app. And that's the one teachers and parents should probably start worrying about.

Annotations
[1] a **humble brag** = phenomenon of people showing off and putting themselves down at the same time
[2] **kinda** (slang) = kind of

3 Texts — Part B: Living in the digital age

Analysing a dystopian novel

1

a) **Card survey** Note down what you associate with reality TV, which is supposed to show the real lives of celebrities or ordinary people who are not always presented in their normal environment, but are confronted with challenges in scenarios developed by TV stations. Consider examples of programmes, typical features, what constitutes their appeal and what is criticized about them. Cluster your cards on the board.

b) Read the prologue of Kerry Drewery's 2016 novel *Cell 7*. Collect clues as to what has happened and what the first-person narrator expects to happen in the future.

c) Language awareness Analyse what you find out about Martha Honeydew, the sixteen-year-old protagonist and narrator. Consider especially her description of her physical reaction and her choice of words in general.

→ **S12:** Checklist: Analysis – prose, p. 352

Cell 7
by Kerry Drewery

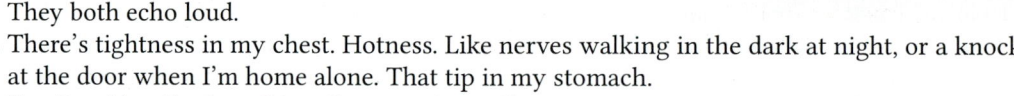

Extract 1

Prologue
There are two sounds in my head.
The bang of the gun through silence.
And my own voice shouting, 'Go!'
They both echo loud.
5 There's tightness in my chest. Hotness. Like nerves walking in the dark at night, or a knock at the door when I'm home alone. That tip in my stomach.
I'm dizzy[1] but I'm breathing. I'm conscious. Alive.
What have I done?
Those words repeat over again.
10 Same, same, same.
The darkness is crushing.
My breath screeches through it; my heart thuds.
I hear a siren in the distance; see headlights, dim.
You could run, I think.
15 'No point,' I reply out loud. 'This is the chance to do something. Change things. Have to.'
Siren's louder now, brighter headlights too.
The headlights turn, drowning me in white. I lift the hand holding the gun and shield my eyes. Blue lights flash on my skin.
On, off, on, off, on …
20 And flash on the body at my feet. Show me red pouring from him.
What have I done?
Still that echo in my head.
'What you had to,' I tell it. 'It was the only choice. Only chance.'
Headlights dip. Dark uniforms pour from cars, talking, ordering. I'm not listening.
25 I drop the gun, rest my hands on my head.
'I did it!' I shout. 'I shot him! I killed Jackson Paige.' I can't tell their reply.
Their eyes on me are full of disgust, handcuffs on my wrists cold as their hearts.
They live in the bubble of the Avenues and the City, let the gloss reflect and not wonder what's outside.
30 I'll die in seven days because I have to, but after that, their bubbles will burst and everyone will know the truth.

Annotations
[1] **dizzy** = feeling as though you are spinning around

Part B: Living in the digital age | Texts

2

a) Read extract 2 of the novel. Compare the news story to what the first-person narrator says about her situation in extract 1.
b) Explain how the plot of the novel is related to the topic of reality TV and how it reflects the notes you made in 1a).
c) Joshua Decker, the news reporter, claims that their country has the "most democratic justice system in the world" (ll. 11-12). Comment on this claim.

Extract 2

News

'The breaking news this morning is the shocking murder of celebrity Jackson Paige. Paige, who won the nation's hearts with his appearances on reality TV and his tireless charity work, was shot metres from where I'm standing here on Crocus Street, in
5 the area of the city known as the High Rises. In a bizarre twist, the culprit[1], who stayed on the scene following the shooting, has already confessed her guilt and been named by police as sixteen-year-old Martha Honeydew.

Honeydew has since been arrested and, in accordance with the Seven Days of Justice law was this morning placed in Cell 1 of death row[2]. This will be a landmark[3] case – Honeydew, at
10 sixteen years of age, is both the first teenage girl to face the death penalty and the first to be tried by our country's unique Votes for All system, the most democratic justice system in the world, where you, the viewer, decide on the fate of the accused.

We'll certainly be following what is most likely to be her final seven days very closely indeed. You can keep up to date via all our usual social media portals, as well as our dedicated
15 twenty-four-hour TV channel, *An Eye for An Eye*. Our show *Death is Justice* – on air every evening from 6.30 p.m. – will be analysing the details of this horrendous crime and the life of the accused, asking what could have led her to become such a cold-hearted killer.

Her willingness to admit her crime may have already reserved her a place in the electric chair when public voting is calibrated[4] and results are given in seven days but, viewers, do not
20 miss your chance to vote on this historic case.

This is Joshua Decker signing off and handing you back to Kristina in the studio.'

Annotations
[1] **culprit** = a person guilty of sth
[2] **death row** = part of a prison where criminals await their execution
[3] **landmark** = groundbreaking, historic
[4] to **calibrate** = to measure exactly

3

a) Martha's case is regularly discussed in the TV show *Death is Justice*. Read extract 3 on p. 94 and find out who considers her guilty and who doesn't and why.
b) Analyse the atmosphere and the characters' attitudes and behaviour in this extract.

→ **S12:** Checklist: Analysis – prose, p. 352

Language support

the atmosphere can be …		attitudes can be …		behaviour can be …	
crazy	calm	arrogant	modest	bossy	timid
relaxed	tense	hard	soft	brash	reserved
warm	cold	superficial	thoughtful	reckless	cautious
cheerful	gloomy	careless	responsible	loud	quiet
hysterical	peaceful	bitter	kind	indifferent	attentive

4

The novel *Cell 7* is set in a society that has not become a reality yet. Discuss whether you see any sense in the use of television or other media as an instrument of engaging the general public in political decision-making as well as in judging criminal cases.

→ **S6:** How to write a discussion/comment, p. 338

Extract 3

6.30 p.m. Death is Justice

[...] KRISTINA: Good evening and welcome to *Judge Sunday*!

The audience applaud.

KRISTINA: As always on *Judge Sunday* we're coming to you live from this historic building in central London – the Old Bailey[1] – which has stood on this spot since the late seventeenth century [...]. Following the phasing out of courts, it's been saved from closure by being transformed into television studios for our very own show *Judge Sunday* [...].

[...] The audience applaud. Kristina's teeth and her diamond necklace glint[2] in the studio's lights.

KRISTINA: Joining us again on tonight's programme is our lovely roving[3] reporter, Joshua Decker.

Wearing a blue designer suit with waistcoat and tie, Joshua bounces into the room, his hand up to wave to the audience as they clap and whistle him. He winks at a few as he passes, takes the hand of one and kisses it with a smile.

[...] Joshua raises a hand to calm the audience.

KRISTINA: Tonight, exclusive to our channel, we are bringing you a panel of experts discussing teen killer Martha Honeydew's case, and helping you to make an informed decision on how to cast your votes. Is she truly guilty as she claims she is? Did she truly steal one of our national treasures from us?

The studio falls quiet. The camera zooms in on Kristina's face – wetness to her eyes, a tremble to her mouth.

JOSHUA: Let's get them on!

Joshua and Kristina step towards the empty lecterns[4].

KRISTINA: At lectern number one we have psychologist to the stars, Penny Drayton!

The audience clap as stocky woman steps out from backstage, waving to the camera as she takes place at the far lectern.

KRISTINA: From the City's serious crime squad – Detective Inspector Hart is at lectern number two.

A broad man in a crisp, blue uniform, shiny epaulettes and a row of medals strides out and takes his place. His expression is blank. His eyes are cold. The applause from the studio audience quietens slightly.

JOSHUA: Bestselling author of *Why Teens Kill*, at lectern number three is Ian Chobury.

Applause picks up slightly as a middle-aged man steps out; the lights reflecting off his bald head and his thick glasses as he briefly nods and waves and stands at the next lectern.

KRISTINA: And finally, at lectern number four, is a face already known to our viewers, and a last minute addition to our panel today, *ex* Supreme Court Judge, Mr Cicero.

Cicero pushes his glasses up his nose as he shuffles out and takes his place, his moustache twitches as he tries to smile. His hands rest on the lectern, his fingers clasped together. If the camera zoomed in on him, it'd see the beads of sweat gathering around his shirt collar.

The applause dies. At either side of the lecterns, Kristina and Joshua take their places at what were once raised witness stands. Each holds a gavel[5] in their hands.

KRISTINA: Cicero, if we could come to you first. This is your second time visiting to discuss the case of Martha Honeydew. Why the interest?

Cicero wipes a hand through his greying hair.

CICERO: I am interested in justice for all. For the victims, yes. The families left behind, but also the accused.

DI HART: The accused? The *accused* forfeited[6] their right to justice when they committed their crime!

CICERO: You're assuming she's guilty when all she is, is accused. What happened to innocent until PROVEN guilty?

DI HART: She is as guilty as they come. My men caught her. She's admitted it. What more do you want?

CICERO (shouting): EVIDENCE! I want EVIDENCE! Proof, for God's sake!

Joshua taps his gavel gently on the wood. The guests stop and turn. He smiles.

JOSHUA: I think our panel are getting a little over excited there, don't you, Kristina?

Annotations
[1] The Old Bailey is the central criminal court in England
[2] to **glint** = to shine
[3] to **rove** = to move around constantly
[4] **lectern** = *Rednerpult*
[5] **gavel** = a wooden hammer as used in courts
[6] to **forfeit** /ˈfɔː(r)fɪt/ = to lose, esp. a right to sth

Part B: Living in the digital age | Advanced texts | 3

The future of news

1
a) Study the diagram about media preferences in the US and describe it.
b) Explain what it reveals about media use in different generations.
c) Name possible consequences for the media and society. Consider how media use may have implications for the media industry, access to information, reaching target groups for products or political messages.

→ **S18:** How to analyse statistics, p. 362

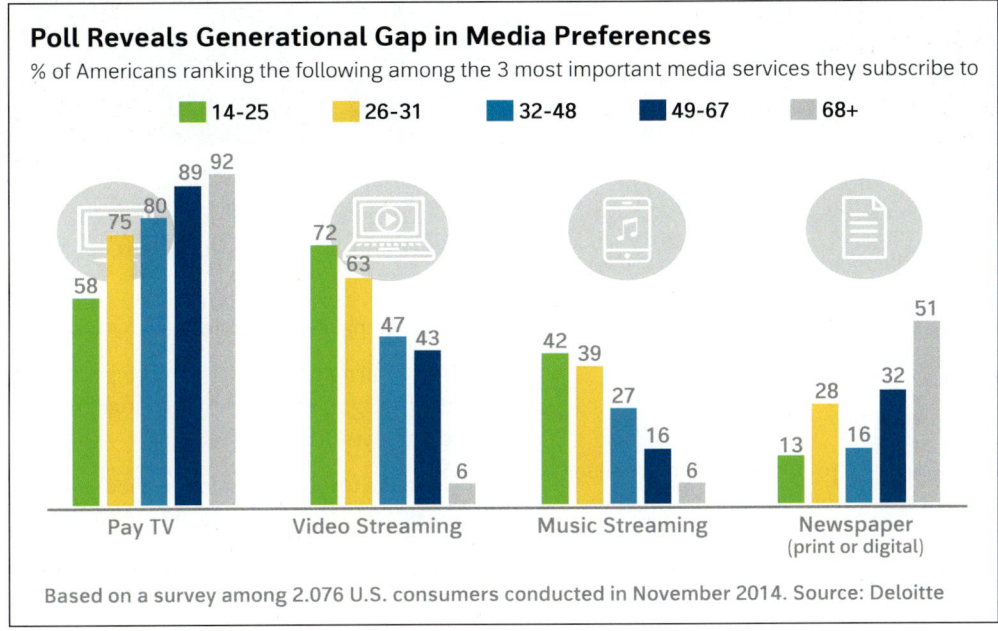

2
a) Read the article on pp. 96-97 and identify the main problem James Harding addresses in his article.
b) List the changes
   • that, according to Harding, have already taken place,
   • that the future may bring.
c) **Placemat**
   1. Note down
      a. which change(s) you consider alarming and why,
      b. what you would do to make sure that as many citizens as possible stay well-informed from reliable sources.
   2. Read your partners' statements and ideas and comment on them.
   3. In your group, agree on the top three solutions to the problems you have identified.
d) Discuss the groups' ideas in class.

Future of News
James Harding, 28 January 2015, BBC

Jerry Seinfeld, the comedian, once said: **"It's amazing that the amount of news that happens in the world everyday always just exactly fits the newspaper."**

Today, it doesn't fit.

There is more information, more readily available, more immediately, in more formats, on more devices and to many hundreds of millions more people than ever before.

And it used to be said that freedom of the press is limited to those who own one.

Today, anyone with an internet connection and a Twitter account can make the news. If you choose, the powers that be are you.

So, how has the internet changed the news?

Infinitely for the better. For anyone interested in reporting the world – finding stories, telling stories, sharing stories – it's all become so much more possible.

We are living at the most exciting time for journalism since the advent of television.

And the internet age has only just begun. By 2025, most people in the UK will likely get their television programmes over the internet. By 2030, possibly everyone will. The TV aerial will have gone the way of the typewriter. [...]

To be sure, technological change is uneven between different parts of the world, different age groups, different communities. But it is going to keep on coming.

If anything, it will accelerate.

The thrilling possibilities of change, though, can't disguise the fact that change is disruptive – and difficult. [...]

Take the local press. As classified[1] and local advertising has moved online, the regional press has suffered.

From the Rocky Mountain News in the US to the Reading Post in the UK, local newspapers have closed.

More than 5,000 editorial jobs were cut across the regional and national press in the UK in a decade.

[...]

International reporters working for US newspapers declined 24% from 2003 to 2010. The amount of airtime network evening newscasts devoted to overseas reporting in 2013 was less than half of what it was in the late 1980s. [...]

A generational change in the way we consume the news is already well under way.

In Sweden, the average age of the nightly news bulletin audience on SVT – its public service broadcaster – is 66.

Meanwhile, a recent survey found that 26% of two-year-olds in Sweden are online at least once a day.

Annotations

[1] **classified advertising** = advertising that is grouped together by subjects, e.g. job adverts

[...]

Who cares? People say access to the news has never been better.

The BBC ran a survey recently. 76% of people agreed that it's easier than it's ever been to know what's going on in the world.

But the medium, as ever, shapes the message. Half a century ago, TV transformed the news. For millions of people, it brought it to life. But television news also put a premium on dramatic pictures, telegenic politicians and snappy soundbites.

The internet will also change the news. It's already happening.

For example, 59% of UK online news users said they had glanced at the news headlines online in the past week, compared to 43% who said they had read longer stories online. [...]

The internet is bypassing the professional reporter. Computers can do what journalists used to, namely compile the football results, produce travel news bulletins and write up company results stories.

The services that used to be essential parts of the news are increasingly automated and available separately online.

And people in power are finding they can speak directly to the public without needing to bother with a reporter's pesky[2] questions. The journalist's competitor is no longer another journalist. Often, it's the subject of the story.

Political parties, celebrities, corporations communicate directly with the public. An era of greater connectivity is not necessarily leading to more accountability.

It is an age of growing information inequality.

Millions of people are online, millions are not. The world is dividing into those who seek the news and a growing number who skim it.

Those searching, those who expect to be found, and those who don't want to know.

To simplify, the information gap between younger people, poorer people and some ethnic minority groups, on the one hand – and older people, richer people and some groups of white people, on the other – is widening.

There is ever more data, more opinion, more freedom of expression, but it's harder to know what's really going on.

Even though people say it's easier to get the news, people are increasingly unsure of the facts and unclear what they mean.

People's knowledge of the key facts when it comes to public policy is astonishingly patchy[3], as shown by an October 2014 Ipsos MORI poll.

For example, the British think 24% of the population are immigrants (almost twice the actual figure of 13%) and believe that nearly 24% of the working age population are unemployed (the real figure is 7%).

This is an uneven age. We see, in places, sagging enthusiasm for democracy, polarisation of opinion, disengagement from society and a crisis of citizenship.

These problems are not the fault of the news media. But journalism – particularly public service journalism – has a responsibility to address them.

The news industry can help determine the kind of connected society we are.

Annotations
[2] **pesky** = annoying
[3] **patchy** = incomplete, inaccurate

---

3 **CHALLENGE**

"The journalist's competitor is no longer another journalist. Often, it's the subject of the story." (ll. 96-98) Find an example of this phenomenon and examine how, in your example, the subject bypasses the journalists.

→ **S9:** How to structure a text, p. 344

Workshop: Step by step — Part C: English as a global language

Webcode
You can download a word list for Part C here:
WES-73644-034

Step by step — Mediation

Preview

In this Workshop, you are going to work on a mediation task. When working on such a task, do not translate the German text literally, but express the relevant content in your own words in English.
Before you start, it is important to fully understand the task in order to identify the following four points:
- who is the addressee?
- what is the situational context?
- what type of text should be produced?
- what aspects of the content should you focus on?

1 Across cultures

Read the instructions below. Match the colours to the four points in the Preview above.

You are taking part in an international youth conference on the role of media in society. On the last day, there will be a panel discussion with young people from different countries on the influence of the media on the way we communicate and how TV and other mass media influence the way we use language. Your task will be to speak about the benefits of the availability of English-language media for young Germans.
As preparation, you have done some research and found the article by Klaus Ungerer.
Write an introductory speech to the panel discussion focusing on
- the way Germans have dealt with the English language up to now,
- changes the author is seeing at the moment.

→ **S19:** How to improve your mediation skills, p. 364

2

Prepare a short checklist for the introductory speech you need to produce. Include points on all relevant aspects of a mediation task. Your checklist may look like this:

checklist		
addressee	young people …	✓
situational context	…	

3

a) Read the article below and take notes on points that are relevant to your task.
b) Identify relevant aspects or examples that might not be understandable without knowledge of German culture and take notes on how you want to explain these to your audience.

→ **S5:** Checklist: Writing a speech, p. 337

4

Write your introductory speech. Include your explanations of culture-specific concepts if necessary.

KLAUS UNGERER

Lustig? Nicht auf Deutsch!

Deutsche Zuschauer erleben die Stars der Film- und Serienwelt nur als bewegte Abziehbilder. Die Synchronisation raubt ihnen den eigenen Ton und die Sprache. Ein Selbstversuch zeigt,
5 **was uns dabei alles entgeht.**

Frankfurter Allgemeine Zeitung, 4. März 2017

Mein Opa hat sein Abitur noch mit knoff und kneff bestritten. Sie hatten Englisch als mündliche Prüfung, so erzählte er manchmal, aber mündliches Englisch hatte im Unterricht nie
10 stattgefunden, damals. Sie hatten die Sprache ungefähr so kennengelernt, wie man einem lateinischen Text gegenübersitzt. Sie hatten sich braverweise die Formen eingepaukt, und mit den Formen gingen sie dann in die mündliche

Prüfung: weiß, wusste, gewusst – knoff, kneff, knoffn. Und so weiter. Es muss eine quälende Sache gewesen sein, die einen zwischen Scham und Lachen zerrissen hätte, und vielleicht wussten es nicht einmal ihre Lehrer viel besser, damals, irgendwo in Südniedersachsen kurz nach dem Ersten Weltkrieg. [...]

Abiturklasse 1920

Müheloses Switchen zwischen den Sprachen

Und auch selbst denkt man nur ungern zurück an die Zeit in Schweden als Austauschstudent: Sie mochten nicht ganz so hochtrabend gebildet sein, die schwedischen Kommilitonen, wie man selbst, ihre Uni mochte verschulter sein – aber mit ihrem jederzeit fließenden Englisch machten sie aus dem deutschen Austauschstudenten binnen Sekunden einen stammelnden Globalisierungsverlierer.

Mühelos switchten sie von ihrer Heimatsprache ins Englische hinüber und zurück, und es mochte ihnen an Rechtschreibung und Grammatikkenntnissen fehlen, doch sie beherrschten das Wunder der Sprache: sich jederzeit auszudrücken, geschmeidig mit jedem kommunizieren zu können. Woran aber liegt es, dass sie im entlegenen, menschenleeren Norden eine solche selbstverständliche Weltläufigkeit entwickeln konnten, derweil der Durchschnittsdeutsche im Herzen Europas als Provinzdepp herangewachsen ist?

Viele Elemente gehen verloren

Ausnahmsweise ist hier eine einfache Antwort möglich. Sie sind da oben so sprachstark und wir so verblödet, weil die Leute in Hollywood dunnemals den Tonfilm erfunden haben, und weil der Tonfilm kurz darauf eine geistige Verfinsterung über uns brachte, von der skandinavische Länder oder auch die Niederlande verschont blieben. In Deutschland wurde immer alles synchronisiert, und synchronisiert heißt: Man nimmt ein Filmkunstwerk voller Schauspieler und Sprache, voller Körperlichkeit, Timing und Sprachwitz. Zieht das alles ab. Behält die Bildspur bei. Und klatscht eine neue, teutsche Tonspur druff. Was da alles verloren geht! Erste Opfer sind seit Urzeiten Dialekt und Soziolekt, unrettbar. Denn wie will man einen Dialekt übersetzen, ohne dass es peinlich wird? Wie soll überleben, was da mitschwingt, wenn in einem amerikanischen Film plötzlich jemand mit britischem Akzent auftaucht? Wie soll man den Graben eindeutschen, der schon sprachlich zwischen einem Afroamerikaner und dem Redneck-Polizisten klafft? Rein ins Hannoversche Bühnendeutsch alles. Perdü, vorbei.

Ein Experiment mit den eigenen Lieblingsserien

[...] Einen Nachmittag lang wage ich das Experiment. Und schaue mir ein paar Lieblingsserien an. Im Original habe ich sie staffelweise gefressen. Jetzt mal auf Deutsch. Schauen wir mal. Hören wir mal. Praktisch unvermeidlich: dass oft der Sprachwitz auf der Strecke bleibt. Viele englische Ausdrücke lassen sich nicht übertragen, mancherlei Anspielungen würden im Deutschen sinnlos verpuffen. [...]

Etwas hat sich geändert

[...] Hoffnung aber ist immer. In meinem Fall ist sie 13 Jahre alt und flitzt nach der Schule am liebsten in ihr Zimmer. Sie guckt Netflix. „Big Bang Theory", „Dr. Who", „Pretty Little Liars". Hat sie alle schon durch. Manchmal taucht sie aus ihrem Zimmer wieder auf, manchmal sprechen wir Englisch. Achte Klasse, wie soll ich sagen? Mühsam holperten wir uns damals durch das englische Gestrüpp, nie werden wir fit sein für die globalisierte Welt. Die Tochter aber spricht fließend, und sie spricht mit bewundernswertem amerikanischem Akzent. Sich das Zeug auf Deutsch reinzuziehen käme ihr nie in den Sinn. Der Uropa hätte seine Freude an ihr. Er würde lächeln – über sich selbst, über kneff und knoff und all das Verpasste.

Workshop: Practice — Part C: English as a global language

Practice: Mediation

→ **S19:** How to improve your mediation skills, p. 364

1 → SUPPORT **D4, p. 303** | Across cultures

You are on a high school exchange in America. Your English teacher asks you to do a presentation about English as the "global language" from a German perspective. After some research, you find the blog post below. Use it to write the beginning of the presentation for your class. Focus on reasons that speak against English as the global language from the author's point of view.

Warum Englisch nicht als Weltsprache taugt

Wer die Welt beherrscht, beherrscht auch die Sprache. [...] Jetzt kommen mir aber auch immer wieder Versuche unter, das Vorherrschen des Englischen mit einer allgemeinen sprachlichen Überlegenheit gegenüber dem Deutschen zu begründen. Einige dieser Argumente greife ich hier auf. [...]

Kürzer = schwieriger zu lernen.

Ganz objektiv lässt sich dagegen sagen, dass englische Formulierungen kürzer sind als deutsche. Und das wird der Sprache auch ständig hoch angerechnet. Zu Unrecht – wie ich meine. Wenn Kürze so erstrebenswert ist, stellt sich nämlich die Frage, warum wir dann nicht gleich Kanji, die chinesischen Schriftzeichen, statt einer Lautschrift verwenden. [...] Wenn Du von Kanji schon gehört hast, wirst Du jetzt vielleicht gleich aufschreien: »Ja, aber von denen gibt es doch Tausende. Wie soll man sich die denn alle merken?« Und ja, da gebe ich Dir recht. Der springende Punkt ist nur: Die Verkürzung im Englischen gegenüber dem Deutschen bekommt man ebenso wenig für lau. Das Deutsche wird gerne für Wortungetüme wie Kraftfahrzeughaftpflichtversicherung [...] kritisiert. [...] Der Vorteil solcher zusammengesetzten Wörter ist aber, dass sie sich einfach herleiten lassen. Man könnte die Kraftfahrzeughaftpflichtversicherung auch einfach Krafag nennen. Aber kein Mensch, der dieses Vokabel nicht stur auswendig gelernt hat, wird dann noch wissen, wovon die Rede ist. Im Englischen ist das der Normalfall, wie ich an folgender »Schweinerei« demonstriere:

pig	wild boar	warthog	swine	pork
Schwein	Wild-schwein	Warzen-schwein	Haus-schwein	Schweine-fleisch

Kürzer = schwieriger zu verstehen.

Kurze Ausdrücke haben noch ein zweites Problem: Sie sind störungsanfällig. [...] Akzente, Radios, lärmende Nachbarn, eine Schießerei vor dem Haus, Pfropfen aus Ohrschmalz im Gehörgang, … irgendetwas trägt immer dazu bei, dass beim Hörenden nicht alles ankommt, was der Sprechende von sich geben wollte. [...] Am Weihnachtstisch kann man »pork« (»Schweinefleisch«) schon mal leicht mit »fork« (»Gabel«) oder »dork« (»Depp«) verwechseln. Um »Schweinefleisch« falsch zu verstehen, muss dagegen schon sehr viel schief gehen. Vielleicht ist ja auch das der Grund, warum es Leute gibt, die Deutsch für witzlos halten – weil man den Cousin beim Weihnachtsessen nicht ungestraft als Depp bezeichnen kann. [...]

Fazit: Englisch kocht auch nur mit Wasser.

Ist Englisch also gut als gemeinsame Sprache aller Länder geeignet? Nein, definitiv nicht. In der Kürze liegt nicht nur Würze, sondern auch ordentlich Pfeffer und zum Sprechen ist die Sprache schlechter geeignet als zum Schreiben. [...] Damit will ich umgekehrt nicht sagen, dass eine andere Sprache besser wäre. [...] Mir fehlt ein ausreichender Überblick, um eine einzelne Fremdsprache wirklich in Relation setzen zu können. Deutsch hat als meine Muttersprache natürlich einen klaren Sympathiebonus, aber ich glaube trotzdem jedem, dass zumindest die deutsche Grammatik schwieriger als in Englisch zu erlernen ist. Als dritte Sprache könnte ich bestenfalls noch auf ein paar Jahre Lateinunterricht verweisen. Aber davon ist außer ein paar pseudointellektuellen Sprüchen nicht mehr viel übrig. Sic transit gloria mundi. [...]

Part C: English as a global language | Texts

The global language of the future

PRE-LISTENING

1

a) Look at the infographic below and describe what they show.
b) Now discuss the implications in class. Consider:
- what you learned
- what you found surprising
- use the diagram to speculate on future global languages

→ **S18:** How to analyse statistics, p. 362

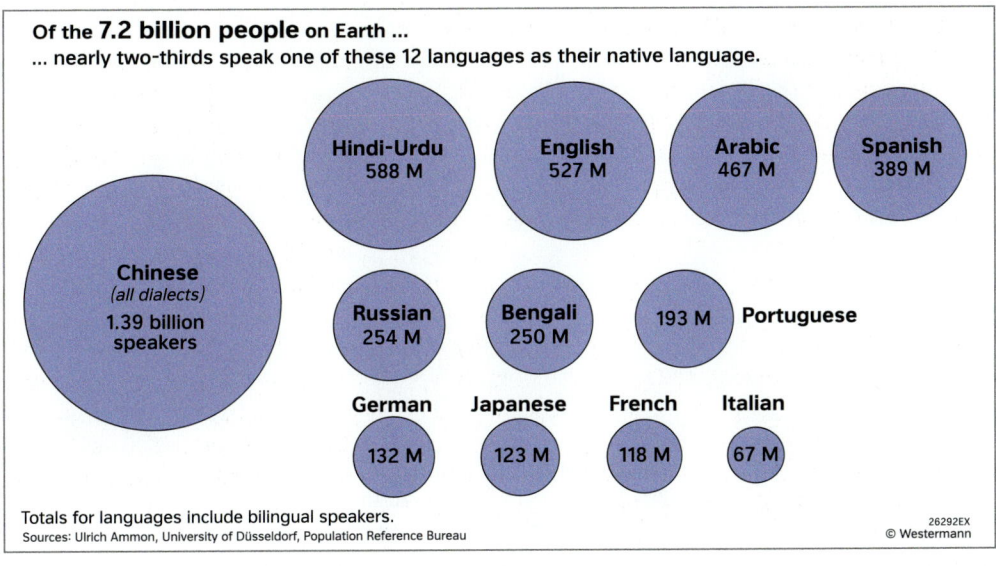

2
In a talk for the British Council, renowned linguist David Crystal uses these terms:

| futurologists | predominantly | "money talks" | air traffic control | to retain | it is not "rocket science" | to diminish | diminution |

If necessary, use a dictionary to look up their meanings. Then speculate about what aspect(s) of the topic "English as a global language" the talk might be about.

→ **S25:** How to work with a dictionary, p. 374

LISTENING

3 ⊙ CD/06

Listen to part of the talk by David Crystal. Then take notes on the following questions:
1. Why, according to Crystal, did English become the global language in the past?
2. What are reasons why it still has this status today?
3. Under what circumstances might English remain the global language in the future?
4. What other three likely scenarios does Crystal describe?

Webcode
You can find the audio file here:
WES-73644-035

→ **S20:** How to listen/ watch effectively, p. 366

WRITING

4

 CHALLENGE Should Mandarin, the predominant Chinese dialect, be made a compulsory subject in European schools? Discuss this question in no more than 300 words.

→ **S9:** How to structure a text, p. 344

Part C: English as a global language

The value of language learning apps

PRE-READING

1 Across cultures
a) Describe the map. Which countries study which languages?
b) In class, interpret the results. Have you got any explanations for them?

The most popular language studied on *Duolingo* in each country

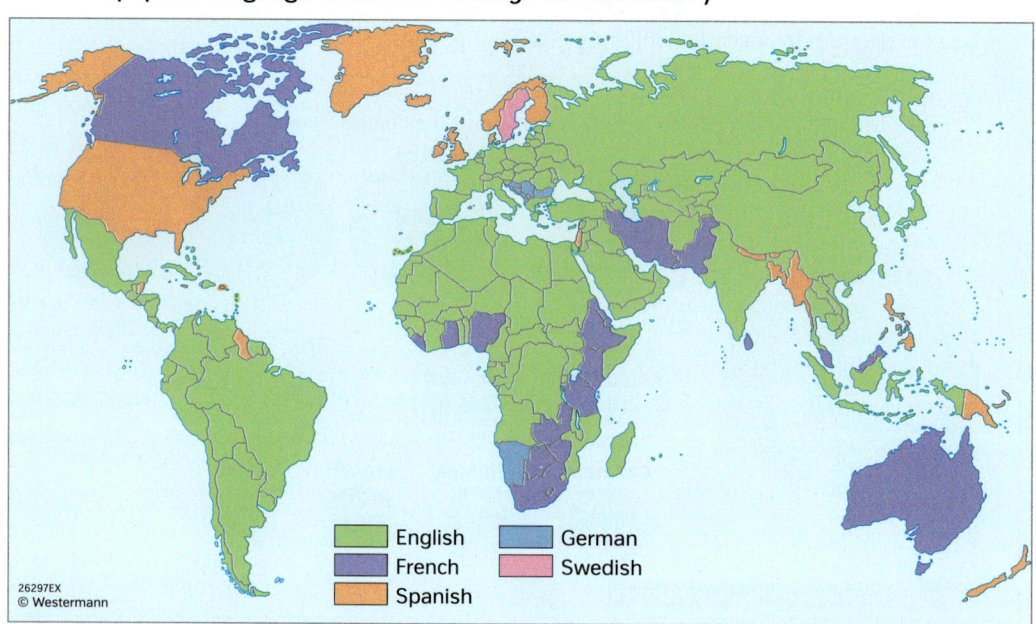

2
Collect advantages and disadvantages of learning a language via an app.

COMPREHENSION

3
Read the text about *Duolingo*, a language learning app.
a) List problems the author encounters while trying to improve his Spanish with *Duolingo*.
b) Describe what, according to the article, an app like *Duolingo* is helpful for.
c) Explain in your own words why, according to this article, it is not possible to become fluent in a language using an app like this.

Are Duolingo Users Actually Learning Anything Useful?

Mike Pearl, 12 January 2017

When I first tried the free language learning app Duolingo, which calls itself "the most popular way to learn languages in the world," I was delighted. I told it that I wanted to beef up my Latin American
5 Spanish, and it launched into a brief quiz that took me on a whirlwind tour of the language. The quiz took me from insultingly basic phrases like "hola," to the stuff I got sick of in 9th grade like "¿Dónde está mi bolígrafo?," to tougher stuff in a few
10 minutes. At the end, I was told I was 65 percent fluent.

That's a grade worth bragging about[1], considering my Spanish is complete trash.

Part C: English as a global language — Advanced texts

Anyone who has ever heard me try to communicate in Spanish knows I barely muddle through it. My attempts at conversation in the language often fail completely; if the other person can speak English, the conversations end up taking place in English instead. I encounter opportunities to speak Spanish every day of my life, but I break out in a cold sweat when I have to – so getting better at speaking my city's second pseudo-official language seemed essential.

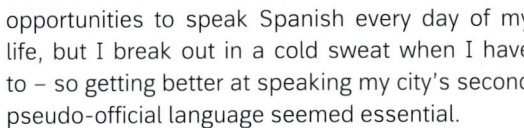

I enjoyed accruing[2] Duolingo's currency, lingots, and got a rush from competing with myself thanks to the app's lauded gamification. I also enjoyed the cartoon graphics and weirdly dark sentences embedded in the lessons ("He can't swim!" "I have no nationality!"). But after a few months with Duolingo, the most popular educational app in iTunes, when it came time to speak Spanish, I hadn't noticeably improved. What gives?[3]

To find out, I checked in with linguists who focus on language acquisition. Most of them weren't into Duolingo at all, nor did they love its more expensive cousins like Wanikani and Rosetta Stone. "Many of us in academia have quite a bit of disdain[4] for the endless series of gadgets and apps that are supposedly going to solve all our problems," Robert M. De Keyser, professor of second language acquisition at University of Maryland's School of Languages, Literatures, and Cultures, told me in an email.

According to Roumen Vesselinov, assistant professor of statistics at Queens College at The City University of New York, "Generally [Duolingo] seems to work." In an experiment commissioned by Duolingo itself, Vesselinov and his team found that using Duolingo for 34 hours is about the equivalent of a one-semester language class. It's an impressive result to be sure.

However, Vesselinov also told me that the evaluation process relied on a text-based online quiz called WebCAPE. "In other studies, with other software packages, we were able to use oral tests," he told me, referring to comparable tests of the language applications Rosetta Stone and Busuu. "You give a recording to evaluators, they listen, and they evaluate your communication skills," he explained, and he said this produces a result that is "more objective." Vesselinov said it "would be nice to test Duolingo for both vocabulary and oral proficiency[5]."

What's more, he said, "the biggest measurable progress is when you start from zero." According to his report, the difference between beginner and advanced progress was "noteworthy" and not "statistically significant," because of the small sample size. But with beginners achieving 9.2 test points of progress on the WebCAPE, and more advanced students achieving a paltry 0.6 points of progress, Vesselinov wrote that, "with [a] larger sample, the result would have been significant."

"It's more difficult when you're at an advanced stage to improve further," he told me point-blank[6]. Since I'm not able to have what I think is a normal conversation, I'm not at what I consider an advanced stage in my Spanish knowledge – but I seem to have reached a plateau. This is most likely because, as MIT linguist Suzanne Flynn told me in an email, apps like Duolingo are "good for learning new vocabulary at best," and don't have "what is needed for true language acquisition to take place – immersion[7] or immersion-like language experiences."

Immersion is, of course, the gold standard of language teaching methods; generally, anyone who teaches a language recommends moving for a while so you can be among native speakers if you want to make real progress. But I'd imagined that, at the intermediate and upper levels, an app like Duolingo (or Rosetta Stone, if I wanted to spend

---

Annotations

[1] to **brag** = to talk proudly about your achievements
[2] to **accrue** = *here:* to collect
[3] **What gives?** *(infml)* = What is going on?
[4] **disdain** = disrespect
[5] **proficiency** = high level of ability
[6] **point-blank** = clearly and directly
[7] **immersion** = *here:* a method of language teaching in which teachers and students use only the foreign language during classes

Part C: English as a global language

more money) could get me close enough, and that I'd only need immersion if I wanted to speak with the panache[8] of a native.

I now know from experience that an app won't even let me successfully eavesdrop[9] on a conversation between two native speakers.

Robert Daland, a UCLA linguistics professor, explained that my ability to form a sentence pieced together from snippets, as learned from Duolingo, isn't even fighting half the battle. "An equally important part of language acquisition – in fact, I would say maybe even a more important component – is perception, the ability to understand what someone means when they say something to you." He said each language comes with unique challenges when it comes to just understanding a normal sentence – things he referred to as "lazinesses or sloppinesses," that make everyday speech baffling to a non-native speaker.

Let's take an example, in English: Go ahead and say the elementary sentence, "It's in that green box over there," out loud. According to Daland, you just confused any non-native speaker by referring to a "greem box." The unwritten rules of spoken English say that when you hear an "m" at the end of green, that's actually an "n," and you've probably never given it a second thought. And it's not just that all languages allow for muddled consonants, he explained. "The way languages allow this is different," and currently, no app really teaches this kind of thing, even though the problems it presents materialize at a very basic level of speech.

"Any kind of strategy that's going to help you learn words is going to [be] beneficial for you in the long run, as long as you're learning frequent and useful words," Daland told me. But I'll never, ever get anywhere close to fluent with Duolingo. "It is going to possibly be a very helpful part of a multi-component program," he said.

Annotations
[8] **panache** /pəˈnæʃ/= when you are doing sth with panache, you are doing it with great confidence

[9] to **eavesdrop** /ˈiːvzˌdrɒp/= to listen to other people's conversations

WRITING

4 → SUPPORT D5, p. 303

 The map in 1 shows that millions of people worldwide try to learn or improve their English using a language learning app. Use your knowledge about learning a language (not necessarily with an app) to write a flyer with useful guidelines for them.

The future of English

1
a) Read the article by Nicholas Ostler and note down the three examples of English as the global language you find most interesting or surprising. Discuss your results in class.
b) Use the article to create an illustrated and annotated timeline of English as a global language. Include Ostler's predictions for the future, too.

NICHOLAS OSTLER

The Guardian, 27 February 2018

Have we reached peak English in the world?

One of Britain's greatest strengths is set to diminish as China asserts itself on the world stage

In China last month, Theresa May attended the launch of the British Council's English is Great campaign, intended to boost interest and fluency in our national language. This might sound like Donald Trump's notorious "Make America great again", but comes in fact from a stronger position. Beyond doubt, the use of English is greater than ever, and far more widespread than any other language in the world. All non-English-speaking powers of our globalised world recognise it as the first foreign language to learn; it is also, uniquely, in practical use worldwide. The British Council reckons that English is spoken at a useful level by some 1.75 billion people, a quarter of the world's population. It is taught from primary level up in all China's schools; it is the working language of the whole European Union.

On the news service France 24, English is used more prominently than French. Its use is required of all airline pilots and control towers, 24/7. And it is seen as an essential cachet[1] for progress in some amazing places: for example, 14 years ago, the prime minister of Mongolia – a country with no historic links to an English-speaking power – decreed it should replace Russian in all schools as part of his aspiration to make Ulaanbaatar a centre for telephone call services. One in six Russians claims to speak it. English is clearly the language of choice for those with global aspirations, whatever their political stance towards Anglo-Saxon powers.

This global acceptance of English, now far beyond the zones of influence of the British empire or the United States' backyard, has effectively grown up in just a century – neatly, and a little paradoxically, since the 1919 treaty of Versailles. In deference[2] to the US, this was the first international treaty written in English; but it also turned out to mark the incipient decline of the world's greatest English-speaking institution, the British empire. From a language point of view, however, British power had the good fortune to be succeeded by its cousin in North America, so that the usual historic lag[3], as political command leads on to linguistic imitation, was disguised. Even as Britain began to decline economically, its established position was reflected by increased take-up of English as the language to learn.

But all this while, especially from the 1920s to the 1990s, the focus of US expansion was changing, moving from North America to the world, leading to influence on trade, engineering, telecommunications, mining, media, science and finance, as the dollar moved to replace sterling as the world's reserve currency. This was followed by the digital information revolution, creating new fortunes based in Silicon Valley at the turn of the 21st century. These were all positive for the world role of English (a role founded by Great Britain), but should have been expected to peak later, in the growth of soft power and the increased popularity of American culture.

When circumstances change, dominant languages fall. And the change is clearly coming It is this lagged growth of English, reflecting US influence hitherto[4], that we are now experiencing. Yet it is happening in a 21st century when other nations, particularly in Asia but also in South America and Africa, are far outpacing the US (let alone Britain and the European Union) in economic growth rates. This is an amazing juncture[5] in world history. And two questions arise. Is the position of English a real asset to the states that speak it natively? And is the language likely to hold this position in the pecking order[6] indefinitely?

Considering the windfall benefits of English as one's own language, some immediate advantages are undeniable. It has given direct access to the

---

Annotations

[1] **cachet** /ˈkæʃeɪ/ = a highly regarded attribute
[2] **deference** = behaviour that shows great respect towards sb
[3] **lag** /læg/ = a period of time between one event and another
[4] **hitherto** /ˌhɪðə(r)ˈtuː/ = until now
[5] **juncture** = *here:* critical point in time
[6] **pecking order** = the order of power in a group

3 Advanced texts — Part C: English as a global language

world's principal medium of communication: good for having an inside track on "news we can use", as well as facilitated access for well-educated anglophones to influential jobs. It has also put us in a position to charge some kind of rent for allowing others admission to this linguistic elite: hence the massive earnings from teaching English as a foreign language (now well over £2bn in the UK alone, reaching £3bn by 2020), and global markets for English-language publishing (£1.4bn in exports in 2015). This is another spin-off from Britain's recent history of dominance, like the siting of the Greenwich meridian, giving daily opportunities for global trades between Asia and America, or the association of investment, and hence global finance, with the City of London.

But special knowledge of a language is an asset that wastes all too soon when it becomes global property. World English will have just a historic connection to Britain or the US, and knowing it well is no longer exclusive to native speakers. Even the short-term windfall advantages came with a moral hazard. Presumption of entitlement can breed complacency at home, as well as resentment abroad – all too evident in the current "negotiations" on Britain's divorce from Europe.

It is hard to credit the vulnerability of a language such as English – which has spread, unbidden and unplanned, far beyond its homeland, and is even claimed to be the "language of freedom". But this in itself is nothing new. Transnational lingua francas, once established, always give off an aura of permanence. Yet when circumstances change, they fall. And the change is clearly coming. And so the natural expectation will be that after the new powers, such as China, India or Brazil, establish themselves economically, politically (and probably militarily), their linguistic and cultural influence too will come to be felt, among those who want to do business with them, and then with one another. But as with all newly dominant languages, there will be a lag.

If centred on China, say, the world may be less enthusiastic for "the hidden hand" of Adam Smith's free markets. If other centres emerge, the result may be more mixed, asserting local Islamic, Buddhist or Hindu traditions. Evolving translation technologies may make languages largely interchangeable, pushing national cultures into the background. Whatever, there will be no special deference to the current English-speaking tradition.

Something like this, after all, is what happened in the 17th century, when the newly global power France won a role for French as a common language for civilised Europe: French – with strong Enlightenment overtones – replaced Latin itself, which had held that role for 15 centuries. In a different way, it is what happened in the 19th century, when the imperial interlopers Russia and Britain abolished Farsi in their Asian domains. Before that, Farsi had been pre-eminent for 800 years as the language of Muslim culture, trade and politics.

For English, therefore, its current peak is likely to be as good as it will ever get, its glory as a world language lasting just a couple of centuries – almost a flash in the pan, not yet comparable with those forerunners Latin or Farsi. And on present form, its fall is likely to coincide with the latest rise of China, whose documented history has run for three millennia. Chinese, too, is great.

Nicholas Ostler is the author of Empires of the Word, and The Last Lingua Franca. He chairs the Foundation for Endangered Languages.

→ **S1:** Checklist: Summary, p. 330

2
a) Read the article by Simon Horobin on p. 107 and summarize the changes in the English language he describes in no more than 80 words.
b) **Language awareness** Look at the different highlighted parts in the article. What kinds of English are they examples of? Sort the words and phrases into categories.
c) **EXTRA** Find more examples for your categories.

category	examples
US English	• "get a cookie", • "I'm good" …
US pronunciation	…
…	…

Part C: English as a global language — Advanced texts

What will the English language be like in 100 years?

Simon Horobin, 10 November 2015

One way of predicting the future is to look back at the past. The global role English plays today as a lingua franca – used as a means of communication by speakers of different languages – has parallels in the Latin of pre-modern Europe.

Having been spread by the success of the Roman Empire, Classical Latin was kept alive as a standard written medium throughout Europe long after the fall of Rome. But the Vulgar Latin used in speech continued to change, forming new dialects, which in time gave rise to the modern Romance languages: French, Spanish, Portuguese, Romanian and Italian.

Similar developments may be traced today in the use of English around the globe, especially in countries where it functions as a second language. New "interlanguages" are emerging, in which features of English are mingled[1] with those of other native tongues and their pronunciations. [...]

So the future for English is one of multiple Englishes.

Looking back to the early 20th century, it was the Standard English used in England, spoken with the accent known as "Received Pronunciation", that carried prestige.

But today the largest concentration of native speakers is in the US, and the influence of US English can be heard throughout the world: *can I get a cookie, I'm good, did you eat, the movies,* "skedule" rather than "shedule". In the future, to speak English will be to speak US English.

US spellings such as *disk* and *program* are already preferred to British equivalents *disc* and *programme* in computing. The dominance of US usage in the digital world will lead to the wider acceptance of further American preferences, such as *favorite, donut, dialog, center*.

What is being lost?

In the 20th century, it was feared that English dialects were dying out with their speakers. Projects such as the Survey of English Dialects (1950-61) were launched at the time to collect and preserve endangered words before they were lost forever. A similar study undertaken by the BBC's Voices Project in 2004 turned up a rich range of local accents and regional terms which are available online, demonstrating the vibrancy and longevity of dialect vocabulary.

But while numerous dialect words were collected for "young person in cheap trendy clothes and jewellery" – *pikey, charva, ned, scally* – the word *chav* was found throughout England, demonstrating how features of the Estuary English spoken in the Greater London area are displacing local dialects, especially among younger generations. [...]

In the online world, attitudes to consistency and correctness are considerably more relaxed: variant spellings are accepted and punctuation marks omitted[2], or repurposed to convey a range of attitudes. Research has shown that in electronic discourse exclamation marks can carry a range of exclamatory functions, including apologising, challenging, thanking, agreeing, and showing solidarity.

Capital letters are used to show anger, misspellings convey humour and establish group identity, and smiley-faces or emoticons express a range of reactions.

Getting shorter

Some have questioned whether the increasing development and adoption of emoji pictograms, which allow speakers to communicate without the need for language, mean that we will cease to communicate in English at all? ;-)

The fast-changing world of social media is also responsible for the coining and spreading of neologisms, or "new words". Recent updates to Oxford Dictionaries give a flavour: *mansplaining, awesomesauce, rly, bants, TL;DR* (too long; didn't read).

Clipped forms, acronyms, blends and abbreviations have long been productive methods of word formation in English (think of *bus, smog* and *scuba*) but the huge increase in such coinages[3] means that they will be far more prominent in the English of 2115.

Whether you Like 👍 or *h8* such words, think they are *NBD* or *meh*, they are undoubtedly here to stay.

Simon Horobin is Professor of English Language and Literature at the University of Oxford.

Annotations

[1] to **mingle** = to mix   [2] to **omit** = to leave out   [3] **coingage** /ˈkɔɪnɪdʒ/ = *here:* a recently created word or phrase

4 Globalization

Webcode
You can download a word list for the Intro and the WordPool here:
WES-73644-036

Webcode
You can find a link to the video here:
WES-73644-037

1

a) Think of your everyday life. Examine what aspects are affected by globalization. Give examples.
b) Collect your ideas in class and organize them in a mind map or diagram. You can use the one on the right or come up with an idea of your own.
c) Watch this video and add more details about the different aspects of globalization to your mind map or diagram.
d) Watch the video again. Concentrate on the words on the left below and match them to their meanings. → **S20:** How to listen/watch effectively, p. 366

1. ramifications
2. interdependent
3. stakeholders
4. affordable
5. remote area
6. freight charge
7. trade barrier
8. tariff
9. quota
10. catalyst
11. direct investments
12. multinational corporations
13. McWorld
14. sufficient
15. white goods

A not too expensive for someone to pay for
B a restriction that makes the international exchange of goods more difficult and expensive
C an event or person that helps to cause a great change
D large electrical goods for the house
E a fixed, limited amount that is officially allowed
F depending on each other
G the results of an action, decision, etc.
H a term that expresses criticism of the worldwide spread of western culture
I sum to pay for the transport of goods
J large companies that are active in many different countries
K people that are involved in a process
L money that is invested directly in a company
M a sum that has to be paid when goods are imported into a country
N enough
O a place far away from bigger cities

Globalization — Intro 4

effects on
- economy:
- politics:
- culture:

GLOBALIZATION

driving factors:

winners:

losers:

Preview

Global responsibility for the environment

The first part of this Theme deals with global environmental problems. In the **Workshop**, you will analyse speeches.

Globalization and the economy

Part B focuses on economic aspects of globalization.

Migration and the world of work

The third part of the Theme focuses on international migration and the world of work. In the **Workshop** you will practice writing comments.

Living in a globalized world

The last part of the Theme deals with different aspects of life in a globalized world. In the **Workshop** you will learn how to tackle speaking tasks.

2
a) Choose a photo. Prepare to describe the photo and explain how it relates to what you have learned about globalization.
b) **Group work**
   - Form groups with experts on different photos. Present the photos to each other, based on your preparation in a).
   - Discuss in your groups if you consider globalization a more positive or a more negative phenomenon based on what you have learned so far.
   - Note down the main points of your discussion.
c) Add any new points to your mind map/diagram.

3
Use your new vocabulary and what you have learned about globalization so far to write a short entry for a young people's encyclopedia in which you explain what globalization is.

A FAST-CHANGING WORLD

Globalization is the term used to describe the process of interaction and integration between people, businesses and governments on a global scale. Recent advances in transportation and communication technologies have allowed it to progress rapidly over the past few decades. Businesses are expanding their operations beyond the borders of their home countries more than ever before, and multinational corporations have come to dominate the world economy. With access to the Internet, television and telecommunication services being widely available, it has never been easier to interact with societies and individuals in geographically and culturally distant places.

MIGRATION

A factor both caused by and driving globalization, especially in recent years, is migration. There are now considerable numbers of economic migrants in many places. Some come from neighbouring countries, like the many Eastern Europeans attracted by better working conditions elsewhere in the EU. Others migrate overseas, like the Indian immigrants who have started to play an important role in the US economy. In addition, masses of people are forced to leave their home countries in search of a new life. Fleeing conflicts and political persecution in their homelands, refugees from the Middle East, Asia and Africa have been entering Europe over the past few years, seeking a safe haven in countries with a very different way of life. With migrants often unable to integrate quickly, and natives in many cases unprepared to accommodate the newcomers, tensions can arise in regions with a significant migrant presence, which makes migration a contested issue. The resentment of migrants felt by some parts of the population has resulted in an increase in political polarization in many countries.

THE DARK SIDE OF GLOBALIZED COMPANIES

Businesses and investors can benefit greatly from collaboration with partners and clients worldwide.
But there are ethical issues involved. As labour forces in countries such as China and Bangladesh are able to mass-produce goods at a low cost, many popular brands outsource the manufacture of their products to factories in such countries. Many western consumers love to purchase the latest version of a particular smartphone or items of clothing that have recently come into fashion, more often than not oblivious to the workers on the other side of the world who have been exploited for their new pair of jeans.

CONSEQUENCES FOR THE ENVIRONMENT

Unprecedented damage to the environment is another effect of globalization. Scientists warn us that the Earth is running out of resources. Plastics pollute the oceans, which is potentially harmful to our health. Climate change is being accelerated by the excessive energy consumption needed to sustain economic expansion. As a result, rising sea levels as well as hurricanes and other extreme weather events could seriously endanger humanity if left unchecked.

A WAY FORWARD?

Globalization is not an inherently negative process. However, the freedom of individuals, corporations and governments to operate on a global scale does not come without its responsibilities. With the well-being of the global population at stake, there must be a collective, worldwide effort to address urgent issues such as mass-migration, take action against the exploitation of workers, and find both short-term and long-term solutions to reverse the damage that has already been done by climate change.

Globalization WordPool

1

Rewrite these sentences using words or phrases from the text that have a similar meaning to the underlined passages.

1. In recent years, extreme weather conditions have reached a level which mankind has never experienced before.
2. As a consequence of these storms, droughts and floods, many people's livelihoods are in danger.
3. Many professors and researchers claim that CO_2 and other gases are mainly responsible for this development.
4. Without the joint effort of people all around the globe, it will be difficult to turn the trend towards higher emissions of CO_2 and other greenhouse gases around.
5. One important factor is the use of fossil fuels like coal, oil and gas, which are the energy resources that keep worldwide production and transport going.
6. Despite the environmental damage caused by fossil fuels, mankind has such an appetite for them that we are approaching their depletion.
7. However, it is highly controversial whether renewable energies can completely replace fossil fuels in the near future.
8. In any case, customers should become more aware of the power they have to bring about change in making industrial production and the supply of energy more environmentally friendly.

2

Complete the grid with the corresponding words. Use a dictionary, if necessary.

noun	adjective	verb
tension	tense	...
...	exploitative	...
...	...	sustain
persecution		...
resentment	...	...
collaboration	...	...
integration	...	...
...	...	pollute

3

Fill in the missing prepositions.

1. Many chemicals that are used in the production of jeans, for example, are harmful **1** the workers' health.
2. After some accidents at clothes factories in South Asia, some major clothing companies have got involved **2** an initiative to improve working conditions.
3. However, it is difficult to take effective action **3** inhumane working conditions in the context of fast fashion.
4. But it is not just workers in developing countries that need to adjust **4** the globalized economy.
5. As many people in the developing countries have access **5** the Internet as well, they increasingly compete **6** workers from the developed world for the same jobs.
6. In addition, many jobs in manufacturing are moved **7** cheaper production facilities in developing countries by the process of outsourcing.

Webcode

You can download the grid here:
WES-73644-038

4

Look at the photos on this double page and find captions for them using phrases from the text on the left.

111

4 Workshop: Step by step — Part A: Global responsibility for the environment

Webcode
You can download a word list for Part A here:
WES-73644-039

→ **S25:** How to work with a dictionary, p. 374

Step by step Analysing a speech

PRE-READING

1

a) **Pair work** Study the infographic and explain the greenhouse effect to your partner.

b) Make sure you know the meaning of the words. If necessary, use a dictionary. Use the words below in a flow chart to present the consequences of climate change.

> flooding | drought | glacier | melting polar icecaps | famine | rising sea level | crop failure | extreme weather conditions | spreading of tropical diseases | heat wave | desertification | changing habitat | health risk

c) **Pair work** Describe your flow chart to a partner. → SUPPORT D1, p. 304

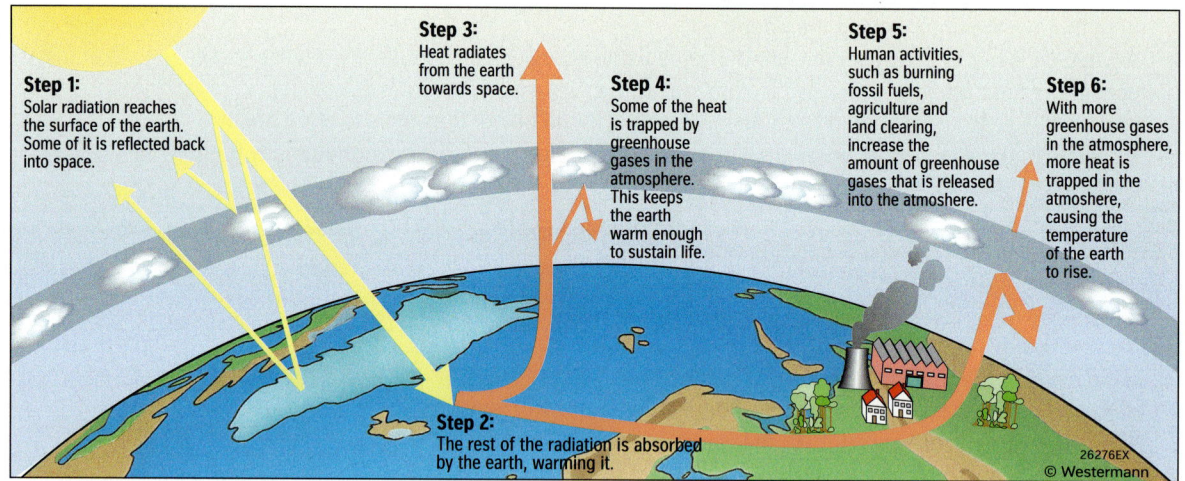

Info

Paris Agreement

The Paris Agreement is an international agreement negotiated by representatives from 196 countries and signed in 2016. It aims to ensure that, in this century, global average temperatures do not increase by more than 2 °C above the temperatures of pre-industrial times.

2 DVD/13

In his documentary *Before the flood*, actor and film producer Leonardo DiCaprio explores the consequences of climate change and what could be done about it.

a) Watch the sequence from the beginning of the documentary and explain why DiCaprio has chosen a famous painting as an introduction to his film.

b) DiCaprio is shown at a UN conference on climate change. Explain why he is invited to speak to the representatives from the different nations.

Webcode
You can find the video here:
WES-73644-040

Webcode
You can find the audio file here:
WES-73644-041

→ **S20:** How to listen/watch effectively, p. 366

COMPREHENSION

3 CD/07

Listen to the speech that the actor Leonardo DiCaprio delivered at the United Nations climate summit after the Paris Agreement had been signed. Sum up the purpose of his speech in one sentence.

Part A: Global responsibility for the environment
Workshop: Step by step

4

Preview

In this Workshop, you will analyse speeches. After listening to a speech to get a feeling for the way it affects the audience, you will work with a transcript of the speech, analysing its structure and rhetorical devices.

ANALYSIS

4 CD/07

Study how DiCaprio uses emphasis to get his message across.
a) Listen again and note down words or phrases which are specially stressed and/or can be considered as keywords of the speech.
b) Use the words on your list to summarize the content of the speech.
c) Choose three adjectives from the box below to describe the way DiCaprio delivers his speech and its effect on the listeners.

> convincing | dramatic | stern | emphatic | poignant | warning | urgent | insistent | impressive | serious | pointed | moving | forceful | beseeching | threatening | matter-of-fact

d) **Pair work** Explain your choice to a partner.

Webcode
You can find the audio file here:
WES-73644-041

→ **S1:** Checklist: Summary, p. 330

5 Language awareness

Read the transcript of the speech. Use the language support to explain the function of the different parts of the speech. → SUPPORT D2, p. 304

→ **S14:** How to analyse a speech, p. 355

Language support

> introduces the topic of his speech by … | draws a historical parallel to … | provides examples of/from … | proves the necessity to/of … | uses the evidence of … to justify … | claims/acknowleges/concedes that … | argues in favour of/against … | concludes his speech by referring back to/by appealing to … | appeals to his audience morally to …

Thank you, Mr. Secretary General, for the honour to address this body[1] once more. And thanks to the distinguished climate leaders assembled here today who are ready
5 to take action.
President Abraham Lincoln was also thinking of bold action 150 years ago when he said, "The dogmas of the quiet past are inadequate to the stormy present. As our
10 case is new so we must think anew and act anew. We must disenthrall[2] ourselves and then we shall save our country."
He was speaking before the US Congress to confront the defining issue of his time –
15 slavery.
Everyone knew it had to end but no one had the political will to stop it. Remarkably, his words ring as true today when applied to the defining crisis of our time – climate change.

20 As a UN Messenger of Peace, I have travelled all over the world for the last two years documenting how this crisis is changing the natural balance of our planet. I have seen cities like Beijing choked[3] by industrial
25 pollution, ancient Boreal forests[4] in Canada that have been clear cut, and rainforests in Indonesia that have been incinerated. In India I met farmers whose crops have been literally[5] washed away by historic flooding.
30 In America I have witnessed unprecedented droughts in California and sea level rise flooding the streets of Miami. In Greenland[6] and in the Arctic I was astonished to see that ancient glaciers are rapidly disappearing
35 well ahead of scientific predictions. All that I have seen and learned on this journey has absolutely terrified me.
There is no doubt in the world's scientific

Annotations
[1] **body** = *here:* a group of people
[2] to **disenthrall** onself from sth / ˌdɪsɪnˈθrɔːl/= *sich von etw freimachen*
[3] to **choke** /tʃəʊk/= to make it impossible to breathe
[4] **Boreal forests** = *nördliche Nadelwälder*
[5] **literally** = *wörtlich; hier zur Bekräftigung*
[6] **Greenland** = *Grönland*

4 Workshop: Step by step — Part A: Global responsibility for the environment

community that this is a direct result of human activity and that the effects of climate change will become astronomically worse in the future.

I do not need to tell you these statistics. You know them better than I do, but more importantly, you know what will happen if this scourge[7] is left unchecked. You know that climate change is happening faster than even the most pessimistic of scientists warned us decades ago. It has become a runaway[8] freight train bringing with it an impending disaster for all living things.

Now think about the shame that each of us will carry when our children and grandchildren look back and realize that we had the means of stopping this devastation, but simply lacked the political will to do so. Yes, we have achieved the Paris Agreement. More countries have come together here to sign this agreement today than for any other cause in the history of humankind – and that is reason for hope – but unfortunately the evidence shows us that it will not be enough.

Our planet cannot be saved unless we leave fossil fuels in the ground where they belong. An upheaval and massive change is required, right now. One that leads to a new collective consciousness. A new collective evolution of the human race, inspired and enabled by a sense of urgency from all of you.

We all know that reversing the course of climate change will not be easy, but the tools are in our hands – if we apply them before it is too late.

Renewable energy, fossil fuels, and putting a price on carbon pollution are beginning to turn the tide[9]. This transition is not only the right thing for our world, but it also makes clear economic sense, and is possible within our lifetime.

But it is now upon you[10] to do what great leaders have always done: to lead, to inspire, and empower as President Lincoln did in his time.

We can congratulate each other today, but it will mean absolutely nothing if you return to your countries and fail to push beyond the promises of this historic agreement. Now is the time for bold unprecedented action.

My friends, look at the delegates around you. It is time to ask each other – which side of history will you be on?

As a citizen of our planet who has witnessed so much on this journey, I thank you all for everything you have done to lay the foundation of a solution to this crisis, but after 21 years of debates and conferences it is time to declare no more talk. No more excuses. No more ten-year studies. No more allowing the fossil fuel companies to manipulate and dictate the science and policies that affect our future. This is the only body that can do what is needed. All of you, sitting in this very hall[11].

The world is now watching. You will either be lauded by future generations, or vilified by them.

Lincoln's words still resonate to all of us here today, "We will be remembered in spite of ourselves. The fiery[12] trial[13] through which we pass will light us down, in honour or dishonour, to the last generation. We shall nobly save, or meanly lose, the last best hope of earth."

That is our charge[14] now – you are the last best hope of Earth. We ask you to protect it. Or we – and all living things we cherish[15] – are history.

Annotations

[7] **scourge** /skɜː(r)dʒ/ = sth that is extremely harmful
[8] **runaway** = out of control
[9] to **turn the tide** = to change a situation for the better
[10] **it is upon you to** = it is your task to
[11] **in this very hall** = precisely in this hall (used for emphasis)
[12] **fiery** /ˈfaɪri/ = like or consisting of fire; *here:* difficult/dangerous
[13] **trial** /ˈtraɪəl/ = *here:* a test; sth that is painful and difficult
[14] **charge** = *here:* responsibility
[15] to **cherish sb/sth** /ˈtʃerɪʃ/ = to treat sb/sth with care because you appreciate sb/sth

Part A: Global responsibility for the environment — Workshop: Step by step

6 Language awareness

In his speech DiCaprio uses several rhetorical devices to convince his audience of the need to act.
a) Study the info box and the examples, then identify more of these devices in DiCaprio's speech. Frequently a combination of rhetorical devices is used to increase the effect on the audience.
b) Explain the function or effect of the rhetorical devices. Refer to the context and the purpose of the speech in order to give a meaningful interpretation. → SUPPORT D3, p. 304

→ **S14:** How to analyse a speech, p. 355

Info

device	definition	example
alliteration	repetition of the initial sound in two or more words to emphasize the phrase and make it more memorable	turn the tide
allusion	reference to a detail of common knowledge, e.g. a historical incident, famous person, song title etc. to draw a parallel or point out similarities	DiCaprio refers to Abraham Lincoln and the issue of slavery.
anaphora	repetition of the first word or phrase of a sentence to emphasize the importance of the statement	You know them …, you know what will happen … You know that …
antithesis/ contrast	the use of opposite ideas to denote a clear distinction/encompass extremes/highlight a certain development	his time – our time honour – dishonour
direct address	to involve the audience directly and give each person the feeling of being referred to individually	My friends, … you
ellipsis	incomplete sentence limited to only a few words which are esssential to the issue	No more excuses.
enumeration/ accumulation	using a list of items/actions to convey an impression of including different groups/ problems/steps to achieve a goal etc., to intensify a picture	I have seen cities like Beijing …, ancient Boreal forests …, and rainforests in Indonesia …
inclusive language	words or phrases that place speaker and audience on the same level and help to identify with the goal	we – our – ourselves all of us
metaphorical language	a word or phrase creating a picture in the reader's mind and triggering associations	Beijing choked by industrial pollution
repetition	repeating certain words to highlight their importance for the purpose of the speech	we must think anew and act anew
rhetorical question	a question which does not expect an answer, but serves as emphasis or to make the audience think	Which side of history will you be on?

7
Use your results from tasks 4-6 to write an analysis of the speech. → SUPPORT D4, p. 304

→ **S9:** How to structure a text, p. 344

115

Workshop: Practice
Part A: Global responsibility for the environment

Practice: Analysing a speech

COMPREHENSION

1 Read the speech Obama delivered at the Paris UN conference on climate change and point out what dangers he envisages.

Nearly 200 nations have assembled here this week – a declaration that for all the challenges we face, the growing threat of climate change could define the contours
5 of this century more dramatically than any other. What should give us hope that this is a turning point, that this is the moment we finally determined we would save our planet, is the fact that our nations share a
10 sense of urgency about this challenge and a growing realization that it is within our power to do something about it.

Our understanding of the ways human beings disrupt the climate advances by the
15 day. Fourteen of the fifteen warmest years on record have occurred since the year 2000 – and 2015 is on pace to be the warmest year of all. No nation – large or small, wealthy or poor – is immune to what this means.
20 This summer, I saw the effects of climate change firsthand in our northernmost state, Alaska, where the sea is already swallowing villages and eroding shorelines; where permafrost thaws and the tundra
25 burns; where glaciers are melting at a pace unprecedented in modern times. And it was a preview of one possible future – a glimpse of our children's fate if the climate keeps changing faster than our efforts to address
30 it. Submerged countries. Abandoned cities. Fields that no longer grow. Political disruptions that trigger new conflict, and even more floods of desperate peoples seeking the sanctuary[1] of nations not their
35 own.

That future is not one of strong economies, nor is it one where fragile states can find their footing. That future is one that we have the power to change. Right here. Right
40 now. But only if we rise[2] to this moment. As one of America's governors has said, "We are the first generation to feel the impact of climate change, and the last generation that can do something about it."
45 I've come here personally, as the leader of the world's largest economy and the second-largest emitter, to say that the United States of America not only recognizes our role in creating this problem, we embrace our
50 responsibility to do something about it.

Over the last seven years, we've made ambitious investments in clean energy, and ambitious reductions in our carbon emissions. [...]
55 The advances we've made have helped drive our economic output to all-time highs, and drive our carbon pollution to its lowest levels in nearly two decades.

But the good news is this is not an American
60 trend alone. Last year, the global economy grew while global carbon emissions from burning fossil fuels stayed flat. And what this means can't be overstated[3]. We have broken the old arguments for inaction. We
65 have proved that strong economic growth and a safer environment no longer have to conflict with one another; they can work in concert with one another.

And that should give us hope. [...]
70 So our task here in Paris is to turn these achievements into an enduring framework for human progress – not a stopgap solution, but a long-term strategy that gives the world confidence in a low-carbon future.
75 Here, in Paris, let's secure an agreement that builds in ambition, where progress paves the way[4] for regularly updated targets [...].

Here in Paris, let's agree to a strong system of transparency that gives each of us the
80 confidence that all of us are meeting our commitments. [...]

Here in Paris, let's reaffirm our commitment that resources will be there for countries willing to do their part to skip the dirty
85 phase of development. And I recognize this will not be easy [...] that's why, this afternoon, I'll join many of you to announce an historic joint effort to accelerate public and private clean energy innovation on a
90 global scale. [...]

Annotations
[1] to **seek sanctuary** = *Zuflucht suchen*
[2] to **rise to sth** = to take on sth that is difficult with enthusiasm
[3] to **overstate** = to exaggerate
[4] to **pave the way for sth** = to make preparations in order to make sth possible or easier

Part A: Global responsibility for the environment — Workshop: Practice

And finally, here in Paris, let's show businesses and investors that the global economy is on a firm path towards a low-carbon future. If we put the right rules and incentives in place, we'll unleash the creative power of our best scientists and engineers and entrepreneurs to deploy[5] clean energy technologies and the new jobs and new opportunities that they create all around the world. There are hundreds of billions of dollars ready to deploy to countries around the world if they get the signal that we mean business[6] this time. Let's send that signal. [...]

And let there be no doubt, the next generation is watching what we do. Just over a week ago, I was in Malaysia, where I held a town hall[7] with young people, and the first question I received was from a young Indonesian woman. And it wasn't about terrorism, it wasn't about the economy, it wasn't about human rights. It was about climate change. And she asked whether I was optimistic about what we can achieve here in Paris, and what young people like her could do to help.

I want our actions to show her that we're listening. I want our actions to be big enough to draw on[8] the talents of all our people – men and women, rich and poor – I want to show her passionate, idealistic young generation that we care about their future.

For I believe, in the words of Dr. Martin Luther King, Jr., that there is such a thing as being too late. And when it comes to climate change, that hour is almost upon us. But if we act here, if we act now, if we place our own short-term interests behind the air that our young people will breathe, and the food that they will eat, and the water that they will drink, and the hopes and dreams that sustain their lives, then we won't be too late for them.

And, my fellow leaders, accepting this challenge will not reward us with moments of victory that are clear or quick. Our progress will be measured differently – in the suffering that is averted, and a planet that's preserved. And that's what's always made this so hard. Our generation may not even live to see the full realization[9] of what we do here. But the knowledge that the next generation will be better off for what we do here – can we imagine a more worthy reward than that? Passing that on to our children and our grandchildren, so that when they look back and they see what we did here in Paris, they can take pride in our achievement.

Let that be the common purpose here in Paris. A world that is worthy of our children. A world that is marked not by conflict, but by cooperation; and not by human suffering, but by human progress. A world that's safer, and more prosperous, and more secure, and more free than the one that we inherited. Let's get to work. Thank you very much.

Annotations
[5] to **deploy** = to put to use
[6] to **mean business** = to be serious about doing sth
[7] to **hold a town hall** (AE) = (referring to politicians) to answer questions from the public at an event
[8] to **draw on** = to make use of a resource
[9] **realization** = putting a plan into action

ANALYSIS

2 Language awareness

Analyse the rhetorical devices Obama uses to draw a convincing picture of the dangers, to give his audience hope and encourage them to take action.

→ **S14:** How to analyse a speech, p. 355

COMMENT

3
a) Watch the trailer of the film *An inconvenient sequel: Truth to power* and describe the development since 2016.
b) CHALLENGE Explain how images are used to comment on the change.

Webcode
You can find a link to the video here:
WES-73644-042

4
Use your knowledge about climate change to comment on US President Donald Trump's decision to pull out of the Paris Agreement.

→ **S20:** How to listen/watch effectively, p. 366

→ **S6:** How to write a discussion/comment, p. 338

4 Texts — Part A: Global responsibility for the environment

Plastic waste – a growing problem

1

a) Read the text and summarize it in one sentence.
b) Take notes to answer the following questions:
  • What is the general problem the article deals with?
  • What are the causes of the problem?
  • What are the consequences?
  • What advice is the reader given?
c) **Pair work** Compare your results and add any aspects to your notes that you may have missed.

The oceans are drowning in plastic — and no one's paying attention

Dominique Mosbergen, 27 April 2017

"We're being overwhelmed by our waste."

Imagine an area 34 times the size of Manhattan. Now imagine it covered ankle-deep in plastic waste – piles of soda[1] bottles and plastic bags, takeout containers[2] by the
5 mile, drinking straws[3] as far as the eye can see.
That's a total of about 19 billion pounds of garbage. And according to one of the best estimates available, that's how much
10 plastic waste ends up in our oceans every year.
"We're being overwhelmed by our waste," said Jenna Jambeck, an environmental engineer who led the 2015 study that
15 determined this staggering number. According to Jambeck's research, this figure is on track to double by 2025 unless something is done, swiftly and at a global scale, to stem the tide of garbage[4].
20 Plastic – a versatile, durable and inexpensive material – has in many ways been a boon to humanity, used in everything from medical equipment to parts of airplanes. But some of the very traits that have made plastics
25 so popular (they're cheap, and therefore easy to throw away) have also made them a growing problem in our landfills and oceans. Today, plastics are the No. 1 type of trash found in the sea. Ocean Conservancy,
30 a nonprofit that organizes an annual coastal cleanup event in more than 150 countries worldwide, said plastic debris[5] makes up around 85 percent of all the trash collected from beaches, waterways and oceans – and
35 that's just the stuff we can see.
There are also untold numbers of extremely small plastic fragments in marine[6] waters. Plastics are non-biodegradable[7] and merely break down into smaller and smaller pieces
40 with exposure to sunlight. These fragments, known as microplastics, are less than 5 millimeters long, or about the size of a sesame seed. Some are microbeads[8], tiny pieces of plastic that are added as exfoliants
45 to health and beauty products, while others come from larger plastic pieces that have degraded over time.
Recent studies have found that microplastics can also get washed out of synthetic
50 clothing, like those made of polyester or acrylic. A 2016 paper concluded that a single cycle of a washing machine could release more than 700,000 microplastic fibers[9] into the environment.
55 [...] So, how does all this plastic waste end up in the oceans?
Some of it comes from ships and offshore oil and gas platforms, but more than 80 percent of plastic waste in the oceans comes
60 from land. Activities like the deliberate dumping of garbage into waterways and water pollution by plastic manufacturers contribute to some of this ocean trash, but mismanaged waste disposal appears to be
65 the primary culprit[10].
In 2010, according to Jambeck's research,

Annotations
[1] **soda** *(AE)* = *Getränk mit Kohlensäure*
[2] **takeout container** = *Verpackung für Essen zum Mitnehmen*
[3] **drinking straw** = *Strohhalm*
[4] **to stem the tide of garbage** = *sich der Müllflut entgegenstellen*
[5] **debris** /ˈdebriː/ = *hier: (verstreuter) Müll*
[6] **marine** /məˈriːn/ = *associated with the sea*
[7] **non-biodegradable** = *nicht biologisch abbaubar*
[8] **microbead** /ˈmaɪkrəʊˌbiːd/ = *small rounded piece*
[9] **fiber** *(Am. spelling)* = *Faser*
[10] **culprit** /ˈkʌlprɪt/ = *the person or thing responsible for something bad*

Part A: Global responsibility for the environment — Texts

over 50 percent of waste in more than 60 countries worldwide was found to be inadequately managed, mostly due to a lack of waste management infrastructure coupled[11] with ballooning[12] populations. [...] Developing nations don't bear all the blame: The United States has an ocean pollution problem, too. The main issue in this country is littering, according to Jambeck. "Even though we do have robust and effective waste management systems, we have litter," she said. "And because our per-person waste generation rate is so high in the U.S., even that small amount of litter contributes to this problem." The United States is one of the world's top five waste-generating developed countries, according to the World Economic Forum.

Litter that consists of single-use plastic products is a particularly troublesome source of ocean garbage – the plastic bag wafting[13] in the wind that finds its way to a storm drain[14]; the potato chip bag forgotten on a beach; the plastic soda bottle washed away in a stream that leads to a river and, finally, the sea.

Worldwide, "single-use packaging is the biggest source of trash" found in or near bodies of water[15], said Ocean Conservancy's Nick Mallos. In 2015, volunteers in the group's International Coastal Cleanup event collected almost 1 million plastic beverage bottles, 800,000 plastic bottle caps[16], and about half a million each of plastic bags and drinking straws – and this was in just a single day. [...]

Ocean Conservancy says plastics are believed to threaten at least 600 different wildlife species. One in three leatherback turtles[17], which often mistake plastic bags for edible jellyfish, have been found with plastic in their bellies. In February, a dead whale beached on Norway's coast had 30 plastic bags in its stomach. Ninety percent of seabirds, including albatross and petrels[18], are now eating plastics on a regular basis. By 2050, that figure is expected to rise to 100 percent.

And it's not just wildlife that's threatened by the plastics in our seas. A growing body of evidence[19] suggests humans are consuming plastics through the seafood we eat. [...] For now, the potential risks to human health posed by this plastic consumption are not totally clear – although preliminary research suggests some plastics could be toxic to humans, and could potentially increase the risk of cancer and liver damage, reproductive[20] problems, and other negative health effects.

With this in mind, experts say that all of us have a critical role to play in mitigating the issue – in ways both big and small. [...] We can all start by thinking twice before we use single-use plastic products – and when we do use them, we should take care to properly dispose of them or recycle.

"The one thing I've learned in doing my research is that population density is a huge driver of ocean pollution, so especially in places with high population densities, our individual choices really do matter," Jambeck said. "Things that may seem mundane[21], like using a reusable bottle or a reusable bag – when taken collectively, these choices really do make a difference. I think it's empowering as a citizen to know that your choices can make an impact."

Annotations
[11] **coupled** = combined and producing a particular effect as a consequence
[12] **to balloon** /bəˈluːn/ = to grow very fast
[13] **to waft** /wɑːft/ = to float through the air
[14] **storm drain** = Gully
[15] **body of water** = Gewässer
[16] **cap** = hier: Deckel
[17] **leatherback turtle** = Lederschildkröte
[18] **petrel** /ˈpetrəl/ = a specific type of seabird
[19] **body of evidence** = all of the evidence taken together
[20] **reproductive** = Fortpflanzungs-
[21] **mundane** /ˌmʌnˈdeɪn/ = not interesting, ordinary

2 Group work
a) Discuss how the information you have gathered relates to your own lifestyle.
b) Language awareness Design a poster or a leaflet to raise awareness about the problems associated with plastic.
  • Think of a catchy headline. Try to use rhetorical devices like an alliteration or a rhyme.
  • Use rhetorical devices, e.g. rhetorical questions, anaphoras, inclusive language, etc.
  • Use visuals like photos or statistics.
  • Conclude with an appeal, suggestion or advice.
c) **Gallery walk** Hang up your leaflets or posters in class. Write comments on the other students' work and stick them on the posters. You can comment on positive aspects and/or make suggestions as to what could be improved.

4 Advanced texts — Part A: Global responsibility for the environment

Preparing to leave planet Earth?

1

T.C. Boyle's novel *The terranauts*, published in 2016, deals with the "Ecosphere experiment".

a) Read the first extract to find out what kind of experiment it is and what motivated it.

b) **CHALLENGE** **Language awareness** The story is told from multiple perspectives. In this extract, Ramsay Roothoorp, the publicity officer, is the narrator. Analyse how T.C. Boyle uses choice of words and stylistic devices to reveal Roothoorp's attitude towards the project.

The terranauts
by T.C. Boyle

Extract 1

The whole notion of the Ecosphere, of eight people confining themselves willingly in a man-made world for twenty-four months, caught the public's imagination precisely
5 *because* of that hook[1], the conceit[2] of voluntary imprisonment – not to mention the Mars connection. If E2 was supposed to be an experiment in world-building, it was also about business, the kind of potentially
10 remunerative enterprise[3] that enticed a man like Darren Iverson to put up his money in the first place. The Earth was running out of resources, global warming was beginning to be recognized as a science fact
15 and not science fiction, and if man was to evolve to play a part in things instead of being just another doomed organism on a doomed planet, if the *technosphere* was going to replace pure biological processes,
20 then sooner or later we'd have to seed life elsewhere – on Mars, to begin with.

Annotations
[1] **hook** /hʊk/= here: attraction
[2] **conceit** /kənˈsiːt/= here: clever and unusual idea
[3] **enterprise** = a new and challenging project

2

a) Read the second extract and outline what happened on the first mission.

b) Analyse how the media and the public are presented. Quote from the text to prove your view.

c) **CHALLENGE** Examine how the narrator, Ramsay Roothoorp, talks about the incident, the mission and the people involved. Explain what this reveals about his character.

Extract 2

[…] one of the crew – Roberta Brownlow – had a medical emergency, the seals were broken, and the deal was off. She was out in
25 the world, your world (what we like to call E1, the original ecosphere) for less than five hours, but even if it had been five minutes, five *seconds*, the whole thing would have collapsed. Because it was the conceit that
30 counted, and couldn't anybody see that?
If they *were* on Mars, she would have died. They all would have died. If not from O₂ depletion[1], then starvation. The fact was, the Mission One crew was to go on to break
35 closure[2] in a panoply of ways during the course of the mission – once the precedent had been set, they all figured[3] why not? – and the public saw through that and labeled the whole thing a sham[4]. Goodbye.
40 Adios. Forget the lessons learned. Forget ecology. Forget modeling[5] and the Intensive Agriculture Biome[6] and the elegant interaction of the wilderness biomes and all
the rest. All that mattered was that the crew
45 had broken closure, reneged on a promise, on the *deal*, and that was laughable, it really was. What did E.O. Wilson say?
If those committed to the quest fail, they will be forgiven. The moral imperative of humanism
50 *is the endeavour alone, whether successful or not, provided*[7] *the effort is honourable and failure memorable.*
Well, he was wrong. There is no forgiveness and there won't be the next time or the
55 time after that and we weren't about to make the same mistake. Tell me: what does closure mean? It means closure. Period[8]. The good news was that Mission Control[9] was on board[10] with that, one hundred percent.
60 Of course they were – learn from your mistakes, right? They did a whole lot of fast back-pedalling and settled into prophylactic mode, as in let's anticipate the problems before they arise. They'd made Gretchen
65 Frost have her wisdom teeth removed,

Annotations
[1] **O₂ depletion** /dɪˈpliːʃ(ə)n/ = lack of oxygen
[2] **closure** /ˈkləʊʒə(r)/ = here: state of being locked in
[3] to **figure** *(infml)* /ˈfɪɡə(r)/ = here: to think
[4] **sham** = sth that is not real, authentic or honest
[5] **modeling** = the making of models, in this case of ecological systems
[6] **biome** /ˈbaɪəʊm/ = an area of the world with a particular climate and a particular combination of animals and plants
[7] **provided** = (only) if
[8] **period** = used to emphasise that there is no more to be said about a topic
[9] **Mission Control** = the group of people observing and controlling the enterprise from the outside
[10] to **be on board with** sth = to support sth, to agree with sth

Part A: Global responsibility for the environment — Advanced texts

and T.T. (Troy Turner) took a course in emergency dentistry, just in case, and we all lauded that. [...]

And, as I said, even if one of us had something catastrophic occur once we were inside – ruptured appendix, gangrene, heart failure – it wouldn't have made an iota of difference[11]. That would be it. Death was as much a part of natural processes as life, and in strictly Darwinian terms[12], practical terms, that is, it would be a boon for the other seven. As it was[13], we'd be hard-pressed[14] to feed ourselves, if the Mission One crew was any indication, and to have one less digestive tract[15] up and working would go a long way toward taking some of the pressure off.

I'm talking theoretically here, of course, and strictly in terms of caloric intake[16] – the loss of any of us would be a public relations disaster and an emotional one too, because we *were* a team and we were dedicated[17] to one another no matter what anybody tells you. [...] I suppose you can never underestimate people's appetite for the sensational – if somebody *were* to die inside, there's no doubt our public awareness factor would shoot up. Simple as that. Not that it was going to happen, but we were prepared for anything. If the eight of us had stopped short of lacerating our palms and taking a blood oath, we'd made our pact nonetheless. Nothing in, nothing out. That was our mantra.

Was Roberta Brownlow's situation unfortunate? Yes, of course it was. And I'm sure you remember the flap[18] over it – furore, really – and how the press came howling after her like hyenas on a scent. Or jackals, I suppose, since hyenas don't howl, do they? She was Mission One's MDA[19], very good-looking, stunning actually, an exemplar of what our species has come to consider the prime breeding stock[20], with a robust figure, abundant hair and teeth like piano keys – the white ones, that is – and she had a way with the press that was just short of flirtatious on the one hand and all business on the other. She was a perfect choice, not simply by way of looks but because she was first-rate at what she did, which, though it involved the least scientific knowledge or discipline, was on some level the most essential function of the crew: to provide food. She wasn't "Supervisor of Field Crops," the title that would go to Diane Kesselring on our mission, but the lion's share of her work went into food production, more than anyone else's. So she was a fit, Roberta Brownlow, and we were all proud of her. (Yes, we: I came aboard, as most people will know, two months before Mission One closure, putting my head down and working support staff till training started for Mission Two). But accidents happen.

Annotations
[11] **it wouldn't have made an iota of difference** /aɪˈəʊtə/ = it would have made no difference at all
[12] **in Darwinian terms** = referring to the scientist Charles Darwin (1809-1882), famous for his theory of evolution by natural selection
[13] **as it was** = already
[14] **to be hard-pressed to do sth** = to have difficulty doing sth
[15] **digestive tract** = *Verdauungstrakt*
[16] **caloric intake** = *Kalorienzufuhr*
[17] **to be dedicated to one another** = to feel responsible for each other's well-being
[18] **flap** = *hier: Aufregung*
[19] **MDA** = *here:* Manager of Domestic Animals, in charge of the animals that would provide the crew with the necessary essential fats and proteins
[20] **breeding stock** = *Zuchtmaterial*

3
Roberta Brownlow was a crew member on the first mission. Consider what it must have felt like to be one of the chosen 8 for mission 1 and finally be the one to blame for its failure. Write an interior monologue. Refer to aspects of her experience as well as her feelings, hopes and worries.

→ **S2:** Checklist: Creative writing, p. 331

4
a) Watch a video about *Biosphere 2*. Say what you find most surprising and most shocking.
b) Note down information on:
- the history of the project,
- the construction of *Biosphere 2*,
- problems associated with life in a closed system,
- the scientific insights gained from the experiment.

Webcode
You can find a link to the video here:
WES-73644-043

→ **S20:** How to listen/watch effectively, p. 366

5 CHOOSE
Use your notes from task 4 to comment on humankind's attempt to do a trial run of life on Mars in order to save humanity from impending ecological disaster.
OR
a) Research national and international biosphere projects on the Internet and give a brief presentation on your findings.
b) Discuss the usefulness of these kinds of experiments in class.

Texts Part B: Globalization and the economy

Globalization and the fashion industry

Webcode
You can download a word list for Part B here:
WES-73644-044

Webcode
You can download the survey questions here:
WES-73644-045

PRE-READING

1

a) Global production and availability of goods has opened up a shoppers' paradise, especially for clothing items. Use the following questions to conduct a class survey on your shopping habits.

1. How often do you shop for clothes?
   ❏ every week ❏ every month ❏ every season

2. Do you follow the latest trends?
   ❏ always ❏ sometimes ❏ never

3. How much do you spend every month?
   ❏ less than €40 ❏ €40-80 ❏ more than €80

4. Are fashion labels important to you?
   ❏ absolutely ❏ not really ❏ not at all

5. How important are the clothes on a person you meet for the first time?
   ❏ essential ❏ not really important ❏ irrelevant

b) Use the results of the survey to discuss how important fashion is in your class.

→ **S6:** How to write a discussion/comment, p. 338

Webcode
You can find a link to the video here:
WES-73644-046

2

a) You are going to watch a video in which the expression "fast fashion" is used. You already know the term "fast food". Note down the advantages and disadvantages of "fast food".
b) Watch the trailer of the documentary "The true cost" and describe the problems it highlights.
c) Watch the trailer again and note down what pictures impress you most. Give reasons.
d) Discuss which features of "fast food" can be attributed to "fast fashion".

→ **S20:** How to listen/ watch effectively, p. 366

3 Pair work

a) Study one of the diagrams each. Present them to each other and decide what information you find most surprising.
b) Use the information to explain the title of the documentary the trailer for which you worked on in task 2: "The true cost – the future is on sale".

Product-Lifecycle Impact of Studied Levi's® 501® Jeans

is equivalent to:

- 32.3 kg of CO_2 • 78 miles driven by the average car in the United States
- 3480.5 litres of water • 53 showers (based on 7 minute showers)
- 400.1 MJ of energy • Powering a computer for 556 hours

The Journey of Levi's Jeans

1. Yarn[1] from the Republic of Korea
2. Fabric is woven[2] and dyed[3] in Taipei, China
3. Fabric is cut in Bangladesh
4. Zippers[4] produced in the Philippines
5. Assembled[5] into jeans in Cambodia
6. Exported to the rest of the world
* Li and Fung coordinates all activities from Hong Kong, China

Annotations
[1] **yarn** = cotton, wool
[2] to **weave** = weben
[3] to **dye** = färben
[4] **zipper** = Reißverschluss
[5] to **assemble** = to put together

122

Part B: Globalization and the economy — Texts

COMPREHENSION

4
Read the article below. Outline the problems Daisy Buchanan depicts and the solutions she offers.

DAISY BUCHANAN   The Guardian, 08 November 2017

The Zara workers' protest shows why fast fashion should worry all of us

With workers for a supplier in Turkey putting notes in clothes complaining over pay, has sexism prevented us from taking industry exploitation seriously?

If I search for #Zara on Instagram, I can see well over 22m posts of people wearing clothing that was bought from the retailer, everywhere from Dublin to Dubrovnik, New York to Newport. If you're reading this in an office, I'd bet you a tenner that someone, somewhere in the building is wearing a Zara shirt or jacket. In the UK, Zara has been a high-street fixture[1] since 1998, and has a growing number of stores. Millions of us have brought the brand into our homes – and so millions of us should be shocked and infuriated by reports that factory workers in Istanbul have been hiding notes in the clothes that they have been producing for one of Zara's suppliers, pleading for help. One note apparently read: "I made this item you are going to buy, but I didn't get paid for it." The workers were reportedly left unpaid after their factory shut down overnight.
Inditex, Zara's parent company, has since promised to reimburse its sub-contractor's[2] workers as soon as possible. But the rise in rampant consumerism remains a worry. The value of the UK fashion industry has jumped to £26bn (up from £21bn in 2009) and fashion bucks[3] broader growth trends – to put it simply, our appetite for new shoes and accessories is growing more quickly than our appetite for food. We know that our love of fast fashion is terrible for the environment. It was estimated that this spring Britons would send 235m pieces of clothing to landfill. Consumer debt levels are reaching an all-time high, and as retailers such as Asos are starting to offer credit options to their young customers, it's scarily easy to spend money we don't have on clothes we don't need.

I wonder whether our failure to address the fast fashion problem is because it affects more women than men, at every level. Even though research conducted earlier this year found that British men typically spend more on their clothes than women, fashion and clothes are routinely dismissed as trivial, feminine interests. Women are exploited and mocked, disproportionately targeted by advertisers and then accused of being frivolous and fluffy for spending their hard-earned money on a shopping trip. That's just at the consumer end. More seriously, it's estimated that, of the estimated 60-75 million garment[4] workers who are employed to make our clothes, 80% are women, working in dangerous conditions and not being paid a living wage, if they're being paid at all. Globally, poverty affects women first. More than 70% of the world's poorest people are women.
In 2013, Rana Plaza, a building in Bangladesh that housed five garment factories, collapsed, killing more than 1,100 people and injuring thousands more. At the time, the tragedy was believed to be a wake-up call, one that would permanently change the way that the goods we consume are produced. Yet just 17 brands have signed the Apparel[5] and Footwear Supply Chain Transparency Pledge, and there has been a spate[6] of fires in garment factories
It's too easy to dismiss the complaints of underpaid workers as a women's problem. When we do this, we don't acknowledge that every

---

Annotations
[1] **high-street fixture** /ˈfɪkstʃə(r)/ = a shop that can be found in many shopping districts
[2] **sub-contractor** = Subunternehmer, Zulieferfirma
[3] to **buck a trend** = to succeed despite a negative general trend
[4] **garment** = a piece of clothing
[5] **apparel** (AE) /əˈpærəl/ = clothes
[6] **a spate of** = a large number of

one of us is part of the solution, regardless of gender. I know many men and women who are horrified by the way so many of our clothes are produced, and are doing their best to consume more carefully, by introducing no-spend months or ensuring that they only ever buy second-hand clothes. However, we need a much more effective solution, and something that can be implemented at a higher level.

A globally agreed, industry-wide minimum wage and safety standards for all workers is imperative[7]. It's important that manufacturers would face serious, punitive consequences for failing to meet these standards. Ultimately the brands must take responsibility for making these changes – but even if consumers can't lead this revolution, we can agitate[8] for it.

The 2015 ethical consumer report shows that the ethical market in the UK has grown to £38bn, meaning that it is now worth twice as much as the tobacco market. The evidence suggests that we care about where our clothes come from, and we don't necessarily want them to be produced as cheaply as possible – not when lives are at stake. I'm not sure that the best way to support these workers is to stop shopping altogether. This action does not address the fact that the fashion industry could potentially be a positive space for women, and provide opportunities for them as skilled workers and consumers. It's vital that we recognise the industry's wider value. Paying the predominantly female workers properly might cut into profit margins, or force us to pay more for our jeans – but it gives workers the chance to lead happier, safer lives, to live in better conditions and to educate their children, which is ultimately going to provide an enormous boost to the global economy.

Annotations
[7] **imperative** /ɪmˈpɛrətɪv/ = urgently necessary
[8] to **agitate** /ˈædʒɪteɪt/ = to be politically active in order to achieve changes

ANALYSIS

5
a) Explain why the author relates the topic of fast fashion exploitation to sexism.
b) Language awareness Examine how she makes her article appeal to young readers.
c) Language awareness Analyse the stylistic devices and choice of words she uses to convince her readers of her views.

MEDIATION

6 Language awareness

→ **S19:** How to improve your mediation skills, p. 364

Imagine you are an exchange student at an Englisch school. Some students are planning a campaign to raise awareness about the consequences of our shopping. You are asked to give a short presentation on the situation in Germany and new ideas about how to improve the situation. In order to do this, follow these steps:
1. Skim the article and find out what it is about.
2. Determine what type of text is expected for your mediation.
3. Read the article carefully, find relevant passages and note down key words and/or key sentences in English.
4. Write your report in English. Remember to stick to the facts and to use a formal register.

Sharing Economy für Kleidung wächst
Wozu Mode kaufen, wenn man sie mieten kann?

Von Anne Kohlick, 19. Januar 2018

60 neue Kleidungsstücke kauft sich jeder Deutsche jährlich. Doch nur ein kleiner Teil des wachsenden Klamottenbergs wird regelmäßig getragen. All das, was man selbst kaum nutzt, könnte man teilen – oder es gar nicht erst kaufen, sondern leihen.

Neu, neuer, am neusten! In einem immer schnelleren Takt verkündet die Modewelt Must-Haves, Dos und Don'ts – nicht nur jetzt zur alljährlichen Fashion Week in Berlin. Das Oberteil, das gestern noch in war, ist morgen schon out. Fast Fashion heißt das Phänomen. Es beschreibt eine Modeindustrie, die Laufsteg-Trends innerhalb kürzester

Zeit in Billigform in die Läden bringt, sodass bei großen Ketten wie H&M oder Zara das Sortiment ständig wechselt: bis zu 24 Mal im Jahr.

Fünf neue Kleidungsstücke kauft der Deutsche pro Monat im Durchschnitt, also 60 pro Jahr. Tendenz steigend: In den Jahren von 2000 bis 2010 hat sich die Zahl der Modeartikel, die wir im Schnitt kaufen, beinahe verdoppelt – die Summe, die wir dafür ausgeben, aber nicht. Von einem T-Shirt, das in Deutschland 29 Euro kostet, gehen laut einer Studie der Clean Clothes Campaign nur 18 Cent an alle Arbeiter, die an dem Kleidungsstück beteiligt waren.

Etwa 40 Prozent der Klamotten, die wir kaufen, ziehen wir dann aber kaum oder gar nicht an. Und schneller als früher wird der Kleiderschrank ausgemistet, Altes aussortiert. Wir nutzen heute unsere Kleidung nur noch halb so lang wie vor 15 Jahren. So landen jährlich eine Million Tonnen Textilien in der deutschen Altkleidersammlung. Doch gegen das Wegwerf-Prinzip der Fast Fashion regt sich Widerstand.

Wohnungen, Motorroller, Haushaltsgegenstände – in vielen Lebensbereichen hat sich die Sharing Economy schon etabliert. Wozu ein eigenes Auto besitzen, wenn man jederzeit eins to go mieten kann? Der Grundsatz „Mieten statt Kaufen" breitet sich jetzt auch in der Modebranche aus. Mit dem Hamburger Unternehmen Tchibo, das neben Kaffee auch Gebrauchsartikel und Textilien verkauft, steigt erstmals eine große Marke in das Mode-Sharing-Geschäft ein.

Am kommenden Dienstag startet Tchibo Share für Baby- und Kinderkleidung. Strampler, Hosen und Pullis, aus denen die Kleinen schnell herauswachsen, kann man dort mieten, statt sie zu kaufen. Eine Jacke soll vier Euro pro Monat kosten, ein Shirt zwei. Zu mindestens 50 Prozent soll die Kleidung aus Biobaumwolle hergestellt sein. Sobald man ein Kleidungsstück nicht mehr benötigt, schickt man es zurück. Dann wird es gereinigt, aufbereitet und an die nächste Familie versandt.

Mit diesem Geschäftsmodell arbeitet der Magdeburger Online-Mietservice Kilenda schon seit

Herbst 2014. Rund 15.000 Kleidungsstücke für Kinder, Schwangere und Stillende sowie Spielzeug bietet das Portal zum Ausleihen an. [...]

Neben der Kinderbekleidung ist Mode-Sharing für festliche Anlässe beliebt. Teure Abendkleider trägt man so selten, dass sich in diesem Fall Leihen statt Kaufen besonders lohnt. Nach dem Vorbild des amerikanischen Anbieters Rent the Runway haben sich auch in Deutschland Portale wie Dresscoded oder Chic by Choice etabliert, die Designerkleider und Accessoires vermieten. Die günstigsten Kleider sind ab 50 Euro zu mieten.

Jacken, Blusen und Hosen, die man auch im Alltag tragen kann, lassen sich online in der Kleiderei leihen. Das Hamburger Start-up bietet seit 2012 eine Mitgliedschaft für 50 Euro monatlich an. Dafür bekommen die Kundinnen jeden Monat ein individuell zusammengestelltes Paket mit vier Kleidungsstücken. Das können sie nach einem Monat wieder zurückschicken oder länger behalten. Gerade arbeiten die Gründerinnen Thekla Wilkening und Pola Fendel an einem Feature, das es Userinnen in Zukunft ermöglicht, eigene Kleider zu vermieten. An neue Kleider kommt man aber auch, ohne Geld auszugeben – auf Kleidertauschpartys zum Beispiel. Die Facebook-Seite Kleidertausch listet kommende Termine bundesweit auf. Berlins größte Tauschparty KleiderWandel organisieren Greenpeace und die Kampagne für Saubere Kleidung seit 2015 jährlich gemeinsam. Zuletzt trafen sich mehr als 1.500 Tauschwillige im vergangenen Herbst im Haubentaucher auf dem RAW-Gelände.

WRITING: SPEECH

7 CHALLENGE

You are a member of an international group that aims to change consumer habits. Use the information you have gathered to write a speech on the dangers and opportunities of globalized trade in clothing and to appeal to your audience to support new appoaches. → SUPPORT D5, p. 305

→ **S5:** Checklist: Writing a speech, p. 337

4 Advanced texts — Part B: Globalization and the economy

Globalization defined – and re-defined

1

In his 1999 book *The lexus and the olive tree*, Thomas L. Friedman, an American journalist and expert on globalization, defined globalization as follows:

"[...] globalization involves the inexorable integration of markets, nation-states, and technologies to a degree never witnessed before – in a way that is enabling individuals, corporations, and nation-states to reach around the world farther, faster, deeper, and cheaper than ever before, and in a way that is also producing a powerful backlash from those brutalized[1] or left behind by this new system."

a) Explain Friedman's definition in your own words.
b) Find examples that illustrate the developments included in Friedman's definition.

Annotations
[1] to **brutalize** sb = to hurt sb

2

In his 2016 book *Thank you for being late*, Friedman refers both to his old ideas of globalization and tries to come up with a new definition.
a) Identify the three stages of globalization developed in *The world is flat*. → SUPPORT D6, p. 305
b) Explain which changes Friedman observes in globalization. → SUPPORT D7, p. 305
c) Compare your findings to Friedman's definition of globalization quoted in task 1. Discuss whether his 1999 definition is still valid or needs to be updated and, if so, how.

Thank you for being late
by Thomas L. Friedman

Annotations
[1] to **step down** = to leave an official position or job

When I wrote *The world is flat* in 2005, the argument was that globalization was once driven by countries – Spain discovering the "New World." Then it was driven by
5 companies – think the Dutch East India Company two centuries ago or Apple today. And now, thanks to all of these digital flows, globalization is being driven by everyone and anyone – small groups, start-ups,
10 individuals, and multinationals – and is fast connecting East and West, North and South, and South and South. So many people can now take advantage of digital globalization and the flows off the supernova, to go global
15 on their own terms. No one has observed this transition more acutely than Jeff Immelt, the longtime CEO of General Electric, who stepped down[1] in 2017.
"I think the world's gone from macro to
20 micro," Immelt said to me in an interview at GE's Boston headquarters in March 2017. During the last forty or fifty years, he noted, globalization was shaped by big platforms created by big governments – like the World
25 Trade Organization or the World Bank. But as he travels the world now, Immelt said he finds that the new globalizers have never heard of the WTO and have no clue who the U.S. ambassador is in their country.
30 "They don't even speak those languages," Immelt said. "They are just globalizing on their own. They use platforms like Alibaba and Tencent and Amazon." These new globalizers are really "good digitally"; the
35 ones in China are all using WeChat and on their own they figure out how to connect "Chinese funding for a power plant in Pakistan with a Canadian export credit."
In this kind of a world, said Immelt, GE
40 now sees itself as a "multilocal" not a multinational. It is pushing down power and opportunity to its local teams all over the world and encouraging them to link up with other teams and opportunities anywhere in
45 the world. "None of them would even know how to bring a complaint to the WTO," added Immelt.
In 2000, 70 percent of GE's revenue was in the United States. In 2017, over 60 percent
50 came from global markets. But this was not by outsourcing. "Outsourcing is yesterday's game," Immelt said in his 2017 annual report. "During the 1980s and 90s, business looked to the emerging markets as a cheap labor

126

Part B: Globalization and the economy — Advanced texts

source. American jobs migrated to countries that welcomed U.S. companies with open arms. American workers lost in the game of wage arbitrage[2]. Chasing the lowest labor costs is yesterday's model."

In today's model there is no over here and over there. "We see substantial opportunity to grow around the world by investing, operating, and building relationships in the countries where we do business," Immelt said. "We partner with Chinese construction companies[3] and leverage[4] their funding to win contracts in Africa and Asia. Our investments have created jobs in China and the U.S., while making GE more competitive." The multinational companies that thrive in the age of accelerations will be those that digitally weave together the optimal production talents, design talents, logistics capabilities, financing, and market sales opportunities that look at every country as both a market and a source of skills. If they don't, their competitors will.

Annotations
[2] **wage arbitrage** /ˈɑː(r)bɪˌtrɑːʒ/ = making a profit by benefitting from low labour costs in one country and selling the product in another
[3] **construction company** /kənˈstrʌkʃ(ə)n ˌkʌmp(ə)ni/ = Bauunternehmen
[4] **to leverage** /ˈliːvərɪdʒ/ = to borrow the necessary capital for an investment, counting on future profits for covering the cost for interest rates and repayment

Backlash – globalization and its discontents

1

 a) In class, collect what you already know about the following people and events. If necessary, search the Internet to expand your understanding of the terms.

> electoral victory of Donald Trump in 2016 | Brexit vote in 2016 | the Midwest of the USA and its economic situation | Marine Le Pen | end of the Soviet Union

b) Read the article below and note down the advantages and disadvantages of globalization.
c) Outline the different developments the author mentions in the context of a "backlash" to globalization.

Column: Why there's a backlash against globalization and what needs to change

John Rennie Short, 30 November 2016

Globalization is under attack. The electoral victory of Donald Trump, the Brexit vote and the rise of an aggressive nationalism in mainland Europe and around the world are all part of a backlash to globalization.

In each instance, citizens have upset the political order by voting to roll back economic, political and cultural globalization. Support for Brexit came in large part from those worried about their jobs and the entry of immigrants. Similarly, the Midwest of the U.S. – the industrial heartland hurt by global competition – was the linchpin of Donald Trump's victory.

But what exactly are these globalizations and why the discontent? A deeper examination of global integration sheds some light[1] on how we got here and where we should go next.

The rise of the globalization agenda
The roots of today's global economic order were established just as World War II was coming to end. In 1944 delegates from the Allied countries met in Bretton Woods, New Hampshire to establish a new system around open markets and free trade. New institutions such as the International Monetary Fund, the World Bank and a precursor to the World Trade Organization were established to tie national economies into an international system. There was a belief that greater global integration was more conducive to peace and prosperity than economic nationalism.

Initially, it was more a promise than reality. Communism still controlled large swaths[2] of territory. And there were fiscal[3] tensions as the new trade system relied on fixed exchange rates, with currencies pegged[4] to the U.S. dollar, which was tied to gold at the time. It was only with the collapse

---

Annotations
[1] to **shed some light on** sth = to help to explain sth
[2] **large swaths of territory** /swɒθs/ = a large area
[3] **fiscal** = *here:* financial
[4] to **peg** sth **to** sth = to fix sth to sth

of fixed exchange rates and the unmooring[5] of the dollar from the gold standard in the late 1960s that capital could be moved easily around the world.
And it worked: Dollars generated in Europe by U.S. multinationals could be invested through London in suburban housing projects in Asia, mines in Australia and factories in the Philippines. With China's entry onto the world trading system in 1978 and the collapse of the Soviet Union in 1989, the world of global capital mobility widened further.

Global transfer of wealth

While capital could now survey the world to ensure the best returns, labor was fixed in place. This meant there was a profound change in the relative bargaining power[6] between the two – away from organized labor and toward a footloose[7] capital. When a company such as General Motors moved a factory from Michigan to Mexico or China, it made economic sense for the corporation and its shareholders, but it did not help workers in the U.S. Freeing up trade restrictions also led to a global shift in manufacturing. The industrial base shifted from the high-wage areas of North America and Western Europe to the cheaper-wage areas of East Asia: first Japan, then South Korea, and more recently China and Vietnam.

As a result, there was a global redistribution of wealth. In the West as factories shuttered[8], mechanized or moved overseas, the living standards of the working class declined. Meanwhile, in China prosperity grew, with the poverty rate falling from 84 percent in 1981 to only 12 percent by 2010.

Political and economic elites in the West argued that free trade, global markets and production chains that snaked across national borders would eventually raise all living standards. But as no alternative vision was offered, a chasm grew between these elites and the mass of blue-collar workers who saw little improvement from economic globalization.

The backlash against economic globalization is most marked in those countries such as the U.S. where economic dislocation[9] unfolds with weak safety nets and limited government investment in job retraining[10] or continuing and lifetime education.

Expanding free markets

Over the decades, politicians enabled globalization through trade organizations and pacts such as the North American Free Trade Agreement, passed in 1994. The most prominent, though, was the European Union, an economic and political alliance of most European countries and a good example of an unfolding political globalization.

It started with a small, tight core of Belgium, France, Italy, Luxembourg, the Netherlands and West Germany. They signed the Treaty of Rome in 1957 to tie former combatants into an alliance that would preclude further conflicts – and form a common market to compete against the U.S.

Over the years, more countries joined, and in 1993 the European Union (EU) was created as a single market with the free movement of goods, people and capital and common policies for agriculture, transport and trade. Access to this large common market attracted former Communist bloc[12] and Soviet countries, to the point where the EU now extends as far east as Cyprus and Bulgaria, Malta in the south and Finland in the north.

With this expansion has come the movement of people – hundreds of thousands of Poles have moved to the U.K. for instance – and some challenges.

The EU is now at a point of inflexion[12] where the previous decades of continual growth are coming up against popular resistance to EU enlargement into poorer and more peripheral[13] countries. Newer entrants often have weaker economies and lower social welfare payments, prompting immigration to the richer members such as France and the U.K.

Annotations
[5] to **unmoor** = *(ein Schiff vom Anker) losmachen*
[6] **bargaining power** = *Verhandlungsposition*
[7] **footloose** /ˈfʊtˌluːs/ = unmarried and not in a relationship; *here:* free
[8] to **shutter** = to close with a shutter, i.e. a cover for a window
[9] **economic dislocation** = *wirtschaftliche Verwerfungen*
[10] **retraining** = *Umschulung*
[11] **bloc countries** = a group of countries with shared political aims
[12] **point of inflexion** = critical moment
[13] **peripheral** /pəˈrɪf(ə)rəl/ = am Rand liegend

Part B: Globalization and the economy — Advanced texts

Cultural backlash

The flattening of the world allowed for a more diverse ensemble of cultural forms in cuisine, movies, values and lifestyles. Cosmopolitanism[14] was embraced by many of the elites but feared by others. In Europe, the foreign other became an object of fear and resentment, whether in the form of immigrants or in imported culture and new ways. But evidence of this backlash to cultural globalization also exists around the world. The ruling BJP party in India, for example, combines religious fundamentalism and political nationalism. There is a rise of religious fundamentalism around the world in religions as varied as Buddhism, Christianity, Hinduism, Islam and Judaism.

Old-time religion, it seems, has become a refuge from the ache of modernity. Religious fundamentalism held out the promise of eternal verities in the rapidly changing world of cultural globalization.

There is also a rising nationalism, as native purity is cast as contrast to the profane[15] foreign. Across Europe from Bulgaria to Poland and the U.K., new nationalisms have a distinct xenophobia. Politicians such as Marine Le Pen in France recall an idealized past as a cure for the cultural chaos of modernity. Politicians can often gain political traction[16] by describing national cultural traditions as under attack from the outside.

Indeed, the fear of immigration has resulted in the most dramatic backlash against the effects of globalization, heightening national and racial identities. In the U.S. white native-born American moved from being the default category to a source of identity clearly mobilized by the Trump campaign.

Reclaiming globalization

Globalization has now become the catchword to encompass the rapid and often disquieting and disruptive social and economic change of the past 25 years. No wonder there is a significant backlash to the constant change – much of it destabilizing economically and socially disruptive. When traditional categories of identity evaporate quickly, there is a profound political and cultural unease.

The globalization project contains much that was desirable: improvements in living conditions through global trade, reducing conflict and threat of war through political globalization and encouraging cultural diversity in a widening cultural globalization.

The question now, in my view, is not whether we should accept or reject globalization but how we shape and guide it to these more progressive goals. We need to point the project toward creating more just and fair outcomes, open to difference but sensitive to cultural connections and social traditions.

A globalization project of creating a more connected, sustainable, just and peaceful world is too important to be left to the bankers and the political elites.

Annotations
[14] **cosmopolitanism** = *Weltoffenheit, Weltbürgertum*
[15] **profane** /prəˈfeɪn/ = not sacred; disrepecting religious things
[16] to **gain traction** = an Boden gewinnen

2

a) Explain the reasons why people in developed countries have objections to globalization.
b) Discuss whether these objections are understandable and/or justified.
c) Comment on this claim: "Although there may be some minor disadvantages, the benefits of globalization for humankind as a whole outweigh them by far."

→ **S6:** How to write a discussion/comment, p. 338

Workshop: Step by step
Part C: Migration and the world of work

Webcode
You can download a word list for Part C here:
WES-73644-047

Step by step Writing a comment

PRE-READING: INTERNATIONAL MIGRATION

1 Across cultures **Card survey**
a) Note down reasons why
  1. you and others may want to leave Germany to spend a few months or longer abroad and
  2. others may leave their home country to move to Germany.
b) Cluster the cards on the board to identify factors that encourage migration.

Webcode
You can find a link to the video here:
WES-73644-048

2
a) You are going to watch a video on global migration. Before watching, read the annotations.
b) Watch the video. Identify its overall message on migration these days. → SUPPORT D8, p. 306
c) Watch the video again and note down information on these aspects:
  • advantages and challenges of immigration for a society
  • types of migration/migrants
  • causes of migration
  • reactions to immigration
d) **Pair work** Compare your notes and add information you may have missed.
e) **Group work** Look at the results of your card survey in task 1 again and discuss to what extent the video reflects your ideas on migration.
f) CHALLENGE Research the current situation of international migration and prepare a short presentation.

Annotations
war in Syria = the Syrian Civil War, which started in 2011 and led to several hundred thousand casualties and millions of war refugees
expansion of the EU = enlargement process of the European Union towards the East that took place in the 2000s
sub-Saharan Africa = territory south of the Sahara desert, i.e. central and southern Africa

COMPREHENSION

3
Read the extract from Hari Kunzru's novel *Transmission*. Describe the changes that are about to happen in Arjun's and his sister Priti's lives and and their family's reaction.

Transmission

by Hari Kunzru

Though he held several class prizes and was once a runner-up in a national computer problem-solving competition, Arjun's certified honours were not as impressive as they ought to have been. He had scored badly in the IIT entrance exams, a failure which his disappointed teachers put down to 'lack of focus' but more accurately was due to focal misdirection, the star comp.sci pupil having got obsessed during the crucial revision period with constructing a database of his all-time favourite films of the 1970s, searchable by name, cast, director, box office takings and personal critical ranking. As a consequence of his passion for cinema, his (entirely genuine, non-bazaar-bought) higher education had been conducted not at one of the prestigious Indian Institutes of Technology, but at North Okhla, a middle-ranking school which had the compensatory advantage, felt more keenly by his mother than by Arjun himself, of allowing him to live at home while he studied.

He was still at home two years after graduation.

'Mummy? Mummy?' He bounded[1] into the hall, almost knocking over Malini the maid, who was carrying a glass of tea.

'Oh, sorry, Malini. Ma, are you there?'

'Yes, Beta[2]. Come through. I'm only resting.' He flung[3] open the door to his mother's bedroom and gave her the news.

'Mummy, I'm going to America!'

He might as well have said *prison* or *be trampled by horses*. Letting out a groan, she buried[4] her head in her hands and burst into tears.

It was to be expected. As an Indian mother, Mrs Mehta's prime directive was to ensure that her first-born son was never more than ten feet away from a source of clean clothes, second helpings and moral guidance. She expected to have to release her child eventually, but only into the hands of another woman, whose family tree had been thoroughly vetted and whose housekeeping could be easily monitored from the vantage point of a chair in the living room of No. 18 Gleneagle House, into which the girl would naturally move. America, unhandily located several thousand miles away, was known to be populated by females who would never dream of starching[5] a collar, and whose well-documented predilection for exposing flesh, drinking alcohol and feeding ground beef[6] to unwitting Hindu boys was nothing short of an international scandal. Hardly the place for her beta, her unmarried 23-year-old baby.

Arjun, who felt he did not really understand emotions as well as he might, made the gestures you make when you are trying to comfort someone. Disconcertingly, when his father came back into the office he started to cry as well. 'My son,' sobbed Mr Mehta, 'America? Oh, my son.' Even Malini was at it. At least Priti, his younger sister, seemed unmoved. She was hopping up and down behind her father's shoulders with impatience. 'What about my news? Is no one vaguely interested in what happened to me today?'

For a long time Mr Mehta had been unable to feel altogether optimistic about his son. Something about the boy emanated muddle, and if thirty-five years of line management had taught him anything, it was that muddle is prejudicial to career success.

News of a job in America was most affecting. His joy was augmented by the thought that finally he had got one back on his brother-in-law. Arvind, the sala[7] in question, was the owner of an aggregates firm, with a contract to supply gravel to the Gujarat State government. He and his preening[8] wife lived in what could only be described as a mansion in one of Ahmadabad's most exclusive colonies[9]. They had dedicated[10] a statue at a local mandir[11]; there was a photo of them standing next to it, with some sadhus[12] and a minister. Their unappealing son Hitesh had for some years been employed by an artificial-flavourings company near Boston. For as long as Mr Mehta could remember it had been Hitesh this, Hitesh that. Hits is topping fifty k. Hits is team-leading a push for a new minty-fresh aroma. And all the while his own fool of a boy never seemed

Annotations
[1] to **bound** = to jump
[2] **beta** *(Hindi)* = son
[3] to **fling sth open** = to open sth quickly
[4] to **bury one's head in one's hands** /ˈberi/= to cover one's face with one's hands
[5] to **starch a collar** = *einen Kragen stärken*
[6] **ground beef** = *Rinderhackfleisch*
[7] **sala** *(Hindi)* = brother-in-law; also used as a mildly insulting term for a man
[8] to **preen** = to try to make oneself more attractive, e.g. by putting on a lot of make-up
[9] **colony** *(Indian English)* /ˈkɒləni/= a group of houses built for a specific purpose, e.g. by a company for its workers, possibly surrounded by fences or walls
[10] to **dedicate** sth /ˈdedɪkeɪt/= *hier: etw stiften*
[11] **mandir** = Hindu or Jain temple
[12] **sadhu** = holy person in Hinduism

Workshop: Step by step

Part C: Migration and the world of work

Annotations
[13] **bananas** /bəˈnɑːnəz/ = crazy
[14] to **chuck sb on the cheek** = jdm. die Wange tätscheln
[15] **New South Wales** = a state on the east coast of Australia
[16] to **be in the hot seat** = here: to be in a difficult position that comes with a lot of responsibility
[17] **nom de guerre** /ˌnɒm də ˈɡeə(r)/= a pseudonym
[18] **beti** (Hindi) = daughter
[19] to **chastise** /tʃæˈstaɪz/= here: to criticize
[20] **Doordarshan** = Indian public broadcaster

able to keep his head out of filmi magazines. But now Amrika! God be praised!

Of all the Mehtas, the one with the best excuse for crying was Priti. She loved Arjun dearly. It was good he had finally stopped being such an idiot, but her parents were only going bananas[13] over him because he was a boy. Why should he get chucked[14] on the cheek for every fart and belch, while she made her way in the world with the bare minimum of encouragement? Since she had passed her communications degree, all her parents appeared to want was to marry her off to the first all-four-limbs-possessing boy who wandered through the door.

As it happened, Arjun was not the only one to have a new job. But did anyone care? Did anyone even notice? Finally, after her parents had phoned almost everyone they knew with her brother's news and her father had put the receiver down at the end of a particularly gratifying call to Ahmadabad, she got to tell them.

'What do you mean you've never heard of Dilli-Tel? They're only the most dynamic call centre in the city!'

She explained the New South Wales[15] connection, how she would be 'in the hot seat[16],' providing service and support to customers of one of Australia's biggest power companies. Her mother asked why she needed a job at all. Wouldn't she rather stay at home? Her father frowned over his spectacles, grappling ineptly with the fundamentals of modern telecoms.

'What?' he asked. 'You mean they call on the telephone here, all the way from Australia?'

'Exactly. These big companies find it cost-effective.'

'Cost-effective? It must be like throwing money down the drain!'

'Daddy, they buy capacity. The customers don't pay. They don't even know they are calling abroad. It's such a great job, Daddy. I'll receive training in Australian language and culture. We all have to be proficient in vernacular slang and accent, and keep day-to-day items of trivia at our fingertips.'

'Trivia?'

'Sporting scores. Weather. The names of TV celebrities. It adds value by helping build customer trust and empathy. As operators, we even have to take on new Australian identities. A nom de guerre[17], the manager calls it. What do you think of Hayley?'

'Namda-what?' spluttered Mr Mehta. 'Now look here, young lady, what all is wrong with your own good name?'

Her mother nodded in agreement. 'Beti[18], I don't like the sound of this at all. It doesn't seem decent. Why can't you tell these Australian fellows to call you Priti or, better still, Miss Mehta? That would be so much nicer.'

Priti had been trying her best. The tears would not stay in any longer.

'I don't believe it. I do something good and you throw it in my face. I hate you! I hate all of you!'

'Don't talk to your father like that,' snapped Mrs Mehta, but she was chastising[19] her daughter's departing back.

Mr Mehta looked towards God and the ceiling. 'This is what comes of too many TV channels. MTV, lady fashion TV, this, that and what all TV. No daughter would have spoken to her father in such a way when we were having Doordarshan[20] only.'

'She's turning into one of these cosmopolitan girls,' said his wife. 'I think we should find a boy for her sooner rather than later.'

ANALYSIS

Analyse how Arjun's and Priti's characters and situation reflect the influence of tradition and the opportunities on the global job market.

→ **S9:** How to structure a text, p. 344

Preview

At the end of the Workshop you will be asked to comment on Arjun and Priti's situation. Before that, you will find out how to structure a comment and how to write an effective introduction.

Part C: Migration and the world of work — Workshop: Step by step

WRITING A COMMENT

5

Read the comment below on whether Mrs Mehta holds modern views concerning women's social roles and identify these structural elements:

1. **introduction:** a few lines that catch the readers' attention and provide necessary background information about the issue to be addressed
2. **thesis statement:** a sentence or two which contain the main idea of your comment
3. **main part:** your arguments that support your thesis statement with evidence, e.g. by giving examples, using background knowledge, etc. (one may also include counterarguments, but should explain why they are not as strong as the ones supporting your view)
4. **conclusion:** briefly repeat your opinion/main idea and key arguments, but use different words and aim for a more general statement; you may also end with a personal reflection, but don't forget to show a connection to your thesis statement

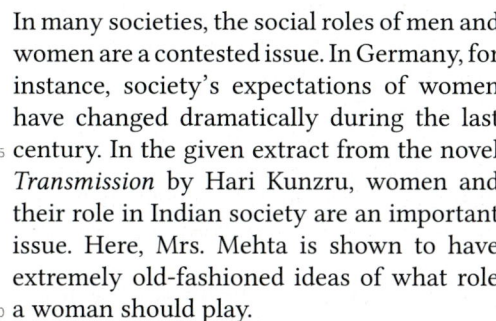

In many societies, the social roles of men and women are a contested issue. In Germany, for instance, society's expectations of women have changed dramatically during the last century. In the given extract from the novel *Transmission* by Hari Kunzru, women and their role in Indian society are an important issue. Here, Mrs. Mehta is shown to have extremely old-fashioned ideas of what role a woman should play.

One of the most poignant illustrations of Mrs. Mehta's rather traditional ideas about a woman's role are her thoughts about the kind of girl she expects her son to marry: she would "naturally" move in with the family and Mrs. Mehta would make sure that she could oversee her housekeeping skills. By stressing this fact, the narrator makes it clear that this is the most important quality Mrs. Mehta expects in her future daughter in law. That this woman will have to give up whatever life she may have had before goes without saying.

Mrs. Mehta's aspirations for her daughter Priti are clear: she suggests that they "find a boy for her sooner rather than later". The main thing Mrs. Mehta seems to want for her daughter is for her to get married. Whom she marries, however, does not seem to be important. Arjun's future wife's family, on the contrary, would have to be "thouroughly vetted". Moreover, it seems to be clear that her parents will look for a husband for Priti and not that she will be able to marry whom she wants or even choose not to marry at all. Mrs. Mehta is worried that her daughter is about to become "one of these cosmopolitan girls", which would apparently be an extremely negative development. This ties in with her attitudes towards women in America: she likens them to predators preying on "unwitting Hindu boys". They are known for "exposing flesh" and "drinking alcohol". The narrator's word choice makes it clear that Mrs. Mehta finds them dangerous and regards them and their supposed lifestyle as the opposite of how a woman should behave.

In conclusion, the extract makes it clear that Mrs. Mehta's views about women's social role are the opposite of modern. She believes that a woman should at all costs get married, that she should aspire to have excellent housekeeping skills and that the lifestyle of American women is detestable.

6 Language awareness

a) Read the text again and note down phrases you can use for your own writing, especially for introducing and linking arguments.
b) Examine the introduction and the strategy the author uses to encourage the reader to read on.
c) Think of other strategies you could use in an introduction to a comment. → **SUPPORT** D9, p. 306

→ **S13:** Checklist: Analysis – non-fictional texts, p. 354

7

Based on the extract from *Transmission*, write a comment on whether the Mehta family represents a modern family that embraces the values and opportunities of a globalized world.

→ **S6:** How to write a discussion/ comment, p. 338

4 Workshop: Practice — Part C: Migration and the world of work

Practice Writing a comment

Webcode
You can find the video here:
WES-73644-049

PRE-READING: MEDIATION

1 ● DVD/14

a) You are taking part in an international students' project on the global economy and have been given the task to add an encyclopedic entry on China to the project website. Watch a German-speaking video on China and its economy. Note down key information on China's political and economic situation.

b) **Pair work** Compare your notes with a partner's.

c) Use your notes to write the encyclopedic entry for the project website.

COMPREHENSION

2

In the 2018 novel *The emperor of shoes* by Spencer Wise, Alex Cohen, a 26-year-old American from Boston, lives in southern China, where his father would like him to take over the family's shoe factory. In the process of learning about his trade, he realizes how the company's success has also been due to his father closely cooperating with corrupt party officials. In addition, Alex becomes aware of the harsh working and living conditions and the workers' exploitation as he grows closer to one of his Chinese factory workers named Ivy, who would like to bring about change in the factory, but also on a larger political scale. Consequently, Alex has to make up his mind about how he is planning to run the family business in the future. Read the following extract in which Alex is summoned to a meeting with Gang, a local government official.

a) Describe the relationship between Alex and Gang and which factors influence it in this situation.
b) Explain how this scene reflects what you have learnt about China in task 1.

The emperor of shoes
by Spencer Wise

Extract 1

"I possess internal information," he said, punctuating each word with the tap of the screw, "that there are crooked nails in your factory."
He tilted his head to see if I was following.
5 "Radicals," he continued, "who want to undermine you. Me. Want to overthrow the Chinese government. You know anything about this sort of thing? These plotters[1]?"
I shook my head. No. And sat in solemn terror.
10 "I need your help," he said.
My mouth was dry. I had to swallow a few times before getting the words out.
"With what?" I asked.
"Finding them." [...]
15 "I chose not to tell your father," Gang continued. "He is my old friend. This would embarrass him. Cause him to lose face. He would blame himself. Feel he did something to bring the radicals inside his plant. So I think of you. Soon you take over
20 for him. You are younger. Stronger. You can help me find the bad elements. Probably a handful of rootless young people with very low IQs. Your generation causing problems again. I let it go at the Honda plant[2] last month – a strike – to show
25 support for the migrant class. But we can't have copycats. This is my purpose with you." [...]
He didn't seem panicked about not having the names. And this feeling – this bright gas flame of a feeling that Gang put in me with his eyes, telling
30 me I was nothing in the big scheme[3], a single nail – and so was he, his look said that too – and it didn't make a bit of difference whose side I took or anybody took because the government, this colossal China machine, rolled on invulnerably
35 and couldn't be stopped.
But he didn't have the names. I leaned back in my chair and reminded myself of this fact. The establishment didn't have everything.
"I protect public harmony. You protect your
40 plant," he said. "These radicals operate in shadow. Lost youth. Created by Western television. False revolutionaries desiring celebrity and fame. For endangering the public, they deserve their tongues cut off."
45 Gang made a fist and set it on the desk. His eyes narrowed. "Find one. A ringleader. Bring me the name of a suspect."

Annotations
[1] **plotter** = *Verschwörer/in*
[2] **plant** = *here:* factory
[3] **scheme** /skiːm/ = a plan, especially one to achieve something dishonest or illegal

Part C: Migration and the world of work — Workshop: Practice

COMPREHENSION

3

Read extract 2 and summarize Ivy and her fellow activist Zhang's plan and Alex's reaction to it.

→ **S1:** Checklist: Summary, p. 330

Extract 2

They came to the cities, slaved away in the factories for their best years and maybe they stayed, but no one really wanted them. In the subway, all the handsome, well-heeled[1] Chinese scooted over, sneaking a few pitying glances at their darker, dirtier country-men in pith helmets[2], holding mattocks[3], covered in tunnel soot, a different species almost, exhausted, their heads rattling against a subway ad, dreaming of high-rises, and the whole thing was enraging. But what could you do about it?

"But this is China," I said. "There's nothing you can do. I mean, they locked up Ai Weiwei for flicking off Tiananmen Gate. The middle finger and he's thrown in jail. You want to start trouble with these people?"

Zhang inhaled sharply with a hiss. "Trouble? No trouble. No violence. We have no army. No weapons. This is not a proper course. We need visibility. Something broadcast. Over internet maybe. A platform. A forum." [...]

"A forum," I said. "Here, at the factory. You're talking about a demonstration, aren't you?"

Zhang waved his hand in front of his face. "I don't like this word."

"But you're saying it. Which means a strike."

"We want to lift the shoe and show the world," he said. "Put it this way."

I turn to Ivy. "Do you agree with this?"

She nodded. "Show the world the solidarity of Chinese workers," Ivy said. "We broadcast speeches. On the internet. YouTube. With VPNs[4] we go around the firewalls." [...]

"Of course you cannot stop factory operation," Zhang said, his clever habit of preemptively arguing your side of things.

"That's right," I said. "Look, I want to support you guys, but I can't stop the lines[5]."

"But maybe for one day this is possible. To give us a forum."

So he really did mean that. I didn't know how to respond. Only I was aware that my mouth was open a little and I hadn't said anything yet. So I forced the words out.

"You know that'd hurt my business. Cost money, jobs."

"We never want to lose jobs." Said Ivy firmly. "We need you in China. Factory jobs are good jobs. Mingong[6] don't want to go back to rice farming." [...]

Ivy shook her head. "No, no. This isn't 'rotten capitalist go home!' The workers are young capitalists. They want money. Want business. Retail or trading booth in Guangzhou. The women are future iron ladies, yes? Who will provide? Not the government anymore. We help make them a path. It's only one day to spare, Alex. One day."

"This is moving ahead," said Zhang. "The real Great Leap Forward[7]." He chuckled again at his own wordplay. "You let us have our YouTube videos, our speeches. Then everyone back to work."

"But what does that accomplish?" I asked. "That I don't understand."

"Big pressure to the top in Beijing." Ivy said. "So when we ask respectfully for what we want, they are forced to give because the pressure of the world is so great on them."

"Democracy," Zhang said in a tone that made it sound like he was clarifying what Ivy said, even though she wasn't talking about democracy. Zhang read this confusion on my face. "Not now, of course. Slowly. It should be the case."

Annotations

[1] **well-heeled** = rich
[2] **pith helmet** /ˈpɪθ ˌhɛlmɪt/ = *Tropenhelm*
[3] **mattock** = *Hacke*
[4] **VPN** (Virtual private network) = a technology that makes it possible to send and receive data across shared or public networks as if one were directly connected to a private network and which can be used to avoid censorship
[5] to **stop the lines** = to stop production (referring to assembly lines)
[6] **Mingong** = migrant workers in China
[7] **The Great Leap Forward** = an economic and social campaign from 1958 to 1962 by the Communist Party of China under Mao Zedong, with the goal of transforming the country from an agrarian economy to a socialist society through rapid industrialization and collectivization; it is widely considered to have caused the Great Chinese Famine

ANALYSIS

4

Analyse how the conversation reflects the challenges of globalization in China.

COMMENT

5

Alex is confronted with many different expectations at the same time – those of his father to continue the company in his spirit, of government officials like Gang and of his lover Ivy and her fellow activists. Write a comment on how Alex should behave in this situation.

Part C: Migration and the world of work

The future of work

PRE-READING: WATCHING

Webcode
You can find a link to the video here:
WES-73644-050

→ **S20:** How to listen/watch effectively, p. 366

1
Watch the video on Microsoft's visions for the future of work.
Round robin Share your first impression with the class.

2
a) Watch the video a second time. Take notes on
   1. what new/advanced technologies the video shows.
   2. how these new technologies affect the lives of the people in the video.

Webcode
You can download the grid here:
WES-73644-051

b) **Pair work** Compare your results with a partner's. Use your notes to fill in the grid:

technology	people affected				
	students	female oceanologist (Kat Liang)	waiter	businesswoman/ boss	businesswoman's father
…	…	…	…	…	…

c) **Pair work:** Collect advantages and disadvantages of the new technologies in the video.
d) Comment on whether you would like to live and work like the people in the video when you leave school.

→ **S6:** How to write a discussion/comment, p. 338

COMPREHENSION

3

→ **S1:** Checklist: Summary, p. 330

Yuval Noah Harari, an Israeli professor of history, published the non-fiction book *Homo Deus* in 2015. Read the extract below and summarize how he sees the future of work. Focus on problems that, according to the author, the next generation will have to deal with.

Homo Deus
by Yuval Noah Harari

In the nineteenth century the Industrial Revolution created a huge new class of urban proletariats, and socialism spread because no other creed managed to answer the
5 unprecedented needs, hopes and fears of this new working class. Liberalism eventually defeated socialism only by adopting the best parts of the socialist programme. In the twenty-first century we might witness the
10 creation of a massive new unworking class: people devoid of any economic, political or even artistic value, who contribute nothing to the prosperity, power and glory of society. This 'useless class' will not be merely
15 unemployed – it will be unemployable.
In September 2013 two Oxford researchers, Carl Benedikt Frey and Michael A. Osborne,

Part C: Migration and the world of work — Texts

published "The Future of Employment", in which they surveyed the likelihood of different professions being taken over by computer algorithms within the next twenty years. The algorithm developed by Frey and Osborne to do the calculations estimated that 47 per cent of US jobs are at high risk. For example, there is a 99 per cent probability that by 2033 human telemarketers and insurance underwriters[1] will lose their jobs to algorithms. There is a 98 per cent probability that the same will happen to sports referees, 97 per cent that it will happen to cashiers and 96 per cent to chefs. Waiters – 94 per cent. Paralegal assistants[2] – 94 percent. Tour guides – 91 per cent. Bakers – 89 per cent. Bus drivers – 89 per cent. Construction labourers[3] – 88 per cent. Veterinary assistants[4] – 86 per cent. Security guards – 84 per cent. Sailors – 83 per cent. Bartenders – 77 per cent. Archivists – 76 per cent. Carpenters – 72 per cent. Lifeguards – 67 per cent. And so forth. There are of course some safe jobs. The likelihood that computer algorithms will displace archaeologists by 2033 is only 0.7 per cent, because their job requires highly sophisticated types of pattern recognition[5], and doesn't produce huge profits. Hence it is improbable that corporations or government will make the necessary investment to automate archaeology within the next twenty years.

Of course, by 2033 many new professions are likely to appear, for example virtual-world designers. But such professions will probably require much more creativity and flexibility than current run-of-the-mill[6] jobs, and it is unclear whether forty-year-old cashiers or insurance agents will be able to reinvent themselves as virtual-world designers (try to imagine a virtual world created by an insurance agent!).

Since we do not know what the job market will look like in 2030 or 2040, already today we have no idea what to teach our kids. Most of what they currently learn at school will probably be irrelevant by the time they are forty. Traditionally, life has been divided into two main parts: a period of learning followed by a period of working. Very soon, this traditional model will become utterly obsolete, and the only way for humans to stay in the game will be to keep learning throughout their lives, and to reinvent themselves repeatedly. Many if not most humans may be unable to do so.

The coming technological bonanza[7] will probably make it feasible to feed and support these useless masses even without any effort from their side. But what will keep them occupied and content? People must do something, or they go crazy. What will they do all day? One answer might be drugs and computer games. Unnecessary people might spend increasing amounts of time within 3D virtual-reality worlds, that would provide them with far more excitement and emotional engagement than the drab reality outside. Yet such a development would deal a mortal blow[8] to the liberal belief in the sacredness of human life and of human experiences. What's so sacred about useless bums[9] who pass their days devouring artificial experiences in La La Land?

Annotations
[1] **insurance underwriter** = someone who provides insurance
[2] **paralegal assistant** /ˌpærəˈliːɡ(ə)l/ = someone who assists a lawyer
[3] **construction labourer** = Bauarbeiter/in
[4] **veterinary assistant** = Tierarzthelfer/in
[5] **pattern recognition** = Mustererkennung
[6] **run-of-the-mill** = gewöhnlich
[7] **bonanza** /bəˈnænzə/ = a situation in which people become very rich very fast
[8] to **deal a mortal blow to sth** = etw den Todesstoß versetzen
[9] **bum** = lazy person

ANALYSIS

4

a) `Language awareness` Analyse Harari's rather bleak view of the future of work and how he uses arguments and stylistic devices to achieve this. → SUPPORT **D10, p. 306**

b) Use your findings to explain this quotation:
"What's so sacred about useless bums who pass their days devouring artificial experiences in La La Land?"

c) Compare Harari's view to the one presented in the Microsoft video. Which scenario for the future do you find more likely? Give reasons.

→ **S13:** Checklist: Analysis – non-fictional texts, p. 354

CREATIVE WRITING

5

Imagine you are a high school job counsellor. Taking into consideration what you have learnt from Harari and the Microsoft video, design a leaflet to help students decide about their future careers.

4 Advanced texts — Part C: Migration and the world of work

Migration between India and the US: Listening

Webcode
You can find a link to the audio file here:
WES-73644-052

Webcode
You can download the grid here:
WES-73644-053

1 Listen to a radio report about Indian immigrants. While listening, complete the grid. You need not write complete sentences. → **S20:** How to listen/watch effectively, p. 366

1	one reason why people leave their home country for America	…
2	reason why many Indians move back to India	…
3	Apurva Koti's age	…
4	how Apurva felt about India at the beginning	…
5	how Apurva feels about India now	…
6	how many Indians move back to India every year	…
7	reason why Apurva's mother has an easier life in India	…
8	one reason why Shirish, Apurva's father, sees no real difference between his job in India and before in the US	…
9	where you can find gated communities like the one where the Kotis live	…
10	what going back to India often meant in the past	…
11	what happens when the children finish high school	…

Globalization and migration in an age of accelerations

1 Read an extract from Thomas Friedman's non-fiction book *Thank you for being late*. Sum up what the critics Friedman refers to say against globalization and migration.

Thank you for being late
by Thomas L. Friedman

While I was writing the original hardcover of this book over the three years ending in the summer of 2016, I was also watching the looming U.S. presidential election out of
5 the corner of my eye and sometimes head-on. Who couldn't? But I never attempted to cover it in this book. I was truly focused on how the three accelerations had evolved and the long-term challenges and opportunities
10 they were generating for people, businesses, and communities. Not surprisingly, though, when I began my book tour – just two weeks after the election of Donald Trump – the question arose whether I thought there was
15 a connection between Britain's decision to leave the European Union, Trump's victory, and the trends that I had written about. My answer was an unequivocal "yes".
For a certain portion of the population in
20 both America and the European Union, the world had indeed – as I worried in chapter 7 – gotten "just too damned fast." The age of accelerations brought on so much automation, immigration, and competition
25 and so many flows of new ideas and mores that a swath[1] of the population began to feel unmoored[2], especially less-educated, working-class whites living in rural areas. The challenge started at the office, where
30 all of a sudden average was over. People discovered that just working hard and playing by the rules was not enough to ensure an average middle-class lifestyle. You had to become a lifelong learner to get a job
35 and hold the job – but too many people were not equipped to make that change. They were prepared to show up, work hard, and do an honest day's labor – but they were

Annotations
[1] **a swath of the population** /swɒθ/ = a large part of the population
[2] **to unmoor** = *(ein Schiff vom Anker) losmachen*

Part C: Migration and the world of work — Advanced texts

quite content to be told what to do and quite sure that if they did what they were told to do well then job security, a decent wage, and the American Dream or British Dream would still be theirs.

At the same time, thanks to the age of accelerations, communities were rapidly going from monocultures to polycultures, due to a surge in migrants and refugees from Latin America to North America and from Africa, Eastern Europe, and the Arab-Muslim world into Western Europe. All of a sudden, the lady at the checkout counter³ was wearing a head covering that was not a baseball cap. And the language she was speaking to her coworkers was not English. The fact is, the European Union expanded too far, too fast, enabling large numbers of Eastern Europeans to flock to London faster than parts of British society could absorb them. The fact is, China's exports to the United States, and illegal immigration from Mexico and Latin America, came too far, too fast for some communities in America to adapt, culturally or economically. These societal changes happened at the same time the market and Moore's law⁴ were accelerating. Without proper surge protectors⁵, some people really get burned.

The British-born writer Andrew Sullivan put it in family terms in a March 31, 2017, essay he wrote for New York magazine: his brother and father both voted in favor of Brexit. "I asked my brother to explain." Sullivan wrote.

"It was really quite simple, he said. He believed that immigration into Britain was happening at too fast a pace. He saw overcrowded schools and hospitals, a groaning transportation system, an acute housing shortage, and a country that has been transformed so fast many of its inhabitants began to not recognize it at all. He wanted immigration to come down to more manageable levels – and, in the last election, he therefore voted Conservative, because that's what the Tories⁶ promised. They pledged to bring immigration down to the tens of thousands a year. But after a year in office, the immigration statistics showed no drop at all: Over 600,000 migrants were still entering the U.K. per year, with a close to 300,000 from the EU, and there was no end in sight. That number was completely unprecedented before 2014, but had stayed on that level for three years in a row. For a comparison, EU immigration into Britain was a mere 44,000 in 1992 and 66,000 in 2003."

And, while all of this was happening, the acceleration of flows was also changing social norms faster than some could adapt. In the United States, this process brought new genders into restrooms, new kinds of couples into marriage, new rules of political correctness onto college campuses and new phrases into the lexicon⁷ [...]

Whatever one might personally feel about all these changes, one would have to be blind, deaf, and dumb⁸ not to see that they came at too rapid a clip⁹ for many white middle- and lower-middle-class men and women in exurbia¹⁰ and rural areas. They looked around, and it seemed like every group had been handed some kind of step stool¹¹ by society to get a leg up in this age of accelerations – except them. And Trump and pro-Brexit politicians spoke to and for them – promising to slow down or reverse some of the changes that were making people so dizzy at school, so unmoored at work and so not-at-home in their communities.

In short, Trump's victory and Brexit were not just economic backlashes, they were also cultural backlashes by white working-class voters who felt they were being forgotten, left behind, and looked down upon all at the same time. Trump and Brexit were their "I am somebody" fist in the face of a system that had threatened their status and their livelihoods.

Annotations

³ **checkout counter** = Kasse (im Supermarkt)
⁴ **Moore's law** = Modell, das besagt, dass die Leistung von Computern exponentiell wächst
⁵ **surge protector** = Überspannungsschutz
⁶ **Tories** = the Conservative Party in the UK
⁷ **lexicon** = the complete vocabulary of a language
⁸ **dumb** (esp AE) /dʌm/ = stupid (offensive: unable to speak)
⁹ **clip** (AE, infml) = speed
¹⁰ **exurbia** = residential areas (especially with rich inhabitants) outside the suburbs of a town
¹¹ **step stool** = Tritthocker, hier: Hilfsmittel

2 Explain the changes in the world of work that Friedman identifies.

3 Write a comment in which you argue for globalization and migration, refuting the critics.

→ **S6:** How to write a discussion/comment, p. 338

Workshop: Step by step   **Part D:** Living in a globalized world

Webcode
You can download a word list for Part D here:
WES-73644-054

Webcode
You can find a link to the video here:
WES-73644-055

→ **S20:** How to listen/watch effectively, p. 366

Step by step   Speaking

PRE-SPEAKING

1

a) Speculate on what issue(s) a non-governmental organization (NGO) called "Global Citizen" might be concerned with.

b) Watch a video that presents what Global Citizen is. Identify the main aims of the organization and how it tries to motivate people to join and take action.

c) List further ways to make the world a better place and name ways to motivate people to get involved.

d) EXTRA Research other NGOs that take action to improve the world. Prepare a three-minute talk on who they are and what they do.

> **Preview**
>
> There are different kinds of speaking exams.
> Usually they are made up of at least two different parts:
> - Interview
> - Monologue
> - Dialogue
>
> In this Workshop, you will learn what to expect and how to cope in these three different settings.

INTERVIEW

Webcode
You can find the audio file here:
WES-73644-056

→ **S20:** How to listen/watch effectively, p. 366

2 CD/08

You and a partner may be asked questions by the teacher in an interview setting.

a) Before you listen to two students answering the following interview question, take notes on how you would answer.

   "*To what extent do you feel like a global citizen? Explain your view.*"

b) Now listen to two students giving their answers. Decide who completed the task better. Give reasons for your decision. → SUPPORT D 11, p. 307

c) **Group work** Divide the class into two groups and listen again.
- One group concentrates on the content of the answers. Decide which points were the most convincing ones in each answer. Compare your results to the points you noted down in a). What could be added to further improve the students' answers?
- Language awareness The other group concentrates on the language. Consider the structure, the use of phrases and words that link different ideas, the choice of words, etc.

d) Present your findings in class and put together a list of the top six tips for answering an interview question like the one above.

3 → SUPPORT D 12, p. 308

Group work (4) In order to practice for an interview situation, work together in groups of four. Divide your group up into two pairs (**A** and **B**). First, **Pair A** asks the questions and **Pair B** answers, then switch roles.

Part D: Living in a globalized world — **Workshop: Step by step**

Pair A

a) Read questions 1-3 that you are going to ask Pair B. Note down possible answers so you know what to expect.
b) Ask Pair B your questions. They will take turns answering.
c) Give Pair B feedback on their answers by comparing them to your notes from a).
d) Now take turns with your partner to answer the questions Pair B has for you.

1. Think of people you are in contact with that were born or live in another country. Describe your relationship to them.
2. Explain whether it matters where you live and come from or whether your background does not play any role at all.
3. Imagine you had to move to another country. Explain how you would feel and which factors might have an influence on your feelings about this development.

Pair B

a) Read questions 1-3 that you are going to ask Pair A. Note down possible answers so you know what to expect.
b) Take turns with your partner to answer the questions Pair A has for you.
c) Now ask Pair A your questions. They will take turns answering.
d) Give Pair A feedback on their answers by comparing them to your notes from a).

1. Describe global problems you worry about. Give reasons for your worries.
2. Explain what you do or think you could do about them.
3. Explain why you would or would not join an NGO like Global Citizen.

4 CD/09
In the monologue part of a speaking exam, you will be asked to give a coherent statement on some material, often a visual. Depending on the task, you may have to present, explain and/or comment on the material.

a) Study photos 1 and 2 on p. 142 and take notes. Follow these steps:
   - Identify the general issue the photos refer to.
   - Explain the connection between the photos. Explain what the photos have in common and to what extent they cover different aspects of the topic.
   - Refer to different aspects of the topic. Make sure that you use the photos as a starting-point and refer to what you see in the photos to explain how they illustrate the general issue.

   „Talk about these pictures. What do they suggest about global eating habits and their consequences?"

b) **Group work** Talk about what you associate with the photos and add any relevant points to your notes.
c) Read the checklist on p. 142, then listen to a student working on the task. While listening, take notes to give feedback.
d) In class, talk about what the student did well and what he could improve.
e) Listen again to note down some useful phrases from the passages he did well.

Webcode
You can find the audio file here: WES-73644-057

→ **S15:** How to describe pictures, p. 358

→ **S20:** How to listen/watch effectively, p. 366

→ **S24:** How to give feedback/peer-edit, p. 372

Workshop: Step by step — Part D: Living in a globalized world

Checklist

Monologue part of a speaking exam

Introduction
- ✓ Describe the general issue depicted in the photos.
- ✓ Refer to at least some elements of the photos to illustrate how they are connected.
- ✓ Refer to elements of the photos to explain connections to general aspects of the topic.

Addressing the topic
- ✓ Explain which aspects of the general issue in question are highlighted by the photos. Refer to relevant details in the photos that are related to the topic in question. Use the photos as a starting-point and do not add information randomly.
- ✓ Incorporate your background knowledge.
- ✓ Describe specifically which part of the photo you refer to (e.g. "In the background …").
- ✓ Use the present progressive for any activities shown in the photos.
- ✓ Make sure that you use suitable connectives (e.g. "That's why …").

Conclusion
- ✓ Sum up your observations and the overall message of the photo.
- ✓ Do not repeat all the points above, but express them in a concise form, also by using different words

1

2

5 Pair work

→ **S15:** How to describe pictures, p. 358

→ **S24:** How to give feedback / peer-edit, p. 372

a) Work on the task below and present the two photos to each other. Follow the steps outlined in task 4. → SUPPORT D13, p. 308
b) Give each other feedback.

"Talk about these pictures. What differences in young people's food consumption and attitudes towards food in a globalized world do they illustrate?"

3

4

Part D: Living in a globalized world — Workshop: **Step by step** 4

DIALOGUE
6 CD/10

In the dialogue part of a speaking exam, you need to discuss a topic with a partner. Although pictures are sometimes part of this task as well, you are not expected to give a detailed description of them. The main focus of the task is to express your views fluently, but also to engage your partner in the discussion and refer to his or her arguments.

Webcode
You can find the audio file here:
WES-73644-58

a) Look at the task and the photos below. Take notes on why or why not each photo represents a more or less important example of globalization in teenagers' lives today.

"You are preparing a presentation on the influence of globalization on teenagers' everyday lives. Agree on the two most relevant pictures."

b) **Language awareness** Listen to an extract from a discussion between two teenagers about the photos. One half of the class concentrates on the arguments they exchange, the other half focuses on the language they use. Take notes.

c) Present your findings in class and talk about how well the two students worked on the task.

d) **Pair work** Now discuss the photos with a partner.

Language support

Keeping up the conversation: Turn-taking

Encouraging your partner to say something
- What do you think about …?/What is your opinion on …?
- Have I understood you correctly that you believe that …?
- Can you think of other examples/arguments that …?
- Do you agree that …?
- Is there anything you would like to add to …?

Referring to your partner's statement
- I see your point, but …
- I agree that …
- What I would like to add to your point about … is that …
- I wouldn't say that …

5

6

7

8

9

10

Workshop: Practice — Part D: Living in a globalized world

→ **S21:** How to succeed in oral exams, p. 367

Practice Speaking

INTERVIEW

1

a) Write down five questions related to the globalization topics you have covered in class on separate cards or sheets of paper. Look at the example in task 2 (p. 140) as a model.
b) Collect the questions in class. Your teacher will check them and hand out a deck of cards/questions to each group.
c) **Group work (4)** Your teacher will give you a deck of cards with questions. Take turns to take over the role of each student (A–D).

Student A:
Take a card. Ask student B and C the question from that card.

Student B:
Answer the question. Try to be as fluent as possible and show your overall knowledge of the topic „globalization".

Student D:
Listen carefully to B's and C's answers. Take notes on language and content to give feedback afterwards.

Student C:
Answer the question. Try to be as fluent as possible and show your overall knowledge of the topic „globalization".

MONOLOGUE

2 Group work (4)

→ **S15:** How to describe pictures, p. 358

→ **S24:** How to give feedback/peer-edit, p. 372

a) Take turns to roll the dice. The number tells you which pair of photos you need to work on.
b) Read the task and look at the photos. Then make your statement. →**SUPPORT** D14, p. 309
c) In the meantime, the other students take notes.
d) Give feedback.

Talk about the photos.
What are the pros and cons of global travel?

Talk about the photos.
What are the pros and cons of the global fashion industry today?

Part D: Living in a globalized world — Workshop: **Practice**

Talk about the visuals.
What are pros and cons of the worldwide use of the Internet today?

DIALOGUE
3 Group work (4)
a) Work in pairs. Take turns to roll the dice. The number tells you which task you need to work on.
b) Read the task. Then start your discussion. → SUPPORT **D15, p. 310**
c) In the meantime, the other students take notes.
d) Give the other pair feedback.

→ **S24:** How to give feedback/peer-edit, p. 372

Globalization – negative aspects
Read the list of worries that are connected with globalization. Agree on one statement that sums up what you fear about globalization. Also talk about your reasons for choosing this statement.

Globalization is a threat because it may lead to …
a) the loss of job opportunities.
b) climate change.
c) the exploitation of workers.
d) pollution and environmental damage.
e) a lack of privacy and data security online.
f) mass migration.

Globalization – positive and negative points
Read the sentences about what globalization means. Agree on one statement that sums up globalization best for you. Also talk about your reasons for choosing this statement.

Globalization is a process which …
a) turns the world into a village.
b) has the potential to make the world a better place.
c) allows people from all over the world to cooperate.
d) spreads poverty and pollution.
e) is beyond our control.
f) people in highly developed countries profit from.

Part D: Living in a globalized world

Globalization – the state of affairs

1

→ **S1:** Checklist: Summary, p. 330

→ **S14:** How to analyse a speech, p. 355

→ **S5:** Checklist: Writing a speech, p. 337

a) Read former US President Barack Obama's farewell speech delivered at the United Nations on 20 September 2016. Sum up his main arguments.
b) Language awareness   Analyse Obama's view and the means he uses to convince the audience of it.   → SUPPORT   D 16, p. 310
c) CHALLENGE   Imagine you were a representative in the United Nations' General Assembly and a critic of globalization. Write a short speech as a reply to Obama's speech in which you deal with some of the issues he raised.

Annotations
[1] **nonproliferation** = limitation of the spread of nuclear weapons
[2] **fault line** = a crack in the earth; *here:* an issue that is likely to cause disagreements
[3] **across vast swaths of** = in a large part of
[4] to **muzzle** = *einen Maulkorb verpassen*
[5] to **quash** /kwɒʃ/ = to use violence to stop political action
[6] to **spur** /spɜː(r)/ = to cause

From the depths of the greatest financial crisis of our time, we coordinated our response to avoid further catastrophe and return the global economy to growth. We've taken away terrorist safe havens, strengthened the nonproliferation[1] regime, resolved the Iranian nuclear issue through diplomacy. We opened relations with Cuba, helped Colombia end Latin America's longest war, and we welcome a democratically elected leader of Myanmar to this Assembly. Our assistance is helping people feed themselves, care for the sick, power communities across Africa, and promote models of development rather than dependence. And we have made international institutions like the World Bank and the International Monetary Fund more representative, while establishing a framework to protect our planet from the ravages of climate change.

This is important work. It has made a real difference in the lives of our people. And it could not have happened had we not worked together. And yet, around the globe we are seeing the same forces of global integration that have made us interdependent also expose deep fault lines[2] in the existing international order.

We see it in the headlines every day. Around the world, refugees flow across borders in flight from brutal conflict. Financial disruptions continue to weigh upon our workers and entire communities. Across vast swaths[3] of the Middle East, basic security, basic order has broken down. We see too many governments muzzling[4] journalists, and quashing[5] dissent, and censoring the flow of information. Terrorist networks use social media to prey upon the minds of our youth, endangering open societies and spurring[6] anger against innocent immigrants and Muslims. Powerful nations contest the constraints placed on them by international law.

This is the paradox that defines our world today. A quarter century after the end of the Cold War, the world is by many measures less violent and more prosperous than ever before, and yet our societies are filled with uncertainty, and unease, and strife. Despite enormous progress, as people lose trust in institutions, governing becomes more difficult and tensions between nations become more quick to surface.

And so I believe that at this moment we all face a choice. We can choose to press forward with a better model of cooperation and integration. Or we can retreat into a world sharply divided, and ultimately in conflict, along age-old lines of nation and tribe and race and religion.

I want to suggest to you today that we must go forward, and not backward. I believe that as imperfect as they are, the principles of open markets and accountable governance, of democracy and human rights and international law that we have forged remain the firmest foundation for human progress in this century. I make this argument not based on theory or ideology, but on facts – facts that all too often, we forget in the immediacy of current events.

Here's the most important fact: The integration of our global economy has made life better for billions of men, women and children. Over the last 25 years, the number of people living in extreme poverty has been cut from nearly 40 percent of humanity to under 10 percent. That's unprecedented. And it's not an abstraction. It means children have enough to eat; mothers don't die in childbirth.

Meanwhile, cracking the genetic code promises to cure diseases that have plagued us for centuries. The Internet can deliver the entirety of human knowledge to a young girl in a remote village on a single hand-held device. In medicine and in manufacturing, in education and communications, we're experiencing a transformation of how human beings live on a scale that recalls the revolutions in agriculture and industry. And as a result, a person born today is more likely to be healthy, to live longer, and to have access to opportunity than at any time in human history.

Moreover, the collapse of colonialism and communism has allowed more people than ever before to live with the freedom to choose their leaders. Despite the real and troubling areas where freedom appears in retreat, the fact remains that the number of democracies around the world has nearly doubled in the last 25 years.

In remote corners of the world, citizens are demanding respect for the dignity of all people no matter their gender, or race, or religion, or disability, or sexual orientation, and those who deny others dignity are subject[7] to public reproach. An explosion of social media has given ordinary people more ways to express themselves, and has raised people's expectations for those of us in power. Indeed, our international order has been so successful that we take it as a given that great powers no longer fight world wars; that the end of the Cold War lifted the shadow of nuclear Armageddon; that the battlefields of Europe have been replaced by peaceful union; that China and India remain on a path of remarkable growth.

I say all this not to whitewash[8] the challenges we face, or to suggest complacency. Rather, I believe that we need to acknowledge these achievements in order to summon the confidence to carry this progress forward and to make sure that we do not abandon those very things that have delivered this progress.

In order to move forward, though, we do have to acknowledge that the existing path to global integration requires a course correction. As too often, those trumpeting the benefits of globalization have ignored inequality within and among nations; have ignored the enduring appeal of ethnic and sectarian[9] identities; have left international institutions ill-equipped[10], underfunded, under-resourced, in order to handle transnational challenges.

Annotations
[7] to **be subject to sth** = *etw. ausgesetzt sein*
[8] to **whitewash** = *here:* to hide negative facts to prevent criticism
[9] **sectarian** = relating to differences between religious groups
[10] **ill-equipped** /ˌɪlɪˈkwɪpt/= *schlecht ausgestattet*

2

a) Choose one of the cartoons and prepare a short presentation on its message.
b) Compare your cartoon's message to that of Obama's speech.

→ **S17:** How to work with cartoons, p. 361

A
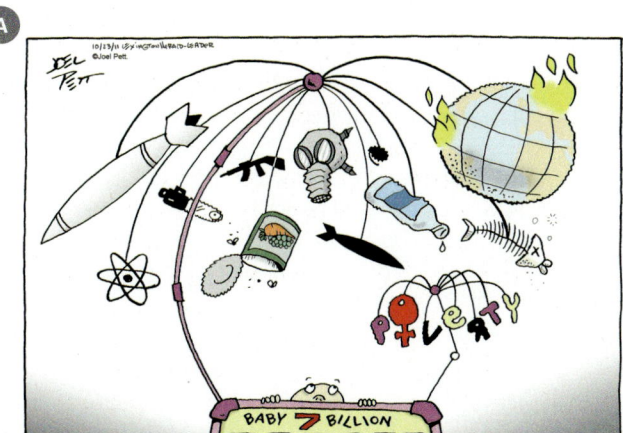

B

Advanced texts — Part D: Living in a globalized world

Effects of globalization: Working with drama

1

a) **Pair work** Talk about what couples can do if they want to have a child. Compare your ideas in class.
b) Read the extract from Vivienne Franzmann's play *Bodies*, written in 2017. Josh and Clem are a white middle-class couple in their forties. Dr Sharma is a doctor in Delhi, India and Lakshmi one of his patients. Find out what the play is about.
c) Explain how the characters feel about the situation they are in.
d) Analyse the character constellation and how it reflects globalization. → **SUPPORT** D 17, p. 311
e) Discuss whether you consider Dr Sharma's services a positive effect of globalization.

→ **S11:** How to work with drama, p. 350

→ **S6:** How to write a discussion/ comment, p. 338

Clem's House/Fertility Clinic Skype

CLEM, JOSH, DR SHARMA and LAKSHMI on Skype.
LAKSHMI *is visible to* CLEM *and* JOSH. CLEM *and* JOSH *are not visible to her.*
    DAUGHTER *watches.*
5 —

DR SHARMA (*Hindi*): *Voh tumhe achi tarah dekhna chatey hain. Line pay aa jao.* [They want to see you properly. Move to the line, please.]
LAKSHMI *moves forward*
DR SHARMA (*Hindi*): *Line pay khadhe ho jao.* [Stand on the line.]
10 CLEM: Lakshmi, can you move forward a little bit please?
DR SHARMA (*Hindi*): *Thodha aage ho jao. Aapne payr line par rakho.* [Put your toes on the line.]
LAKSHMI *puts her toes on the line.*
CLEM: Thank you, Lakshmi.
15 DR SHARMA (*to* CLEM): Is she clearly visible to you?
CLEM: Yes, that's fine.
DR SHARMA (to LAKSHMI, *Hindi*): *Is taraf mudh jao.* [Turn to the side.]
LAKSHMI *turns to the side.*
JOSH: I can't really see anything there. (*To* CLEM) Can you?
20 DR SHARMA: She is just twelve weeks, remember.
CLEM: Of course. She'll barely show, so it's not really —
JOSH: She's a lime[1].
 —

JOSH: It's happening. It's actually fucking happening. Sorry about the
25   swearing, doctor, it's just —
DR SHARMA: You're excited.
JOSH: Can you tell her to push it out.
 —
    Push her belly out.
30 CLEM (*to* JOSH): Don't be so —
DR SHARMA: Yes, I can ask her.
CLEM: Don't ask her to do that. (*To* JOSH) That's so —
JOSH: Okay, don't ask her. Veto that.
DR SHARMA: I can ask her —
35 JOSH: Sorry. No, don't. That was stupid of me.
 —

Annotations
[1] to **be a lime** *(infml)* = to be of high quality

DR SHARMA: We are very pleased with the baby's progress. And Lakshmi is excellent.
–
40 She's made friends with the other ladies in the centre. It's a very supportive environment. They take –
JOSH: Can you ask her to turn to the left a little bit?
DR SHARMA (*Hindi*): *Bayen hath ki taraf mudho.*
45 [Turn to the left.]
LAKSHMI *turns to the left.*
JOSH: God, you can really … Clem, look …
–

DR SHARMA: Is there anything else you'd like to ask her?
50 JOSH: Tell her that she's made us the happiest people ever. Tell her that.
DR SHARMA (*Hindi*): *Yeh kahtey hain ki tumney inko bahut khush kiya hai.* [He says that you've made them very happy.]
LAKSHMI *smiles.*
She is pleased.

55 JOSH: Do we have the date for the caesarean[2]?
DR SHARMA: We are not quite there yet, so –
JOSH: Obviously, we'd like to book the flights sooner rather than later.
DR SHARMA: Of course.
JOSH: So as soon as you know the date, you'll let me know.
60 DR SHARMA: Yes, of course.
CLEM *looks at* DAUGHTER.
CLEM: Can you ask her something for me?
DR SHARMA: Of course.
CLEM: Can you ask her how she feels?
65 DR SHARMA (*Hindi*): *Tumhara kaysa haal hai?* [How do you feel?]
LAKSHMI (*Hindi*): *Main Khush hun.* [I am happy.]
DR SHARMA: She is happy.
DAUGHTER *motions for* CLEM *to ask again.*
CLEM: I mean, how does it feel having our baby growing inside her?
70 DR SHARMA: It is tiring for her, but she's –
CLEM: No, I mean, how does she feel with our baby growing inside her rather than her own, what is that like for her?
DR SHARMA: She is looking forward very much to giving you your child.
CLEM: Can you ask her how she feels about having our child inside her?
75 JOSH: Why are you –
CLEM: Ask her, please.
DR SHARMA (*Hindi*): *Yeh puchti hai ki tumhain kaysa lagta hai ki inka bacha tumhorey ander badh raha hai.* [She wants to know what it is like having their baby grow inside of you?]
80 LAKSHMI (*slowly, English*): Happy to make dreams come true.
–
JOSH: That's lovely. Thank you, Lakshmi.

Annotations
[2] **caesarean** /sɪˈzeərɪən/ = *Kaiserschnitt*

5 Britishness

Webcode

You can download a word list for the Intro and the WordPool here: WES-73644-059

1 Placemat

a) Imagine you had to illustrate "Germanness" or German traditions and culture for a textbook to be used in British schools. What kind of images or photos would you choose? Write down what you think should be shown.
b) Compare your ideas with your partners' and agree on a final list of the top five images.

→ **S15:** How to describe pictures, p. 358

2

a) The pictures above illustrate aspects of British traditions and culture. Identify the aspect(s) depicted in each photo. If you are in doubt, ask your classmates.
b) **Pair work** Choose the one that appeals to you most and tell your partner why you chose that photo.
c) **Group work (4)** Compare these pictures with those that you might have chosen to illustrate German traditions and culture: which photo(s) do you find are closest to your own background and which differ most?

Webcode

You can find the audio file here: WES-73644-060

3 ⊙ CD/11

The Guardian asked people from all over the UK what being British means to them.
a) Read Nadia Hussain's statement and listen to the statements of the other people. Note down how they define Britishness.

Nadia Hussain, 32	Alan Ward, 65	Ross Purdie, 24	Moses Gittens, 48	Manish Gajjar, 40
…	…	…	…	…

Britishness — Intro 5

Nadia Hussain:
My parents came here from Pakistan in 1974. I was born in Forest Gate, east London, in 1979, and have four brothers and sisters. I experienced a lot of racism growing up. The racial groups – white, black, Asian – tended to keep in their own groups. It was really weird. But I love the East End, and wouldn't change it for the world. Our neighbours are white, and we love them to bits. I still live with my parents, and because of our cultural background I can only break away when I get married. I'm not a strict Muslim, but I do carry my faith close to my heart, and I'd be unlikely to marry outside it; the culture clash would be too great. Britain is moving too fast and has lost its sense of Britishness. It's obsessed by money, and social bonds are breaking down. My parents always make us have a meal together in the evening. That's been lost in this generation. Respect for teachers has also been lost. I'm proud to be British, but the country isn't as strong as it was. Our educational system is deteriorating, unemployment is rising, and I worry about the future.

b) **Pair work** Compare your notes with a partner's and add missing aspects to your own.

c) **Pair work** Tell each other which person you would like to talk to and what you would ask that person. Come up with five questions.

Preview

British identity
The first part of this Theme is about different aspects of British identity. In the **Workshop**, you will analyse a newspaper article.

The monarchy and the political system
The second part of the Theme is about the monarchy and the political system in Britain. In the **Workshop**, you will write an opinion piece for a newspaper.

The many faces of Britain
The third part of the Theme focuses on multiculturalism in British society. In the **Workshop**, you will analyse modern poetry.

WordPool — Britishness

BRITISH IDENTITY

What makes Britain British? Is there an exact mix of social roles, ethnicities and religions that makes the country the way it is? Maybe it's the countryside or the food? National identity consists of all of these things and more, shaped by a complex, shared heritage that is developing continuously.

Britain consists of four nations: England, Northern Ireland, Scotland and Wales. These nations are spread over two islands, but together they form the United Kingdom. While each nation has its own individual identity, British identity consists of them all combined. British identity is therefore about fluidity and flexibility. Many people have moved to Britain over the years and they have all brought their foods and customs with them, meaning that nowadays an Indian curry could be considered just as British as a plate of fish and chips. (Though even that was probably introduced by Jewish immigrants from Spain and Portugal!)

THE MONARCHY AND THE POLITICAL SYSTEM

Britain is both a monarchy and a democracy. Interestingly, Britain does not have a written constitution. Instead, political documents like The Magna Carta (1215) and the Bill of Rights (1689) have helped to shape the political system. While the Magna Carta was an effort to limit the king's power over the people, the Bill of Rights reinforced the rights of parliament and its members, transforming the country into a constitutional monarchy.

Generally, the people decide how the country is run. Their sovereignty finds expression in general elections, when the electorate votes for the members of the House of Commons, one of the two chambers of parliament. The other chamber, the House of Lords, is not voted for by the people, but has only very limited powers.

The monarch inherits his or her position and acts as head of state in Britain. Although the king or queen has a lot of responsibilities, e.g. formally appoint the Prime Minister, who will then form a government, the real power lies with parliament.

Who should be allowed to vote has caused concern for centuries. When the term "parliament" was first used in 1236 to refer to the people running the country, representatives weren't voted for by the people. It wasn't until 1258 that voting was introduced, and even then it was mainly for wealthy, male landowners. While over the centuries, more and more men were granted the vote, it was only in 1928 that the government gave all women over 21 without distinction the right to vote. Today any citizen of Britain over the age of 18 is entitled to vote in elections.

THE MANY FACES OF BRITAIN

Britain has always been multicultural. People have moved to the UK for centuries and will almost certainly continue to, creating a population of different backgrounds, ethnicities and religions. Since the Roman invasion of 55 BC, Vikings, Normans, Flemings, Africans, Eastern Europeans, Asian and American people, and many more have moved to Britain, leaving their descendants to form today's population. While much of this is down to specific historical events (a number of Africans, for example, came to Britain as seamen and soldiers during the First World War), much is also down to very different individual reasons. Everyone who comes to Britain makes a contribution; the economy benefits from wider spending and future generations are brought up in a place where hopefully everyone will be valued equally. However, gaps between the upper classes, the bourgeois middle classes and the poorer lower classes have long been seen as unjust by many. Younger people with more egalitarian viewpoints in particular claim that this is one of Britain's most severe problems.

Britishness — WordPool 5

1
Choose from the highlighted words in the text to complete the following sentences.
1. The new Chancellor of the Exchequer was determined to cut public ▢ and reduce debts.
2. Only the lawful ▢ of the monarch is allowed to become king or queen.
3. The Prince of Wales praised the team's ▢ to British sports.
4. The Commonwealth countries have greatly influenced Britain's cultural ▢.
5. One reason that British people voted for Brexit is that they were afraid of losing their national ▢ to the European Union.
6. The result of the Brexit referendum has been the subject of great ▢ for many people, particularly to those in the financial sector.
7. A great ▢ is needed to make people trust the government again.
8. Many countries lack both democratic traditions and a strong ▢, which often encourages corruption in politics.

2
Rewrite the sentences using the highlighted verbs from the text instead of the underlined verbs.
1. As a democratically elected head of state he <u>has</u> immunity from prosecution.
2. It was not until after the First World War that British women were <u>given</u> the vote.
3. In former times, only the eldest son <u>was left</u> the property of his father after the latter's death.
4. The majority of British people <u>appreciate</u> the monarchy and all it stands for.
5. The Prime Minister has the right to <u>choose</u> his cabinet after winning an election.

3
a) Copy the grid and fill in the missing parts of speech.

verb	noun	adjective
...	1) contributor 2) contribution	contributory
to distinguish	...	1) distinct 2) ...
...	1) election 2) ...	1) electable 2) elect
...	1) inheritance 2) ...	hereditary
to concern	concern	concerned

Webcode
You can download the grid here:
WES-73644-061

b) Find words from the grid to match these definitions.
1. someone who writes articles for a newspaper or magazine
2. all the people who are allowed to vote
3. to separate into classes or categories
4. when something is passed on from one generation to another by reason of birth
5. anxious or worried

c) Take the parts of speech with two alternatives, e.g. elect/electable. Complete the following sentences using one of the two alternatives given in the grid.
1. He was surprised by the size of his ▢ after his parents died. He had not realized how rich his parents were.
2. Stopping global warming would be the greatest ▢ that could be made to future generations.
3. At the next ▢ the Conservatives are expected to lose a number of seats in Parliament.
4. There is a ▢ possibility that Queen Elizabeth will continue to reign as long as she can. She is unlikely to abdicate.
5. The politician's youthful appearance made him an extremely ▢ candidate.

5 Workshop: Step by step — Part A: British identity

Webcode
You can download a word list for Part A here:
WES-73644-062

Step by step Analysing a newspaper article

PRE-READING

1

a) Look up the words on the right. Then write a very short story of exactly 50 words and with a happy ending using all of them.

to entrench | myth | warped | hostile

b) Read the headline of the article below and speculate:
- on the direction this article is going to take
- what myths about British culture the author Afua Hirsch might refer to

c) Write a speech bubble for the young man in the centre of the photo holding the English flag. Compare them in class.

COMPREHENSION

2

a) Read the article and write down the author's central idea in one sentence.
b) **Pair work** Compare your sentences and decide which is more precise.
c) **Pair work** Tell each other what really surprised you in this article and what did not surprise you at all.
d) **Pair work** Talk about the connection between the Brexit referendum and ethnic minorities living in Britain as outlined in the article.

Annotations
[1] **warped** /wɔː(r)pt/ = strange
[2] to **flaunt** /flɔːnt/ = to show sth in order to be admired
[3] Europe's main human rights organization

AFUA HIRSCH

The Guardian, 25 May 2017

Brexit is entrenching some dangerous myths about 'British' culture

Britain has always had a warped[1] sense of its own history, excluding ethnic minorities. Now a survey suggests this is becoming something more hostile and alarming

Britain First and EDL protesters stage a demonstration in London.

— headline
— standfirst or subheading
— caption
— date of publication
— photo or illustration
— paragraph

There is something deeply ironic about the wave of nostalgia sweeping political discourse in modern Britain. On the one hand, it harks – increasingly since the Brexit vote – back to the age of empire. "A small island perched on the edge of the European continent became a leader of world trade," is how international trade secretary Liam Fox fondly described that epoch to a group of Commonwealth trade ministers. On the other, the supposed humanitarianism that accompanied that age has been swiftly forgotten.

While the empire was founded on racist beliefs about the supposed inferiority of the people it subjugated, humanitarianism was its proudly flaunted[2] justification. This was manifested perfectly in Winston Churchill, who was able to boast of killing "savages" in Sudan, while also playing a leading role in creating the international humanitarian norms that many consider one of the great accomplishments of the 20th century. It's only a matter of time before Britain's membership of the Council of Europe[3] – along with the rest

154

of the European institutions developed by patriotic Brits who are keen to avoid a repeat of war – faces the same fate as our membership of the EU. […]

In Britain something specific is happening. A survey found that more than half of British people feel hostile not just to refugees, but to ethnic minorities – many of them British people themselves – already living here. This can be put down to various perceived economic and social threats – a quarter think immigrants take away jobs, and a third that they remove more from society than they contribute. But more sinister is its generality. More than half of the British people surveyed felt that people from ethnic minorities threatened their "culture".

This one finding says so much. It confirms what we all know, that "British culture" is perceived as something white. This was the dog-whistle[4] narrative of the Brexit referendum campaign – apart from the appeal to imperial greatness, there was the demand to "get our country back". Few said explicitly that this meant make our country white again. But some heard it nevertheless. It was surely part of the reason for the spike in racist attacks after the result, and why a cabbie[5] told me I'd "be off home soon" as I rushed around on a referendum-related news story.

It was also the reason why, according to an Opinium[6] poll, ethnic minority British people are now less likely to identify as British since the EU referendum. Instead, many are more likely to claim the identity of their ethnic minority heritage. British people who are not white feel less British now because that hostility is palpable[7], because there is an agenda of regressing to a time, before the European Union, that many remember not for the joys of complete sovereignty, but for the absence of protection from racism in the workplace, or at the hands of the police, or for being openly chased in the streets by white racists.

Multicultural history: The Great Mosque on Brick Lane in London used to be a Protestant church and a synagogue.

The idea that British "culture" is somehow opposite to the presence of ethnic minorities is a historical nonsense. Many of our most iconic cultural traditions are the products of immigration – such as fish and chips, an innovation of Jewish refugees from Portugal. Roads and cities were built by the Romans, banks were founded by Huguenots, a royal household established by a broad cross-section of European aristocracy. There were Africans in Britain, it's now widely accepted, before there were any "English". No society ever has a perfect grasp of its history, and that doesn't matter, it's perceptions that count, and the harm that they cause. Britain's sense of self has become so warped, so divorced from reality, that it is demonising[8] its visible minorities, including the 6 million or so British people of minority heritage among them. In this context, when I hear politicians appeal to patriotism, I feel very nervous. Not because there is anything wrong with patriotic feeling – like populism, it's a term that only becomes malign[9] by its context. But because I know only too well what that current context is. And thanks to the findings of widespread hostility towards the impact of ethnic minority people on British culture, so should everyone else.

Annotations
[4] dog-whistle messages are political messages that are aimed at certain parts of the population
[5] cabbie (infml) = cab/taxi driver
[6] name of a British company that conducts opinion polls
[7] palpable /ˈpælpəb(ə)l/ = when sth is palpable, you can sense it easily
[8] to demonise/demonize = to say that sb or sth is very bad although they are not
[9] malign /məˈlaɪn/ = bad

body

Workshop: Step by step — Part A: British identity

Preview

In this Workshop you will be asked to analyse a newspaper article. In order to do so, you will need to look closely at the following aspects:
- structure
- line of argument
- rhetorical devices

ANALYSIS

3 Language awareness

Study the info box and decide which type of article it is.

Info

Types of articles

News article: The main focus of a news article is on factual information and therefore it provides mainly answers to the who, what, where, when, why and how of an incident.

Feature article: It is an article that explores a news story in depth. Its main purpose is not to tell you what has happened, but to look at the wider context of a news story. The author's opinion may shine through, but it should always be based on the analysis of the situation, not a personal attitude or bias.

Opinion piece: In this type of article the author clearly expresses his or her view on a certain issue. The style of writing may be argumentative, entertaining, biased or evaluative. Opinion pieces can be sub-divided into:
- **Editorial:** This article is always written by the paper's editor or senior editorial staff. It is clearly marked as an editorial and usually unsigned.
- **Column:** This article may be written by a regular or a guest columnist. Such pieces may be strongly opinionated, and the opinion expressed is that of the writer and not (necessarily) of the paper.

4

Match the parts (1-7) of the article on pp. 154-155 with the corresponding points (A-G).

Structure and line of argument:
- A topic sentence: states what the paragraph is about
- B conclusion: referring back to the beginning/to the main argument
- C appeal: a serious, urgent, or heartfelt request; a call for action

Language and rhetorical devices:
- D juxtaposition: placing two or more things side by side to compare or contrast them
- E quoting experts/authorities: to lend credibility to the argument
- F facts and figures: to give credence to the points made
- G examples: illustrating or supporting the main arguments

1	2	3	4	5	6	7
…	…	…	…	…	…	…

5 Language awareness

→ **S13:** Checklist: Analysis – non-fictional texts, p. 354

→ **S9:** How to structure a text, p. 344

 Examine how the author tries to convince the reader of this view:

"The idea that British "culture" is somehow opposite to the presence of ethnic minorities is […] nonsense" (ll. 74-76).

Refer to structure, line of argument and rhetorical devices.
You may start like this: *In her article … Afua Hirsch criticizes …* → **SUPPORT** D 1, p. 312

COMMENT/DISCUSSION

6

In class, discuss whether this quotation could be applied to Germany and German culture.

Part A: British identity   **Workshop: Practice**

5

Practice **Analysing a newspaper article**

PRE-READING

1
a) **Group work (3)** Tell each other what you know about Brexit.
b) Look up Brexit in an online encyclopaedia and write down five essential keywords on cards.

c) Describe the cartoon and identify its symbols. Then talk about their effect and the message of the cartoon.
d) **Pair work** Compare the message of the cartoon with your five keywords from b).
e) Look at the article from *The Observer* on pp. 158-159 and point out the structural elements of a newspaper article.

→ **S17:** How to work with cartoons, p. 361

COMPREHENSION

2
a) Read the article and note down the author's main arguments in keywords.
b) **Pair work** Compare your notes and also talk about what you think of the arguments.

ANALYSIS

3 Language awareness

Analyse the article. Refer to structure, line of argument, and language.   → **SUPPORT** D 2, p. 312

→ **S13:** Checklist: Analysis – non-fictional texts, p. 354
→ **S9:** How to structure a text, p. 344

Workshop: Practice — Part A: British identity

23 October 2016

The Observer view on Britain becoming mean and narrow-minded
Observer editorial

The post-referendum political debate has been besmirched by racism, bigotry[1] and hatred

Tracy Brabin, newly elected MP for Batley and Spen, who was heckled[2] by far-right demonstrators.

Annotations
[1] **bigotry** /ˈbɪɡətri/ = the practice of having strong prejudices against certain people
[2] to **heckle** = to shout at sb in public
[3] **byword** = a typical example of sth
[4] British film director, who has won many awards
[5] **brutish** = cruel
[6] **emboldened** = to be given more confidence

Just four years ago, Britain proudly projected the image of an open, tolerant, confident nation onto the international stage. We luxuriated in the glow of an Olympic opening ceremony that drew together the best of British: from Shakespeare to *EastEnders*; the Queen to James Bond; the NHS to the internet.

It featured Dizzee Rascal and Rowan Atkinson, Arctic Monkeys and the London Symphonic Orchestra. It was, according to writer Jonathan Freedland, "a byword[3] for a new approach, not only to British culture but to Britishness itself. Politicians would soon be referring to it, using it as shorthand for a new kind of patriotism that does not lament a vanished Britain but loves the country that has changed." It was hailed abroad and Britain, it seemed, had shown itself to the world as a vibrant, open, confident, multicultural country.

That all seems like a long time ago.

Over the last few weeks, the image of a country celebrated by the genius of Danny Boyle[4] is being replaced by one marked out by narrow minds and mean spirits. What has happened to us? The messages being sent across the world is that foreign students are not welcome and that British firms will have to list foreign workers. [...]

It seems that some in politics and the press have misinterpreted the referendum result as a justification for an alarming shift in our political discourse. The referendum created a popular mandate for Britain to leave the European Union and demonstrated public appetite for a more controlled approach to immigration. It was not a mandate to descend into a brutish[5] politics – and a brutish public discourse fanned by the lie factories of Fleet Street. The discourse is built on the assumption that we are a country with hostile views towards those who do not hail from these shores. That is not true. Politics has never felt meaner-spirited. We have seen the home secretary announce plans to force companies to disclose how many foreign workers they employ. MPs have called for dental checks to determine the age of refugees, even as the British Dental Association declared this inaccurate and unethical; and sections of the press have been attacked by Microsoft for using an inaccurate "fun app" to "prove" that child refugees are adults. The prime minister has reinforced the message that international students are a drag, not a boost, for Britain. And those who voted Remain and dare to scrutinise the government's position on Brexit are now deemed unpatriotic and undemocratic.

It seems those politicians and commentators who flirted with xenophobia and bigotry in the referendum campaign have been emboldened[6]. Theresa May's government has done nothing to challenge the tone of discourse. She once described the Tories as the "nasty party⁷" – it would be a shame if she is the prime minister who oversees the rise of the "nasty country". But that is what is happening. As Seema Malhotra says on other pages today: "The post-Brexit debate is becoming less reasoned, more toxic and more intolerant. Language matters and political rhetoric has consequences."

It is true that public concern about immigration has risen, particularly since the wave of European immigration after the EU expanded eastwards in 2004 and the financial crisis. But such concerns cannot be allowed to obscure the fact that Britain is, on the whole, a tolerant, diverse and successful society. There is a small segment of the population – the thinktank British Future puts it at one in 10 – who endorse nakedly racist views. But racist attitudes have sharply declined over the last 30 years. The World Values Survey rates Britain as one of the most racially tolerant countries in the world. An analysis of public attitudes by the campaign group Hope Not Hate finds that England is a more tolerant and confident multicultural society in 2016 than in 2011. The proportion of the English population broadly positive about immigration has risen to 38%; and the proportion most hostile to immigration – whose attitudes are driven by opposition to ethnicities and religions other than their own – has shrunk from 13% to 7%. The biggest chunk – 42% – are concerned about the economic impact of further immigration or have concerns about its impact on cultural identity.

The majority position in England can be characterised as tough, but pragmatic: 60% favour only allowing in migrants who help the economy. This is reflected in the lack of public support for government policy to reduce the number of international students: one poll suggests 87% of the British public would like to see the same number, or more, international students when they are given information about the economic benefits.

No matter: the government seems determined that the rest of the world hear the message that Britain is no longer the country it used to be. The world has started to notice. *The Times of India* has condemned the government's approach, declaring: "Other countries like Canada and Australia are much more welcoming." The Irish ambassador has made similar noises. The irony is that we need to be projecting precisely the opposite image to make a success of Brexit. We need friends and cordial relations with as much of the international community as possible. […] Britain needs a government prepared to lead a responsible and honest public conversation on immigration and integration, while challenging the racism and bigotry of a small minority. Instead, by assuming the 52% who voted Leave⁸ will embrace her government's policies on foreign students and child refugees, Mrs May is committing the same sin she has been quick to attribute to the liberal elite: patronising and belittling voters concerned about immigration. In doing so, she betrays her misunderstanding of who we are as a country.

Annotations
⁷ **nasty** = mean, very unpleasant
⁸ name of the campaign in Britain to leave the EU

4
Compare the two opinion pieces that you have read. Use at least six of the following words and phrases:

> whereas | in contrast to | while | on the other hand | however | on the contrary | in/by comparison with | as opposed to | whilst | likewise | similarly | as distinct from | conversely

5 Texts — Part A: British identity

Listening

1 CD/12

You will hear statements made by six people from Britain on the question "What does being British mean?"
Match each statement (1-6) with the corresponding headline (A-G). There is one more answer than you need.

		Headline
1	...	A Honouring the past
2	...	B Variety and typical food
3	...	C Living with what is there
4	...	D Not showing any feelings
5	...	E Like a strong and fierce animal
6	...	F Different people, different views
		G Being able to deal with something unpleasant or annoying

Webcode
You can find the audio file here:
WES-73644-063

→ **S20:** How to listen/watch effectively, p. 366

Viewing

2
a) Watch the video "Stephen Fry welcomes you to Heathrow" and say which aspects of Britishness he talks about.
b) **Group work (4-6)** Talk about which aspects you would include in a video that welcomes visitors to Germany and note down your ideas.
c) **EXTRA** Produce a video in English welcoming visitors to Germany.

Webcode
You can find a link to the video here:
WES-73644-064

Mediation: Differences in humour

3 Pair work
English people sometimes joke that "German humour is no laughing matter". Talk to your partner about how you understand that pun and whether you agree or disagree with this sentiment.

4
 You are currently spending a year abroad at an English comprehensive school. Your year is doing a project on humour around the globe. You have decided to outline the information on humour and the Germans, as described in the interview.
Write a blog entry for the school website.

→ **S19:** How to improve your mediation skills, p. 364
→ **S7:** Checklist: Writing a blog post, p. 340

„Wir sollten Ernst und Humor häufiger mischen"
Warum die Deutschen als humorlos gelten

23. März 2014, FOCUS Online

Die Deutschen haben nicht gerade den Ruf, viel Spaß zu verstehen. Woher kommt dieses Klischee – und hat es einen wahren Kern? FOCUS-Online-Experte Rainer Stollmann erklärt die Geschichte
5 der deutschen Ernsthaftigkeit.

FOCUS Online: Herr Stollmann, sind die Deutschen wirklich so humorlos, wie oft behauptet wird?
Rainer Stollmann: Ja. Vorurteile sind selten ohne jeden Wirklichkeitsbezug. Die Deutschen sind
10 humorlos, weil sie Romantiker sind. Die Romantik war die deutsche Epoche, die andere Völker so nicht kennen. So wie die Renaissance italienisch und der Barock spanisch ist. Der wichtigste Begriff der Romantik ist „Sehnsucht". Wer sich vor Sehnsucht
15 verzehrt und gern Weltschmerz empfindet, lacht nicht.

FOCUS Online: Das ist nun aber schon 200 Jahre her.

Rainer Stollmann: Stimmt, aber in der klassisch-romantischen Epoche wurde die Ernsthaftigkeit geboren, die noch heute als Markenzeichen deutscher Kultur auf der Welt gilt, besonders in der „ernsten" Musik und der Philosophie. Hegel war völlig humorlos. Gegensätze, über die Engländer gelacht hätten, dachte er ohne jeden Anflug von Heiterkeit durch und entwickelte so die „Dialektik". Einer, der seine „Logik" mit dem Satz „Das Sein und das Nichts sind dasselbe" anfängt, ist Engländern und Franzosen suspekt.

FOCUS Online: Es gab aber auch im 19. Jahrhundert große deutsche Humoristen, zum Beispiel Wilhelm Busch, der im Grunde den Cartoon erfunden hat.

Rainer Stollmann: Manches an Wilhelm Busch ist genial, anarchisch, hochkomisch. Aber der größere Teil seines Werkes, den wir heute nicht mehr kennen, ist spießig. Nehmen wir einmal die großen nationalen Klassiker: Shakespeares Stücke können Sie fast alle, auch „Romeo und Julia", als Tragödie oder als Komödie inszenieren, ohne die Substanz zu verletzen. Bei Schiller und Goethe, die Shakespeare doch das Wasser reichen können, geht das nicht. In der deutschen klassischen Hochliteratur gibt es eigentlich nur zwei Komödien: Lessings „Minna von Barnhelm" und Kleists „Der zerbrochene Krug". Die Deutschen wurden zuerst in der Kultur zu einer „Nation", so dass sie diese ungeheuer ernst nehmen. Die Engländer wurden ökonomisch eine Nation, die Franzosen politisch.

„Max und Moritz, diese beiden ..." –
der Gipfel deutschen Humors?

FOCUS Online: Sie sprechen von Hochkultur, aber inzwischen gibt es doch auch in Deutschland eine Unterhaltungskultur.

Rainer Stollmann: Zu den ersten Formen einer deutschen Popularkultur gehörten etwa die Grimmschen Märchen. Wie man den Märchensammlungen anderer Völker entnehmen kann, waren Märchen ursprünglich Geschichten zum Lachen. Das, was heute der Witz ist, waren vor 500 Jahren die Märchen. So sehr ich die Brüder Grimm verehre: Sie haben den Märchen das Lachen entzogen, indem sie den berühmten „Grimm-Sound", den Märchenton, die „Kinder- und Hausmärchen" erfanden – also etwas Naives und Innerliches, eben Romantisches.

FOCUS Online: Seit den Brüdern Grimm hat sich einiges getan.

Rainer Stollmann: Wir haben Heinz Erhardt, Otto Waalkes, Loriot und Helge Schneider und ebenso gute Satire-Zeitschriften und einige Fernsehproduktionen wie andere Länder. Aber das Vorurteil, dass die Deutschen humorlos seien, führt dazu, dass kein Engländer und kein Franzose Loriot kennt, obwohl der mit aller englischen und französischen Komik mithalten kann. Dagegen hat das deutsche Publikum – zumindest im Westen – Charlie Chaplin, Buster Keaton, Laurel und Hardy, Mr. Bean, Monty Python, Jacques Tati und Louis de Funès, der so eine Art französischer Heinz Erhardt ist, im Fernsehen ausführlich kennengelernt. Das deutsche Durchschnittspublikum kennt mehr internationale Komik als andere Fernsehnationen.

FOCUS Online: Das heißt, wir sind doch nicht so humorlos?

Rainer Stollmann: Loriot hat die Frage einmal sehr schön beantwortet: Die Deutschen, sagte er, lachen genauso gern wie alle anderen, aber sie trennen Ernst und Humor schärfer. Die Deutschen warten auf ein Signal zum Lachen. Loriot hat das bedauert. Sie müssten Humor und Ernst mehr mischen, also einfach mal an der Stelle lachen, wo eigentlich ein ernstes Gesicht gemacht werden müsste. [...]

5

a) **Pair work** Read each other's blog entries and give feedback.
b) Talk about Stollmann's view of Germans and humour and say why you agree or disagree with him.

→ **S24:** How to give feedback/peer-edit, p. 372

Advanced texts Part A: British identity

6 Across cultures

a) **Group work (4)** Read Stollmann's last answer again. Discuss whether the following situations should be taken with more humour in Germany:
- the train you need to take is an hour late
- the yoghurt you bought turns out to be spoiled
- your best friend forgot your birthday
- your favourite football team has lost an important match
- your neighbour's dog mistakes your bicycle for a tree
- your brother/sister always steals your favourite food from the fridge

b) Talk about what you could say or do to make light of the situations in a).

c) How would the situations be dealt with in other cultures? Exchange your experiences.

7

a) Find English jokes online and share your favourite ones in class. Make sure not to hurt anyone's feelings or be rude.

b) Talk about where you see the biggest difference between English and German humour.

Advanced texts Englishness

PRE-READING

1

a) **Pair work** Explain to each other the differences between England, Britain and the United Kingdom.

b) Read the headline of the article on the next page and look at the photos. Then speculate about the direction the article is going to take.

COMPREHENSION

2

a) Read the article and see whether your speculations in 1b) were correct.
b) Outline the major differences between Britishness and Englishness as described in the article.
c) Use a map to locate all the different regions mentioned.

ANALYSIS

3

→ **S13:** Checklist: Analysis – non-fictional texts, p. 354

Examine the features and characteristics of the New Englishness. → SUPPORT D 3, p. 312

COMMENT

4

→ **S6:** How to write a discussion/comment, p. 338

Comment on the author's opinion that all the New Englishness "can promise is the past, and there can be no hope or glory in that." (ll. 150-152)

162

Part A: British identity — Advanced texts

What It Means to Be English in 2017

As Brexit Britain fractures, UKIP are hoping to make a revival of Englishness their version of "Make America Great Again".

Angus Harrison, 27 February 2017

According to a poll released by YouGov last month, nearly a fifth of people in the UK define themselves as English as opposed to British, up five percent from 2015. This comes in the wake of a decision to leave the European Union, driven in large part by English voters, at a time when UKIP's new leader, Paul Nuttall, has promised his party will seek to challenge Labour by espousing this newly reawakened English nationalism. "The next big issue that's going to come up in British politics beyond Brexit is Englishness," he told the Telegraph.

Englishness as a standalone identity has always struggled to articulate itself. During the 20th century it was largely subsumed into Britishness. England's cultural behemoths, from The Beatles to the Sex Pistols, emerged draped in Union Jacks rather than St George's flags. It was Britpop and Madchester; never "the English Invasion". Aside from a tournament once every two years, when the four nations split up to experience their own footballing disappointments, English people tend to identify themselves locally – as Cornish[1] or Scouse[2], say – instead of under any kind of shared nationhood.

Britishness, meanwhile, is going from strength to strength. In recent years it's been reborn as a brand – the cult of *Keep Calm and Carry On* sold to shy-Tory 20-somethings who think the Queen is "cute". Bolstered by the 2012 Olympics, this is a cuddly, meme-friendly national identity of *Very British Problems*[3] and "21 Things British People Miss When They Move To America". This deeply privileged universe of Marmite[4] and umbrellas has allowed Britishness a place in the new millennium, repositioning the Union Jack as a symbol of complaining about weather rather than the banner of colonisation and genocide.

[…]

Englishness has long struggled to define itself against the competing national characters of Scotland, Wales and Northern Ireland. It's an oft-trod line of argument among beleaguered Englanders that "Welsh people are allowed to celebrate St David's day, but if we celebrate St George we're told we're racist!" While this suggestion of a discriminatory disparity is largely imagined, it is true that Northern Ireland, Wales and Scotland have all become increasingly influential political characters in their own right, leaving England gasping for meaning. Talk of parliamentary devolution[5] has all too easily conflated England with London, and as such misunderstood Englishness as an assumed, self-confident, dominant identity – a misunderstanding that fails to appreciate the suburban stretches and satellite towns in as much need for definition as the Scottish highlands.

[…]

Scotland is a rival now far more than a partner. When the SNP aren't campaigning

Annotations
[1] **Cornish** = coming from Cornwall
[2] **Scouse** /skaʊs/ (*infml*) = coming from the area around Liverpool
[3] a popular book and TV series on typically British behaviour
[4] brand name of a British vegetable spread
[5] **devolution** = the process of transferring power from a central government to regional governments

Advanced texts — Part A: British identity

Annotations

6 **defiant** /dɪˈfaɪənt/ = refusing to follow a person or rule

7 name of a London-based radio station

8 **bumper sticker** = sticker that is attached to the rear of a car, usually bearing some kind of slogan or message

for their own independence, they are moving to oppose the Brexit they never voted for in the first place. They fly their flag and extol their virtues defiantly[6], which has sent England into an existential crisis – for if the Union falls apart, what will become of the shapeless patch of rock in the middle? Scotland has forced England to manufacture a reactionary identity of its own.

The English patriotism of 2017 doesn't fly a flag. Instead, it complains loudly about not being allowed to fly one. It is not the sound of throats rattling in common song; rather, it's the drone of MPs debating whether or not England should have its own national anthem. It's the call to reinstate crowns on pint glasses. It is a national identity built on strongly worded letters of complaint and LBC[7] phone-ins.

The New Englishness [...] is a celebration of everything it hates, defined by all the wrong it sees. The New Englishness is a tabloid patriotism of outrage and injustice, far more comfortable working in negative space than it is in celebration. It is anti-EU, anti-political correctness, anti-Muslim, anti-Scottish independence, anti-vegan, anti-globalisation [...].

Tellingly, England's newly awakened patriotism is also old. The results of Viceland's census of 18 to 35-year-olds strongly indicated that young people don't care about nationalism, with a quarter of respondents registering themselves as 0 out of 10 in terms of how patriotic they are. YouGov has published statistics which follow a similar model, revealing in 2015 that patriotism significantly declines with each generation. It is the old, then – the same old who drove Britain out of the European Union – who are at the beating heart of England's new patriotic zeal. They have no interest in contemporary England; their passion comes instead from a longing for the past, and a conviction that they are somehow being censored from revelling in it. In a strange turn of events, declaring love for Queen and country has become an anti-establishment sport.

[...]

The New Englishness [...] is a national pride that simply wants to be noticed – a self-aware patriotism that lionises the idea of England without ever substantiating its qualities. It is nothing but a bumper sticker[8], a campaign banner, a defence mechanism and a political tool.

Depressingly, we're going to be hearing a lot more about this English patriotism over the coming years. UKIP are likely to make England's awakening their "Make America Great Again" as they pick up seats in the forgotten corners of the nation, like nightclub crawlers preying on the broken-hearted. The Conservatives will have no problem aping this in order to stay afloat, and many Labour MPs are calling for Labour to rediscover the socialist patriotism carved out by Orwell in the 1940s. It would be a mistake to dismiss this renewed patriotic fervour as racist or backwards, but that doesn't mean we should blindly accept this facsimile of pride as a positive thing.

If the New Englishness is the fightback of forgotten communities, then it is a national identity borne out of an inherently political place – a volksgeist of resentment – not a cultural or a spiritual one. All it can promise is the past, and there can be no hope or glory in that.

Listening: "Hybrid identities"

5 ⊙ CD/13

Listen to BBC reporter Ritula Shah talking to Scottish chef Tony Singh. While listening, note down the correct answer (a, b, c or d).

1. **Where was Mr Singh born?**
   - a. Aberdeen
   - b. New Delhi
   - c. Edinburgh
   - d. West Indies

2. **What makes his restaurant special is that it**
   - a. has a Sikh chef.
   - b. has a peculiar fireplace.
   - c. offers Indian-Scottish food.
   - d. is located in a special part of Scotland.

3. **The stories Mr Singh's grandfather heard about Scotland included**
   - a. God's country.
   - b. national heroes.
   - c. a reference to Pakistan.
   - d. a famous Scottish drink.

4. **According to Mr Singh, his identity is influenced by his**
   - a. ancestors.
   - b. Scottish accent.
   - c. traditional Sikh dress.
   - d. religion and place of birth.

5. **Growing up, Mr Singh ate traditional Punjabi food, sometimes mixed with Scottish**
   - a. fish.
   - b. pork.
   - c. beef.
   - d. lamb.

6. **Haggis Pakora partly consists of**
   - a. fish eggs.
   - b. chips.
   - c. exotic fruits.
   - d. meats.

7. **Which of the following titles fits what you have heard so far best?**
   - a. All things spicy
   - b. Culinary Scotland
   - c. Fusing effortlessly
   - d. Cooking Sikh style

Tony Singh

Webcode
You can find the audio file here:
WES-73644-065

→ **S20:** How to listen/watch effectively, p. 366

6 ⊙ CD/14

a) Now listen to the second part of the radio programme. While listening, note down the correct answers. You need not write complete answers.

The census
1. Year of census

Findings
2. Group most likely to call themselves British
3. More likely to choose "English"
4. More likely to choose "British"
5. One possible reason for findings
6. Reason given by Ms Shah

Saratha Rajeshwan
7. Main reason why immigrants came to Britain
8. Two aspects that make her British
9. Two countries that make up her Asian background
10. Her concept of Britishness

Webcode
You can find the audio file here:
WES-73644-066

b) Explain in your own words why in Britain many people with an immigrant background find it easier to identify as British rather than English.

c) **EXTRA** **Across cultures** Do you have a "hybrid identity", i.e. feel at home in two or more cultures? Reflect on the reasons why this might or might not be the case for you. If you don't have an immigrant background, ask someone who has and write about their reasons.

Introduction to the political system of the United Kingdom

1 Read the following information on the political system of the United Kingdom. Identify three aspects you find most surprising or particularly interesting.

2 Across cultures
Point out three major differences to the German political system, e.g. look at how members of parliament are elected.

Monarchy and the political system

Britain may be one of the few countries in Europe that still has a monarchy, but at the same time it is the oldest democracy in the world. However, Britain has never had a written constitution in its history. Instead the political system is based on a number of documents that are linked to important events in British history and may be considered as essential steps on the way to democracy.

The Magna Carta (Great Charter) 1215

As the earls and barons in the Middle Ages were often dissatisfied with the way their kings governed the country, they frequently rebelled against decisions they did not agree with. In 1215 they made King John sign a document that limited the king's power and protected their own privileges. Although this charter was originally designed for the nobility only, the rules that granted the barons more rights would later come to apply to everyone.

The term "parliament" was first used in 1236 to refer to meetings the king held with his barons and high-ranking representatives of the church in order to seek their advice. In 1258, the barons wanted regular meetings of parliament three times a year and demanded that parliament should not only include the barons and earls, but also 12 non-noble representatives chosen from the counties. Since 1327 the representatives of the counties and of the towns had met as a permanent part of parliament, and from 1332 on they met separately in their own chamber. This became known as the House of Commons.

The Bill of Rights 1689

The Bill of Rights of 1689 was yet another constitutional document that limited the powers of the crown while reinforcing the rights of parliament: it contained rules for freedom of speech in parliament, required the king to convene meetings with parliament at regular intervals and established immunity for members of parliament so that they did not have to fear retributions from the king if they voiced their criticism or made controversial claims.

Later developments

Up to the end of the 19th century the people entitled to vote in parliamentary elections were a small group of men who were mainly rich landowners. Their main concern was to protect their own interests, i.e. to protect their property against taxation and the interference of the state as well as against the consequences of social unrest.

But the industrial revolution brought about many changes. People moved from the country, where agriculture was in decline, to the big cities where factories needed large workforces. Yet, the growth of the urban population was not immediately reflected in parliament: small villages of historic importance might still have two representatives in parliament, while urban areas like Manchester or Birmingham were not represented at all. The growing importance of the big cities and their population called for a change in the distribution of seats in the Commons and reforms concerning the right to vote were essential achievements in the development of parliamentary democracy in the 19th century.

Women, however, were still not allowed to vote at the beginning of the 20th century.

Part B: The monarchy and the political system — Facts

Women in the early 20th century demonstrated for their right to vote.

As they had the same duties as male citizens concerning taxation and the law, they felt entitled to the same political rights as men. The women who fought for their right to vote in the early 20th century were called suffragettes. Apart from peaceful demonstrations they also resorted to militant methods of campaigning until most women over 30 were granted the right to vote in 1918. Still, it took another ten years before all women gained the right to vote at the age of 21.

Today, parliament is an essential part of UK politics. Its main roles are:
- examining and challenging the work of the government (scrutiny)
- debating and passing all laws (legislation)
- enabling the government to raise taxes

There are two Houses: the House of Commons and the House of Lords.

The House of Commons
Currently the UK is divided into 650 parliamentary constituencies, each of which is represented by one member of parliament (MP) in the House of Commons. Each constituency has roughly the same number of voters (approximately 68,175) even if the area of the constituencies may vary considerably.

The House of Lords
The House of Lords is the second chamber of the UK parliament, often referred to as the Upper House. Currently, it has about 760 members. In contrast to the House of Commons they are not elected, but are either high-ranking members of the Church of England, life peers who are appointed by the Queen following the recommendation of the leaders of political parties, or hereditary peers, who have inherited the title. Since parliamentary reform in 1999 only 92 hereditary peers at the most are permitted to sit in the Lords. The House of Lords is independent from the elected House of Commons. Its main function is to examine and revise the work of the government thereby sharing the task of shaping laws and checking the government's legislation.

General elections
General elections are generally held every five years. Voters elect the members of parliament for their constituency who represent their interests and concerns in the House of Commons. The political party that wins a majority of seats normally forms the government.

First-past-the-post voting
MPs are elected in a first-past-the-post voting system. Voters put a cross (X) next to their favoured candidate on the ballot paper. The candidate with the most votes in a constituency is elected to represent it, while all the other votes in that constituency count for nothing (winner-takes-all). This system is considered by many people to be unfair because voters who did not vote for the winning candidate are not represented in parliament and the number of seats smaller parties get nationally does not reflect their full share of the national vote.

In the media you will find different phrases to refer to central government such as Downing Street or simply Number 10, the official home and the office of the Prime Minister; Westminster which stands for Parliament; and Whitehall, the road in central London where many government buildings are located and which is used to refer to British governmental administration.

The House of Commons in session.

Workshop: Step by step — Part B: The monarchy and the political system

Step by step Writing an opinion piece

Preview

This Workshop will enable you to write an opinion piece. In order to do that you need
- relevant factual information
- to know how to structure an article
- appropriate language to persuade your readers.

GATHERING FACTUAL INFORMATION

1
a) Read the article (A), study the statistics from 2015 (B) and watch the video (C). Make up your mind how you intend to argue in your article to answer the question whether the British monarchy still has its place in modern society.

b) Extract the arguments most useful for your article and paraphrase them. Include arguments opposing your own view as you will need to refute them in your article.
Here is an example:

Americans would not stand for this. Why do Britons? The case against hereditary appointments in public life is straightforward: they are incompatible with democracy and meritocracy, which are the least-bad ways to run countries. Royalists say this does not matter because the monarch no longer "runs" Britain. Yet in theory, at least, she has considerable powers: to wage war, sign treaties, dissolve Parliament and more.

arguments against the monarchy	arguments for the monarchy
• to inherit a public office is undemocratic (ll. 12–13)	• the monarch has no real political power (ll. 15–16)
• …	• …

c) Look at your list of arguments and number them according to their persuasive potential with number 1 being the strongest argument.
d) Decide which arguments you need to include in your article and which are interesting but not vital.

A

The British crown

Should Britain abolish the monarchy?

8 September 2015, The Economist

On September 9th, Queen Elizabeth II will become the longest-serving monarch in Britain's history. Below, […] Economist writers argue for different futures for the British crown.

5 **The case against the monarchy**
America's 2016 election has been cancelled. The White House has announced that in the interests of political stability the next president and all future ones will be chosen using the British model. […]

10 Americans would not stand for this. Why do Britons? The case against hereditary appointments in public life is straightforward: they are incompatible with democracy and meritocracy, which are the least-bad ways to run countries. Royalists say this does 15 not matter because the monarch no longer "runs" Britain. Yet in theory, at least, she has considerable powers: to wage war, sign treaties, dissolve Parliament and more.
[…]
20 The second pitfall[1] is subtler: in the belief that the monarchy forms some kind of constitutional backstop against an overmighty Parliament, Britain is strangely relaxed about the lack of serious checks on its government. […] It is true

Part B: The monarchy and the political system
Workshop: Step by step

that monarchs can, as a last resort, stand up for the nation: royalists cite the example of King Juan Carlos of Spain, whose televised address to the nation in 1981 helped prevent a coup. But the more one believes that the head of state's role really matters, the more serious a problem it is that the monarch is chosen using a mechanism as dodgy[2] as inheritance.

Opinion polls and healthy sales of commemorative junk[3] suggest that Britons and foreigners alike love the Windsors. But the royals may not be entirely good for the country's image abroad, or its view of itself. Britain still has a reputation as a snooty, class-obsessed place. [...] [It] would be stronger if its head of state were elected. And if the winner were Elizabeth, then good for her.

The case for the monarchy

Ipsos MORI has been tracking opinion on the monarchy for the past 20 years, and the responses have been remarkably consistent over that time. By a margin of well over three to one, respondents have favoured keeping the institution over turning Britain into a republic. It is hard, in fact, to find any political question on which the British people are more united, except perhaps their dislike of politicians. [...]

Those who would like to scrap[4] a popular monarchy need to be able to show that there is a significant demand for a change (which there is not) or that the institution does significant harm, which is just as hard to do. It is accused of being expensive [...]. An alternative, elected head of state would not be cost-free either.

The monarchy is accused of entrenching[5] elitism and the class system, but it is a fantasy to imagine that those things would vanish in a republic; they certainly have not in America, while the monarchies of Denmark, Sweden and Norway are among the most meritocratic and egalitarian in the world. It is accused of damaging democracy because (on paper) the Queen retains vast constitutional powers. But this ignores the fact that there is not the remotest chance that she or her successors would actually use them [...].

On the other hand, it is just as plausible to assert that there are benefits to a monarchy, on top of the (hard to quantify) economic ones. At a time when most government institutions everywhere are unpopular and even hated, any part of the state which people still actually like is a rare plus, something not to be discarded[6] lightly. [...]

And the case for modest reform

Critics of Britain's monarchy will often say that if you were starting a 21st-century democracy from scratch[7] you wouldn't dream of having an hereditary head of state. Though this is undoubtedly true, it is also true that the history of the past 50 years shows that starting democracies from scratch is very hard. Successful democracies grow out of an historical experience that is specific to the nations involved, and British democracy has grown up entangled[8] with the monarchy. [...]

The fact that a monarchy is not intellectually justifiable does not mean that it does not have a stabilising role. This may be particularly true in Britain, a composite nation. [...]

But to keep Britain's monarchy does not entail keeping it in its current form. Its entangled history of democracy and monarchy has left Britain with a highly centralized constitution that locates the nation's sovereignty in "the king in parliament" – a situation that gives the leader of the majority party in the legislature a disturbingly large part of the power that was once vested[9] entirely in the monarchy. This situation could be remedied[10] quite easily by keeping the crown but changing its constitutional basis to one along the lines of that most excellent of countries, Belgium. Belgium is a popular monarchy. Its constitution makes clear that sovereignty rests in the people; the King (or Queen, though it has yet to have one) – who is King of the Belgians, a people, not Belgium, a territory – becomes monarch not by right, but by taking an oath to uphold the people's constitution.

A change to the British constitution which made the kingdom's various peoples sovereign and the head of state the guardian of that sovereignty, not the source of it, would be a welcome plank in the more general programme of reform that the British state clearly needs. [...]

Annotations
[1] **pitfall** = a tricky problem
[2] **dodgy** /ˈdɒdʒi/ (*infml*) = suspect, not quite right
[3] **junk** (*infml*) = rubbish
[4] to **scrap** = to abolish
[5] to **entrench** = to establish firmly
[6] to **discard** = to throw away
[7] **from scratch** = from the very beginning
[8] **entangled** = very closely connected
[9] to **vest** = to give power
[10] to **remedy** = to make better

Workshop: Step by step — Part B: The monarchy and the political system

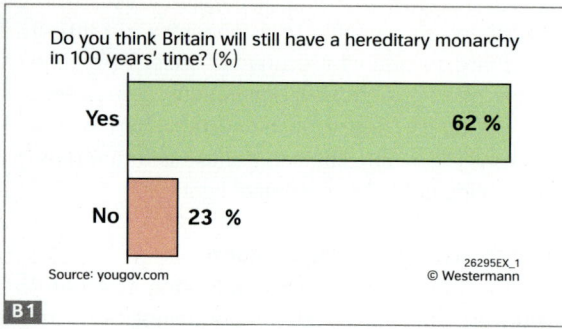

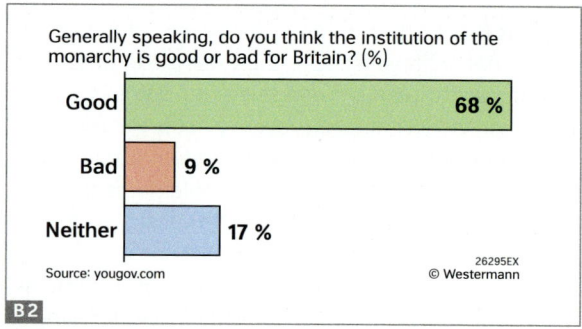

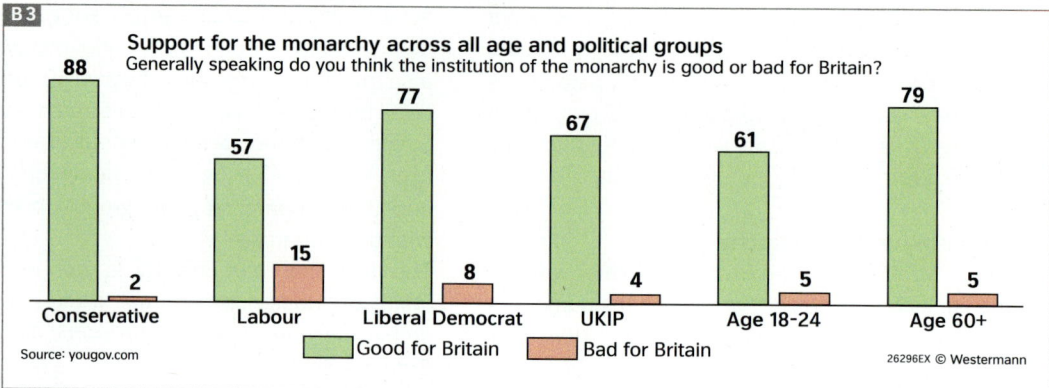

Webcode
You can find a link to the video here:
WES-73644-068

🎬 David Starkey: "How history will judge Queen Elizabeth II"

FINDING A HEADLINE

2

The headline of an opinion piece has several functions:
- to grab the reader's attention
- to address a certain group of readers
- to deliver a message

This can be done by asking a question, by being provocative, or by making a promise of useful information.

Here is an example: ***Britishness – nothing but an empty word?***

a) Find three possible headlines for your article and write them down.

b) **Pair work** Present your three headlines to each other and explain in which direction you intend your article to go. Give each other advice on which headline best suits your intention.

WRITING THE INTRODUCTION

3

Similar to the headline, the introduction should also catch the reader's attention. Start your article with a thesis-like statement. You can ask a question, use a quote, or you can summarize what the whole opinion piece is about. Clearly state your argument with regard to the question whether the British monarchy still has its place in modern society. The rest of your column will be based on supporting this opinion.

Here is an example:

Britishness – nothing but an empty word?
Our daily life is full of words with thousands of them floating around without us thinking twice about them. One of the more shallow and indeed empty ones is the word Britishness. This might come as

Part B: The monarchy and the political system   **Workshop: Step by step**

a surprise to members of a nation that has long seen itself as one homogeneous group united by common values and century-old traditions.

a) Examine how this introduction catches the reader's interest.
b) Write your introduction.
c) **Pair work** Read your partner's introduction and give him/her a detailed feedback according to the criteria mentioned above.
d) Rewrite your own introduction with the help of your partner's feedback.

→ **S24:** How to give feedback/peer-edit, p. 372
→ **S8:** How to improve your text, p. 341

Checklist

The main body of an opinion piece
✓ Present the strongest opposing argument first. Make sure you identify the groups who oppose you. State their opinions objectively, using accurate facts or quotations. Do not use slander.
✓ It is fine to state positive things about the opposing side, if they are based on facts. If you neglect to present valid or strong arguments of your opponents, your opinion piece will appear biased and uninformed.
✓ Present your reasons/evidence to directly refute the opposition. Utilize facts and quotations from other sources which support your opinion. Offer alternative answers or solutions to the arguments of your opponents.
✓ Now present your own arguments starting with your strongest one. Whatever your reasons are, make sure to clearly come down on one side of the argument; there is no room for grey areas here. Begin this section with a linking device (see task 4 in Workshop Part A, p. 159), to clearly flow from their argument to yours.

WRITING THE MAIN BODY

 4 Language awareness

a) Study the rhetorical devices on p. 115. Write down an example for each rhetorical device that you would like to use in your article.
b) Write the main body of your article:
 • consider the points in the checklist
 • make good use of the language support for structure
 • use rhetorical devices

Language support

Structure
Pointing out opposing arguments:
Opponents of this idea claim/maintain/argue that …
Those who disagree/are against these ideas may say/assert that …
Another argument/point/reason that is often put forward is …

Refuting the opposing idea:
After seeing this evidence, there is no way one can agree with this idea.
Some may say that …, however …
Whereas A claims …, it is important to note that …

In contrast to A's point of view, it has to be said that …
As opposed to …, I definitely believe that …

Reaching the turning point and presenting your own ideas:
However, you have to consider/to take into consideration that …
On the other hand, I am convinced/certain that …
As far as I am concerned, …
Looking at the two sides, I have to say/I strongly believe …
I would also like to point out that …

Workshop: Practice   **Part B:** The monarchy and the political system

WRITING THE CONCLUSION

5

Conclude your article with a punch. A note-worthy statement will engrave the column into the reader's mind. Use quotations or a question to make the readers think hard. (e.g. *If we do not take care of our national heritage and valued traditions, then who will?*)
- a) Write your conclusion.
- b) **Pair work** Swap your conclusion with a partner, read it and say in your own words which position your partner has taken. See whether your partner got the gist of your message correctly.

PROOFREADING

6

→ **S8:** How to improve your text, p. 341

Proofread your work. A great piece is not great if it is riddled with spelling, grammar and punctuation errors. Have someone in your class look over your work: two minds are always better than one.

Practice Writing an opinion piece

PRE-WRITING

1

→ **S25:** How to work with a dictionary, p. 374

- a) Look up the word "devolution" in a dictionary.
- b) **Pair work** Talk to each other and speculate about possible advantages and disadvantages of devolution generally and for Britain.
- c) Carry out an online research on "devolution in Britain" and take notes.
- d) Compare your findings with your speculations from b).

WRITING

2 Language awareness

Write an opinion piece on whether devolution can be seen as a means to keep the United Kingdom united. In order to do that, follow the steps on pp. 168-172.
- Use your research results and decide which arguments you are going to use in your article.
- Find a headline and write an introduction that grabs the reader's attention and delivers a clear message.
- Write the main body and the conclusion.
- Proofread your article.

GIVING FEEDBACK

3

- a) Read at least three other articles that your classmates wrote and say whose should be read out in class.
- b) Give detailed feedback on the article that is read.

→ **S24:** How to give feedback/peer-edit, p. 372

Part B: The monarchy and the political system | Texts | 5

Analysing a feature film: *The Queen*

PRE-VIEWING

1
Study the chart and explain the roles of the prime minister and the monarch.

The UK system of government

Judiciary
The UK Supreme Court
- 12 professional judges
- it upholds the law
- it represents the rule of law

The Crown
The Monarch
- ceremonial head of state/ represents UK internationally
- upholds traditions
- gives Royal Assent[2] to Acts of Parliament[3]

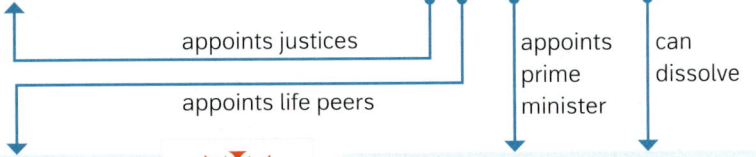

appoints justices   appoints prime minister   can dissolve
appoints life peers

Appointed legislature
The House of Lords
- approx. 760 members (life peers, Anglican bishops, 92 hereditary peers)
- life peers can be recommended by the prime minister, leaders of opposition parties or a commission and are appointed by the crown
- it amends and approves bills[1]

The Executive
The Government
- the leader of the party with most MPs in the Commons becomes **prime minister** (head of the government)
- the prime minister appoints approx. 20 ministers/ heads of government departments to the **cabinet**
- it puts forward laws

Elected legislature
The House of Commons
- MPs are elected from 650 constituencies (in first-past-the-post electoral system every five years)
- the party with the most MPs forms the government
- it designs, amends and approves bills

Electorate
(all men and women over the age of 18)

elects

Annotations
[1] **bill** = a law that is proposed to the legislature
[2] **Royal Assent** = the monarch's formal approval of an act
[3] **Act of Parliament** = a law passed by the British parliament that, in principle, cannot be overruled by any other political body

COMPREHENSION/ANALYSIS

2 DVD/15
The film *The Queen* covers a time span in 1997 when 43-year-old Labour candidate Tony Blair had just won the election and become prime minister. Soon after his election, the death of Princess Diana brings about a serious crisis for the British monarchy.

a) Watch extract 1 from the film *The Queen*. Describe the first meeting between Prime Minister Tony Blair and the Queen.
b) Observe the body language of the Queen, Blair and his wife. Discuss what it reveals about their feelings and attitudes. → SUPPORT D 4, p. 313
c) Compare the PM's and the Queen's constitutional roles (see chart) to the way their relationship is depicted in the scene.

Webcode
You can find the video here:
WES-73644-069

173

5 Texts — Part B: The monarchy and the political system

Webcode
You can find the video here: WES-73644-070

3 Pair work · DVD/16

After Diana's death, the Queen, who is staying at Balmoral Castle in Scotland with her family, does not address the public in a statement or go to London where Princess Diana's coffin is kept at Buckingham Palace before the funeral. The Queen has decided this death is a family matter rather than a state affair. Besides, the Queen has been brought up not to show her emotions in public. This behaviour, however, is not understood by the public and consequently seems to threaten the monarchy. Tony Blair spends almost a week trying to convince the Queen of the necessity to come to London and acknowledge Diana's achievements. Eventually the Queen agrees. Her speech is sent to Downing Street, but before it is broadcast live, one of Blair's spin doctors changes some of the wording.

In order to analyse the sequence of extract 2, work with a partner. The viewing log may help you.
a) Watch the extract and note down what happens in the scenes.
b) Note down what cinematic devices are used and explain their function in the context of the scene. Of course you cannot document every single detail of the camera work but certain devices stand out and produce a special effect.

→ Go to the info box on pp. 87-88 for an overview of cinematic devices.

Webcode
You can download this viewing log here: WES-73644-071

EXAMPLE OF A VIEWING LOG:

scene	action	cinematic devices	function/effect
in front of Buckingham Palace	…	…	…
in the Prime Minister's office	…	…	…
in front of Buckingham Palace again	…	close-up of Queen's face and reverse angle shots of letters to Diana	…

c) Compare and discuss your results.

4
Music is rarely used in this film, but it accompanies the second scene in front of Buckingham Palace. Describe the music and explain why it is used in this particular scene. → SUPPORT D 5, p. 313

5
→ S16: Checklist: Analysis of a film scene, p. 359

Analyse to what extent the use of cinematic devices supports the message the director wants to convey about the monarch's predicament. Use your results from 3 and 4.

COMMENT

6
"Ever since Diana, people want glamour and tears … the grand performance … and I'm not very good at that. I prefer to keep my feelings to myself … foolishly I believed that's what the people wanted from their Queen … duty first, self second. It's how I was brought up."

Use the quotation from the film as a starting point to discuss what you consider important in the role of a modern monarch.

Part B: The monarchy and the political system — Advanced texts

Britain's constitution

1
a) Read the article from the British Library website and sum up the nature of the British constitution in one sentence.
b) Explain what the particular nature of the British constitution means for
   1. the relationship between parliament and the courts and
   2. the role of the monarch.

2 CHOOSE
Work on either of the tasks below.
When once asked by a student what the British constitution was, former head of the British civil service Robin Butler answered: "It is something we make up as we go along." Discuss Butler's view.
OR
"Britain needs a written constitution." Comment on this claim.

 S6: How to write a discussion/comment, p. 338

Britain's unwritten constitution

Robert Blackburn, 13 March 2015

[...] For most people, especially abroad, the United Kingdom does not have a constitution at all in the sense most commonly used around the world – a document of fundamental importance setting out
5 the structure of government and its relationship with its citizens. All modern states, saving only the UK, New Zealand and Israel, have adopted a documentary constitution of this kind, the first and most complete model being that of the United
10 States of America in 1788. However, in Britain we certainly say that we have a constitution, but it is one that exists in an abstract sense, comprising a host of diverse laws, practices and conventions that have evolved over a long period of time. [...]

15 **Features of Britain's unwritten constitution**
There are a number of associated characteristics of Britain's unwritten constitution, a cardinal one being that in law Parliament is sovereign in the sense of being the supreme legislative body. Since
20 there is no documentary constitution containing laws that are fundamental in status and superior to ordinary Acts of Parliament, the courts may only interpret parliamentary statutes. They may not overrule or declare them invalid for being contrary
25 to the constitution and "unconstitutional". [...]
Another characteristic of the unwritten constitution is the special significance of political customs known as "conventions" [...]. These are unwritten rules of constitutional practice, vital to our
30 politics, the workings of government, but not committed into law or any written form at all. The very existence of the office of Prime Minister, our head of government, is purely conventional. So is the rule upon which he or she is appointed, being
35 whoever commands the confidence of the House of Commons (the majority party leader, or head of a coalition of parties).
The Monarchy is one of the three components of Parliament (shorthand for the Queen-in-
40 Parliament) along with Commons and Lords. In legal theory, the Queen has absolute and judicially unchallengeable power to refuse her assent to a Bill passed by the two Houses of Parliament. However, convention dictates the precise opposite
45 and in practice she automatically gives her assent to any government Bill that has been duly passed and agreed by Parliament. [...]

Should the UK have a written constitution?
[...] If a written constitution for the future is to
50 be prepared, it must be one that engages and involves everyone, especially young people, and not simply legal experts and parliamentarians. Some of the mystique and charm of our ancient constitution might be lost in the process, but a
55 written constitution could bring government and the governed closer together, above all by making the rules by which our political democracy operates more accessible and intelligible to all.

Workshop: Step by step | **Part C:** The many faces of Britain

Webcode
You can download a word list for Part C here: WES-73644-072

Step by step Analysing modern poetry

Preview

In this Workshop you will learn how to analyse modern poetry. You will look closely at form and content.

PRE-READING

1

 Find out about the different ethnic and migrant groups that are part of German society. Take these aspects into consideration:
- countries of origin
- reasons for coming to Germany
- their contributions to the German way of life
- problems of integration

2

Multiculturalism means different things to different people.
a) Think about what it means to you and write a short definition.
b) Compare your definition with two of your classmates' and point out differences and similarities.
c) Read the two definitions below and compare them with your own.

A I see no incompatibility between multiculturalism and Britishness. Britishness must be part of multiculturalism.
For a long time the UK has been a multicultural state composed of England, Northern Ireland, Scotland and Wales, and also a multicultural society ... made up of a diverse range of cultures and identities […].
In other words, dual identities have been common, even before large scale immigration.
[…] To be British means that we respect the laws, the parliamentary and democratic political structures, traditional values of mutual tolerance, respect for equal rights ...
But Britishness does not mean a single culture. Integration is the co-existence of communities and unimpeded movement between them, it is not assimilation.
Britishness is a strong concept but not all embracing.

PROFESSOR SIR BERNARD CRICK - Chair of the 'Life in the UK' report which led to the new citizenship tests

B There are two ways in which people interpret multiculturalism.
The first one is the more common way and that is every culture has the right to exist and there is no over-arching thread that holds them together.
That is the multiculturalism we think is so destructive because there's no thread to hold society together. […]
There is another way to define multiculturalism which I would call diversity where people have their own cultural beliefs and they happily coexist – but there is a common thread of Britishness or whatever you want to call it to hold society together. […]

RUTH LEA - Director of the Centre for Policy Studies, a centre-right think tank

COMPREHENSION

3

Poets often write poems about subjects that matter to them. Many of Benjamin Zephaniah's poems centre on the topic of living in a multicultural society.
a) Read his poem "The British" and look up words you are unfamiliar with.
b) "Talking to the text": copy the text. Then write speech bubbles into the text, thus "talking" to it. You can find two examples on the next page. You can note down your observations, questions, or feelings you get from the poem as you read.

→ **S10:** How to work with poetry, p. 347

Webcode
You can download the text of the poem here: WES-73644-073

Benjamin Zephaniah

c) Talk to your partner about your speech bubbles and comment on his/hers. Also talk about the frame or pattern of the poem and pay special attention to how the poem begins and ends.
d) Poetry only really comes to life when it is read out loud. First read the poem aloud to yourself. Then listen to the poem read out loud by at least three of your classmates.

The British (serves 60 million)

Take some Picts, Celts and Silures *(Who are they?)*
And let them settle,
Then overrun them with Roman conquerors.
Remove the Romans after approximately 400 years
Add lots of Norman French to some
Angles, Saxons, Jutes and Vikings, then stir vigorously.

Mix some hot Chileans, cool Jamaicans, Dominicans,
Trinidadians and Bajans with some Ethiopians, Chinese,
Vietnamese and Sudanese. *(Reminds me of tea.)*
Then take a blend of Somalians, Sri Lankans, Nigerians
And Pakistanis,
Combine with some Guyanese
And turn up the heat.
Sprinkle some fresh Indians, Malaysians, Bosnians,
Iraqis and Bangladeshis together with some
Afghans, Spanish, Turkish, Kurdish, Japanese
And Palestinians
Then add to the melting pot.
Leave the ingredients to simmer.
As they mix and blend allow their languages to flourish
Binding them together with English.
Allow time to be cool.
Add some unity, understanding, and respect for the future,
Serve with justice
And enjoy.

Note: All the ingredients are equally important. Treating one ingredient better than another will leave a bitter unpleasant taste.

Warning: An unequal spread of justice will damage the people and cause pain. Give justice and equality to all.

Benjamin Zephaniah

4 Language awareness **Pair work**

Poets use poetic devices to achieve a particular effect. Breaking up the poem into formal poetic components enhances your understanding of the poem's overall theme, tone, and/or general purpose.
On the following page you find a list of questions focusing on the elements **speaker**, **tone**, **language and imagery**, **structure** and **sound and rhythm**. They help you understand and analyse the poem.
a) Choose ten questions from the list that best apply to your poem.
b) Answer the questions you chose and take notes. Make sure to be specific about the function of each element you write about. Here is an example for a love poem by British poet Wendy Cope: Who is the speaker addressing? ➝ *a long-time lover, possibly husband or wife; this becomes clear in l. 5: "Our love is old and sure, not new and frantic"*

Workshop: Step by step — Part C: The many faces of Britain

Speaker: Who "tells" the poem?
- Does the poem give any clues about the speaker's personality, the point of view, age, or gender?
- How is the speaker involved in the poem?
- Who is the speaker addressing?

Tone: What mood or attitude does the poem express?
- What is the poem trying to do? (e.g. making a point, praising something, moving someone to action, simply expressing an emotion such as love, joy, disappointment, sadness)
- What is the speaker's mood? Is the speaker angry, sad, happy, cynical?
- Does the mood change as the poem progresses?

Language and imagery: Which words are used and what is their effect?
- How would you characterize the poet's word choice? Is it formal or conversational?
- What are the connotations of particular words?
- What images does the poet draw? Why were they chosen? (e.g. if a fox is mentioned, is it to refer to someone's character or a time of day?)
- What devices does the poet use to compare one thing to another? Metaphors, similes, personification, symbols or analogies?
- Are certain images repeated, or are there clusters of words with similar connotations?
- What sensory experiences are evoked by the images?

Structure: What does the organization of the poem express?
- How is the poem divided up?
- Are there individual stanzas or sections?
- How are the sections or stanzas related to each other?
- Does the poem follow a formal poetic structure such as a sonnet, haiku, ode?
- Does it follow the structure of a different text or is there a lack of structure?
- What does the form tell you about the poet's attitude towards the subject? (e.g. with a free form the poet might want to express that the subject itself is chaotic and out of control)

Sound and rhythm: How does the poem's "music" affect its meaning?
- Does the poem rhyme?
- Is there a definite pattern of rhymes?
- Does the poem have an identifiable rhythm arranged in the meter (e.g. iambic pentameter)?
- Which words slow the reader down? Which ones hurry the reader along?
- How would you characterize the sound of the poem? Melodic? Hectic? Dissonant?
- How does the sound of the poem enhance its meaning?

ANALYSIS

Now that you have read the poem several times, talked about your first impressions and also answered several analysis questions, you can prepare for writing a coherent analysis of the poem.

a) Look through your notes and mark those that are most insightful. Think in terms of cause and effect and look for relationships within the poem itself. For example, if you see a pattern of imagery which suggests something about the speaker's attitude, look at other areas of the poem for more evidence along the same lines.
b) Now write a thesis statement.
c) **Group work (4)** Read your thesis statement to your group and give feedback on the others' statements. If necessary, revise your own thesis statement.

Info

Thesis statement

A thesis statement is a statement, NOT a question, that sets forth the basic argument of a writer or speaker, who then proves it.

You need to ask yourself how you can make the information you have gathered on the poem work to prove your thesis statement. Your thesis statement must argue a point. Instead of simply saying that a poet uses certain poetic devices, you must give some indication in your thesis as to how those devices work and what they do to the poem's meaning.

Here is an example for a famous Shakespeare poem:
In Shakespeare's sonnet 18 the speaker compares his lover to a summer's day in order to praise his lover's superior beauty.

Part C: The many faces of Britain | **Workshop: Step by step**

6

Now write your analysis. While writing, keep the following points in mind:

→ **S9:** How to structure a text, p. 344

1. **The first paragraph**
   Your first paragraph should make your reader comfortable with the poem by:
   - identifying the poet
   - offering a brief, general description of the poem
   - leading into the thesis and development of the argument

   Sonnet 18 by William Shakespeare is one of the most famous poems in the English language. Throughout the 14 lines the speaker compares his lover to a summer's day in order to praise his lover's superior beauty.

2. **Organization of the essay**
   To organize your text, you can choose between these two models:

linear presentation	non-linear presentation
You go through the poem chronologically to show how an image, for example, changes in significance from line to line or stanza to stanza.	You go back and forth within the poem to draw attention to cycles or other patterns in the poem.

   Always remember to keep your thesis in sight!

3. **Strong paragraphs**
   At the beginning of each paragraph, tell your reader the focus of your argument in that paragraph by starting with a topic sentence. The rest of the paragraph should address your claim with convincing evidence.

   In the opening line the speaker seems to almost be teasing and the speaker's uncertainty in his attempt to compare his lover with a summer's day becomes apparent. To convey …

4. **Backing up with evidence**
   Try incorporating your evidence into a "sandwich" of information which will allow your reader to receive the full impact of the lines. Before the quotation, describe the evidence in terms of the poem. Where is it located in the poem? Is it part of a pattern? Let your reader know what he or she should be looking for. After the quotation, if the passage is particularly difficult to understand, you should explain problematic syntax or vocabulary.

5. **The conclusion**
   In your conclusion you can emphasize crucial ideas, raise questions about the poem, or connect the poem to other literary works or experiences. This is where you can offer your interpretation of the poem, which by now should be convincing to your reader. You may raise new ideas in a conclusion, provided that they are solidly linked to the development of your argument.

7

Have your partner look at your analysis and do the same for him/her. These questions may help you to give advice on what to improve: is the essay well structured? Is the thesis statement convincing?

→ **S24:** How to give feedback/peer-edit, p. 372

CREATIVE WRITING/MEDIATION

8 Across cultures

a) Write a similar poem in German about the Germans, applying Zephaniah's main idea.
b) Read your poem aloud in class.

Workshop: Practice — Part C: The many faces of Britain

Practice: Analysing modern poetry

PRE-READING

1 DVD/17

Webcode — You can find the video here: WES-73644-074

Watch part of a poetry recital with the sound turned off. Talk about your first impressions in class, considering the following questions: What might the presenter be talking about? What might his attitude be? What do his gestures and facial expressions hint at?

COMPREHENSION

2 DVD/18

Watch and listen to the whole recital with sound. Write down in one sentence what the poem is about.

Webcode — You can find the video here: WES-73644-075

3 This poem by John Agard is titled "Listen Mr Oxford don". Do some research and write down what is commonly associated with someone who is an "Oxford don".

ANALYSIS

4 → SUPPORT D 6, p. 313

Write a poetry analysis, using the skills you have learned in the step by step part.

Annotations

[1] **creole** = a creole language is a mixture of a European language and one or more other languages. It is spoken as the first language by a people
[2] **Me not no** = double negatives to express negative meaning → I am not
[3] **de** = the
[4] **I ent** = I don't
[5] **yu** = your
[6] **dem** = they
[7] **to serve time** = to go to prison
[8] **I rekking** = I think/ believe it to be
[9] **wit mih** = with my
[10] **mek dem** = make them
[11] **I ent serving** = I am not going to serve

> **Info**
>
> ### Caribbean English
>
> From the 1700s, thousands of people from Africa were transported as slaves to the British islands in the Caribbean. As a result a new form of English developed: Caribbean English. In its most extreme form, it can be very difficult to understand for outsiders. There are a number of elements that characterize Caribbean English. The lack of the verb "to be" in statements such as *she dreaming*, where Standard English requires *she's dreaming*, is typical of the type of structure that occurs in a creole[1] language. Similarly, verbs might not always carry a tense marker as in the statement *Him tell me dat yesterday* for *He told me that yesterday*.

Listen Mr Oxford don

Me not no[2] Oxford don
me a simple immigrant
from Clapham Common
I didn't graduate
I immigrate

But listen Mr Oxford don
I'm a man on de[3] run
and a man on de run
is a dangerous one

I ent[4] have no gun
I ent have no knife
but mugging de Queen's English
is the story of my life

I don't need no axe
to split up yu[5] syntax
I don't need no hammer
to mash up yu grammar

I warning you Mr Oxford don
I'm a wanted man
and a wanted man
is a dangerous one

Dem[6] accuse me of assault
on de Oxford dictionary
imagine a concise peaceful man like me
dem want me serve time[7]
for inciting rhyme to riot
but I rekking[8] it quiet
down here in Clapham Common

I'm not a violent man Mr Oxford don
I only armed wit mih[9] human breath
but human breath
is a dangerous weapon

So mek dem[10] send one big word after me
I ent serving[11] no jail sentence
I slashing suffix in self defence
I bashing future wit present tense
and if necessary
I making de Queen's English accessory to my offence

John Agard

COMMENT

5 Language awareness

→ **S6:** How to write a discussion/ comment, p. 338

In the poem Agard challenges the view that Standard English is the correct form of English, and other forms of English are of a lesser status. Comment on this view.

Part C: The many faces of Britain Texts 5

Scottishness

1
Read the article on p. 182.
a) Describe the connection Lebby Campbell feels to her clan.
b) Explain what is meant by "ancestral tourism" and how "ancestral tourists" differ from other tourists.
c) Examine the importance of ancestral tourism for the Scottish economy.
d) Imagine you are Lebby Campbell and keep a travel diary. Write a diary entry for one of her days in Scotland.

2
The United Kingdom is made up of four countries: England, Scotland, Wales and Northern Ireland. National identity – as opposed to a British identity – is particularly strong in Scotland.
a) In 2018 the BBC conducted a survey on national identity in Scotland. Look at the graph showing some of the results and name the main aspects making someone Scottish according to the survey.
b) Skim the article on p. 182 again and compare the concept of Scottishness in the article with the survey results.

→ **S18:** How to analyse statistics, p. 362

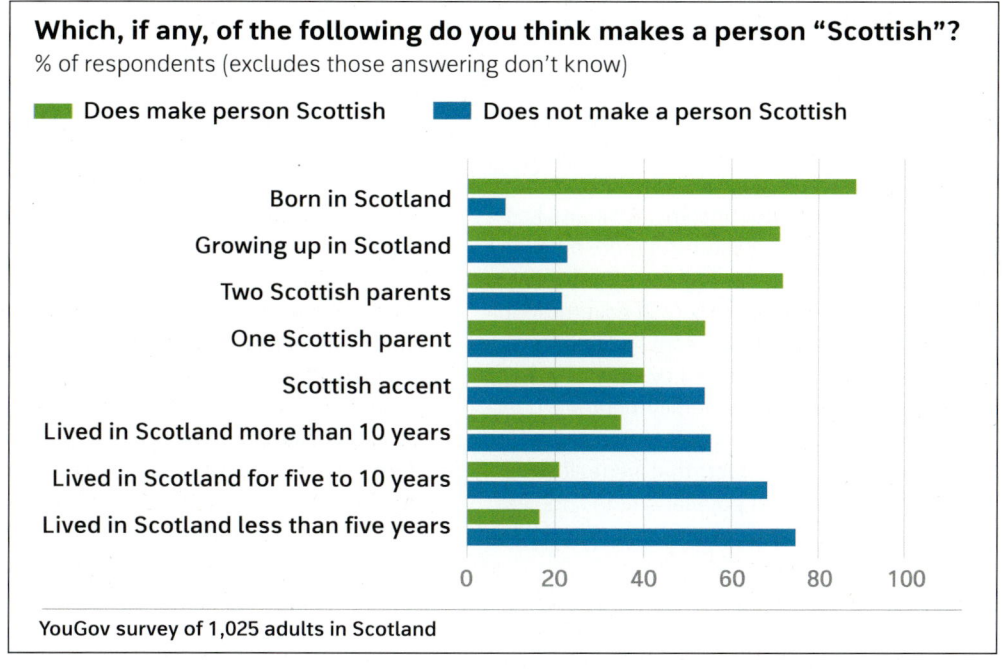

3 Across cultures Group work
a) Discuss what makes someone German.
b) Compare your ideas to the views of national identity you dealt with in task 2.

Part C: The many faces of Britain

The business of being Scottish: Are you one of 50 million?

It doesn't matter if the last person in the family to set foot in Scotland was a great-great-grandfather: many descendants are feeling a pull to visit the country ... and spend money.

Lennox Morrison, 25 May 2017, BBC special

Lebby Campbell's heart swelled[1] as she strolled through Inveraray Castle on the mountain-fringed shores of Loch Fyne. Although she was in the Scottish Highlands, thousands of miles from her home of Charleston, South Carolina, the 34-year-old administrative assistant felt a sense of belonging.

"You read about the history of your ancestors, but when you get there and you're on Campbell lands, it brings it all to life," she says. "Everything hit home. I felt a sense of pride and awe[2] and a real connection with my ancestors."

The axes and broadswords displayed beneath a ceiling studded with the family crest[3] made her think of blood spilt in bygone[4] battles, Campbell says. The emotional pull she feels to this place is the driver behind what the industry calls "ancestral tourism" – and in a small country such as Scotland, it's a valued source of income. Scotland has a population of 5.4 million. But more than 50 million people worldwide have a family link to the country, and the Scottish government wants to attract more of them to visit. [...]

Ancestral tourism isn't a new concept. [...] But today, researching family heritage has become simpler. The internet has made it so much easier, in fact, that genealogy is now one of the most popular online hobbies globally.

Family dollar

Drawn mainly from the United States, Canada, Australia and New Zealand – historical destinations for Scottish emigrants – ancestral tourists are an economic boon[5] for the nation. In the first nine months of 2016, visitors from these nations generated a total of £524m ($678m) for the Scottish economy – and for almost 50% of them, an ancestral connection was one of the reasons for making the trip, according to a recent study by VisitScotland.

Typically, ancestral tourists stay longer than other travellers and disperse throughout the country on itineraries[6] linked to family history, bringing income to places beyond the classic sightseeing routes [...]. They also often travel outside July and August, so their spending comes outside the high season. [...]

In the six years since [Christine] Woodcock began leading Canadians of Scottish descent across the Atlantic, she has seen interest grow hugely, she says. "Regardless of how many generations back the connection is, the minute they step on Scottish soil they have an overwhelming sense of belonging, a feeling that they've come home," she says of her clients. [...]

For centuries, Scots have left their homeland – some in a spirit of adventure and discovery, but many more fleeing poverty or oppression. [...]

Personal touch

While much research about family roots can be done online, on Scottish soil the story can be fleshed out[7]. And in a country where distances are not great, it's easy to follow the trail to the church one's grandparents, great-grandparents or earlier generations belonged to, and to the town, village or glen[8] where they lived. [...]

For Lebby Campbell, the family connection is many generations distant, but the connection to her clan is very much alive. (For many centuries, up to the 1746 Battle of Culloden, Scotland was run by the clan system – clan meaning "family" or "children" in Gaelic). Through the Clan Campbell Society, Lebby has made friends at home in South Carolina, as well as in New York City and further afield. "We call ourselves 'kinsmen'. I'm part of a big worldwide family," she says.

Voice aglow, she describes meeting current clan chief Torquhil Campbell, 13th Duke of Argyll – as he manned[9] the cash desk in the gift shop of Inveraray Castle, his ancestral home. "I felt like a 13-year-old meeting Justin Bieber. It was surreal," she says. [...]

Annotations

[1] to **swell** = to become larger than usual
[2] **awe** = feeling of great respect
[3] **crest** = symbol showing a family's high standing and long history
[4] **bygone** = past
[5] **boon** = great gain
[6] **itinerary** = plan of a journey
[7] to **flesh out** = to add more detail, esp. to a story
[8] **glen** = Scottish term for a valley
[9] to **man** = *here:* to operate

Part C: The many faces of Britain | Advanced texts | 5

Class

1 Across cultures **Placemat**
a) Write down social groups that you think exist in Germany.
EXAMPLES: *the elite, academics, …*
b) Talk about your ideas in your group and agree on at least three social groups.

2
Traditionally, UK society is thought to consist of three groups: working class, middle class and upper class. However, in 2011, British sociologists Mike Savage and Fiona Devine together with the BBC carried out a survey of people around Britain. After studying the data, they developed a set of seven class categories that reflect British society today.

Annotations
[1] **home counties** = the English counties near London, such as Kent or Sussex

→ **Solution,** p. 392

a) Study the descriptions of the seven classes and compare this class system to your ideas about German society in 1.
b) Arrange the seven classes from the BBC study from the highest to the lowest.
c) Compare your order with the actual one. Find possible reasons for the ranking. Consider reasons that are related to:
- the people's financial/economic status
- the social contacts
- free-time/cultural activities

New affluent workers
Percentage of population: 15 %
Average age: 44
- economically secure, but not well off
- have high scores for emerging culture (e.g. watching sport, using social media)
- less interested in highbrow culture (e.g. classical music, theatre)
- often have working class background
- many live in old manufacturing centres of UK

Traditional working class
Percentage of population: 14 %
Average age: 66
- many own their own home
- tend to mix socially with people like themselves
- less interested in emerging culture (e.g. going to gym, using social media)
- this group has oldest average age
- jobs in this group include lorry drivers and electricians

Established middle class
Percentage of population: 25 %
Average age: 46
- enjoy a diverse range of cultural activities
- socialize with a broad range of people
- many work in management or the traditional professions
- most have middle-class backgrounds
- many live outside urban areas

Precariat
Percentage of population: 15 %
Average age: 50
- tend to mix socially with people like themselves
- tend not to have a broad range of cultural interests
- jobs in this group include cleaner and van driver
- more than 80 % rent their home
- many live in old industrial areas

Elite
Percentage of population: 6 %
Average age: 57
- UK's biggest earners
- score highest for social, cultural and economic factors
- many went to private school and elite universities
- this group is exclusive and very hard to join
- many live in London and the home counties[1]

Technical middle class
Percentage of population: 6 %
Average age: 52
- tend to mix socially with people like themselves
- work in research, science and technical occupations
- more interested in emerging culture, (e.g. using social media) than in highbrow culture (e.g. classical music)
- often have mainly middle-class backgrounds
- many live in suburban locations

Emergent service workers
Percentage of population: 19 %
Average age: 34
- youngest of all class groups
- have highest scores for emerging culture (e.g. watching sport, using social media)
- socialize with a broad range of people
- jobs include chefs and production assistants
- many live in inexpensive locations in cities like Liverpool and Newcastle

5 Advanced texts — Part C: The many faces of Britain

3
a) Divide the class into two groups. Choose one character profile each, study it and decide which social class the profile belongs to.
b) **Pair work** Present your character to someone from the group that worked on the other character and explain which social class he is in.

Lee Armstrong
- 23, grew up in Gateshead and went to state school
- Rejected university to get a job, works in digital marketing and earns £24,000 a year
- Owns a three-bedroom semi in central Gateshead
- Likes computer games, social networking, watching sport, playing sport, going to the pub, listening to pop music and eating in nice restaurants
- Doesn't go to the theatre, art galleries, museums or listen to classical music
- Friends from secondary school and work

Kevin Henderson
- 23, grew up in Dagenham and went to state school
- Went to university, now works with adults with learning disabilities and earns £18,000 a year
- Still lives with parents in Dagenham
- Likes socializing with friends, going to see all types of live music, art galleries, the theatre and museums
- Not interested in computer games or watching TV
- Wide network of friends from school, university and work

4 Jigsaw
The online journal *Spiked Review* published an interview with sociologist Mike Savage, one of the people behind the Great British Class Survey in 2018.
1. In groups of three, work on a different part of the interview each. Note down the most important information.
2. Get together with other students who have worked on the same part of the interview. Present your findings to each other and add the findings of the others to your notes.
3. Get back into your original groups and present the information about the three parts of the interview to each other. Then sum up the most important information from the interview in a few bullet points.

Annotations
[1] to **hark back to** = to remind one of the past

Social class in the 21st century
2 February 2018

Spiked Review: In your recent work, you've developed a seven-class schema. Why did you move away from the more familiar, middle- and working-class, bourgeois and proletarian, distinction? And why is there this fragmentation?
Mike Savage: Those old terms, middle class and working class, really hark back[1] to an industrial society. The categories then were concerned with the divisions between manual occupations (working class) and non-manual occupations (middle class or lower middle class). And the assumption was that your occupation was the key defining feature of your class.
And I think that way of thinking about class has become a bit outdated. [...] [T]here is an increasing range of factors that influence your situation in life. So, it's not just the money you earn from your job, it also includes your inheritance, the money in your home, your savings, and also your education and qualifications. [...]
Spiked Review: How do you assess the relations between the classes? Is there a widening

division between top and bottom? A bunching and blurring together in the middle?

Savage: That's exactly right. Our big argument […] is that the old model used to be focused on upper, middle and working class with the big dividing lines in the middle. But what we're saying now is that the top levels are pulling away, the elite people are much better off than they were 30 or 40 years ago […]. People at the bottom aren't much better off, possibly even worse off because benefit levels haven't really always kept up with inflation and so forth. So you see the two extremes pull apart, with the elite being a lot more elite compared to the precariat than used to be the case. And the middle is much more confused and fuzzy […].

Spiked Review: Your work draws on French sociologist Pierre Bourdieu, particularly his three ideas of capital – economic, cultural and social. How do the latter two – the cultural and social – confer[2] advantage on some and disadvantage others?

Savage: The idea of capital for Bourdieu is that you have capital if that capital can convey advantages vis a vis other people. So if you've got a certain kind of capital, you are put in a position in which you are advantaged, and those advantages can be accumulated and passed on. And obviously we know about economic capital, we know that people with more money have got more advantages. You can convert[3] economic capital into a better quality of life. But Bourdieu was very important in saying that it's not just a matter of money […]. There's also cultural capital, and the argument goes that people who are […] taught in their home to value art and culture, then they're better able to convert their interests into educational achievements – that is, they're able to do better in school and university. This means that those qualifications can be turned into better jobs. […] And then social capital is the idea that your social networks are an important resource which might allow you to gain certain advantages. […] If you went to an elite university and know lots of elite people in different walks of life, like a top judge, a top bank manager and a top doctor, you're better placed to use those connections to benefit your own interests. So Bourdieu is really arguing that across these three categories of capital – economic, cultural and social – you can see how different sorts of advantages play out for certain people who've got the right kind of capital. […]

Spiked Review: Education, especially higher education, has long been championed as a way to overcome rigid class divisions – that is, more people into universities, therefore more cultural, social and economic capital accrued[4] by more and more people. Why do you think this has been unsuccessful? Has the higher education sector created class divisions within itself, between, for example, elite universities and middle-ranking universities, etc?

Savage: Yeah, you're absolutely right. There is this belief that education would get rid of class divisions and allow people with the right talents to get the right educational outcomes. But in fact what's happened is that as education has become more competitive (it's more difficult to get into the top universities, and more important to do well at school), only a few people can get into Oxford and Cambridge, to give an example – and it's those people who can mobilise all their advantages who are best placed to do that. So if you can mobilise private tutors, if you can mobilise parents who are very supportive with a huge house so you can study undisturbed without being stressed by the TV, and if you go to the best school and know the right friends who know the tips on to how to get into Oxford and Cambridge, you're more likely to get in. So a competitive education system allows those people with the most advantages to do well. I don't think it's a conspiracy – it's not as if the elite are trying to keep top educational institutions for their own kind (though that occasionally happens); it's more just that the most advantaged people will tend to do well. […] So, it is the case that education has acted to create the same class inequalities, rather than erode them.

5 Across cultures

a) **Pair work** Compare Professor Savage's findings about British society with your ideas concerning social classes in Germany (task 1). Focus on what Savage says about what generally defines one's class and the role of education. Would you say that the situation in Germany is similar or quite different?

b) Discuss your findings in class.

Annotations
[2] to **confer** = to give
[3] to **convert** = to change into
[4] to **accrue** /əˈkruː/ = to build up

Advanced texts — Part C: The many faces of Britain

The North-South divide

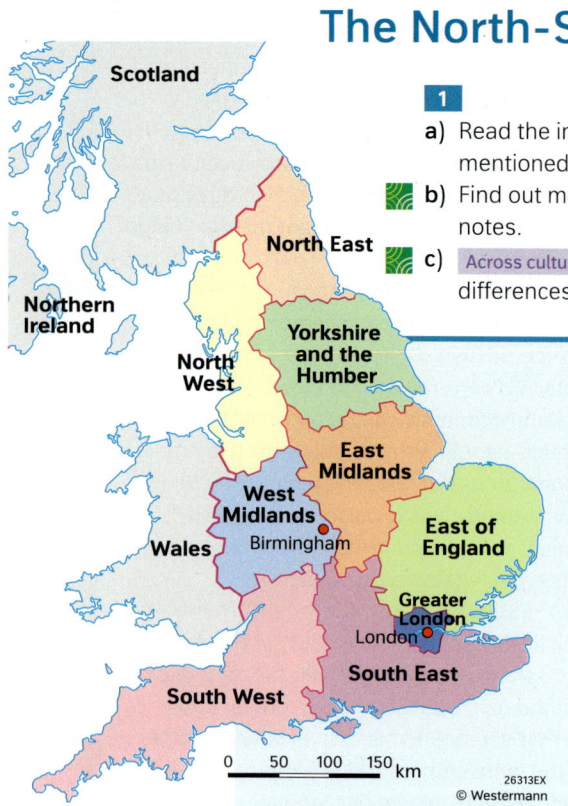

1
a) Read the info box on the North-South divide and identify the areas mentioned on the map of England.
b) Find out more information on the North-South divide in England and make notes.
c) **Across cultures** Compare the situation with what you know about regional differences in Germany. Look up some facts and figures online if necessary.

Info

The North-South divide in England

The North-South divide refers to social, cultural and economic differences between the Northern English regions (the North East, the North West, Yorkshire and the Humber) and regions of Southern England (the South East, the South West, and Greater London). The status of the East and the Midlands with Birmingham as the second largest city in Britain is unclear. Generally speaking, the North is perceived as poor, disadvantaged and deprived whereas the South – and particularly London – is seen as rich, privileged and advantaged. Indices to describe the average make-up of the two areas are income, employment, health, education, skills and training, housing conditions, and crime. The following show some indication of the North-South divide:

- health conditions are worse in the North, despite the fact that spending on health care is higher in the North. Dying early, for example, is 20 per cent more likely for those who live in the northern areas of the country and rates of obesity are also considerably higher in the North.
- house prices are higher in the south, particularly in the South East and London.
- average earnings are significantly higher in the South and South East.
- northern accents are an impediment when applying for well-paid or academic jobs because they are perceived as an indication of backwardness.
- government spending. The North of England has seen £59 billion less in transport spending compared to London over the last ten years.

Webcode
You can find the video here:
WES-73644-076

→ **S20:** How to listen/watch effectively, p. 366

2
a) Watch Toby Campion recite his poem "From the Midlands".
b) **Pair work** Share your first impressions of the poem.
c) Listen to the poem again and note down the characteristics of the Midlands as expressed by the poet.
d) Compare the message with the information you gathered in 1.

→ **S1:** Checklist: Summary, p. 330

3
Sum up the main aspects of the North-South divide as mentioned in the article on p. 187.

→ **S13:** Checklist: Analysis – non-fictional texts, p. 354

4 **Language awareness**
Analyse the author's position and the means used to convince the reader.

→ **S6:** How to write a discussion/comment, p. 338

5
"But this is a division we are all guilty of reinforcing." (l. 72)
Comment on this claim, considering ways to improve the situation.

The North-South divide is getting worse – because London is sucking all opportunity from the rest of the UK

A damning report released earlier this week suggested that dying early is 20 per cent more likely for those who live in the northern areas of the country – no wonder it's so quiet up here

Juliette Bretan, 11 August 2017,
The Independent

[...] The statistics revealed that while the mortality rates in England have improved overall, there is a clear distinction between the statistics from the north and south of the country: those aged 35 to 44, for example, are a whopping[1] 49 per cent more likely to die suddenly if they reside in the north. And crucially, the report doesn't actually specify the cause of these disparate figures – which makes living up north, in effect, a death sentence.

Well, maybe – or, maybe not. The problem with this kind of research is that it fails to take into account the complex nature of the north-south divide; with latent similarities between both sectors rejected in favour of an archaic us vs them dichotomy. The team based their findings on a physical barrier, on a "geography [which] divides the English population into two approximately equal halves", using the traditional "line drawn between the Wash and the Severn Estuary" to demarcate north and south; a strategy which is all well and good if this dividing line was not as frequently and fiercely contested as reality has it. [...] In truth, to concur with anyone about the precise coordinates of the north-south divide is like asking Donald Trump and Kim Jong-un to settle their beef with the flip of a coin.

This may, at least, be of some comfort to those of us living in northern areas – but we can't wholly disregard the statistics of the report either. Nuances must be taken into account when we consider the north-south boundary; which, though elusive[2] and mercurial[3], does exist in some form – making efforts to reduce the divide difficult to manage. Take transport, for example. According to figures released last week, "the north of England has seen £59bn less in transport spending compared to London over the last 10 years". For those of us stranded up here, with a seemingly-endless convoy of tractors lying between our homes and blessed civilisation, this may seem terribly unjust; a case of yet more anti-northern discrimination. [...] The north-south divide has existed since the 19th century at least, and still, no vast improvements have been made to reset the balance. Though government spending across the country is relatively equal, private-sector growth has historically been centred on London, meaning underlying economic inequalities remain. [...]

Babies are less likely to be breastfed by their mothers if they live in the north. Schools in northern areas receive less funding than their southern counterparts, while schoolchildren in the north have fallen behind by the age of five. Schools in the south-east are also sending nearly 50 per cent more students to Oxbridge than the national average. The disparity in arts funding is also considerable, with £700m needed to bridge the division. And the wage gap, too, is alarming: the average wage of a working woman in Camden is £560 a week, while Hartlepool has an average of £252. Though house prices may be lower in the north, research has suggested that "the same number of new homes are being built in London as every city region in the so-called 'Northern Powerhouse' combined". Then there is the charity study based on inspections taken by the Quality Care Commission which revealed 15 of the 20 worst areas for social care were in the north. And finally, there are the reports which suggest those in the north-west have the lowest life expectancy of 77.9 years, while those in the south-east have the highest at 80.5.

But this is a division we are all guilty of reinforcing. Question any university student on their future plans and the dream is always London, never Blackpool. Internships are often available only in the city; and the flow of graduates is always north-to-south, never the other way round. It's London or nothing.

"But I love the north!" A friend from Hammersmith sighs. "It's so quiet!"

Maybe that's because everyone up here is stuck indoors for want of public transport; or trying to find better wages; or in a month-long queue for a GP appointment. Or dead.

Annotations

[1] **whopping** /ˈwɒpɪŋ/ = gigantic   [2] **elusive** = not easy to grasp   [3] **mercurial** = unpredictable

6 The American experience

①  ②  ③  ④

Webcode

You can download a word list for the Intro and the WordPool here: WES-73644-077

1

a) What comes to mind when you think of America? Write down five potential endings to this sentence opening:
   America is a country that/where/without/in which …
b) Compare the different results in class.
c) **Pair work** Use the ideas collected in class to complete the mind map.

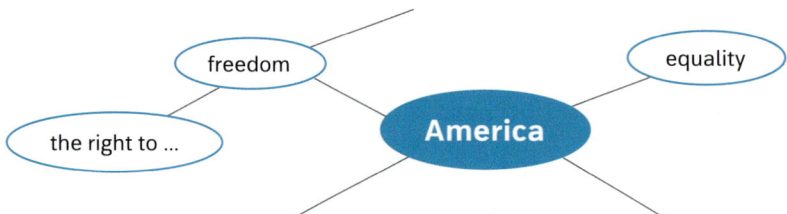

The American experience — Intro 6

Preview

The American Dream
The first part of this Theme deals with the still influential concept of the American Dream. In the **Workshop**, you will practise analysing cartoons.

Culture wars
Part B focuses on a set of social and ideological conflicts often referred to as culture wars. In the **Workshop**, you will work on listening tasks.

African American experiences
The last part of the Theme focuses on the experiences of African Americans and their struggle for equality.

2
a) **Pair work** Take turns describing what you can see in the pictures.
b) **Pair work** Identify the central themes and relate them to the categories from 1c.
c) Share your thoughts in class.

3
The Irish musician Bono once said: America is not just a country, it's an idea.
a) Based on what you already know about the US, comment on this statement in no more than 250 words.
b) **Pair work** Read your partner's comment and talk about the similarities and differences between your texts.
c) Share your thoughts in class.

Tip
If you need some help, you can read the text on the next page.

189

WordPool: The American experience

A GREAT NATION
The USA is one of the most politically influential countries in the world. Today, it is widely regarded as a superpower, boasting the world's largest economy and possessing the world's most powerful military. The USA plays a leading role in global politics, exercising great influence in organisations such as NATO and the United Nations. Contemporary US popular culture transcends borders, with American music hits and Hollywood blockbusters entertaining audiences in countries across the globe.

AMERICAN WAR OF INDEPENDENCE
It all started with 13 British colonies that were established in the 17th and 18th centuries at the North American Atlantic coast. Between 1775 and 1783, these colonies fought for their independence against the Kingdom of Great Britain. In 1776, American statesman Thomas Jefferson wrote the Declaration of Independence, a document announcing that the 13 colonies at war with Britain were no longer under British rule. Five years after the war ended, the constitution of the United States was adopted.

A LAND OF IMMIGRANTS
During the USA's first few decades of independence, the population of the country did not exceed 10 million. Today American citizens number well over 300 million. One of the main reasons for this huge rise in population is the country's history of immigration. In a trend spanning over two centuries, successive generations of immigrants have been leaving their mark on the country. The first waves of newcomers were largely European migrants, leaving behind their homelands to start a new life in the New World. During the course of the 20th century, more and more Latin Americans, especially Mexicans, entered the country, many of them illegally. Most recently, there has been a large influx of immigrants from India and China seeking employment in the services and technology sectors. What unites the vast majority of these immigrants is their search for a better life in the United States – their quest for the so-called *American Dream*.

THE AMERICAN DREAM
Perceptions of the American Dream have changed over time. However, the basic idea is still more or less the same – namely that anybody in America, regardless of their circumstances at birth or their place in society, can achieve success, happiness and prosperity as long as they work hard. Both historically and contemporarily, America has been seen by many as a land of opportunity, where all hardworking citizens can reap the benefits of their efforts.
However, for millions of hopeful Americans today, traditional ideals such as home ownership and financial stability will remain but a dream. Immigrants are similarly in many cases disillusioned by the lack of upward economic mobility.

AN AMERICAN NIGHTMARE?
In spite of the magnanimous statements made in the Declaration of Independence, the USA has had a history troubled by slavery, civil war, racism and inequality. Even Thomas Jefferson's claim 'that all men are created equal' is contradictory to the reality of his lifestyle: he was a slaveholder. In the 1860s, there was such marked polarization between the pro-slavery southern states and the predominantly anti-slavery northern states that the southern states separated from the US. President Abraham Lincoln, who advocated the abolition of slavery, led the North in a bloody civil war with the South. During the course of the conflict, the southern states lost ground and eventually lost the war. Slavery was abolished by the 13th constitutional amendment. However, racist sentiments continued to linger in the South as well as in other parts of the country, resurfacing as antagonistic attitudes towards the civil rights movement in the mid-20th century.
Even today, after the passing of the 1964 Civil Rights Act and much necessary social reform, there are still widespread cultural, racial and class-based divisions in American society. Frequent clashes between young African American males and US police officers are a source of controversy, with the police often being accused of racism.

The American experience — WordPool

1
Complete the grid with the correct verbs and/or adjectives. Use a dictionary, if necessary.

noun	adjective	verb
prosperity	...	...
effort	...	
upward mobility	...	...
controversy	...	
slavery		...
division	...	...

→ **S25:** How to work with a dictionary, p. 374

Webcode
You can download the grid here:
WES-73644-078

2
Find nouns derived from the following verbs and adjectives. If necessary, use a dictionary.
1. to lose ground
2. to abolish
3. constitutional
4. contradictory
5. predominantly
6. antagonistic

→ **S25:** How to use a dictionary, p. 374

3
Now make sentences using eight of your new words from tasks 1 and 2. Ideally your sentences should be related to the topic *The American experience*.

4
Read the text on the left and find words that are synonyms for the following words:
1. affluence
2. disagreement
3. conflict
4. to exceed
5. to do away with
6. to support
7. opposed
8. mainly
9. hostile

5 Language awareness
Some words are often used together and are considered the "right way" to say something, even though other combinations are technically possible. For example, a native speaker of English would always use the word "tea" with "strong", never with "potent" or "powerful".
These popular compositions are called collocations. In the text on the left, different examples of collocations can be found, e.g. "to exercise influence". Use the collocations from the text to complete the sentences below. The underlined words help you find the correct collocations in the text.

The USA is a country of immigrants. Millions have come to the country, hoping ⟨1⟩ success and happiness. Many newcomers have been able to live the American Dream, ⟨2⟩ the benefits of their hard work. Some have even risen to prominence, ⟨3⟩ great influence as powerful politicians or ⟨4⟩ their mark in other fields. Quite a few famous Hollywood actresses, actors and film directors were born outside the US. Nonetheless, they have become an integral part of an entertainment industry whose influence ⟨5⟩ national borders and has a truly global impact.

6 Part A: The American Dream

The American Dream

1
a) Think about your own dreams for the future and write down five keywords to describe them.
b) **Pair work** Talk to your partner about your dreams and what might be necessary to achieve them.

2
a) Watch a video about the American Dream. Note down how the people define it.
b) **Pair work** Compare your results with a partner's.
c) **Pair work** With your partner, come up with categories into which you can sort your notes.

Webcode
You can find a link to the video here:
WES-73644-080

Webcode
You can download a word list for Part A here:
WES-73644-079

3 Read the text below. Taking into account both the information from the text and the illustration above, draw a timeline of the different concepts of the American Dream.

4 Across cultures
Having studied the definitions of the American Dream, compare them with your own dreams.

Definitions of the American Dream
The authors of the United States' Declaration of Independence (1776) held certain truths to be self-evident: "that all Men are created equal, that they are endowed by their Creator with certain unalienable[1] Rights, that among these are Life, Liberty and the Pursuit of Happiness." This sentiment could
5 be considered the foundation of the American Dream.
In James Truslow Adams' book *The Epic of America*, published in 1931, we find an expanded version of the Founding Fathers'[2] vision. Adams wrote that the American Dream is "that dream of a land in which life should be better and richer and fuller for everyone, with opportunity for each according to ability or achievement. [...] It is not a dream of motor cars and high wages merely, but a dream of
10 social order in which each man and each woman shall be able to attain to the fullest stature of which they are innately capable, and be recognized by others for what they are, regardless of the fortuitous circumstances of birth or position."

Manifest Destiny
The ideology of Manifest Destiny, widespread, could be regarded as the dark side of the American
15 Dream. Especially in the 19th century, many Americans were convinced that God had blessed the growth of the American nation and expected it to expand. Secure, then, in the knowledge of their cultural and racial superiority, they felt bound to 'enlighten' the nations that were not fortunate enough to have God's blessing. There was a strong belief in the virtue of the American people and that it was their destiny to impose their – mainly puritan – way of life on others.

20 ### The development of the American Dream
In the course of history the concept of the American Dream evolved, depending on the people concerned and what they were looking for in pursuit of their happiness. The homesteaders[3] who left the big cities of the east dreamed of happiness on their own piece of land in an unknown wilderness. The many immigrants who came to the United States in the 19th and 20th centuries dreamed of
25 freedom in the land of opportunities. And the veterans of World War II desired to settle down, to have a home, a car and a family after having fought for their country.
Nowadays, many argue that the American Dream has become the pursuit of material prosperity – that people work more hours to get bigger cars and fancier homes, but have less time to enjoy their prosperity. Others say that the American Dream is beyond the grasp of the working poor who must
30 work two jobs to ensure their family's survival.

Annotation
[1] **unalienable** sth that is unalienable cannot be taken away from or denied to someone
[2] **Founding Fathers** = the group of men who led the American Revolution, some of whom are also responsible for the Declaration of Independence
[3] **homesteaders** = American settlers moving west in the 1860s

Part A: The American Dream   **Workshop: Step by step**   6

Step by step Analysing a cartoon

Preview

Cartoons are often used to make a critical comment on a serious issue in a humorous way. In this Workshop you will learn how to analyse cartoons. A cartoon analysis often involves three steps:
1) Description
2) Interpretation
   - analysing visual and textual elements
   - explaining the message of the cartoon
3) Comment
   - commenting on the effectiveness/persuasiveness of the cartoon and/or
   - commenting on the central message of the cartoon

Depending on the task, step 3 (comment) may be left out.

DESCRIPTION

1
a) Describe the cartoon.
b) **Pair work** Read your description to a partner and listen to his/her description. If necessary, add further details to your own description.

→ **S17:** How to work with cartoons, p. 361

Annotation
cake mix = Backmischung

Language support

Interpreting cartoons
The expression on the woman's face shows …
This could mean that …
This suggests …
By presenting …, the cartoonist …
The topic/issue addressed by the cartoon is …
The figure(s) represent(s)/ symbolize(s) …
The caption suggests/implies/ underlines …
The cartoonist ridicules/draws attention to/caricatures …
The … is a caricature of…
The message is accentuated by …

INTERPRETATION

2
a) On the basis of your description of the cartoon, interpret the relevant elements. The info box on the next page may help you. → **SUPPORT** D1, p. 314
b) Use your interpretation of the elements of the cartoon to state its central message. To do so, it may help you to answer these questions:
   - What problem(s) does the cartoon illustrate?
   - What is the cartoonist's opinion on the situation?
c) **Pair work** Compare your answer with a partner's and add any points to your interpretation that you may have missed.
d) Use the language support to write the interpretation part of the cartoon analysis.

→ **S17:** How to work with cartoons, p. 361

193

6 Workshop: Step by step — Part A: The American Dream

> **Info**
>
> ## Persuasive techniques used in cartoons
>
> **Symbolism**
> Cartoonists often use simple objects to express larger themes or concepts. These objects are called symbols. Identify the symbols in a cartoon and what they are supposed to represent.
>
> **Exaggeration**
> Cartoonists sometimes exaggerate certain physical features of people or things. Look out for any characteristics that appear to be overdone, e.g. facial features or items of clothing, and suggest what the cartoonist might be trying to say.
>
> **Labelling**
> Cartoonists sometimes label items in their cartoons to make it clear what these items represent. Try to explain why the cartoonist might have labelled a particular person or object and decide whether the label makes the significance of the object any clearer.
>
> **Analogy**
> An analogy is the comparison of one thing with another similar thing in order to explain it. Often a complicated matter or situation is compared with a simpler, more relatable one. Identify the main analogy in the cartoon and what two situations the cartoonist is comparing. Does this analogy make the cartoonist's point any clearer?
>
> **Irony**
> Irony is the strange and often amusing aspect of a situation that is very different from what you would expect. Cartoonists can use irony to express their viewpoint on an issue. If the cartoon contains any examples of irony, think about what the irony is intended to emphasize. Does the irony help express the cartoonist's viewpoint more effectively?

COMMENT

3 Give your opinion on the cartoon and its message.

a) **Pair work** Discuss the following questions with a partner:
- How effective is the cartoon's portrayal of the message?
- How well does the cartoonist get the message across?
- What is your opinion regarding the cartoon's central message?

b) **CHOOSE** Write the comment part of your cartoon analysis. Decide whether you want to comment on the persuasiveness of the cartoon, i.e. on how good a job the cartoonist has done

OR

whether you want to give your opinion on the cartoon's central message.

4 Compare the definitions of the American Dream you dealt with on the facts page (p. 192) with the American Dream as depicted in the cartoon.

Language support

Commenting on the message of a cartoon

In my opinion …
As I see it …
I agree / disagree with …
As opposed to … I believe that …
In contrast to …, I …
While there is no doubt that …, I must say …

Part A: The American Dream — **Workshop: Practice**

Practice: Analysing a cartoon

1 Jigsaw

a) Home groups: Work in groups of four. Each member works on one of the cartoons below.
  - Describe the cartoon.
  - Interpret the cartoon:
    - Analyse the visual and textual elements.
    - State the message of the cartoon.
  - Comment on the message of the cartoon.

→ **S17:** How to work with cartoons, p. 361

b) Expert groups: Compare your results with other students who have worked on the same cartoon.

c) Prepare and practise a short presentation of your cartoon. Divide your presentation into parts for description, analysis and a comment on the cartoon's central message.

d) Go back to your home group and present your cartoon to the rest of the group.

> **Info**
>
> **White picket fence**
> The white picket fence has iconic status, symbolizing the ideal middle-class suburban life and thus the American Dream. But today some people associate picket fences with what they regard as the more negative aspects of this lifestyle.

1. "I BEGUN LIKE YOU, WITH NOTHING BUT MY BARE HANDS. LOOK AT ME NOW! ONLY 25 YEARS LATER, I'M BEGGING WITH MY OWN HAT! GEEZ, I LOVE THIS COUNTRY! EVERYBODY CAN MAKE IT HERE!"

2.

3.

4.

2
Now write a full analysis of your cartoon.

→ **S17:** How to work with cartoons, p. 361

6 Texts — Part A: The American Dream

The American Dream in a political speech

1 Read former First Lady Michelle Obama's speech and outline her experiences concerning the American Dream.

→ **S14:** How to analyse a speech, p. 355

2 Language awareness
Analyse her use of stylistic devices in order to illustrate her idea of the American Dream.
→ **SUPPORT** D2, p. 314

3 Across cultures
Pair work Compare her view with what you know about the American Dream.

First Lady Michelle Obama speaks at the Democratic National Convention in Charlotte, N.C.

4 September 2012

Over the past few years as First Lady, I have had the extraordinary privilege of traveling all across this country.
5 And everywhere I've gone, in the people I've met, and the stories I've heard, I have seen the very best of the American spirit.
I have seen it in the incredible kindness and warmth that people have shown me and my
10 family, especially our girls.
I've seen it in teachers in a near-bankrupt school district who vowed to keep teaching without pay.
I've seen it in people who become heroes at
15 a moment's notice[1], diving into harm's way to save others … flying across the country to put out a fire … driving for hours to bail out a flooded town. […]
You see, Barack and I were both raised by
20 families who didn't have much in the way of money or material possessions but who had given us something far more valuable – their unconditional love, their unflinching sacrifice, and the chance to go places they
25 had never imagined for themselves. […]
And when my brother and I finally made it to college, nearly all of our tuition[2] came from student loans and grants.
But my dad still had to pay a tiny portion of
30 that tuition himself.
And every semester, he was determined to pay that bill right on time, even taking out loans when he fell short.
He was so proud to be sending his kids to
35 college … and he made sure we never missed a registration[3] deadline because his check was late.
You see, for my dad, that's what it meant to be a man.
40 Like so many of us, that was the measure of his success in life – being able to earn a decent living that allowed him to support his family.
And as I got to know Barack, I realized that
45 even though he'd grown up all the way across the country, he'd been brought up just like me.
Barack was raised by a single mother who struggled to pay the bills, and by
50 grandparents who stepped in when she needed help.
Barack's grandmother started out as a secretary at a community bank[4] … and she moved quickly up the ranks … but like so
55 many women, she hit a glass ceiling[5].
And for years, men no more qualified than she was – men she had actually trained – were promoted up the ladder ahead of her, earning more and more money while
60 Barack's family continued to scrape by[6]. […]
Like so many American families, our families weren't asking for much.
They didn't begrudge anyone else's success or care that others had much more than
65 they did … in fact, they admired it.
They simply believed in that fundamental American promise that, even if you don't start out with much, if you work hard and

---

Annotations
[1] **at a moment's notice** = without much warning or time to prepare
[2] **tuition** (AE) /tjuːˈɪʃ(ə)n/ = the money you must pay to receive an education
[3] **registration** = the process of signing up for college
[4] **community bank** = a smaller bank, typically locally owned
[5] **glass ceiling** = a barrier to career progress for members of a disadvantaged group
[6] **to scrape by** = to just have enough money to live on

do what you're supposed to do, then you should be able to build a decent life for yourself and an even better life for your kids and grandkids.

That's how they raised us ... that's what we learned from their example.

We learned about dignity and decency – that how hard you work matters more than how much you make⁷ ... that helping others means more than just getting ahead yourself.

We learned about honesty and integrity – that the truth matters ... that you don't take shortcuts⁸ or play by your own set of rules ... and success doesn't count unless you earn it fair and square⁹.

We learned about gratitude and humility – that so many people had a hand in our success, from the teachers who inspired us to the janitors who kept our school clean ... and we were taught to value everyone's contribution and treat everyone with respect.

Those are the values Barack and I – and so many of you – are trying to pass on to our own children. [...]

So when it comes to rebuilding our economy, Barack is thinking about folks like my dad and like his grandmother.

He's thinking about the pride that comes from a hard day's work.

That's why he signed the Lilly Ledbetter Fair Pay Act¹⁰ to help women get equal pay for equal work.

That's why he cut taxes for working families and small businesses and fought to get the auto industry back on its feet.

That's how he brought our economy from the brink of collapse to creating jobs again – jobs you can raise a family on, good jobs right here in the United States of America. [...]

Because Barack knows what it means when a family struggles.

He knows what it means to want something more for your kids and grandkids.

Barack knows the American Dream because he's lived it ... and he wants everyone in this country to have that same opportunity, no matter who we are, or where we're from, or what we look like, or who we love.

And he believes that when you've worked hard, and done well, and walked through that doorway of opportunity ... you do not slam it shut behind you ... you reach back, and you give other folks the same chances that helped you succeed. [...]

I love that for Barack, there is no such thing as "us" and "them" – he doesn't care whether you're a Democrat, a Republican, or none of the above ... he knows that we all love our country ... and he's always ready to listen to good ideas ... he's always looking for the very best in everyone he meets. [...]

And he reminds me that we are playing a long game¹¹ here ... and that change is hard, and change is slow, and it never happens all at once.

But eventually we get there, we always do.

We get there because of folks like my Dad ... folks like Barack's grandmother ... men and women who said to themselves, "I may not have a chance to fulfill my dreams, but maybe my children will ... maybe my grandchildren will."

So many of us stand here tonight because of their sacrifice, and longing, and steadfast love ... because time and again, they swallowed their fears and doubts and did what was hard.

So today, when the challenges we face start to seem overwhelming – or even impossible – let us never forget that doing the impossible is the history of this nation ... it's who we are as Americans ... it's how this country was built. [...]

If farmers and blacksmiths could win independence from an empire ... if immigrants could leave behind everything they knew for a better life on our shores ... if women could be dragged to jail for seeking the vote ... if a generation could defeat a depression, and define greatness for all time ... if a young preacher could lift us to the mountaintop with his righteous dream¹² ... and if proud Americans can be who they are and boldly stand at the altar with who they love ... then surely, surely we can give everyone in this country a fair chance at that great American Dream.

Because in the end, more than anything else, that is the story of this country – the story of unwavering hope grounded in unyielding struggle.

Annotations

⁷ **how much you make** = how much money you earn

⁸ to **take shortcuts** = to take steps in order to do something more quickly

⁹ **fair and square** = in an honest way, without cheating

¹⁰ The **Lilly Ledbetter Fair Pay Act** was the first bill signed into law by US President Barack Obama in 2009. The law makes it easier for people to file an equal-pay lawsuit.

¹¹ to **play a long game** = to work towards a goal in a somewhat distant future

¹² an allusion to civil rights leader Martin Luther King and his famous "I have a dream" speech (1963)

6 Advanced texts | Part A: The American Dream

American nightmare?
Working with newspaper articles

1 CHOOSE

Work on one of the two following opinion pieces.
Read the article "Is the American Dream killing us?" and outline the writer's view on the significance of the American Dream today.
OR
Read the article "Trump is killing the American Dream" and outline what the writer believes has happened to the American Dream.

ROBERT J. SAMUELSON   Washington Post, 2 April 2017

 Is the American Dream killing us?

It isn't often that economics raises the most profound questions of human existence, but the recent work of economists Anne Case and Angus Deaton
5 (wife and husband, both of Princeton University) comes close. You may recall that a few years ago, Case and Deaton reported the startling finding that the death rates of non-Hispanic middle-aged
10 whites had gotten worse — they were dying younger.

The results were startling because longer life expectancies have been a reliable indicator of improvement in the human
15 condition. In 1940, U.S. life expectancy at birth was 63 years; by 2010, it was 79 years. The gains reflect medical advances (drugs, less invasive surgery), healthier lifestyles (less smoking) and safer jobs
20 (less physically grueling factory work). These trends were expected to continue.

But in a new paper, Case and Deaton confirm and extend their findings. In the new century, mortality — that is, dying
25 — has increased among middle-aged non-Hispanic whites, mainly those with a high school diploma or less. By contrast, life expectancy is still improving among men and women with a college degree.
30 It's also increasing among blacks and Hispanics, whose mortality rates have traditionally exceeded whites'.

The conclusions largely corroborate the work of conservative scholar Charles
35 Murray. In a 2012 book — "Coming Apart: The State of White America, 1960-2010" — he argued that the country was splintering along class lines as well as racial and ethnic lines. Like Case and
40 Deaton, he focused on people without a college degree. Some political analysts have attributed President Trump's victory to support from this angry group. The main causes of rising death rates
45 among non-Hispanic whites 50 to 54, men and women, are so-called "deaths of despair" — suicides, drug overdoses and the consequences of heavy drinking. Since 1990, the death rate from these
50 causes for this group has roughly doubled to 80 per 100,000. These deaths offset[1] mortality gains among children and the elderly, leading to a fall in overall U.S. life expectancy in 2015, Case and Deaton say.
55 Why? That's the mystery. Trying to answer takes us afield[2] from economics to questions usually left to literature. How do people judge themselves? What do they expect from life? How do they deal
60 with disappointments and setbacks?

One theory attributes the spike in deaths of despair to growing income inequality. There would be fewer suicides, drug overdoses and alcohol-related deaths if
65 incomes were distributed more equally, the argument goes. People take out their frustrations and anger by resorting to self-destructive behavior.

Annotations
[1] to **offset** /ˈɒf.set/ = ausgleichen
[2] **afield** /əˈfiːld/ = a long distance away

198

Part A: The American Dream — Advanced texts

Although this sounds plausible, Case and Deaton are skeptical. They don't discount it entirely but think the argument is oversold³. They point out that, in many places and among many populations, growing income inequality has not increased death rates. For example, American blacks and Hispanics are living longer despite growing economic inequality. In Europe, slow economic growth and more inequality have not led to higher death rates.

Instead, Case and Deaton advance a tentative⁴ theory — they emphasize tentative — that they call "cumulative⁵ deprivation⁶." The central problem is a "steady deterioration in job opportunities for people with low education."

One setback leads to another. Poor⁷ skills result in poor jobs with low pay and spotty⁸ security. Workers with lousy jobs are poor marriage candidates; marriage rates decline. Cohabitation⁹ thrives, but these relationships often break down. "As a result," write Case and Deaton, "more men lose regular contact with their children, which is bad for them, and bad for the children."

To Case and Deaton, these "slow-acting and cumulative social forces" seem the best explanation for the rise in death rates. Because the causes are so deep-seated, they will (at best) "take many years to reverse." But even if their theory survives scholarly¹⁰ scrutiny, it's incomplete. It misses the peculiarly American aspect of this story.

The proper question may be: Is the American Dream killing us?

American culture emphasizes striving for and achieving economic success. In practice, realizing the American Dream is the standard of success, vague though it is. It surely includes homeownership, modest financial and job security, and a bright outlook for our children. When striving accomplishes these goals, it strengthens a sense of accomplishment and self-worth.

But when the striving falters and fails — when the American Dream becomes unattainable — it's a judgment on our lives. By our late 40s or 50s, the reckoning is on us. It's harder to do then what we might have done earlier. We become hostage to unrealized hopes. More Americans are now in this precarious position. Our obsession with the American Dream measures our ambition — and anger.

Annotations
³ to **oversell** /ˌəʊvə(r)ˈsel/ = to give an argument too much weight
⁴ **tentative** /ˈtentətɪv/ = careful, uncertain
⁵ **cumulative** /ˈkjuːmjʊlətɪv/ = overall
⁶ **deprivation** /ˌdeprɪˈveɪʃ(ə)n/ = not having enough of something
⁷ **poor** = *here:* bad
⁸ **spotty** = with gaps in between
⁹ **cohabitation** /kəʊˌhæbɪˈteɪʃ(ə)n/ = *here:* living together without being married
¹⁰ **scholarly** /ˈskɒlə(r)li/ = wissenschaftlich

KASHANA CAULEY New York Times, 22 January 2018

B

Trump is killing the American Dream

When I was growing up, the American Dream meant you had a house with a white picket fence, 2.5 children and a dog. I'm from a small city in Wisconsin, which has a well-regarded state university system that an overwhelming majority of my peers expected to and did attend. The promise of that university education was why the people I grew up with believed in the dream.

We made fun of the white picket fence part, which seemed stiff and boring to our 1990s teenage tastes. We cracked bad jokes about the best way to split the third kid in half. I lived in a white, straight, Christian city, but my friends who didn't fit in those boxes and I believed in the dream too. My parents had fled there from a larger, dangerous city and worked their way up from apartments to a spacious house on the edge of town. Many of my friends were children of immigrants who had covered longer distances to achieve the same goal. Our parents had bettered themselves. We could too.

The American Dream has been endangered for some decades now. I'm not the first person to point that out, and President Trump's policies aren't the first set of developments that have called it into question. The long decline of labor unions and the rise of automation,

Advanced texts — Part A: The American Dream

among other things, have made it harder for many people to afford a picket fence or 2.5 kids.

But the Trump administration's racist and classist policies are hastening the demise of the American Dream. His cruel, unnecessarily hard-edged approach to immigration enforcement goes after law-abiding, taxpaying residents. That, along with the recent tax cut on the rich that will be funded by the middle and lower classes, and Education Secretary Betsy DeVos's lack of interest in public education, all serve as proof that the dream is dying.

Mr. Trump's immigration policies are yanking the dream from many aspiring Americans. In 7-Elevens[1] undergoing sudden immigration raids. In ICE[2] detention centers where a 12-month-old baby was kept separately from his asylum-seeking parents. In the news that President Trump plans to deport 60,000 people to Haiti and 200,000 to El Salvador, the most dangerous country in the world. All that, along with the 800,000 "Dreamers"[3] allowed to live here under the Deferred Action for Childhood Arrivals program who are waiting on Congress and the courts to see if they will be permitted to stay. [...]

Since he used a vulgar term to describe Haiti and African countries and argued that America should be trying to attract immigrants from Norway instead, it's clear that Mr. Trump doesn't see black and brown immigrants as welcome in this country.

The new tax bill, in addition to imposing a tax increase on the working and middle classes over time, allows for private school parents to take up to $10,000 a year from tax-free 529 savings accounts[4] to pay tuition, while capping[5] the deduction for state and local taxes at $10,000, which reduces public school funding.

Secretary DeVos has chosen to ignore public schools in favor of promoting more expensive, restricted-entry private and charter schools[6]. [...]

Though upward economic mobility is limited in this country, and how much money your parents make is highly correlated with how much you'll make, people who go to college still make more money and have better careers than those who don't. So the twin punch of taking funding away from public K-12 schools[7] and encouraging for-profit colleges to continue to defraud students will undeniably limit people's futures.

The American Dream is being yanked out of people's hands as they are physically shipped elsewhere, in many cases separated from the families that have always been a key part of this vision. It's being taken out of their pocketbooks[8] as the debt that will be incurred by the permanent tax cuts for the rich. It's being stolen by diminishing opportunities to obtain a quality public education.

The American Dream was never a perfect vision, insofar as it tended to exclude minorities and disparage the poor. But it encouraged us to see ourselves and our neighbors with love and potential, two values that are desperately needed in a diversity-rich country. And Americans still believe in it. A survey last August found that 36 percent of American adults believe their family has achieved the dream, defined as "freedom of choice in how to live," "a good family life" and "retiring comfortably." An additional 46 percent believe they are "on their way" to achieving it.

If we lose it, we run the risk of turning into a hostile, bitter people convinced that we cannot better our own circumstances, and that any neighbor who appears to have more than we do or is otherwise different from us is to blame.

Annotations
[1] **7-Elevens** = a chain of small shops
[2] **ICE** = U.S. Immigration and Customs Enforcement, agency which enforces the US immigration laws
[3] **"Dreamers"** = name given to undocumented immigrants who were still children when they entered the USA
[4] **529 savings accounts** = bank accounts used to save money for the future education of a child, supported by the state
[5] to **cap** = to put an upper limit on the amount of
[6] **charter school** = school that receives money from the government but runs independently from the state system
[7] **K-12 schools** = publicly funded primary and secondary schools
[8] **pocketbook** (AE) = wallet

2
In class, compare how the two opinion writers assess the concept of the American Dream today.

→ **S6:** How to write a discussion/comment, p. 338

3
Based on your knowledge, comment on the validity of the American Dream today.

Part A: The American Dream — Advanced texts

Let America be America again – a poem

1 Read the poem written by the famous African American poet Langston Hughes and briefly sum up the view of the American Dream as expressed in the poem.

Let America Be America Again

Let America be America again.
Let it be the dream it used to be.
Let it be the pioneer on the plain
Seeking a home where he himself is free.

5 (America never was America to me.) [...]

O, let my land be a land where Liberty
Is crowned with no false patriotic wreath[1],
But opportunity is real, and life is free,
Equality is in the air we breathe.

10 (There's never been equality for me,
Nor freedom in this "homeland of the free.")

Say, who are you that mumbles in the dark?
And who are you that draws your veil across the stars?

15 I am the poor white, fooled and pushed apart,
I am the Negro bearing slavery's scars.
I am the red man[2] driven from the land,
I am the immigrant clutching the hope I seek –
And finding only the same old stupid plan
20 Of dog eat dog, of mighty crush the weak. [...]

Yet I'm the one who dreamt our basic dream
In the Old World while still a serf of kings,
Who dreamt a dream so strong, so brave, so true,
That even yet its mighty daring sings
25 In every brick and stone, in every furrow turned
That's made America the land it has become.
O, I'm the man who sailed those early seas
In search of what I meant to be my home –
For I'm the one who left dark Ireland's shore,
30 And Poland's plain, and England's grassy lea,
And torn from Black Africa's strand[3] I came
To build a "homeland of the free."

The free?
Who said the free? Not me?
35 Surely not me? The millions on relief[4] today?
The millions shot down when we strike?
The millions who have nothing for our pay?
For all the dreams we've dreamed
And all the songs we've sung
40 And all the hopes we've held
And all the flags we've hung,
The millions who have nothing for our pay –
Except the dream that's almost dead today. [...]

Sure, call me any ugly name you choose –
45 The steel of freedom does not stain.
From those who live like leeches on the people's lives,
We must take back our land again,
America!

50 O, yes,
I say it plain,
America never was America to me,
And yet I swear this oath –
America will be!

55 Out of the rack and ruin of our gangster death,
The rape and rot of graft[5], and stealth, and lies,
We, the people, must redeem
The land, the mines, the plants, the rivers.
The mountains and the endless plain –
60 All, all the stretch of these great green states –
And make America again!

Annotations
[4] **on relief** = receiving unemployment benefit
[5] **graft** (AE) = illegally giving sb money to gain an advantage in business or politics

2 Analyse the poem, taking into account the structure and stylistic devices used.   → **S10:** How to work with poetry, p. 347

3 The poem was written in 1935. Comment on how far the views expressed in the poem are still relevant today.

Annotations
[1] **wreath** /riːθ/ = a ring-shaped arrangement of flowers and leaves
[2] **red man** = an old-fashioned and now offensive term for a person of Native American origin
[3] **strand** = *here:* shore

Part B: Culture wars

Facts

Webcode
You can download a word list for Part B here:
WES-73644-081

Contested issues in a diverse country

1
a) **Pyramid discussion** Agree on the four most controversial political and social issues in Germany right now.
b) Explain briefly why these issues are so controversial and, if possible, name groups that support each side of the debate on these contemporary hot topics.

2
→ **S15:** How to describe pictures, p. 358

a) Describe what you can see in the pictures.
b) Explain which controversies affecting American society are highlighted in the photos.
c) Across cultures Compare the issues you can identify in the photos to your list from task 1. Say which similarities and which differences surprise you the most.

3 Group work (4)
a) Read the text on pages 203-205 and work on one of the maps (1-4). Each student should work on a different map. → **SUPPORT** D3, p. 315
   1. State what the map shows.
   2. Describe the map in greater detail.
   3. Sum up your findings.
b) Present your maps to each other.
c) Compare your findings. Look out for striking similarities and differences between different parts of the US.
d) Use your findings to colour in and label a blank map of the United States. Highlight regions and their characteristic features.

Webcode
You can find a blank map you can use here:
WES-73642-082

Part B: Culture wars — Facts

Culture wars
The US is a very diverse country in which different groups of people hold very different views on a variety of issues. In 1991, sociologist James Davison Hunter detected two distinct groups within American society who held opposing views over a number of hotly debated issues. He used the term "culture wars" to refer to this general polarization within society.

The colonial past
Much of the diversity and antagonism in the US stems from the country's historical development. The starting point for mass immigration from Europe were the thirteen British colonies along the Atlantic Coast, which declared their independence from British rule in 1776 and thus formed the core of what was to become the United States of America. The strong influence of European culture can still be felt today, especially in the former New England and Middle Colonies, as many inhabitants are of European ancestry, including, for example, people of Irish and Italian descent. With the westward movement, more and more land was colonized and incorporated into the United States, especially in the 19th century. Immigrants of similar ethnic backgrounds tended to settle in the same areas, with Germans and Scandinavians concentrated mainly in the Midwest and, in general, the states close to the Canadian border.

The flag and the national anthem
Both the flag and the national anthem are linked to the nation's early past. In the flag, the vertical stripes represent the thirteen British colonies that declared their independence in 1776, whereas the stars in the top left hand corner represent the fifty constituent states of the nation today. "The Star-Spangled Banner" has been the national anthem of the United States since 1931. The lyrics, however, were composed by Frances Scott Key during the War of 1812 which the young republic fought against Great Britain.
In the United States, the national anthem and flag are given considerable importance. There are certain protocols to be followed by US citizens, soldiers and athletes at events where the anthem is played, and there are codes of etiquette surrounding the handling and flying of the flag. The "Flag Code", which is part of a federal law, establishes very particular restrictions and standards of respect to be observed when handling the flag. At American football games the athletes and team personnel are required to stand when the national anthem is played. During the anthem, players must also face the flag, hold their helmets in their left hand and refrain from talking.

Race
With the arrival of European settlers, the Native Americans were stripped of their land by the colonists and pushed further and further west into remote regions with often infertile land. Many of these regions were later turned into reservations which are still the home of many underprivileged Native Americans.
Many settlers, especially in the Southern Colonies, set up huge plantations to produce rice, tobacco and cotton for the European market. In order to cope with the work to be done on those plantations, millions of slaves were imported from Africa in the 17th and 18th centuries. When the controversy over the abolition of slavery reached its climax, the young republic became deeply divided, resulting in the Civil War (1861-1865) between the anti-slavery Union states of the North and the pro-slavery Confederate states of the South. Although the Union states under President Abraham Lincoln eventually won and millions of slaves across the United States were freed, the situation of African Americans remained one of ongoing racial discrimination. The civil rights movement of the 1950s and 1960s was crucial in fighting inequality and allowing a prosperous black middle class to develop. Nevertheless, the situation of African Americans is still characterized by a higher risk of unemployment, poverty, crime and imprisonment.
Recent controversies over flying the Confederate flag as a symbol of racism and the excessive use of police force against black people highlight that the racial conflicts of the past still have an impact on the present, particularly in the South.

Info

The Thirteen Colonies
New England Colonies:
Massachusetts (part of which is now Maine), New Hampshire, Rhode Island, Connecticut, Vermont (became a state in 1791, fomerly disputed area between New York and New Hampshire)

Middle Colonies:
New York, New Jersey, Pennsylvania, Delaware

Southern Colonies:
Maryland, Virginia (West Virginia seceded in 1861), North Carolina, South Carolina, Georgia

6 Facts Part B: Culture wars

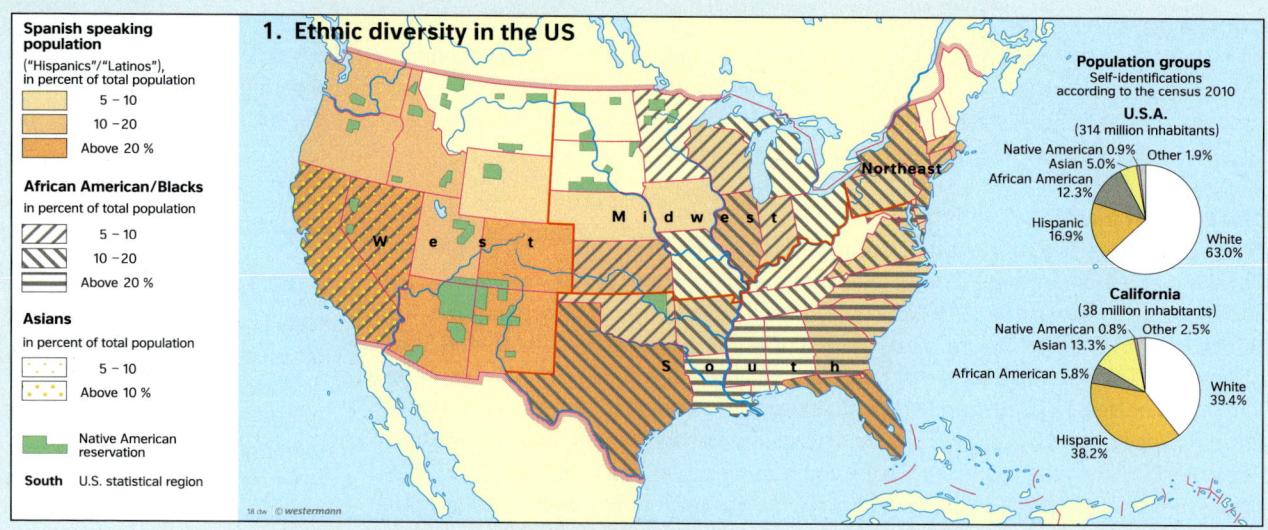

1. Ethnic diversity in the US

Immigration and the multicultural society

The United States has attracted millions of immigrants over the centuries with the promise of a better life and, as the Declaration of Independence says, the "pursuit of happiness". Whereas the vast majority of immigrants came mainly from Europe up to the middle of the 20th century, it has – since then – been largely Hispanics from Latin America and Asians who have made the US their new home, often undocumented. Not only have they added further diversity to North America's multicultural society, but the illegal status of many Latino immigrants in particular has put the issues of border control and the conditions for naturalization on the political agenda.

2. Average religiosity (2013)

Info

Second Amendment to the US Constitution (1791):

"A well regulated militia being necessary to the security of a free state, the right of the people to keep and bear arms shall not be infringed."

Religion

America's image as a safe haven for those suffering from poor living conditions or persecution in their home countries has always had strong religious overtones, which is exemplified by terms like "Promised Land" and "God's Own Country", as applied to the US.

Many settlers emigrated to America because they had been persecuted for religious reasons in their home countries. The best-known example of this were the Puritans, a group of very pious Protestants that enforced high moral standards in their congregations and rejected worldly joys as standing in the way of a religious life. As many 17th-century settlers in the newly-founded British colonies had a Puritan background, their views had a strong impact on the moral code of the colonial society in general. Its effects can still be felt today, for example in the very prudish attitude towards sexuality or nudity in large parts of American society. All in all, religion plays a far more important role in people's everyday lives than it does in European states. Churches also form an important element of social

Part B: Culture wars | Facts

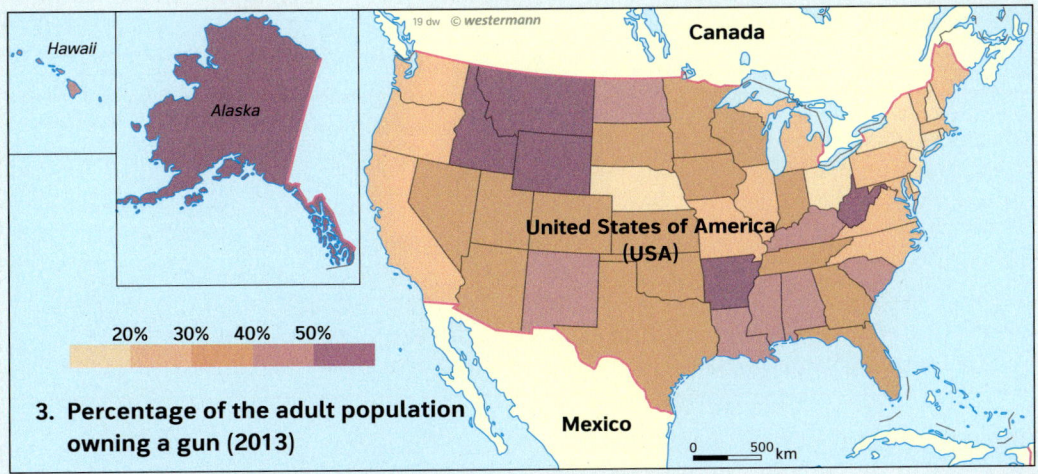

3. Percentage of the adult population owning a gun (2013)

life in communities in general. They are often the hub of many non-religious activities as the US is a country in which clubs (Vereine) are not as common as in Germany, for instance. Furthermore, as social welfare provided by the state is much less comprehensive in the States than in Europe, mutual support and charity work is another field where churches play an important role.

Conflicting interpretations of civil rights
Although freedom and equality are among the values widely accepted by Americans across the political spectrum, there is much less agreement on what these abstract terms mean in real life. Whereas, for example, some people fiercely defend their right to bear arms as a constitutional right, others argue for stricter gun control and question whether the Second Amendment actually constitutes an unconditional right to gun ownership. Similarly, the Supreme Court's decision in 2015 to give members of the LGBT community the right to marry like everyone else came as a shock to many conservative Americans and was regarded as an attack on their family values.

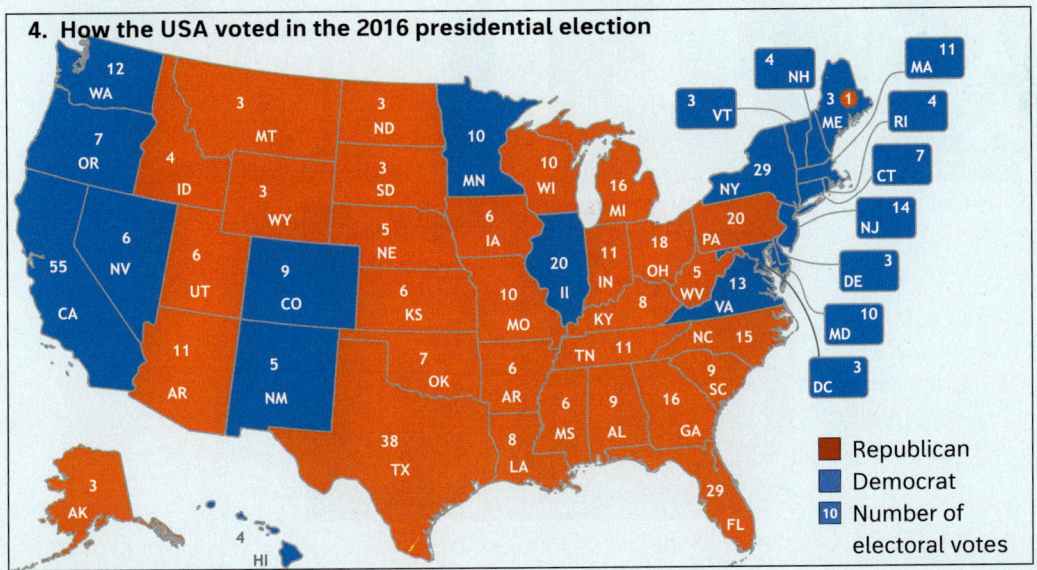

4. How the USA voted in the 2016 presidential election

WA = Washington
OR = Oregon
CA = California
ID = Idaho
MT = Montana
UT = Utah
AR = Arizona
NV = Nevada
WY = Wyoming
CO = Colorado
NM = New Mexico
ND = North Dakota
SD = South Dakota
NE = Nebraska
KS = Kansas
OK = Oklahoma
TX = Texas
MN = Minnesota
IA = Iowa
MO = Missouri
AR = Arkansas
LA = Louisiana
WI = Wisconsin
IL = Illinois
KY = Kentucky
TN = Tennessee
MS = Mississippi
MI = Michigan
IN = Indiana
AL = Alabama
OH = Ohio
GA = Georgia
FL = Florida
WV = West Virginia
VA = Virginia
NC = North Carolina
SC = South Carolina
PA = Pennsylvania
NY = New York
VT = Vermont
NH = New Hampshire
ME = Maine
MA = Massachusetts
RI = Rhode Island
CT = Connecticut
NJ = New Jersey
DE = Delaware
MD = Maryland
(DC = District of Columbia; not part of any state)
AK = Alaska
HI = Hawaii

The political divide
The rather aggressive way of discussing political issues is largely due to the fact that there is a long-standing rivalry between two major parties: the more conservative Republicans and the more liberal Democrats. As most states clearly lean to one of the major parties, in many presidential campaigns it is often a handful of "swing states" which most of the campaigning is focused on.

6 Workshop: Step by step — Part B: Culture wars

Step by step Listening

> **Preview**
>
> In this Workshop you are going to practise working on listening tasks. In an exam, you will usually encounter one of these formats:
> - short answers: You are to answer questions, often in the form of notes, with the help of the listening text.
> - table completion: You are asked to complete a table by adding missing information.
> - multiple choice: You have to choose one of usually three or four options.
> - multiple matching: For a listening text with several speakers, you have to match the speakers to statements that are given, in other words decide who said what.

PRE-LISTENING

1

Recently "taking a knee" has made headlines in the US. You need to look at the different definitions of the term first in order to find out what is behind it.
Read the following three different definitions of the phrase "to take a knee" and match them with the appropriate picture.

1. to take a temporary break from an activity
2. when the quarterback in American Football drops to one knee immediately after receiving the ball, thus automatically ending the play
3. to kneel instead of standing up during the National Anthem to protest against police brutality, racism or discriminatory practices

1

2

3

LISTENING

2

Webcode
You can find a link to the audio file here:
WES-73644-083

a) You are going to listen to a radio program called "On point" about politics and the National Football League (NFL). Before you start listening, read the info box on how to work on a listening task below.

Part B: Culture wars | **Workshop: Step by step**

6

Listening – Before you listen

Before you start listening to a recording, make sure that you are ready for what you are going to hear. Usually, you already have a fairly good idea of what kind of recording you can expect after following the steps below.

1. Read the instructions carefully. It often tells you what **kind of listening text** it is, e.g. a lecture, a call-in show, a podcast. This could give you a clue as to **the number of speakers** you are likely to hear and the **kind of language** to expect, e.g. formal (speech) or informal (call-in show) as well as the variety of English (American/British/Australian/… English).

Info

2. In addition, the instructions as well as the overall context of the listening task hint at the **topic** of the listening text. You probably have heard of the topic before or already worked on it in class. Therefore you may know what the people are likely to talk about and be familiar with a lot of the relevant vocabulary.

EXAMPLE:
Listen to a speech by former US President Bill Clinton to students at Harvard University on the issue of racial inequality.
- speech (→ rather formal; use of stylistic devices)
- one native speaker of US English
- racial inequality (→ different opportunities for different ethnic groups)

b) Now listen to the recording twice. While listening, answer the following questions. You need not write complete sentences.

→ **S20:** How to listen/watch effectively, p. 366

1. What are the players protesting against by taking a knee?
2. President Trump spoke at a rally.
   a When did the rally take place?
   b Where did it take place?
3. What does Trump equate kneeling with?
4. What is Trump's demand for NFL owners?
5. What was the reaction to it?
6. What did the owner of the Dallas Cowboys threaten players with who kneel?
7. What does the American civil rights activist Al Sharpton accuse Jerry Jones of?
8. Why could Jones' statements be considered contradictory?
9. When did Colin Kaepernick start the protest?
10. How did his form of protest develop at the beginning of the season?
11. What did Donald Trump instruct Vice President Pence with in case players should kneel?
12. Why should Pence not have been surprised by kneeling players?
13. Why does the interviewee think that Trump and Pence acted unwisely?
14. What indicates that the NFL is reluctant to deal with the matter constructively?

COMMENT

3

a) Explain which different sides there are to the conflict and what the contested issue is in the program you listened to.
b) Justify whether you would call this conflict a culture war.
c) **Pair work** Discuss whether the football players are justified in choosing this form of protest. One of you argues for, the other one against it.

4 Across cultures

a) In this picture you see the German football team Hertha BSC Berlin taking a knee before a match on 14 October 2017. Think of possible reasons.
b) This form of protest has its origin in the US where it has been used mainly by black people to protest against discrimination and violence against black people. In class, share your thoughts on Hertha BSC taking a knee.

207

Workshop: Practice — Part B: Culture wars

Practice: Listening

PRE-LISTENING

1

a) Finish the following sentence: *An intellectual is someone who …*
b) Share your definitions of an intellectual in class.

LISTENING

Webcode
You can find a link to the audio file here: WES-73644-084

→ **S20:** How to listen/watch effectively, p. 366

2

You are going to listen twice to a radio program called "Allergy to intellectualism" about the age-old American dispute over intellect. While listening, choose the one correct answer a, b, c, or d.

1. John F. Kennedy
   a is critical of research.
   b promises to fund education.
   c is critical of a group of people.
   d speaks out against intellectuals.

2. Archie Bunker is
   a a fictional character.
   b an expert on queens.
   c an icon of his generation.
   d a fan of John F. Kennedy.

3. The WNYC reporter wanted to explore the topic further because he
   a is a Trump supporter.
   b noticed something unexpected.
   c is afraid of terrorism and immigration.
   d expected to understand the resentment.

4. Fiori Napolitano
   a comes from an island.
   b is a professional driver.
   c wants things to be different.
   d is skeptical of Donald Trump.

5. According to Fiori, intellectuals are missing
   a a brain.
   b knowledge.
   c a proper job.
   d good judgement.

6. Anti-intellectualism is critical of
   a a certain attitude.
   b a specific scientific field.
   c learning about the world.
   d people who want to learn things.

7. The character from the movie thinks intellectuals are
   a vain.
   b impolite.
   c snobbish.
   d embarrassing.

8. Which definition of intellectuals comes closest to Omatoso's?
   a They construct engines.
   b They pay attention to details.
   c They reflect on human affairs.
   d They speak their minds carefully.

9. The main argument of the program is that
   a America is in need of more intellectuals.
   b President Trump made life a lot harder for intellectuals.
   c intellectuals are often seen as out of touch with reality.
   d intellectuals are extremely useful to society as a whole.

COMMENT

3

a) **Pair work** Discuss what the consequences are when a society becomes "allergic" to intellectualism.
b) Across cultures In class, discuss whether an "allergy to intellectualism" can also be detected in German society.

Part B: Culture wars — Texts

The two sides in the US culture wars

1

a) Read the article "Confederate flag is a symbol of America's culture wars".
b) **Across cultures** In the text, the author asks you to take on the perspective of two very different Americans. Outline what, according to the text,
  - might be objectionable for the "professional black woman living in Washington, D.C." (ll. 6-7).
  - could be hard to grasp[1] for the "50-year old white man living somewhere in the Deep South" (ll. 55-56).
c) Taking these aspects into account, name reasons for the "culture wars" in the article.

The Confederate Flag: A contentious symbol

Annotations
[1] to **grasp** = *here:* to understand

MATT K. LEWIS   The Daily Telegraph, 27 June 2015

Confederate flag is a symbol of America's culture wars

American Way: Society is changing rapidly – from Rachel Dolezal to gay marriage – and both sides need to take a breath and see things from the other's
5 **perspective**

Pretend for a minute you're a professional black woman living in Washington, DC. During your lifetime, things have mostly improved. But everywhere, vestiges of the
10 past still haunt you. Living in Washington, DC, you probably have to take Jefferson Davis highway once in a while – a road named after the president of the Confederacy. That's just one of the daily
15 reminders.
In the wake of the horrific shooting of nine African Americans at the Emanuel AME church in Charleston, South Carolina, last week, I talked with Crystal Wright,
20 who blogs at a site called Conservative Black Chick, about calls to remove the Confederate flag. "I'm a black woman and I was raised in the South," she told me, "so as a black person, regardless of
25 politics, [the flag] bothers me."
"You know, when I go home to Richmond … to visit my family, I see the Confederate flag in people's yards[1]," she continued. That doesn't bother her. What does
30 bother her is seeing the flag flying in public spaces. "It represents a period in American history that one set of Americans – white Americans from the South – wanted to own blacks as
35 property," she said.

Count me among the many Americans who agree the Confederate flag has no place on public property. Sure, to some Americans it symbolises a Southern
40 tradition – but to many more Americans, it's a very personal symbol of slavery and lynching and segregation.
To understand this, Ms Wright encourages white folks to engage in a sort of role-
45 play – to imagine what it would have been like to be a slave. I suspect this is a healthy intellectual exercise. […]
But putting yourself in the other guy's shoes is a two-way street. And since
50 I'm speaking to a predominantly British audience here, I thought it might be healthy to continue this game of role-play.
Now, pretend for a minute that you're a
55 50-year old white man living somewhere in the Deep South[2]. You cast your first vote for Ronald Reagan[3] in 1984. As a kid, your favourite show was the Dukes of Hazzard[4], which featured a car called
60 The General Lee. […] Today, your way of life is under attack – and this (by far) transcends the Confederate flag. You're experiencing what feels like a radical cultural revolution.
65 You grew up being taught to respect authority – and now the police and the military are increasingly coming under attack. Then-candidate Barack Obama mocked people who "cling to guns and
70 religion". But you grew up around guns – both for hunting and protection. And

Annotations
[1] **yard** (*AE*) = garden (*BE*)
[2] **the Deep South** = the states in the southern US that were historically the most dependent on plantations and, therefore, on slavery
[3] **Ronald Reagan** /ˈreɪɡən/ = President of the United States from 1981 to 1989
[4] **The Dukes of Hazzard** = an American comedy series that ran from 1979 to 1985

Texts   Part B: Culture wars

Annotations

[5] Research has established a link between playing football and concussions, early onset dementia and degenerative brain disease. Therefore, some medical experts have discussed a ban on high school football and former US President Barack Obama has said that if he had a son, he is not sure he would allow him to play football.

[6] **Caitlyn** (formerly **Bruce**) **Jenner** = winner in the decathlon at the 1976 Olympics, came out as a transgender woman in 2015

you grew up attending church every Sunday. Now Christianity and guns are both under attack all of a sudden. Some are even suggesting Walmart shouldn't sell guns anymore.

Friday night football was another huge part of your life. Today, there's talk about banning high school football – and your own president declared that if he had a son, he's not sure he'd even let him play.[5]

Bruce Jenner – you know, the man who was considered the greatest athlete in the world when you were 10 years old? – now goes by the name Caitlyn.[6] (More astonishingly, your kids scold you when you refer to "him" and not "her.")

You turn on the TV and hear about a woman named Rachel Dolezal, a white girl who unilaterally decided to become black. The assumption, I suppose, is

Rachel Dolezal, appears on the "Today" show

that nothing is permanent. The once immutable concepts of gender and race are now fluid.

You grew up being taught that homosexuality was a sin. On Friday, the Supreme Court ruled that gay couples have the right to marry in all 50 states. In what seems like a matter of minutes, the Confederate flag has been replaced by the gay rights rainbow flag. The smoky bar you used to go to drown your sorrows is now "a smoke-free environment".

You're not sure when it happened, but all of a sudden, Bruce Jenner is a woman,

The White House celebrates same-sex marriage ruling

marriage is for two men, and Rachel Dolezal is black.

Institutions you grew up with are being torn down, almost overnight. Behaviour which was once completely normal is now considered politically incorrect, or even intolerant.

Some of these changes are clearly good; some of them will probably lead to problems down the road. Either way, it's all happening very rapidly. And I think we can expect there to be major political reverberations – just as there were during the 1960s.

What we need now is to come together. While some Americans are hoping to finally cast off the vestiges of bigotry that have prevented them (and us) from realising the American Dream, others simply want to preserve American traditions and institutions that, while certainly not perfect, are deeply ingrained in American culture.

There are good, decent people on both sides of this culture war (even if the people leading both sides are too often less than noble). It is only through compassion and understanding that we can empathise with the men and women on both sides of this clash. Only then can we achieve a more perfect union.

→ **S13:** Checklist: Analysis – non-fictional texts, p. 354

2

a) Analyse how the author uses the structure of his article to support his message that "only through compassion and understanding" can America "achieve a more perfect union" (ll. 132-133, 135-136) and make the text more convincing. → **SUPPORT** D4, p. 315

b) Analyse how the author uses stylistic devices and choice of words to get his message across. → **SUPPORT** D5, p. 316

→ **S4:** Checklist: Letter to the editor, p. 336

3

Write a letter to the editor in which you comment on Matt Lewis's article.

Part B: Culture wars | Advanced texts

Mediation: Gun culture

1 Across cultures → **S18:** How to analyse statistics, p. 362
a) Analyse the statistic.
b) Speculate on possible reasons for the differences between Germany and the US.

2 Across cultures
You take part in a school exchange with a high school in California. Your social studies teacher asks you to give a presentation on the issue of gun laws in Germany compared to the American situation. You find the following interview on the *Deutschlandfunk* website and want to use it for a comparison of the legal situation in the two countries. Write a script for your presentation.

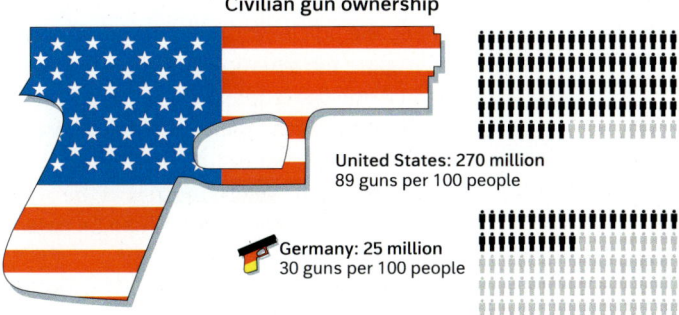

Civilian gun ownership

United States: 270 million
89 guns per 100 people

Germany: 25 million
30 guns per 100 people

→ **S19:** How to improve your mediation skills, p. 364

Ex-Schützenfunktionär: Waffenrecht in Deutschland und den USA vergleichbar

Sandra Schulz (Deutschlandfunk): Jetzt [...] diskutieren die USA wieder um eine Verschärfung des Waffenrechts. Alle bisherigen Vorstöße waren ohne Ergebnis geendet, zerschellt am Widerstand der mächtigen Waffenlobby. Wie ist das eigentlich in Deutschland? [...] Die Verhältnisse in Deutschland seien nicht vergleichbar mit den USA, heißt es immer wieder. Nicht ganz so sieht es Otto Obermeyer, Rechtsanwalt in Bonn und bis 1996 Vorsitzender des Bundes Deutscher Sportschützen. Jetzt ist er am Telefon. Guten Morgen, Herr Obermeyer!

Otto Obermeyer: Guten Morgen!

Schulz: Sie sagen, die Sicherheitsverhältnisse in Deutschland seien nicht besser als in den USA. Warum?

Obermeyer: Es ist ja grundsätzlich so, dass man zum Beispiel die Waffe, mit der dieser Täter in den USA jetzt diese Kinder erschossen hat, in Deutschland genauso erwerben kann wie in den USA – als Sportschütze. [...]

Schulz: Herr Obermeyer, helfen Sie uns auf die Sprünge: Der Waffenbesitz ist doch hier in Deutschland vergleichsweise streng reguliert. Es gibt schlichtweg in Deutschland auch gar nicht so viele Menschen, die eine Waffe haben. Inwiefern haben wir da amerikanische Verhältnisse?

Obermeyer: Also erst mal ist es so, dass bei uns ein Sportschütze ja Schusswaffen erwerben kann. Das ist unbestreitbar. Und wenn Sie Sportschütze werden wollen, müssen Sie im Jahr 18-mal auf einem Schießstand geschossen haben, und schon haben Sie Ihre erste Waffe. Sie dürfen natürlich nicht vorbestraft sein, aber das ist in den USA auch so. Also es ist sehr leicht bei uns, über einen Sportschützenbedarf an Schusswaffen zu kommen.

Schulz: Aber die Sportschützen sagen ja, das sei nun mal ihr Sport, und es wird auch immer wieder gesagt, Sportler dürften nicht unter Generalverdacht gestellt werden. Was ist daran falsch?

Obermeyer: Das ist ja vollkommen richtig. Man kann die Sportschützen nicht unter Generalverdacht stellen. Darum geht es ja auch gar nicht. Nur so zu tun, als sei bei uns alles hundertprozentig besser als in den USA, ist einfach nicht richtig. Wie gesagt, jeder Sportschütze kann bei uns die gleichen Waffen kaufen wie in den USA, auch solche schrecklichen Waffen wie dieses halbautomatische Gewehr, mit dem die Kinder erschossen wurden. Das ist so! Übrigens war die Mutter von diesem Täter auch eine Sportschützin.

Schulz: Jetzt ist hierzulande das Waffenrecht ja immer wieder verschärft worden, eben nach den Amokläufen von Erfurt und Winnenden. Waren das aus Ihrer Sicht denn wenigstens Schritte in die richtige Richtung?

Obermeyer: Ja, was zweifellos vernünftig war, waren die strengeren Aufbewahrungsrichtlinien. Dass also wirklich nur der Sportschütze selber an die Waffe kommen kann und nicht irgendwelche anderen Personen. Das ist ganz klar bei uns besser als in den USA.

6 Advanced texts — Part B: Culture wars

US society today: Culture wars or class war?

1
a) Read the article written by sociologist James Davison Hunter and outline his main argument.
b) Compare the situation in the last four decades, as Hunter describes it, to the present situation and name the reasons the author gives for this development.
c) Explain the consequences of this new polarization that Hunter calls attention to.

→ **S13:** Checklist: Analysis – non-fictional texts, p. 354

→ **S6:** How to write a discussion/comment, p. 338

2 Across cultures **CHALLENGE**
Discuss whether similar trends can be detected within German society.

JAMES DAVISON HUNTER   The Washington Post, 12 September 2017

How America's culture wars have evolved into a class war

It is tempting to see the Unite the Right rally last month in my hometown of Charlottesville and the counterprotests it inspired[1] as yet another tragic — albeit, violent and racist — episode in the culture wars. Indeed, history has long been a source of conflict in the culture war. [...]
Yet, while there are elements of the ongoing culture wars present in the debate over Confederate statues, the rally of white nationalists in Charlottesville reveals how the culture wars have evolved and metastasized[2] into a class war with several sprawling[3] components, far different from the one Karl Marx[4] might have predicted. Much of this evolution has to do with a widening gap between members of America's middle class.
The cultural conflict of the last four decades has mostly taken place within the white middle class, mainly between the aspiring lower-middle and the comfortable upper-middle classes. But the cleavage[5] between highly educated professionals and the less educated, nonprofessional, lower middle and working classes has widened in recent years, producing new tensions, as Richard Reeves has documented in his book "Dream Hoarders."
Overlaying the cultural divisions of yesteryear are new and strikingly different ones. This is the heart of the new culture war: Where the culture wars of the last several decades were fought over sexuality, religion and family, today's culture wars offer a new set of cultural

Right-wing demonstrators clash with counter-protesters in Charlottesville, Virginia

battles linked with shifting economic circumstances, including globalization, immigration and the changing boundaries of legitimate pluralism.
What's driving the wedge between[6] these separate segments of the middle class? While the professional class has fared well[7] in the recovery from the Great Recession[8], the lower middle class has lost ground. Wages are stagnating for middle and low wage workers, union membership and its traditional benefits are on the decline, income inequality is on the rise, and manufacturing jobs have been lost to technology and other countries. Thus those in the lower end of the middle class have grown increasingly estranged from their counterparts in the professional class as they have watched their opportunities and hopes for a better life grow more distant and, in some cases, disappear.
What is more, these members of the lower middle class see many of the values and beliefs they live by — once perceived as honorable in their own communities

---

Annotations
[1] Several hundreds of extreme right-wing demonstrators assembled on 11/12 August 2017 in Charlottesville, Virginia after the city council decided to demolish a statue of Confederate general Robert E. Lee. One attendee of the rally drove a car into a crowd of counterprotesters, killing one and injuring many more.
[2] to **metastasize** When cancer spreads in the body, it metastasizes.
[3] to **sprawl** = wuchern
[4] **Karl Marx** (1818–1883) German economist and political theorist, author of *The Communist Manifesto* and *Das Kapital*.
[5] **cleavage** = here: division
[6] to **drive a wedge between** = to cause division or unfriendliness between
[7] to **fare well** = to be successful
[8] **the Great Recession** = a period of economic decline during the early 21st century, affecting the US mainly from 2007 to 2009

212

— ridiculed as bigoted, homophobic, misogynist, xenophobic and backward[9] by a relatively privileged and powerful elite. According to a study entitled "The Vanishing Center of American Democracy" conducted by the Institute for Advanced Studies in Culture (which I lead), about 8 of 10 Americans with less than a college degree believe that "political correctness is a serious problem in our country, making it hard for people to say what they really think" compared with 5 of 10 of the well-educated. Likewise, 7 of 10 of the less educated believe that "the most educated and successful people in America are more interested in serving themselves than in serving the common good" compared to just over 4 of 10 of college or postgraduate educated[10] Americans. [...]

Another feature of our new culture wars is our crisis of legitimation, the very kind of crisis that troubled postwar[11] German social theorists when they attempted to make sense of the rise of Hitler and prevent a similar historical nightmare from occurring. A growing majority of Americans believe that their government cannot be trusted, that its leaders (and the leadership class more broadly) are incompetent and self-interested, and that as citizens, they personally have little power to influence the powerful institutions or circumstances that shape their lives. Survey research shows that this distrust has grown and even hardened.

Unsurprisingly, this crisis, too, follows a class pattern. The poorly educated are one and a half times more likely than the college educated to hold the highest levels of distrust of the government; nearly three times more likely to be highly cynical of politicians; and over twice as likely to express the highest levels of alienation from the political process. Among the poorly educated who are religiously conservative, the levels of distrust, cynicism and alienation are even higher.

As a result, the credibility of the political establishment, conservative and liberal — its governing philosophies and ideals, its institutional authority, and its leadership — has been depleted. Most significantly, the idea that one can find truth in the words of politicians or that there are even agreed-upon truths to which politicians could be held to account[12] has largely vanished. [...]

Whatever else the culture war of the last several decades accomplished, it unquestionably contributed to the intensification of this legitimation crisis. On any issue, from abortion to same-sex marriage, what was considered reasonable and justifiable governance and policy for one side came to be viewed as irrational and indefensible by the other. The resulting political discourse has been less about persuasion and compromise than about demonizing the opposition through overstatement and hyperbole.

Antagonistic public discourse is hardly new in American history. What is new are assorted media platforms that favor the sensational over the substantive, the superficial over the serious, and the visceral over the thoughtful. To be sure, there are still journalists committed to objectivity and truth. But the relentless pursuit of ratings[13], market share[14], and advertising dollars by the media establishment predisposes it in ways that guarantee a debased public discourse into the future.

We want to believe that the tragic insults to liberal democracy today — whether in the White House or the streets of Charlottesville — are atypical, and that soon, reason and good sense will again prevail. Yet the candidacy and presidency of Donald Trump are not an aberration, but a reflection of the political estrangement of our times. So is the authoritarian impulse we see bubbling up from the fringes[15]. Genuine democratic freedom has become an opportunity for carefully staged political theater, the end[16] of which is the denial of democratic freedom. The culture wars we fought before have given way to[17] a new and worrying confrontation, the stakes[18] of which feel darker and higher.

Annotations
[9] **backward** (*AE* = backwards *BE*) = opposed to change
[10] **college or postgraduate educated** = *mit Hochschulabschluss*
[11] **postwar** = refers to the period after the Second World War
[12] to **hold** sb **to account** = to hold sb responsible
[13] **ratings** = *Einschaltquoten*
[14] **market share** = *Marktanteil*
[15] **the fringes** = *here:* the political extremes
[16] **end** = *here:* goal
[17] to **give way to** = to be replaced by
[18] **stakes** = the things that can be gained or lost

Facts **Part C:** African American experiences

Webcode
You can download a word list for Part C here:
WES-73644-085

African Americans and the struggle for equality

Read the text on African Americans and their struggle for equality (pp. 214-215).

Signing of the Declaration of Independence, painting by John Turnbull

The Declaration of Independence

The American Declaration of Independence was issued on 4 July 1776. Fifteen months earlier, war had broken out between the American colonies and Great Britain over the question whether the British government could impose taxes on the colonies although they were not represented in the British Parliament. The text of the Declaration was aimed at justifying the break with the monarchy by emphasizing the failure of the monarch to protect the fundamental rights of man. The authors of the Declaration, most prominently Thomas Jefferson, claimed that a king would naturally lose his rights to govern if he attempted to restrict those rights.

Even more revolutionary than independence for many of the colonists were other claims put forward in the Declaration, namely that "all men are created equal" and have "unalienable rights" to "life, liberty and the pursuit of happiness". Many colonists believed that such rights should only be granted to specific people – they certainly did not believe in universal rights. Jefferson himself was a slave owner and his definition of "all men" referred to white property owners. However, the fundamental principles he set down in the Declaration were hugely significant and formed the basis for all claims of equality by following generations.

Slavery and the Civil War (1861-1865)

Within a hundred years, the unity of the American states, as expressed in the Declaration of Independence, was put to a severe test. The American Civil War (1861-65), or War of Secession, divided the new nation. Although there were a number of causes of the war between the Northern (Union) and Southern (Confederate) states, the most fundamental issue was that of slavery.

With the exception of New York City, the institution of slavery had never taken hold in the Northern colonies, because the climate was not favourable to the development of plantation agriculture. During the revolutionary war (1775-83) many slaves had fled their Southern masters to join the British army, with a promise of freedom. Most of the Northern states subsequently abolished slavery. In the Southern states, however, slavery was the basis of power of many of the revolutionary leaders, such as George Washington and Thomas Jefferson. The contradiction between owning slaves and the claims of the Declaration of Independence that "all men are created equal" was solved by denying that slaves were people at all but rather possessions. They were declared to be genetically inferior to white people, in line with racist prejudices.

In the course of the 19th century, thousands of people began to move westwards and take away land of the indigenous Americans to establish farms. These small farmers in the West were critical of slave labour in the South because they feared the competition of cheap labour. Meanwhile, Northern industrialists complained that slavery prevented the spread of factories. The anti-slavery movement gained momentum during this time. Many supporters were ex-slaves who had managed to escape or had been freed at some time. It soon, however, became clear that the South was not going to abolish slavery willingly. In fact the Southern states were keen to increase the number of pro-slavery states in the West. Even if not all of the Republican Party were in favour of abolition, they were determined not to allow slavery to spread any further.

So when the Republican candidate, Abraham Lincoln, was elected president in 1860, South Carolina left the Union and was followed by ten other Southern states. This move led to the start of civil war in April 1861, initially with the intention of winning back the Southern states. However, it soon became clear that only by destroying slavery could the Union be prevented from falling apart. Thousands of slaves fled to the North to fight against their former masters. After the victory of the Union against the Confederacy in 1865 the 13th Amendment to the Constitution finally abolished slavery.

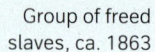

Group of freed slaves, ca. 1863

Part C: African American experiences **Facts**

6

Segregation, Jim Crow and the Ku Klux Klan

The abolition of slavery did not, however, mean equal rights for African Americans. Soon after the end of the war the Southern states passed the so-called Jim Crow laws which effectively segregated black and white people in all areas of society including churches, hospitals, theatres and schools. Black people continued to have the worst jobs and the poorest standard of education. African Americans also found it difficult to register to vote because the majority could not afford to pay the Poll Tax and/or they could not pass the reading test. If a black person actually passed these tests, they would then be threatened and attacked so that they would not vote. This intimidation was often carried out by members of the Ku Klux Klan, an organization which was very active in the South but also in the Midwest and West. They were responsible for the deaths of many black people by lynching, and since they often had connections to influential people in society, it was difficult to stop them. In the state of Georgia, 135 black people were lynched between 1924 and 1925 alone.

The civil rights movement

The Second World War was a turning point in the history of race relations. Many black Americans fought for their country in the war, even though they were segregated from white soldiers in the US army. After the war, President Harry S Truman attempted to pass laws against lynching and the Poll Tax, but his plans were rejected by Congress. He was, however, able to abolish segregation in the armed forces.

In the 1950s and 1960s African Americans took things into their own hands and began to fight for equal rights. The most famous leader of the civil rights movement was a young Baptist[1] minister from Alabama, Dr Martin Luther King, Jr. He was in favour of peaceful protest by means of sit-ins and boycotts and opposed the use of violence. In December 1964 Martin Luther King was awarded the Nobel Peace Prize, but in 1968 he was assassinated by a white man.

Parallel to King's peaceful civil rights movement, Malcolm X became the figurehead of the Black Power movement. He and others believed that peaceful resistance would not lead to equality and advocated more violent means. There were a number of race riots in the 1960s, e.g. in New York in 1964 and in Los Angeles in 1965, in which many people were injured or killed. Malcolm X was shot dead in 1965 but more radical groups such as the Black Panthers continued to fight for equality.

One lasting success of the civil rights movement was a series of important laws that were passed in the 1960s, giving black people legal equality, at least on paper:

The Civil Rights Act (1964) outlawed segregation in schools, public places or jobs.
The Voting Rights Act (1965) outlawed practices such as literacy tests, which had prevented many black people from voting up until this time.
The Fair Housing Act (1968) banned discrimination in housing.

Martin Luther King, Jr.

Annotations
[1] **Baptist** = a branch of protestant Christianity

Black lives matter

Some progress has definitely been made in the situation of black people in America since the 1960s. The "Black is Beautiful" movement of the late sixties and early seventies aimed to make African Americans more proud of being black, and since then more and more black people have enjoyed success in the world of politics, sports and entertainment. One of the greatest success stories has been that of Barack Obama, who became the first black President of the United States in January 2009.

However, racial inequality is still a fact. Poverty is more widespread among black Americans and many black people still face prejudice and discrimination in their everyday lives. Moreover, the number of incidents of police violence against members of the black population, in particular against young black men, has increased greatly in the last few years. As a protest against the police shootings of unarmed black youths, three young black women started the "Black Lives Matter" campaign in 2013 to draw attention to racial discrimination by the police. The campaign has attracted thousands of followers, in particular via social media, including many celebrities.

215

6 Facts — Part C: African American experiences

→ **S6:** How to write a discussion/comment, p. 338

2 Pair work
Take these quotations as a starting point to discuss the question of race relations in America today.

> *We hold these truths to be self-evident, that all men are created equal, that they are endowed by their Creator with certain unalienable Rights, that among these are Life, Liberty and the Pursuit of Happiness.*
> From: The Declaration of Independence, 4 July 1776

> *In a way, the American Negro is the key figure in this country; and if you don't face him, you will never face anything.*
> Author James Baldwin, 1961

> *I was raised by parents who taught me to love and respect people regardless of their race or background, so I am saddened and frustrated by the divisive rhetoric and racial tensions that seem to be getting worse as of late. I know this country is better than that, and I can no longer stay silent. We need to find solutions that ensure people of color receive fair and equal treatment AND that police officers – who put their lives on the line every day to protect us all – are respected and supported.*
> Former basketball player Michael Jordan, 25 July 2016

3
a) Read the beginning of the poem *America* by the African American poet James M. Whitfield and add one more line to the poem.

America (1853)
America, it is to thee[1],
Thou[2] boasted land of liberty,—
It is to thee I raise my song,

Info

James M. Whitfield (1822-1871)
Born in New Hampshire, the African American poet James Monroe Whitfield was active in the abolitionist movement. In many of his poems, he advocates against slavery or criticizes the hollowness of the promises of the American Dream.

Annotations
[1] **thee** (*archaic*) = you (object)
[2] **thou** (*archaic*) = you (subject)

b) Go to p. 392 to find out with what line Whitfield ended his poem. Comment on the main idea of the poem.

4 Group work
Do some research on one of these aspects of the civil rights movement and prepare a short presentation. Include information on the significance of the event/person/group of people for the civil rights movement. Use visuals to make your presentation more attractive.

Court case Brown v. Board of Education of Topeka
Rosa Parks & Montgomery Bus Boycott
Martin Luther King, Jr. and his March on Washington
Little Rock Nine
Sit-ins
Freedom Riders
Malcolm X
Civil Rights Act/Voting Rights Act/Fair Housing Act
Black Panthers

Part C: African American experiences | Texts | 6

Poems about the African American experience

1 Pair work
a) From the five poems on pp. 217-218, choose the poem that appeals to you most. Explain your choice.
b) Outline the theme of the poem.
c) Explain what you learn from this poem about the African American experience.

→ **S10:** How to work with poetry, p. 347

2 CHALLENGE Language awareness
Examine the stylistic devices employed by the poet to enhance the meaning of the poem you have chosen. Consider form, word choice and imagery.

3
Comment on the message of your poem.

→ **S6:** How to write a discussion/comment, p. 338

4
a) Talking to the poem: Write a short text, e.g. a poem, in which you respond to the message of the poem you have worked on.
b) EXTRA Prepare a presentation on your poem. Include some information on the poet and incorporate your short text from a) in your presentation. Give your presentation to the class.

5 EXTRA
a) Practise reading your poem out loud.
b) Present and perform your poem to the class.
c) After all the groups have finished, choose the best performance.

A I, Too (1926)
by Langston Hughes (1902-1967)

I, too, sing America.

I am the darker brother.
They send me to eat in the kitchen
When company comes,
5 But I laugh,
And eat well,
And grow strong.

Tomorrow,
I'll be at the table
10 When company comes.
Nobody'll dare
Say to me,
"Eat in the kitchen,"
Then.

15 Besides,
They'll see how beautiful I am
And be ashamed—

I, too, am America.

B We Own the Night (1961)
by Amiri Baraka (born LeRoi Jones, 1934-2014)

We are unfair[1]
And unfair
We are black magicians
Black arts we make
5 In black labs of the heart

The fair are fair
And deathly white

The day will not save them
And we own the night

Annotations
[1] **fair** = light in colour; just

C Harlem (1951)
by Langston Hughes (1902-1967)

What happens to a dream deferred?

Does it dry up
like a raisin[1] in the sun?
Or fester like a sore—
5 And then run[2]?
Does it stink like rotten meat?
Or crust and sugar over—
like a syrupy sweet?

Maybe it just sags
10 like a heavy load.

Or does it explode?

Annotations
[1] **raisin** = Rosine
[2] to **run** = *here:* to spill a liquid

Part C: African American experiences

D Feeding the Lions (1966)
by Norman Jordan (1938-2015)

They come into
our neighborhood
with the sun
an army of
5 social workers
carrying briefcases
filled with lies
and stupid grins
Passing out relief
10 checks
and food stamps
hustling from one
apartment to another
so they can fill
15 their quota
and get back
before dark.

E Nikki-Rosa (1968)
by Nikki Giovanni (born 1943)

childhood remembrances are always a drag[1]
if you're Black
you always remember things like living in Woodlawn
with no inside toilet
5 and if you become famous or something
they never talk about how happy you were to have
your mother
all to yourself and
how good the water felt when you got your bath
10 from one of those
big tubs that folk in chicago barbecue in
and somehow when you talk about home
it never gets across how much you
understood their feelings
15 as the whole family attended meetings about Hollydale
and even though you remember
your biographers never understand
your father's pain as he sells his stock
and another dream goes
20 And though you're poor it isn't poverty that
concerns you
and though they fought a lot
it isn't your father's drinking that makes any difference
but only that everybody is together and you
25 and your sister have happy birthdays and very good
Christmases
and I really hope no white person ever has cause
to write about me
because they never understand
30 Black love is Black wealth and they'll
probably talk about my hard childhood
and never understand that
all the while I was quite happy

Annotations
[1] to **be a drag** = to be annoying

Part C: African American experiences Texts **6**

Brothers:
Working on a short story

1
Look at the photo and think of a caption.

2
Read the extract from the short story written by James Baldwin in 1957 and outline the situation.

3 Language awareness → SUPPORT D6, p. 317
Analyse the means the author employs to achieve a profound impact on the reader.

4
"And the world ain't changed." (l. 106) Against the background of the short story extract and the situation of African Americans today, discuss this statement.

→ **S13:** Checklist: Analysis – non-fictional texts, p. 354

→ **S6:** How to write a discussion/ comment, p. 338

Sonny's Blues
by James Baldwin

"I want to talk to you about your brother," she said, suddenly. "If anything happens to me he ain't going to have nobody to look out for him."
5 "Mama," I said, "ain't nothing going to happen to you or Sonny. Sonny's all right. He's a good boy and he's got good sense."
"It ain't a question of his being a good boy," Mama said, "nor of his having good sense.
10 It ain't only the bad ones, nor yet the dumb ones that gets sucked under." She stopped, looking at me. "Your Daddy once had a brother," she said, and she smiled in a way that made me feel she was in pain. "You
15 didn't never know that, did you?"
"No," I said, "I never knew that," and I watched her face.
"Oh, yes," she said, "your Daddy had a brother." She looked out of the window
20 again. "I know you never saw your Daddy cry. But I did-many a time, through all these years."
I asked her, "What happened to his brother? How come nobody's ever talked
25 about him?" This was the first time I ever saw my mother look old.
"His brother got killed," she said, "when he was just a little younger than you are now. I knew him. He was a fine boy. He
30 was maybe a little full of the devil[1], but he didn't mean nobody no harm." Then she stopped and the room was silent, exactly as it had sometimes been on those Sunday afternoons. Mama kept looking out into the
35 streets.
"He used to have a job in the mill," she said, "and, like all young folks, he just liked to perform on Saturday nights. Saturday nights, him and your father would drift
40 around to different places, go to dances and things like that, or just sit around with people they knew, and your father's brother would sing, he had a fine voice, and play along with himself on his guitar.
45 Well, this particular Saturday night, him and your father was coming home from some place, and they were both a little drunk and there was a moon that night, it was bright like day. Your father's brother
50 was feeling kind of good, and he was whistling to himself, and he had his guitar slung over his shoulder. They was coming down a hill and beneath them was a road that turned off from the highway. Well,
55 your father's brother, being always kind of frisky, decided to run down this hill, and he did, with that guitar banging and clanging behind him, and he ran across the road, and he was making water behind a
60 tree. And your father was sort of amused at him and he was still coming down the hill, kind of slow. Then he heard a car motor and that same minute his brother stepped from behind the tree, into the
65 road, in the moonlight. And he started to cross the road. And your father started to run down the hill, he says he don't

Annotations
[1] **a little full of the devil** = always causing trouble

know why. This car was full of white men. They was all drunk, and when they seen your father's brother they let out a great whoop and holler and they aimed the car straight at him. They was having fun, they just wanted to scare him, the way they do sometimes, you know. But they was drunk. And I guess the boy, being drunk, too, and scared, kind of lost his head. By the time he jumped it was too late. Your father says he heard his brother scream when the car rolled over him, and he heard the wood of that guitar when it give, and he heard them strings go flying, and he heard them white men shouting, and the car kept on a-going and it ain't stopped till this day. And, time your father got down the hill, his brother weren't nothing but blood and pulp."

Tears were gleaming on my mother's face. There wasn't anything I could say. "He never mentioned it," she said, "because I never let him mention it before you children. Your Daddy was like a crazy man that night and for many a night thereafter. He says he never in his life seen anything as dark as that road after the lights of that car had gone away. Weren't nothing, weren't nobody on that road, just your Daddy and his brother and that busted guitar. Oh, yes. Your Daddy never did really get right again. Till the day he died he weren't sure but that every white man he saw was the man that killed his brother." She stopped and took out her handkerchief and dried her eyes and looked at me. "I ain't telling you all this," she said, "to make you scared or bitter or to make you hate nobody. I'm telling you this because you got a brother. And the world ain't changed." I guess I didn't want to believe this. I guess she saw this in my face. She turned away from me, toward the window again, searching those streets. "But I praise my Redeemer," she said at last, "that He called your Daddy home before me. I ain't saying it to throw no flowers at myself, but, I declare, it keeps me from feeling too cast down to know I helped your father get safely through this world. Your father always acted like he was the roughest, strongest man on earth. And everybody took him to be like that. But if he hadn't had me there-to see his tears!"

She was crying again. Still, I couldn't move. I said, "Lord, Lord, Mama, I didn't know it was like that."

"Oh, honey," she said, "there's a lot that you don't know. But you are going to find out." She stood up from the window and came over to me. "You got to hold on to your brother," she said, "and don't let him fall, no matter what it looks like is happening to him and no matter how evil you gets with him. You going to be evil with him many a time. But don't you forget what I told you, you hear?"

"I won't forget," I said. "Don't you worry, I won't forget. I won't let nothing happen to Sonny."

My mother smiled as though she was amused at something she saw in my face. Then, "You may not be able to stop nothing from happening. But you got to let him know you's *there*."

Being black in Germany: Mediation

→ **S19:** How to improve your mediation skills, p. 364

1 Across cultures

Dealing with the topic "African American experiences" in class and having spent an exchange year in the United States yourself, you have often wondered what life is like in Germany for people from a mixed-race background. Now you have come across the book *Das deutsche Krokodil – Meine Geschichte* by Ijoma Mangold, a well-known German journalist and literary critic – son of a German mother and a Nigerian father. In the chapter *African Americans* he describes his reaction when he is referred to as "Afrodeutscher" for the first time in his life.

You decide to write an article for your American school magazine in which you outline Mangold's personal view and experiences which seem to be very different from those of African Americans in the United States.

Das deutsche Krokodil
by Ijoma Mangold

Wer heute arabisch ausschaut, wird leicht ungnädig angeguckt, eine Form gereizter Gruppenverurteilung, der ich nie ausgesetzt war: Ich gehörte keiner Minderheit an, ich war eine Singularität. Ein
5 Individuum, das wegen eines afrikanischen Vaters, der ansonsten keine Rolle spielte, anders aussah. Dort, wo mir diese Singularität genommen werden sollte, reagierte ich verschnupft.

In den siebziger und achtziger Jahren ist mir, von
10 Nora abgesehen, nur ein anderer Mensch begegnet, der irgendwie auch in meine Kategorie fiel. Er hieß Kofi, besuchte eine andere Schule, und doch war öfter von ihm die Rede, er galt als klug, selbstbewusst, charismatisch, und sein Vater kam aus
15 Ghana. Wir kannten uns nur flüchtig, und vermutlich hielt ich auch eher auf Abstand, aber einmal, es muss um 1989 gewesen sein, kam er auf mich zu und fragte, was *meine Wurzeln* seien. Ich sagte es ihm, und er erzählte daraufhin von einem Club
20 oder Verein, so ganz verstand ich es nicht, in dem sich Afrodeutsche zusammentäten, ob mich das interessieren würde. Wir teilten ja eine Erfahrung.

Das hatte ich noch nie gehört: Afrodeutscher? Was sollte das sein? Kofi war, wie gesagt, ein feiner,
25 keineswegs distanzloser Mensch, aber dass er da plötzlich einen solchen Begriff aus dem Hut zauberte, der auch noch etwas mit mir und meinem Leben zu tun haben sollte, das empfand ich nicht nur als Übergriff, sondern fast als Bedrohung. Ich
30 war doch der, dessen Plädoyers für den Vernunftstaat Preußen alle wohlwollend lauschten, zumal ich weder blond noch blauäugig war und keiner alarmiert sein musste, das könne aus der falschen Ecke kommen. So hatte ich mich eingerichtet. Und
35 jetzt trat Kofi auf und bot mir eine völlig andere Gemeinschaft an, in der ich mich überhaupt nicht wiedererkannte. Wenn man erst einmal begänne, mich als Afrodeutschen zu sehen, wäre ich ja eines, für das ich mich bisher gehalten hatte, ganz sicher
40 nicht mehr, nämlich Deutscher. Was sollte dadurch gewonnen sein? Von Kofis freundlichem Angebot, kam es mir vor, ging eine Gefahr für mich aus. Darauf konnte ich mich auf keinen Fall einlassen, das musste ich von mir weisen. Kofi spürte meine Ver-
45 haltenheit und drang nicht weiter in mich.

Als ich meinen Freunden erzählte, was Kofi gesagt hatte, lachten sie empört auf: Das sei ja völlig lächerlich! Ich sei Deutscher, die Hautfarbe spiele keine Rolle, das hätten Leute wie Kofi nur noch
50 nicht begriffen! Empört waren sie, denke ich heute, weil Kofis Angebot unausdrücklich einen Mangel oder Missstand voraussetzte: Zusammentun musste man sich als Afrodeutscher ja nur, wenn den Afrodeutschen in diesem Land Unrecht ge-
55 schähe. Das sahen meine Freunde (und ich) allerdings keineswegs so: Sie hatten mich ja nie, auch nicht hinter vorgehaltener Hand, als Nichtdeutschen behandelt, sie hatten mich nie ausgegrenzt. Einen Minoritätenschutz hatte ich infolgedessen
60 nicht nötig.

Erst Jahre später erfuhr ich, dass Kofi mit seiner Band Advanced Chemistry einer der Begründer des deutschen Hiphop geworden war. „Fremd im eigenen Land" hieß der Song, mit dem sie 1992 ih-
65 ren Durchbruch feierten. Ich glaube, das Lied war wichtig, um eine bestimmte Erfahrung festzuhalten, und wenn ich es mir heute anhöre, bin ich beeindruckt, wie geschickt Advanced Chemistry die Frage nach dem Anderssein mit den Mordan-
70 schlägen auf die Asylbewerberheime in Rostock-Lichtenhagen verknüpfte, mit welch sicherer Hand sie überhaupt ihr Thema, fremd im eigenen Land zu sein (und als latente Drohung zu fragen, ob die Radiosender dieses Lied wohl spielen werden), er-
75 fasste und pointierte. Aber damals war das einfach nicht meine Erfahrung. Ich hatte mich nie fremd im eigenen Land gefühlt, sondern immer gut aufgehoben.

Oder machte ich mir etwas vor? War ich blind für
80 die Ausgrenzung, die mir widerfuhr? Aus Harmoniesucht? Verdrängte ich das Unangenehme, um glücklich leben zu können? Wollte ich den Rassismus nicht wahrnehmen aus Angst, meine Lebensblase könnte sonst platzen?

85 Manchmal sagten die Leute: „So deutsch wie du – das gibt's ja gar nicht!" Worin sich unausgesprochen und gewiss nur halb reflektiert die moderne Einsicht ausspracht, wonach Deutschsein nicht in den Genen, sondern im Kopf steckt.

90 War ich überassimiliert, deutscher als jeder Deutsche?

Advanced texts | **Part C:** African American experiences

The last day in the life of Martin Luther King: Working with a play

1

The Mountaintop by Katori Hall is a one-act play set in the Lorraine Motel in Memphis, Tennessee. In it, Hall creatively reimagines Martin Luther King's last night. The play deals with a fictitious encounter between King and Camae, a young chambermaid who, towards the end of the play, turns out to be an angel sent by God to take King "to the other side".
Read the first extract from the play and outline what you learn about the situation and the characters.

The Mountaintop
by Katori Hall

Extract 1

Lights up. Night. 3 April 1968. Room 306, the Lorraine Motel, Memphis, Tennessee. The outside street lights project the shadows of rain sliding down the pane on to the walls.

5 *The motel room door creaks open. The rain pours outside. Enter* DR. MARTIN LUTHER KING, JR. *Tired. Overwrought. Wet. He is ready to take his shoes off and crawl into bed. He coughs. He is hoarse. He stands in the doorway, the red and*
10 *yellow motel sign casting a glow on to his face. He yells out of the door into the stormy night.*

KING. Abernathy[1], get me a pack of Pall Malls, when ya go. Naw. Naw. Naw. I said Pall Malls. I don't like those Winstons you smoke. You
15 can call me siddity[2] all you like, I want me a Pall Mall. Pall Malls, man! Don't be cheap. Be back soon, man. I'm wanting one. Bad. That's right … That's right …

He closes the door. He locks the deadbolt. Click. He
20 *chains the door. Rattle. Then he pulls the curtain tight over the window. He walks around in the darkness, but he knows the lay of the room[3] well. He turns on a lone lamp that instantly illuminates the room. Water stains pockmark the walls. Bright*
25 *orange and fading brown sixties decor accent the room. The carpet is the color of bile. He loosens his tie. Unbuttons his shirt. Coughs.*

An opened briefcase lies on one of the two full beds, covered with rumpled peach sheets. He picks
30 *up his sermon papers from the bed.*

(Reading.) 'Why America is going to Hell …'
He goes into the bathroom.
'Why America is going to Hell …'
We hear him urinate. He flushes the toilet. He
35 *walks back into the room.*

They really gonna burn me on the cross for that one. 'America, you are too ARROGANT!'
He goes to the nightstand and checks the empty coffee cups.
40 What shall I say … what shall I say …
He goes to the black rotary phone[4] on the night stand between the beds. He dials.
America … Ameri —
He stops. In complete silence: unscrews the receiver.
45 *Checks the phone for bugs[5]. None there. Screws the receiver back. Checks the night stand. None there. Sighs. Dials again.*

Room service? There's not any more room service tonight? When did it stop? Last week?
50 We were here last week and y'all[6] were still serving room service till midnight. Been always able to get me a cup of coffee when I wanted it. Needed it. Pardon? I just want a coffee. One cup. *(Pause.)* Thank you! Got
55 to do some work before I go to bed. You can bring it on up. Room 306. *(He smiles a broad smile.)* Yes, we call it the 'King-Abernathy Suite' too. I appreciate that, sir. We thank you for your prayers, sir. We're not gonna stop.
60 These sanitation workers gonna get their due. I'm here to make sure of that. Yes, sir! My autograph, sir? *(Beat.)* Uhhh … I don't give those out. I only give thanks. Sorry, sir. Yes. It'll be right up? Five minutes? Thank you
65 kindly. Kindly.

Annotations

[1] **Ralph Abernathy** = civil rights activist and pastor of a Baptist Church in Montgomery, Alabama
[2] **siddity** *(AE, slang, outdated)* = acting as if you are better than someone else
[3] **the lay of the room** = the way the room is arranged
[4] **rotary phone** = old-fashioned phone that works by turning a dial on the front to the right numbers
[5] **bug** = *here:* tiny hidden microphone used to spy on people
[6] **y'all** *(AE, infml)* = you all (used to address a group of people)
[7] allusion to the patriotic song "My country, 'tis of thee" [*archaic* = it is of you]

Part C: African American experiences — **Advanced texts**

He hangs up. He gives the phone a 'what the fuck was that about' look.

'America, America, my country 'tis of thee …'⁷

He begins to take off his shoes.

70 'My country who doles out constant misery —'

He smells them.

Wooooh! Sweet Jesus. I got marching feet and we ain't even marched yet! […]

75 *He throws himself back on the bed. There is a knock at the door. He rushes to go and answer. He undoes the deadbolt, then the chain.*

Reverend, about time, man. The store ain't but down the street —

80 *Enter CAMAE, a beautiful young maid. She stands in the doorway, one hand holding a newspaper over her head to catch the rain, the other balancing a tray with a cup of coffee.*

CAMAE. Room service, sir.

85 KING. That was fast.

CAMAE. Well, I been called Quickie Camae befo'.

He is taken aback, stunned by her beauty. She waits and waits and waits. He snaps out of it.

90 KING. Where are my manners? Come on in.

He steps aside. She walks in. Dripping over everything.

CAMAE. Where would you like me to put this?

KING. On the table over there.

95 *She sets the tray on the downstage table, bending slightly at the waist. KING appreciates his view. Beat. She looks back; he looks away.*

KING. How much is that gonna cost?

CAMAE. Folk down there say it's on the house.
100 For you. It like this yo' house, they say. So you ain't gotta pay them. But you can pay me a tip⁸ for gettin' my press 'n curl⁹ wet out in this rain.

She holds out her hand. He smiles and pulls money
105 *from his billfold.*

KING. You new?

CAMAE. First day, sir.

KING. That's why. I haven't seen you before. Stayed here plenty a' times, but I've never
110 seen your face.

CAMAE. I done seen yo's befo' though.

KING. Oh, have you?

CAMAE. Of course. On the TV down at Woolworth's¹⁰. You like the Beatles.

115 KING. Wish folks would listen to me like they listen to the Beatles.

CAMAE. Mmhm. 'Specially white folks.

KING *laughs, then breaks into a fit of coughs.*

CAMAE. Sound like you needin' some tea, not
120 no coffee. You got a cold?

KING *(straining)*. Just done got to getting hoarse. Shouting.

CAMAE. And carryin' on.

KING. No, not carrying on. Testifying. […]

125 CAMAE. You need anythang else 'fore I go?

KING. Actually … if you got a cigarette …

CAMAE. Cigarettes *and* coffee? That ain't a diet befittin' of¹¹ a preacher.

KING. 'Judge not and ye shall not be judged.'¹²

130 CAMAE. Honey, I hears that. I guess if you was at home you'd be eatin' mo' right.

KING. I suppose. […]

The phone rings.

KING. Excuse me.

135 CAMAE. Well, I'll just be on my —

He motions for her to stay. Then puts on his 'KING voice'.

KING. Dr. King, here. *(Voice shifts.)* Oh, Corrie. Yes. I did call. You didn't pick up. Oh. You
140 were at a meeting. Oh. It went fine. Not as many people there, but … it was enough. I am getting hoarse, I know. Yes, I'm drinking my tea. I'm drinking tea right now.

He looks at CAMAE, who snickers. He motions for
145 *her to be quiet.* […]

2

Take a close look at the stage directions and analyse their function. What do they contribute to the understanding of the scene and the characters? → **S11:** How to work with drama, p. 350

> **Info**
>
> **Stage directions**
> - may include details about the setting and the characters, like their age, race, clothing
> - indicate how the playwright wants his/her lines to be performed (giving the actors information on feelings, body language and facial expressions, for example)

Annotations
⁸ **tip** = *Trinkgeld*
⁹ **press 'n curl** = hairstyle worn by many black women in the US
¹⁰ **Woolworth's** = a chain of department stores
¹¹ **befittin' of** = appropriate for
¹² alludes to a quote from the Bible

Advanced texts — Part C: African American experiences

3 Read extract 2. Outline Camae's ideas and King's reaction to her speech.

Extract 2

KING. So if you were me, what would you do?

CAMAE. Really? You wanna know what lil'[13] old me would do?

KING. Yes.

5 CAMAE. You really wanna know what I'd do?

KING. Yes. I. Do.

Beat.

CAMAE. Can I borrow yo' jacket?

KING. Sure.

10 CAMAE. And yo' shoes?

He hands them to her. She puts them on. She stands on top of one of the beds. KING *looks on in awe. She steadies herself. Throughout her speech* KING *is her congregation, egging her on*[14] *with* 15 *well-timed sayings like,* 'Well!' 'Preach!' *or* 'Make it plain!'

CAMAE. (*with a 'King' voice*) Chuuch! We have gathered here today to deal with a serious issue. It is an issue of great paponderance[15]
20 — you like that? — paponderance! It is a matter of importance more serious than my overgrown mustache: *how do we deal with the white man?* I have told you that the white man is our brother. And he should be
25 treated as such. We touch our brother with the softest of hands. We greet our brother with the widest of smiles. We give our brother food when he is hungry. But it is hard to do this when our brother beats his fist upon our
30 flesh. When he greets us with 'Nigger' and 'Go back to Africa', when he punches us in our bellies swelling with hunger. Abel was slain by his brother Cain[16] and, just like the Biblical times, today the white man is killing
35 his Negro brethren[17], shackling his hands, keeping us from rising to the stars we are boooooouuuuund to occupy. We have walked. Our feet swelling with each step. We have been drowned by hoses. Our dreams being
40 washed away. [...] To this I say, my brethren, a new day is coming. I'm sick and tired of being sick and tired, and today is the day that I tell you to KILL the white man! (*Sotto voce*[18].) But not with your hands. Not with your guns. But
45 with your miiiind! (*Back to regular voice.*) We are fighting to sit at the same counter, but *why*, my brothers and sisters? We should build our own counters. Our own restaurants. Our own neighborhoods. Our own schools. The
50 white man ain't got nothin' I want. Fuck the white man! Fuck the white man! I say, FUCK 'em!

CAMAE *looks to* KING *sooooo embarrassed.*

CAMAE. I AM SO SORRY! Preacher, Kang.
55 Oooooooo. I just can't control my mouth.

KING. Obviously, neither can I. [...]

KING. That's what you would have me say?

CAMAE. Why not?

KING. 'Fuck the white man'? (*Long heavy beat.*) I
60 likes that. I think that'll be the title of my next sermon.

CAMAE. Ooooooo! Folks ain't gone know what to do with that.

KING. Amen! Fuck 'em!

65 CAMAE. I never thought I'd hear you say that!

KING. Ooooo! They got me so tired, Camae. All this rippin' and runnin', rippin' and runnin' around this entire world, and for what? FOR WHAT? White folks don't seem to want to
70 listen. Maybe you're right. Maybe the voice of violence is the only voice white folks'll listen to. (*He coughs.*) I'm tired of shoutin' and carryin' on, like you say. I'm hoarse.

He grabs CAMAE's *flask and drinks.*

75 KING. Sometimes I wonder where they get it from. This hatred of us. I have seen so many white people hate us, Camae. Bombin' folks' homes. Shootin' folks ... blowin' up children.

CAMAE. Make you scared to bring a Negro child
80 into this world the way they be blowin' 'em up.

KING. Yes, Camae! They hate so easily, and we love too much.

CAMAE. Last time I heard you was preachin'
85 'everybody the same'. Negro folk. White folk. We all alike.

KING. Well, at the most human level we are all the same.

Annotations
[13] **lil'** = little
[14] to **egg** sb **on** = jdn anstacheln
[15] **paponderance** = a made-up word
[16] In the Bible, Cain, the first-born son of Adam and Eve, murdered his brother Abel.
[17] **brethren** (*archaic*) = brothers
[18] **sotto voce** /ˌsɒtəʊ ˈvəʊtʃi/ = in a very quiet voice

Part C: African American experiences — **Advanced texts**

CAMAE. What one thing we all got in common?
Beat. He searches hard to come up with an answer.
KING. We scared, Camae. We all scared. Scared of each other. Scared of ourselves. They just scared. Scared of losin' somethin' that they've known their whole lives. Fear makes us human. We all need the same basic things. A hug. A smile. A —
CAMAE. Smoke?
KING *(frustrated).* Which I could use one more of. Where is that niggah wit' my pack? [...]

4

a) Analyse the function of dramatic dialogue and stage directions in this scene. How are they used to characterize Camae and Dr. King and to understand their respective views on race relations.

→ **S11:** How to work with drama, p. 350

Info

Dramatic dialogue

Typical elements of spoken language are:
- short, incomplete sentences (ellipses) to heighten the tension, e.g. in a conflict/in a situation of mutual enthusiasm or support
- unfinished sentences when a person is interrupted or hesitates
- talking at cross purposes to show a lack of understanding/to ignore a person's contribution
- colloquial language
- repetition to emphasize a keyword or make a distinction/to mirror an attempt at finding the right words

Pauses (*beat*):
Depending on the situation or context they can be interpreted as
- hesitation
- speechlessness due to shock or embarrassment
- an attempt to choose words carefully so as not to sound insulting or provocative

Pace:
A quick exchange of short questions and answers or statements and retorts speeds up the pace and might suggest
- liveliness and shared enthusiasm
- a controversy
- an attempt to discourage
- an increasingly tense atmosphere

Extended contributions by the characters slow down the pace and might indicate
- a relaxed/respectful atmosphere
- interest in the story told/the information provided

Register/level of speech:
Formal register with words of French or Latin origin or technical terms and complex sentence structure may be used to:
- suggest a higher social class and/or educated background
- reveal a pretension to superiority

Colloquial language/informal register may suggest:
- a lower social class
- a relationship among friends
- an attempt to bridge the gap between people of different social standing

A change in register might indicate:
- a change in a character's mood
- growing annoyance or disrespect
- imitating/assuming a specific role/parodying/trying to be funny

b) **CHALLENGE** **Language awareness** Analyse the characters' use of language.

5 **CHOOSE**

Comment on Camae's and Dr. King's views on race relations.
OR
Comment on this statement from a review of the play: "Katori Hall's creative reimagining of King's last night has energy, humour and moral gravity."

→ **S6:** How to write a discussion/comment, p. 338

6 **EXTRA** Dramatic reading (group work)

a) In groups of 3 (2 actors + director) and based on your findings from tasks 2 and 4, practise a dramatic reading of one of the two extracts.
b) Perform your dramatic reading to the class.
c) Give feedback and explain which interpretation was the most convincing.

→ **S24:** How to give feedback/peer-edit, p. 372

7 Postcolonial experiences

1888

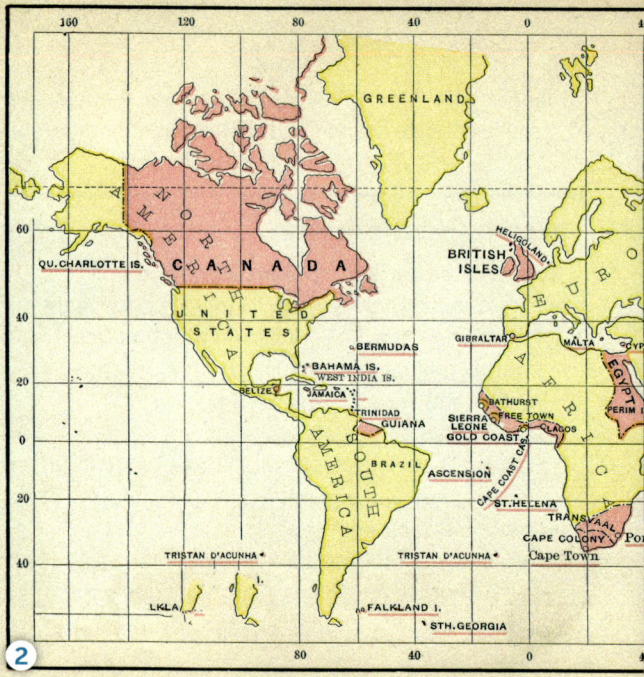

Webcode
You can download a word list for the Intro and the WordPool here:
WES-73644-086

1
Look at the map above and read the quotations.
a) Use the map to explain the quotations.
b) Note down any questions you would like answered.

We hold dominion over palm and pine[1]

from a poem by British author Rudyard Kipling (1865-1936)

... this vast empire on which the sun never sets[2], and whose bounds nature has not yet ascertained.

George Macartney (1737-1806), British statesman and diplomat.

Powerful, prosperous, peace-loving, with the seas all round us and the Royal Navy on the seas ...

Violet Bonham Carter (1887-1969), British politician and author

Rule Britannia!
Britannia, rule the waves!
Britain never never never shall be slaves.

lyrics of a patriotic song written by James Thompson (1700-1748) and Davis Mallet (1703-1765)

Annotations
[1] **pine** = tree that has needles instead of leaves
[2] to **set** (sun) = to go down

2
a) Watch a video clip on the history of the British Empire and try to find answers to any questions you had in 1b.
b) Watch again and put the following sentences in a chronological order.

Webcode
You can find a link to the video here:
WES-73644-087

1. In the 19th century, the British Empire continued to grow in Asia and Africa.
2. In the 17th century, some colonies were set up along the coast of North America and in the Caribbean.
3. The British monarchs Henry VII and Elizabeth I sent ships to explore the coast of North America.
4. By 1922 the British Empire was at its height and ruled over 25% of the world's population.
5. At the end of the First World War, the Treaty of Versailles (1918) awarded further territories to Britain.
6. Having defeated the French and the Dutch in a number of wars, Britain became the most important colonial power in 18th-century Europe.
7. During the American War of Independence, thirteen North American colonies declared their independence from Britain.

Postcolonial experiences | Intro

7

3 1902

3 Think-pair-share
Choose one of the two cartoons 1 and 3 above and analyse it. → **S17:** How to work with cartoons, p. 361
- Note down your own ideas.
- Compare your ideas with those of a partner and reach an agreement on the following points:
  – description of the cartoon
  – message
- Now talk to two students who have chosen the other cartoon and present your results to each other.
- In your groups, discuss the views of colonialism expressed in the cartoons.

4
a) Read the following definition of postcolonialism and explain it in your own words.
  The term postcolonialism refers to the effects of colonization on cultures and societies. On the one hand, the term has a chronological meaning and is used by historians to signal the end of colonialism and the beginning of a new historical period. On the other hand, the scientific field of postcolonial studies explores what is often termed the postcolonial present, i.e. the lasting legacy of colonialism both in the former colonies and the mother countries in contemporary times.

b) From what you know about Great Britain, think of possible legacies of colonialism in Great Britain and in the former colonies today.
  → **SUPPORT** D1, p. 318

Preview

India
The first part of the Theme is about India. In the **Workshop** you will learn how to write an interior monologue.

Nigeria
Part B focuses on Nigeria. In the **Workshop** you will practice analysing characters.

Multicultural Britain today
Part C deals with the legacies of colonialism in Britain. In the **Workshop** you will analyse a screenplay.

THE RISE OF THE BRITISH EMPIRE

At its prime around 1900, the British Empire was the largest empire in history. With the unmatched power of its Royal Navy, Britain was able to exercise control over territories all across the globe and came to be known as 'the empire on which the sun never sets'. During the 17th and 18th centuries, England and later Britain was only one colonial power among many and the emancipation of thirteen North American colonies from British rule in the late 18th century was a massive blow to British dominance. However, after the French defeat in the Napoleonic Wars, Britain was able to rise to almost unrivalled world domination during the 19th century and especially in the age of imperialism in the decades leading up to the First World War.

INDIA

India was Britain's most important colony. At the start of the colonization process stood the British East India Company, a private enterprise that established a number of trading posts in India. However, over time it took control of more and more of the country, enforcing its control by military means. Popular resistance led to a massive rebellion in 1857, which was crushed after a year. As a consequence, the British East India Company was dissolved and the British government took over control of the country.

In 1947, India became independent from Britain. However, unwavering tensions between Hindus and Muslims could not be overcome and led to the partition of the country into two independent countries, India and Pakistan. Today's India is a land of contradictions. The country is marked by extreme disparities: between more traditional rural areas and fast-growing cities, extreme poverty and massive wealth, staggering progress in many areas and the persistence of conservative social norms. One example is the caste system, which sustains the oppression of the Dalit, who are still marginalized. Moreover, women are yet to gain an equal role in society, with female employment levels still very low.

COLONIALISM IN AFRICA

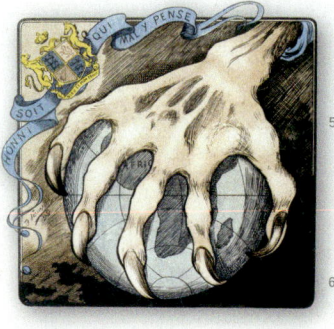

By the 15th century, European powers had already started establishing trading posts along the West African coast. During the second half of the 19th century, the Europeans massively expanded their spheres of influence, finally holding sway over most of the continent towards the end of the century.

In the 1860s, the British tightened their grip over the territory which is now Nigeria so that more and more of the different peoples populating the region had to submit to British dominion. Apart from economic and military endeavours, missionary activities were another crucial factor in the colonization process.

THE LEGACY OF COLONIALISM

After the Second World War, and especially in the 1960s, many colonies gained their independence.

In independent Nigeria, the legacy of colonialism can still be felt in many areas: the ethno-religious tensions between the predominantly Muslim north and the Christian south, as well as the dominance of British and multinational oil companies in the Niger delta region where many people feel exploited and oppressed, are at least in part a consequence of British imperial rule. However, the aftermath of colonialism can also still be felt in Britain. For example, many people have immigrated from the former colonies since the mid-20th century.

Postcolonial experiences — WordPool 7

1
Read the definitions and find the corresponding words highlighted in the text. More words are highlighted than you need.
1. a group within the social hierarchy, e.g. of India
2. a vast territory of different countries which are governed by the same ruler
3. situation or consequence that exists due to events that happened in the past
4. gaining political or legal rights that people did not have before
5. political freedom from the control of another country's government
6. official power to govern a country and its people
7. term referring to the political system of colonialism, often used with a negative connotation
8. inequalities in age, rank, wealth or living conditions
9. period of time after a catastrophic event such as a natural disaster, accident or war, when people still have to deal with the consequences

2
a) Learning a new word can open up a whole range of new words when you consider the word family. Use the given words to extend your vocabulary by filling in the grid. Work with a dictionary if necessary. Sometimes more than one word is possible, especially when prefixes are added.

b) Use six of the new words in meaningful sentences about colonialism or the postcolonial era.

noun	verb	adjective
colony	to colonize	colonial
colonialism	to decolonize	postcolonial
colonization		
...	to progress	...
...	to oppress	...
employment	...	...
resistance	...	...
...	to exploit	...
...	to populate	...
...	to submit	...
...	to marginalize	...

3
Many words are often used in a particular combination. These are called collocations. Find the collocations by combining 1-10 with A-J. In some cases, you will need to insert *of* or *to*.

1	rural	A	influence
2	colonial	B	system
3	to exercise	C	rule
4	sphere	D	norms
5	to hold of/to	E	domination
6	social	F	area
7	caste	G	independence
8	to gain	H	colonialism
9	aftermath	I	sway
10	to submit	J	control

Webcode
You can download the grid for task 2 here: WES-73644-088

4
Read the following text and fill in the missing words from the box in the correct form. There are more words than you need.

During the time of the British Empire, colonies were of great economic relevance: not only did the people have to ⟨1⟩ to British rule, the colonists also ⟨2⟩ the natural resources of the countries. This explains why after gaining ⟨3⟩, many former colonies found it hard to establish a productive industrial sector. As a ⟨4⟩ of colonialism, social injustice often prevailed. Today a new ruling class often profits from globalization, while a great part of the population in many former colonies is ⟨5⟩, especially in ⟨6⟩ areas. As the gap between rich and poor widens, regional ⟨7⟩ provide further obstacles to nation-wide progress and development. In countries that are ⟨8⟩ by many different ethnic and religious groups, a particular attempt to connect to their own cultural heritage is a crucial part of ⟨9⟩.

emancipation
to marginalize
disparities
tension
to submit
to exploit
empire
independence
legacy
to populate
rural

229

Workshop: Step by step — Part A: India

Webcode
You can download a word list for Part A here:
WES-73644-089

Webcode
You can find a link to the video here:
WES-73644-090

→ **S20:** How to listen/watch effectively, p. 366

Step by step Writing an interior monologue

PRE-READING

1

a) Watch the video clip about India. Use adjectives from the box to describe your first impression of the country.

overwhelming	chaotic	exotic	overpopulated
diverse	busy	colourful	awe-inspiring
unpredictable	magnificent	poverty-ridden	wealthy

b) Watch the video a second time and take notes on these themes:
- history
- society
- religion
- culture

2
You are going to work on the short story "Death on Facebook" by Claude Forthomme.

a) **Pair work** Consider the title in the context of Indian society and sketch a plot outline for a short story.

b) **Group work** Discuss your ideas with another pair.

COMPREHENSION

3

a) Read the first part of the short story and describe the conflict between Anamika and her brother.

b) Point out what the conflict reveals about Indian society.

c) Compare your results with your own ideas for a possible plot (task 2).

Death on Facebook
by Claude Forthomme

Extract 1

"Anamika, don't deny it! I saw you on Facebook." He pulled out the pictures he had downloaded and threw them on her desk.

"You were at that despicable party. No mistake, 5 that's you!"

She didn't bother to look. She kept her head low and he glared at her shiny black hair pulled back in a modest bun at the nape of her delicate neck. All he could see of her face was an expanse of white 10 forehead, as smooth as porcelain. At least, she had the decency to wear a sari[1]. It was the one their mother had given her when she had left home to study in Mumbai. He recognized the green silk, it came from the same material their mother used for 15 her own dress.

"Who's this Vikram?" He growled. That was the name that was tagged on his face in the picture. "Vikram Chaudhry is his name, right? I'm waiting for an explanation!"

20 "There isn't any." Her voice was so low he could hardly hear.

"What do you mean? You're sitting on this man's knees. And here you're in his arms about to kiss him. Who's he?"

25 She shrugged. "He's a doctor at the Hospital."

"A doctor? You think that's a good excuse? I bet his real name isn't Chaudhry ..." He paused and glowered before adding with force: "He's trying to hide the fact he's a Dalit[2]. That's what they all do 30 ... He's a Dalit, isn't he?"

No answer.

Her brother sighed. "With that face he's not a Brahmin[3], that's obvious! He looks so ... dark, how could you? Anamika, I can't believe you were in 35 that filthy boy's arms, drinking wine!"

"It wasn't wine. I don't drink."

"That's not the point and you know it. Father and Mother are furious."

"Vikram is perfectly respectable. He does cancer 40 research, he's brilliant. And he wants to marry me!"

"Marry you?" He stopped again and frowned. "Never. He cannot marry you. You're a Brahmin and don't forget it!" A pause. He stared at his big

---

Annotations

[1] **sari** = traditional Indian piece of clothing for women: a very wide, long piece of cloth worn wrapped around the waist and draped over the shoulder

[2] **dalit** = a member of the "untouchable" caste in India, the lowest of the castes

[3] **brahmin** = a member of the priest caste in India, the highest of the castes

sister. He had been so proud of her when she had gone to study in Mumbai – the new generation reaching out to the world, and his sister was part of it. What a mistake ... "Our parents were too good with you, too lenient" he continued. "They should never have let you attend the Hospital College. This fixation of yours with medicine. Ridiculous. It's not the kind of work any woman belonging to our family should ever get into. I told them something bad would happen to you. I was sure of it."

"You told them?" She was amazed. Here was treason! He used to look up to her. Ever since childhood, she had been convinced they were on the same wave length. She didn't recognize her sweet Adinah, the math prodigy, the computer techie, the clever boy in the family. When she had left home four years ago, he was in the habit of navigating the Internet half the night, making their mother angry. She'd admonish him over breakfast. "Adinah, my boy, you're blue under the eyes! You must get some sleep or you'll never grow to be a strong, healthy man like your father!"

She and Adinah would exchange winks behind her back. Their mother was always objecting to new ideas. Not surprisingly: she was the pillar of the home, the guardian of traditions. That was her role in the family.

When Anamika had decided to attend the famous college linked to the Tate Memorial Hospital, all hell had broken loose. As expected, their mother had made it sound like a desperately sinful place on the other side of the planet – as if it were in America.

Fortunately her father had come to the rescue. "With the Deccan Queen train it's only three and half hours away," he pointed out. "Anamika can come home every week-end!" Anamika knew there was an implicit order in that apparently innocent remark.

She had tried to keep up her end of the bargain and come to the family homestead in the old city of Pune as often as she could. But now that college was finished, she had been overwhelmed with work at the Hospital. She welcomed the extra work: she knew it meant her real career had started at last – she was doing what she had always wanted to do. What she was meant to do in her life. It was exhilarating. In the last few weeks, she hadn't found the time to go back home. She hadn't even thought of it.

Then there was Vikram. The work at the hospital and a new life opening up with Vikram, everything came together.

Adinah stood up. "You have to come home with me," he said, his voice cold.

"I won't." He didn't understand, there was just too much to do at the Hospital. It was too important, people were sick, people needed her.

"Oh, but you are coming home. That's why I'm here, you're coming with me. Now."

"I'm not."

He shrugged. "Pack your things. There's no time to lose. The train leaves in an hour. At 5:10 sharp." He looked for her luggage and saw a couple of suitcases piled up in a corner. He threw the bigger one on the bed and opened it with a flourish.

For the first time since he'd come, she turned her face up to him but remained seated on the chair. Her little brother could scream as much as he liked, she wasn't going home with him.

"Get moving, pack!" He was so angry he choked on his words.

She still didn't move. He walked across the room and slapped her on the face, hard.

She stood up and walked away, applying the cool palm of her hand to her burning cheek. It helped. She looked out the window. The panes were dirty but she had a direct view of the street below. Few people wandered about, it was the usual quiet before the rush hour. She loved that street with the small shops.

She loved Mumbai, she was going to miss it.

"Adinah, what has gotten into you? We used to be friends!" she murmured. He repeated, his tone icy. "Get moving. Pack!"

There was no point in answering. Her brother didn't know, couldn't understand what it meant to be committed to work, to fall in love and know this man was the right one, the only one to share everything with. Adinah would say that kind of love was a degenerate Western idea. A Brahmin could never love someone from a lower caste. Adinah was clever with a computer, he could navigate Internet and come across her on Facebook, but he was still a Brahmin at heart. And she had better behave like one too. It was a simple matter of honor.

"What are you looking at?" he asked, his voice cracking with irritation."

"Nothing."

"Ok, if you're not going to pack, I'll do it for you!" he said, grabbing her clothes out of the wardrobe as if they were rags. He threw them in the suitcase and within seconds had made a mess of them. She stared at the rumpled clothes overflowing onto the bed and the floor.

"Let me do it" she said.

Workshop: Step by step Part A: India

ANALYSIS

4

Read the info box on the Indian caste system and explain Adinah's reaction to his sister's relationship with Vikram Chaudhry.

> **Info**
>
> ### The caste system
>
> Despite laws that aim to create equality, the caste system still has a strong impact on Indian society. The system is believed to go back about 3000 years and splits up Hindus into four groups according to their work and birth: the Brahmins (the priestly class); the Kshatriyas (the ruling, administrative and warrior class); the Vaishyas (the class of artisans, traders, farmers and merchants); and the Shudras (manual workers). There are also people who fall outside the system, including tribal people and the Dalits, who used to be known as "untouchables".

> **Preview**
>
> At the end of this Workshop, you will be asked to write an interior monologue from the perspective of Adinah, Anamika's brother. To be able to do this, you will first have to find out what kind of person Adinah is.

WRITING: INTERIOR MONOLOGUE

5

To find out more about Adinah's character, read the first part of the short story again and answer the following questions. In many cases, the answers will not be in the text. This means you have to answer them convincingly using your imagination. You can use some of your answers later as part of your interior monologue.

Tip
Work together with a partner to understand Adinah better. One of you plays the role of Adinah and the other one asks him these questions. When all the questions are answered, switch roles. You can also come up with additional questions of your own.

- What is his relationship with his sister? What was it like in their childhood days?
- How did he feel when Anamika was allowed to go to Mumbai to study medicine? What did he think about his parents' reaction to her plans?
- How did he feel when he spotted Anamika with a strange man on Facebook?
- Why did he show the photo to his parents? Was he sent by them or did he go to Mumbai on his own accord?
- What went through his mind while travelling to Mumbai?
- What makes him so aggressive? Consider his sister's behaviour as a medical student and in this particular situation.
- How does he look upon Vikram and his career?
- What does he not understand, or not want to understand, about Anamika's life?
- How does he define his own role? How does he justify his actions? Will they affect his position in the family?

6

After the quarrel with his sister, the scenes of their confrontation are still vivid in Adinah's mind.

→ **S2:** Checklist: Creative writing, p. 331

a) Write his interior monologue and include:
  - references to his childhood days with Anamika,
  - recollections of his feelings when first seeing her photo on Facebook,
  - his emotions when confronting her,
  - thoughts about his behaviour and his role.

Remember that an interior monologue reveals the thoughts going through a person's mind. It has similar elements to spoken language like questions, elliptical, or unfinished, sentences and exclamations.

→ **S24:** How to give feedback/peer-edit, p. 372

b) **Peer editing** Exchange your text with a partner's. Consider the questions in 5 to decide whether Adinah's views are presented convincingly.

Part A: India   **Workshop: Practice**

Practice: Writing an interior monologue

COMPREHENSION

1
a) Read part 2 of the short story and sum up what happens.
b) Describe how Anamika's mother is presented. Consider both her initial appearance when Anamika returns home and her final sentence.

Extract 2

The train ride was longer than Anamika remembered it. Her brother didn't speak and neither did she. When they reached home, night had fallen.
5 For the first time, it didn't feel like home to her.
The air, redolent[1] with the smell of spice and flowers, was warm and moist as usual at this time of year and it was the only
10 thing she recognized. The house? No, it was not welcoming. She could feel the tension even before crossing the threshold. Her parents both stood at the foot of the stair like guardians of the temple, scowling, their
15 faces a rigid mask of disapproval.
She didn't listen to her father's speech. She closed her eyes. She wished she could close her ears. All she heard was the conclusion. "You will stay in your bedroom until such
20 time as you see the light," he said. "In the meantime, we shall look for a suitable man for you to marry!"
Her brother threw her luggage in her room and her mother locked her in.
25 She had never been locked in her own bedroom before. She had a fit of rage[2]. She grabbed the door knob and shook it with all her might. It wouldn't budge. Then she hammered the door until her fists hurt. She
30 screamed and scratched her face.
If only she'd had the courage, she would have gouged[3] her eyes. She didn't have that kind of courage. She passed her hand on her face and saw it was full of blood. She
35 went to the water basin, washed herself and looked into the mirror. The scratches on her cheeks stood out, wisps of wet hair clung to her face, she looked like a witch.
She couldn't stop her tears. They kept
40 flowing out, in silence. Ah, the angel face Vikram had loved was no more. She would never see him again. What was the point of living?

She hardly ate, rarely moved out of bed.
45 The only person who looked after her was her mother – who always locked the door after tending to her. "Your father has found someone willing to marry you!" she said one day. "You must eat and look good for
50 him!" But Anamika shook her head and wouldn't eat.
Her mother began to worry. The girl was too thin, she looked like a scarecrow. Who would ever accept to take her as a wife?
55 Then she noticed something worse: after a month her daughter still showed no sign of menstruation. Might she be pregnant? What a scandal! No, this was inconceivable.
One morning, she found Anamika retching[4]
60 helplessly over the water basin, her legs shaking. "What's the matter?" she asked.
"I'm feeling nauseous[5] …" whispered Anamika, her forehead glistening with perspiration.
65 "Are you pregnant?"
Anamika shrugged.
She took her daughter by the shoulders and swung her around, like a rag doll. "Are you pregnant?" she screamed. Anamika's silence
70 drove her mad. "You made love with that swine, didn't you?"
"Why won't you answer, you slut! You made love with him, I know you did! I'm a woman, I can tell!"
75 She pushed her hard and Anamika fell on the bed, sprawled across the rumpled sheets. "We had found a husband for you and now you've made it impossible! No one will ever want you, you are as dirty as a Dalit!" She
80 wailed[6], wringing her hands. "How could you, my one and only daughter, the light of my eyes!" and she ran out of the room, locking the door.
What was she to do now? This planned
85 marriage was a good one, the father of the groom had already sent a lavish gift of

Annotations
[1] **redolent** /ˈred(ə)lənt/ = here: filled with a particular smell
[2] **fit of rage** = *Wutanfall*
[3] to **gouge** sb's **eyes out** = *jdm die Augen ausstechen*
[4] to **retch** = *würgen*
[5] **nauseous** /ˈnɔːziəs/ = feeling as if you will be sick
[6] to **wail** = to make a long high-pitched sound

Workshop: Practice — Part A: India

sweets. How was she to tell her husband? There was no question Anamika's father had been too soft with her. It was all his
90 fault. He had let her do whatever she pleased. Anamika wasn't like Adinah who could be both a good Brahmin and a clever student of Western technology. Anamika was bound to trip[7] and fail.
95 And now, there was no coming back to an earlier, happier time. There was no remedy. Or perhaps there was one.

She repaired[8] to the largest room in the house, the one in the center where a sacred
100 picture had been hung high, a six-foot picture of *Venkateshwara*, the Vishnu god. She looked up at him and he frowned down on her, fierce and ready to combat sin. She let the god's vibrations flow down to her.
105 For a long time she stood immobile, waiting for her resolve[9] to gather strength. She could feel it coming.

She said a prayer of thanks and grabbed the biggest silk pillow she could find. She
110 climbed up to her daughter's bedroom, unlocked the door and found the young woman still lying on the bed, facing the wall.

That made it easier.
115 She pushed the pillow down on her head and smothered[10] her. "Your soul is saved", she murmured in her ear.

Annotations
[7] to **trip** = to fall because you caught your foot on sth
[8] to **repair to** = to move to
[9] **resolve** /rɪˈzɒlv/ (*no pl*) = determination
[10] to **smother** sb /ˈsmʌðə(r)/ = to kill sb by covering their face so that they cannot breathe

ANALYSIS

2

Many short stories focus on a single event, introduce a limited number of characters, open abruptly and conclude with a surprise ending. Frequently the incident described represents a turning point in the main character's life. Evaluate how these aspects are realised in "Death on Facebook".

→ **S12:** Checklist: Analysis – prose, p. 352

WRITING: INTERIOR MONOLOGUE

3

After her deed Anamika's mother leaves the room and returns to the sacred picture of the god Vishnu. She keeps thinking about her daughter. Imagine her state of mind and write her interior monologue. Consider her feelings about her daughter and about her deed. → **SUPPORT** D2, p. 318

→ **S2:** Checklist: Creative writing, p. 331

COMMENT

4

"Death on Facebook" was written by Claude Forthomme, a non-Indian writer. She grew up on three different continents and worked as an economist for the United Nations in different countries for 25 years. Bearing in mind the definition of postcolonialism on p. 227, discuss whether her short story can be regarded as postcolonial literature.

→ **S6:** How to write a discussion/comment, p. 338

Part A: India | Texts

Women in India

COMPREHENSION

1
Read the article below and sum up the main information. Focus on these aspects:
- the goal of the project and how successful it has been so far,
- the problems the women working in the train station had to deal with and how they coped,
- the situation at the train station before the women took up their jobs and what has changed since then.

→ **S1:** Checklist: Summary, p. 330

Full steam ahead: India's first women-run train station blazes a trail[1]

Annie Banerji, 10 October 2018, Reuters

As Chandra Kala heard the blaring horns of a train, she quickened her pace, zig-zagged and elbowed across a teeming[2] platform while hauling[3] a sack of wheat, a suitcase and a backpack.

She placed the luggage inside a carriage just as the train began to chug[4] out of Gandhi Nagar railway station, which in February became India's only major terminal where women run the show.

Kala is a rare female porter in the conservative, desert state of Rajasthan in western India, and one of about 40 women holding positions traditionally held by men.

"Earlier, I used to feel very shy," said Kala, a widow with two children. "How should I speak to passengers, how can I lift luggage? It all felt very weird."

She had taken over her husband's porter job when he passed away[5] last year, and she now supports her children from her earnings of about 3,000 rupees ($40) a week.

"It does not feel weird any more," said Kala. "It feels really good."

From ticket sellers and conductors, to station managers and cleaners, these trailblazers are upending sexist views and providing hope in a country where women are slowly vanishing from the workplace.

India is one of the world's fastest growing major economies but the rate of female employment is startlingly low, in large part due to social prejudices and general disapproval of working women.

At least 20 million women – the combined population of New York, London and Paris – have left the workforce of Asia's third-largest economy since 2005, World Bank data shows, with only 27 percent now employed.

The Gandhi Nagar initiative is part of efforts by the state-run railway – India's biggest employer – to empower women in its workforce of 1.3 million people.

Indian Railways officials are planning to replicate the all-women staff model in other stations, according to Tarun Jain, a spokesman for the railways ministry.

The experiment has also created a financial windfall[6], according to Jain, who said Nagar station has experienced "record earnings" since women took over.

Each year, millions of tourists flock to ancient fortresses and camel-back desert safaris in Rajasthan, which is also home to some of India's poorest villages where age-old customs like purdah[7], or veiling[8], often dictate a woman's life.

At Gandhi Nagar station in the state capital of Jaipur, 25 trains pass through every day with about 7,000 commuters – mostly from conservative rural and tribal areas – witnessing women carrying out jobs many have only seen men do before.

Bewildered, surprised and even upset, many gawked at[9] the women when they first took over the station and often undermined their authority, asking for a "male manager", according to Neelam Sharma, a reservation supervisor.

"Some people reacted quite angrily," said Sharma, adding that passengers would say things like, "We do not know how any work will get done here."

However, as the months rolled by, Sharma said commuters were pleased to see improvements

---

Annotations
[1] to **blaze a trail** = to do sth that has never been done before; to set an example
[2] **teeming** = crowded
[3] to **haul** = to drag or carry sth heavy, often with difficulty
[4] to **chug** = to make the sound of an engine
[5] to **pass away** = to die
[6] **windfall** = an amount of money that one gets without expecting it
[7] **purdah** /ˈpɜː(r)də/ = practice of hiding women from the public and requiring them to cover parts of their body
[8] **veiling** = wearing a veil to cover one's face
[9] to **gawk at** sb = to stare at sb in shock

7 Texts — Part A: India

at the station, including faster service, smaller queues, better information and cleanliness.

"Now those same people come to us and really appreciate us and say things like, 'Madam, we really like coming here, our work gets done quicker', and, 'The men did not explain things to us properly,'" Sharma said.

"Passengers are quite happy now." [...]

Members of the team credit this success to their motivation to prove themselves in what is commonly considered a male bastion.

"[We] are giving our 100 percent efforts," said station master Angel Stella, sitting behind a control panel with color-coded track lines and buttons that send signals to incoming trains in order to prevent accidents.

But it was not easy getting to this point, she said. The women, who were mostly transferred from stations in smaller towns, had to overcome their own doubts and fears of running a station by themselves.

They had to get comfortable working night shifts and working in positions of responsibility traditionally held by men, said Stella.

"We were scared and we thought, 'How will we do this?'"

It was also a challenge for those who lived with their children or in-laws[10] to strike the balance between work and family, Stella added.

To ensure their comfort and safety, authorities equipped the station with CCTV cameras, deployed an all-women police force, installed sanitary pad vending machines, and created a temporary daycare.

Female employees said they hope to inspire young girls passing through the station, and trigger a change among people who think a woman's place is at home.

Annotations
[10] **in-law** = sb you are related to through marriage

WRITING AN INTERVIEW

2 Across cultures **Pair work**

Imagine you have the chance to interview one of the women working at the train station. Note down questions for an interview with one of them and also her possible answers. To do so, explore the situations that are described in more detail. You can add a more emotional quality to your answers or include references to life experiences that will make the interview more personal, but your answers must relate to the information provided by the article.

a) To prepare the interview, use your knowledge about the status of women in India to formulate questions.
b) Find convincing answers to your questions in the text. If necessary, use the given details to write a more personal account.
c) Read the first part of the checklist on interviewing strategies and write an introduction to your interview.
d) Read the remaining tips and use them to complete your written interview.
e) **EXTRA** Act out your interview.

Checklist

Interviewing strategies

- ✓ A good interview is the result of serious research and certain conversational strategies. To start the interview the journalist usually uses his/her research to introduce both the topic and the person he/she is going to talk to.
- ✓ Remember that an interview is not simply a series of isolated questions and answers. It is quite similar to a conversation and consequently relies on certain conversational strategies, such as:
  - leading up to a question, e.g. by presenting some facts, referring to a specific situation or incident, giving a provocative or critical account etc.
  - responding to an answer by showing agreement or disagreement, providing support, revealing surprise, doubt or a different view, or by drawing a parallel.
  - linking up to what has been said before when moving on to the next question.
- ✓ Evidently an answer can trigger new questions to clarify certain points. At any rate every answer calls for a response from the interviewer before the next question is presented.

Part A: India | **Advanced texts**

India's caste system today

COMPREHENSION

1
a) Language awareness Read the headline of the article and identify the topic. Explain what the choice of words reveals about the author's attitude.
b) Read the text and determine what type of article it is. Give reasons.

2
a) Describe the situation of dalits in modern India as depicted in the article.
b) Outline the author's plea.
c) Point out how the author links the problem of the caste system to the historical achievements of independence.

MARI MARCEL THEKAEKARA

The Guardian, 15 August 2016

India's caste system is alive and kicking[1] – and maiming[2] and killing

The country is celebrating the 70th anniversary of its independence from Britain. But for its 'untouchables', oppression and
5 violence are still an everyday reality.

It's 15 August 2016, and in India we're celebrating the 70th anniversary of our independence. Flags wave. There's the usual huge Independence Day parade
10 in the capital.
But the celebrations bring out both pride and anguish. All of us imbibed[3] the "freedom struggle" stories as children. We were taught to be proud of our country's prolonged battle
15 against colonialism, of the martyrs who gave their blood for India. We showed the world how to shed the shackles of imperialism. And we spread the doctrine of non-violence at a time when it seemed an impossible
20 dream. What's not to be proud of?
But for those who work with our poorest, most marginalised groups, to ask some loaded[4] questions is almost mandatory. What does freedom mean? Free to be
25 mercilessly thrashed for doing a job thrust forcibly on you, such as skinning dead cows, your destiny because that's the caste you were born into? "It's our curse," dalits have said to me.

30 As I write this, the dalits (India's most oppressed group, our "untouchables") are doing a special "freedom" march to Una, a small town in Gujarat where last month four young men were brutally beaten up
35 with iron rods by a mob of cow vigilantes for skinning dead cows. These young men are from the "chamar" or leather tanning caste. Even now, if ordered to move a carcass – and that means any dead animal
40 ranging from cows to goats to dogs or cats – they are compelled by societal norms to do so, regardless of whether they've earned a doctorate in economics or history. The unwritten rule: once a chamar, always
45 a chamar. Yes, we've come a long way economically, but our feudal system is alive and well. And not just kicking. It's maiming, raping and killing, too.

Annotations
[1] **alive and kicking** = still in existence and doing well
[2] **to maim** = to injure sb severely so that part of their body no longer works correctly
[3] **to imbibe** = to take in enthusiastically
[4] **loaded** = belastet, heikel

7 Advanced texts — Part A: India

As millions of Indians celebrate Independence Day, the Times of India ran a story about Ovindra Pal, a dalit man who despite having a master's in history, was forced to work in his father's trade, skinning bovine carcasses. Understandably, Pal is bitter, as are thousands of dalits who have painstakingly inched up the education ladder but still can't find a job commensurate with their skills and qualifications.

All Indians, whether Christian, Muslim, Parsi[5], Buddhist, Jain[6] or Hindu, carry some vestiges of the caste system in them. Caste and casteism[7] have been carried to every corner of the globe to which the Indian diaspora migrated. Our caste prejudices manifest themselves most clearly in the matrimonial newspaper columns, where prospective brides and grooms of all religions are sought for traditional marriage alliances. Caste and skin colour are the most important criteria for admitting a strange woman into that most intimate circle, the home and the family. The woman who will bring forth children to perpetuate the line must almost always be fair-skinned and of the same caste. The exceptions to this rule are very rare.

My plea this Independence Day is very basic, and echoes that of the marchers in Gujarat for justice and equality. I don't care if people continue to choose whom they eat with or to whom they marry their daughters and sons. Change, after all, comes slowly. But we do need to stop the prevailing culture of total impunity which allows murderers and rapists of our nation's poorest people to flaunt their crimes, knowing they can get away with anything.

In India, justice for the poor and powerless is the exception rather than the rule. Our much maligned media cry themselves hoarse, but the powerful continue to strut around their crime scenes protected by politicians and corrupt bureaucrats.

For how many centuries more will we continue to allow heinous caste crimes to go unpunished? It makes a mockery of everything our freedom fighters died for.

Must dalits fight alone? Or can decent Indians stand with them? Our more enlightened business leaders, socially conscious Bollywood actors, and our few decent politicians should organise a different freedom celebration. We can and must begin a campaign against casteism. Only then, when the medieval practice of untouchability and caste is honestly a thing of the past, can we truly celebrate India's freedom.

Annotations
[5] **Parsi** = member of a Zoroastrian community who migrated to India in the 7th century; Zoroastrianism worships a single creator god and is one of the world's oldest religions
[6] **Jain** = follower of an ancient Indian religion (Jainism)
[7] **casteism** = a hatred or intolerance of people of different (usually lower) castes

ANALYSIS

3
→ **S13:** Checklist: Analysis – non-fictional texts, p. 354

a) Language awareness Analyse the stylistic devices used by the author to describe the freedom fight against British imperialism.
b) Analyse the structure of the article.

COMMENT

4 CHOOSE
→ **S6:** How to write a discussion/comment, p. 338

The author describes the Indian caste system as "maiming and killing". Discuss to what extent this can be applied to the individual as well as to Indian society as a whole.
OR
Discuss to what extent the caste system can be considered an obstacle to true Indian freedom.

Part A: India — Advanced texts

7

Colonial India: Working with a feature film

1 DVD/19

In 1924 the British author E.M. Forster published his novel *A Passage to India* in which he depicts colonial India, where British civil servants enforce British values and culture. As the ruling class, the British mainly set themselves apart in an insular community without any social contact with the Indian population. In 1984 the novel, which is considered one of the most important works in English literature, was made into a film.

Miss Quested, a young school teacher, travels to India with Mrs Moore, to meet her fiancé Ronny, Mrs Moore's son, who is a civil servant in Chandrapore, India. Their arrival in Mumbai (at the time known as Bombay) is a special occasion, since the viceroy, the King's representative in India, is travelling on the same ship.

Watch the first extract from the movie.

a) Describe Miss Quested and Mrs Moore's arrival in Mumbai.
b) Outline how British dominance is presented and characterize the Indian reactions.

→ **S20:** How to listen/watch effectively, p. 366

Webcode
You can find the video here:
WES-73644-091

Info

The British Raj

British colonial rule in India is referred to as the British Raj (raj meaning "rule" in Hindi). The phrase is applied to the period from 1858 to 1947, when Great Britain controlled wide areas of the Indian subcontinent directly, or indirectly through indigenous rulers under British supervision. The time is also referred to as the Indian Empire.

2 DVD/20

Miss Quested and Mrs Moore have to travel to Chandrapore by train. On the train they meet Mr Turton, the chief administrator of Chandrapore, Ronny's superior, and his wife.

a) Watch extract 2 and state what their conversation is about.
b) Point out the different attitudes and expectations concerning British life in India and explain how facial expressions are used to underline them.
c) Describe the long shots outside the train and how they contrast with the presentation of the situation inside the train. Explain how these cinematic devices are used as metaphors for British rule in India.
d) The word "Sahib", master, was especially used as a title of authority for white government officials in India. Identify the speakers of the two statements and discuss the attitudes revealed by them.
   1. "Ronny has become a proper Sahib. Just the type we want …"
   2. "Might Ronny really have turned into a Sahib?"

Webcode
You can find the video here:
WES-73644-092

3 DVD/21

a) Watch extract 3 and describe how Indian and British life in India are contrasted.
b) The two Indians in black suits, Dr. Azis and his friend, have returned from university in England, where they studied medicine and law. Point out how they feel about the British and relate their comments to the presentation of the British in the scene.

Webcode
You can find the video here:
WES-73644-093

4

Discuss why at the time of its publication Forster's novel *A Passage to India* was not received very well by the British public.

→ **S6:** How to write a discussion/comment, p. 338

239

Part B: Nigeria

Nigeria past and present

→ **S15:** How to describe pictures, p. 358

Webcode
You can download a word list for Part B here:
WES-73644-094

1
Nigeria has the highest population in Africa and its economy is largely based on oil. Yet in 2018 the human development index (HID), which is used by the United Nations to measure progress, ranked Nigeria 148 out of 189 countries worldwide. With an estimated 87 million people, i.e. about half the population, living on less than 1.90$ a day, Nigeria now has the largest number of people worldwide living in extreme poverty.

a) Locate Nigeria on the map on the left.
b) Across cultures Describe the photos. Assess what impression they give of Nigeria.
c) Pair work Discuss to what extent the photos reflect the economic situation of Nigeria.

2
a) Read the text on Nigeria's history and draw a timeline of the most important events.
b) Look at the map and describe the most important differences between the regions.

Pre-colonial and colonial times

For centuries, the territory of modern-day Nigeria has been populated by hundreds of different ethnic groups. The biggest among these are the Yoruba (in the west), the Fulani and Hausa (in the north) and the Igbo (in the south-east). Since the unification of Nigeria as a British colony in 1914, these different ethnic groups have been in constant rivalry with each other. They have had different religious beliefs and have generally had very little in common.

In the 19th century, the British began Christian missionary activity in Southern Nigeria, which led to the Christianisation of large parts of the Igbo and Yoruba populations. The missionaries built schools in the area and sent teachers to help with reading and writing. However, at the same time the missionaries imposed their language and culture on the indigenous population, which helped to destroy parts of the native social structure.

By the end of the 19th century, Britain controlled the whole of the territory which makes up modern-day Nigeria, but keeping the vast territory under control remained a major problem. Only by introducing "indirect rule", where local chiefs maintained considerable power, was it possible to appease the north. Meanwhile, in the south the British government exercised control directly. As a result, the ethno-religious differences between the Muslim north and the Christian south became

Part B: Nigeria Facts

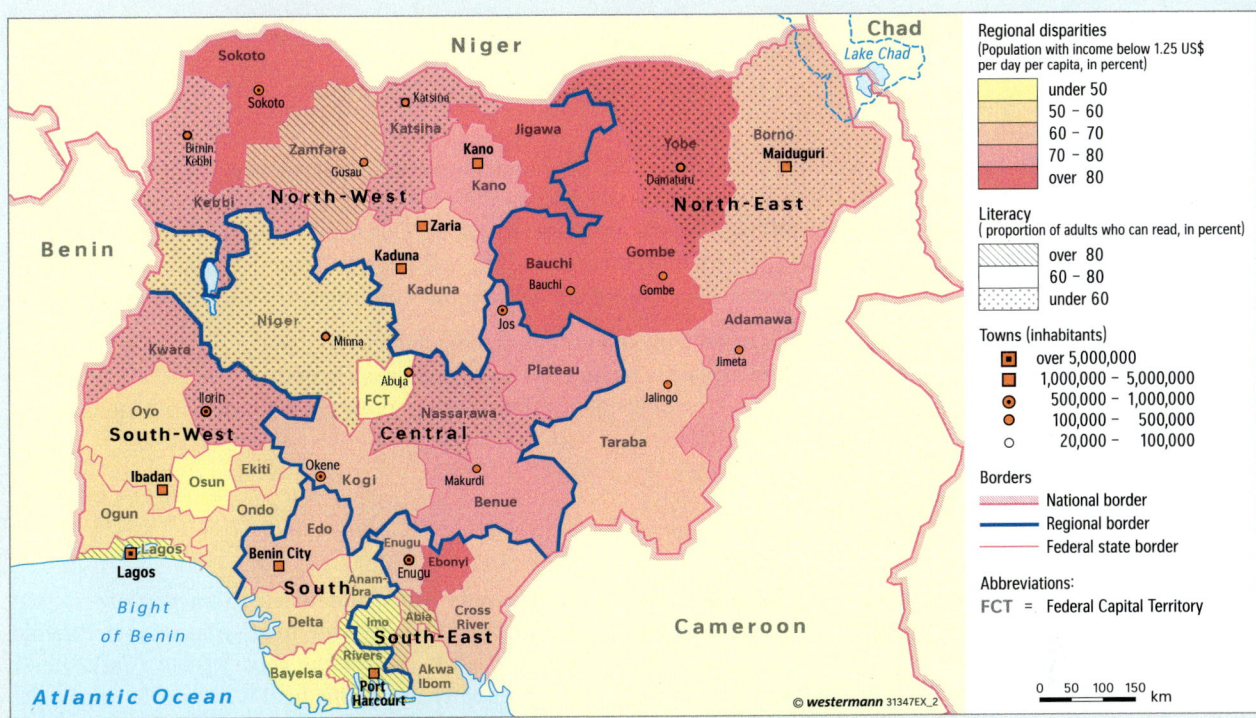

more obvious, with the northern Hausa and Fulani peoples able to keep many of their local social structures and the southern Igbo and Yoruba peoples having to submit to direct British rule.
When oil was discovered in the south-east of the country in 1956, the colonial government granted Shell British Petroleum a monopoly to produce oil. Multinational and, above all, British companies continue to dominate the oil sector in Nigeria to this day.

Independence and ethno-religious conflicts
In October 1960, Nigeria gained full independence from Britain, but hostilities among the different Nigerian ethnic groups have been a feature of independent Nigeria from the start until the present day. Various civil and military governments were unable to ease the ethnic tensions between the north and the south, which led to the massacre of thousands of Igbo people in the north in 1966. This resulted in a mass migration of Igbo people back to their "homeland" in the southeast and eventually triggered the breakaway from Nigeria of the Igbo region calling itself the Republic of Biafra in 1967. After a bloody civil war, the Biafran forces had to surrender in 1970 and the region was reintegrated into Nigeria.

But the problems still remain. There have been frequent changes between military and civil governments, but no government has succeeded in overcoming the ethno-religious hostility between the different groups and assuring a lasting peace and national identity for all Nigerians.
One example of recent religious conflict has been the activities of the radical Islamic group Boko Haram, which has been involved in around 30,000 killings in the last decade. The group's first known attack occurred in 2003 and they have been active ever since, being responsible for kidnappings, killings and political disturbances. The most high-profile act was the 2014 kidnapping of 276 teenage girls from a boarding school in northern Nigeria. This sparked global outrage and a social media campaign (#bringbackourgirls), headed by celebrities like Michelle Obama. UNICEF estimates that Boko Haram has kidnapped more than 1,000 children in north-eastern Nigeria since 2013.
Nigeria has the largest population in Africa and is the seventh most populous country in the world. It offers a bigger market than most African countries put together and is one of the 'Next Eleven' (N-11) countries which are expected to have the largest economies in the 21st century. However, at the present time, the economy cannot create jobs fast enough to keep up with the growth in population. So many highly-skilled Nigerians and students are leaving their country.

7 Workshop: Step by step — Part B: Nigeria

Step by step Analysing characters

COMPREHENSION

1

In her novel *Americanah*, published in 2013, Chimamanda Ngozi Adichie tells the story of Ifemelu and Obinze, who fall in love at university. But as the political situation in military-ruled Nigeria becomes increasingly difficult, Ifemelu emigrates to the US. Due to a stricter US immigration policy following 9/11, Obinze cannot join Ifemelu in the US and goes to Britain instead. When his visa expires, he is forced to return to Nigeria, where he eventually becomes rich and successful.

→ **S6:** How to write a discussion/ comment, p. 338

a) Read extract 1 from the novel and outline Obinze's relationship to Ifemelu.
b) Describe the setting and explain what impression of Nigeria is created.
c) Across cultures Discuss how the description relates to your previous impression of Nigeria.

Americanah
by Chimamanda Ngozi Adichie

Extract 1

When Obinze first saw her e-mail, he was sitting in the back of his Range Rover in still Lagos traffic, his jacket slung over the front seat, a rusty-haired child beggar glued outside his window, a hawker
5 pressing colourful CDs against the other window, the radio turned on low to the Pidgin English news on Wazobia FM, he skimmed the e-mail, instinctively wishing it were longer. *Ceiling[1], kedu?[2] Hope all is well with work and family. Ranyinudo*
10 *said she ran into you some time ago and that you now have a child! Proud Papa. Congratulations. I recently decided to move back to Nigeria. Should be in Lagos in a week. Would love to keep in touch. Take care, Ifemelu.*
15 He read it again slowly and felt the urge to smooth something, his trousers, his shaved-bald head. She had called him Ceiling. In the last e-mail from her, sent just before he got married, she had called him Obinze, apologized for her silence
20 over the years, wished him happiness in sunny sentences and mentioned the black American she was living with. A gracious e-mail. He had hated it. He had hated it so much that he Googled the black American — and why should she give him
25 the man's full name if not because she wanted him Googled? — a lecturer at Yale, and found it infuriating that she lived with a man who referred on his blog to friends as "cats", but it was the photo of the black American, oozing intellectual cool in
30 distressed[3] jeans and black-rimmed glasses, that had tipped Obinze over, made him send her a cold reply. *Thank you for the good wishes, I have never been happier in my life*, he'd written. He hoped she would write something mocking back — it was so
35 unlike her, not to have been even vaguely tart in that first e-mail — but she did not write at all and when he e-mailed her again, after his honeymoon in Morocco, to say he wanted to keep in touch and wanted to talk sometime, she did not reply.
40 The traffic was moving. A light rain was falling. The child beggar ran along, his doe-eyed expression more theatrical, his motions frantic: bringing his hand to his mouth, again and again, fingertips pursed together. Obinze rolled down the
45 window and held out a hundred-naira note. From the rear-view mirror, his driver, Gabriel, watched with grave disapproval.
"God bless you, oga[4]!" the child beggar said.
"Don't be giving money to these beggars, sir,"
50 Gabriel said. "They are all rich. They are using begging to make big money. I heard about one that built a block of six flats in Ikeja!"
"So why are you working as a driver instead of a beggar, Gabriel?" Obinze asked, and laughed, a little too heartily. He wanted to tell Gabriel that his
55 girlfriend from university had just e-mailed him […] His phone rang and for a confused moment he thought it was Ifemelu calling from America.

Annotations
[1] **Ceiling** = nickname Ifemelu had given him when they were a couple
[2] **kedu?** (*Igbo*) = how are you?
[3] **distressed** = made to look old and worn
[4] **oga** = Nigerian word meaning boss or sir

Preview
In this Workshop, you will focus on analysing characters in fictional texts. To do so, you will start by collecting information on the different aspects of a character's personality. Then you will write a characterization.

242

Part B: Nigeria   **Workshop: Step by step**   7

2

The characters in a novel are presented in a way that makes the reader sympathize or even identify with them. There are minor characters who are only sketched rather than presented in detail and there are the protagonists who the author focuses on. These characters are usually complex and develop throughout the novel, whereas minor characters are often rather one-dimensional. Obinze is one of the protagonists. Read extract 2 and sum up what you find out about his life.

→ **S1:** Checklist: Summary, p. 330

Extract 2

On Lekki Expressway, the traffic moved swiftly in the waning rain and soon Gabriel was pressing the horn in front of the high black gates of his home. [...] Inside was the furniture imported from Italy, his wife, his two-year-old daughter, Buchi, the nanny Christiana, his wife's sister Chioma, who was on a forced holiday because university lecturers were on strike yet again, and the new housegirl, Marie, who had been brought from Benin Republic after his wife decided that Nigerian housegirls were unsuitable. The rooms would all be cool, air-conditioner vents swaying quietly, and the kitchen would be fragrant with curry and thyme, and CNN would be on downstairs, while the television upstairs would be turned to Cartoon Network, and pervading it all would be the undisturbed air of well-being. He climbed out of the car. His gait was stiff, his legs difficult to lift. He had begun, in the past months, to feel bloated from all he had acquired – the family, the houses, the cars, the bank accounts – and would, from time to time, be overcome by the urge to prick everything with a pin, to deflate it all, to be free. He was no longer sure, he had in fact never been sure, whether he liked his life because he really did or whether he liked it because he was supposed to.

"Darling," Kosi said, opening the door before he got to it. She was all made-up, her complexion glowing, and he thought, as he often did, what a beautiful woman she was [...]

She laughed. The same way she laughed, with an open, accepting enjoyment of her own looks, when people asked her "Is your mother white? Are you a half-caste[1]?" because she was so fair-skinned[2]. It had always discomfited him, the pleasure she took in being mistaken for mixed-race.

"Daddy-daddy!" Buchi said, running to him in the slightly off-balance manner of toddlers. She was fresh from her evening bath, wearing her flowered pyjamas and smelling sweetly of baby lotion.

"Buch-buch! Daddy's Buch!" He swung her up, kissed her, nuzzled her neck and, because it always made her laugh, pretended to throw her down on the floor.

"Will you bathe or just change?" Kosi asked, following him upstairs, where she had laid out a blue caftan[3] on his bed. He would have preferred a dress shirt or a simpler caftan instead of this, with its overly decorative embroidery, which Kosi had bought for an outrageous sum from one of those new pretentious fashion designers on The Island[4]. But he would wear it to please her.

"I'll just change," he said.

"How was work?" she asked, in the vague, pleasant way that she always asked. He told her he was thinking about the new block of flats he had just completed in Parkview. He hoped Shell would rent it because the oil companies were always the best renters, never complaining about abrupt hikes[5], paying easily in American dollars so that nobody had to deal with the fluctuating naira.

"Don't worry," she said, and touched his shoulder. "God will bring Shell. We will be okay, darling."

The flats were in fact already rented by an oil company but he sometimes told her senseless lies such as this, because a part of him hoped she would ask a question or challenge him, though he knew she would not, because all she wanted was to make sure the conditions of their life remained the same, and how he made that happen she left entirely to him.

Annotations
[1] **half-caste** = person of mixed race or ethnicity
[2] **fair-skinned** = having (relatively) light skin
[3] **caftan** = a long robe or tunic
[4] **The Island** = an area in Lagos separated from the mainland by a channel
[5] **hike** = increase in price

ANALYSIS: CHARACTERIZATION

3

a) Copy the grid on the next page. Use a complete A4 page.
b) Read both extracts from the novel again. Add quotes from the two extracts that match the different aspects of Obinze's personality to the second column of the grid.
c) Explain what the quotes reveal about Obinze (third column).

→ **S12:** Checklist: Analysis – prose, p. 352

243

Workshop: Step by step — Part B: Nigeria

aspect	quote	interpretation
1. Outward appearance physical features/clothes/body language	"He [...] felt the urge to smooth something, his trousers, his shaved-bald head." (extract 1, ll. 15-16)	well-groomed person; gesture suggests need to reassure himself; agitation upon receiving message
2. Character traits e.g. modesty, courage, uncertainty	...	...
3. Behaviour How a character acts gives an impression of his/her motives, abilities or moral standing.	...	...
4. Mood the emotional state of a character	...	...
5. Language e.g. correct or incorrect use of grammar, simple or sophisticated vocabulary, colloquial language; reflects a character's social background, education, attitudes, etc.	...	...
6. Family/social background	...	...
7. Relationship with others how a character interacts with others and is perceived by them	...	...

Webcode
You can download the grid for task 3 here: WES-73644-095

→ **S12:** Checklist: Analysis – prose, p. 352

4 Use your grid and the information from the info box below to write a characterization of Obinze.

> **Info**
>
> ## Types of characterization
> A character in a fictional text may be presented in different ways:
>
> | **Telling technique:** direct characterization | **Showing technique:** indirect (dramatic) characterization |
> |---|---|
> | The reader is told directly and explicitly about the character's looks, traits and attitudes. This can be done by the narrator, the character himself/herself or other characters. | The reader may be able to infer character traits from a character's actions, clothing, body language, interactions with others and the language he or she uses. |
> | **EXAMPLE:** When described as feeling "the urge to smooth something, his trousers, his shaved-bald head" (extract 1, ll. 17-19), Obinze is presented as a well-groomed man who cares about his appearance. | **EXAMPLE:** The description of Obinze as feeling "the urge to smooth something, his trousers, his shaved-bald head" (extract 1, ll. 15-16) suggests a need to reassure himself, which reveals his agitation upon reading Ifemelu's message. |

WRITING: DISCUSSION

→ **S6:** How to write a discussion/comment, p. 338

5 It is not untypical for Nigerian novels to deal with the experience of former expats on their return from the US or Great Britain. Discuss to what extent the question of identity is dealt with in the two extracts from the novel.

Part B: Nigeria   **Workshop: Practice**

7

Practice Analysing characters

PRE-READING

1
Shortly before her return to Nigeria, Ifemelu is at a hairdresser's for African hairstyles where she has her hair braided by Aisha, a young woman from Ghana. Read their conversation and explain Aisha's reaction to Ifemelu's plans.

Extract 3

"I live in Princeton."
"Princeton." Aisha paused. "You student?"
"I've just finished a fellowship[1]," she said, knowing that Aisha would not understand
5 what a fellowship was, and in the rare moment that Aisha looked intimidated, Ifemelu felt a perverse pleasure. Yes, Princeton. Yes, the sort of place that Aisha could only imagine, the sort of place that
10 would never have signs that said QUICK TAX REFUND[2]; people in Princeton did not need quick tax refunds.

"But I'm going back home to Nigeria," Ifemelu added, suddenly remorseful. "I'm
15 going next week."
"To see the family."
"No. I'm moving back. To live in Nigeria."
"Why?"
"What do you mean, why? Why not?"
20 "Better you send money back. Unless your father is big man? You have connections?"
"I've found a job there," She said.
"You stay in America fifteen years and you just go back to work?" Aisha smirked[3].

Annotations
[1] **fellowship** = being employed by a university or another academic institution as a researcher
[2] **tax refund** = Steuerrückerstattung
[3] to **smirk** = grinsen

COMPREHENSION

2
Before she starts her new job in Nigeria, Ifemelu is invited to her new boss's home. Her best friend Ranyinudo accompanies her. Read extract 4 from the novel and outline how Ifemelu perceives Nigeria and its people after her return from the US.

Extract 4

Ifemelu had found the listing[1] on *Nigerian Jobs Online* – "features[2] editor for leading women's monthly magazine". She edited her résumé, invented past experience as a staff
5 writer[3] on a women's magazine ("folded[4] due to bankruptcy" in parentheses), and days after she sent it off by courier, the publisher of *Zoe* called from Lagos. There was, about the mature, friendly voice on the other end
10 of the line, a vague air of inappropriateness. "Oh, call me Aunty Onenu," she said cheerfully when Ifemelu asked who was speaking. Before she offered Ifemelu the job, she said, tone hushed in confidence,
15 "My husband did not support me when I started this, because he thought men would chase me if I went to seek advertising." Ifemelu sensed that the magazine was a hobby for Aunty Onenu, a hobby that meant
20 something, but still a hobby. Not a passion. Not something that consumed her. And when she met Aunty Onenu, she felt this more strongly: here was a woman easy to like but difficult to take seriously.

25 Ifemelu went with Ranyinudo to Aunty Onenu's home in Ikoyi. They sat on leather sofas that felt cold to the touch, and talked in low voices, until Aunty Onenu appeared. A slim, smiling, well-preserved woman,
30 wearing leggings, a large T-shirt and an overly youthful weave, the wavy hair trailing all the way to her back.
"My new features editor has come from America!" she said, hugging Ifemelu. It was
35 difficult to tell her age, anything between fifty and sixty-five, but it was easy to tell that she had not been born with her light complexion, its sheen was too waxy and her knuckles were dark, as though those folds
40 of skin had valiantly resisted her bleaching cream. "I wanted you to come around before you start on Monday so I can welcome you personally," Aunty Onenu said.
"Thank you." Ifemelu thought the home
45 visit unprofessional and odd, but this was a small magazine, and this was Nigeria, where boundaries were blurred, where work blended into life, and bosses were called

Annotations
[1] **listing** = an advert, e.g. for a job
[2] **feature** (journalism) = an in-depth newspaper or magazine article
[3] **staff writer** = sb who is employed by a newspaper or magazine as a writer
[4] to **fold** = to close

245

Workshop: Practice — Part B: Nigeria

Mummy. Besides, she already imagined taking over the running of *Zoe*, turning it into a vibrant, relevant companion for Nigerian women, and – who knew – perhaps one day buying out Aunty Onenu. And she would not welcome new recruits in her home. [...]

A steward in white, a grave, elderly man, emerged to ask what they would drink.

"Aunty Onenu, I've been reading back issues of both *Glass* and *Zoe*, and I have some ideas about what we can do differently," Ifemelu said, after the steward left to get their orange juice.

"You are a real American! Ready to get to work, a no-nonsense person! Very good. First of all, tell me how you think we compare to *Glass*?"

Ifemelu had thought both magazines vapid[5], but *Glass* was better edited, the page colours did not bleed[6] as badly as they did in *Zoe*, and it was more visible in traffic; whenever Ranyinudo's car slowed, there was a hawker pressing a copy of *Glass* against her window. But because she could already see Aunty Onenu's obsession with the competition, so nakedly personal, she said, "It's about the same, but I think we can do better. We need to cut down the profile interviews and do just one a month and profile a woman who has actually achieved something real on her own. We need more personal columns, and we should introduce a rotating guest column, and do more health and money, have a stronger online presence, and stop lifting[7] foreign magazine pieces. Most of your readers can't go into the market and buy broccoli because we don't have it in Nigeria, so why does this month's *Zoe* have a recipe for cream of broccoli soup?"

"Yes, yes," Aunty Onenu said, slowly. She seemed astonished. Then, as though recovering herself, she said, "Very good. We'll discuss all this on Monday."

In the car, Ranyinudo said, "Talking to your new boss like that, ha! If you had not come from America, she would have fired you immediately."

"I wonder what the story is between her and the *Glass* publisher."

"I read in one of the tabloids that they hate each other. I am sure it is man trouble, what else? Women, eh! I think Aunty Onenu started *Zoe* just to compete with *Glass*. As far as I'm concerned, she's not a publisher, she's just a rich woman who decided to start a magazine, and tomorrow she might close it and start a spa."

"And what an ugly house!" Ifemelu said. It was monstrous, with two alabaster angels guarding the gate, and a dome-shaped fountain sputtering in the front yard.

"Ugly *kwa*? What are you talking about? The house is beautiful!"

"Not to me." Ifemelu said, and yet she had once found houses like that beautiful. But here she was now, disliking it with the haughty confidence of a person who recognized kitsch.

"Her generator is as big as my flat and it is completely noiseless!" Ranyinudo said. "Did you notice the generator house on the side of the gate?"

Ifemelu had not noticed. And it piqued her. This was what a true Lagosian should have noticed: the generator house, the generator size.

Annotations
[5] **vapid** /ˈvæpɪd/ = having no intelligence or imagination
[6] to **bleed** = *abfärben*
[7] to **lift** (*infml*) = to steal

ANALYSIS

3 Analyse how Ifemelu is presented in the extract and write a characterization. → SUPPORT D3, p. 319

→ **S12:** Checklist: Analysis – prose, p. 352

COMMENT/CREATIVE WRITING

4 CHOOSE   Across cultures

Before returning to Nigeria, Ifemelu frequently heard her family's worries, "Will you be able to cope?" and had been irritated by the implication that "she was irrevocably altered by America". Discuss to what extent her family's worries were justified.

OR

 Use your knowledge of life in Nigeria and of Ifemelu's story to write an article for a women's magazine in which she describes her return to her home country, the difficulties she encountered and her feelings about her decision.

→ **S6:** How to write a discussion/comment, p. 338

→ **S2:** Checklist: Creative writing, p. 331

Nigerian poetry

1

Literature is often used as a means of expressing and defining identity. For a country like Nigeria, which has seen years of colonialism and is home to about 200 tribes and 300 languages, this is particularly true.

a) Consider the title of the poem "Let Our Voices Ring" by Efe Paul Azino and speculate on its message.

b) Listen to Efe Paul Azino reading his poem. To what extent have your speculations been fulfilled? Examine what the tone reveals about the poet's feelings.

c) Read the poem and decide who the speaker refers to as "we". Prove your point by quoting the respective lines.

Webcode
You can find a link to a recital of the poem here:
WES-73644-096

→ **S10:** How to work with poetry, p. 347

2

a) State which lines impressed you most. Explain why.

b) Explain what impression is conveyed by the image in lines 17–18.

c) Focus on lines 20–25 and 34–36 and outline their meaning in detail.

d) **Language awareness**
Analyse the poetic devices and the choice of words Azino uses in these lines to highlight the wrongs of the colonial past and the need to overcome it.

→ **S10:** How to work with poetry, p. 347

Let our voices ring
by Efe Paul Azino (born 1979)

Let our voices ring
soft and strong
a million rainbow tongues
pushing our songs through the wind
5 let our stories dance out in step with the moon
let them boom from hamlets[1] in Soweto[2]
rise through the sprawls[3] of Cairo
straddle[4] the contradictions of Lagos
let them tell of sweat and fear:
10 of backs bent to carry dreams too heavy for legs to bear
of old men whose visions of the future tether[5] us to the past
let our voices come accompanied by Djembes[6], talking drums and all that jazz
let our stories speak of sex:
of probing[7] tongues & grinding thighs against the Nairobi[8] heat
15 of love that rises from the ashes of defeat
in Kigali[9]
tapestries[10] of our humanity
woven into beautiful colors of difference and diversity
this is who we are
20 children of histories punctuated by conferences
divided by cartographers in Berlin
defended by storytellers in Makarere[11]
united by this struggle to prove, and be
something more than the soft underbelly
25 of a world perched on the edge of a knife
and it's to these voices we turn, time and again
to remind us that we get past the pain
that we have once chiseled out[12] beauty from mountains of self-doubt
through the dark tunnels of despair these stories will lead us out
30 in Twi[13], in Swahili[14], in Yoruba[15]
whatever the languages of our imaginations
let our voices never stop ringing
let our feet dance up spirits
let our pens conjure the ancient wisdom of the ancestors
35 excavate memories to find the civilizations we once built
before the barbarians barged through the doors
for we are a people too,
a universe of multiple dreams written into history
written out of war
40 written to the sound of thunder,
written in lightning
written, by million rainbow voices that never stop ringing

Annotations
[1] **hamlet** = a settlement smaller than a village
[2] **Soweto** = township in South Africa, now part of Johannesburg
[3] **sprawl** = *Ballungsraum*
[4] to **straddle** = to exist on both sides of sth
[5] to **tether** /ˈteðə(r)/= to tie
[6] **Djembe** = a West African drum
[7] to **probe** = to examine
[8] **Nairobi** = the capital of Kenya
[9] **Kigali** = the capital of Ruanda
[10] **tapestry** /ˈtæpɪstri/= a strong cloth with pictures or designs woven into it
[11] **Makarere** = a neighbourhood in Uganda's capital city Kampala
[12] to **chisel out** /ˈtʃɪz(ə)l/= to shape sth (normally made of stone) with a metal tool
[13] **Twi** = dialect spoken in southern and central Ghana
[14] **Swahili** = language spoken in parts of East Africa
[15] **Yoruba** = language spoken in Nigeria and other parts of West Africa

7 Texts — Part B: Nigeria

Webcode
You can find a link to a recital of the poem here:
WES-73644-097

Annotations
[1] to **unravel** /ʌnˈræv(ə)l/ = to come apart
[2] **rock bottom** = the very bottom, lowest possible point
[3] to **discard** /dɪsˈkɑː(r)d/ = to throw away
[4] **scar** = a mark left on your body after an injury has healed

→ **S10:** How to work with poetry, p. 347

3
a) Read the first six lines of the poem "Becoming" by Titilope Sonuga and describe what kind of situation is depicted.
b) Explain what emotions you associate with this kind of situation and give reasons.
c) Read the rest of the poem and examine who is addressed by the speaker.
   → **S10:** How to work with poetry, p. 347

4
a) Explain the overall message of the poem.
b) Analyse how the choice of the initial setting helps the poet to underline that message.
c) Describe a scenario lines 13–17 might refer to.
d) [Language awareness] Analyse the literary devices Sonuga uses to make her message more urgent.

5 [Across cultures]
Write a dialogue between the speaker and the addressee of the poem. Make sure elements of the poems can be recognized in your text.

→ **S2:** Checklist: Creative writing, p. 331

Becoming
by Titilope Sonuga (born 1985)

When the world unravels[1] before you
and even your dreams are crumbling stones
when everything you dare to touch
is set on fire
5 and all around you is ash and smoke
remember this
rock bottom[2]
is a perfect place for rebuilding
Remember that you are your mother's daughter
10 your grandmothers answered prayers
a whole bloodline of women who bend
in response to raging winds
there is nothing broken here
nothing damaged or discarded[3]
15 each scar[4] is a badge of honor
every misstep is a victory dance
waiting to happen
You are a woman becoming
learning the complicated language
20 of forgiveness
the intricate lessons of the universe
Your heart is just a muscle
it needs exercise
and you were born for this sort of heavy lifting
25 you were born one part saint
one part warrior woman
Loving yourself without shame
is the most important thing
you will ever have to fight for

The danger of a single story: Viewing

Webcode
You can find a link to the video here:
WES-73644-098

→ **S20:** How to listen/ watch effectively, p. 366

1
a) Watch the first part of a talk given in 2009 by Nigerian author Chimamanda Ngozi Adichie and say how it is related to African identity.
b) Watch again and collect all the examples of "single stories" Adichie presents.
c) Explain what danger Adichie wants to illustrate with her examples.

2
Sum up this extract from Adichie's talk in your own words.

> Her default position toward me, as an African, was a kind of patronizing, well-meaning pity. My roommate had a single story of Africa. A single story of catastrophe. In this single story there was no possibility of Africans being similar to her in any way; no possibility of feelings more complex than pity; no possibility of a connection as human equals.

3
Analyse the strategies Adichie uses to win over her predominantly white audience and to make them accept her view.

Oil production in the Niger Delta

1

In his novel *Oil on water*, published in 2010, Nigerian author Helon Habila depicts the journey of two Nigerian journalists, Rufus and Zaq, who are trying to find the kidnapped wife of a white oil executive in the oil-polluted Niger Delta. The continued resistance against the oil companies and the pollution have produced a society marked by violence, corruption and the everyday struggle for survival. Rufus has studied journalism and returns from college in Port Harcourt to proudly present his certificate to his parents.

a) Read extract 1 from the novel and outline the living conditions Rufus finds his family in.
b) Describe how their current life has changed both the mother and the father and explain why Rufus's father does not want him to stay.
c) Analyse how the author reveals the effect of social decline in the description of Rufus's mother.

→ **S12:** Checklist: Analysis – prose, p. 352

Info

Oil production in the Niger Delta

The extraction of oil in the Niger Delta region started towards the end of British colonial rule, when Shell was allowed to explore the region for oil. Other multinational companies have followed. Between 1976 and 1991 alone, nearly 3000 oil spills have led to massive environmental damage and robbed local farmers and fishers of their livelihoods. In 1990 inhabitants of the region formed the Movement for the Survival of the Ogoni People (MOSOP) to fight the oil companies. When nine leaders of the movement were put on trial in 1995 and later executed, this radicalized many activists, who formed new more militant groups. These groups try to drive the oil companies away using military force. In recent years their activities have disrupted oil production on a large scale, which has had a massive impact on the Nigerian economy.

Oil on water
by Helon Habila

Extract 1

Here I was with my certificate, going back home, leaving Port Harcourt[1] for good, I hoped. But when I at last located my family, it was not where I had left them, in the
5 town where I was born and raised. I found out that after moving to a succession of smaller houses, they had finally moved to a town called Junction, whose economy rode on the back[2] of the two asphalt roads
10 that neatly divided the town into four equal parts. My mother looked thinner, tired, and she didn't talk very much. She had appeared briefly excited at my return, hugging me and asking me questions about my time
15 in Port Harcourt; then, as if that display of emotion had drained her of her little reserve of energy, she retreated to the kitchen, not to cook but to stare into the flames in the hearth. My father, on the other hand, was
20 full of energy, almost fidgety[3] with it, unable to sit still.
– Come.
He took me to a large barn at the back of the house. Even before he opened the door I
25 could smell the petrol, and when he turned on the light I saw more than ten drums, most of them empty. We sat on two wooden stools in a clear space between two drums.
– Now that you have your certificate, what
30 are your plans?
He hadn't even touched the certificate. He had only glanced at it and nodded distractedly.
– I don't know. I'll look around and maybe
35 open a photo shop –
– No, not in this town. There's nothing here. He pointed at the empty oil drums.
- This is the only business booming in this town. I buy from little children. I buy cheap
40 and I sell cheap to the cars that come here at night. Emmanuel, John's father, is my partner. You remember your friend John? Well, Emmanuel has proved himself to be a true friend. He's the only one of my former
45 colleagues whom I can still call a friend. He came up with this plan. We started the

Annotations
[1] **Port Harcourt** = large city in the Niger Delta region in southern Nigeria
[2] to **ride on the back of** sth = to rely on sth completely
[3] **fidgety** = unable to stay still

7 Advanced texts — Part B: Nigeria

whole thing with his savings. It's not a bad business, really. We get by, we give the police a little something to look the other
50 way, but sooner or later they'll get greedy. They'll arrest us, or take over the whole business themselves. I don't want you to be here when that happens. There's nothing for you here. Go back to Port Harcourt. You're smart. Talk to your master. You'll find
55 something. And when you do, don't forget us. Don't forget your mother and especially your sister.
All I could ask, after he had finished speaking, was, Where do the children get
60 the petrol you buy from them?

– They come to me with their little gallons and I don't ask them where they get it.
In the two days I spent at home before returning to Port Harcourt, I saw how much
65 my father had changed. He had turned his back on religion, and now smoked and drank *ogogoro*[4] almost non-stop. He left home early in the morning in a pick-up truck to go to the bush, where he and his partner bought
70 the petrol from the kids, and he returned home only after midnight, often drunk. The house stank of petrol and cigarettes. He said he smoked just to kill the petrol smell.

Annotations
[4] **ogogoro** = a West African alcoholic drink

2 Language awareness — Pair work

a) Imagine you are a journalist and that you want to write an article about the children who are providing the petrol that Rufus's father is selling. Write a headline and several subheadings for your article. Give special consideration to the wording and the effect you want to create.

b) Explain to another pair what effects you want to create with your headline and subheadings and give each other feedback.

→ **S24:** How to give feedback/peer-edit, p. 372

3

Having returned from his venture to find the kidnapped woman, Rufus meets Mr Floode, her husband, to report back to him.

a) Read extract 2 and describe how Mr Floode experiences the situation.
b) Outline his view on Nigeria, its potential and the violence and compare it to that of Rufus.

Extract 2

A British woman had been kidnapped by rebels in the Nigerian Delta, an attempt to make contact was spoiled by an unplanned military intervention, and now it was
5 doubtful if Isabel was still alive. Some oil companies had already stopped sending expatriate workers to the region, and were even thinking of shutting down their operations because the cost was becoming
10 higher than they could bear, and this possibility was already causing a tension in the oil market, with prices expected to rise in response.
He turned off the TV.
15 – It's like a circus. I can't go out, not even to the office, reporters stalk me everywhere, and the funny thing is I don't even know what to tell them, I don't know what's happened to her. That's why I wanted Zaq
20 to go in there and find out. [...]
– Mr Floode –
– Call me James.
– James, there really isn't anything to report.

– But what did you see? What do you think?
25 Is she alive or not? [...]
He picked up a bell from a side table and rang it loudly. Then, as if unable to keep away from the news, he turned on the TV again. The screen was filled by a blown-up
30 photo of a smiling Isabel, and behind her was a crowded street, a bridge, and far in the distance the iconic Big Ben clock tower. Next, there was a shot of picketing[1] youths holding placards in front of an oil-company
35 building in Port Harcourt. This segment[2] was accompanied by a long, rote-like[3] voiceover about poverty in Nigeria, and how corruption sustained that poverty, and how oil was the main source of revenue, and how
40 because the country was so corrupt, only a few had access to that wealth.
Floode turned off the TV and turned to me.
– Such great potential. You people could easily become the Japan of Africa, the USA
45 of Africa, but the corruption is incredible.
I said nothing, looking to the door to see if

Annotations
[1] to **picket** = to prevent other workers from entering your place of work during a strike
[2] **segment** (news) = a short piece of news
[3] **rote** = sth learnt word-for-word but not understood

250

Part B: Nigeria — Advanced texts

the maid[4] was coming in answer to Floode's ring. He warmed to this topic, scratching his chin vigorously as he spoke.

– Our pipelines are vandalized daily, losing us millions ... and millions for the country as well. The people don't understand what they do to themselves ...
– But they do understand.
– What?
– Have you ever heard of a town called Junction?
– No. I don't think so ...
– I'm from there. Almost five years ago I came home from Lagos after graduating from journalism school and found half the town burned down. The newspapers said the villagers brought it upon themselves by drilling[5] into the pipelines to steal oil ...
– Yes, I have heard of that, isn't that a place called Jesse?
– That is a different place. There are countless villages going up in smoke daily. Well, this place, Junction, went up in smoke because of an accident associated with this vandalism, as you call it. But I don't blame them for wanting to vandalize the pipelines that have brought nothing but suffering to their lives, leaking into the rivers and wells[6], killing the fish and poisoning the farmlands. And all they are told by the oil companies and the government is that the pipelines are there for their own good, that they hold great potential for their country, their future. These people endure the worst conditions of any oil-producing community on earth, the government knows it but doesn't have the will to stop it, the oil companies know it, but because the government doesn't care, they also don't care. And you think the people are corrupt? No. They are just hungry, and tired.
– Hmm, well. I've read about it before. A tragedy. But it does illustrate my point –
– No, actually, it illustrates my point.

Annotations
[4] **maid** = a woman employed to do housework
[5] to **drill** = to make a hole in sth using an electric tool
[6] **well** = a hole in the ground from which you can get water

4
After his meeting Rufus comments on his meeting with Mr Floode. As a critical journalist he uses his own experience to reflect upon Mr Floode's attitude towards Nigeria. Write his commentary.

→ **S8:** How to improve your text, p. 341

Nollywood – Nigeria's dream factory

1
As a popular medium, film fulfills many different functions. Choose the three functions from the list below that you find most relevant. Give examples from your experience to justify your views.
- to educate the viewer by offering role models
- to entertain
- to manipulate people to adopt a certain attitude or behaviour
- to convey an authentic impression of historic events
- to open up new worlds to the audience beyond their personal experience
- to portray social problems
- to confront the audience with the harsh realities of life
- to create empathy and enable the viewer to understand conflicts on an emotional level
- to promote consumerism

2
a) The Nigerian film industry, which produces more than 1500 films per year, is called Nollywood. Explain the term.
b) Watch the trailers of three Nollywood films and discuss which functions each film fulfills.

Webcode
You can find the trailers here:
WES-73644-099

3
In her book *Nollywood – the making of a film empire*, published in 2017, Emily Witt explores the development of the Nigerian film industry from the very beginning to the present. In the introduction to the book, Femi Oduagbemi, the founder of a documentary film festival in Lagos and producer of a popular soap opera, presents his view of the different phases and of their importance for Nigeria.

251

7 Advanced texts — Part B: Nigeria

a) Read the text and explain how Oduagbemi sees the films of colonial times.
b) Describe how the Nigerian film industry started and outine how the difficult political situation and the technological development contributed to its success.
c) Explain to what extent Nigerian films have altered the perception of Nigeria in the world according to Oduagbemi.
d) Consider Oduagbemi's reference to Nollywood as "our voice", "our documentary", "our answer to colonialism". Discuss to what extent the development of Nollywood can be seen as an essential aspect of emancipation.

→ **S6:** How to write a discussion/comment, p. 338

Annotations
[1] **narrative** = story
[2] **to move** = *here:* to sell
[3] **perfect storm** = an unusual or unlikely combination of events that bring a powerful or significant result
[4] **to commission** = to formally ask sb for a piece of their work
[5] **to wipe** = to delete
[6] **principal** = *here:* employer

Up until the last twenty to thirty years the history and culture of African communities were the narratives[1] of the colonialists. Those narratives, quite frankly, beyond not
5 being accurate, beyond not being authentic, were political.

Now: cinema is political. Every cinema is political. The only way cinema works for you is if you are in charge of it. Every
10 colony used cinema – whether in the genre of documentary or the genre of drama – they used cinema to what? To alter behaviour. They used cinema to explain that it was civilised to use knives and forks to
15 eat, as though the natives were not eating before they came. There was a replacement therapy and film was the tool. If you knew a god before they came, cinema was able to give you a greater god, and a better
20 god, and explain to you why your god was rubbish. If you dressed a certain way before they came, they were able to use cinema to assure you that what the queen approved as gentlemanly was a suit. Film allowed you to
25 be able to show, to tell, to wow, to entertain – while indoctrinating. Unless you were in control of that, your story was at risk. Your story was told by someone else.

When Nollywood started out in the 1980s,
30 the executive producers were actually merchants who sold videotapes. Someone had the brilliant idea that the way to move[2] these videotapes was to put something on them. Now, at that time, locally produced
35 soap operas were very popular on NTA, the Nigerian Television Authority. And a videotape salesman named Kenneth Nnebue thought to himself, if I could get one of these guys who made the soap opera at NTA to
40 make me something like a soap opera, then we'll move the sales of the tapes. It turned out to be brilliant. But also at that time, like a perfect storm[3], security was an issue, the military regime was in place, and people
45 wanted to stay at home. The tape players were new, and it was a sign of elitism to be able to watch a film in your own house. The cinemas were going down. We grew up in a time where we could go to cinemas and
50 our mothers didn't care where we were. But cinemas were dying, there was crime in the streets, the military were out there … you know what I mean. So how did the tapes move? The merchants commissioned[4] the
55 soap opera producers: Make me what was essentially an episode, write and direct it for me, and put it on tape. It moved the tapes. What they didn't sell, they wiped[5], and made another film.

60 The way to distribute it was simple: The tapes were simply placed in every electronics shop. It was at that time mostly urban, essentially sold in Lagos. And then, guess what? The house girls and house
65 boys who came from the village and lived with their principals[6] in Lagos found it to be something to watch when madam and *oga* [Yoruba for "sir" or "boss"] were not at home. In that boring period during the
70 day when there was nothing happening, they slotted in the tape. The stories were representations of those things that were present-day realities: big houses, lots of cars, house girls, madam, *oga*. The stories were all
75 about those experiences.

From the 1990s to the 2000s, the industry began to expand. The limits of the experience of the house girl in Lagos were exhausted, but she had a local life in the village. The stories moved to the village; the people who were the consumers began to become the storytellers. And in 1990 to 2000 the whole concept of spiritualism – otherworldliness – emerged. We began to take on the point of view of the house girl, who believed that the unseen controlled the seen. In the village she had mythology, she had *juju*[7] to deal with. You get it? So the stories all became the house girl that brought *juju*, the house girl that took madam's husband.

The way that the movies were distributed also changed. The film left the urban and began to go into the rural areas. The girls, when they go home for their holidays, or to go and see mama that is sick, took along with them videos of Nollywood. By then the story was also now relevant to those down there. They understood the otherworldly thing, they understood all of that. And they embraced it.

By 2000 the VHS[8] was at the end. The VHS machine disappeared. Everything became cheaper. There was this video-CD thing, where you could now have one film, two films, three films, in one. VCDs came and they were cheaper. Everybody had the player, including mama in the village, including the grandma, and then the ownership of Nollywood shifted from the makers to the consumers. And that's when a young man who was working with a new cable[9] company decided that, you know what? This is something that needs to be put on cable. [...]

By bringing it on TV he gave it a value. In giving it value those people who were wiping could licence content. That's when Nollywood became international. [...]

From 2000 to 2010, a few things are beginning to come together. A star system is emerging: looking for storytelling in a formal sort of way is emerging; a class of writers and filmmakers and cameramen. There is a certain consciousness now that what we are doing actually has a meaning. It was at that same time that festivals began to be interested in what is this activity in this Nigeria, and curiosity. Remember, suddenly out of nowhere, a country is producing dramatic features[10] in the thousands. So it turns out that academia is interested. Some festivals are interested. Everybody's asking now, What's this activity?

What they discovered, which was quite shocking, was that it was, how shall I say it? It grew on its own steam. Its originators were Nigerians, its performers were Nigerians, its audience were Nigerians. Why? They all shared a certain one common thing: the Nigerian experience.

So the 2000s were the time where we were all seeking an understanding, both internally and externally, of this thing. There were a lot of crises in trying to define what it is. The people who were doing it didn't have the formal education of film. [...]

They told urban tales people lived and swore by[11]. And the first thing to grow was not their storytelling capacity, it was their audience. That really was what made Nollywood unique across the world. The audience grew, before the birth, before those driving it. The audience embraced it even before the owners knew what it was. And you know what was even more interesting? The audience chose it before international foreign stuff. And that's enough for you to understand my constant conversation about Nollywood being documentary. It was the answer to colonial narratives. [...]

It was from Nollywood you knew about the power structures of our communities, our consideration of spirituality, a very important component of who we are. Respect for our elders. The morality of our environment. How we looked at things like death, things like life. Our respect – all of those things that basically define who we are began to be evinced[12] with those films. So whatever its imperfection, Nollywood, in 2000 to 2010, became our voice, and thus our documentary. We did not need you to create a space for us.

There were a lot of films in Nigeria through the years, but none spoke our voice. None recognized our existence as a distinct civilization, a distinct aspiration. We were just defined in one single ... you know what they call poverty porn? The little boy starving with big inflated[13] stomach defined our narrative. Well guess what? It was from Nollywood that people first realized that we build houses with huge big columns and we could afford it.

Annotations
[7] **juju** = magic
[8] **VHS** = video cassette
[9] **cable** = (*here:*) cable TV
[10] **feature** = *Spielfilm*
[11] to **swear by** sth = to believe in or depend on sth
[12] to **evince** = to express or show clearly
[13] **inflated** = *aufgebläht*

Part C: Multicultural Britain today

Webcode
You can download a word list for Part C here:
WES-73644-100

Immigration to Britain

In the late 19th and early 20th centuries, a number of British colonies started to acquire greater autonomy. In 1931 the British Commonwealth was founded as an organization for these territories to maintain some ties to Britain as they moved towards independence. The Commonwealth took on its present shape after the Second World War following the independence of India and Pakistan.
5 The London Declaration of 1949 modernized the community and declared all member states to be free and equal.

Following the end of the Second World War, Britain was suffering from a massive shortage of workers. The British Nationality Act of 1948 gave all Commonwealth citizens free entry into Britain. This encouraged immigration from Commonwealth countries, particularly from the Caribbean, India
10 and Pakistan.

But not everyone was happy to see the new arrivals. As immigration increased, so did racial tensions, fostered by competition for housing and jobs. Race riots occurred frequently in the 1950s, culminating in the Notting Hill riots in 1958, which lasted a week. Eventually, the government responded with the Race Relations Act (1965), forbidding discrimination on the grounds of skin colour, race, ethnic
15 background or nationality. However, private boarding houses and shops were excluded from this legislation and advertisements for rooms often contained the words "No Coloured".

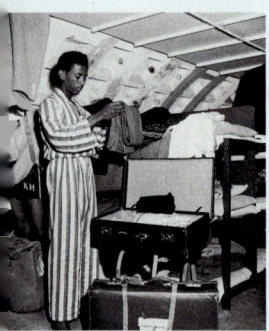

Immigration continued in the 1950s and 1960s and by 1971 the immigrant population numbered over 3 million. In the late 1960s and in the 1970s, East African Asians also sought refuge in Britain. They came from Kenya and Uganda and were no longer welcome in those African countries. The
20 increasing number of immigrants led to right-wing protests led by the Conservative politician Enoch Powell. Although he was expelled from the party, he gained support from around the country, particularly in areas with a high proportion of immigrants.

In 1972 the government introduced new immigration restrictions, whereby British passport holders born overseas could only settle in Britain if they had a work permit and a parent or grandparent born
25 in the UK. This made immigration more difficult for non-white Britons born overseas.

From the 1980s until 2000, refugees began arriving from Eastern Europe in growing numbers. In 2004 ten new countries joined the European Union, which meant that people from these countries could move to Britain, which many did, seeking employment in the UK.

The origin of today's multicultural society in Britain is the immigration of the 20th century. Immigrants
30 did not only come to work, but brought their culture with them. One example is the Notting Hill Carnival, a celebration of Caribbean culture which takes place every year and attracts thousands of people. Descendants of immigrants are also firmly established in all areas of public life, including politics, sports and the media. The current Mayor of London, the Labour politician Sadiq Khan, comes from a working-class British Pakistani family. London alone is home to citizens of over 90
35 countries from all around the world.

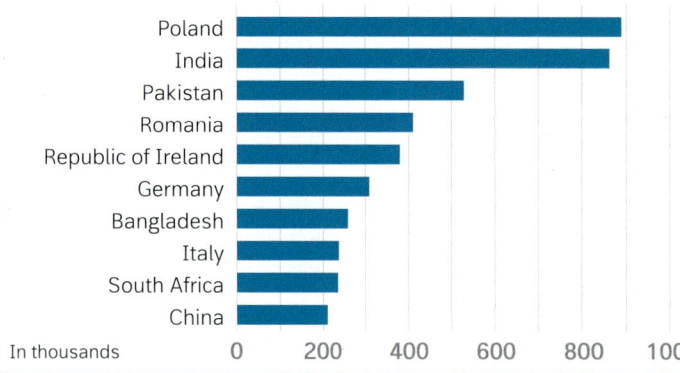

Most common countries of birth for immigrants to the UK 2017/18 (In thousands)

1

a) Read the text about immigration to the UK and interpret the statistic in light of what you have learned.
b) State what surprises you, if anything.
c) **Across cultures** Research the most common countries of birth for immigrants to Germany and compare the data to the numbers for the UK.

→ **S18:** How to analyse statistics, p. 362

Part C: Multicultural Britain today **Workshop: Step by step**

Step by step Working with a screenplay

PRE-READING

1 ● DVD/22

a) Watch the beginning of the film "My son the fanatic" (1997) without the sound and talk about your first impressions.

b) **Group work (6)** Watch it again without the sound and concentrate on one of the characters each:
- Parvez (the Asian father)
- Minoo (the Asian mother)
- Farid (the Asian son)
- Mr Fingerhut (the white father)
- Mrs Fingerhut (the white mother)
- Madelaine (the white daughter)

Based on the facial expressions and gestures of your character, note down your thoughts on how he/she feels in this particular situation.

> **Webcode**
> You can find the video here: WES-73644-101
>
> → **S20:** How to listen/watch effectively, p. 366

> **Preview**
> In this Workshop you will learn how to analyse a screenplay (film script). This will involve looking at
> - the setting/location
> - the plot/storyline
> - the language the characters use
> - character development
> - the creation of suspense

THE SETTING

2

Read the extract from the screenplay, written by Hanif Kureishi, who is also the author of the short story the film is based on. A screenplay is the blueprint that producers, actors and directors use to translate a story from page to screen. It is in many ways similar to the script of a play.
Find information in the screenplay about the setting (place and time) in this scene and describe it in one or two sentences.

> **Language support**
> The opening scene is set/located in ….
> The opening scene of the film takes place in …
> The camera first shows the viewer a shot of ….
> The characters are then shown ..

EXT. FINGERHUT HOUSE. DAY
A large modern house in the country, surrounded by land.
INT. LIVING ROOM. FINGERHUT HOUSE.
5 DAY
In the living room. MRS FINGERHUT, prim¹, snobbish, middle class, has been entertaining the assembled group for some time, as FINGERHUT is late.
10 *The atmosphere is strained. MRS FINGERHUT's daughter MADELAINE, PARVEZ, MINOO and their son FARID – all in their best clothes – sit on hard chairs. PARVEZ is both terrified and ecstatic to be*
15 *there.*
MRS FINGERHUT puts down a photograph album she has been showing everyone.

MRS FINGERHUT
Madelaine was a delightful girl.
20 *(Pause.)*
She still is, of course.
(MADELAINE and FARID, both uncomfortable, glace at one another.)

PARVEZ
25 *(Smiling at her.)*
And a little bit plumpish² at times … as you said, twice.

MINOO
Rice is very good.
30 *(MRS FINGERHUT looks bewildered.)*
For reducing diet.

PARVEZ
Cricket is excellent. Farid was Captain. I

Annotations
¹ **prim** = formal, aware of social expectations
² **plumpish** = not slim, carrying extra body weight

Workshop: Step by step — Part C: Multicultural Britain today

Annotations

[3] **to go whole hog** = to do sth as fully as possible

[4] **kissingly** = schmeichelnd, sich einschleimend

[5] **to make a face** = to show one's feelings (usually disgust or dislike) by changing one's facial expression

warned, don't you ever go professional, career is over in five years. MRS FINGERHUT – Hilda – this boy of ours, I can assure you he is all-round-type; going whole hog[3], but not on field!

MINOO
Oh yes. But in garden?

PARVEZ
(*To* MINOO, *sharply*)
One minute.
(*To* MRS FINGERHUT)
At school he carried the prizes home. Now at college he is … he is top student of year.

MADELAINE
Not difficult.
(MRS FINGERHUT *looks at* MADELAINE, *who scratches*. FARID *smirks. They sit there a moment: tense.*)

EXT. FINGERHUT HOUSE. DAY
Fingerhut's chauffeur-driven car turns into the drive, stopping beside Parvez's battered taxi, which FINGERHUT *regards with aversion as he walks past it. The house dogs rush towards him, barking.*
INT. LIVING ROOM. FINGERHUT HOUSE. DAY

PARVEZ
(*Hushed voice*)
The Chief Inspector.

MRS FINGERHUT
(*Going to the door*)
About time.

PARVEZ
The law never sleeps at night.
(*Looks at* FARID, *who is cringing.*)
Perhaps a career in the police would be guaranteed for you.
Let me mention it to Chief Inspector.

FARID
Papa.

PARVEZ
Leave the matters of business opening to me. Put on cheerful face – blast it! – this is happiest occasion of my life.

MINOO
(*In Urdu, subtitled*)
I want the toilet.

PARVEZ
(*In Urdu, subtitled*)
Not again. They'll think we're Bengalis.

MINOO
They couldn't tell the difference between a Pakistani and a Bengali. We're all –
(MINOO *is halted by the expression on* PARVEZ's *face.*)

FINGERHUT *grandly enters the room and looks around at everyone.* PARVEZ *goes to him, kissingly*[4].)

Cut to FINGERHUT *and* PARVEZ *together.* FARID *watches this, embarrassed and repelled.*

PARVEZ
I will arrange all engagement party details personally. Our tradition is beautiful in this respect.
(FINGERHUT *appears to make a face*[5].)
You enjoy our food when I bring it personally to police station.
(*Leaning closer*)
Chief Inspector, please inform me absolutely in confidence: Farid is top police material, isn't he?

FINGERHUT
Isn't he training to be an accountant?

PARVEZ
Law and order might be more reliable. Crime is everywhere out of control, wouldn't you confirm?
(*Looking at* FARID, *who is cringing.*)
My boy says the same.

FINGERHUT
He would know, would he?

Cut to:

PARVEZ
(*To* MINOO)
Get camera. Now is moment!

Cut to: (*To* FINGERHUT)
Please, sir, would a pose be all right for private use exclusively?
Fingerhut appears to nod.

Part C: Multicultural Britain today — **Workshop: Step by step**

125 (*To MINOO*)
Bring champagne, too.
(*MINOO pulls a camera and a bottle of champagne out of a bag.*)
Cut to: A photograph is being taken, by
130 *the chauffeur, of the whole group. MRS FINGERHUT stands next to PARVEZ, who has his arm around FARID. MADELAINE is beside FARID. MINOO and CHIEF INSPECTOR FINGERHUT.*
135 *We see all the faces. There is a flash. Other photographs, in other combinations. And finally, PARVEZ and FARID together – both drinking champagne, clinking glasses, PARVEZ laughing to himself.*

THE PLOT

3
Summarize what happens in this scene.
a) Begin with an opening sentence which states the general theme. → **SUPPORT** D4, p. 321
b) Note down in your own words what happens.
c) Write a summary of the plot.

→ **S1:** Checklist: Summary, p. 330

ANALYSIS: LANGUAGE

4
Screenplays are visually similar to drama scripts but there are some differences in layout. Read the info box and find examples from the text for each of the terms.

Info

The language and layout of a screenplay

term	function	typescript
scene heading / slugline	tells the reader when the scene takes place (time) and where (location): indoors (INT. = interior) or outdoors (EXT. = exterior)	capital letters; Interior and Exterior abbreviated
action lines	similar to stage directions in a play; can give more information about setting and atmosphere, but also about the characters, their gestures, facial expressions etc.	italics
character names	tell the character when he/she speaks	written in capitals letters with the dialogue lines below
dialogue/lines	the words spoken by the actors	

5 CHALLENGE
Language awareness   There are also differences between drama scripts and screenplays concerning language:
- Drama scripts focus on the words the actors will speak, they are mainly about what the audience will hear.
- Screenplays are mainly concerned with what the audience will see. A lot is shown through the characters' actions and not told through their words. The use of language tends to be economical.

Look carefully at the language in this screenplay and find examples to prove these points.

Workshop: Step by step — Part C: Multicultural Britain today

ANALYSIS: CHARACTERS

6 ● DVD/23

Webcode
You can download this grid here:
WES-73644-102

a) Go through the screenplay and collect information about the characters from the action lines. Then explain their context.

character	action lines	line	explanation
Parvez	terrified and ecstatic	14	• Parvez is terrified because he feels out of his depth in this middle-class home with the snobbish Mrs Fingerhut. • He is ecstatic because …
…	…	…	…

Webcode
You can find the video here:
WES-73644-103

b) In 1b) you speculated on the characters' feelings in this scene. To what extent does the screenplay support your conclusions?

c) Watch the scene again with sound and note down how the actors use the information from the action lines in the screenplay to express their emotions.

→ **S20:** How to listen/watch effectively, p. 366

7 EXTRA CHOOSE

Write a short characterization of one of the characters, using your results for a).

→ **S9:** How to structure a text, p. 344

OR

Language awareness Look closely at Parvez and Minoo's use of language and explain how and why it differs from the other characters in this scene.

8 Across cultures **Hot Seat**

The first scene in the film hints strongly at the cultural differences between the two families.
- With these cultural differences in mind think of questions you would like to ask the characters in this scene.
- Take turns to sit in the 'Hot Seat'.
- The first question asked determines which character you are.
- Answer the questions from that character's point of view.

ANALYSIS: SUSPENSE

9

At the end of each scene, the reader should never quite be able to guess what will happen next. There should be enough suspense to keep them interested.

a) Does Kureishi succeed in creating suspense at the end of this first scene? Give reasons for your answer.

b) Speculate on the story development after this scene. What clues are you given?

COMMENT

10

Discuss to what extent the events depicted in this scene can be seen as a positive example of multiculturalism in Britain. → SUPPORT D5, p. 321

→ **S6:** How to write a discussion/comment, p. 338

Part C: Multicultural Britain today — Workshop: Practice

Practice: Working with a screenplay

PRE-READING

1 Look at these two film stills. Explain what they reveal about the development of Farid's character and his relationship to his father.

→ **S15:** How to describe pictures, p. 358

PLOT

2 Parvez takes Farid to his friend Fizzy's restaurant where he had planned to hold the reception after Farid and Madelaine's wedding.
Read the extract from the screenplay and outline the plot in this scene.

EXT./INT. FIZZY'S RESTAURANT. NIGHT
As FARID and PARVEZ *walk up to and enter the restaurant* PARVEZ *straightens his tie and looks critically at* FARID, *as if he were a schoolboy; he even reaches out and attempts to brush his hair.* FARID *moves away in annoyance.*

PARVEZ
It has been so long since we had a real enjoyable chatterbox[1]!
(*Indicates front of restaurant*)
5   What a magnificent joint! Bloody old Fizzy has done good.

INT. FIZZY'S RESTAURANT. NIGHT
As they go in:

FIZZY
10   (*Approaching them with two glasses of champagne*)
What a handsome big man he has grown into! Is he good?

(FARID *waves away the champagne as*
15   PARVEZ *drinks his.*)

PARVEZ
(*into* FIZZY's *ear*)
Lately he has been having some funny ideas we must straighten out!

20 **PARVEZ**
If I'd know it was free I would have missed lunch!
(*He leans forward and says confidently*)
I tell everyone, eat here and you'll never
25   be constipated[2] again!
(*The* WAITER *comes over with plates.*)

WAITER
We will bring a good selection.

PARVEZ
30   This is my only son.
(*To* FARID)
Have a beer with dad.
(FARID *shakes his head, and the* WAITER *goes.*)

Annotations
[1] **chatterbox** = *here:* chat
[2] **constipated** = *verstopft*

Workshop: Practice — **Part C:** Multicultural Britain today

FARID
35 Don't you know it's wrong to drink alcohol?
(FARID *is looking at him steadily. PARVEZ bangs his glass down on the*
40 *table and laughs dismissively.*)
It is forbidden. Gambling too.

PARVEZ
I am a man.

FARID
45 You have the choice, then, to do good or evil.

PARVEZ
I may be weak and foolish, but please inform me, am I really, according to you,
50 wicked?

FARID
If you break the law as stated then how can wickedness not follow? You eat the pig. In the house.

PARVEZ
55 A bacon butty[3]? Tasty! You loved them too.

FARID
(*A little shiftily*[4])
60 Perhaps. I didn't force mother to eat it.

[…]

FARID
Papa, there is a wise maulvi[5] from Lahore[6]. He is a good man and we
65 have invited him to offer us a little instruction. Can he stay a few days?
(*Without thinking, PARVEZ picks up his whisky and drinks, then raises his drink approvingly at a waiter.*)

PARVEZ
70 In our house?

FARID
(*Excessively polite*)
If you would give permission.
75 (*FARID sees PARVEZ give a little confused and perfunctory nod. Some waiters bring more food and drink. PARVEZ's mouth is messy with food, and he drops keema*[7] *and dall*[8] *onto his*
80 *trousers.*)

PARVEZ
That is what the money was for? You're not going anywhere?

FARID
85 (*Shaking his head*)
He can stay?

PARVEZ
(*Nods*)
Our house is open. Why haven't you
90 told me about this interest?

FARID
(*Shiftily*)
The irreligious find belief difficult to comprehend. Those who love the sacred
95 are called fundamentalists, terrorists, fanatics.

PARVEZ
And that's why you've left Madelaine? Her father, Chief Inspector Fingerhut of
100 the police force –

FARID
(*Sighing*)
Papa –

PARVEZ
105 I don't want this anti-Fingerhut face!

FARID
But you are reminding me of something disgusting! Surely you grasped how ashamed I was, seeing you toadying[9] to
110 Fingerhut.
(*PARVEZ stares at him, a handful of chapatti*[10] *at his mouth.*)

FARID
The girl is okay. But Fingerhut … Do you
115 think his men care about racial attacks? And couldn't you see how much he hated his daughter being with me, and how … repellent he found you? I never want to see those people again.
120 (*PARVEZ is in shock, drinking, shaking his head to clear his brain, and looking around the restaurant, as if for assistance. He is starting to get drunk.*)

PARVEZ
125 (*Watching FARID*)
All right. If this is reality, that I am disgusting, that I have never been a good man, and never done anything

---

Annotations

[3] **butty** = sandwich
[4] **shifty** = untrustworthy
[5] **maulvi** = a Muslim religious scholar
[6] **Lahore** = a city in the Pakistani province of Punjab
[7] **keema** = traditional Indian dish of ground meat, often cooked as a curry
[8] **dall** = traditional Indian vegetarian dish
[9] **to toady to** sb = to flatter sb
[10] **chapatti** = traditional South Asian bread

Part C: Multicultural Britain today — **Workshop: Practice**

worthwhile, I must face it. After all, you have observed me for a long time.
(*Pause.*)
But tonight I am determined to get one good thing. Tell me that at least you are keeping up with your studies.

FARID
Papa, there are suffering men in prison who require guidance.

PARVEZ
What guidance? If they're inside they must be fools!

FARID
I have never met men more sincere and thirsty for the spirit. And accountancy … it's just capitalism and taking advantage. You can never succeed in it unless you go to the pub and meet women.
(PARVEZ *starts to yell. Customers look around at him. Waiters and* FIZZY *stand watching concernedly.*)

PARVEZ
Fool, you're beginning to irritate my arse! What's wrong with women?!

FARID
Many lack belief and therefore reason. Papa, the Final Message is a complete guidance.

PARVEZ
You donkey's dirty arse, this evening you have shown me something –

FARID
This is the true alternative to empty living from day to day … in the capitalist dominated world we are suffering and I am telling you, the Jews and Christers[11] will be routed[12]! You have taken the wrong side!

PARVEZ
One thing, one thing I know –

FARID
Papa, please, it is not too late! I beg you to seek Allah's forgiveness for your mistakes!

PARVEZ
Please, boy, don't go too far with this thing!

FARID
No. It is you who have swallowed the white and Jewish propaganda that there is nothing to our lives but the empty accountancy of things … of things … for nothing … for nothing.

PARVEZ
I am swallowing nothing but Fizzy's dinner, and it will give me indigestion now.
(*By mistake he sweeps a dish from the table.*)
But a wasp has gone into your gullet!
(FIZZY *rushes over to see what the commotion is.*)

FIZZY
Mayor is sitting over there! Eat!

PARVEZ
I have lost my appetite! The boy is massacring my life!
(PARVEZ *is choking and distraught.*)

Annotations
[11] **Christer** = offensive term for a Christian
[12] to **rout** = to defeat, destroy

ANALYSIS

3
a) [Language awareness] Analyse how the language of the screenplay (dialogue, action lines) underlines the development in the relationship between Parvez and Farid.
b) Compare the views of father and son concerning British mainstream society.

COMMENT

4 DVD/24 CHOOSE
Watch part of the scene in the film and comment on both the director's and the actors' interpretations of the screenplay.
OR
CHALLENGE Discuss to what extent film is a suitable medium to highlight the challenges of a multicultural society. You may refer to other films or TV series you know.

Webcode
You can find the video here:
WES-73644-104

Webcode
You can find links to some trailers here:
WES-73644-105

Part C: Multicultural Britain today

Multicultural Britain: Working with cartoons

→ **S17:** How to work with cartoons, p. 361

→ **S24:** How to give feedback/peer-edit, p. 372

1 Pair work (2)
a) Analyse one cartoon each.
b) Present your analysis to your partner and give each other feedback.
c) In class, discuss the way multiculturalism in Britain is expressed in the cartoons.

① "Good morning. Nice queue! You've all passed!"

②

Multicultural Britain: Working with a blog post

1
a) Read the following blog post and choose the best title for it from these three options. Explain your choice.
 1. Why multicultural communities are what makes London (and Britain) great – and why we must protect them
 2. How multicultural communities are disappearing from London and the role of financial development
 3. Where multicultural communities flourish most and increase diversity

b) Read the blog post again and note down the blogger's arguments in favour of a multicultural society.

→ **S6:** How to write a discussion/ comment, p. 338

2
Comment on the blogger's views on the French ban of the burqa.

Part C: Multicultural Britain today — Texts

Jermain Jackman, 27 January 2016

Whilst competing on *The Voice*, Tom Jones gave me the nickname 'The Singing Politician', which is due in no small part to growing up in one of the most multicultural communities on the planet.

I spent my childhood in Hackney[1]: an amazing smorgasbord[2] of ethnicities that includes Irish travellers[3], West Indian, African, Indian, Chinese and White British communities (and that's just the tip of the iceberg). Although pitted as a fairly 'edgy' area by some; I can't imagine a more enriching place in which to learn how to become an adult.

Just popping for a casual shopping trip in the area is like going around the world and back again: from the incredible fusion of West Indian and Western food and delicious world spices at Ridley Road Market, to the fascinating Jewish communities at Stamford Hill. [...]

My family are of Guyanese descent, so naturally I've adopted many cultural traditions from the country. But my family's customs are by no means the only ones that I embraced whilst growing up in the area. For example there's a large Turkish community in the borough[4], and one of my fondest childhood memories is learning how to speak the language at school.

There are several studies suggesting that multiculturalism makes us smarter and more creative; and I can attest that being part of such a varied community provided me with some amazing opportunities whilst growing up – such as being elected in to the Diversity Office for the Hackney Youth Parliament, or learning the ropes[5] at the Artist Development Program at the Hackney Empire[6]. The experience I gained from meeting and talking to such a varied group of people has made me the person I am today: much more than anything that could be gleaned from a text book.

This sense of sharing and learning from the world's cultures applies to the whole of London: from the curry houses of Tooting to the canals of Little Venice. But London (and the country, for that matter) is rapidly changing. And not for the better.

All around the capital, high rise council flats that have been home to so many for so long are now seen as eyesores[7]; whilst new million pound flat developments are being built just around the corner. Whole communities are losing this very sense of multiculturalism that is essential to their identity, as they are priced further and further out of London.

Whilst it's fantastic that there's been so much investment in more disadvantaged boroughs of London, it's hard to deny that this is for the benefit of a privileged few – not the people who have lived there for years and made the area what it is today. Put simply: if an area is going to be developed, it needs to be for the benefit of the whole community, not just those with money to spend.

And there are similar concerns brewing with self-expression too. France's headline grabbing ban on the burqa[8] is prompting debates about whether we should adopt the same policy, for example – so where do we draw the line? When will it become unacceptable to watch a certain film, or like a particular band? We should be embracing these cultural differences (as we have been for years), not shying away from them.

What makes Britain (and London) 'Great' is that it houses such a tolerant culture that accepts and embraces people from all walks of life. It also isn't afraid to adopt traditions and lessons learned from these cultures, and then transform them into something that is inherently 'British'. This very sense of tolerance and diversity is on the line, and as a nation I fear we risk losing ourselves.

Annotations
[1] **Hackney** = an area of London
[2] **smorgasbord** = *here:* variety
[3] **Irish travellers** = ethnic group from Ireland who frequently move from place to place instead of living somewhere permanently
[4] **borough** /ˈbʌrə/ = area or neighbourhood
[5] to **learn the ropes** = to learn how sth works or how to do sth
[6] **Hackney Empire** = theatre in Hackney
[7] **eyesore** = sth very ugly
[8] **burqa** = a piece of clothing worn by women that covers the body and face

Part C: Multicultural Britain today

British intercultural experiences: Watching a video

→ **S10:** How to work with poetry, p. 347

1
Read the poem which is recited in the video you are going to watch and explain its message.

There's a saying at home, that home is where the heart is.
But if home is where the heart is,
Then I must come from a broken home.
For my heart is split, across the world, across the sea.

5 Half in the cold familiar land I'm headed to and half in the land that I am leaving.
The land where I really want to be, the land of family and sun
And of sunlight and sea.

And I know, of course I know
That my heart is beating in my chest.
10 But it feels that there are parts of it
That are separate from the rest.
That I've given pieces away to friends and family
As freely as gifts.

So if home is where the heart is
15 Then my home is split.
'Cos my heart has been given out
Bit by bit.

Webcode
You can find a link to the video here:
WES-73644-106

→ **S20:** How to listen/ watch effectively, p. 366

2
Watch the video and answer the questions below in a few words.

1. What is Zahra Dadd's project about?
2. How does Serena describe British society?
3. What is life about according to Harry (Haroon)?
4. What is important to Saffiyah concerning her cultural heritage?
5. What is the main advantage of having a multicultural background according to Zahra?
6. How does Saffiyah describe the practice of Islam in Pakistan and Bosnia?
7. How does Harry feel when he is with his family?
8. What is Jumoke and Abian's dilemma?
9. How does Zahra define her Britishness?
10. What makes Britain great, according to Jumoke?

Part C: Multicultural Britain today — Advanced texts

A Jamaican immigrant's story

1 Hortense is a young Jamaican woman who marries Gilbert Joseph, a young Jamaican man whom she hardly knows, in order to start a new life in London in 1948.
Read the following excerpt from the novel *Small Island* by Andrea Levy, published in 2004, and summarize briefly what happens to Hortense at the Education Authority.

→ **S1:** Checklist: Summary, p. 330

Small Island
by Andrea Levy

Gilbert Joseph looked wide-eyed on me to exclaim, 'Wait, is that your wedding dress you have on there?'
So I tell him, 'At last I have an occasion that
5 warrants such a fine dress.'
The silly care free countenance slipped from his face with such force it bump on the floor. He make me feel sorry for the words. His bottom lip protruding with their harshness. His eye
10 displaying sorrow. I thought to apologise for that quick tongue. But then he start cussing[1] – sucking on his teeth, and cha, cha, cha on me like a ruffian. So I paid him no mind.
Ah, even the sun was shining. Only a weak light but
15 enough to raise my spirits higher than this stupid man's worry. My two letters of recommendation each contained words that would open up the doors of any school to me. Despite the slow start at the school for scoundrels in Half Way Tree, my
20 headmaster had seen fit to call my teaching skills proficient. Looking for the meaning of the word in the English dictionary, I was honoured to see he thought me expert. Miss Morgan, the formidable principle at my college, declared me highly
25 capable. And a highly capable expert I felt. This was the day I was going to present myself for a position as a teacher at the offices of the education authority and no pained-face, fool-fool man was going to imperil my elation.
30 Gilbert's explanation for how I might travel to this place called Islington took him more than an hour. The man insisted I take a note, and proceeded to deliver his instruction in one babble of turn-left-turn-right-no-wait-go-straight-on. The only lull[2]
35 in this breathless litany occurred when he asked, 'You write this down?' I am not a writing machine. Was it little wonder that when the man finally finish the only note I had written on the paper was the word 'bus'?
40 'This is the only thing you write?' He said.
'You speak too fast,' I told him.

It was with one long, agitated breath that he blew the words into my face,
"Come. I will go with you."
45 Anyone hearing Gilbert Joseph speak would know without hesitation that this man was not English. No matter that he is dressed in his best suit, his hair greased, his fingernails clean, he talked (and walked) in a rough, Jamaican way. Whereas I, since
50 arriving in this country, had determined to speak in an English manner. It was of no use to imitate the way of speaking of those about me, for too many people I encountered spoke as a Cockney[3] would. All fine diction lost in a low-class slurring garble[4].
55 No. To speak English properly as the high-class, I resolved to listen to the language at its finest. Every day my wireless[5] was tuned to the most exemplary English in the known world. The BBC, The Light Programme – *Women's Hour, Mrs Dale's Diary,*
60 *Music While You Work*, and of course the news. I listened. I repeated. And I listened once more. To prove practice makes perfect, on two occasions a shop keeper had brought the item requested without repetition from me. With thanks to that
65 impeccable English evidenced on my wireless, I was understood easily.
But Gilbert was still sucking on his teeth. Every two bells[6] the man said 'cha' and could not, no matter how I tried, stop himself exclaiming, 'Nah, man,'
70 with every utterance. I worried that the refined and educated people at the education authority might look aghast at me if Gilbert Joseph were anywhere near. But I have to confess: 'Hortense, "bus", is not enough instruction to see you delivered safely.' So
75 I agreed. 'Okay,' I told him. 'You may accompany me.'
It was a fine establishment. Brick-brown and ageing with all the dignity of learning. The building stately imposed itself on the rundown street with
80 as imperial a demeanour as Miss Morgan in front of we girls. With trepidation my heart beat like fluttering wings. Gilbert walking in front of me

Annotations
[1] to **cuss** = to swear
[2] **lull** = pause or break
[3] **Cockney** = a person from the East End of London, usually working-class
[4] **garble** = unclear speech
[5] **wireless** = radio
[6] **every two bells** = very often

placed his hand on the shining brass of the door. 'You can leave me now,' I told him.

'What, you no wan' me come in?' The man look on me in that same pained manner.

'No, thank you. I will be fine.'

'I wait here for you, then.'

'There is no need for you to darken up the place. I can find my way now.'

'What is there to find? I get you here.' He was trying my patience. So I told him politely that perchance[7] the education authority would want to show me the school at which I would be working. It might take some time and I did not want to disrupt his day further. The man look on me for a long while. Then, quietly, he said, 'Hortense, this is not the way England work.' I then informed him that a teacher such as I was not someone to be treated in the same way as a person in a low-class job. He just shake his head on me and say, 'You won't listen to me, will you? I wait for you.' There was no persuasion that could dislodge this man from the step. [...]

Three women, sitting neatly at desks perused me as I came through the door. In a puppet dance all three quickly glanced to each other then returned to staring on me.

'Good day,' I said.

Two dropped their heads returning to their business as if I had not spoken, leaving just an older woman to ask, 'Yes, do you want something?' This woman smiled on me – her countenance gleaming with so much joy that I could do nothing but return the welcome. Her beaming smile was so wide I had trouble stretching my own lips to match the delight. She bathed me in this greeting for several moments before breath sufficient enough for a reply returned to me.

'I am a teacher,' I said, intending to carry on with some further explanation. But I was startled to find myself timorous in this woman's friendly presence. My voice faltered into a tiny squeak. I took a moment to cough into my hand. Having composed myself I began again. 'I am a teacher and I understand this is the place at which I should present myself for a position in that particular profession.' Through this woman's warm smile I detected a little confusion. Too well bred to say 'What?' she looked a quizzical eye on me, which shouted the word just as audibly. I repeated myself clearly but before I had completed the statement the woman asked of me sweetly, 'Did you say you are a teacher?'

'I am,' I said. My own smile was causing me some pain behind my ears but still I endeavoured to respond correctly to her generosity. I handed her the two letters of recommendation which I had taken from my bag in anticipation of their requirement. She politely held out her slim hand, took them, then indicated for me to sit. However, instead of studying the letters she merely held them in her hand without even glancing at their contents.

'What are these?' She asked with a little laugh ruffling up the words.

'These are my letters of recommendation. One you will see is from the headmaster at –'

Interrupting me, her lips relaxed for just a moment before taking up a smile once more, 'Where are you from?' she asked. The letters were still held in mid-air where I had placed them.

'I am from Jamaica,' I told her.

She was silent, we both grinning on each other in a genteel way. I thought to bring her attention back to the letters. 'One of the letters I have given you is from my last post. Written by the headmaster himself. You will see that –'

But once more she interrupted me: 'Where?'

I wondered if it would be impolite to tell this beguiling woman to read the letter in her hand so all her questions might be answered. I concluded it would. 'At Half Way Tree Parish School,' I told her.

'Where's that?'

'In Kingston, Jamaica.'

She leaned back on her chair and instead of opening the letters she began playing with them – flicking the paper against her fingers. 'And where did you train to be a teacher?' she asked me.

Her comely smile belied the rudeness of her tone. And I could not help but note that all gladness had left her eye and remained only at her mouth. 'I trained at the teacher-training college in Constant Spring, under the tutelage of Miss Morgan.'

Annotations

[7] **perchance** /pə(r)'tʃɑːns/ = by chance, possibly

'Is that in Jamaica?'

'Yes.'

It was relief that tipped her head to one side while she let out a long breath. I eased myself believing everything was now cleared between us. Until, leaning all her ample charm forward, she told me, 'Well, I'm afraid you can't teach here,' and passed the unopened letters back to me.

I was sure there had been some misunderstanding, although I was not clear as to where it had occurred. Perhaps I had not made myself as understood as I could. 'If you would read the letters,' I said, 'one will tell you about the three years of training as a teacher I received in Jamaica while the other letter is concerned with the position I held as a teacher at –'

She did not let me finish. 'The letters don't matter,' she told me, 'You can't teach in this country. You're not qualified to teach here in England.'

'But …' was the only sound that came from me.

'It doesn't matter that you were a teacher in Jamaica,' she went on, 'you will not be allowed to teach here.' She shook the letters at me. 'Take these back. They're of no use.' When I did not take them from her hand she rattled them harder at me. 'Take them,' she said, so loud she almost shouted. Her smile was stale as a gargoyle. My hand shook as it reached out for the letters.

And all I could utter was 'But –'

'Miss, I'm afraid there really is no point in your sitting there arguing with me.' And she giggled. The untimely chortle made my mouth gape. 'It's not up to me. It's the decision of the education authority. I can do nothing to change that. And, I'm afraid, neither can you. Now, I don't mean to hurry you but I have an awful lot to do. So thank you for coming.'

Every organ I possessed was screaming on this woman, 'What are you saying to me?'

She went back about her business. Her face now in its normal repose looked as severe as that of the principal at my college. She picked up a piece of paper, wrote something at the top. She looked to another piece of paper then stopped, aware that I was still there.

'How long is the training in England?' I asked her.

'Goodbye,' she said, pointing a finger at the door.

'Must I go back to a college?'

'Really, miss, I have just explained everything to you. You do speak English? Have you not understood me? It's quite simple. There is no point you asking me anything else. Now, please, I have a lot to do. Thank you.'

And she smiled on me – again! What fancy feigning. I could not stand up. My legs were too weak under me. I sat for a little to redeem my composure. At last finding strength to pull myself up, I told this woman, 'I will come back again when I am qualified to teach in this country.'

'Yes,' she said, 'you do that. Goodbye.'

As I stood she rolled her eyes with the other women in the room. But I paid them no mind. I fixed my hat straight on my head and adjusted my gloves. 'Thank you and good day.' I called to them all, as I opened the door to leave. Each woman returned that pantomime greeting as if I had meant it. I opened the door and walked through. Suddenly everything was dark. I was staring on a ladder, a mop and a broom. I put out my hand and touched shelves stacked with bundles of paper. For one moment I wondered how I would find my way out through this confusion. Only when my foot kicked against a bucket did I realise I had walked into a cupboard. I had stepped with all the confidence I could grasp, while the women watched me.

All three were giggling when I emerged from the dark of the closet. One behind a hand, another with a sheet of paper lifted up so I might not see. The older woman was, of course, smiling but pity encircled the look. 'It's that door,' she said, pointing her spiky finger at the other wooden opening. I thanked her, bade them all good day once more and passed through the correct exit, untroubled by the sound of their rising laughter.

2

Examine Hortense's attitude towards her life in Britain and compare it with Gilbert's.

→ **S12:** Checklist: Analysis – prose, p. 352

3

In the evening, Hortense writes home to her best friend in Jamaica and expresses her feelings about her new life. Write that letter.

→ **S2:** Checklist: Creative writing, p. 331

4 Across cultures

Comment on the situation Hortense finds herself in and consider whether contemporary immigrants to Germany have better chances.

→ **S6:** How to write a discussion/ comment, p. 338

8 Shakespeare

1 Henry V

2 Richard III

3 Hamlet

4 Othello

→ Solution, p. 392

Info

Tupac Amaru Shakur (1971-1996) was an American rapper and actor who sold over 75 million records worldwide. He was murdered, possibly by a rival rapper.

Webcode

You can download a word list for the Intro, WordPool and Facts pages here: WES-73644-107

→ **S6:** How to write a discussion/comment, p. 338

1 Who said it: Tupac or Shakespeare?

a) The rapper Tupac used to say that he was influenced by William Shakespeare. Read the quotations and say whether they are from Tupac or Shakespeare. How many did you get right?

1. Time and the hour run through the roughest day.
2. If you can make it through the night, there's a brighter day.
3. We must remember that tomorrow comes after the dark.
4. Tomorrow, and tomorrow, and tomorrow creeps in this petty pace from day to day.
5. If music be the food of love, play on.
6. Fear is stronger than love.
7. Cowards die many times before their deaths.
8. A coward dies a thousand times, a soldier dies but once.
9. You cannot escape fate. Just as you rose you shall fall, by my hands.
10. It is not in the stars to hold our destiny but in ourselves.

b) Say what strikes you when you compare the two writers.

2

a) Look at the photos above of productions of some of Shakespeare's most famous plays and speculate on their themes.

b) **Group work** Choose a play you would like to find out more about.
- Hang up the photos in different parts of the classroom.
- Go to the play you are most interested in.
- With the other students interested in the play, do some research to find out more about it.
- Prepare a short presentation on your play and give it in front of the class.

c) Discuss to what extent the themes of the plays are still relevant and/or inspiring for you today.

Shakespeare — Intro 8

Macbeth 5

6 Romeo and Juliet

8 The Taming of the Shrew

Twelfth Night 7

3
Pair work Read the following quotations taken from some of the above plays.
a) Say what you think Shakespeare is trying to tell us.
b) Rewrite the quotations in your own words.

1. *All the world's a stage
And all the men and women merely players;
They have their exits and their entrances;
And one man in his time plays many parts.*

2. *I am the one who loved not wisely but too well.*

3. *What's in a name? That which we call a rose
By any name would smell as sweet.*

4. *The course of true love never did run smooth.*

5. *Some are born great, some achieve greatness, and some have greatness thrust upon them.*

6. *The labour we delight in physics[1] pain.*

Annotation
[1] **physics** = cures

c) Discuss whether you agree with the views expressed in the quotations.

4
a) Watch this video, which is concerned with one of the most famous quotations of all time. Identify the quotation and the play.
b) Referring to Shakespeare's plays, the famous actor Simon Russell Beale claims, "You can do what you like with it." Examine to what extent the video supports this view.

→ **S20:** How to listen/watch effectively, p. 366

Preview

Shakespeare and the world that made him
First of all, you will learn something about Shakespeare's life and the time in which he lived.

Shakespeare's sonnets
In the **Workshop** and the rest of this part of the Theme, you will get to know some of Shakespeare's poetry.

Shakespearean drama
Part B focuses on Shakespeare's plays. In the **Workshop**, you will look closely at *Romeo and Juliet*.

Webcode
You can find a link to the video here:
WES-73644-108

A GIANT OF LITERATURE

Throughout as well as beyond the English-speaking world, William Shakespeare needs no introduction. During his lifetime a renowned playwright and poet in London, Shakespeare is today recognized as a giant of English literature and poetry, his works continuing to entertain and inspire audiences four centuries after his era, all over the world.

Shakespeare's literary opus includes at least 37 plays, many of which are some of the most famous plays in literary history. He was also a prolific poet, and famously composed a series of 154 sonnets, as well as two long narrative poems. While his sonnets deal primarily with the theme of romantic love, his plays fall into three main categories, namely tragedy, comedy and history. He also wrote plays that merged tragic and comic themes, known as tragicomedies.

SHAKESPEAREAN DRAMA

Shakespeare's tragedies generally follow the downfall of a protagonist or anti-hero at the hands of fate. In these plays, a fault or weakness in the protagonist's character, known as a tragic flaw, plays a part in bringing about his ruin. In the case of Othello, it is his jealousy that dooms him. Similarly, it is Macbeth's ambition to be crowned king that leads to his demise. Guilt is a recurring theme in Shakespearean tragedies, usually experienced by the protagonist as a result of his sinful or unjust actions.

Before focusing on tragedies, Shakespeare wrote historical plays and comedies. The historical plays tended to focus on English monarchs, offering portrayals of each monarch in agreement with the sentiments of the era. His comedies were somewhat formulaic, usually involving a rather complicated plot, an intelligent servant, and ridiculous costumes and props. Romantic love usually also played a part, albeit under far more light-hearted circumstances than in the tragedies.

Shakespeare wrote most of his plays in blank verse, which is a poetic form consisting of unrhymed iambic pentameter. The language in his plays and his poetry is full of wordplay and stylistic devices, and even some neologisms which have become commonplace vocabulary in modern standard English. The language of his plays contains jokes and puns which Elizabethan audiences would have found very witty, if not outrageously funny.

Dialogue between multiple characters makes up most of the text in his scripts, but Shakespeare also frequently employed the soliloquy – a lengthy monologue delivered by a lone character, either to drive the plot forward, to explain something important to the audience, or for dramatic effect. Juliet confesses her love for her beloved in a soliloquy – the iconic 'Wherefore art thou Romeo?'

SHAKESPEARE'S CONTINUING IMPORTANCE

Successive generations of literary critics and scholars have studied and commented on Shakespeare's works, continuing to produce fresh interpretations of the texts and coming up with various theories as to the inspiration behind his writings. Greek tragedies, as well as the writings of his contemporaries in England and Europe, appear to have influenced his work. It is possible that in some cases, he modified and retold stories originally conceived by other writers. He, too, has been a monumental source of inspiration for later generations: there have been numerous literary, theatrical and cinematic adaptations of his work. Some of the inspiring speeches delivered by characters in his plays are still lauded today as feats of oratory force and eloquence.

During his time, many members of society did not actually deem acting or the theatre to be respectable ways of making a living. Aspects of the industry were regarded as blasphemous, subversive to societal harmony, and a source of disorder in the land. Nevertheless, there was demand for his work, and Shakespeare spent almost three decades of his life writing plays. He died in 1616 in his hometown of Stratford-upon-Avon and was buried in the same church where he had been baptized in 1564.

Shakespeare WordPool 8

1
Find literary terms in the text that match the following definitions.
1. a monologue by one character alone on stage addressed to the audience.
2. a person who writes drama.
3. lines of unrhymed poetry, usually in iambic pentameter
4. clever and often amusing use of language in a verbal exchange between characters
5. a style of writing verse in lines of ten syllables with the emphasis on every second syllable
6. a poem consisting of fourteen lines with a specific structure and rhyme scheme
7. a weakness in the main character of a play leading to his or her downfall
8. the leading character in a novel or a play

2
Replace the underlined words with some of the highlighted adjectives from the text without changing the meaning. More words are highlighted than you need.
1. In *The Taming of the Shrew* the characters Katherina and Petruchio are famous for their <u>clever and amusing</u> verbal exchanges.
2. <u>16th century</u> playwrights such as William Shakespeare were certainly familiar with the Great Chain of Being, which organized the world into a fixed order with God at the top.
3. Theatre companies built their playhouses and performed outside the city boundaries because the Council of London aldermen believed that they were <u>dangerous and rebellious</u>.
4. William Shakespeare was the son of a <u>worthy</u> citizen of Stratford upon Avon, who was a prosperous businessman and later a member of the town council.
5. It is Othello's passion of jealousy which causes him to murder his <u>treasured</u> Desdemona.
6. William Shakespeare is one of the world's most popular playwrights and his words and characters continue to be <u>uplifting</u> for actors and audiences worldwide.

3
Complete the sentences below using the verbs in the box. There are more verbs than you need.

> to bury
> to inspire
> to make a living
> to involve
> to modify
> to retell
> to confess one's love
> to compose

The movie *West Side Story* **1** the classic tale of Romeo and Juliet. The story is set in New York City in the 1950s and the original plot of two feuding families **2** so that the Montagues become the Jets and the Capulets become the Sharks. Maria (Juliet) **3** working in a bridal shop and longs for more excitement in her life. This comes when she meets Tony (Romeo) at a school dance. Although he is a member of the rival gang, it is love at first sight. They **4** for each other and plan to run away together. However, tragedy strikes and Tony is killed. Unlike in the original play, in which the two lovers **5** side by side, Maria survives, a broken figure.

4
a) Match these opposites. There is one more word than you need in the second column.

1 innocence	A disorder
2 original	B demand
3 offer	C plot
4 choice	D guilt
5 order	E adaptation
6 dialogue	F downfall
7 ascent	G soliloquy
	H fate

b) Correct the wrong statements using some of the words from a).
1. Othello was convinced of Desdemona's innocence, so he killed her.
2. Those people in the audience who were familiar with Shakespeare realized that the performance was an original because the setting and plot had been changed.
3. In the 16th century many people believed that it was fate that determined their lives.
4. Hamlet begins his famous dialogue with the line "To be or not to be."
5. His enemies wished strongly for his ascent and were granted this wish in the last act.
6. There are many good Shakespearean actors on demand, but few of them are as outstanding as Sir Lawrence Olivier.

Shakespeare and the world that made him

Shakespeare's life

In April 1564 William Shakespeare was born in Stratford-upon-Avon, about 150 kilometres north-west of London. Very little is known for certain about his life. He married in 1582 and had three children. By 1592, he had risen to prominence in London as an actor and a playwright. He
5 joined *The Lord Chamberlain's Men*, the most successful company of actors, two years later and shortly thereafter became a shareholder in the company. In 1610 Shakespeare apparently retired to his hometown Stratford-upon-Avon, where he died on 23 April 1616.

The political background

When Shakespeare was born, England was ruled by Queen Elizabeth I from the Tudor dynasty. After
10 Elizabeth died in 1603, James I inherited the throne, starting the fateful Stuart dynasty, which joined the thrones of England and Scotland but ultimately threw England into a period of religious and political turmoil ending in civil war and the execution of James' son, King Charles I.

The Elizabethan Age

Under Elizabeth I (reigned 1558-1603), the last of the Tudor monarchs,
15 England enjoyed a period of relative peace and prosperity. Her father, Henry VIII, had broken with Rome and the Catholic Church and made himself Supreme Head of the Church in order to divorce his first wife. But it was Elizabeth who finalized this process and created the Church of England or Anglican Church, which was a compromise incorporating
20 the doctrine of the Reformation with the concept of Catholicism, i.e. the universal church of Jesus Christ. It was a compromise that many were prepared to accept, although there was still opposition from many Catholics, who refused to deny the authority of the Pope, and the Puritans, radical Protestants who were opposed to the new church's rituals, which
25 were still largely Catholic in nature.

James I inherits the throne

Elizabeth never married and was depicted as the Virgin Queen. There was no lack of marriage proposals, but Elizabeth refused them all. This made the succession a problem and parliament was keen to prevent religious and political unrest. King James VI of
30 Scotland, who was the son of Elizabeth's cousin Mary Stuart, inherited the throne as James I of England (reigned 1603-1625), thus joining the crowns of Scotland and England. Unlike his Catholic mother, he had been brought up as a radical Protestant.
Under James' reign, religious and political opposition to the crown reached new heights. James I had a more autocratic approach to monarchy and emphasized his right to rule
35 by divine right, i.e. as God's representative on earth. Catholic rebels planned to reinstate Catholicism but failed in their attempt to blow up Parliament at its opening ceremony in 1605.
Puritan opposition to the crown was based on their dissatisfaction with the Elizabethan settlement. They sought to ban Catholic practices from the Church of England and were opposed
40 to the control of the church through the monarchy. The Puritans became a major political force in Parliament since many of them were successful in the growing commercial world.

Parliament

Both Elizabeth and James were dependent on Parliament financially since only Parliament could impose taxation. The English Parliament was made up of two chambers: the House of Lords, consisting of the nobility and the clergy, and the House of Commons. Whereas the Lords inherited their seats, the Commons were voted for in elections, although only very few people were allowed to vote.

The Elizabethan world view

The Elizabethans had a view of the universe very different from ours. They believed in a hierarchical order of the universe in which all creation was ranked in an unalterable order from God to the angels down to man and from there further down to the animals, plants and minerals. The Elizabethans pictured the world as a 'great chain of being'. Those higher in the chain possessed understanding and, accordingly, had more authority and responsibility than the lower beings. Every being was thought to have its place within this chain, which was a functioning system as long as every being knew its place and fulfilled its destined duty for the rest of the chain. God was at the top of the chain, he alone possessed divine attributes. The angels were a purely rational or spiritual class linked to man in the class below by understanding.

The Elizabethans had an analogical world view relating God and man. This meant that hierarchy and order in the political world were extremely important. As God was the ruler of the macrocosm, the monarch was the ruler of the political world, his position derived from God. The divine right of kings implied that rebellion was a sin not only against the state but against heaven itself.

Next to the king or queen in the social order came the nobility followed by the knights and gentlemen. The poor were at the bottom of the chain. By analogy the father was the head and ruler of the family. Children were brought up to fear and respect their parents. Women had few rights. The authority of the father was recognized as part of the overall social order.

The concept of an ideal order was taken for granted by the ordinary educated Elizabethan. Believing in it firmly, they were terrified of disorder. Chaos meant cosmic anarchy to them, whereas to us chaos only means some sort of confusion.

The Great Chain of Being

The doctrine of the four elements, an ancient belief that all matter was made up of earth, water, fire and air, also shaped the Elizabethan world view. Man himself was formed by the combination of the four elements: in ascending hierarchical order, these were earth and water, both tending to fall to the centre of the universe, and air and fire, both tending to rise. The elements, in a mixed state, shaped man's temperament. Each element possessed two qualities which combined into a 'humour' or human temperament: earth (cold and dry: melancholy), water (cold and moist: phlegmatic), air (hot and moist: sanguine), fire (hot and dry: choleric).

Workshop: Step by step — Part A: Shakespeare's sonnets

Webcode
You can download a word list for Part A here: WES-73644-109

Step by step: Analysing a Shakespearean sonnet

PRE-READING

1 Pair work

Note down what images you would use to describe someone you love. Here are some examples:

My lover is a day I can't forget
(American singer-songwriter Cuco)

You light up my life. 'Cause, baby, you're a firework
(American singer Katy Perry)

My love is like a red, red rose
(Scottish poet Robert Burns)

COMPREHENSION

Webcode
You can find a link to a recital here: WES-73644-110

2
a) Listen to a recital of Sonnet 18 and talk about your first impressions in class.
b) **Pair work** Now read the sonnet and paraphrase it line by line in everyday English.

Annotations
l. 1 **thee** = you (object)
l. 2 **thou art** = you are
     temperate = calm, even-tempered
l. 4 **hath** = has
     date = duration
l. 6 **complexion** = skin colour
     to **dim** = to become less bright
l. 7 **fair** = beautiful
l. 8 **untrimmed** = stripped of ornament
l. 9 **thy** = your
l. 10 **ow'st** = own, possess
l. 12 **eternal lines** = immortal verses
      to time thou grow'st = you become part of time (and therefore exist forever)

Sonnet 18

Shall I compare thee to a summer's day?
Thou art more lovely and more temperate:
Rough winds do shake the darling buds of May,
And summer's lease hath all too short a date:
5 Sometime too hot the eye of heaven shines,
And often is his gold complexion dimmed;
And every fair from fair sometime declines,
By chance, or nature's changing course, untrimmed;
But thy eternal summer shall not fade,
10 Nor lose possession of that fair thou ow'st,
Nor shall death brag thou wander'st in his shade,
When in eternal lines to time thou grow'st:
    So long as men can breathe or eyes can see,
    So long lives this, and this gives life to thee.

ANALYSIS

3 Language awareness

a) Say what you like about Shakespeare's language.
b) Explain what differences to today's English you notice. You can use the info box below.

Info

Shakespeare's language

Like other poets of his time, Shakespeare experimented with language. Any kind of wordplay and especially puns were extremely popular with the Elizabethan audience. He also made up many new words and introduced them into the English language, although in some cases, a word may have existed before Shakespeare but was never recorded. Shakespeare also modified existing words by changing their function, e.g. using verbs as if they were nouns or making verbs out of nouns by adding prefixes, e.g. "to unhair". Some words have changed their meaning since Shakespeare's time, others are not used any more and with still other words, we just do not know what they may have meant in Shakespeare's day.

The words "thou", "thee" and "thy" as opposed to "you" and "your" are used frequently. To put it very simply, in 1600 "you" was polite, more formal usage whereas "thou" was more familiar. Depending on the social context, "thou" could imply either closeness and friendship or it could mean contempt and even be insulting. Shakespeare's language may at first seem quite difficult to understand and very different from today's English. But once you have familiarized yourself with his language, you will get the gist of it, although you may not understand every single word. So if there are some passages which you just do not understand, why not turn to your neighbour and ask "Hast thou done thy homework? Hast thou understood these lines?"

Part A: Shakespeare's sonnets — Workshop: Step by step

8

4
Sonnet 18 can be read as an argumentative text, leading to a logical conclusion. Analyse the logical train of thought in the sonnet step by step.

lines	interpretation
1	opening of the train of thought in the form of a rhetorical question; direct address of the beloved
2	affirmative answer to the question: The speaker claims that the beloved is …
3–6	evidence to support the claim of line 2: summer is …
…	…

→ **S10:** How to work with poetry, p. 347

Webcode
You can download this grid here:
WES-73644-111

5 Language awareness
Although the sonnet follows a logical train of thought, it also has a great poetic impact. What makes Shakespeare's language poetic? In order to find out, analyse the language and imagery. Use the info box below to find examples of stylistic devices and their effects. → **SUPPORT** D1, p. 322

→ **S10:** How to work with poetry, p. 347

Info

Stylistic devices

element	definition and example	effect
alliteration	words beginning with the same letter or sound, e.g. "false forgeries" (Sonnet 138)	helps to enrich the poetic effect
allusion	sth that is said and refers to another person or subject in an indirect way, e.g. "a King who took us to the mountaintop" (former US President Barack Obama in a speech, alluding to Martin Luther King)	to arouse the reader's interest
anaphora	the repetition of identical words or phrases at the beginning of a sentence or a line, e.g. "Nobody hurt you. Nobody turned off the light" (We Remember Your Childhood Well, by Carol Ann Duffy)	to emphasize a thought or a claim
antithesis	the opposition of ideas, words or phrases, e.g. "Fair is foul, and foul is fair" (*Macbeth*)	to express and underline conflict, or to heighten the intensity of feeling
ellipsis	leaving out words deliberately, e.g. "Therefore I'll lie with her, and she [will lie] with me" (Sonnet 138)	to give a statement more emphasis or to make a text stylistically more conversational/lively
metaphor	a word or phrase used to describe sb/sth else in a way that is different from its normal use, e.g. "the eye of heaven" (Sonnet 18)	to create an image in the reader's mind which makes the description more powerful
extended metaphor	a metaphor extended over several lines, e.g. "All the world's a stage, and all the men and women merely players" (*As You Like It*)	engages the audience intellectually
onomatopoeia	words that sound like their meanings, e.g. the word "cuckoo"	to add emphasis and make a text more lively
parallelism	the repetition of sentence structure, e.g. "Some say thy fault is …, Some say thy grace is …" (Sonnet 96)	may be used to contrast certain aspects or viewpoints
personification	representing objects, concepts, etc. as humans, e.g. "Make war upon this bloody tyrant Time" (Sonnet 16)	to underline certain qualities in an object, concept, etc.
repetition	deliberately repeating words or phrases	to enrich meaning and emotional appeal
rhetorical question	a question which expects no answer, e.g. "Shall I compare thee to a summer's day?" (Sonnet 18)	direct address of the reader, often intended to influence him or her
simile	a word or phrase that compares sth to sth else using the words *like* or *as*, e.g. "My love is like a red, red rose" (A Red, Red Rose, by Robert Burns)	to create an image in the reader's mind which makes the description more powerful

Workshop: Step by step — Part A: Shakespeare's sonnets

→ **S10:** How to work with poetry, p. 347

6 → SUPPORT D2, p. 322

Analyse the structure of the sonnet. Consider the following:
- number of lines
- rhyme scheme
- stanzas
- turning point
- rhythm

Info

Sonnets

A sonnet is a **fourteen-line poem** with conventional demands as to its structure and rhyme scheme. A sonnet can be divided into **quatrains** (four lines) and **tercets** (three lines) or **quatrains** (four lines) and a **couplet** (two lines).

There are different types of sonnets:
The **Italian (Petrarchan) sonnet** consists of two quatrains and two tercets, often with a turn or change of theme in the two tercets.

The **English (Shakespearean) sonnet** consists of three quatrains and a couplet, often with a turn or change of theme in the couplet. The turn can come before the couplet, usually at line 9.

Structure of poems		
element	definition	example
blank verse	unrhymed lines with a five-beat rhythm (iambic pentameter)	"So foul and fair a day I have not seen." (*Macbeth*)
enjambment	one line continuing onto the next	"Let me not to the marriage of true minds Admit impediments." (Sonnet 116)
free verse	poetry without a regular rhythm or rhyme	
iambic pentameter	five stressed (/) syllables alternating with five unstressed (x) syllables, giving a ten-syllable line	x / x / x / x / x / "No longer mourn for me when I am dead" (Sonnet 71)
metre	the pattern of stressed and unstressed syllables	
rhythm	the pace or "movement" of a poem; the rhythm is determined by the metre and by the length of sentences	
rhyme	the repetition of sounds, usually at the end of two or more lines	And then my heart with pleasure fills, And dances with the daffodils. (I wandered lonely as a cloud, by William Wordsworth)
rhyme scheme	the pattern created by the repetition of sounds at the end of lines	The rhyme scheme of Shakespeare's sonnets is abab cdcd efef gg.
stanza/verse	a section of a poem consisting of a group of lines	

COMMENT/CREATIVE WRITING

7 CHALLENGE CHOOSE

→ **S6:** How to write a discussion/ comment, p. 338

Discuss whether the claim of the last two lines is still valid today.

OR

Write your own declaration of love. → SUPPORT D3, p. 322
- Choose the lyrical form (e.g. sonnet, song, rap, free verse) that will best express your feelings.
- Choose your own addressee. This need not be a person. You might want to address your text to e.g. your hometown, your most cherished childhood memory, a hobby you particularly enjoy, your favourite music group – anything you love.
- Language awareness Include a variety of stylistic devices.

8 EXTRA

Learn Sonnet 18 by heart. Be prepared to recite it to your class.
Think about how you personally want to speak the lines. What words do you want to stress? Why?

Practice: Analysing a Shakespearean sonnet

1 Group work (3 or 4)

a) Exchange your ideas about one of the two sonnets. You may prefer to have a discussion which is completely unstructured, although it is sometimes helpful to have some kind of framework to help you start off a discussion. Here is a possible framework:
- What is your general impression of what this sonnet is about?
- Who is speaking? To whom?
- Which words, phrases or lines appeal to you the most?
- Is there a dominant image, or a variety of images?
- Which words or lines do you find difficult?
- What is the sonnet's tone or mood?
- Is there a point where the mood or meaning changes?

b) In your groups, work on the following tasks:
1. **Comprehension:** Say in a few sentences what the poem is about.
2. **Comprehension/Analysis:** Paraphrase and examine the sonnet line by line.
3. **Analysis:** Analyse the imagery.
4. **Analysis:** Compare this sonnet with Sonnet 18. Explain why this is/is not a typical sonnet/love poem.
5. Present your findings to the class.

→ **S10:** How to work with poetry, p. 347

1 Sonnet 116

Let me not to the marriage of true minds
Admit impediments. Love is not love
Which alters when it alteration finds,
Or bends with the remover to remove:
5 O, no! it is an ever-fixèd mark,
That looks on tempests and is never shaken;
It is the star to every wandering bark,
Whose worth's unknown, although his height be taken.
Love's not Time's fool, though rosy lips and cheeks
10 Within his bending sickle's compass come;
Love alters not with his brief hours and weeks,
But bears it out even to the edge of doom.
 If this be error and upon me proved,
 I never writ, nor no man ever loved.

Annotations
l. 2 **impediment** = obstacle
l. 3 **alteration** = change (in the beloved)
l. 4 **bends ... remove** = changes when the other person's love changes
l. 5 **mark** = light to guide seamen, lighthouse
l. 7 **bark** = ship
l. 8 **Whose ... be taken** = the star's (astrological) influence is not known, although the star's "height" (altitude) may be used for navigation
l. 10 **his** = Time's
sickle = tool for cutting grass
compass = *here:* range of the sickle
l. 12 **bears it out** = lasts
doom = doomsday, day of the Last Judgement

Webcode
You can find a link to a recital of the sonnet here:
WES-73644-112

2 Sonnet 130

My mistress' eyes are nothing like the sun;
Coral is far more red than her lips' red;
If snow be white, why then her breasts are dun;
If hairs be wires, black wires grow on her head.
5 I have seen roses damasked, red and white,
But no such roses see I in her cheeks;
And in some perfumes is there more delight
Than in the breath that from my mistress reeks.
I love to hear her speak, yet well I know
10 That music hath a far more pleasing sound;
I grant I never saw a goddess go;
My mistress when she walks treads on the ground.
 And yet, by heaven, I think my love as rare
 As any she belied with false compare.

Annotations
l. 5 **damasked** = of the colour of the damask rose, i.e. bright pink
l. 11 **go** = walk
l. 13 **rare** = valuable
l. 14 **belied** = wrongly praised

Webcode
You can find a link to a recital of the sonnet here:
WES-73644-113

8 Texts — Part A: Shakespeare's sonnets

Pop sonnets

1

Erik Didriksen is an American author who transforms the lyrics of pop songs into sonnets. You are now going to work on one of his pop sonnets.

a) Read the lyrics of Taylor Swift's song (1) and the sonnet (2) that was created from it. Outline the theme of both texts in one or two sentences.
b) Comment on the adaptation of the song. How convincing is it?
c) **CHOOSE** Rewrite a pop song in the form of a sonnet.
   OR
   Rewrite a sonnet in the form of a pop song or a modern poem or a rap.

→ **S6:** How to write a discussion/comment, p. 338

1 We Are Never Ever Getting Back Together
by Taylor Swift

I remember when we broke up the first time
Saying, "This is it, I've had enough," 'cause like
We hadn't seen each other in a month
When you said you needed space. (What?)
5 Then you come around again and say
"Baby, I miss you and I swear I'm gonna change, trust me."
Remember how that lasted for a day?
I say, "I hate you," we break up, you call me, "I love you."

Ooh, we called it off again last night
10 But ooh, this time I'm telling you, I'm telling you

We are never ever ever getting back together,
We are never ever ever getting back together,
You go talk to your friends, talk to my friends, talk to me
But we are never ever ever ever getting back together

15 Like, ever …

I'm really gonna miss you picking fights
And me, falling for it screaming that I'm right
And you, …

2
My mem'ry gazes back on young romance
and on its twilight throes, when first you left;
you claim'd we needed absence to advance,
yet for togetherness, we'd been bereft.
5 You soon returned, your face forlorn and drawn
and from your lips hung promises to change;
then, by the morrow, all those oaths were gone
and once again we found ourselves estranged.
The cycle never breaks; our sordid tales
10 end always with ellipses, not full stops.
When yesternight our courtship freshly failed,
you saw the cue to take it from the top.
   But now that we are once again apart,
   I swear you shan't again reclaim my heart.

Annotations
l. 2 **throe** = painful fight
l. 4 **bereft of** sth = robbed of sth
l. 5 **forlorn** = in despair
l. 7 **the morrow** = tomorrow
l. 12 to **take** sth **from the top** = to do sth again
l. 14 **shan't** = shall not, will not

Part A: Shakespeare's sonnets — Advanced texts

Relating Shakespeare's sonnets to the place you live

1

Think about the place where you live. What location would you choose as a setting for any of Shakespeare's sonnets?

a) To get some ideas, watch one or two of the video clips which relate Shakespeare's sonnets to the urban poetry of New York City.

b) Choose either one of the sonnets dealt with in class or another one that appeals to you personally. Describe the setting you would choose or film it on your mobile and synchronize it with a reading of the sonnet.

Webcode
You can find a link to the videos here: WES-73644-114

Discussion of Sonnet 66

1

a) Read the sonnet and identify the theme.
b) Explain how the theme differs from the ones you have read before.
c) Note down the message of the sonnet in your own words.
d) Discuss whether the theme of the sonnet concerns us today.

→ **S10:** How to work with poetry, p. 347

→ **S6:** How to write a discussion/comment, p. 338

Sonnet 66

Tired with all these, for restful death I cry:
As to behold desert a beggar born,
And needy nothing trimmed in jollity,
And purest faith unhappily forsworn,
5 And gilded honour shamefully misplaced,
And maiden virtue rudely strumpeted,
And right perfection wrongfully disgraced,
And strength by limping sway disablèd
And art made tongue-tied by authority,
10 And folly (doctor-like) controlling skill,
And simple truth miscalled simplicity,
And captive good attending captain ill:
    Tired with all these, from these would I be gone,
    Save that, to die, I leave my love alone.

Annotations
l. 2 **As to behold** = for example to see
desert = a deserving person
l. 5 **gilded honour** = noble dignity
l. 6 **strumpeted** = made a prostitute
l. 8 **limping sway** = misdirection, here: weak government
l. 10 **doctor-like** = like a pompous and ignorant teacher

The theatre in Shakespeare's time

The playhouses
In 1576 the first purpose-built playhouse, called *The Theatre*, was erected in Shoreditch, north of the river Thames. In the following years, more theatres were built, with *The Globe* opening in 1599. Playhouses drew big audiences of more than a thousand spectators, but they were not popular with everyone. The officials who ran the City of London thought that they were noisy and attracted undesirable people. This explains why a number of playhouses were built outside the city walls on the south bank of the river, outside the control of city officials. Here other forms of entertainment, such as animal baiting, taverns and brothels, would also be found.

Plays were performed in daylight because there was no artificial lighting apart from candles. This meant that the audience could see each other, which made the whole experience a more communal one than today.

All outdoor playhouses had a central yard that was open to the sky and a raised stage, which protruded into the yard. There was a roof over the stage called 'the heavens' and a trapdoor on the stage led to 'hell'. Behind the stage was the 'tiring house', a backstage area where the actors dressed and waited for their entrances. There were roofed galleries around the yard with seats for those who could afford to pay more than a penny.

The reconstructed *Globe Theatre* in London, opened in 1997

The audience
For many people, theatre was the main form of entertainment. In 1600 about 15 to 20% of people who lived within reach of London's theatres were regular play-goers. The theatre was not only a middle-class or aristocratic form of entertainment. Many members of the middle class were in fact Puritans and opposed to the theatre. A large part of the audience was made up of skilled workers, artisans, clerks, apprentices and women. The entrance fee for the central yard or 'the pit', as it was called, was a penny and affordable for many, although not the very poor. The spectators in the pit were called the 'groundlings' because they stood on the ground. Gentlemen of various degrees would occupy the two-penny or three-penny seats in the gallery and members of the nobility sat in seats at the side of the stage, in the shilling rooms.

The audiences were not rowdy and misbehaved as the city council believed and must have had a higher level of understanding to enjoy the plays. It would appear that on the whole they listened carefully, applauding or laughing at the appropriate moments.

A performance at the reconstructed *Globe Theatre*

The companies
The construction of Elizabethan theatres was dependent on entrepreneurs such as James Burbage, who put up the capital and ran the theatre companies which performed there. Each company was named after its aristocratic or royal patron, e.g. *The Lord Chamberlain's Men* or *The King's Men*. A company consisted of eight to ten 'sharers', performers and sometimes writers who bought into the company and shared the profits. Other actors, musicians, etc. were hired on contract. When Burbage built *The Globe*, Shakespeare became a shareholder and his company moved there.

Companies performed six days a week, putting on a different play each day. The demand for new plays was high. When James I became king in 1603, he and his family became patrons of three main theatre companies. This meant regular and lucrative performances in the royal palaces but also gave the court some influence over the theatre.

The actors
Acting was not considered to be a respectable profession. Women were not allowed to perform on stage and young boys took on the roles of women. It was believed that because actors made a living pretending to be someone they were not, they could not be trusted. The Puritans even believed that theatres could be subversive and upset the natural order of things: common men dressed up as kings and boys as women, thus overturning social distinctions. But for those involved, acting was a serious art, requiring talent and imagination, since there were very few props and special effects in comparison with modern day productions.

Part B: Shakespearean drama — Workshop: Step by step

Step by step: Working with Shakespearean drama

PRE-READING

1

a) Read the prologue to the play *Romeo and Juliet* and note down what clues the audience is given about the play they are about to watch.

b) Analyse the structure of the prologue.

> Two households, both alike in dignity,
> In fair Verona, where we lay our scene,
> From ancient grudge[1] break to new mutiny[2],
> Where civil blood makes civil hands unclean.
> 5 From forth the fatal loins[3] of these two foes
> A pair of star-cross'd[4] lovers take their life;
> Whose misadventured[5] piteous overthrows[6]
> Do with their death bury their parents' strife.
> The fearful passage of their death-mark'd love,
> 10 And the continuance of their parents' rage,
> Which, but their children's end, nought[7] could remove,
> Is now the two hours' traffic[8] of our stage;
> The which if you with patient ears attend,
> What here shall miss, our toil shall strive to mend.

Annotations
[1] **grudge** = hatred
[2] **mutiny** = hostility
[3] **loins** = parts of the body used to create and bear children
[4] **star-cross'd** = destined by the stars to be unlucky
[5] **misadventured** = unfortunate
[6] **overthrow** = disappointment
[7] **nought** = nothing
[8] **traffic** = business

2 EXTRA DVD/25

a) **Group work** Consider how you would film the prologue. Think about
- setting,
- cast,
- costumes,
- music.

b) Watch the beginning of the film from 1997 in which Leonardo DiCaprio and Claire Danes play Romeo and Juliet. What do you find surprising? Compare it with your ideas.

→ **S20:** How to listen/watch effectively, p. 366

Webcode
You can find the video here:
WES-73644-116

Preview

In this Workshop, you will work on one of the most famous scenes in Shakespeare's plays, "the Balcony Scene" (Act II, Scene 2) from *Romeo and Juliet*. You will have a close look at the plot, the language Shakespeare uses and the characters.

COMPREHENSION: UNDERSTANDING THE PLOT

3

Since Shakespeare did not work with readers in mind but for the actors who performed his plays and the audience, most of whom could not read anyway, it makes sense to watch the play performed before reading it.

a) **Pair work** Watch this performance of the balcony scene performed by the Royal Shakespeare company. Talk about the feelings it evoked in you.

b) Watch it again and note down
- the couple's dilemma,
- how they plan to resolve it.

c) **Pair work** Compare your findings with those of a partner.

Webcode
You can find a link to the video here:
WES-73644-117

→ **S20:** How to listen/watch effectively, p. 366

8 Workshop: Step by step — Part B: Shakespearean drama

4
Now read part of the scene and put these sentences into the correct order.

1. Romeo begins to swear his love for her but she stops him, worried that everything is happening too quickly. He is able to reassure her and they confess their love for each other again.
2. The Nurse calls Juliet and she goes inside briefly. When she returns she says she will send someone to Romeo the next day to find out if he wants to marry her.
3. Juliet confesses her love for Romeo, but she is worried that he may not be telling the truth about his feelings or think that she is too easily won.
4. Romeo, who is hiding in the Capulet garden, is overjoyed when he realizes that Juliet is on the balcony.
5. Juliet, believing she is alone, professes her love for Romeo and at the same time her sorrow that he is a Montague.
6. Romeo reveals himself and surprises Juliet by agreeing to her wish for him to cast off his name.

Capulet's Garden. Enter **ROMEO**
JULIET *appears above at a window.*

ROMEO. But soft[1], what light through yonder window breaks?
5 It is the east and Juliet is the sun!
Arise, fair sun, and kill the envious moon,
Who is already sick and pale with grief
That thou her maid art far more fair than she.
Be not her maid, since she is envious;
10 Her vestal livery is but sick and green[2],
And none but fools do wear it. Cast it off.
It is my lady, O, it is my love!
O that she knew she were!
She speaks, yet she says nothing; what of that?
15 Her eye discourses[3], I will answer it.
I am too bold: 'tis not to me she speaks.
Two of the fairest stars in all the heaven,
Having some business, do entreat her eyes
To twinkle in their spheres[4] till they return.
20 What if her eyes were there, they in her head?
The brightness of her cheek would shame those stars,
As daylight doth[5] a lamp. Her eyes in heaven
Would through the airy region[6] stream so bright
25 That birds would sing and think it were not night.
See how she leans her cheek upon her hand
O that I were a glove upon that hand,
That I might touch that cheek!

JULIET. Ay me!
30 **ROMEO.** She speaks.
O, speak again, bright angel, for thou art
As glorious to this night, being o'er my head,
As is a winged messenger[7] of heaven
Unto the white-upturned[8] wondering eyes
35 Of mortals that fall back to gaze on him
When he bestrides[9] the lazy-puffing clouds
And sails upon the bosom of the air.

JULIET. O Romeo, Romeo! Wherefore[10] art thou Romeo?
40 Deny thy father and refuse thy name;
Or, if thou wilt not, be but sworn my love,
And I'll no longer be a Capulet.

ROMEO. [*Aside.*] Shall I hear more, or shall I speak at this?

45 **JULIET.** 'Tis but thy name that is my enemy:
Thou art thyself, though not a Montague.
What's Montague? It is nor hand, nor foot,
Nor arm, nor face, nor any other part
Belonging to a man. O, be some other name.
50 What's in a name? That which we call a rose
By any other name would smell as sweet;
So Romeo would, were he not Romeo call'd,
Retain that dear perfection which he owes[11]
Without that title. Romeo, doff[12] thy name,
55 And for that name, which is no part of thee,
Take all myself.

Annotations
[1] **soft!** = He tells himself to speak quietly.
[2] **Her vestal ... green** = reference to the dress worn by the Vestal virgins in ancient Rome, who served the virgin priestess of the goddess Vesta, whose insistence on a life of chastity for her virgin priestesses is not healthy according to Romeo
[3] **Her eye discourses** = Her eye speaks to me. Note that it also sounds like 'Her I discourses' in the sense of 'her self'.
[4] **spheres** = paths or orbits of the stars
[5] **doth** = does
[6] **the airy region** = the upper air
[7] **winged messenger** = angel
[8] **white-upturned** = turned up so that the pupils can hardly be seen
[9] **bestrides** = stands on or walks across sth
[10] **wherefore** = why

ROMEO.   I take thee at thy word.
Call me but love, and I'll be new baptis'd;
Henceforth I never will be Romeo.

60 **JULIET.** What man art thou that, thus bescreened[13] in night,
So stumblest on my counsel[14]?

ROMEO.   By a name
I know not how to tell thee who I am:
65 My name, dear saint, is hateful to myself,
Because it is an enemy to thee
Had I it written, I would tear the word.

JULIET. My ears have yet not drunk a hundred words
70 Of thy tongue's uttering, yet I know the sound.
Art thou not Romeo, and a Montague?

ROMEO. Neither, fair saint, if either thee dislike.

JULIET. How cam'st thou hither, tell me, and wherefore? [...]

75 **ROMEO.** By love, that first did prompt me to enquire.
He lent me counsel[15], and I lent him eyes.
I am no pilot[16], yet, wert thou as far
As that vast shore wash'd with the furthest sea,
80 I should adventure for[17] such merchandise.

JULIET. Thou knowest the mask of night is on my face,
Else would a maiden blush bepaint[18] my cheek
For that which thou hast heard me speak tonight.
85 Fain[19] would I dwell on form[20]; fain, fain deny
What I have spoke. But farewell compliment[21].
Dost thou love me? I know thou wilt say 'Ay[22]',
And I will take thy word. Yet, if thou swear'st,
Thou mayst prove false. At lovers' perjuries[23],
90 They say, Jove[24] laughs. O gentle Romeo,
If thou dost love, pronounce it faithfully:
Or if thou thinkest I am too quickly won,
I'll frown, and be perverse[25], and say thee nay,
So thou wilt woo[26]: but else, not for the world.

95 In truth, fair Montague, I am too fond;
And therefore thou mayst think my 'haviour[27] light[28]:
But trust me, gentleman, I'll prove more true
Than those that have more cunning to be
100 strange[29].
I should have been more strange, I must confess,
But that thou overheard'st, ere I was 'ware[30],
My true-love passion: therefore pardon me;
And not impute this yielding[31] to light love
105 Which the dark night hath so discovered[32].

ROMEO. Lady, by yonder blessed moon I vow,
That tips with silver all these fruit-tree tops –

JULIET. O, swear not by the moon, the inconstant moon,
110 That monthly changes in her circled orb[33],
Lest that[34] thy love prove likewise variable.

ROMEO. What shall I swear by?

JULIET.   Do not swear at all.
115 Or if thou wilt, swear by thy gracious self,
Which is the god of my idolatry[35],
And I'll believe thee.

ROMEO.   If my heart's dear love –

JULIET. Well, do not swear: although I joy in
120 thee,
I have no joy of this contract[36] to-night:
It is too rash, too unadvised, too sudden;
Too like the lightning, which doth cease to be
Ere one can say 'It lightens.' Sweet, good night!
125 This bud of love, by summer's ripening breath,
May prove a beauteous flower when next we meet.
Good night, good night! as sweet repose and rest
Come to thy heart as that within my breast

130 **ROMEO.** O, wilt thou leave me so unsatisfied?

JULIET. What satisfaction canst thou have to-night?

Annotations
[11] **owes** = owns;
[12] **doff** = put off, remove
[13] **bescreened** = hidden
[14] **So stumblest on my counsel** = comes so unexpectedly upon my secret thoughts
[15] **He gave me counsel** = He [i.e. love] gave me some advice
[16] **pilot** = navigator of a ship
[17] **I should adventure for** = I would come, however great the danger
[18] **bepaint** = colour
[19] **Fain** = gladly, willingly
[20] **dwell on form** = give time to formal ceremonies
[21] **Farewell compliment** = goodbye to formality
[22] **Ay** = yes
[23] **perjuries** = false statements, lies
[24] **Jove** = another name for the Roman god Jupiter, king of the gods
[25] **perverse** = unwilling to give in
[26] **woo** = try to win sb's love
[27] **'haviour** = behaviour
[28] **light** = immoral, lustful
[29] **have more cunning to be strange** = are more skilled at being reserved
[30] **ere I was 'ware** = before I was aware of your presence
[31] **impute this yielding** = take the fact that I return your love to mean that I am easily won
[32] **Which the dark ... discovered** = which you have discovered thanks to the darkness of the night
[33] **circled orb** = sphere, orbit
[34] **Lest that** = unless, in case
[35] **idolatry** = worship of a physical object or false god
[36] **contract** = marriage vows

Workshop: Step by step — Part B: Shakespearean drama

ROMEO. The exchange of thy love's faithful vow for mine.
135 **JULIET.** I gave thee mine before thou didst request it:
And yet I would[37] it were to give again.
ROMEO. Wouldst thou withdraw it? for what purpose, love?
140 **JULIET.** But to be frank[38], and give it thee again.
And yet I wish but for the thing I have:
My bounty[39] is as boundless as the sea,
My love as deep; the more I give to thee,
The more I have, for both are infinite.
145 **NURSE** *calls within.*
I hear some noise within; dear love, adieu!
Anon[40], good nurse! Sweet Montague, be true.
Stay but a little, I will come again.
Exit **JULIET** *above.*
150 **ROMEO.** O blessed, blessed night! I am afeard.
Being in night, all this is but a dream,
Too flattering-sweet to be substantial.

Re-enter **JULIET** *above.*
JULIET. Three words, dear Romeo, and good
155 night indeed.
If that thy bent of love be honourable[41],
Thy purpose marriage, send me word to-morrow
By one that I'll procure to come to thee[42],
Where and what time thou wilt perform the rite[43];
160 And all my fortunes at thy foot I'll lay
And follow thee my lord throughout the world.

Annotations
[37] **would** = wish
[38] **frank** = generous
[39] **bounty** = warm generosity
[40] **Anon** = soon, in a little while
[41] **If that ... honourable** = if your love is honourable in its intentions
[42] **one that I'll procure to come to thee** = a messenger I will send to you
[43] **the rite** = marriage

ANALYSIS: LANGUAGE

Webcode
You can find a link to the video here:
WES-73644-118

5 Pair work: Dramatic reading

a) Read the following info box, then watch the video. Note down what you learn about iambic pentameter.

Info

You should for the following reasons read Shakespeare aloud:

- Shakespeare wrote for theatre-goers, who watched the play and listened to the lines.
- The spoken word was the only means of communication for most people, since the majority of the population could not read or write.

- Most of Shakespeare's plays are written in blank verse. The iambic pentameter of the lines gives them a rhythm when they are spoken.
- Shakespeare uses many different registers for his characters, e.g. the street language of the poor, the passionate language of lovers, the pretentious language of rulers etc. These are more obvious if the lines are spoken.

b) Use the tips from the video to prepare a dramatic reading of lines 1-80, one of you as Juliet and one as Romeo. Also use the checklist.

Checklist

Dramatic Reading

Before you start
- read any annotations for this part so that you understand the text,
- consider who is speaking to whom and what they want,
- think about which words should be stressed to best convey the meaning.

While you are reading
- don't stop when you reach a word you don't know,
- do not automatically pause at the end of each line but pay attention to the punctuation. Pause briefly when there is a comma, and a longer time for a full stop.

Part B: Shakespearean drama   **Workshop: Step by step**

6

a) At the beginning of this scene Romeo is a teenager who has just fallen madly in love. The imagery in his language reflects this state of mind. Look at Romeo's first speech (lines 3-28) and complete the grid.
→ SUPPORT D4, p. 323

quotation	imagery/ interpretation	effect
But soft, what light through yonder window breaks? It is the east and Juliet is the sun!	metaphor: Juliet = sun	...
...	...	...

b) Find examples from Juliet's lines (119-144) to illustrate her feelings for Romeo. What images does she use to express those feelings? Compare them with Romeo's use of imagery. → SUPPORT D5, p. 323

Webcode
You can download the grid here: WES-73644-119

ANALYSIS: CHARACTERS

7

An analysis of Shakespearean characters needs to take into account what kind of play they appear in. *Romeo and Juliet* is a tragedy. In many Shakespearean tragedies, the hero's "tragic flaw" or inner weakness is the main cause of his downfall. Therefore, it is important to look for both strengths and weaknesses in the main characters. However, in *Romeo and Juliet*, fate also plays a major role. They are "star-cross'd lovers" right from the beginning and their fate is predicted in the prologue.

a) Look at the following list of adjectives and choose those which most appropriately fit
  • Romeo   • Juliet   • both of them.
  Look up any words you are not familiar with in a dictionary.

→ **S25:** How to work with a dictionary, p. 374

Language support

impulsive	impetuous	passionate	naïve	courageous	obedient	disobedient	strong-willed
hesitant	independent	headstrong	determined	immature	intense	emotional	vulnerable
rebellious	cowardly	inexperienced	cautious	innocent	modest	pragmatic	sensible	romantic

b) Find evidence in the scene to support your choice. → SUPPORT D6, p. 324
c) Despite the role of fate it is possible to recognize weaknesses in Romeo's character, which helped to bring about their downfall. Discuss
  • which character trait is most likely to be Romeo's "tragic flaw",
  • whether Juliet might be considered to be the more mature of the two lovers.
  Use quotations from the scene to support your arguments.

→ **S11:** How to work with drama, p. 350

→ **S6:** How to write a discussion/ comment, p. 338

8 Speed dating
• Form two groups. One group is Romeo, one Juliet.
• Write down at least five questions you (as Romeo or Juliet) would like to ask Romeo or Juliet.
• Sit in two rows facing each other.
• Ask and answer the questions of the person opposite you.
• After two minutes all Romeos move one place to the left.
• Ask the next Romeo/Juliet questions.
• Continue until you have talked to five Romeos/Juliets.
• Choose the partner you find most convincing and tell him/her why.

COMMENT/CREATIVE WRITING

9 CHOOSE

You are an actor/actress and have read that a new production of *Romeo and Juliet* is being planned. Write a letter to the director explaining why you are perfect for the role of Romeo/Juliet.
OR
The English playwright and contemporary of Shakespeare, Ben Jonson wrote that Shakespeare was "not of an age but for all times". Discuss this view, referring to the scene from *Romeo and Juliet*.

→ **S3:** Checklist: Formal letter, p. 334

→ **S6:** How to write a discussion/ comment, p. 338

Workshop: Practice — Part B: Shakespearean drama

Practice Working with Shakespearean drama

PRE-READING

 S15: How to describe pictures, p. 358

1 Look at this picture from a production of the play. Romeo is in the centre. Describe his role.

COMPREHENSION

 S1: Checklist: Summary, p. 330

2 Read the following excerpt from Act III, Scene 1 and summarize the plot. Romeo and Juliet have been secretly married. Later, Benvolio and Mercutio, two Montagues, meet Tybalt, a Capulet and Juliet's cousin, on the streets of Verona. Tybalt is angry that Romeo attended a Capulet ball and has challenged him to a duel.

Enter **ROMEO**

TYBALT. Well, peace be with you, sir: here comes my man[1].

MERCUTIO. But I'll be hanged, sir, if he wear
5 your livery:
Marry, go before to field, he'll be your follower;
Your worship in that sense may call him 'man'.[2]

TYBALT. Romeo, the hate I bear thee can afford
No better term than this, – thou art a villain.

10 **ROMEO.** Tybalt, the reason that I have to love thee
Doth much excuse the appertaining[3] rage
To such a greeting: villain am I none;
Therefore farewell; I see thou know'st me not.

15 **TYBALT.** Boy, this shall not excuse the injuries
That thou hast done me; therefore turn and draw.

ROMEO. I do protest, I never injured thee,
But love thee better than thou canst devise[4],
Till thou shalt know the reason of my love:
20 And so, good Capulet, – which name I tender
As dearly as my own, – be satisfied.

MERCUTIO. O calm, dishonourable, vile submission!
Alla stoccata carries it away.[5]
25 [*Draws*]
Tybalt, you rat-catcher, will you walk[6]?

TYBALT. What wouldst thou have with me?

MERCUTIO. Good king of cats, nothing but one of your nine lives[7]; that I mean to make bold
30 withal[8], and as you shall use[9] me hereafter, drybeat[10] the rest of the eight. Will you pluck your sword out of his pilcher[11] by the ears[12]? Make haste, lest mine be about your ears ere it be out.

Annotations

1. **my man** = Tybalt means 'just the man I am looking for', but Mercutio playfully develops the idea that 'man' can also indicate a male servant.
2. **Marry go ... call him 'man'.** = The only way Romeo would ever be Tybalt's 'follower' or 'man' is if he followed him to the duelling ground, having accepted his challenge.
3. **appertaining** = justified, understandable
4. **devise** = imagine
5. **Alla stoccata carries it away.** = An appeal to the sword wins the day. "Alla stoccata" is Italian for "To the sword".
6. **will you walk?** = will you go somewhere with me where we can fight?
7. **your nine lives** = an allusion to the nine lives that a cat is said to have
8. **to make bold withal** = to take the liberty of ending
9. **use** = treat
10. **drybeat** = put an end to
11. **pilcher** = a negative term for the case of a sword
12. **ears** = handle of a sword
13. **put thy rapier up** = lower your sword

Part B: Shakespearean drama — Workshop: Practice

35 **TYBALT.** I am for you.
[*Drawing*]
ROMEO. Gentle Mercutio, put thy rapier up[13].
MERCUTIO. Come, sir, your *passado*[14].
They fight
40 **ROMEO.** Draw, Benvolio; beat down their weapons.
Gentlemen, for shame, forbear this outrage!
Tybalt, Mercutio, the prince expressly hath
Forbid this bandying[15] in Verona streets.
45 Hold, Tybalt! Good Mercutio!
TYBALT *under* **ROMEO**'s *arm stabs* **MERCUTIO**[16], *and flies with his followers* […]
Exeunt **MERCUTIO** *and* **BENVOLIO**
ROMEO. This gentleman, the prince's near ally,
50 My very friend, hath got his mortal hurt
In my behalf; my reputation stain'd
With Tybalt's slander, – Tybalt, that an hour
Hath been my kinsman[17]! O sweet Juliet,
Thy beauty hath made me effeminate
55 And in my temper[18] soften'd valour's steel[19]!
Re-enter BENVOLIO
BENVOLIO. O Romeo, Romeo, brave Mercutio's dead!
That gallant spirit hath aspired the clouds[20],
60 Which too untimely here did scorn the earth[21].
ROMEO. This day's black fate on more days doth depend;
This but begins the woe[22], others must end.

BENVOLIO. Here comes the furious Tybalt back
65 again.
ROMEO. Alive, in triumph, and Mercutio slain!
Away to heaven, respective lenity[23],
And fire-eyed fury be my conduct now!
Re-enter **TYBALT**
70 Now, Tybalt, take the villain back again,
That late thou gavest me; for Mercutio's soul
Is but a little way above our heads,
Staying for thine to keep him company:
Either thou, or I, or both, must go with him.
75 **TYBALT.** Thou, wretched boy, that didst consort[24] him here,
Shalt with him hence.
ROMEO.   This shall determine that.
They fight; **TYBALT** *falls*
80 **BENVOLIO.** Romeo, away, be gone!
The citizens are up[25], and Tybalt slain.
Stand not amazed: the prince will doom thee death[26],
If thou art taken: hence, be gone, away!
85 **ROMEO.** O, I am fortune's fool[27]!
BENVOLIO.   Why dost thou stay?
Exit **ROMEO**

Annotations

[14] **your** *passado* = let me see you make a thrust with your sword
[15] **bandying** = fighting
[16] Romeo has rushed between them to part them. Tybalt then aims a blow at Mercutio, the sword passing under Romeo's arm.
[17] **that an hour … kinsman** = who, by my marriage with Juliet, has only just become my relative
[18] **temper** = character, personality; blacksmiths also 'temper' steel by immersing it in cold water when it is hot
[19] **soften'd valour's steel** = softened Romeo's formerly brave and steadfast character

[20] **hath aspired the clouds** = has been sent to heaven
[21] **Which too … earth** = left the earth too soon
[22] **woe** = misery
[23] **respective lenity** = gentleness that is respectful
[24] **consort** = accompany
[25] **are up** = are in a state of commotion
[26] **will doom thee death** = will condemn you to death
[27] **fortune's fool** = The Elizabethans believed that everyone's destiny was dictated by Fortuna, the goddess of luck, fate and fortune.

ANALYSIS

3 Language awareness Examine the changing roles Romeo plays in this scene and analyse how Shakespeare's language underlines them. → SUPPORT D7, p. 324

→ **S11:** How to work with drama, p. 350

COMMENT/CREATIVE WRITING

4 CHOOSE
Comment on Romeo's description of himself as "fortune's fool".
OR
Write Romeo's letter to Juliet explaining what happened in this scene from his point of view.

→ **S6:** How to write a discussion/comment, p. 338

→ **S2:** Checklist: Creative writing, p. 331

Texts Part B: Shakespearean drama

Love at first sonnet

1

Look at this film still of Romeo and Juliet's first meeting and describe how you perceive the two characters' feelings in this situation.

→ **S15:** How to describe pictures, p. 358

2

a) Read the text below and watch a video illustrating how Romeo and Juliet begin "talking in sonnets" when they speak to each other for the first time in Act I, Scene 5. This is called a shared sonnet. The lines are spoken alternately by two characters.

Webcode
You can find a link to the video here: WES-73644-120

→ **S20:** How to listen/watch effectively, p. 366

b) Analyse the pilgrim metaphor in Romeo and Juliet's "shared sonnet". → SUPPORT D8, p. 324

→ **S10:** How to work with poetry, p. 347

Annotations
[1] **profane** = dishonour
[2] **mannerly devotion** = proper worship
[3] **palm** = inside of the hand
[4] **palmer** = pilgrim

ROMEO. *Taking JULIET's hand*
If I profane[1] with my unworthiest hand
This holy shrine, the gentle sin is this:
My lips, two blushing pilgrims, ready stand
5 To smooth that rough touch with a tender kiss.

JULIET. Good pilgrim, you do wrong your hand too much,
Which mannerly devotion[2] shows in this;
For saints have hands that pilgrims' hands do touch,
And palm[3] to palm is holy palmers'[4] kiss.

10 **ROMEO.** Have not saints lips, and holy palmers too?

JULIET. Ay, pilgrim, lips that they must use in prayer.

ROMEO. O then, dear saint, let lips do what hands do.
They pray: grant thou, lest faith turn to despair.

JULIET. Saints do not move, though grant for prayers' sake.

15 **ROMEO.** Then move not while my prayer's effect I take.
He kisses her

3

a) At the end of the play, the two lovers die. Do you know what exactly happens? Talk about it in class.

b) After they have kissed for the first time at the end of their shared sonnet, Romeo says to Juliet, "Thus from my lips, by thine, my sin is purged." Explain how this line foreshadows the tragic end of their love story.

4

Pair work Act out the scene.

Part B: Shakespearean drama — Advanced texts

8

The seven ages of man

1
Watch a video clip of a famous Shakespearean soliloquy and list the seven ages of man according to Shakespeare. Note down a few key words about each one.

→ **S20:** How to listen/watch effectively, p. 366

Webcode
You can find a link to the video here:
WES-73644-121

2
Comment on Shakespeare's view that life is like a play.

3 CHOOSE
Write a modern version of this speech for men.
OR
Write a modern version of this speech for women.

→ **S5:** Checklist: Writing a speech, p. 337

> **Info**
> **Soliloquy**
> A soliloquy is a typical element of Shakespearean drama. It is a monologue which gives the audience access to a character's mind, revealing his or her innermost thoughts and motives. Some famous examples could be described as internal debates.

Listening: Could Shakespeare survive in Hollywood?

1 CD/15
Listen to the following programme on whether Shakespeare could survive in Hollywood and answer the questions about it in a few words.
1. How many cinema and TV adaptations of Shakespeare have been made?
2. Name two sources of income Shakespeare would have today.
3. Why would Shakespeare need a lawyer if he were a contemporary writer?
4. Why is the US TV series *Deadwood* considered to be Shakespearean?
5. What would Shakespeare need in order to get a contract with a TV company?
6. What aspect of many Shakespearean plays might not go down too well with modern audiences?
7. How much would Shakespeare earn every year according to *Forbes* magazine?

Webcode
You can find the audio file here:
WES-73644-122

→ **S20:** How to listen/watch effectively, p. 366

Shakespeare retold: The Taming of the Shrew

PRE-READING
1 Round robin
Talk about how you would define a 'good' husband and a 'good' wife.
- Are there differences between them in your opinion?
- How do your ideas compare with the expectations of society in general?

THE ORIGINAL PLAY
2
The Taming of the Shrew is a comedy about gender roles. Katherina, the shrew, is a witty and sharp-tongued woman who refuses to get married. However, her father insists unrelentingly that she marry before her younger sister, Bianca. Katherina finally agrees to marry Petruchio, a clever but rough man who "tames" her and makes her into a "model wife", or so it seems. At a banquet to celebrate three marriages at the end of the play, Petruchio suggests a contest to determine the most obedient wife. Katherina wins with the following controversial monologue which is open to interpretation.

Read the monologue on p. 290 and outline Katherina's arguments in favour of male supremacy.

Advanced texts — Part B: Shakespearean drama

KATHERINA
Fie[1], fie! Unknit that threat'ning unkind brow
And dart not scornful glances from those eyes
To wound thy lord, thy king, thy governor.
5 It blots thy beauty as frosts do bite the meads[2],
Confounds thy fame[3] as whirlwinds shake fair buds,
And in no sense is meet[4] or amiable.
A woman moved[5] is like a fountain troubled,
10 Muddy, ill-seeming, thick, bereft of beauty,
And while it is so, none so dry or thirsty
Will deign to[6] sip or touch one drop of it.
Thy husband is thy lord, thy life, thy keeper,
Thy head, thy sovereign, one that cares for thee,
15 And for thy maintenance commits his body
To painful labor both in sea and land,
To watch the night in storms, the day in cold,
Whilst thou liest warm at home, secure and safe,
And craves no other tribute at thy hands,
20 But love, fair looks and true obedience –
Too little payment for so great a debt.
Such duty as the subject owes the prince,
Even such a woman oweth to her husband.
And when she is froward[7], peevish[8], sullen, sour,
25 And not obedient to his honest will,
What is she but a foul, contending rebel
And graceless traitor to her loving lord?
I am ashamed that women are so simple
To offer war where they should kneel for peace;
30 Or seek for rule, supremacy and sway
When they are bound to serve, love and obey.
Why are our bodies soft and weak and smooth,
Unapt[9] to toil and trouble in the world,
But that our soft conditions and our hearts
35 Should well agree with our external parts?
Come, come, you froward and unable worms!
My mind hath been as big as one of yours,
My heart as great, my reason haply[10] more,
To bandy[11] word for word and frown for frown.
40 But now I see our lances are but straws,
Our strength as weak, our weakness past compare,
That seeming to be most which we indeed least are.
45 Then vail your stomachs, for it is no boot,
And place your hand below your husband's foot:
In token of[12] which duty, if he please,
My hand is ready, may it do him ease.

PETRUCHIO
50 Why, there's a wench![13] Come on and kiss me, Kate.

Annotations
[1] **Fie** /faɪ/ = expression of outrage
[2] **meads** /miːdz/ = areas of grass
[3] **Confounds thy fame** = makes you look bad
[4] **meet** = appropriate
[5] **moved** = angry, agitated
[6] **Will deign to** = will bring themselves to
[7] **froward** = difficult to deal with, stubborn
[8] **peevish** = in a foul mood
[9] **Unapt** = unsuited
[10] **haply** = by chance, perhaps
[11] **to bandy** = to quarrel, argue
[12] **In token of** = as a gesture of
[13] **Why, there's a wench!** = There, that's my girl!

3

→ **S6:** How to write a discussion/comment, p. 338

There have been many different interpretations of Katherina's last speech on stage. From your knowledge of Shakespeare's women, e.g. Juliet, discuss which interpretation is most likely in your opinion.
- Katherina pretends to be "tamed" in order that she and Petruchio win the bet. This would suggest a certain mutuality and equality between them.
- Petruchio's brutal methods (e.g. lack of food and sleep) have tamed Katherina into submission and she is the "good" wife she is expected to be.
- Katherina's speech is meant ironically. Katherina is telling the audience what they want to hear but not what she believes herself.
- Katherina is the victim of a deal between her father and Petruchio and her speech is full of bitter resignation.

Part B: Shakespearean drama — Advanced texts

A MODERN ADAPTATION IN NOVEL FORM

4 Shakespeare has been the source of inspiration for a great deal of modern literature. Anne Tyler's novel *Vinegar Girl*, published in 2016, is an example. Read the summary of the novel and discuss how convincing the plot is.

→ **S6:** How to write a discussion/comment, p. 338

Underappreciated, forthright and opinionated, Kate Battista longs for a life beyond looking after the household for herself, her father (an eccentric and adventurous scientist) and her pretty younger sister. Things at work aren't perfect either, where she is constantly told to be more diplomatic and patient with the parents of the pre-school children who adore her.

Meanwhile, her father is seeking a solution to his own problem. He's finally reached an academic breakthrough that could reverse years of unproductivity. However, his lab assistant, Pyotr, who has been a brilliant asset and essential to his research, is close to being deported from the country.

His idea of how to keep Pyotr in the country legally is scandalous, and he needs Kate's assistance. She cannot believe it and is so angry that he could ask anything more of her, however eventually she agrees to marry Pyotr.

5 Read the extract from the novel and outline Kate's arguments on behalf of men.

Vinegar girl
by Anne Tyler

She was conscious of Pyotr's eyes on her – of everybody's eyes – and of Uncle Barclay's highly entertained expression and Aunt Thelma's tensed posture as she watched for the first possible chance to break in and put an end to this. But Kate focused solely on Bunny. "Treat your husband any way you like," she said, "but I pity him, whoever he is. It's hard being a man. Have you ever thought about that? Anything that's bothering them, men think they have to hide it. They think they should seem in charge, in control; they don't dare show their true feelings. No matter if they're hurting or desperate or stricken with[1] grief, if they're heartsick or they're homesick or some huge dark guilt is hanging over them or they're about to fail big-time at something – 'Oh, I'm okay,' they say. 'Everything's just fine.' They're a whole lot less free than women are, when you think about it. Women have been studying people's feelings since they were toddlers[2]; they've been perfecting their radar – their intuition or their empathy or their interpersonal whatchamacallit[3]. They know how things work underneath, while the men have been stuck with the sports competitions and the wars and the fame and success. It's like men and women are in two different countries! I'm not 'backing down,' as you call it; I'm letting him into my country. I'm giving him space in a place where we can both be ourselves. Lord have mercy, Bunny, cut us some *slack*[4]!"

Bunny sank onto her chair, looking dazed. She might not have been persuaded, but she was giving up the fight, for now.

Pyotr rose to his feet and placed an arm around Kate's shoulders. He smiled into her eyes and said, "Kiss me, Katya."

And she did.

Annotations
[1] **stricken with** = affected by a serious problem
[2] **toddler** = very small child
[3] **whatchamacallit** /ˈwɒtʃəməˌkɔːlɪt/ = a word you cannot remember at the moment
[4] to **cut** sb **some slack** = to be less strict with sb

6
a) Compare the arguments put forward in the original and the modern version.
b) Comment on the arguments put forward by Katherina and Kate Battista.

→ **S6:** How to write a discussion/comment, p. 338

Advanced texts — Part B: Shakespearean drama

→ **S5:** Checklist: Writing a speech, p. 337

7 CHOOSE

From a Shakespearean/Elizabethan point of view, write a speech on what constitutes a 'good' husband. How should he treat his wife?

OR

Write a speech on what problems women have in present-day society.

Webcode
You can find the video here:
WES-73644-123

A MODERN FILM ADAPTATION

8 DVD/26

The BBC production *Shakespeare retold: The Taming of the Shrew* is set in present-day London. Katherine Minola is an opposition MP, who is instructed to find a husband to make her more electable.

→ **S20:** How to listen/watch effectively, p. 366

a) Watch the video clip and say how convincing you find the actress's version of Katherina's final monologue.

→ **S6:** How to write a discussion/comment, p. 338

b) Discuss the relevance of Shakespeare's gender theme today.

Henry V: Shakespeare for managers

→ **S14:** How to analyse a speech, p. 355

1

a) Read the following speech, given by King Henry V in Shakespeare's historical play of the same name and explain its message.

→ **S6:** How to write a discussion/comment, p. 338

b) Imagine you had been a soldier in Henry's army. Comment on how inspiring you would have found his motivational strategies.

Once more unto the breach[1], dear friends, once more;
Or close the wall up with our English dead.
In peace there's nothing so becomes[2] a man
5 As modest stillness and humility:
But when the blast of war blows in our ears,
Then imitate the action of the tiger;
Stiffen the sinews, summon up the blood,
Disguise fair nature with hard-favour'd rage;
10 Then lend the eye a terrible aspect[3];
Let pry through the portage[4] of the head
Like the brass cannon; [...]
Now set the teeth and stretch the nostril wide,
Hold hard the breath and bend up every spirit
15 To his full height. On, on, you noblest English.
Whose blood is fet[5] from fathers of war-proof[6]!
Fathers that, like so many Alexanders[7],
Have in these parts from morn till even[8] fought
And sheathed their swords for lack of argument:
20 Dishonour not your mothers; now attest
That those whom you call'd fathers did beget[9]
   you. [...]
And you, good yeoman[10],
Whose limbs were made in England, show us here
25 The mettle of your pasture[11]; let us swear
That you are worth your breeding; which I doubt not;
For there is none of you so mean and base,
That hath not noble lustre in your eyes.
30 I see you stand like greyhounds in the slips[12],
Straining upon the start. The game's afoot:
Follow your spirit, and upon this charge
Cry 'God for Harry, England, and Saint George!'

Annotations
[1] **breach** = breach in the city walls
[2] **becomes** = suits
[3] **aspect** = gleam
[4] **portage** = porthole, meaning eye socket
[5] **fet** = descended
[6] **of war-proof** = who have proved themselves in a war
[7] **Alexanders** = reference to Alexander the Great, who conquered a huge empire in a short time
[8] **even** = evening
[9] **beget** = create/father a child
[10] **yeoman** = ordinary soldier
[11] **The mettle of your pasture** = the fine character you developed working the land
[12] **in the slips** = on their leads

2

Now read the excerpt from Richard Olivier's book *Inspirational leadership* and name the mistakes managers often make when trying to motivate their employees.

Inspirational leadership
by Richard Olivier

FIRST STEPS – FIRST BLOCKS
That's the whole scene. One speech. It could easily be taken as a stirring beginning to the conflict. The only clue that this is not so is that little word, "more": "Once more unto the breach …"

Henry has started out with a very reasonable strategy; land at Harfleur in August with 10,000 troops, take it in a week, push on through France and take Paris by Christmas. Sounds sensible enough, except that, like many big projects, things don't quite work out the way they were planned at Head Office. The fact is that at the beginning of Act 3 Scene 1 Henry and his troops have been outside Harfleur for three months, during which time they have lost 2,000 troops. Another 3,000 are ill, and the remaining 5,000, as you might imagine, are not keen to head back into "that breach".

COMMON MISTAKES
Now Henry needs to motivate the demoralised troops. There are several key features to the speech, many of which elude modern managers. In workshops, we often give people the opportunity of role play motivating their "troops" out of their first blocks. If I were to paraphrase a typical first response to this challenge, it would sound something like the following: "Right you lot. Thanks for coming to the meeting, although I am sure you all know why it has been necessary to call it. I gave you a target when we started; to take this town in a week. It is now three months, three months later, and you have still not achieved it. You are way behind schedule and severely over budget. What's more, I am sure it has not escaped your notice that 20% of you are dead, and another 30% have called in sick. What the hell is going on?"

At which point the "troops" are about as keen to fight as they would be to jump off a cliff. All the speaker has done is to remind the listeners of what has gone wrong.

Henry's troops have been living in a marsh[1] for three months, watching their mates die, believe me they know what is wrong. What they need is something that can change their energy and create a different result.

The first thing Henry does is to include himself in the conversation: "Once more unto the breach, dear friends …" When was the last time you were three months behind delivery on an important project and your boss called you dear friend? If there is no inclusion then there is separation. You and Them. […]

He requires a different energy than in peacetime, but he also reminds them that if they succeed they will be one step nearer to peace. We keep asking for more energy, more commitment, better results faster without any let up[2] or time for rest and relaxation. This is simply not sustainable and can quickly cause burn out. It implies that if the troops meet the target in the short term we will give them a bigger target in the long term. Where's the motivation in that? Don't punish people who work hard and get results.

THE RIGHT IMAGE CHANGES THE ENERGY
The key to re-motivation is effective use of imagery. Henry does not simply tell his troops where to go (they know that already), he tells them how they can be successful when they get there: "… imitate the action of the tiger …"

The language itself serves to wake people up. If you then actually try to put the images into the body, it doubles the effect. This is a very similar idea to the "active imagination" techniques used in psychology. "See" the desired results, then think what energy you need to achieve it, then imagine doing it, then do it. […] If you really take the image on board it will change your energy. The right change of energy can change the result.

Annotations
[1] **marsh** = area of soft wet land
[2] **let up** = pause

3 **Language awareness** Olivier says that if you want to motivate people the effective use of imagery is essential. Think of a situation you might experience, e.g. as the captain of a sports team, a class representative etc. Briefly describe the situation and write a short speech using motivational imagery.

→ **S5:** Checklist: Writing a speech, p. 337

Diff section

1 The individual and society
Part A: Irish identity

Workshop: Step by step

D1 SUPPORT FOR TASK 4 (P. 24)

Match the following features to the various narrative perspectives and modes of presentation they represent. This may improve your understanding of each method's advantages and disadvantages. Note that some points may apply to for more than one category.

EXAMPLE: 1B, 2 …

1. allows the author great freedom to follow the lives of various characters and switch between them
2. gives the reader important background information without narrating it in detail
3. restricts the story to the experiences of a single person
4. allows the reader to identify easily with one character
5. may cause the reader to be misguided by a character's flawed perception of events
6. introduces the reader directly and comprehensively to a character's inner life, including all the random associations and ideas that may come to the character's mind
7. allows the characters to present themselves and their actions in their own words and in detail
8. often gives the reader an advantage over the characters when it comes to knowing about what has happened and what may happen in the future
9. conveys an important moment very vividly
10. makes it easier to cover longer periods of time and various settings efficiently
11. is often characterized by a flow of observations, thoughts and ideas that seem confusing and disconnected and therefore difficult for the reader to follow

A first-person narration
B third-person narration – omniscient narrator
C third-person narration – selective narrator
D telling/panoramic mode of presentation
E showing/scenic mode of presentation
F stream of consciousness

Workshop: Practice

D2 SUPPORT FOR TASK 4 (P. 26)

a) Read these short extracts from novels and short stories. Identify the narrative perspective and the mode of presentation used in each extract.

Extract 1

Sister Imelda
by Edna O'Brien

We had returned from our long summer holiday and we were all wretched. The convent, with its high stone wall and green iron gates enfolding us again, seemed more of a prison than ever – for after our spell in the outside world we all felt very much older and more sophisticated, and my friend Baba and I were dreaming of our final escape, which would be in a year. And
5 so, on that damp autumn evening when I saw the chrysanthemums and saw the new nun intent on prayer, I pitied her and thought how alone she must be, cut off from her friends and conversation, with only God as her intangible spouse.

The next day she came into our classroom to take Geometry. Her pale, slightly long face I saw as formidable, but her eyes were different, being blue-black and full of verve.

Extract 2

The Gathering
by Anne Enright

The house knows me. Always smaller than it should be; the walls run closer and more complicated than the ones you remember. The place is always too small.
Behind me, my mother opens the sitting room door.
5 "Will you have something? A cup of tea?"
But I do not want to go into the sitting room. I am not a visitor. This is my house too. I was inside it, as it grew; as the dining room was knocked into the kitchen, as the kitchen swallowed the back garden. It is the place where my dreams still happen.
10 Not that I would ever live here again. The place is all extension and no house. Even the cubby-hole beside the kitchen door has another door at the back of it, so you have to battle your way through coats and hoovers to get into the downstairs loo. You could not sell the place, I sometimes think, except as a site. Level it and start again.
15 The kitchen still smells the same – it hits me in the base of the skull, very dim and disgusting, under the fresh, primrose yellow paint.

Extract 3

Music at Annahullion
by Eugene McCabe

"Thanks very much," Annie said to herself. She hooked a griddle over the glow of sods to warm a few wheaten scones. She could maybe mention it quiet like, give it time to sink. He might rise to it after a while maybe, or again he might know what she was up to and say nothing. [...]
5 "Only Petey Mulligan the shopboy. He kep' sayin' 'Jasus' every minute to see poor George nod and bless himself, and then he winked at me, much as to say 'mad frigger, but we're wise' ... too old-fashioned by half."
Teddy was quiet for a minute and then said: "Religion puts people mad."
"No religion puts them madder."
10 He thought about this. He hadn't confessed for near forty years, lay in bed of a Sunday with rubbishy papers Liam wouldn't use to light fires. Sometimes they had bitter arguments about religion and the clergy. Liam and Annie never missed Mass.

b) To write your analysis, you can use this language support:

> **Language support**
>
> **Analysing the narrative perspective of a novel**
> The story is told by an omniscient/a first-person/selective third-person/ unreliable narrator.
> The first-person/third-person narrator is involved in the story as a protagonist/a minor character.
> The narrator presents the story from a limited/an unlimited point of view.
> The narrator possesses some insight into the consciousness/thoughts and feelings of one character/several characters.
> With the help of the …. narrative perspective, it becomes clear/is revealed/the reader is made to feel/experience …

Diff section

Part B: Canadian identity

Workshop: Step by step

D3 SUPPORT FOR TASK 5 (P. 37)

If you need help, you can copy this grid to which some of the information has already been added.

name	category	information from the text/quote	interpretation
Martha	personal details	"Martha was only a little girl" (l. 1)	She does not fully understand what is going on.
	character	"Trusting, affectionate and with a ready smile" (ll. 15-16)	Martha is described as a happy child.
		…	She appears naive and innocent.
Mary	personal details	belongs to one of Canada's First Nations (l. 52)	…
	character	dresses her daughter up for the trip (ll. 22-24)	…
		…	…
Trader	personal details	had served in the armed forces during the war (ll. 40-41)	This could mean that he has a tough character.
	character	…	…
Pilot	personal details	white, ex-air force (ll. 40-41)	…
		married to … (l. 53-54)	He is likely to have some understanding of indigenous culture.
	character	thinks it's wrong to take children from their parents (ll. 59-61)	…
		"and if he didn't do it, someone else would snap up the business." (ll. 63-64)	He is rather pragmatic.

Webcode

You can download the grid here:
WES-73644-124

D4 SUPPORT FOR TASK 7 (P. 37)

When writing a scene from a different point of view, it is important to decide which register is appropriate. The register will depend on the age and background of the narrator.
Look at the following two paragraphs. They are possible openings for a change of perspective in this scene.

1.
I was just a kid when these guys came and took me away. People talked about this place called school, but I thought only bad kids went there. And I wasn't bad. I tried real hard to be good. School scared the life out of me.

2.
She was a pretty young girl with beautiful, black eyes, who was quite small for her age. I could tell she was terrified of the plane because she hid behind her mother. I felt extremely sorry for that poor child, separated from her parents at such an early age and sent to an institution.

Diff section

a) Identify the points of view from which they are written.
b) Look for differences in language:
   - find examples of informal/colloquial language (vocabulary, grammar, short forms, etc.), e.g. *real hard*.
   - find examples of more formal language, e.g. *terrified*.
c) Rewrite the first paragraph in a more formal register.

Workshop: Practice

D5 SUPPORT FOR TASK 3 (P. 39)

The second extract from the novel is set some ten years later, when Martha returns home for good. The years at school have transformed the happy, affectionate child we met in the first extract from the novel.

a) Choose five expressions from the language support box to describe Martha at the age of 16 when she returns home and find appropriate evidence in the text to support your choice.
b) Use the expressions you have chosen to explain the changes Martha has experienced and how this affects her relationship to her mother.

EXAMPLE:

Martha is traumatized by the abuse she received from Father Antoine. As her mother refused to believe or help her, Martha is full of pent up anger.
She ...

Language support

to be	traumatized/abused/troubled by sb or sth
	caught between two cultures
	full of pent up anger
to feel	betrayed/rejected by sb
	like an outcast/outsider
	abandoned/forsaken/neglected by sb
	hostile/antagonistic towards sb or sth
to become	despondent towards/dispirited by sth
to lose/to lack	faith/trust in sb

D6 SUPPORT FOR TASK 4 (P. 39)

Before rewriting this extract from Martha's mother Mary's perspective, you need to analyse her character. This will influence the way she recounts the events.

Look at the following situations from the extract 2:
- Mary refused to respond to her daughter's accusations about Father Antoine.
- Mary complained that she couldn't support her daughter financially.
- Mary made fun of Martha's attempt to speak her native language.
- Mary criticized Martha's attempts to help in the house.
- Mary refused to support Martha when she became ill.

What do these situations suggest about Mary? Choose one or more of the words in the box to describe her character in these situations. When you make your decision, take into account the possible motives for her behaviour. Write one or two sentences to explain each situation.

Language support

ashamed | bewildered | callous | confused | contemptuous | derisive | egoistic | hardened | heartbroken | heartless | ignorant | indifferent | insecure | money-grabbing | out of her depth | suspicious | uneducated | unkind | unsympathetic

EXAMPLE:

Mary's refusal to respond to the abuse suffered by Martha suggests that she is a heartless mother. Although she is dependent on the money she gets from the state, this does not justify her unsympathetic attitude towards her daughter's situation. On the other hand ...

Diff section

2 Science and technology
Part A: Chances and risks

Workshop: Step by step

D1 SUPPORT FOR TASK 6 (P. 53)

If you want to summarize a text, it helps to understand the structure of the text first.
a) Divide the text into paragraphs.
b) Very briefly summarize each paragraph.
c) Now explain how the paragraphs are linked fluidly, i.e. describe the logical structure of the text. Use this grid:

Webcode
You can download the grid here:
WES-73644-125

lines	content	structure
ll. 1–18	Power and wealth, which today are in the hands of many, may in the future only belong to those who create the algorithms.	one possible scenario, contrasted with the situation today
ll. 19–31	Algorithms may …	an alternative scenario
ll. 32–50		possible consequences of second scenario
…	…	…

d) Write the summary. You can start like this:
In this extract from the non-fiction book "Homo Deus" by Yuval Noah Harari, the author focuses on what might happen if more and more jobs are taken over by algorithms. Power and wealth may … Another possibility would be that …

Part B: Literary visions of the future

Workshop: Step by step

D2 SUPPORT FOR TASK 1B (P. 62)

Complete the sentences and use them to describe the atmosphere in the scene.

The use of dark colours The lack of natural light The melancholy music The fact that the scene is set in an operating theatre at a hospital The use of close-ups of faces expressing pain and showing tears welling up in the characters' eyes The medium shot of Tommy's body on the operating table The lack of direct conversation The flashback to her childhood days	reveals suggests emphasizes points out draws the viewer's attention to the fact hints at a key feature of the plot, namely creates the impression provides the reader with an inkling	that something terrible/deeply sad/… is about to happen, namely … that the two characters are having a terrible experience because … that the story is set in a society that seems to be characterized by … that the characters feel under intense pressure that … that the situation is tense/tragic/… because …

298

Diff section

D3 SUPPORT FOR TASK 5B (P. 65)

Another part of the grid has been filled in for you.

quotation	type of device	interpretation	concrete function/effect
"We'd been in the pavilion ... that afternoon" (ll. 2-6)	the meaning of the place	The pavilion is usually associated with a positive and carefree experience loved by the students for the games they can play there, etc.	The narrator creates a carefree and light-hearted atmosphere here.
...	...	It seems like the rain will never end, thus keeping the students huddled together under the roof instead of allowing them to leave the pavilion in order to play a game of rounders, i.e. enjoy themselves.	The atmosphere begins to change, becoming somewhat tense.

D4 SUPPORT FOR TASK 6 (P. 65)

a) Here are some words you can use for describing the atmosphere. See if you understand them and check a dictionary for the ones you do not know.

b) Place the words into groups of positive and negative adjectives.

> alarming | awkward | bustling | cheerful | depressing | dismal | dynamic | eerie | energetic | gloomy | grim | harmonious | hopeful | hopeless | idyllic | inviting | light-hearted | nightmarish | nostalgic | pessimistic | playful | relaxed | scary | sentimental | tense | threatening | uncanny | uncomfortable | warm | welcoming

c) You can use these phrases to explain how the narrator uses certain techniques to create a particular atmosphere:

Language support

> to create a(n) ... atmosphere with the help of ...
> to build up a(n) ... atmosphere through the use of ...
> to make the reader feel ...
> to draw the reader's attention to ...
> to connect/contrast/... the outside world with ...
> to instill a feeling of ... in the reader
> to convey the impression that ...

Webcode

You can download the grid here:
WES-73644-126

D5 SUPPORT FOR TASK 7 (P. 65)

Before you start working on task 7, consider the following aspects and note down to what extent they help to justify Miss Lucy's decision to tell the student's about their fate:
- the emotional and psychological impact of this information on both the guardians and the students,
- the guardians' responsibility for the students' well-being,
- possible consequences the revelation may have for the donation programme,
- the role of the state in the context of this programme,
- Miss Lucy's motivation behind revealing this information.

Diff section

Workshop: Practice

D6 SUPPORT FOR TASK 3 (P. 66)

Before you start working on task 3, you may use the tips and questions listed below to take notes for your analysis.

Checklist

Atmosphere:

1) **The characters:**
   - What mood are they in? e.g. "I was keen to regain the carefree, almost silly mood" (ll. 1-2)
   - Has it changed or is it changing in the scene?
   - How does their behaviour influence the overall impression of the situation?
     e.g. "we both stopped talking until they'd gone further up the slope and out of earshot." (ll. 54-55)

2) **The setting:**
   - Where are the characters and what is said about the place?
     e.g. "It would have made a nice spot in the summer for an ordinary family to sit and eat a picnic." (ll. 11-13)
   - What could be its significance or (symbolic) meaning?
   - How does the weather relate to the topic of the characters' discussion?

Language:
choice of words / imagery:
- ✓ What do the words used by Kathy and Tommy reveal about the way they experience the situation?
  e.g. "But the point is, whoever decides, Madame or whoever it is, they need something to go on." (ll. 83-85)
- ✓ What does the language used by the narrator to describe the characters and the situation convey?
  e.g. "a steeply climbing path" (l. 6); "they've been stoking it up" (l. 26)

Diff section

Advanced texts

What is the true meaning of equality?

D7 SUPPORT FOR TASK 3B (P. 73)

a) Before you write your analysis, look at the examples and complete the grid with explanations of the effect/function.

b) Add more examples to each part. Watch out for:
- use of language: rhetorical devices (e.g. metaphors, similes, alliteration, climax), choice of words (e.g. emotive language, positive/negative connotations, superlatives)
- elements of the plot that tell you something about the society

Webcode

You can download the grid here:
WES-73644-127

example	effect/function
1. Use of language	
"blindingly beautiful" (l. 228)	alliteration: emphasizes how distorted her looks usually are and how impressive her appearance is once the handicaps have been removed
"feel like something the cat drug in" (l. 45)	…
"a tremendous pair of earphones, and spectacles with thick wavy lenses" (ll. 165-166)	…
"That was a real pretty dance" (l. 34); "so's you can rest …" (ll. 84-85); "kind of wore out" (l. 95), "a few of them lead balls" (l. 98)	Hazel's speech is characterized by small grammatical errors typical of American everyday speech. By having her speak like this, the narrator …
…	…
2. Elements of the plot	
"All this equality was due to the 211th, 212th, and 213th Amendments to the Constitution, and to the unceasing vigilance of agents of the United States Handicapper General." (ll. 6-10)	a legal framework that defines equality on the level of a constitutional amendment (not just a law); a government official who is in charge of pursuing any kind of violation with determination and strictness ("unceasing vigilance")
"And George, while his intelligence was way above normal, had a little mental handicap radio in his ear. He was required by law to wear it at all times. It was tuned to a government transmitter. Every twenty seconds or so, the transmitter would send out some sharp noise to keep people like George from taking unfair advantage of their brains." (ll. 20-27)	…
"'I forget,' she said. 'Something real sad on television.' […] 'It's all kind of mixed up in my mind,' said Hazel." (ll. 279-282)	…
…	…

Diff section

3 The media
Part A: Opinion-makers

Advanced texts

Filter bubbles and echo chambers

D1 SUPPORT FOR TASK 1C (P. 82)

1. Find a headline for your article that attracts attention:
   - ask a question, e.g. *Are we too naive?*
   - use a quote, e.g. *'It's madness', says football coach*
   - state the main point, e.g. *Politician angered by media coverage*
   - state an argument or opinion, e.g. *Teenage well-being matters to all of us*
   - if you're confident, you can try a play on words, e.g. *Big Bang Theory: Why Germans love their fireworks on New Year's Eve*

2. Structure your article:
   - briefly explain how the filter bubble works.
   - state its advantages according to the video.
   - state its disadvantages according to the video.
   Use your own words.

3. Find an ending to your article that neatly rounds off what you have written. You can:
   - refer back to your heading, e.g. *And that is why teenage well-being is a matter that concerns us all.*
   - sum up the main idea of your text, e.g. *All in all, … To sum up …*
   - end with a question, e.g. *The question remains whether …*

Part B: Living in the digital age

Workshop: Step by step

D2 SUPPORT FOR TASK 2D (P. 86)

Here is an example of a character fact file:

Webcode
You can download the grid here:
WES-73644-128

(character name)	what you notice in the film	what it tells you about the character and the plot
general information: age, outward appearance, job/education, family background	…	…
actions/behaviour	…	…
interaction with other characters /relationships	…	…
thoughts/feelings/motivation	…	…

Diff section

D3 SUPPORT FOR TASK 3C (P. 87)

Language support

Describing film stills and their effect on the viewer

The still	conveys	an impression of	distance/proximity.
The position of the people	suggests	a feeling of	inferiority/superiority/dominance/weakness.
The facial expression	indicates	a relationship characterized by	isolation/loneliness.
The camera angle	reveals		love/affection/joy/pride/respect/admiration/indifference.
The lighting	illustrates	an atmosphere of	
The field size	highlights	an air of	tension/fear/aggression/conflict/shock/disgust.
	intensifies	the importance of	the viewer's disbelief/surprise.

Part C: English as a global language

Workshop: Practice

D4 SUPPORT FOR TASK 1 (P. 100)
This checklist can help you:

Checklist

Mediation
✓ Identify
  • addressee,
  • situational context,
  • topic,
  • type of text/register.
✓ Note down the information from the German text which you need for your presentation.
✓ Note down the words and expressions which have no direct English equivalent.
  • Decide whether you need them for your presentation.
  • If so, find a way to explain them in English so you can include the information.

Advanced texts

The value of language learning apps

D5 SUPPORT FOR TASK 4 (P. 104)
You can start like this:
1. *Use technology:*
   • *switch on English subtitles when you watch a film*
   • *download …*
   • *…*
2. *Spend time in*
   • *…*
   • *…*
3. *Read*
   • *…*
   • *…*

Diff section

4 Globalization
Part A: Global responsibility for the environment

Workshop: Step by step

D1 SUPPORT FOR TASK 1C (P. 112)

Language support

as a consequence/consequently/as a result … | due to … | is/are caused by … | the ramifications/repercussions are … | … trigger/cause/lead to …

D2 SUPPORT FOR TASK 5 (P. 113)

Here are two examples:

A As an introduction, DiCaprio refers to legendary American President Abraham Lincoln, who had to deal with an existential threat to his nation's unity in his time. DiCaprio then applies Lincoln's words – that an existential crisis makes it necessary to adopt new ways of thinking and acting – to the present, thus drawing a historical parallel between slavery and the American Civil War and climate change.

B DiCaprio begins the main body of his speech by providing examples from around the globe to prove the need for a united stand against climate change.

D3 SUPPORT FOR TASK 6B (P. 115)

Here are two examples:

A DiCaprio uses metaphorical language when he describes Beijing as "choked by industrial pollution" (ll. 24-25), illustrating the imminent dangers in a drastic way. This personification presents an image of a person unable to breathe, which may eventually lead to their death. The verb "choke" used in the passive also suggests that this death is inflicted on the inhabitants who have become the helpless victims of industrial processes.

B By using Lincoln's plea "we must think anew and act anew" (ll. 10-11), in which the word "anew" is repeated, DiCaprio lays particular emphasis on his claim that the current situation of climate change calls for a completely new approach and for immediate action. With the inclusive pronoun "we", DiCaprio involves all the members in his audience and motivates them to leave old theories behind and to act on the basis of newly gained insights.

D4 SUPPORT FOR TASK 7 (P. 115)

Tip:
When you write your analysis, it is helpful to focus on the literary devices used by the author rather than working through the speech chronologically. For example, write a paragraph on DiCaprio's use of enumeration in which you include all the instances where he employs this device. This approach helps you to present a more focused analysis and avoid unnecessary repetitions.

Diff section

Part B: Globalization and the economy

Texts

Globalization and the fashion industry

D5 SUPPORT FOR TASK 7 (P. 125)

When writing a speech, it is important to follow these steps:

Checklist

- ✓ Determine the goal of your speech.
- ✓ Consider your audience (age, attitudes) as well as the event/venue at which you are talking, since they determine the appropriate register.
- ✓ Structure your speech:
  - → Start with an **introduction** that will attract your listeners' attention, e.g. with an anecdote/the presentation of the current situation leading up to a rhetorical question.
  - → Present your arguments in the **main part**: You can choose
    - a chronological order (organizing your arguments in a sequence in time),
    - a climactic order (leading from the least important to the most important argument),
    - a topical order (giving different aspects equal importance).
  - → Finish with a **conclusion** which concisely summarizes your view, maybe leading to an appeal, a call to action, to a warning or an expression of hope for the future.

Advanced texts

Globalization defined – and re-defined

D6 SUPPORT FOR TASK 2A (P. 126)

Copy the grid and complete it with the help of the information of the first part of the extract.

The three stages of globalization:			
stage of globalization	1	2	3
main driving force/agent	…	…	…
typical developments/effects	…	…	…
size of the world	L ("macro")	M	S ("micro")

Webcode

You can download the grid here:
WES-73644-129

D7 SUPPORT FOR TASK 2B (P. 126)

Explain the old and new forms of globalization. Consider the following notions related to each form of globalization.

"Old globalization": WTO, World Bank, outsourcing, multinational

"New globalization": globalizing on their own, no over here and over there, multilocal, age of accelerations

305

Diff section

Part C: Migration and the world of work

Workshop: Step by step

D8 SUPPORT FOR TASK 2A (P. 130)

Before you watch the video, complete these sentences with words from the box that are taken from the video.

> demographic | displaced people | famine | make a moral case | refugees

1. Many Western countries are currently undergoing ▢1 change because of aging populations.
2. ▢2 have been forced to leave their home for any number of reasons, whereas ▢3 have fled their home country to escape from war or persecution.
3. Climate change has resulted in temperature rises around the world, which has resulted in bad harvests and therefore sometimes even ▢4.
4. You need good arguments to ▢5 for a change in immigration policy.

D9 SUPPORT FOR TASK 6C (P. 133)

If you find it difficult to think of other strategies, take a look at these alternative introductions to the comment and identify the strategies used here.

A Getting married or staying single, becoming a housewife or an entrepreneur – there are so many roles a woman can play in today's society. By contrast, for Mrs Mehta, a character in Hari Kunzru's novel *Transmission*, it is clear what a woman should aspire to be. She holds extremely traditional views regarding a woman's social role.

B You know what it's like: you have to be slim and sexy, a loving mother, caring wife and at the same time an ambitious career woman. It's not easy being a woman in today's society. How different are the views of Mrs Mehta, a character in Hari Kunzru's novel *Transmission*, concerning what a woman should be like, and how limited in comparison. Her views are extremely conservative.

Texts

The future of work

Webcode
You can download the grid here:
WES-73644-130

D10 SUPPORT FOR TASK 4A (P. 137)

The following grid can help you because it displays the way Harari presents his arguments. Copy the grid and complete it. Then use it as a framework for your analysis.

| Harari's central message: in the future, many people will become … (ll. 9-15) | argument: 47 per cent of jobs in the US are at a high risk of disappearing within the next twenty years (ll. 16-25). | strategy: numbers, quotes from experts (ll. 16-40) ──────── rhetorical device: enumeration of examples (ll. 25-40) ──────── register: rather formal/ scientific | quote: "For example, there is a 99 per cent probability that by 2033 human telemarketers [..] will lose their jobs to algorithms. [...] Waiters – 94 per cent. Paralegal assistants – 94 per cent. Tour guides – 91 per cent. Bakers – 89 per cent. [...] And so forth." (ll. 25-40). | effect: statistics, expert opinion and technical terms suggest reliability; readers get the impression that these are FACTS rather than mere PREDICTIONS |

Diff section

Harari's central message: in the future, many people will become ... (ll. 9-15)	argument: new professions will come into existence, but they will require a highly skilled and creative workforce and not be suitable for many of today's workers (ll. 51-60)	strategy: examples (ll. 52-60) _____ rhetorical device: contrast, irony (ll. 57-60) _____ register: ...	quote: "and it is unclear whether forty-year-old cashiers or ..." (ll. 56-57)	effect: ...
	argument: ... (ll. 61-63)	_____ _____		
	argument: ... (ll. 75-82)	_____ _____		

Language support

	The author puts forward the argument that ...	To support his argument, Harari uses ...	This can be seen in this example: "..." (ll. ...)/The statement "..." (ll. ...) supports ...	The effect on the reader ...

Part D: Living in a globalized world

Workshop: Step by step

D11 SUPPORT FOR TASK 2B (P. 140)
Use the following phrases to give feedback to how the speakers in 2b) answered the question.

	content	language, structure and presentation
🙂	• The first/second speaker included a lot of different/specific/well-explained/relevant/... arguments such as ... • By referring to ..., the ... speaker showed a profound/deep/differentiated/... understanding of the issue/question.	• The first/second speaker used varied expressions/specific topic-related vocabulary/... • The sentence structure was varied and sophisticated, but still very easy to understand, for example when ... • The answer was well structured/The ideas were linked well, for example when ... • You could follow the line of argument easily because ... • The speaker spoke fluently and used his/her voice to emphasize certain points, for example ...
😐	• There was a number of good arguments such as ..., but not all points were directly relevant to the question, for example ...	• The speaker's statement included some topic-related words, but in general ... • All in all, the statement was easy to understand, but it lacked more complex sentence structures/specific vocabulary/...

Diff section

	content	language, structure and presentation
	• The speaker had some understanding of the topic, for example when he/she referred to …, but he/she should have mentioned other points as well such as …	• In some parts, for example when the speaker referred to …, the answer was fluent, but there were too many pauses/slips/… in the rest of the answer, especially … • The speaker used hardly any connectives to make it clear …
	• The points the speaker referred to do not really address what the question asked him/her to focus on. She/He should have talked about … • Some points were not directly relevant to the question, for example …	• The language the speaker used was fairly simple, for example … • It lacked specific vocabulary to deal with the topic, for example … • The sentence structure was very basic and repetitive because the speaker always used sentences like … • The answer was just a disconnected list of ideas which lacked a clear structure. You could notice that, for example, when … • The way the speaker expressed himself/herself sounded a bit German and not very natural, for example …

D12 SUPPORT FOR TASK 3 (P. 140)

Language support

Structuring your answer	Explaining points
First of all, … Secondly, … What seems most important to me is that … As a consequence, … That's why … By contrast, … However, … What one shouldn't forget is that … Finally, … All in all, …	In order to illustrate this, one could mention … … is a typical example of this. From what I know/have experienced/…, …. According to some experts, … … serves as evidence for/that …

D13 SUPPORT FOR TASK 5 (P. 142)

Tips for talking about the photos:

- take a close look at what kind of people are presented in the photos. What is their ethnic background? Where do they live? What seems to be their social status? Are they rich or poor? How do these factors influence their eating habits?
- focus on the kind of food they are eating in the photo. Is it a basic meal? Is it sufficient to keep you going or is it too much? How healthy is the food? Can the people in the photo provide themselves with the food they need? What can you guess about the environmental impact of the food (production, packaging, etc.)?
- consider the wider implications of the photo with regard to current issues of eating habits in a globalized world:
    → sufficient and fair distribution of resources
    → health issues
    → environmental issues
    → food supplies as an example of wealth or poverty

Diff section

Language support

Introduction
What the photos have in common is that they both deal with …

Whereas … in the first picture, the second photo shows …

The … in the first picture expresses a critical attitude towards …

The … in the second picture convey(s) a (positive/negative/…) image of …

The photos are connected to the question of …

Addressing the topic
As the most prominent elements/As the central themes of the photos suggest, the topic under discussion here is …

The … in the foreground/background/… of the first/second photo makes the viewer aware of …

The way the people in the photo are acting/eating/… suggests that …

The background/the setting of the first/second photo conveys the impression that …

In the light of current trends of globalization, the photos allude to the issue of …

Whereas the first picture is closely connected to the opinion that …, the second photo expresses a more critical/optimistic view of …

Going beyond the content of the photos, one can refer to other trends in the field of …

Conclusion
All in all, the photos address the issue of …

To my mind, it is a very controversial issue because …

In my view, there is no way around changing our attitude towards …/making people more aware of …

Workshop: Practice

D14 SUPPORT FOR TASK 2B (P. 144)
These prompt cards can help you to talk about the photos and answer the question.

Photos
- Consider the chances you have to travel and see the world nowadays. Think of various means of transportation, accommodation, communication, the time you need to reach any location around the globe as well as the costs.
- Consider what you may gain from such trips in terms of cultural experiences, sightseeing, understanding of social and political situations, etc.
- Consider the opportunities tourism may provide to businesses and the workforce in countries around the globe.
- Consider the downsides of the ever-growing number of travellers and their journeys. Think of the environmental impact, but also how tourism may affect the local culture and infrastructure.

Photos
- Consider what fashion companies offer you nowadays. Think of how many clothes you can choose from, how much they cost, how often new lines of clothing are introduced into the market, etc. Consider how this influences your shopping habits.
- Consider what these developments mean for the working conditions in the countries where your clothes are produced, e.g. wages, health and safety as well as environmental standards.
- Think of ways the situation could be improved.

Photos
- Consider ways in which the Internet and other media have made communication, the exchange of information, messages, goods, etc. easier – not only locally, but internationally.
- Think of risks that are involved in our dependence on the Internet, how much we reveal of ourselves online and who has access to our data and can use the Internet to influence us.

Diff section

> **Language support**
>
> This photo reminds me of …/conveys an impression of …
> As the … in the picture illustrates, …
> The … in the photo makes me think of …/could be connected to …/…
> The topic has wider implications in addition to what is expressed in the photo, for example …
> If you compare the photos, it becomes clear that …
> Although it is not clearly expressed in the photos, one should not forget that …
> Although the first photo suggests that …, the other one clearly shows that …

D15 SUPPORT FOR TASK 3B (P. 145)

> **Language support**
>
> | Agreeing | Disagreeing |
> |---|---|
> | You're absolutely right with that point. | You seem to miss the point that … |
> | That's exactly how I see it. | I don't understand why … |
> | That's a good point. | I'm sorry, but I disagree. |
> | I couldn't have said it better. | I see it rather differently. |
> | That's what I was thinking too. | To my mind, there are other arguments that seem much more important. |
>
> **Helping someone join the conversation**
>
> What's your view on this?
> Is there anything to add?
> Which statement do you like best?
> I like …/My favorite is … What do you think?

Texts

Globalization – the state of affairs

D16 SUPPORT FOR TASK 1B (P. 146)

Find examples of the following devices and interpret their function.
- use of superlatives (grammatically, e.g. "best", and with regard to meaning, e.g. "perfect")
- enumeration
- emotive words
- metaphor/metaphorical language
- short and clear sentences
- alliteration
- parallelism
- contrast
- use of statistics
- use of concrete examples
- allusion (e.g. to the Bible, to the audience's background knowledge)

> **Language support**
>
> **Phrases to express function**
>
> to allude to sth | to convey sth | to draw attention to sth | to emphasize/underline/stress sth | to express sth | to make his audience see/understand/become aware of/… sth | to point out sth | to refer to sth | to support his view that …

Diff section

Advanced texts

Effects of globalization: Working with drama

D17 SUPPORT FOR TASK 1D (P. 148)

To prepare for your analysis, note down how the following elements influence your understanding of the scene. Find suitable examples from the extract.

Webcode

You can download the grid here:
WES-73644-131

	element	meaning	example
Dr Sharma	talking to Lakshmi in Hindi	…	…
	translating for Josh and Clem	…	…
	what he tells Josh and Clem and how he reacts to their questions and wishes	…	…
Josh and Clem	asking Lakshmi to move in a certain way for them	…	…
	sometimes disagreeing over what to say and ask	…	…
Lakshmi	her reaction/behaviour when being presented on Skype	…	…
In general	how the characters see their own role	…	…
	how much control each character has	…	…
	how much respect each character shows to the others	…	…

Diff section

5 Britishness
Part A: British identity

Workshop: Step by step
D1 SUPPORT FOR TASK 5 (P. 156)

Language support

> The use of … is highly effective/ineffective because …
>
> Illustrating her point by … is a powerful/a persuasive/a forceful/a potent/an efficient/ misleading/biased/ ineffective/weak strategy because …
>
> By …, the author gives weight/lends credibility to her arguments.
>
> The author's strategy to use …, makes her arguments quite compelling/convincing/ persuasive/forceful/unreasonable/doubtful/unconvincing.

Workshop: Practice
D2 SUPPORT FOR TASK 3 (P. 157)

Prepare for your analysis: Notetaking
After you have identified the author's main argument(s), it is helpful to take notes on how the author tries to convince the reader of their view. As you progress through the text, consider all three aspects: structure, line of argument and language.

Structure your analysis: Introduction – main part – conclusion

1. **Introduction:** State what you have discovered through your analysis of the article.
   EXAMPLE: *The editorial's point that the public discourse in Britain has changed into … is supported by the article's structure, line of argument and language.*

2. **Main part:** P-E-A
   Divide your analysis into paragraphs and follow this structure as you write your paragraphs:
   P – Point: state the point you are trying to make.
   E – Evidence: provide examples from the text to support your point.
   A – Analysis: explain what the examples mean with regard to your argument.

   EXAMPLE: *One of the ways the author underpins their message is by contrast. At the beginning of the article, for example, …. This is to show how quickly the public discourse has changed and that …*

3. **Conclusion:** Concise summary
   Summarize the main findings of your analysis.
   EXAMPLE: *To sum up, there are three main ways through which the author tries to convince the reader of their view. First, …*

Advanced texts
Englishness

D3 SUPPORT FOR TASK 3 (P. 162)
As you examine the features and characteristics of the "New Englishness", try to group them into categories and provide an example for each category. A table might help you to organize your ideas before writing.

category	example
origin	referendum, …
supporters	…
alternative concept to	Scottishness, …
…	…

Diff section

Part B: Monarchy and the political system

Texts

Analysing a feature film: *The Queen*

D4 SUPPORT FOR TASK 2B (P. 173)

Language support

body language	feeling/attitude
bowing | curtseying | extending a hand | frowning | grinning | raising an eyebrow | shrugging shoulders | smiling | standing to attention	arrogant | cocky | condescending | defiant | disdainful | full of anticipation | in awe | indifferent | insecure | nervous | reassuring | self-assured | self-confident | sheepish | superior | over-zealous

D5 SUPPORT FOR TASK 4 (P. 174)

Language support

rhythm and pace		mood
fast	slow	boisterous | cheerful | playful
frantic	monotonous	hesitant | mysterious | sad | sentimental | solemn | sorrowful | yearning
dissonant	harmonious	aggressive | eerie | scary | threatening
choppy	flowing, smooth	

Part C: The many faces of Britain

Practice

D6 SUPPORT FOR TASK 4 (P. 180)

Thesis statements are not easy to write but they are really helpful in keeping your analysis focused. It is important to keep the thesis statement short. Ideally, it should only consist of one sentence.

When forming a thesis statement, it is helpful to consider the following points:
1. Be clear about your thesis. Before you write it, organize your idea in a way that suits you, e.g. using visuals such as charts, maps or webs.
2. Although the thesis statement might only be a single sentence, still think of it as two parts. When analysing a poem, for example, one part of your thesis statement makes a claim about the message/meaning of the poem, the other part about how the message/meaning is conveyed.
   EXAMPLE: *In William Wordsworth's poem "My heart leaps up" the importance of childhood is emphasized by making the way a child sees the natural world fundamental to one's existence.*
3. When you have formulated your thesis statement, ask yourself if it fulfils the following criteria:
   • Does your thesis statement make a claim, i.e. answer a question not pose a question?
   • Is it specific enough, i.e. not too general or vague? The following example would be too vague: *The poem "My heart leaps up" by William Wordsworth deals with childhood in an interesting way.*

Ideally, you should have a someone else read your thesis statement. If they're clear about what you are trying to argue and would be interested to read a more detailed analysis, you're good to go!

Diff section

6 The American experience
Part A: The American Dream

Workshop: Step by step

D1 SUPPORT FOR TASK 2A (P. 193)

Look at the different elements used in the cartoon below. Then finish the interpretations of the elements.

"Remember, son, what doesn't kill you, makes you poorer."

1. The appearance of both father and son is slightly exaggerated. The father is depicted as a rather traditional businessman in a striped suit, and his son looks quite studious and appears to be wearing a school uniform. This suggests that he is attending a private school in America. They stand for …
2. The charts hanging in the father's office also appear to be over the top. They emphasize that the father is a businessman. All of the charts display a downwards trend. This symbolizes that …
3. The caption is meant ironically. The saying normally goes "what doesn't kill you, makes you stronger". By replacing "stronger" with "poorer" the cartoonist turns the advice a parent might give to their child on its head. This means …

Texts

The American Dream in a political speech

D2 SUPPORT FOR TASK 2 (P. 196)

One way to analyse a longer speech is to break it down into different parts and to take notes on each part.

Below is a grid with the different sections of Michelle Obama's speech. For some of the parts there are notes on the rhetorical devices she uses and the function they have. Complete the notes on the remaining parts.

Diff section

section	rhetorical device(s)	function with regard to the American Dream
ll. 1-18	• use of pronoun 'I' • repetition/parallelism ("I have seen … I have seen …") • emotive language/word field: heroes	• credibility that American Dream still exists • American Dream has to do with emotions and with what people achieve in difficult situations
ll. 19-73	…	…
ll. 74-92	…	…
ll. 93-108	• parallelism ("That's why …That's how") • amplification ("jobs …good jobs") • …	…
ll. 109-123	…	• emphasis on shared experience, on community • …
ll. 124-141	…	…
ll. 142-170	• allusion ("lift us to the mountaintop") • …	…

Webcode
You can download the grid here:
WES-73644-132

Part B: Culture wars: Tearing apart the US?

Facts

D3 SUPPORT FOR TASK 3A (P. 202)

Language support

1. The map depicts/shows/deals with/reveals …

2. The colours that are used indicate … • With the use of various colours, it becomes clear … • The states in blue are the ones that … • The darker the shade of green, the more … • Most of the states that … can be found … • States that … are mainly located in … • States that are close to/border on … seem to be/tend to be … • States with the highest/lowest rate of … are …, which cover the north/west/east/south/… of … • The state of … seems to be an exception as …

3. All in all, the map highlights that …/helps to explain why …/emphasizes a divide between states … and those …

Texts

The two sides in the US culture wars

D4 SUPPORT FOR TASK 2A (P. 210)
Divide the article up into different parts. For each part, briefly state its content and explain its function for the text. The info box and language support may help you. You can start like this:

Part 1 (ll. 6-15):
- *surroundings in Washington, D.C. (especially Confederate flag) seen through the eyes of a black woman*

Diff section

- function: to get readers to see potentially offensive symbols/reminders of slavery in everyday life through the eyes of a black person; evoke compassion/understanding

Part 2 …

Info

The structure of an article

Besides obvious elements like the heading, subheading and possibly an introduction, it is often helpful to look at the structure of the main part of an article.

Firstly, identify the individual parts and their function.

Decide if a part:
- is informative
- aims to provoke emotion
- provides evidence
- presents examples
- shares the author's opinion
- offers possible solutions to a problem

Do the paragraphs focus on:
- facts?
- personal statements?

After you have looked at the individual parts, you should also pay attention to the way they have been arranged by the author:
- have the parts been arranged to show a contrast between two points of view?
- are the arguments arranged cumulatively or does the text begin with the strongest argument?

Please note: you don't normally find all of these functions in one text.

Language support

The article/speech/report/review/commentary/… consists of … parts that show …
The article/speech/report/review/commentary/… begins/starts with …
The main part includes/is comprised of …
The conclusion consists of/contains/incorporates …
In the first/second/… paragraph the readers learn about …
The readers are informed about/are shown/are persuaded …
… is described/presented/introduced/touched upon/explained/commented on/discussed in detail.
Examples are used/Images are evoked/Experts are quoted/… to illustrate the topic/to back the main idea/to prove …

Webcode
You can download the grid here: WES-73644-133

D5 SUPPORT FOR TASK 2B (P. 210)

Look at the quotes in the grid and read the corresponding passages in the article on pp. 209-210 again. Complete the grid by naming the rhetorical devices or explaining their function in the text.

	quote	rhetorical device	function
1	"vestiges of the past still haunt you" (ll. 9-10)	…	negative connotation (ghosts, the long dead come back to life …) to underline the unpleasant experience of still being confronted with the evidence of slavery in your everyday life
2	"under attack" (l. 61), "radical" (l. 63), "revolution" (l. 64), "being torn down" (ll. 108-109)	choice of words/word field: war/revolution/violent conflict	…
3	"very rapidly" (l. 116), "major political reverberations" (ll. 117-118)	choice of words: intensifying expressions	…

Diff section

	quote	rhetorical device	function
4	"under attack" (l. 61), "under attack" (ll. 67-68), "under attack" (l. 74)	…	emphasizes how radical the change in society seems to be for some people
5	"you know, the man who was considered the greatest athlete in the world when you were 10 years old?" (ll. 82-84)	direct address	…
6	"While some Americans are hoping to finally cast off the vestiges of bigotry that have prevented them (and us) from realising the American Dream, others simply want to preserve American traditions and institutions that, while certainly not perfect, are deeply ingrained in American culture." (ll. 121-128).	…	shows that these concepts, while certainly linked, do not necessarily mean the same in different contexts or for different people
7	"Only then can we achieve a more perfect union." (ll. 135-136)	allusion to the preamble of the US Constitution	…

Part C: African American experiences

Texts

Brothers: Working on a short story

D6 SUPPORT FOR TASK 3 (P. 219)

Language support

The use of a first-person narrator has the effect of …
… takes the reader right back to the time when …
The strong bond between the father and his brother is expressed by …
The contrast between … and … makes the events appear even more …
The mother's narration of the events is very powerful. This is due to …
While telling the story, the mother is very …That way the reader …
Through the characters' use of slang, the author manages to …

Diff section

7 Postcolonial experiences

Intro

D1 SUPPORT FOR TASK 4B (P. 227)

In 1948, the *Windrush* carried immigrants from the Caribbean to Britain

Language support

Colonialism has contributed to …
Britain's contemporary society reflects …
Certain aspects of Britain's contemporary culture can be attributed to …
One important effect of Britain's colonial past is …
Politically and economically, Britain …
Britain's former colonies have profited/suffered as a result of …
Whereas British rule was responsible for … it was also …
Former British colonies have been burdened with …

Part A: India

Workshop: Practice

D2 SUPPORT FOR TASK 3 (P. 234)

When you write an interior monologue, it is important to consider:
- a person's character
- their emotions in a certain situation
- their language, i.e. the way they would talk

To prepare writing Anamika's mother's interior monologue, consider these steps:

1. **Analysing a character**

The reader is introduced to Anamika's mother in the first part of the story. The following questions may help you to get to know her better:
- what impression of her is created from the start?
- what is her social standing?
- why does she want to prevent Anamika's departure to Mumbai?
- how does she see the role of a good woman in society?
- what is her self-image? How does she see her role in the conflict?
- how does she feel about her way of "solving" the problem?

2. **Becoming aware of a character's emotions**
a) Study the list of adjectives describing feelings and use a dictionary to look up any words you do not understand.

> annoyed | appalled | apprehensive | ashamed | cheated | compassionate |
> considerate | deceived | desperate | determined | devastated | disgraced | disgusted |
> disrespected | empathic | enraged | frustrated | full of foreboding | furious |
> honourable | humiliated | justified | mournful | obliged | proud | relieved | reproachful

b) Imagine how Anamika's mother must have felt in each of the following situations and choose an adjective from the list in a) that best reflects her feelings:
- when she sees Anamika turn into a beautiful young woman
- when her daughter is leaving for Mumbai to study medicine
- when Anamika does not come home regularly anymore

- when Adinah shows her the photo of Anamika and Vikram on Facebook
- when Anamika is brought back by her brother
- when she locks up her daughter
- when she finds out that Anamika is pregnant
- when she finds a "solution" to her problem

c) Discuss your choice with a partner.
d) Add a thought bubble to each situation in which you reveal the mother's feelings, her hopes, her worries, her evaluation of the respective situation.

Use your ideas for the mother's interior monologue but remember that you are looking at the events in hindsight.

3. Considering the appropriate language
a) When you study the mother's language, you will find that her way of addressing Anamika is rather contradictory. Read the following quotes and decide what they reveal about Anamika's mother and her relationship to her daughter.

> "You made love with that swine!"

> "Why don't you answer me, you slut?"

> "How could you, my one and only daughter, the light of my eyes!"

b) Since an interior monologue represents the thoughts that go through a person's mind, the language you use is that of spoken English. Consequently, you can use:
- elliptical sentences (sentences which are incomplete and can consist of only one or two words)
- questions that can also be incomplete
- admonitions addressed to oneself (what one should or shouldn't have done)
- accusations against others
- exclamations
- harsh language to reveal despair or disapproval

Note down one or two examples for each category that fit the context and could be part of the interior monologue you are going to write.

Part B: Nigeria

Workshop: Practice

D3 SUPPORT FOR TASK 3 (P. 246)
To prepare for writing a characterization, consider these steps:

1. Gathering information about a character
When collecting information for the characterization of a fictional character, you will come across:
- explicit statements about the character = direct characterization
- descriptions in which a person's character traits, behaviour and attitudes are implied and must be figured out = indirect characterization

Compare the two quotes from the text and identify direct and indirect characterization. Explain what the quotes reveal about Ifemelu and point out the difference.

A She already imagined taking over the running of *Zoe* [...] perhaps one day buying out Aunty Onenu.

B "You are a real American! Ready to get to work, a no-nonsense person."

Diff section

2. Organizing the information

Each of the following (shortened) quotes from extract 4 tells you something about Ifemelu's character traits, her behaviour and attitudes – be it directly or indirectly.

1. She invented past experience as a staff writer on a women's magazine.
2. Ifemelu felt that the magazine was a hobby for Aunty Onenu. Not a passion. Not something that consumed her.
3. Ifemelu thought the home visit unprofessional.
4. *Glass* was better. But because she could already see Aunty Onenu's obsession with the competition, she said: "It's about the same, but we can do better."
5. "We need to … We need more … we should …"
6. "[We should] stop lifting foreign magazine pieces. Most of your readers can't go to the market and buy broccoli, because we don't have it in Nigeria, so why does this month's *Zoe* have a recipe for cream of broccoli soup?"
7. "Talking to your new boss like that!"
8. "And what an ugly house!" [And] yet she had once found houses like that beautiful.
9. … with the haughty confidence of a person who recognized kitsch.
10. And it piqued her. This was what a true Lagosian should have noticed.

They are listed chronologically as they occur in the text. In your analysis, however, it is not helpful to present your findings in this order. Instead you should group them in clusters.

a) Use the categories in the grid to reorganize the quotes. Some quotes may be sorted into more than one category, e.g. "We need to … We need more … we should …"

aspect	quote	interpretation
1. Outward appearance	…	…
2. Character traits	…	…
3. Behaviour	…	…
4. Mood	…	
5. Language	…	
6. Family/social background	…	
7. Relationship with others	..	

b) Take each quote and note down what it reveals about Ifemelu. The adjectives from the box may help you.

> adventurous | ambitious | calculating | candid | committed | critical | daring | dedicated | determined | diplomatic | direct | dishonest | energetic | fearless | honest | important | inconsiderate | inhibited | introverted | judgmental | judicious | outspoken | passionate | perceptive | persevering | professional | self-assured | self-conscious | self-critical | sensible | sensitive | submissive | superior | trustworthy | unconventional | unreserved | valiant

EXAMPLE:

2. Character traits	Ifemelu felt that the magazine was a hobby for Aunty Onenu. Not a passion. Not something that consumed her.	Ifemelu is very perceptive and critical as she immediately realizes a lack of dedication in her future employer; this lack is evidently contrary to her own passionate and dedicated attitude towards her work.

c) Find further examples from the text.

Diff section

3. Writing the characterization
When writing your characterization, follow this structure.

Introduction: state who you are writing about and what the focus of your analysis is. Include terms like protagonist, round character, direct or indirect characterization.

Main part: present your findings in a structured way, the categories of characterization can help you.

Conclusion: sum up the essence of your analysis/your results in a general statement which should be poignant and precise.

Language support

Introduction
After returning from the US, Ifemelu, the protagonist of the novel, tries to find her place in her home country Nigeria. In this extract, it becomes obvious that …

Main part
Ifemelu is presented/described/characterized as …
When she … it becomes obvious/clear/is revealed that …
The fact that … highlights/reveals/illustrates that …
Her thoughts concerning …/criticism of …/assessment of … suggest/indicate/hint at …

Conclusion
From the analysis of Ifemelu's character, we can conclude that …
In conclusion, Ifemelu can be seen as/regarded as …

A view of the well-to-do neighbourhood *Ikoyi*, where Aunty Onenu lives

Part C: Multicultural Britain today

Workshop: Step by step

D4 SUPPORT FOR TASK 3A (P. 257)
You can start your opening sentence like this:
The opening scene shows a meeting between … at the …

D5 SUPPORT FOR TASK 10 (P. 258)

1. To prepare for your discussion, go through the scene again and note down what can be seen as a positive example of multiculturalism and what contradicts this idea. Add quotes from the text where necessary.
   EXAMPLE:
   positive: forthcoming marriage between a man from an Asian family and a white woman; …
   negative: tense atmosphere between the families ("The atmosphere is strained", l. 10), …

2. Before you start writing your discussion, it is important to know what line of argument you wish to follow. Ask yourself whether the scene can been seen as a positive example of multiculturalism or whether the meeting of different cultures is depicted rather negatively. Formulate your position towards the question in a thesis statement.

3. When writing your discussion, present arguments from both sides. Use telling examples from the screenplay to support the arguments (these can be action lines as well as parts of the dialogue). However, it should be clear throughout your discussion where you're heading, i.e. what position you have. In your conclusion, you should sum up the evidence and restate your thesis.

321

Diff section

8 Shakespeare
Part A: Shakespeare's sonnets

Workshop: Step by step

D1 SUPPORT FOR TASK 5 (P. 275)

EXAMPLE:
The speaker employs the metaphor "the eye of heaven" (l. 5) to refer to the sun, thus stressing the importance of the sun. In the same line, however, he criticizes the sun for being too hot, thereby emphasizing his beloved's perfection in comparison.

Language support

The sonnet employs the imagery of …
The dominant image is …/the dominant imagery is of …
The image which runs through this sonnet is of …
The images (of …) are contrasted with (images of) …
The metaphor of … is used to …
The speaker addresses …
The (opening) words … establish a … tone which …
Throughout the sonnet, … is repeated
The poem creates/evokes/conveys a sense of/an impression of …

D2 SUPPORT FOR TASK 6 (P. 276)

Language support

The sonnet contains a turn/a change of theme/thought/mood …
The poem is divided into/is composed of/consists of …
The … quatrain contains … images of …
The … quatrain raises the question …
The couplet draws a conclusion …
The concluding couplet claims that …
The couplet contradicts the …
The sonnet is written in iambic pentameter.
The rhythm of the sonnet is varied/flexible/unvaried.
The poet varies the sonnet structure.

D3 SUPPORT FOR TASK 7 (P. 276)

For the declaration of love, you might want to use some of these (over)emotional words:

nouns and expressions	adjectives
agony | anguish | bitterness | desire | despair | disgrace | distrust | fever | fire | flame | grief | joy | loss | lust | pain | passion | remorse | resentment | shame | sorrow | tender love | trust | undivided love | yearning	adorable | anxious | betrayed | bitter | brilliant | cheerful | cruel | dearest | deceitful | desperate | destructive | devoted | delightful | desirable | dishonourable | divine | everlasting | evil | excellent | extraordinary | false | faultless | fiery | foolish | frantic | furious | generous | gentle | glorious | graceful | hateful | heartfelt | heavenly | honourable | hopeless | ideal | immortal | incomparable | inspiring | jealous | joyful | longing | lovely | loving | malicious | miserable | mournful | painful | passionate | perfect | pleasant | precious | pure | remorseless | resentful | rude | shameful | sincere | sinful | sorrowful | stubborn | superficial | sweet | tearful | treacherous | triumphant | troubled | truthful | unfaithful | vain | vicious | virtuous | worried | wretched | youthful

Part B: Shakespearean drama

Workshop: Step by step

D4 SUPPORT FOR TASK 6A (P. 285)

To help you with the task, the grid has been further filled in. Try to get into the swing of Shakespeare's language and fill in the rest.

Webcode
You can download the grid here:
WES-73644-134

quotation	imagery/interpretation	effect
But soft, what light through yonder window breaks? It is the east and Juliet is the sun!	metaphor: Juliet = sun	Romeo stresses that Juliet is the light in his life and since she is like the sun he cannot live without her.
Be not her maid, since she is envious. Her vestal livery is but sick and green, And none but fools do wear it. Cast it off.	personification of the moon as a jealous rival of the sun; the moon's demand for virginity is unhealthy and should be ignored	Romeo's sexual attraction towards Juliet is underlined.
Two of the fairest stars in all the heaven, Having some business, do entreat her eyes, To twinkle in their spheres till they return.	personification of two stars and Juliet's eyes: two of the brightest stars ask Juliet's eyes to replace them for a while	…
What if her eyes were there, they in her head? The brightness of her cheek would shame those stars, As daylight doth a lamp.	If the two stars replaced her eyes, her cheeks would be brighter than these stars. This difference is compared to the difference in brightness between daylight and the light of a lamp.	…
…	…	…

D5 SUPPORT FOR TASK 6B (P. 285)

Complete the grid with regard to Juliet's feelings for Romeo.

Webcode
You can download the grid below here:
WES-73644-135

quotation	imagery/interpretation	effect
It is too rash, too unadvised, too sudden;	parallelism: Juliet uses three parallel structures to describe how their promises to each other have been made.	She stresses that they have not given their promises of love enough thought.
Too like the lightning, which doth cease to be Ere one can say 'It lightens.'	simile: she compares their exchange of promises to a flash of lightning.	Juliet underlines the rashness of their agreement and thus puts forward her own doubts.
This bud of love …may prove a beauteous flower when we next meet.	…	…
My bounty is as boundless as the sea, My love as deep;	…	…
the more I give to thee, the more I have,	…	…

Diff section

D6 SUPPORT FOR TASK 7B (P. 285)

EXAMPLE:
Both characters can be described as naive. They expect that their love has a future (see, for example, Juliet's claim "And follow thee my lord throughout the world", l. 148), even though it is clear that the family feud is likely to come between them.

Workshop: Practice

D7 SUPPORT FOR TASK 3 (P. 287)

Look at Romeo's lines from the scene. Examine to what extent they illustrate his role as a lover and peacemaker versus his role as a loyal but impulsive friend.

1. I do protest, I never injured thee,
   But love thee better than thou canst devise, (ll. 17-18)

2. Till thou shalt know the reason of my love:
   And so, good Capulet, – which name I tender
   As dearly as my own, – be satisfied. (ll. 19-21)

3. O sweet Juliet,
   Thy beauty hath made me effeminate
   And in my temper soften'd valour's steel! (ll. 53-55)

4. Alive, in triumph, and Mercutio slain!
   Away to heaven, respective lenity,
   And fire-eyed fury be my conduct now! (ll. 66-68)

Texts

Love at first sonnet

Webcode
You can download the grid here:
WES-73644-136

D8 SUPPORT FOR TASK 2B (P. 288)

The pilgrim metaphor running through Romeo's and Juliet's shared sonnet might not be easy to understand at first. It can help to break up the sonnet and study the meaning of the individual parts, before writing an analysis of the metaphor as a whole.

shared sonnet	meaning
If I profane with my unworthiest hand / This holy shrine, the gentle sin is this: / My lips, two blushing pilgrims, ready stand / To smooth that rough touch with a tender kiss.	
Good pilgrim, you do wrong your hand too much, / Which mannerly devotion shows in this; / For saints have hands that pilgrims' hands do touch, / And palm to palm is holy palmers' kiss.	
Have no saints lips, and holy palmers too?	
Ay, pilgrim, lips that they must use in prayer.	
O, then, dear saint, let lips do what hands do. / They pray: grant thou, lest faith turn to despair.	
Saints do not move, though grant for prayers' sake.	
Then move not while my prayer's effect I take.	

Common mistakes

In this section, you will take a look at some of the most common mistakes which non-native speakers make when they learn English. Typically, confusion can arise when using adjectives and adverbs, punctuation and so-called false friends. Most mistakes are easy to avoid if you know what to look out for.

Adjectives and adverbs

Using adjectives and adverbs in English can often pose a stumbling block for German speakers. This is because the German language often does not have a separate adverb form: the adjective and adverb forms usually look the same. In English, however, it is essential to differentiate between the two and to use the correct form.

THE FORMATION OF ADVERBS

- Most adverbs are formed by adding *-ly* to the adjective:
  quick – *quick**ly***

- Sometimes the spelling changes:
  adjectives ending in *-y*:   *easy* – *eas**ily***
  adjectives ending in *-ic*:   *fantastic* – *fantastic**ally***

- Add *in a … way* to adjectives already ending in *-ly*:
  friendly – **in a friendly way**

Watch out for these exceptions. You should memorize them.
- The adjective is *good*. The adverb is *well*.
  She is a **good** player. She plays **well**.

- Some words are both adjectives and adverbs, e.g. *fast, hard, straight, late* and *right*.
  This is a **fast** train. (= adjective) It goes really **fast**. (= adverb)

- Some adjectives form adverbs that have a different meaning, e.g. *hard, fair* and *late*.
  hard (= *hart* in German) ≠ *hardly* (= *kaum*)
  fair (= *fair* in German) ≠ *fairly* (= *ziemlich*)
  late (= *spät* in German) ≠ *lately* (= *in letzter Zeit*)

  He works really **hard**. ≠ He **hardly** works at all.

USING ADJECTIVES AND ADVERBS

Adjectives tell you what something or someone is like. Adverbs tell you how something is done. It is important to consider what type of word you are describing in a sentence before choosing an adjective or an adverb.

- Use an *adjective* to modify nouns:
  Sandra is a **quiet** person.   (**adjective** + noun)

- Use an *adverb* to modify verbs:
  Bill speaks **quietly**.   (verb + **adverb**)

- Adverbs are also used to modify adjectives and other adverbs:
  Henry is an **extremely** close friend.   (**adverb** + adjective)
  Jane laughs **incredibly** loudly.   (**adverb** + adverb)

Common mistakes

Watch out for these exceptions and memorize them:
- Use an adjective to modify verbs that tell you how someone/something is, e.g. *be, taste, feel, sound, look, appear, seem, smell, become* and *get*.
  *The weather is **great**.*
  *The food smells **good**.*

- Some verbs can be used with either an adjective or an adverb, depending on whether the noun or the verb is modified.
  *The customer looked **angry**.* (the adjective *angry* says something about the noun *customer*)
  *He looked **angrily** at the waiter.* (the adverb *angrily* gives information about the verb *looked*)

- Remember: If the verb can be replaced with a form of *to be*, you must use an adjective.
  *The customer **looked** angry.* ➡ *The customer **was** angry.* ➡ adjective

COMPARISON OF ADVERBS

You have probably already got the hang of forming the comparative and superlative of adjectives. This differs when using adverbs. Make sure to form them correctly:

- The suffixes *-er* and *-est* are added to adverbs with one syllable: *fast, fast**er**, fast**est***
- For adverbs ending in *-ly*, *more* and *most* are used: *easily, **more easily, most easily***
- Some adverbs have irregular comparative and superlative forms:
  *badly, **worse, worst***
  *well, **better, best***
  *little, **less, least***

1
Look at the following sentences. Check if you need an adjective or an adverb. Complete the sentences with the correct forms.

a) That soup looked [1] (delicious). I really wanted to try some! Mum told me to dish it up [2] (careful), so I didn't make a mess. She should have told me not to eat it too [3] (quick). It was still [4] (fair/hot).

b) You'll never believe what happened to Tom Jones at work! He's been [1] (wrong) accused of stealing ideas from someone else. He seems [2] (innocent) to me. He works [3] (independent) and ever so [4] (creative) – he doesn't need to steal people's ideas. It's just [5] (total/unfair)!

c) You look [1] (tired). – I know. I [2] (hard) slept last night. Things have become [3] (real/difficult) at work. My boss always looks at me [4] (critical), and he [5] (rare) praises me. In the past, he used to tell me how [6] (good) I was doing my job. I have no idea what's different now!

d) My son threw the ball [1] (high) into the sky, and it [2] (sudden) disappeared amongst the treetops. Normally, I'm not really a [3] (courageous) person. However, I [4] (brave) climbed to the top and fetched the ball down. My heart was beating so [5] (fast).

2
Look at the following text. Can you spot the mistakes? Correct them and rewrite the text.

It's no wonder Tom didn't improve his marks. He hard worked on his presentation! Although he chose the visuals real good, he often spoke too quick. To make things more badder, he made his teacher angrily by arriving lately. He was prepared poor, and that's why he stuttered constant throughout the presentation. As a result, his teacher didn't mark him as high as he had hoped.

Common mistakes

Punctuation

Punctuation is another area which leads to Germans making mistakes in their English. Therefore, it is important that you are familiar with the correct usage of commas, colons and apostrophes among others. In English, the wrong use of such punctuation can sometimes change the entire meaning of a sentence, making it difficult to understand.

COMMAS

The rules regarding when to use commas in English are less strict than in German. Reading a sentence out aloud, with or without commas included, can often help you to place commas correctly in the sentence. In some cases, however, the rules are very specific and differ from German.

- **Relative clauses**

    There are two kinds of relative clauses: *non-defining* and *defining relative clauses*.
    Non-defining relative clauses give additional information that is not essential to understanding the main clause. The sentence would still make sense if a non-defining relative clause was left out.

    This is my friend Julian, **who is on exchange from Germany**.

    Remember: always use a comma to separate the non-defining relative clause from the main clause.

    Defining relative clauses give essential information about the nouns they define. The sentence would not necessarily make sense if you left them out.

    Janet is the girl **who is sitting next to your brother**.

    Remember: never use a comma to separate a defining relative clause from the main clause.

- **Two main clauses**

    In German, two main clauses can be separated by a comma. If conjunctions like *und* or *oder* are used, the comma is optional.

    Das Konzert ging weiter, die nächste Band kam auf die Bühne.
    Entweder ich gehe morgen[,] oder ich gehe erst nächste Woche.

    In English, two main clauses can only be separated by a comma if the second sentence starts with a conjunction like *and, or, but* or *so*.

    The teacher collected all exam papers, **but** *some of the pupils hadn't quite finished*.

    If there is no conjunction between the two main clauses, you have to use a full stop or a colon to separate them.

    The teacher collected all exam papers. Some of the pupils hadn't quite finished.

COLON

In English, colons are most commonly used for introducing lists or second main clauses. These second main clauses often explain or expand the previous ones.
Remember: in British English, the first word after a colon should not be capitalized even if it introduces a complete sentence. Only use a capital letter if the first word is a proper noun or an acronym.

David has four pets: **t***wo dogs, a cat and a mouse.*
He was sacked from his job: **t***he company realized he had missed all of his deadlines.*
He knows all about different diseases: **A***IDS is one of them.*

In American English, you may find other examples of capital letters after a colon.

Common mistakes

APOSTROPHES
In English, apostrophes are used in short forms and to denote possession.

- Use an apostrophe in short forms of verbs/pronouns to indicate the missing letters. Here are some examples:

    verbs: *I've* = *I have*
    she's = *she is* or *she has*
    he'll = *he will*

    pronouns: *let's* = *let us*

    Remember: only use short forms in spoken or informal written English. They should be avoided in formal written English.

- Use an apostrophe in genitive forms to denote possession, e.g. *Jane's dog, the children's food*.

    Remember: when the last letter of the noun itself is an *-s*, you should add an apostrophe and another *-s* (e.g. *Thomas's car*). In colloquial English, an apostrophe is sometimes simply added on the end (e.g. *Thomas' car*).

    Remember: in plural nouns ending with an *-s*, the apostrophe comes right after the *-s*, e.g. *the pupils' uniform*.

3
Look at the relative clauses. Are they defining or non-defining? Decide if there should be a comma or not.
a) We watched the film **?** which you had told me about.
b) The Spanish restaurant in Normanton **?** which everybody is talking about **?** is very good.
c) I love your new car **?** which is a great size.
d) She visited a place **?** which she had never been to.

False friends

False friends are pairs of words from German and English which look or sound similar to a word in the other language but have completely different meanings. Speakers can often get confused by these pairings. Of course, there are no rulings to avoid this confusion. Instead, it is important to memorize the word pairs.

English word	German translation	False friend in German	English translation of false friend
apart	auseinander	apart	distinctive
art	Kunst	Art	sort, kind, type
bald	glatzköpfig, kahl	bald	soon
body	Körper	Body (*Kleidung*)	bodysuit
box	Schachtel	Box	loudspeaker
brand	Marke	Brand	fire
caution	Vorsicht, Warnung	Kaution	security deposit
chef	Koch	Chef	boss
confession	Beichte, Geständnis	Konfession	denomination

Common mistakes

fatal	tödlich, verhängnisvoll	fatal	disastrous
herd	Herde	Herd	cooker
high school	weiterführende Schule	Hochschule	university
Roman	römisch	Roman	novel
sea	Meer	See	lake
spot	Fleck, Pickel, Punkt	Spott	ridicule
to wink	zwinkern	winken	to wave

4

Look at the list above. Explain the following misunderstandings.

a) *A German woman is leaving for the hairdresser's. She says to her English boyfriend, "Bye, darling. I'll be back bald." Her boyfriend replies, "Oh, no! Please don't."*

b) *A German man walks into a shop for electric goods. He says to the shop assistant, "I'd like to buy a herd." The shop assistant answers, "I'm sorry, Sir. The pet shop is next door."*

5

Pair work Write a short dialogue like the ones above in which false friends lead to a misunderstanding.

6

Look at these false friends. Some are in English and some in German. Use a dictionary or the Internet to find out why they are false friends.

pickle   Aktion
fabric   Rente

Skills section

S1 Checklist: Summary

A summary is for someone who has not read a text and needs to know the essence of what it is about. The readers of your summary do not expect you to go into detail; instead they want a short version of the text. Therefore, a written summary only gives a general idea of what the text is about and the most important information.

Dos	
	Before writing:
	✓ Read the text carefully and highlight key words and/or key sentences.
	✓ Divide the text up into parts or subsections.
	✓ Find an appropriate sentence or keywords to summarize each subsection.
	Writing an introduction:
	✓ The introductory sentence of your summary should include the author, title, type of text, the place and date of publication, and the main idea. In other words, you need to answer these wh-questions:
	→ **Who** is the author?
	→ **When** was the text published?
	→ **Where** was it published?
	→ **What** type of text is it?
	→ **What** topic does the text deal with? State the underlying problem or conflict, and not simply its content.
	Writing the main part:
	✓ The main part of your summary connects the highlighted passages and the summaries or key words of the subsections.
	✓ Focus on the essentials/on basic facts.
	✓ Use the present tense.
	✓ Use your own words.
	✓ Use formal language.
	✓ Use connectives to link your sentences.
Don'ts	✗ Don't include irrelevant details.
	✗ Don't use the present progressive.
	✗ Don't use quotations or direct speech.
	✗ Don't give your personal opinion.
	✗ Don't start analysing the text.
	✗ Don't try to create suspense.

Language support

Introduction:
- The short story/novel/article/poem/… "[title]" …
- The extract from the short story/novel/… "[title]" by [author] …
- … written by [author] in [year] …
- … written by [author] and published in [source] in [year] …
- … deals with/is about/shows/illustrates …

Stating the topic/purpose of a text:
- The text/story … is about/shows/presents/ depicts/alludes to/refers to/criticizes/ targets/comments on/exposes the fact that/the problem of …

Main part:
- According to the author, …
- The author believes/claims/emphasizes/ states/points out …
- From the author's point of view, …
- The author is of the opinion that …

S2 Checklist: Creative writing

A. Continuation of a prose text

When you are asked to continue a prose text you have read, it is important that you write in a similar way as the author. Pay attention to the author's style and the developments in the story. Decide if your continuation is plausible and fits in with what has happened before.

Dos	

	Content:
	✓ Stay in line with the plot and atmosphere.
	→ You are not entirely free as you are expected to show in your text production that you have digested the original text. You have to use the information from that text as a basis for a plausible sequel.
	→ Mention certain features (places, details of landscape or weather) that have been introduced.
	→ Make sure you present the characters in a way that does not contradict their previous behaviour unless this change in character is part of your story.
	→ If possible refer back to events in the text you have dealt with.
	
	Point of view (narrative perspective):
	✓ Adopt the same narrative perspective:
	→ First-person narrator
	→ Third-person narrator
	  • Omniscient (knowing and commenting on all the characters' thoughts and feelings, foreshadowing future events etc.)
	  • Limited (having insight into one of the characters' thoughts and feelings only)
	
	Language:
	✓ Stay in line with the author's style and try to imitate it.
	→ Consider the amount of descriptive as opposed to dramatic passages that mainly consist of dialogue.
	→ Use either long, elaborate sentences or short simple ones like the author.
	→ Employ imagery (symbolic or metaphorical language) if it occurs in the original text; you need not always think of new images but pick up the ones used and extend them.
	→ Adopt the author's use of language to place a character in a particular social class or reveal his/her emotions.

Skills section

B. Change of perspective

You may be asked to consider the fictional situation from the point of view of a different character, writing
- a dialogue
- a diary entry/an interior monologue
- a letter to a friend

Dos	**Content:** ✓ Consider the relationship between the characters involved, their age, their social standing, the way they might be personally affected by what has happened. ✓ For your character, imagine how he/she feels in the circumstances. ✓ Decide how he/she would comment → on the situation or conflict, → on other characters and their behaviour. **Language:** ✓ Age, relationships to other characters, social class and profession determine the way a person speaks. ✓ Make sure you use an appropriate register (formal, informal, colloquial, scientific, educated etc.). ✓ Emotions may alter a person's behaviour and speech. ✓ Use typical elements of spoken language like exclamations, incomplete sentences (ellipses), questions, etc.
Don'ts	✗ Don't stray from the original text you were given. ✗ Don't create an entirely new universe. ✗ Don't quote when you refer back to instances in the original text, but make the references part of your own narrative.

C. Change of narrative perspective

You may be asked to rewrite an extract from a novel or short story using a different narrative perspective. In this case your text will be mainly based on the same content but you will have to modify it according to the narrative perspective you have to work with. All the information above about changing perspective is relevant here as well, but there are also other things you have to bear in mind.

a) First-person narrator

When you are asked to retell a story as a first-person narrator, first determine what the character from the extract who has now become the narrator is like. In the original text, identify how he/she experiences the situation and how he/she would talk about it. Even though you have to keep the main elements of the plot, you can rearrange them to include the narrator's thoughts and feelings or comments he/she might make. Depending on the character, his/her age and social background, the style you have to use will differ, e.g. with snappy and clipped colloquial wording for a teenager or a more elaborate choice of words and sentence structure for a parent, teacher, judge etc.

b) Third-person narrator: omniscient or limited

As an omniscient narrator you can look inside all the characters in the extract: you know their thoughts and feelings. You might even know how the story will end and provide some foreshadowing. However, the elements that you include should be in keeping with the original text.

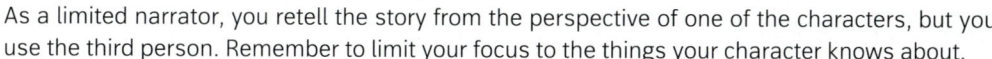

Skills section

As a limited narrator, you retell the story from the perspective of one of the characters, but you use the third person. Remember to limit your focus to the things your character knows about.

Dos	**Content:** ✓ Use the tense of the original text. ✓ As a first-person/third-person limited narrator → determine the narrator's character, → include his/her views, feelings, thoughts about the incident or conflict dealt with in the extract or the people involved, → limit your text to what he/she actually knows or experiences, → include speculations or hopes and worries where he/she has no obvious knowledge, → stay within the framework of the original text. ✓ As an omniscient narrator → refer to thoughts and feelings of all characters, → add comments and judgements on what is happening or on the characters' behaviour and the possible outcome of the narrative. **Language:** ✓ As a first-person narrator → adapt your style to the narrator's character, consider age, social background, emotional state, etc. → use elements of spoken language. ✓ As a third-person narrator (limited or omniscient), you are quite free in what kind of language you use.
Don'ts	✗ Don't invent things that are not linked to the original text. ✗ Don't simply imitate the style of the original text.

Language support

When a **first-person narrator** is telling the story, features of spoken language like questions, incomplete sentences or exclamations are often included:
- Why on earth haven't I …?
- How could X do this?
- Seriously?/The nerve!/Brilliant!

When an **omniscient/limited narrator** is telling the story, the feelings and thoughts of the narrator/different characters can be presented. Phrases to describe feelings may be helpful:
- X felt/was lonely/misunderstood/relieved/overwhelmed/…
- X often thought that …/wondered why …/doubted if …/underestimated …
- X had lost all self-respect/hope/inhibitions.
- To his/her relief/surprise/annoyance …

An **omniscient narrator** might comment or hint at a future outcome or include judgements:
- It was obvious/to be expected/proved inevitable that …
- It was only much later that he/she found out/understood …
- This would prove to be a problem when …

S3 Checklist: Formal letter

There are many different types of formal letters that you could be expected to write, e.g. a letter of request, a letter of inquiry, a letter of complaint, a letter of application (often called a covering letter). Whatever kind of letter it is, the response you get will greatly depend on the way the letter is written. Formal letters are generally precise and to the point, without unnecessary detail. It is also important that you adopt the right tone, i.e. it should sound business-like rather than emotional. Finally you must also think about the layout of your letter and the type of language you use. The language used in this type of letter should not be chatty and personal but rather formal and reserved.

Before you start writing you should first ask yourself:
- Who am I writing to?
- Why am I writing?
- What do I need to tell them?
- What do I want them to do?

Dos	**Before writing:** ✓ Observe the rules for the layout of a formal letter (see next page). ✓ Use formal language. ✓ Choose a more formal font for your letter or email if you use a computer, e.g. *Times New Roman* or *Arial*. ✓ Draft and edit your letter or email before you send it. Poor grammar and punctuation or spelling mistakes do not make a good impression. ✓ Plan the structure of your letter to include the following parts: **Salutation and introduction:** ✓ Address the person you are writing to correctly: → If you know the person's name write: *Dear Ms* (for a woman whose marital status is not known) *Mrs, Mr, Dr Smith*, etc. → If you do not know the person's name: *Dear Sir or Madam,* ✓ Start the first sentence with a capital letter. ✓ State the purpose of your letter in the first paragraph. ✓ Refer to any correspondence that may already have taken place. **Main part:** ✓ Organize your ideas into paragraphs. ✓ Include important and/or relevant details such as exact names, dates and addresses, e.g. where you saw the job advertised, when and where you bought the defective goods etc. ✓ Keep to the point and avoid unnecessary details. ✓ Be polite and tactful. **Conclusion and ending:** ✓ Outline how you expect the recipient to react, e.g. send you information, give you a refund, reply to your application etc. ✓ End the letter in the appropriate way: → *Yours sincerely* if you address them by name in the salutation → *Yours faithfully* if you use *Sir or Madam* in the salutation ✓ Type your full name and sign the letter by hand.
Don'ts	✗ Don't write your name above the address. ✗ Don't use inappropriate or informal language, e.g. slang, short forms, abbreviations, ...

Skills section

Language support

Say why you are writing:

to reply:
- In response to your letter of September 23rd …

to complain:
- I am writing to express my dissatisfaction with …
- Unfortunately, I am forced to write this letter in order to complain about …

to inquire:
- I am writing to inquire about the possibility of …
- I would be very grateful if you would send me further information about …
- Would you kindly tell me how …?

to apply:
- I wish to apply for the post of …
- I am writing to apply for …
- With reference to your advertisement in the Daily News of March 3rd, I should like to apply for the position of …

Say how you expect the recipient to reply to …

your complaint:
- Under the circumstances, I feel an apology should be offered.
- I would be grateful if you could deal with the problem as soon as possible.
- I must insist that you refund me my money immediately.

your inquiry:
- I would like to thank you in advance for your assistance.
- Please accept my thanks for your help.

your application:
- I look forward to hearing from you.
- I will be glad to supply you with any further information you may require.
- I have attached/enclosed the following documents.

The example formal letter below details the general layout that your letter should conform to.

The address of the person you are writing to should be on the left.

Say why you are writing the letter in the first paragraph.

In the last part of the letter, say how you expect the recipient to reply.

End the letter in an appropriate way.

Write your address and email in the top right-hand corner or on the left above the recipient's address.

Leave a line and write the date below your address.

The main part of the letter should include any other necessary information.

68, Wood Lane
Romford RM12 8JY
sgoodenough@internet.com

November 1, 2018

Ms Diane Poole
Personnel Department
Debenhams Ltd.
Romford RM10 6NX

Dear Ms Poole,

With reference to your advertisement in the Romford Recorder of October 24th, I would like to apply for a summer job in your Department Store. My final examinations finish on June 23rd and I will be available to start work any time after that date.

I am just completing my final year at Hornchurch Grammar School and have applied to do Business Studies and French at Bristol University in October. Meanwhile, I would like to gain some experience in a large organization such as yours, and of course earn some extra money to help finance my university course.

Having worked in a local supermarket on Saturdays for the past two years, I have gained a lot of experience in dealing with customers. I also greatly enjoy working in a team and was always a popular member of any group presentation at school because I always do my share of the work. In my last year at school I was a prefect and also captain of the hockey team, which shows I have a sense of responsibility towards others. My teachers have always considered me to be a reliable and conscientious student.

I have attached my CV and will be glad to supply you with any other information you require, for example, the names of referees. Thank you for considering my application.
I look forward to hearing from you soon.

Yours sincerely,

S. Goodenough

Sandra Goodenough

S4 Checklist: Letter to the editor

Readers of newspapers often write a letter to the editor to comment on something they have read, usually in the hope that the letter will be published in the newspaper. When writing a letter to the editor, take the aspects for writing a formal letter into account. Use formal language, but include strong statements. Before you start writing the letter, you will need to note down important facts and points from the text you are reacting to. Note down any other ideas you have and arrange all of them in a logical order.

Dos	**Introduction:** ✓ Start with *Sir,* or *Madam,* ✓ Leave out any introductory or closing remarks with which you show your politeness or personal interest. Concentrate on the point you are trying to make. ✓ Name the article you refer to at the beginning of your letter. ✓ Give the reason why you are writing the letter, i.e. what you support/criticize/would like to comment on about the article. **Main part:** ✓ Follow a clear line of argument and stick to the most important point(s). ✓ Explain why you share or oppose the author's point of view. ✓ Support your arguments with evidence and examples. **Conclusion:** ✓ End with a strong statement that sums up your position and/or says what you expect from future articles on the issue. ✓ Just sign your name and state your place of residence at the end.
Don'ts	✗ Don't use *Yours sincerely/faithfully* at the end. ✗ Don't quote from the original article unless it is absolutely necessary. ✗ Don't retell the article and explain it to the editor, but explain your view.

Language support

Starting the letter:
- I am writing to you in response to the article …
- Having read your article …, I would like to point out …
- In the article …, the author … claims that …
- The article … by … raises the question of whether …

Expressing your opinion in the main part of the text:
- I would like to congratulate you on …
- I personally believe that …
- I could not have put it better myself.
- It is beyond doubt that …
- You are absolutely right when you say …/I utterly agree with you that …
- I wholeheartedly endorse …
- As a firm believer in …/As a supporter of …, I totally agree/I see no reason why …
- Although I understand why …, I cannot accept the overall conclusion that …
- I see the author's point, but I still feel that …
- I think … is mistaken if he/she believes …
- What you need to keep in mind is …
- I would question the argument that …
- Your author overlooks the fact that …

Ending with a strong statement:
- The question can no longer be whether …, but …
- However, doesn't the evidence I have cited prove that …?
- All in all, there can be no doubt that …
- Ultimately, what matters is (that) …

S5 Checklist: Writing a speech

When you give a speech, you are aiming to get people to agree with your views. As your speech will only be heard and not read by your audience, you have to be careful how you present what you have to say. Speeches are meant to be spoken, so your language should not be too formal. You may use short forms and contractions like *don't, we're, haven't, I'm*, etc.

It may help you to read out loud to yourself what you have written to check whether your style creates the desired effect.

Dos	Plan the structure of your speech to include the following parts:
	Introduction:
	✓ Directly address the audience at the beginning.
	✓ Begin your introduction with an "attention-getter" to capture your audience's attention, e.g. a story, a rhetorical question, a quotation.
	✓ Clearly state the topic of your speech and your personal stance on it.
	Main part:
	✓ Explain the topic/problem.
	✓ Quote facts and people to persuade your audience.
	✓ Show your emotional involvement and appeal to the emotions of the audience.
	Conclusion:
	✓ Briefly highlight your main points and end with something strong, e.g. an appeal for support.
	✓ Show that the speech has ended, e.g. by thanking your audience for listening.
Don'ts	✗ Don't put too many ideas in your speech, but give the listeners two or three important things to remember.
	✗ Don't just read the speech out loud to your audience.
	✗ Don't use expressions that are too complex.
	✗ Don't write very long sentences – listeners must be able to follow your point.
	✗ Don't use modifiers, e.g. *might be, possibly, probably, more or less* – you must be very direct and specific to be convincing.

Language support

Introduction:
- Address the audience: *Ladies and gentlemen, Fellow students, My friends, Members of …, My fellow countrymen,* etc.

Main part:
- Relate your speech to your listeners. Use receiver-including pronouns and words like *we, us, our, my friends,* etc.
- Use connectives to structure your speech: *firstly, finally,* etc.
  Link the different points by using phrases such as: *Having discussed … it is now appropriate to mention …*
- Use adverbial phrases to underline your own convictions and win over the audience: *undoubtedly, certainly, undeniably, definitely, indeed, paradoxically, surprisingly, strangely enough, primarily, first and foremost, above all,* etc.
- Include rhetorical questions like: *Don't we all agree/want to …?*
- Include stylistic devices like repetition, exaggeration/hyperbole, alliteration, etc.

Conclusion:
- *Finally, fellow friends of the environment, …*
- Clearly indicate the end of your speech: *Thank you for your attention, ladies and gentlemen.*

S6 How to write a discussion/comment

Many tasks require you to write an argumentative text. Often, this is to be in the form of a discussion or a comment. For both kinds of tasks you will have to state your opinion on a given question. In a discussion, you will need to weigh up arguments in favour of both sides of a debate in order to come to a well-founded conclusion, whereas a comment allows you to focus more on your opinion. But if it helps your case, you can also include arguments for the other side.

		discussion	comment
preparation	1	Know what your line of argument is before you start writing. To accomplish this, prewrite or brainstorm your ideas on paper until you have developed a working thesis.	
	2	Write a rough outline that begins with a thesis statement. A thesis statement is an argument that you want to prove. Three to five facts or examples that support your thesis must follow next in the outline. The last item must be a conclusion that essentially restates the thesis.	
introduction	3	The first sentences should be an interesting introduction that presents the problem your argumentative essay will discuss. The last sentence of the paragraph should clearly state the thesis or the basic question, argument or problem.	
main part	4	**First line of argument** Look at the problem from one side (e.g. the side of those in favour, the arguments for a particular question). Write a handful of paragraphs – at least three – that support your thesis. If you are making an argument about a literary text like a novel or poem, you can select quotes from the text that support your argument. If you are discussing a political controversy, choose reasons that bolster your claim, and find relevant quotes and statistics to cite.	4 **Your line of argument** Look at the problem from your point of view. Refer to at least three aspects of the topic and say what your position is on these. Do not forget to give plausible reasons for what you think. Support your view by means of examples, statistics, relevant quotes etc. **[5 Other lines of argument (optional)]** Although not strictly necessary for a comment, it might be useful to also refer to views of an issue that are in opposition to your position. It might help to prove your point when you show that you are able to think of counter-arguments and how you deal with them. But again: plausible reasons supported by evidence are essential.
	5	**Second line of argument** Then consider the problem from a different side (e.g. the side of those against, the arguments against a particular question). Address any counterclaims in the main body of your argument as well. For example, if your argument is in favour of capital punishment, refute commonly held beliefs about why capital punishment is either morally wrong or ineffective. Counterclaims might not apply in a literary argumentative essay, but usually do in one about politics.	

Skills section

	note: • Instead of discussing first arguments in favour and then arguments against, you may also contrast each argument for with an argument against the issue right away. • The examiner does *not* expect you to consider *every* argument there is. So, instead of listing, say, twelve different points, it is a good idea to concentrate on about three, preferably the most important aspects and discuss these in detail.
conclusion	6 Conclude your comment/discussion with a paragraph that sums up the evidence presented and restates the thesis. Here you say which side or perspective makes more sense or is more justified to you. You may, at this point, also add personal feelings about the topic, say how you see the topic in the context of other related issues and/or give an outlook on how the issue in question might develop in the future. In any case, mere repetition of arguments must be avoided!

Language support

Introduction
- *The text/book raises the question of …/ introduces the problem of …*
- *The problem/issue that is touched upon here is …*
- *The statement/text illuminates the basic problem/dilemma of …*

Lines of argument: my point of view
- *Considering the fact that …*
- *Another important point/factor/argument is …*
- *You also have to take into consideration that …*
- *I am convinced (that) …*
- *Above all, it is important to note …/it must be said …/one cannot ignore (that) …*
- *to be in favour of sth*
- *to (strongly) support/oppose sth*
- *to argue for/against sth*

Lines of argument: balancing points of view
- *On the one hand …, on the other hand …*
- *Whereas A …, B …*
- *In contrast to A, B …*
- *From B's point of view, however, …*
- *Looking at the problem from A's side, you have to admit that …*
- *Supporters/Opponents of …. argue/might argue that …*
- *Another argument/point/reason that is often put forward is …*
- *Others maintain/claim/assert that …*

Personal conclusion
- *I rather agree/disagree with …*
- *As opposed to …, I definitely believe that …*
- *In my opinion, …/As I see it, …/ Personally, …*
- *As far as I am concerned, …*
- *Finally, I would like to point out that …*
- *Taking into account what has been said so far, I …*
- *Having considered the different arguments, I …*
- *Looking at the two sides, I have to say …*
- *To sum up, I am of the opinion that …*
- *To come to a final conclusion, I think …*

S7 Checklist: Writing a blog post

In an exam, you may be asked to write a blog post. A blog is a regularly updated website run by an individual or a group. Blog posts are usually written in a personal, informal or conversational style to engage with readers. It is important to keep in mind who you are writing for. Your target group determines what you write about and how you do it.

Dos	**The structure:** ✓ Give the blog post an eye-catching title that will grab the readers' attention. This is the first thing they see. It will help them decide if it is of interest to them. ✓ Outline the main point in the first paragraph. This will help readers decide whether they want to read on. ✓ Put the details in the following paragraphs. ✓ Add background information if necessary. ✓ End with a conclusion that invites comments or reactions from your readers and other bloggers. ✓ Add your name if you wish to. **Your style:** ✓ Write in a friendly and informal style. ✓ Use first person *I*. ✓ Try to include references to your own experience. ✓ Describe rather than tell. For instance, instead of saying you thought a book was great, try to explain why you enjoyed it. ✓ Use vivid words, conjunctions and modifiers to make the reading more interesting and to improve the flow. ✓ Keep your sentences short and simple. ✓ Always be polite, informative and respectful of other cultures and opinions. ✓ Ask your readers to respond to what you have written. ✓ On the next page, you will find some useful phrases, but make sure your blog post has a personal touch.
Don'ts	✗ Don't be overly negative. ✗ Don't try to impose your beliefs on others. ✗ Don't be rude or impolite. ✗ Don't waffle. ✗ Don't include links to commercial sites or inappropriate materials. ✗ Don't give specific names, places, addresses or contact details.

Skills section

Language support

Introducing a topic
- *In this blog, I'm going to be discussing ...*
- *Today, I want to address ...*
- *It seems that everybody is talking about ... at the moment.*
- *Today's topic is ...*

Introducing an opinion
- *I think/believe/reckon/find ...*
- *As far as I'm concerned, ...*
- *I've been thinking about this over the last few days and ...*
- *I've got to be honest, I think ... is fantastic.*
- *I'm not a massive fan of ...*

Adding further detail
- *But that's not all.*
- *But what's more, ...*
- *That's all well and good, however, ...*
- *Nonetheless, there's a whole other side to this.*
- *Let's not forget ...*

Concluding
- *Whichever side of the debate you're on, I'm sure you'll agree this is a really interesting subject.*
- *That's where we are at the moment, but we'll have to watch how this develops in the future.*
- *Just to sum up this week's post, ...*

S8 How to improve your text

Once you have written your text, read it carefully again and check whether you have considered the criteria listed below. Revise your text accordingly.

a) **Content:**
   - Has your text taken all aspects of the assignment into consideration?
   - Have you given evidence to support your arguments?
   - Have you referred adequately to the text that has to be analysed (lines, quotations)?
   - Have you avoided repetitions?

b) **Structure and logical order:**
   - Are the following parts included?
     - introduction, introductory sentence
     - main part, divided up into several paragraphs
     - conclusion
   - Is the text clearly structured and therefore easy to follow with the help of visible paragraphs and a clear order of arguments or examples?

c) **Language and style:**
   - Have you used the correct tense, e.g. the simple present tense in a summary?
   - Have you used the correct language, e.g. formal language in a letter to the editor?
   - Are your sentences complete and not too long or complicated?
   - Have you avoided waffling, i.e. excluded all unnecessary words?
   - Have you varied your vocabulary by using synonyms? Look at the language support on the next page for some ideas.
   - Do you use connectives effectively to make your text coherent? Again, the language support will help you.

Language support

Synonyms: certain adjectives and nouns
You should ban the following words from your range of vocabulary – at least when writing a formal text like an analysis or characterization:

SAD   HAPPY   NICE   BAD   INTERESTING   SITUATION

Use some of these synonyms instead:
- For "sad" people you could use: *downcast, depressed, downhearted, dejected, dispirited, frustrated, discouraged, sorrowful*
- For a "sad" atmosphere you could use: *dark, gloomy, dismal, dreary, depressing, desolate, melancholy, hopeless, cheerless, bleak*
- For "happy" people you could use: *cheerful, contented, relaxed, pleased, delighted, light-hearted, merry, lively, vivacious, animated, buoyant, spirited*
- For "nice" people you could use: *amiable, kind-hearted, good-natured, gentle, congenial, easy-going, pleasant, sympathetic*
- For a "nice" atmosphere you could use: *cheerful, relaxed, pleasant, harmonious, idyllic, picturesque, familiar, friendly, warm*
- For "bad" people you could use: *despicable, contemptible, loathsome, hateful, detestable, reprehensible, awful, vile, mean, repulsive, horrible, dreadful, terrible*
- For "interesting" you could use: *appealing, exciting, fascinating, remarkable, significant, captivating, intriguing, attractive*
- For "situation" you could use: *circumstance, case, state of affairs, condition, predicament, position, dilemma*

Language support

Synonyms: "author"
Depending on the type of text you are writing about, use one of these synonyms instead of the word "author":
- literary texts: *novelist, playwright, poet, writer*
- newspaper articles: *journalist, reporter, columnist, writer, essayist*

Varying your vocabulary: "the author says"
Similarly, you should avoid writing "the author says", but use more precise alternatives instead. Here are several examples of verbs you could use:

The author …
- *refers to …*
- *alludes to …*
- *talks about/mentions …*
- *addresses the issue of …*
- *examines …*
- *raises the question of whether …*
- *weighs up the arguments …*
- *is in two minds about …*
- *blames sth/sb …*
- *criticizes …*
- *reproaches sb for …-ing …*
- *rejects (the idea of) …*
- *abandons the idea of …-ing …*
- *opposes the idea of …-ing …*
- *refutes the argument …*
- *claims/maintains/argues that …*
- *assumes/supposes/presumes that …*
- *asserts …*
- *believes …*
- *states …*
- *insists …*
- *emphasizes …*
- *sides with …*
- *backs up his argument with …*
- *is in favour of …-ing …*
- *puts forward another argument …*
- *doubts …*
- *attacks/accuses sb of …-ing …*
- *leaves … unanswered …*
- *avoids this issue …*
- *does not consider …*

Skills section

Language support

Connectives

Use some of these connectives to ensure that your text continues to flow for the reader:

- Connectives to show sequence:
  firstly, secondly, thirdly
  next
  consequently
  previously
  simultaneously
  afterwards
  subsequently
  finally
  later
  before
  Firstly, ... In addition, ...
  Equally important, ...

- Connectives to show time:
  soon
  then
  by this time
  as soon as
  meanwhile
  presently

- Connectives to compare different aspects:
  in comparison
  furthermore
  likewise
  similarly
  moreover
  in addition
  additionally
  otherwise
  On the one hand, ... On the other hand, ...

- Connectives to give specific examples:
  for example
  for instance
  in this case
  specifically
  with regard to
  that is to say that
  For example, ... Also ... In addition, ...

- Connectives to contrast:
  in contrast
  whereas
  nonetheless
  however
  on the contrary
  nevertheless
  although
  conversely
  despite this
  in spite of the fact that
  regardless
  even though

- Connectives to signal conclusion:
  in conclusion
  therefore
  as a result (of this)
  in short
  generally
  all in all
  because of this
  evidently

S9 How to structure a text

When analysing a text or commenting on an issue, for example, you should not only pay attention to the content and the correct use of language (grammar, choice of words, etc.), but also to the structure of your text.

In order to write a well-structured text, you should follow the structure of introduction – main part – conclusion. Make sure that you plan how to present your ideas effectively in a sequence of paragraphs before you start writing.

Moreover, you should make the relationships between your points clear by using connectives, e.g. to express cause and effect or to point out contrasts and contradictions.

Apart from creative writing tasks, which require you to follow the specific criteria for the kind of text you need to produce (e.g. a newspaper article or a letter), there are basically three types of texts you may be asked to write, especially in an exam context:

1. comprehension (e.g. Describe/State/Outline/Summarize/…)
2. analysis (e.g. Analyse/Examine/Compare/Explain/…)
3. argumentative writing (e.g. Comment on/Assess/Discuss/…)

Below are some tips to help you structure your texts for all three general text types.

INTRODUCTION			
general tips	**comprehension**	**analysis**	**argumentative writing**
Refer back to the task, if necessary.	• Give the general information on the text at hand (e.g. author, title, etc.). • State the issue the text deals with.	• Make a general statement that sums up what you are expected to find out.	• Make it clear what makes the issue you discuss topical or controversial. • Explain its relevance with regard to the text at hand, if possible or necessary. • Express your general view on the issue.
	Example: Summarize White Mike's encounter with Lionel and Jessica.	Example: Analyse White Mike's character in the passage at hand.	Example: Discuss whether a gap year is worth taking after school.
	The extract from chapter 23 of Nick McDonell's novel *Twelve*, first published in 2002, deals with how White Mike becomes aware of the destructive nature of the drug Twelve and its consequences.	Although White Mike is an experienced drug dealer, his acute observation and ability to empathize make him start to realize that he cannot cope with the effects Twelve has on his job as a dealer.	Thousands of students decide to take a year off from education once they have graduated from school and do not want to start studying straight away. As the article "Why Malia Obama is right to take a gap year" has suggested, a gap year may provide valuable experiences. However, I do not believe that travelling the world for a year, which is what most people seem to do, is of much benefit for your personal development or your career.

Skills section

	MAIN PART		
general tips	comprehension	analysis	argumentative writing
Divide the text up into paragraphs that each deal with one aspect. Link ideas and paragraphs, e.g. with connectives and participle constructions.	• Present the relevant content in your own words.	Follow this structure in your paragraph writing: • P - Point: an introductory sentence that outlines the point you are trying to make in this paragraph so that the reader immediately knows what you are referring to • E - Evidence: examples from the text (including quotations) – in an argumentative text also arguments and examples that you know from other contexts – that can be used to prove your point (P) • A - Analysis: explanation of your examples/quotations/arguments to make it clear which function your evidence (E) has in proving your point (P). Express your general view on the issue.	
	Example: Summarize White Mike's encounter with Lionel and Jessica.	Example: Analyse White Mike's character in the passage at hand.	Example: Discuss whether a gap year is worth taking after school.
	Having been called by Jessica, White Mike is joined by another more professional dealer, Lionel, to meet her. Feeling uneasy in Lionel's company, White Mike walks to the meeting point at 91st Street where he already notices Jessica from a distance.	White Mike empathizes with Jessica and tries to establish some kind of relationship with her. At one point he "tries to look her right in the eye but can't catch her gaze". As White Mike is aware of Jessica's inexperience in dealing with that kind of situation and her strong urge to buy Twelve, he hopes to make her focus on the deal and not come across as an easy victim for Lionel. By trying to make eye contact, he hopes to keep her focused and possibly guide her through the situation without losing respect and dignity.	What kind of activity you do in your time abroad needs to be chosen wisely if it is to be relevant beyond your gap year. If you intend to become a doctor, it might be a good idea to volunteer in a hospital or nursing home. Similarly, those interested in a career in social work or education are more likely to profit from spending some time in a nursing home or school. As a consequence, the choice of a subject for your university studies or your apprenticeship is bound to be a more informed one and you may already gain practical experience in a field that will come in handy when approaching relevant topics at university.

Skills section

	CONCLUSION		
general tips	**comprehension**	**analysis**	**argumentative writing**
Refer back to the opening paragraph, if possible, at least implicitly.	• Usually, no conclusion is necessary unless you need to lead over to the analysis.	• Summarize the most important findings concisely without repeating all the details and using the same words again.	• Draw a conclusion by weighing up the pros and cons and stating your opinion clearly.
	Example: Summarize White Mike's encounter with Lionel and Jessica.	Example: Analyse White Mike's character in the passage at hand.	Example: Discuss whether a gap year is worth taking after school.
	As it has become clear above, White Mike is the character that connects Jessica as a high-school student who is roughly his age and Lionel, who represents the drug dealing part of White Mike's life. In order to see how White Mike's character deals with this particular situation, his behaviour deserves a closer analysis.	All in all, White Mike displays a more sensitive side as he realizes how much a person like Jessica is changing as a consequence of taking and demanding more Twelve. Furthermore, he is aware of his own role as someone linking two very different worlds he is not part of – Jessica's circle of wealthy teenagers and Lionel's world of violence and crime.	All in all, I strongly believe that a gap year needs to be filled with meaningful activities to justify taking a one-year break. Partying for a year in the sun is definitely not worth postponing your studies for, whereas internships or social work can be justified both with regard to career opportunities and personal development.

S10 How to work with poetry

Many students feel insecure when asked to analyse a poem. However, working with poetry can be very rewarding. The following tips will help you to read, enjoy and work successfully with poetry.

Step 1: First reading

The aim of the first reading is to get a general sense of what the poem is about. At this stage you should not worry if you do not understand all the lines but concentrate on your first impressions. Try to identify the topic/subject of the poem. If possible, listen to someone read the poem out loud in order to get a feeling for the rhythm of the poem. If there is no recording, read it out loud to yourself or to a partner.

Listen to this reading of the poem "Fire and Ice" by Robert Frost and read two first impressions.

> The poem appears to be about the end of the world and whether this will be caused by fire or by ice.

> The poem is concerned with the destruction of the world either by fire or by ice.

Step 2: Studying the poem

a) Annotations

While studying the poem you should keep **a set of notes**. Preferably these notes should be **annotations** on and around the poem itself. If you are not allowed to write in the book, make a large copy of the poem, on which you

- underline or highlight key passages or words.
- write down short explanations of your thoughts and interpretations.
- use question marks **?** or wavy lines ~~~ to mark passages that you find difficult to understand.
- use exclamation marks **!** to show that you agree with or are impressed by an idea in the poem.
- use different colours to highlight recurring ideas or emotions.

Annotations	*Poem*	*Form*
Theme of the poem, end of the world/destruction of mankind?	**Fire and Ice** Some say the world will end in fire, Some say in ice.	Three different rhymes.
The contrast between fire and ice.	From what I've tasted of desire I hold with those who favor fire. !	Lines of four or eight syllables.
What does the narrator mean by "tasting desire"? Reference to Frost's own romantic experiences?	But if it had to perish twice, I think I know enough of hate To say that for destruction ice	End-stopped lines (lines 1,2,4,5,9)
The poet thinks the end of the world will most likely come as a result of fire. I agree that it is more likely than an ice age.	Is also great And would suffice. <div align="right">Robert Frost</div>	enjambment (line 7)

b) Form and rhythm

What makes a poem a poem and not a piece of prose? Look what happens if Robert Frost's lines are written as prose.

Some say the world will end in fire. Some say in ice. From what I've tasted of desire I hold with those who favor fire. But if it had to perish twice, I think I know enough of hate to say that, for destruction, ice is also great and would suffice.

Skills section

The language remains but the poetic effect is lost. **Form** and **rhythm** are necessary to transform the lines into a poem.

- **Form** refers to the type of poem, e.g. sonnet, and the way it is organized. Poems are usually organized in groups of lines called **stanzas**. Many poems are organized into stanzas of equal length (3 or 4 lines). Contemporary poems, however, often contain stanzas of varying lengths, without a formal pattern.
- The **rhythm** of a poem refers to the way its sound pattern is organized. It is determined by its stressed and unstressed syllables and by punctuation.

> The poem "Fire and Ice" is not organized into stanzas of equal length but consists of nine lines of either four or eight syllables. The form is what makes this poem so special.
>
> Sóme sáy the wórld will énd in fíre
> Sóme sáy in íce
> From whát I've tásted óf desíre
> I hóld with thóse who fávor fíre.
>
> If you listen to the poem again, you should be able to detect a rhythm. The stressed syllables are marked with ´.
>
> Many of the lines can be read as **iambic**. That means that an unstressed syllable is followed by a stressed syllable. But this rhythm is not consistent. In the first two lines the poet makes a point of stressing the two different views on the destruction of the earth. By using and stressing the word "some", he underlines that this is not a personal view but rather a universal truth.
>
> The poet also employs the following poetic techniques, which affect the rhythm:
>
> - **End-stopped lines** in lines 1,2,4,5 and 9. The lines end in a comma or a full stop creating a natural pause and slowing down the speed.
> - The **enjambment** in line 7 has the opposite effect. By continuing the idea into a new line, the pace of the poem is increased. The reader cannot comfortably pause at the end of the line.

c) Language

Having identified the theme of the poem and studied its form and rhythm, you should then look more closely at the language.

1. Choice of words

The poet's choice of words determines his/her style and adds to the meaning of a poem. The choice of vocabulary in a poem will depend to a certain extent on its theme. It may be **formal** or **informal**, **simple** or **complex**, **straightforward** or **ambiguous**.

> The poem "Fire and Ice", written in 1923, employs formal language to pursue the theme of the destruction of the world, a topic of scientific debate at the time. Some scientists believed that the world would end as a result of explosions of fire from its core. Some scientists believed that an ice age would destroy all living things. Frost states this clearly in the first two lines. The language is straightforward and concise, underlining the scientific nature of the subject matter.

However, the poem also employs **connotations** and **imagery**, introducing a more emotional side to the topic.

- The **connotations** of a word are the **associations** it evokes.
- **Imagery** refers to any aspect of a piece of writing that appeals to the reader's senses. It also refers to the use of comparisons, specifically **similes**, **metaphors** and **personifications**.

> In this poem, Frost associates passionate desire with fire and hatred with ice. He thus creates the image of the world as a relationship, which may be destroyed by too much passion or fire or alternatively by icy indifference and hatred. The metaphorical view of the two elements begins in the first two lines and is developed over the whole poem.

2. Grammar and syntax

When analysing the language of a poem, it is also important to look at grammar and syntax (the way the words are arranged).
- Are there any **questions**, **commands** or **exclamations**? To what effect?
- Is the normal **word order** changed in order to emphasize certain words? To what effect?
- Are certain structures repeated (**parallelism**)? To what effect?
- Is the poem written in the **first person** (I, me)? What feelings and attitudes does the narrator convey?

> The use of parallelism in the first two lines "Some say ..." underlines that only two options are open as far as the final cause of the destruction of the world is concerned. The narrator, introduced in line 3, initially refers to his own experience of desire and maintains that fire is more likely to be the cause of destruction. However, he finally admits that the world could just as easily end in ice, revealing his own experience of hate.

3. Sound

The sound of a poem is not just determined by its rhythm but also by the vocabulary used. The following techniques can create a musical effect, making the poem easier to read but there are often other important effects. It is not enough just to identify the techniques, you must also explain their effect.
- **Rhyme:** It is not difficult to identify rhymes but more difficult to talk about their effects. Rhyme can give a poem momentum as well as an evenness of tone. Poems <u>without</u> a regular rhyme scheme are called **free verse**.
- **Alliteration:** This is when two or more words begin with the same sound, e.g. favor fire.
- **Assonance:** This is the rhyming of vowel sounds within two or more words, e.g. hold with those.

> The poem "Fire and Ice" incorporates three sets of interwoven rhymes. Each line ends with an -ire, -ice, or -ate rhyme. The rhymes bring particular words together that are important for the meaning/message of the poem. "Desire" not only connotes "fire", it also rhymes with it. "Hate" is "great" in the sense of excessive or huge and thus the final message that hatred can also cause destruction is drummed home and further emphasized by the rhyme of "ice" and "suffice". The use of alliteration in line 4, "favor fire" and assonance in line 5, "hold with those" both accentuates the narrator's initial preference for destruction by fire and contrasts strongly with the final message of the last four lines, which come as quite a shock.

Skills section

S11 How to work with drama

Together with poetry and prose, drama is one of the three main literary genres. Drama is a representation of people in conflict with each other and the world around them, which is intended to be performed on stage. It relies on dialogue, interaction and set design.

Types of plays

Tragedies like the famous plays *Romeo and Juliet* or *Hamlet* by William Shakespeare explore human nature and end in a **catastrophe** due to the tragic hero's misjudgement or hubris, causing his/her own death and that of others.

History plays like *Henry V* use historical events to analyse the machinations of politics and warfare, revealing their impact on people's lives. Thus, history plays comment indirectly on the political situation of the time.

Comedies entertain audiences by making them laugh at the quirks and follies of everyday life. But in spite of all the confusion in a comedy, which might also expose and criticize the shortcomings of society, there is no catastrophe but rather a **happy ending**.
Comedy, especially as **social satire**, is a device used to expose corruption and the foolishness of the individual or to unmask current problems and dangerous trends in society.

A special variety of postwar drama is the **theatre of the absurd**, which illustrates the problem of dysfunctional communication, i.e. the inability to communicate in a meaningful way. Its aim is to shock us out of our complacency and to suggest that our world cannot be rationally comprehended.

Structure

A play is divided into **acts** and **scenes**. While in the ancient Greek tradition the action had to take place in one day and one place (**unity of time, place and action**), even some 400 years ago the inventive playwright William Shakespeare used subplots and switched between different locations on his stage.

Normally, the development of the plot follows a certain structure. In the **exposition** the main characters, the setting and the topic/conflict are introduced. During the **rising action** suspense builds up due to unexpected obstacles, complications or a clash of conflicting interests and controversial attitudes. This leads up to the **climax**, which is the point of highest tension and can consequently also be referred to as the **crisis**. The **falling action** shows how the conflict is resolved and leads to the final part, the **resolution** or **denouement**.

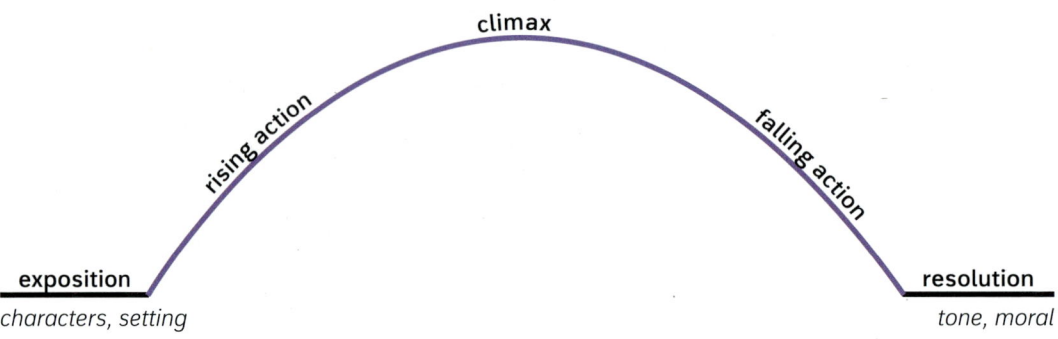

Skills section

Dramatic devices

The script of a play – or a film – is meant to come alive on stage – or on set. The text consists of dialogue and monologue and the stage directions, which help the actors to interpret and perform the play.

The characters are defined by what they say and do. Their ideolect, the language typical of an individual speaker, reveals a lot about their class and education (e.g. by grammatical incorrectness, lower class slang, sophisticated vocabulary), their personality, their mood (e.g. by an aggressive/ polite/reserved/enthusiastic choice of words) and their role (e.g. domineering/hesitant/intimidated/ uncertain, indicated by pauses, incomplete sentences or repetition).

Dramatic devices	
Dialogue	The verbal exchange between two or more characters
Monologue	A long speech or statement by a single character without any interruption
Soliloquy	Alone on stage, the character voices his innermost thoughts and feelings. Just think of Hamlet's famous words "To be or not to be".
Aside	With several characters present, one of them makes a comment or hints at a plan in a way that makes it obvious that the others cannot hear what is said. This is often used to create suspense by giving the audience some idea of further complications in the plot.
Dramatic irony	Relies on the audience knowing more about the course of action than a character on stage and consequently leads them to anticipate what traps he might fall into or what relevance his seemingly unimportant words have.
Reported action	The theatre is a limited space and sometimes details about what happened years ago or in a different place are necessary to explain a character's behaviour or motives or their relationship to others. This can be achieved by characters telling the story and providing the relevant background information.
Comic relief	A favourite device of Shakespeare's, this is a means of breaking the tension and giving temporary relief in a serious or tragic situation by introducing an amusing scene, a comic remark or incident.

Analysis

Plot	Character	Devices
• What is the main problem/ conflict? • How is the conflict introduced? How does it develop? How is it resolved? • What creates suspense? • Are there any subplots? How are they linked to the main plot?	• How is a character presented in the stage directions? • What does his/her ideolect reveal? • How does the character interact with others? • What does the dialogue reveal about the role he/ she is assuming?	• What type of register/what choice of words is used by the individual characters? • How are pauses/volume/ interruptions used? • Does the audience know more than a character on stage? • Is there additional information about past events/experiences and what is its relevance?

Skills section

S12 Checklist: Analysis – prose

When analysing a prose text, i.e. an extract from a novel or a short story, you will be likely to work through the text chronologically, but when writing your analysis, it is often more advisable to use a topical order. As the task usually requires a focus on a particular aspect, such as stylistic devices or choice of words, characterization or narrative perspective, it is more helpful to present your results on individual aspects in clusters or groups. This allows you to combine passages that are taken from different parts of the text but are closely related, and to rearrange them in a way that suits your analysis best.

Consequently, you should plan your text carefully before you start writing your analysis. You should decide which passages are most relevant to the task and what they illustrate so that you can group similar points together. Put them in a logical order that makes your analysis flow naturally. For a characterization, for example, it would be advisable to start with general information on a character like age and family background before you move on to other aspects such as attitudes and feelings. Once you have decided on an outline for your analysis, make sure your answer follows the structure of introduction – main part – conclusion (see pp. 344–346).

Do not just consider the content, but always examine the language used by the author and explain what it reveals about the narrator or a character or what effect it is supposed to have on the reader. Pay attention to features such as narrative techniques, choice of words and stylistic devices.

Dos	✓ Begin with a central claim that forms a first conclusion on the task, e.g. in the case of a characterization, what a character's central character trait appears to be. ✓ Structure your text logically and divide it into paragraphs. ✓ Organize your analysis around the specific aspects you are asked to focus on (unless the task specifically asks you to work on the development and chronology of the text). ✓ Always combine findings on language/structure and content/message. ✓ Quote from the text to support your findings or refer to the text in your own words. ✓ Use the present tense. ✓ Use connectives to link your ideas. ✓ Use formal and neutral language. ✓ End with a conclusion that does not only sum up your findings, but also refers back to the task and states your results on a more abstract level.
Don'ts	✗ Don't use the past tense. ✗ Don't just paraphrase the text you are analysing. ✗ Don't speculate – your findings must be based on evidence from the text. ✗ Don't write about every detail.

Skills section

Language support

Writing about characters:
- The frequent use of direct characterization creates a convincing/clear/positive/negative picture of …/helps the reader to …
- X is directly characterized by …
- The direct characterization by family and friends
  → seems/appears to be controversial/contradictory/…
  → shows/reveals different sides of X as each of them perceives X in his/her own way/in an individual way.
- X is mainly characterized indirectly by/through his/her …
- From the way he/she addresses …/reacts to …/behaves when … we can infer/conclude that …
- The protagonist seems/appears to be …
- X's behaviour/the way he/she speaks/dresses/… suggests that …
- As X is presented/described as …, it becomes clear/it is emphasized/it is highlighted that …
- X's reaction/comment/… reveals/makes the reader feel/believe/understand that …

Writing about narrative perspective:
- By granting the reader access to the character's/characters' mind(s), the narrator draws attention to/makes the reader see/feel …
- Due to the first-/third-person narration (with a limited/omniscient point of view), it is (not so) easy for the reader to identify with …
- As the story is told by …, the reader knows more/does not know more than the character(s) in the story …
- The reader needs to be careful not to take all he/she reads for granted as he/she experiences the development through the main character's eyes …

Writing about atmosphere/choice of words/stylistic devices:
- The author makes use of/uses … to create a/an … atmosphere.
- The use of short forms and colloquial language in direct speech suggests that …
- The simple short sentences in this passage quicken the pace of the action in order to …
- By incorporating a lot of direct speech in this part of the chapter, the narrator manages to …
- The author uses metaphorical language to … /employs stylistic devices to …
- The author's use of stylistic devices underlines/enhances the arguments/message of the text.
- The stylistic device/metaphor/… brings out/emphasizes/underlines/supports/affirms the message …
- to examine/explain/analyse the stylistic devices

S13 Checklist: Analysis – non-fictional texts

When analysing non-fictional texts, i.e. a newspaper article or a speech, you need to look at the analysis task very carefully in order to decide whether you should analyse the text in the order in which it is written or by focusing on a certain aspect.

If you are asked to work on the line of argument, it is advisable to follow the structure of the text and see how the author/speaker moves from one point to the next. If, however, the task requires you to analyse the use of stylistic devices, for instance, it makes more sense to structure your findings according to the different types of devices that are used – no matter in which order they appear.

Take your time to plan your text carefully before you start writing. Decide how to divide your findings up into paragraphs. Your answer should have a coherent structure, consisting of an **introduction**, **main part** and **conclusion** (see pp. 344-346).

Apart from the overall structure, consider the different strategies and devices the author/speaker may use to inform/influence/convince or entertain the reader or – in the case of a speech – the audience. Similarly, the author's point of view and the type of text can have a significant impact on the way a text is written. So watch out for the way facts and opinions are combined, to what extent the text is biased and what the ultimate goal of the article or speech is.

However, it is not sufficient just to identify these devices. Analysing a text means that you have to explain why these devices are used and what the desired effect on the reader is.

Dos	✓ Begin with a central claim. In order to do this, keep the central message or problem of the text in mind, but also the task you are working on. Your central claim should set out what you expect to find in your analysis, e.g. what a speaker's overall aim and strategy is in a speech. ✓ Structure your text logically and write in paragraphs. ✓ Analyse the text either in the order in which it is written or according to each of its various aspects in turn – depending on what fits the task best. ✓ Give examples of important stylistic devices, rhetorical strategies, choice of words and structure (included in your analysis as direct or indirect quotations), explain them/their meaning and analyse their effect on the reader. ✓ Always combine findings on language/structure and content/message. ✓ Use the present tense. ✓ Use connectives to link your ideas. ✓ Use formal and neutral language. ✓ End with a conclusion that not only sums up your findings, but also refers back to the task and states your results on a more abstract level.
Don'ts	✗ Don't use the past tense. ✗ Don't only paraphrase the text you are analysing. ✗ Don't just state that a certain stylistic device is used, but explain its function. Refer only to those devices that you can use as evidence for what you claim. ✗ Don't speculate – you must use evidence from the text to support your findings. ✗ Don't write about every detail. Choose evidence carefully and concentrate on the examples that reveal the most about the author's intention; you can mention similar examples without going into too much detail.

Skills section

Language support

Writing about language/style:
- *formal/informal/colloquial/vulgar/ academic/clear/objective/vivid/... language*
- *complex/simple sentences*
- *a serious/friendly/humorous/ironic/ polite/rude/critical/optimistic/... tone*
- *The style of the text is plain/condensed/ vivid/pompous/artificial/...*

Writing about stylistic devices:
- *The author uses metaphorical language to ...*
- *The author employs stylistic devices to ...*
- *The author uses figures of speech to ...*
- *The stylistic devices underline/enhance the arguments/message of the text.*

- *The stylistic device supports/affirms the author's/the text's message.*
- *The stylistic device/metaphor/... brings out the message ...*
- *to examine/explain/analyse the stylistic devices*
- *to make a comparison ...*

Writing about choice of words:
- *to use emotive adjectives/adverbs that ... to appeal to the readers' emotions*
- *to express ideas in a more informal or colloquial way in order to ...*
- *to associate ... with positive/negative words such as ... in order to ...*
- *the ... connotations of words like ... are meant to make the reader ...*

S14 How to analyse a speech

There are many types of speeches that are delivered on numerous different occasions to different types of audiences. The type of speech a speaker makes depends on the occasion and the objective. Speeches can aim to inform, to persuade or to entertain. Often speeches are a mixture of all three, e.g. the intention of a political speech may be primarily to convince the audience of a particular policy, but it will probably also include important information and might well be entertaining at times, in order to maintain the audience's attention. There is no point in speaking to an audience that does not listen. In your English classes you are more likely to be confronted with political speeches, e.g. a president making a particular statement.

Step 1: Identifying the speaker's objective

The first thing you should do before planning your speech analysis is to decide what the speaker wants to achieve with his/her speech. Read the speech and try to identify the purpose of the speech. The following questions will help you:

- **When and where** is the speech delivered?
  → on a social occasion? in honour of someone/something? in a political context? in public? in private?
- **Who is the speaker?** What can you find out about him/her?
  → a politician? a public figure? a private individual? an entertainer?
- **What kind of audience** is it?
  → small or large? members of the media? politicians? people who share a common goal? representatives of a particular group?
- **What general theme** is covered by the speech?
  → Is it political, cultural, scientific, economic? Is it concerned with biographical information and/or personal achievements?

Skills section

- **What kind of language** does the speaker use?
  → Is it emotional, powerful, graphic? Can you detect humour, irony, or satire? Does the speaker employ stylistic devices?

Tip: If you have the opportunity to **listen to the speech or even watch the speech being delivered** you should do so. The tone of voice of the speaker, the emphasis of certain words, lowering and raising of the voice, will give you good insight into his/her objective.
If a video of the speech is available, you can also take facial expressions and gestures into account.

One of the most famous speeches ever made was by Martin Luther King on 28 August 1963 in Washington D.C. Read the first lines of the speech and try to answer the questions about it. You may have to do some research.

I Have A Dream

I am happy to join with you today in what will go down in history as the greatest demonstration for freedom in the history of our nation. Five score years ago, a great American, in whose symbolic shadow we stand today, signed the Emancipation Proclamation. This momentous decree came as a great beacon light of hope to millions of Negro slaves who had been seared
5 in the flames of withering injustice. It came as a joyous daybreak to end the long night of their captivity.
But one hundred years later, the Negro still is not free. One hundred years later, the life of the Negro is still sadly crippled by the manacles of segregation and the chains of discrimination. One hundred years later, the Negro lives on a lonely island of poverty in the midst of a vast
10 ocean of material prosperity. One hundred years later, the Negro is still languished in the corners of American society and finds himself an exile in his own land. And so we've come here today to dramatize a shameful condition.

Step 2: Planning and writing your analysis

A speech analysis should adhere to the structure you are familiar with and consist of an **introduction**, a **main body** and a **conclusion**.
The following checklist outlines the information you should include in each part.

Checklist

Introduction
✓ Name the speaker and, if relevant, his/her position.
✓ Say when, on what occasion and to whom the speech was delivered.
✓ Identify the theme/topic.
✓ Specify the purpose of the speech (briefly).

Main body
✓ Outline the structure of the speech.
✓ Summarize the speaker's main arguments.
✓ Quote examples of stylistic devices and strategies employed by the speaker and explain their function.

Conclusion
✓ Sum up your conclusions.
✓ If necessary put the speech into its historical context.
✓ Depending on the task, give your personal opinion on whether the speech succeeds in fulfilling the speaker's objectives.

> **Language support**
>
> **Introduction**
> - The speaker, … , a civil rights leader, makes/gives/delivers the speech during a demonstration in …/in an election campaign in the year …
> - The speech is made/delivered to an audience of …/The speaker faces an audience of …
> - The speaker addresses the topic/theme of …
> - His/Her purpose/aim/objective is to persuade/convince the audience/to explain the necessity for …
>
> **Main body**
> - In the first few lines the speaker informs the audience/argues that/puts forward the idea of …
> - He/She continues by expanding his/her arguments on/offering further proof of …
> - About halfway through the speech he/she appeals to the audience by …
> - The scientific evidence cited in lines … offers a powerful argument on behalf of …
> - Throughout his/her speech … employs a number of stylistic devices to underline/illustrate/emphasize his/her point of view.
> - In lines … the repeated use of 'we' is a strong appeal to the audience to …
> - A recurring/much-used/frequently employed stylistic device is the use of … in order to emphasize …
>
> **Conclusion**
> - In general I have come to the conclusion that ….
> - All in all the speaker convincingly argues his/her case on behalf of …
> - Martin Luther King's speech on … was a landmark in the struggle for …
> - The speaker has not achieved his/her objective as far as I am concerned.
> - His/Her arguments fail to convince me/overcome my doubts about …
> - Despite the extensive use of rhetorical strategies, the speaker does not succeed in …

In the *Glossary: literary terms* at the end of your textbook, you can find definitions of different stylistic devices.

Step 3: Proofreading

Very few pieces of writing are printed exactly the way they were first written. A first draft needs to be revised and improved. That may mean changing the order of paragraphs or arguments or including more quotations or references to the text.
In an exam situation you won't have time to redraft a whole piece of writing but you can proofread it. The final read should concentrate on spelling, punctuation and grammar.
You should try to identify your own weaknesses and look for mistakes in these areas, e.g. the wrong use of commas and other punctuation or word order.

Skills section

S15 How to describe pictures

Pictures often say more than words and may be used in many different ways to illustrate a topic. There are many different types of pictures and it is important that you follow these steps when working with them:
- Identify and name the kind of picture you are asked to describe in your introductory sentence.
- Describe the different elements in the picture in detail.

Finally, you may be asked to speculate on a particular aspect of the picture or give your own interpretation.

> 1. **Opening sentence.**
>   *e.g.* This picture shows an advertisement for OMEGA watches in cooperation with the James Bond film *Skyfall*.

> 2. **In the foreground** you can see a watch by the exclusive brand OMEGA.

> 3. **In the top left-hand corner** is the title of the Bond film, *Skyfall*. Below it you can see the famous 007 logo.
>   Next to it at the top you can read OMEGA in capital letters. Below this there is a much smaller subtitle: "James Bond's choice".

> 4. **On the right-hand side** you can see actor Daniel Craig as Britain's most famous agent James Bond. He is wearing a jacket, a scarf and gloves. The expression on his face is serious.

> 5. **The background** of the advertisement is the London skyline.

> 6. **In the centre** you can see the British flag, the Union Jack.

> 7. **In the bottom right-hand corner** there is a reference to the brand OMEGA and its logo, the Greek letter omega.

> 8. **Speculation or interpretation.**
>   Possible questions you could ask yourself are:
> - What do you associate with James Bond?
> - What might be the reason for choosing Bond for the advertisement?
> - What is suggested about Bond and Britain by the words/slogans?
> - What is the message of the advertisement?
> - What is the (intended) effect?
> - What atmosphere is created and how is this achieved?

Language support

Different types of pictures and artists
- advertisement, caricature, collage, drawing, film still, illustration, (oil) painting, photograph portrait, poster, sketch, watercolour,
- graphic designer, artist, portrait painter, photographer

Describing where to find different elements
- In the top right-hand/left-hand corner
- In the foreground/background
- At the top/bottom
- In the middle/centre
- On the left/right

Speculating
- It would appear that the advertisement is part of a campaign to …
- It seems likely/probable that …
- One might assume that …

- The choice of slogan/photograph might mean that …
- It seems to be the intention of the artist to …
- The body language of the central figure suggests …

Interpreting
e.g. atmosphere, tone, etc.
- The atmosphere created by the colours is …
- There is a certain humorous/mocking/critical/light-hearted tone about the …
- The choice of … underlines the intention of the artist/graphic designer/photographer to …
- The painting captures the feeling of …
- The serious/loving/hateful expression on the face of the figure on the right corresponds with/contrasts strongly with …

S16 Checklist: Analysis of a film scene

In order to analyse a film scene, it is necessary to watch the scene multiple times. What and how much you are expected to analyse depends on the task you are given. Sometimes you will have to analyse a film scene as a whole, often in the context of the complete film. In other cases, your task may only be to analyse how stylistic devices are used in a scene. During the viewing process, you should keep a **viewing log**. Having a viewing log makes it easier for you to remember and refer back to important points during the writing process.

A viewing log may look like this:

scene	action	cinematic devices	function/effect
…	…	…	…

You can find an overview of cinematic devices and their primary functions on pages 87-88. When you write your analysis, you can use the checklist on the next page.

Skills section

Dos

Introduction
- ✓ Refer back to the task.
- ✓ Name the film, its director and the year it was released.
- ✓ In the introduction, it often makes sense to make a central claim that sums up what you are going to prove in your essay.

Main part
- ✓ Present your points in a well-structured and logical way. Guide your reader through your text and express connections between points in the text explicitly.
- ✓ Divide your main part up into meaningful paragraphs. Decide whether those paragraphs will reflect a chronological analysis of the excerpt or represent certain aspects or focal points.
- ✓ Within those paragraphs, it usually makes sense to follow the structure Point – Evidence – Analysis: a point you want to make, evidence to support the point and an analysis of the evidence (see S9: How to structure a text, p. 344)
- ✓ For an analysis of a film scene as a whole, you should include and combine
  - an analysis of the dialogue,
  - an analysis of the action,
  - an analysis of images (like objects, landscapes that have metaphorical meaning etc.)
  - an analysis of the camera operations and
  - an analysis of other important cinematic devices (like music, lighting, etc.).
- ✓ For an analysis of a film scene as a whole, you might want to consider
  - how the scene moves the action forward and creates suspense,
  - if/how it represents a turning point,
  - whether it shows a new/important character trait of a protagonist or
  - introduces something new (character, conflict, etc.) or
  - defines the relationship between characters.
- ✓ For an analysis of a scene as a whole, put your findings into a broader context if necessary, i.e. explain them in the context of the complete film: use your knowledge about the plot, the characters etc.

Conclusion
- ✓ Refer back to your introduction.
- ✓ Summarize your most important findings concisely.

Don'ts
- ✗ In the conclusion, do not repeat every single detail of your findings.
- ✗ In the conclusion, do not introduce new details.

Language support

The scene conveys/suggests/indicates/reveals/highlights …
The character's position/stance/facial expression suggests/indicates/reveals/seems to reveal …
The music intensifies/emphasizes/has the effect of …/evokes a feeling of …/creates a(n) … atmosphere.
The sound effects intensify/emphasize/have the effect of …/evoke a feeling of …/create a(n) … atmosphere.
The setting suggests/indicates/has the effect of …/evokes a feeling of …
The use of colour underlines/has the effect of …/creates a(n) … atmosphere.

Skills section

S17 How to work with cartoons

Cartoons are often used to make a critical comment on a serious issue in a humorous way. They are often published in newspapers or magazines. In order to understand the cartoon it is important to look at the details, and you should consider the connection between the picture, the punch line and any speech bubbles.

Issue
Before you study the cartoon in detail, decide what the issue is.

Presentation of characters
Are the characters in the cartoon caricatures of real people like politicians or other persons of public interest, or do they stand for a particular group?

Scene/Setting
What is the situation depicted in the cartoon? Where is it set? Who are the characters involved? What are they doing?

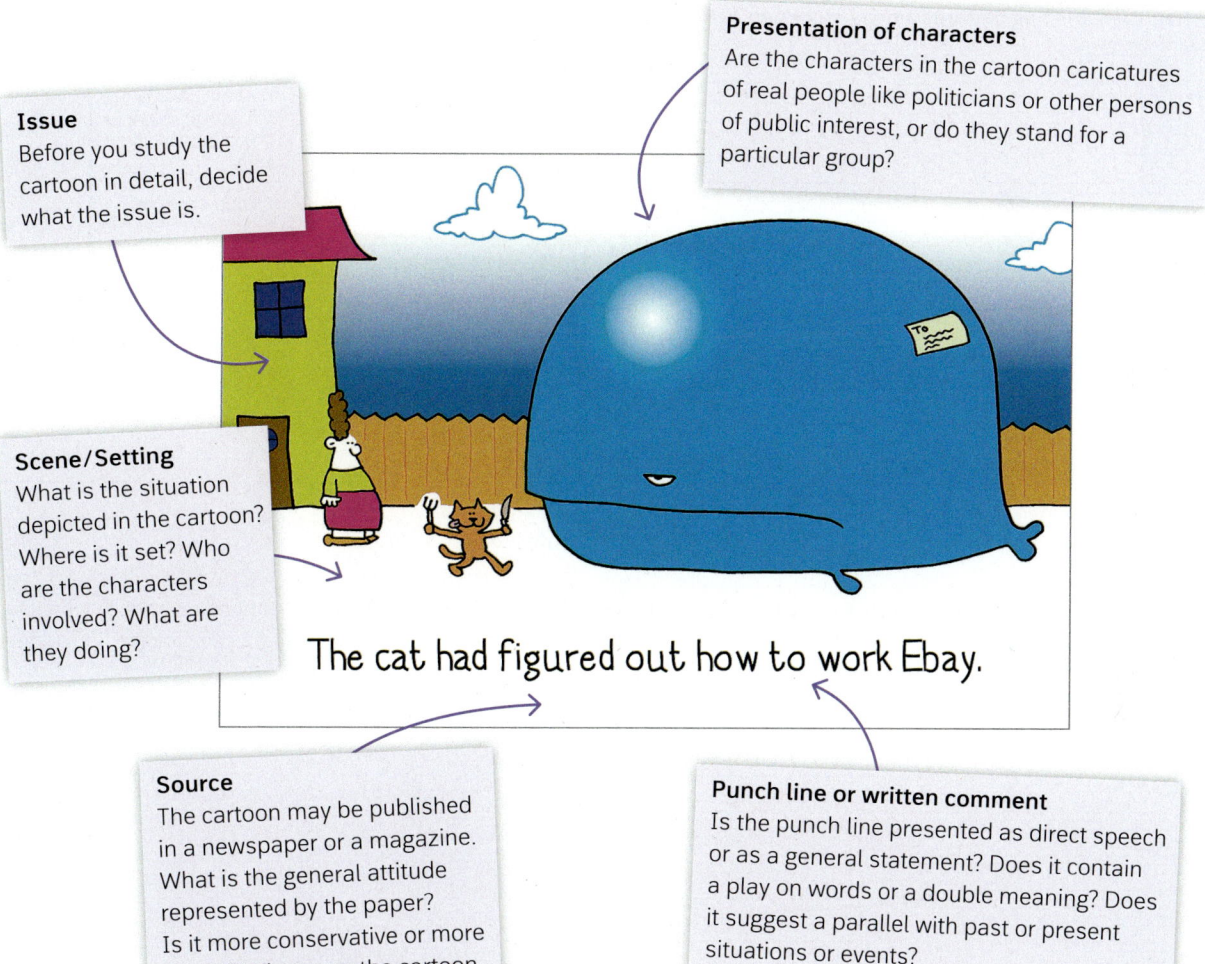

Source
The cartoon may be published in a newspaper or a magazine. What is the general attitude represented by the paper? Is it more conservative or more liberal? When was the cartoon first published?

Punch line or written comment
Is the punch line presented as direct speech or as a general statement? Does it contain a play on words or a double meaning? Does it suggest a parallel with past or present situations or events?

Language support

Describing cartoons	Interpreting cartoons
• At the top/bottom of the cartoon … • In the foreground/background … • On the right/left … • In the centre … • In the top/bottom right-hand/left-hand corner … • The cartoonist shows … • There are … in the picture. • The situation reminds one/me/you of … • The cartoon describes …	• The topic/issue addressed by the cartoon is … • The figures represent/symbolize … • The caption suggests/implies/underlines … • The cartoonist ridicules/draws attention to/caricatures … • The … is a caricature of … • The message is accentuated by …

Skills section

S18 How to analyse statistics

Statistics can appear in different forms. Usually, they take one of the forms below:

bar chart

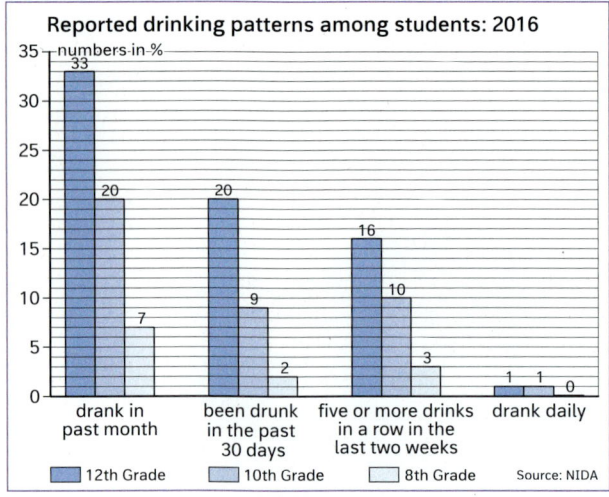

pie chart

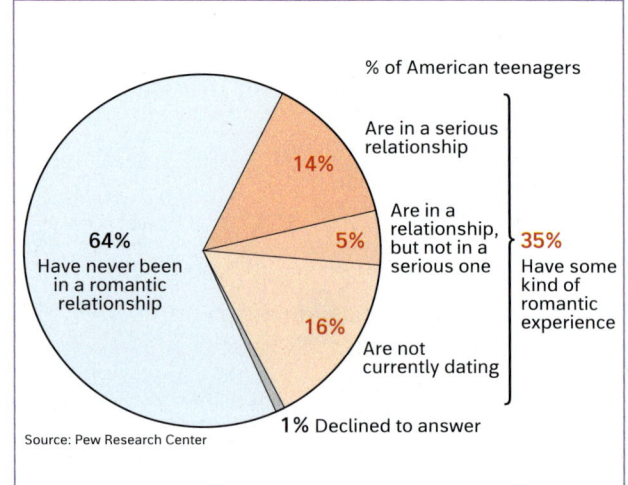

line graph

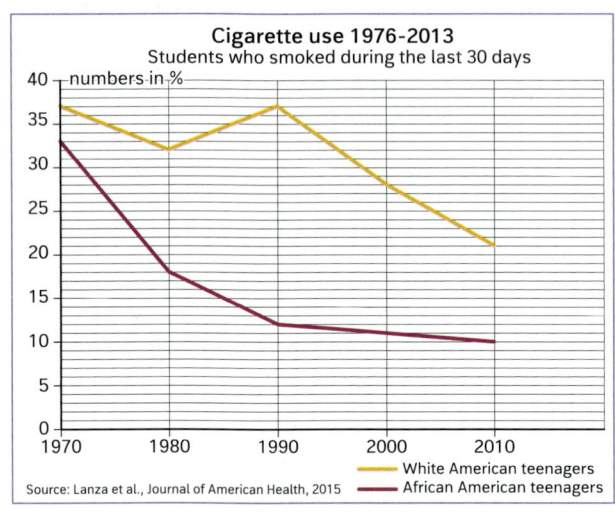

table

Among adult American smartphone owners, % who use...			
	Messaging apps	Auto-delete apps	Anonymous apps
Men	31	24	4
Women	27	23	7
18-29	42	56	10
30-49	29	13	6
50+	19	9	<1
Highschool or less	28	24	5
Some college	25	27	8
College+	33	21	4
Less than $50K/year	28	27	5
$50.000+	29	22	6
Total	29%	24%	5%

Survey conducted March/April 2016   Source: Social Media Update 2016, Pew Resaerch Center

Studying the figures

1. Before you start analysing statistics, make sure you study the graph/chart/table carefully. Find out what the statistics are about.

2. Study the legend and the figures and check if they are absolute numbers or percentages. Pay special attention to the way the figures are presented visually to make sure that proportions are represented accurately, for example.

3. Look for general trends or noteworthy figures or correlations. What you can find out depends largely on the type of visualization. Pie charts and bar charts usually deal with the relative size/importance of data, line graphs and tables often emphasize certain developments including peaks and troughs in trends.

362

Skills section

Language support

Describing and interpreting the figures

Introduction:
- How are the figures presented?
- What is the graph/chart/table about?
- What is the source (author/date of publication) of the figures?

- *The graph/chart/table shows/presents/ provides information on/deals with ..., covering a period of ...*
- *The topic/subject/theme of the graph/chart/ table is ...*
- *It is taken from/The source of the data is ...*
- *The graph/chart/table was published by ... on ...*

Description:
- How do the figures develop?
- What is the highest/lowest point?
- What are the most striking points?
- Are there any irregular figures?
- If there are figures to compare, are there any similarities/differences?

- *The horizontal/vertical axis shows ...*
- *There is a considerable/steady/sharp/slight/ marked increase/decrease in the number of ...*
- *The number/amount/proportion of ... has changed slightly/clearly since ...*
- *After 1980 ... rose dramatically/soared.*
- *The numbers drop/fall/decrease ...*
- *The figures remain constant/steady ...*
- *The figures reach a peak/a trough in ...*
- *In ..., X reached its lowest point at 21%/peaked at 37%.*
- *The downturn began in ...*
- *The average figure for ... is ...*
- *The pie is subdivided into segments that represent ...*
- *The chart/graph/table reveals/shows that ...*
- *The numbers for ... are about twice as high as those ...*
- *The ... with the highest frequency/number of ... is ...*
- *Compared to ...*
- *Nearly half of ...*

Conclusion and evaluation:
- What general conclusion can be drawn from the figures?
- What could be reasons for the figures?
- How can the figures be related to each other?
- What can be predicted on the basis of these figures?
- How do the figures relate to what you know about the topic? Are they objective or biased?

- *All in all/By and large, the statistics for ... reveal/show/... that ...*
- *This development clearly shows/indicates that ...*
- *It seems likely/unlikely that the figures for ... will (not) continue to ...*
- *Against the background of ..., the figures/ results are (not) very surprising/revealing/ enlightening ...*
- *The data confirms/contradicts/is (not) consistent with ...*
- *The graph/chart/table conveys a false/one-sided impression because ...*

S19 How to improve your mediation skills

You are very likely to be confronted with situations where people who do not speak German need your help because some information they need is only available in German.
Such situations are very similar to those that you find in mediation tasks.

Step 1: Understanding the task

Before you start working on a mediation task, make sure that you fully understand what is required from you. Mediation does not mean translating the German original word for word.

a) What is the type of text you need to produce?

In the example below, you can see that the German original is an article, but the text you should produce is an email. This means that you must change the way the information is presented to you in German. In order to do this, you need to remember what is typical of that particular kind of text. In the case of an email, you should first address your partner, introduce your email stating the reason for it, (e.g. by referring to the given situation), write a main part which includes the relevant information from the text and finish your email appropriately.

> Together with an English and a Polish partner school, your school is working on a Comenius project about immigration to Europe. You are a member of your school's Comenius group and you have found the following article in the German magazine Der Spiegel. Use the information given here to write an email in English informing the other partners about immigration laws and the conclusions drawn by the magazine.

b) What information is needed?

Read the task carefully to find out what information is needed. Certain passages or elements of the German text are likely to be irrelevant to the task. You should leave this information out in your text.

c) Who is the addressee?

In a mediation task, another factor that should influence the way you deal with the text is the addressee that is mentioned in the task. Select the aspects that are relevant for the addressee. Explain relevant terms that your addressee would otherwise not understand. If you write a text for teenagers, your text should be less formal and technical than if you were writing about a difficult topic for experts in a particular field, for example.

d) What style and register should you use?

Choose the style and register that fits the text type you have to produce (e.g. an email, letter, speech).

Step 2: Working on the task

a) Reading

- Highlight all the information relevant to the task (see Step 1b).
- Make notes in English.
- Remember that you are not supposed to write a word-by-word translation of passages from the text. If you decide that the translation of a certain expression is necessary to do the task properly, do not get stuck looking for a literal translation of a German expression. Sometimes it doesn't exist and you can paraphrase the idea you want to express. For example, there may be a German idiomatic expression like "das Zeitliche segnen" which you cannot translate directly. So you need to find either an English idiom that has a similar meaning or go for a more neutral expression, for example "to die".

b) Writing the English text

- Arrange the information you highlighted and noted down in a logical order that fits the type of text you are expected to write. Structure it in such a way that it is easy to understand for the people who are supposed to read your text.
- As stated above, you shouldn't translate the German text word for word. It is important that all the relevant information is presented clearly. Leave out anything that is not related to the task, also leave out any personal comments unless the task invites you to include them.
- Be careful with expressions and concepts that are very specific to German and Germany. You may have to include an explanation to someone from abroad. For example, a text may include references to people or institutions that most Germans know, but people from abroad do not know. So you need to add a short explanation: *Many Germans watch <u>the news programme "Tagesschau" at 8 o'clock at night on ARD,</u> <u>which is a public TV channel.</u>*

c) Editing the text

- Make sure that you have included all the relevant information required by the task and not used anything that goes beyond it.
- Check that your text fits the criteria of the type of text that the task has asked you to produce.
- Don't forget that the style and register of the text must suit the addressees that the text is intended for. If necessary, make some changes to style and register.
- Check your text for grammatical correctness and the right choice of words.

Skills section

S20 How to listen/watch effectively

Learning a foreign language properly is impossible without learning to listen and sometimes also watch effectively. Listening and viewing comprehension tasks, however, can take very different forms as you may have to listen to a dialogue, a speech, a song or watch an interview, a news report, an episode from a TV series, etc. The situations – whether it's in parliament or a family context – vary as much as the accents or pace of the speakers.

a) **Before listening/viewing**
- Make sure you read the task carefully.
- Think about the topic you have been discussing in class. If there are photos, headings, additional texts, study them so that you already have some ideas of what the listening text or the video may be about.
- Consider the context of the situation. Where are the people? What do people typically do or talk about in such a situation?
- Think about your expectations and assumptions concerning the video or audio clip. What do you think will happen? What will you see or hear?

b) **While listening/viewing**
- When you listen to an audio or video clip for the first time, listen for gist, i.e. the main ideas. Key words that are repeated several times may help you work out what the clip is about.
- While listening/watching, keep the task in mind and try to remember where in the clip there are relevant passages you should concentrate on when you listen to or watch it for a second time.
- Aim to understand the general message; don't worry if you can't make out every word. If you listen to a clip a second time, you will notice that you understand a lot more. You will then be able to work out the meaning of words from the context or from similarities they have with other words you know in English (e.g. high – height, clean – cleanliness), German or another language (e.g. to deny so. sth. – French: dénier).
- In video clips, gestures and body language can help you to understand the content. The body language of the people speaking, for example, tells you a lot about their feelings and thoughts and thereby can help you to figure out the meaning of unknown words.
- Try to think ahead. What might happen next? What might the speakers say? How are the people possibly going to act? Make predictions.

c) **After listening/viewing**
- Answer the key questions: **Who? Where? When? What? Why?**
- Note down important facts, key words and words you didn't understand.
- Were your guesses right? Did the people do or say what you expected them to? Correct your assumptions based on what you have heard or seen.
- If you are not quite sure whether you understood everything, try to guess what the people could have said by using all the information you got with the help of visual and/or acoustic hints.
- Look up key words that you think are essential for the understanding of the clip. Try to guess other words you don't know by using all other available information.
- If you hear or watch the clip again, set yourself an aim: What do you want to focus on?

d) **Working on the task**
- Use a pencil to take notes or, if it is a multiple-choice test, mark the correct answers.
- Add to your notes when you listen again.
- If it is not a test, check with your partner to see if you understood the same things.

S21 How to succeed in oral exams

Oral exams can be rather intimidating. In order to overcome your fears and to be able to prepare, it is important that you know what to expect in the exam and what the examiner expects of you.

In all oral examinations marks will be given both for the **content** of your answers and your **language competence**.

Content
The exam may be based on topics you have studied in class. In this case you can prepare by noting down useful information and learning it.
You will in many cases get one or more spontaneous "prompts" to start you talking about a particular topic. These are likely to be visuals such as pictures, cartoons etc., in some cases short texts. You will be expected to use these "prompts" together with your own knowledge to give a short talk or presentation (**monologue**) or as the basis for a discussion (**dialogue**). In an **interview** you may have to react spontaneously to questions without preparation or prompts.

Language competence
A good way to make sure that your discourse runs fluently is to use **discourse markers**. These words and phrases help the listener to follow what the speaker is saying by signalling certain aspects of speech. The following discourse markers are common in everyday speech.

so – marks the beginning of a new part of conversation
well – marks a change in focus
right/OK/if you like – mark a response/an agreement
I mean/you know/as I say – mark explanations or re-phrasings
actually – marks a different point of view or the introduction of a new aspect
anyway – marks a shift in topic

Look at the following short discussion:
A: So, I think the first picture is concerned with the consequences of cyber-bullying.
B: Well, that could be the case but it could also just show the importance of social networking.
A: Right. That's what I think, too. But it can still be misused.
B: Actually, I think misuse is not as widespread as many people believe. I mean, most of us don't send threatening texts to our classmates, do they?
A: OK, I suppose you have a point. Anyway, I think we should change the subject and move on to the next topic.

You can also use discourse markers to sequence what you say.

Language support

Beginnings are often introduced by:
- First (of all), ...
- For a start, ...
- Firstly (more formal)

Endings may be signalled by:
- Last of all, ...
- To sum up, ...
- Finally, ...
- In the end, ...

Further points may be introduced by:
- On top of that, ...
- What's more, ...
- Next/Second(ly)/Third(ly)

Skills section

Apart from ensuring that you speak fluently, it is also important not to make too many mistakes. Although no one expects you to be flawless, bear in mind these two points:
- Try to avoid basic grammar mistakes. Know your own weaknesses and practice structures that you have difficulty with, or avoid these structures if they cause you too many problems.
- Concentrate on communicating your ideas successfully. Do not express yourself in a too complicated way. Learn some useful phrases to structure your answers.

Parts of the exam

Usually, an oral exam consists of two or all of the following parts:

1. Interview

This is the most spontaneous type of oral exam and it is not always possible to prepare for it. The examiner is interested in how you can respond spontaneously to his or her questions on a particular topic that will usually be revealed shortly before the interview begins.
The important thing is to keep calm and to listen carefully to the examiner's questions before you answer. Here are some tips:

Checklist

- ✓ If you do not quite understand, ask the examiner to repeat or rephrase the question:
  I'm not quite sure whether I have understood you/the question. Would you mind repeating it, please?
- ✓ If you are not immediately sure about your answer, try to win some time by using phrases such as:
  Let me just think about that for a moment. • As I was saying …
  or by rephrasing or repeating the question:
  You asked me whether …. Personally, I …
- ✓ If it is a partner exam and the other student has to answer the same questions as you, you can refer to what the other candidate has said and agree or disagree with it:
  Actually there isn't very much I can add to what the other candidate has just said. I completely agree with him/her that …
  But generally, you should always try to add aspects of your own.

2. Monologue

In this kind of exam, you will be expected to demonstrate that you can speak coherently for some time on a particular topic. This usually takes the form of a short presentation based on some visual prompts such as photographs and a leading question.

Here is an example:
Talk about these pictures. What do they reveal about the importance of social media in the communication between young adults?

In many cases, you will have little or no time to prepare so that you will have to be able to present your topic quite spontaneously. Here are some tips:

Checklist

- ✓ If you are given time to prepare, use it well. Read the task and look at the pictures carefully (noting down useful information and your own ideas).
- ✓ Structure your talk e.g. by using phrases from the language support on the next page.
- ✓ Begin your talk by referring in detail to the pictures/material you have been given but then move on to include other relevant information or opinions while answering the leading question.
- ✓ Remember the examiner is interested in hearing what you have to say in the relatively short time given. Make sure you use that time effectively, avoiding long periods of silence, but do not "waffle", i.e. spend a lot of time talking about irrelevant aspects. Keep to the point.

3. Dialogue

In this kind of examination, you will have a conversation or a discussion with one or two other candidates based on prompts such as short texts or pictures and a leading question.
Here is an example:
Talk about which of the media in the following pictures have had the greatest impact on society.

Often you will be asked to come to some kind of agreement with the other examinee(s).
The examiner expects you to show the following oral skills:

Checklist

- ✓ listening actively to what the other person says
- ✓ keeping a conversation going
- ✓ reacting to what the other person says by taking turns, agreeing and/or disagreeing
- ✓ stating your own view clearly
- ✓ clarifying and asking for clarification if something you or the other person says is not immediately clear
- ✓ making suggestions and compromises in order to reach an agreement

Language support

Active listening You can use certain discourse markers to show that you are listening and are interested in what is being said.	• *Absolutely.* • *Really?* • *You don't say.* • *I see.* • *Exactly.* • *Sure.*
Keeping a conversation going Sometimes it is necessary to actively involve the person you are talking to, or bring him/her back into the conversation.	• *So what do you think?* • *What makes you so sure?* • *Wouldn't you say so?*
Agreeing and disagreeing It is more idiomatic in speaking to use phrases which are not too direct, especially when disagreeing	• *That's just what I think/how I see it.* • *Well, I'm not sure about that.* • *You could be right, but …* • *I see your point but …*
Stating your own view clearly It is possible to say "in my opinion/view", but in spoken English this sounds rather formal.	• *I'd say …* • *If you ask me, …* • *From my point of view …* • *I'm sure/convinced that …* • *As I see it …*
Clarifying if someone doesn't understand your point	• *What I really mean is …* • *In other words …* • *What I'm trying to say is …*
Asking for clarification if you do not understand another person	• *I'm sorry, I didn't quite understand what you mean.* • *When you talk about …, do you mean …?*
Making suggestions/compromises	• *What about …?/How about …?* • *What do you think about …?* • *Well, I suppose that's a possibility.* • *Why not?*

Skills section

S22 How to stage a debate

A debate is a good way of discussing varied opinions which argue for or against an idea. Through the format of a debate, different opinions and evidence can be shared and considered. The goal of the debate may be to convince the other side of your point of view, or to reach a common consensus through compromises.

Here is some help:

Step 1: Choosing a motion

Identify a clear topic or motion where there is a division of opinion. In these circumstances, the different groups can argue either for or against it. An example of such a motion would be:

"Driverless cars should save their driver and passengers at all costs."

Step 2: Splitting into two groups

Usually, two groups are formed based on common arguments both for and against the motion. However, the people in a single group do not necessarily have to share the exact same motivations or reasoning for their choice of argument. Bringing in different ideas is part of the debating process.

Step 3: Preparing your arguments

Each side of the argument has time to prepare their arguments. Part of a debate is finding weaknesses or flaws in the opposition's argument. Therefore, it is important that you research beforehand and identify evidence which will support your claims. In the same way, you can anticipate what the other side's arguments will be and prepare arguments against their ideas.

Step 4: Having the debate

The group supporting (or putting forward) the motion begins the debate by making an opening statement. This should summarize the key reasons why they are arguing for the topic. Afterwards, the spokesperson for the other side makes a similar opening statement. At this point, the debate really begins. Each group takes it in turns expressing their ideas, as well as exposing weaknesses in their opponent's thoughts.

Step 5: The results of the debate

To conclude the debate, a final vote is held in which everyone involved votes for or against the original motion. At this stage, group members are allowed to vote independently. That is to say that they might have been convinced by the opposition's side of the argument and vote with them on the issue.

Language support

We strongly believe that …	In my opinion, …
We are firm believers that/in …	If you ask me, …
We support the motion proposed here today because …	In my experience, …
It is our view that …	I'd like to point out that …
	Personally, I feel/think/believe/suggest …
	As far as I'm concerned, …
On the contrary, …	Just to be clear, I believe …
I agree to a certain extent but …	
He/she claims that … but …	To recap the main points, …
It is unjustifiable to say that …	In summary, …
	To conclude our side of the debate, …

S23 How to quote

When referring to/working with a text, you need quotations from that text to support your statements and findings with evidence.

You can quote directly or indirectly, and you can integrate quotations into your own sentences or quote passages to back up what you have said in your own words.

Language support

You may ...	Examples
1) ... quote indirectly from a text, i.e. say something that can be found in the text in your own words. This is often used when stating facts that need no in-depth interpretation. To show that you haven't quoted directly from the text, use "cf."[1].	• Ed works as a taxi driver and plays cards with his friends Audrey and Marvin on a regular basis (cf. p. 40).
2) ... integrate direct quotes into your own sentence. But be careful: Don't change the meaning of the quotation, and make sure the resulting sentence is grammatically correct. To show that you are quoting directly from the text, use inverted commas.	• Ed comes from one of the parts of the town where the poorer, less educated people live, which he himself describes as a "dirty secret" (p. 41).
3) ... quote a short passage or sentence directly to back up what you have already said in your own words. Again, use inverted commas to show that it is a direct quotation.	• Ed states clearly that he is not content with his life: "No real career. No respect in the community. Nothing." (p. 40).

Annotations
[1] **Cf.** = is short for the Latin word *confer*, which means *compare*

Checklist

When you quote from a text, ...
- ✓ don't quote very long passages. Quotes should underline or support what you have to say, not say it for you.
- ✓ don't use quotes simply to fill paper space – they must refer to your findings.
- ✓ quote the exact wording and punctuation from the text. If you leave something out or change something to make it fit into your sentence, you have to indicate that clearly by using [...]. You may only make minor changes and mustn't alter the meaning of your quote.
- ✓ don't use quotations to retell a text or story.
- ✓ make sure the quotes are meaningful – don't quote the first two words followed by "...".
- ✓ always refer to lines or pages (l. 1/ll. 5-7/p. 8/pp. 8-9, etc.). Use "l." for one line, "ll." for more than one line, "p." for one page and "pp." for more than one page.
- ✓ you should set off the quoted passage further away from the left-hand margin if the quoted text is more than two or three sentences long.

S24 How to give feedback/peer-edit

Giving constructive feedback is a helpful way to improve the quality of your own and of your classmates' work.

A. Feedback on a presentation

Make sure that the feedback you give …

- is worded in such a way that your classmates can accept it without being embarrassed.
- is objective and not personal.
- focuses more on the corrected form and does not dwell on the mistake.
- highlights the use of good language.

Language support

Here are some phrases you can use to give positive feedback on a presentation by your classmates:
- What I really liked was that you …
- What really impressed me was …
- I particularly liked …
- I think it was a good idea to …
- You managed to …

If you need to be more critical, these expressions can help you:
- The explanations/facts given were not (quite) correct.
- What could be improved is …
- I would have liked to learn more about …
- I missed information about …
- You did not manage to …

B. Peer-editing

A good method of improving your writing is peer-editing. It means working with someone from your class to help you to improve, revise and edit each other's writing.

When editing a text check the following aspects:

- **Topic:** Check whether the writer stays on topic. Information that is not relevant should be left out.

- **Choice of words:** Make sure the writer uses interesting words and not too many "overused" words (e.g. *really, very, nice, interesting*). A writer should also use language which is appropriate for the relevant text type (e.g. register, thematic vocabulary, etc.).

- **Sentences:** Check for sentences that are either too long or too short. A good writer also uses linking words to join his/her sentences.

- **Text structure:** A good text should be well organized and easy to understand. An introduction should immediately grab the reader's attention.

Skills section

When peer-editing a text, you should keep three aspects in mind:

- **Compliments:** The most important rule of peer-editing is to BE POSITIVE!
  Always start with compliments. Remember, you are helping to improve someone else's work. First tell the writer what you think he/she did well. Here are some phrases you can use to give positive feedback:

  This was fun to read because …
  I liked the way you …
  My favourite part was … because …
  I think you used a lot of good details.

- **Suggestions:** Make suggestions by giving some specific ideas about how to improve the piece of writing. Remember to try and stay positive and always try to provide constructive criticism.

  For example, don't say to your partner:
  This paragraph doesn't make any sense.
  Tell him/her: *If you add more details after this sentence, it will be clearer.*

  Rather than saying: *Your choice of words was boring*, say:
  Instead of using the word 'good', maybe you can use the word 'exceptional'.

- **Corrections:** Only after you and your partner have agreed on how to change your pieces of writing can you actually start with the final step in the peer-editing process: making corrections.

  Swap your texts and check your partner's work for:
  - spelling mistakes
  - grammar mistakes
  - missing punctuation

Checklist

Here is some advice on how to spot mistakes:
- ✓ Read the text more than once and concentrate on one aspect at a time, e.g. spelling mistakes.
- ✓ If you have typed your text on the computer, use the spellchecker in Word.
- ✓ After you have finished writing your text, take a break before you check it for mistakes.
- ✓ Reading "backwards", i.e. from end to beginning, might do the trick to spot mistakes.

Skills section

S25 How to work with a dictionary

Many tasks, especially reading and writing tasks, involve the use of a dictionary. There are **monolingual dictionaries**, which provide definitions in English and **bilingual dictionaries**, which give you the German equivalents. Most of the time you will be using a bilingual dictionary.

A. English – German

When working with texts you may not always understand all the words, so you will need to refer to a dictionary. The use of the dictionary, however, may be determined by the situation you are in.

- Don't look up every single word you don't know but apply the **strategies** you have learnt to **understand words from the context** first.
- **Limit the number of words to look up** as using the dictionary is quite time-consuming.
- Depending on the task you are given it may be necessary to **check all the words you don't understand**. If you read a novel or a longer text of course you will need to use your strategies of understanding words from the context, from cognates, etc. But sometimes you need to get a detailed understanding of the text.
- Having gone to the trouble of finding the word, try and use it to build and **extend your active vocabulary**.
  → Decide if the word may be useful for later use.
  → Collect the words you have selected in word fields.
  → Add collocations or idioms to avoid possible mistakes in the future.
  → Use the newly acquired words and phrases in your homework/written texts. This is the best way to remember them.

How to look the word up properly
- Make sure you look the word up in its **correct spelling** or you may end up with an incorrect translation. Examples of this are: *board-bored, fair-fare, sail-sale*.
- Determine whether the word you are looking up is a noun, a verb, an adjective, etc. and read the corresponding part of the entry. With verbs, make sure you look for the infinitive.
- There may still be different meanings. Read the complete entry and decide which translation fits the context of your text best.
- Avoid mistakes by checking what grammatical construction is needed with the word you want to use, for example *used to* **do** as opposed to *get used to* **doing**.

The phonetic transcription shows you how to pronounce a word correctly. It not only reflects the sound but also gives you the intonation of a word, which may be different depending on the function of the word (e.g. pre'sent v – 'present n).

n, vi, vt, adj tell you what type of word it is (noun, verb, etc.). If there are abbreviations you don't understand, check the explanations in the dictionary.

The headword helps you to find the word more easily.

chest [tʃest] n 1. *(torso)* Brust f, Brustkorb m; **to fold one's arm across one's ~** die Arme vor der Brust verschränken – 2. *(trunk)* Truhe; *(box)* Kiste – 3. *(treasury)* Schatzkästchen

The different meanings of a word are listed under numbers. Make sure that you read the whole entry to find the meaning that fits the context.

Expressions in bold letters give you examples of how to use the word correctly in typical phrases or idioms (e.g. "heavy: ~ accent, with a ~ heart").

B. German – English

When writing texts you will, with time, want to make your phrasing more precise, varied and differentiated.

Typical needs

- **Spelling:** You are not sure how the English word you want to use is written.
  → Check for changes in spelling in different grammatical contexts.

- **Vocabulary:** You want to use a particular word.
  → Make sure you have the correct German spelling. For example: The word *Widerspruch* will be hard to find if you think it is spelt with *ie*.
  → Read through **all** the possible meanings and consider the specific lexical area in which you want to use the word. For example: The German word *Bank* can mean either *bank* or *bench* in English.
  → If collocations are given, try to use the whole phrase or a parallel construction in your own text.

- **Style variation (synonyms/antonyms):** When writing a text and editing it you will find that you have repeated certain words.
  → Use the definitions of the German word you have looked up to find other ways in English of expressing it.

Internet dictionaries
/dict.leo.org/
/www.dict.cc/

It may seem the quickest route to use an Internet dictionary, but this often is the quickest way to making lots of mistakes: Internet dictionaries often offer a one-to-one translation which may not always fit. So don't go for the first option but check carefully in which context the respective word can be used.

Tip: Since you will have to work with a non-digital dictionary in your exams, you should practise working with one in class and at home.
- You will start to get quicker at finding words.
- You will start to get more confident in choosing the right meaning.
- You will get used to benefitting from the additional information the dictionary offers you.

Practising scientific writing: The *Facharbeit*

In many German states, students write a *Facharbeit* or another special term paper to practise their researching and writing skills. Each state and school will have different rules and preferences. In some schools this *Facharbeit* has to be written in English, for instance. Always ask your teacher about these preferences to ensure that you produce a well-written paper. Your teacher ought to be your primary source of assistance throughout the process of identifying a topic, structuring an argument and finally writing your *Facharbeit*. However, some general guidelines do apply.

A. FINDING A TOPIC

At many schools, you will be required or encouraged to find and research your own topic. Some restrictions may apply: for instance, you may have to pick a topic relevant to your studies in class. Make sure that you have a genuine interest in your chosen topic. Writing a *Facharbeit* is a long process and this interest will keep you motivated.

In English, several fields might offer good topics:

- a work of literature or art, such as a novel, film, play
- a writer or a poet and their work
- a comparison of a novel or a play and its film adaptation
- a historical event or time in an English-speaking country and its impact on today's society or its representation in a literary work
- challenges in today's society in English-speaking countries
- varieties of English (regional dialects, slang etc.)
- …

B. NARROWING IT DOWN

Once you have found an area or field that you are interested in, you should focus on a precise theme for your *Facharbeit*. For any topic, it is essential that you make it your own and decide which aspects should be highlighted in your work. A precise question enables you to focus on an important element of your topic.

Ask yourself what exactly it is you want to find out in your paper, and whether you are able to answer the question in the number of pages you are required to write: *Shakespeare and his plays* is a topic for a multi-volume book, not for a single essay. Even *Shakespeare and the film versions of his plays* is still too broad a topic. It would be better to choose a specific play and its film adaptation. You should narrow it down even further by looking at a special scene or one or two central characters and their representation in both the original play and the filmic adaptation. An example of a suitable topic would be *A comparison of the balcony scene in the play 'Romeo and Juliet' with classic and modern filmic representations*. A suitable question could be: *How is the balcony scene represented in the original play and subsequent filmic adaptations? What are the possible reasons for the different representations?*

C. RESEARCHING YOUR TOPIC

After successfully identifying a topic, you should research it as comprehensively as possible through the use of sources. Consider different sources and ask your teacher for help finding the most important ones. There are different kinds of sources. This overview can give you an idea of where to start:

- books: fictional (primary sources) or non-fictional (secondary sources)
- articles from professional journals
- newspaper articles
- Internet sources
- other documents
- interviews with experts or others

Checklist

Always make sure that a source that you want to use is reliable. You should check …
- ✓ that the author of any source has published multiple times in his/her field and thus knows what he/she is talking about.
- ✓ that Internet sources have a reliable author. The official website of a newspaper or university is more reliable than a private website.
- ✓ that universities stock the source in their libraries or that the source has been quoted in other publications.
- ✓ that your teacher agrees that the source is appropriate.

When you have found enough material on the topic, read through the sources and take notes. Check out the Workshop *Understanding and summarizing texts* on pages 50-54 for useful reading strategies. It is helpful to note down at least the main arguments any given source contains on your topic. Summarize these main points, link them to other ideas you have found and add your own thoughts and ideas. Make sure that you work with the sources you find, as well as developing your own understanding of the topic at hand. Only doing one or the other is not enough.

It is essential that you note down precisely where you find your information so that you can later reference it correctly in your essay: always write down the title of the source and the author's name, as well as page numbers if applicable. You can use another colour to highlight your own thoughts.

D. STRUCTURING YOUR PAPER

Once you have studied the available material for your topic, it is time to structure your *Facharbeit*. You can change the order of your argument as well as add to or delete from your original structure at any point. However, it is essential that you begin with a structure to use as a guideline for your writing process.

Every *Facharbeit* has an introduction, a main part and a conclusion. The main part should be divided into several shorter sections that look at different aspects of the main topic. Keep in mind that every section requires content, even if it is just a sentence or two outlining what will follow.

Taking the example from above, your structure may look something like this (the points in **bold print** can be found in any *Facharbeit*):

1. **Introduction**
2. **Main part**
    2.1 *Romeo and Juliet* and the significance of the balcony scene
    2.2 The balcony scene in the play
    2.3 The balcony scene in two filmic adaptions of the play
    2.3.1 The balcony scene in Zeffirelli's *Romeo and Juliet* (1968)
    2.3.2 The balcony scene in Luhrmann's *Romeo and Juliet* (1996)
    2.4 Comparison of the play and the filmic adaptations
3. **Conclusion**

E. WRITING YOUR PAPER

At this point, you are ready to begin writing your *Facharbeit*. It is highly recommended that you start by writing the main part and add both the conclusion and the introduction at the end. This is what you should be doing in the three parts of your essay:

- introduction: introducing your topic and outlining what you are going to do
- main part: presenting your argument analytically and with source-based evidence
- conclusion: drawing your points together to summarize and complete your argument

Introduction
In the introduction, you should answer the questions *What do I want to find out? Why?* Make sure that you thoroughly explain your motivation for writing the paper. You should also outline how you want to answer your question by summing up the essay's structure. Do not include elements that are irrelevant at this point. For instance, writing Shakespeare's biography when writing about *Romeo and Juliet* would not be of any use here.

Main part
In the main part of your essay, you should present both your sources and your own findings and analyse them to answer your question. Ideally, the main body should be split into sections which will enable your argument to flow. You should also use direct and indirect quotes from your sources here (see below).
As you write the main part, you might have to readjust your initial structure and change the sequence of different sections. You can also add or skip certain points or slightly shift your focus as you delve deeper and deeper into the topic. Essentially, there is no one right way of presenting your main body. The most important thing is that your argument remains consistent and flows.

Conclusion
In the conclusion, you should answer your original question by summarizing and linking your findings from each section together. Point out what your research shows and how that answers your central question. You should avoid including new points that were not in the main body. However, it is useful to outline how your findings could lead to the discussion of another topic in a future essay.

F. QUOTES AND BIBLIOGRAPHY
Quotes
The main body of your paper must contain both direct and indirect quotes. This is evidence that you have read and acknowledged important works regarding your topic and credited the authors of these works. Check out *How to quote* on page 371 for general help with this.
Since you are likely to cite from various sources, you should provide short bibliographical information after each quote. There are several referencing systems you can use for this. Ask your teacher which referencing system you should use. It is essential that you stick to one and do not mix them.
For example, you want to quote from page 193 of a book called *Shakespeare on film* by Maurice Hindle. It is the second edition of the book. The publishing company Palgrave Macmillan published it in London and New York in 2015.

- Systems like the one recommended by the *Modern Language Association* (MLA) place relevant information in parentheses and add these after the quote. This is called **in-text citation**. Usually just the name of the author and a page number is given:

   The author talks about this in detail (Hindle 193).

- Other systems like the Chicago style use **footnotes** to include bibliographical information. In this case, you would usually add more information about the book:

   The author talks about this in detail.[5]

---
[5] Maurice Hindle, *Shakespeare on film*, 2nd ed. (London/New York: Palgrave Macmillan, 2015), 193.

Bibliography

The bibliography at the end of your *Facharbeit* contains a list of all the sources that were quoted in your work. It is presented in alphabetical order, using the last names of the authors. Apart from the author's name, the full title of the source should be given, as well as its publisher and usually the place and date of publication. Ask your teacher for more specific instructions if you have used sources like websites or interviews.

As stated, there are different systems for presenting this information. Stick to the one you used for quoting. In most systems, the entry for our example will look something like this:

Hindle, Maurice. *Shakespeare on film*. 2nd ed., London/New York: Palgrave Macmillan, 2015.

G. ELEMENTS OF THE FINAL VERSION

In addition to the points outlined above, your final piece should contain a title page and a table of contents. In many states, you are required to add a declaration that you have worked on the paper alone and have cited all your sources properly. In some cases, you may also need an annex with pictures and transcripts of interviews you conducted. Here is a list of all the necessary elements:

- title page
- table of contents
- **the actual essay: introduction, main part, conclusion**
- bibliography
- declaration
- annex

All pages should be numbered in Arabic numerals (1, 2, etc.), starting with the title page and ending with your declaration. Do not print page numbers on the title page and the table of contents; just count them as pages. If you have an annex, you should number its pages with Roman numerals (i, ii, etc.).

H. HOW YOUR TEACHER WILL GRADE YOUR PAPER

As you know, each state and school has different requirements for writing a *Facharbeit*. However, all teachers will check certain points when grading a *Facharbeit*, such as:
- if you have a clearly thought-out central question that you manage to answer in the end
- if the structure of your essay is convincing
- if you did extensive research on the topic (and your sources show this)
- if you combined original thoughts with knowledge you acquired from other sources
- if your work is methodologically correct (citing, numbering points etc.)
- if your paper contains all the necessary sections
- if your English is correct and idiomatic and you use the correct (academic) register
- if your argument flows

I. NOW GET STARTED!

One more piece of advice: make sure that you start early! All that researching, structuring and writing takes time. Do not forget to include time to revise your paper. It will be obvious if you have not allowed enough time to read through and improve your essay before submitting it.

Good luck and enjoy writing your *Facharbeit*!

Glossary

Literary terms

	literary term	definition	example
A	act	One of the parts that a play is divided into. Each act is divided into two or more scenes.	
	action	everything that happens in a fictional text; events that form part of a play or film	
	addressee	the person to whom something is addressed	
	alliteration	emphasis that occurs through the repetition of initial consonant letters of two or more neighbouring words	"bigger box", "red rose"
	allusion	a reference to a familiar or famous historical or literary figure or event	
	analogy	similarity between two things	"'Tis with our judgments as our watches, none go just alike, yet each believes his own." *(Alexander Pope)*
	anaphora	the repetition of identical words or phrases at the beginning of a sentence or a line	"Nobody hurt you. Nobody turned off the light … Nobody locked the door."
	antithesis/contrast	a contrast between two things; denotes the opposing of ideas by means of grammatically parallel arrangements of words, clauses or sentences so as to produce an effective contrast	"It used to be hot, it becomes cool. It used to be strong, it becomes weak." *(Malcolm X)*
	antonym	a word that means the opposite of another word	night – day, wet – dry, hot – cold
	atmosphere	the feeling or mood created by the author, through the description of events, setting, etc.	"For a moment, a cloud drifted past the moon and the sky turned greenish gray."
B	bias	A prejudice in favour of or against one thing, person or group. It is a tendency to hold a certain point of view at the expense of other alternatives. An article is biased if information is presented in a one-sided way and based on personal opinion rather than facts.	
	blank verse	unrhymed lines with a five-beat rhythm (iambic pentameter)	"So foul and fair a day I have not seen." (Macbeth)
	body language	the movements or positions of your body that show other people what you are thinking or feeling	
C	caption	words printed near or on a picture that explain sth about the picture; a joke that is printed underneath a humorous drawing or photograph	
	caricature	a presentation in which sb's/sth's features are exaggerated to produce a comic or grotesque effect	
	character	a person who takes part in the action of a fictional text	

Glossary

	literary term	definition	example
	characteri-zation	The way in which a writer creates characters in a book, play, film etc. The author may present his characters in two ways: directly by describing them (explicit/direct), or indirectly through their actions, thoughts or feelings and words (implicit/indirect).	"I was too lazy at school." "Audrey always sits opposite me, no matter where we play." ➡ She seems to be interested in the narrator.
	close-up	a full-screen shot of a person's face or other body part or object; to reveal a character's emotions by showing their facial expressions; to draw attention to an object	
	conclusion	the final part of a speech, an article or a piece of writing	
	conflict	the disagreement between opposing forces which is the basis of the plot of a story or a play	
	connotation	an additional idea or emotion that a word suggests to you that is not part of its usual meaning	
	content	the information a text contains	
D	dialogue	the words that characters speak in a fictional text, play or film	
	direct address	when the audience is spoken to in the second person	"Ask not what your country can do for you – ask what you can do for your country." *(John F. Kennedy)*
E	ellipsis	leaving out words from a sentence that can be understood from the context in order to avoid repetition and to give a statement more emphasis	"Anyone's guess."
	empathy	the ability to understand how someone feels because you can imagine what it is like to be them	
	end-stopped line	when a phrase or sentence is the same length as the line containing it	"To be, or not to be, that is the question." *(William Shakespeare)*
	enjambment/ run-on line	a structure/construction in which a thought or statement in one line runs into the next	"To the Mind's gaining that prophetic sense / Of future change, that point of vision, whence / May be discovered what in soul ye are."
	enumeration	a listing of words or phrases	
	establishing shot	a shot that provides an overview of a scene/setting, to introduce the viewer to a new location or situation	
	euphemism	word used for sth unpleasant to make it sound less unpleasant	"to pass away" instead of "to die"

Glossary

	literary term	definition	example
	exclamation	something that you say suddenly and loudly because you are surprised, impressed, angry etc.	
	extended metaphor	a metaphor extended over several lines	"All the world's a stage, / and all the men and women merely players" (As You Like It)
	eye level shot	the camera looks straight at a person or object, to provide a neutral view	
F	facial expression	how a person uses his/her face to show what he/she is feeling	
	fiction	A piece of writing that comes from a writer's imagination. Fiction is not factual but may be sometimes based on facts, real experiences or people the writer has known.	
	flashback	a scene that shows what happened in the past and thus interrupts the chronological order of the plot	
	fore-shadowing	the technique of hinting at future events in such a way that the reader/viewer is prepared for them or can even anticipate them	
	free verse	a poem with no regular metre or rhyme	"What you recall are impressions; we have the facts. We called the tune." (Carol Ann Duffy)
	full shot	a view of the entire figure of a person, to show a person in action or to give an impression of how the characters are related to each other	
G	genre	a particular style used in cinema or writing which can be recognized by certain features, such as subject matter, theme, type of characters, etc.	comedy, thriller, horror, romance
	gesture	how a person uses his/her body to communicate messages	frowning, shaking a fist, folding one's arms across one's chest
H	haiku	three-line poem with five syllables in the first line, seven in the second and five syllables in the final line; Japanese in origin	
	headline	the title of a cartoon, a newspaper article, etc.	
	high-angle shot	the camera looks down on a person or object, to make a person/object seem smaller, less important, inferior	
	hyperbole/ exaggera-tion	representing (something) as being larger, greater, better, or worse than it really is	"We've heard this complaint a thousand times."
I	iambic pentameter	metre of five stressed syllables alternating with five unstressed syllables, giving ten-syllable lines	

Glossary

	literary term	definition	example
	imagery	use of vivid or descriptive language to represent objects, actions or ideas	
	inclusive language	including the audience to create a sense of unity or identity	"we", "my friends", "fellow countrymen"
	interior monologue	an expression of the thoughts and feelings passing through a character's mind	
	introduction	the part at the beginning of any text	
L	line	a unit of verse ending in a visual or typographic break	
	line of argument	the views that an author takes on a certain issue and how he/she goes about supporting them	
	long shot	a view of characters or a setting from a distance, to provide an overview	
	low-angle shot	the camera looks up at the person or object, to make a person/object seem more powerful/important, superior or even intimidating	
M	main part/ body	the body/main part of a book or document, not including the introduction, conclusion or the notes	
	medium shot	a view of a person down to his/her waist, to give an impression of a person's looks and behaviour, often used to present two people in conversation	
	message	the main idea that you want people to remember from a speech, advertisement, article, poem, etc.	
	metaphor	Two ideas that are not normally linked are compared in a metaphor without using "as" or "like". This creates an image in the reader's mind and makes the description more powerful.	"They blazed a trail toward freedom through the darkest of nights." *(Barack Obama)*
	metre	the pattern of stressed and unstressed syllables	
	monologue	part of a literary work in which only one character speaks (as opposed to a dialogue)	
	mood	the feeling that the writer tries to evoke	excitement, anger, sadness, happiness, pity, …
N	narrative	any writing that tells a story	
	narrator	A usually fictitious person who tells the story in a novel or film. The story can be told by a first-person or a third-person narrator. The narrator can be a character in or outside the story. The third-person narrator can be omniscient (knowing everything about the characters), selective (perceiving and knowing the same things as one character), or an observer narrator who merely reports the events without having access to the thoughts and feelings of the characters.	

Glossary

	literary term	definition	example
	non-fiction	texts that provide facts about real events, things or people	newspaper article, university lecture, political speech, etc.
	novel	A fairly long fictional prose narrative. Normally it has a plot which develops through the actions, speech, and thoughts of its characters.	
O	onomato-poeia	words that sound like their meanings	the word "cuckoo"
	outward appearance	of or relating to the outside of the body	"I have dark hair, half-tanned skin, coffee brown eyes."
	over the shoulder shot	the camera looks at a character from behind another character's back, to show two people in conversation and draw attention to a character's reaction to what is being said	
	overlay	the technique of putting a transparent image over another one to combine two images at the same time, to add information that the viewer needs in order to understand the scene better or to create a visual effect that reminds the viewer of a different context	
P	pace	the speed at which sth happens or is done	
	panning shot	the camera moves horizontally, e.g. from left to right, to follow an object or person	
	paragraph	a section of a piece of writing that begins on a new line and contains a group of several interrelated sentences	
	parallelism	the repetition of a sentence pattern	"… look at you. Look at us …"
	personifi-cation	A thing, an idea or an animal is given human attributes. Non-human objects are portrayed in such a way that we feel they have the ability to act like human beings.	"When well-appareled April on the heel / Of limping winter treads." *(William Shakespeare)*
	plot	a series of related events that make up the main story in a book, film, etc.	
	poetry	A literary piece of writing characterized by musical (such as rhythm and rhyme) and literary elements (such as metaphor or simile). Poems are divided into lines and often grouped into stanzas.	
	point of view	the relation in which the narrator stands to the story, a mental viewpoint or attitude	
	point of view shot	a scene is filmed as if looking through a character's eyes; to experience a situation as if part of the scene	
	protagonist	the main character in a fictional text	

Glossary

	literary term	definition	example
Q	quote/quotation	words from a book, play, film etc. that you use in a piece of writing	"To be, or not to be" is a famous quote from Shakespeare's tragedy Hamlet.
R	register	the degree of formality in language use: formal, neutral, informal, colloquial, familiar, intimate	formal: "I must say I'm not particularly fond of his films."; neutral: "I've never liked his films."; familiar: "God, I can't stand his films."
	repetition	words or phrases that are used more than once in a text, catching the reader's attention	"I have fought against white domination and I have fought against black domination."
	reverse-angle shot	a shot in a sequence of point of view shots in which the other character's perspective is shown, to allow the viewer to perceive how a conversation develops on both sides	
	review	a report in a newspaper, magazine or online in which a critic gives his views on a new film, novel, etc.	
	rhetorical question	an assertion in the form of a question which strongly suggests a particular response	"The tribe's code of behavior was broken. The new faith could not keep the tribe together. How could it?"
	rhyme	the repetition of sounds usually at the end of two or more lines	"You've lost your head. / If that's how easily you're led"
	rhyme scheme	the pattern created by the repetition of sounds at the end of lines	abab, abba, aabb, etc.
	rhythm	The pace or "movement" of a poem. The rhythm is determined by the metre and by the length of lines.	
S	scene	a part of an act in a play or film in which events happen in the same place or period of time	
	script/screenplay	a written description of the dialogue and action of a play or film, including basic camera directions	
	setting	the place and time at which the action of a fictional text takes place	
	short story	A work of fiction which usually deals with one or two major characters and one major conflict. The elements of a short story are character, plot, setting and theme.	
	simile	a comparison of two ideas, usually linked by "as" or "like"	"Like a magic kingdom that belonged only to Grace and her mother."
	social background	The social background describes various facts about a person, including how he/she was raised and what ethnic group he/she belongs to.	

Glossary

literary term	definition	example
soliloquy	monologue in a Shakespeare play which gives the audience access to a character's mind, revealing his or her innermost thoughts and motives	Hamlet's famous soliloquy starting with "To be or not to be …"
sonnet	A poem consisting of 14 lines. Various forms have been created. A Shakespearean sonnet consists of three four-line verses (or quatrains) followed by a two-line verse (or couplet).	
speaker	the voice that speaks in a poem, from whose perspective the poem is written	
special effects	an unusual piece of action in a film for which particular technical equipment is used	
stage directions	Notes in a play telling the actors how to speak and act. They also say what the characters and the stage should look like and where and when the action takes place.	ARCHIE *(proud)*. […] BETH *(disappointed)*. […] *Everyone hesitates, suddenly embarrassed.*
stanza	a section of a poem consisting of a group of lines	
stereotype	A stereotype is a simplified and generalized understanding, usually of a person or a group of people, based on what you expect from them or have experienced with them. It is a kind of image that immediately arises in your imagination as soon as you hear a name, for example.	Germans wear leather trousers.
still	a photograph taken from one of the scenes in a film	
stress	a stressed syllable is one which has the most emphasis when it is spoken	In "emphasis" the first syllable ("em") is stressed.
structure	the organization of the elements of a text	
style	the special, often personal and individual way in which a writer expresses ideas depending on personal factors and the type of text he/she is writing	
stylistic device	technique used to convince the reader/listener of the author's idea	repetition, enumeration, irony, exaggeration, metaphor
subheading	the title of one section of a longer piece of writing	
suspense	a feeling of excitement or worry that makes a reader curious about the outcome of a fictional text	
symbol	sth concrete that also carries an abstract meaning	the colour white symbolizes innocence, a dove symbolizes peace

Glossary

	literary term	definition	example
T	tension	the feeling evoked by the conflicts of a fictional text	
	tilting shot	the camera moves vertically, i.e. upwards or downwards, to follow an object or person	
	theme	the main idea the writer wants to present	
	tone	the tone the author uses to convey his/her attitude towards the subject	ironic, sarcastic, serious, sentimental, humorous
	tracking shot	the camera follows a person or object	
	tragic flaw	in a Shakespearean tragedy, the hero's inner weakness which leads to his downfall	
	trailer	a short filmed advertisement for a film	
	trait	a particular quality in someone's character	
	turning point	the point at which the action takes a different, often unexpected direction	
V	verse	a section of a poem consisting of a group of lines	
Z	zooming in/ zooming out	the camera moves closer to or further away from a person or object, to draw attention to a detail or connect a detail to its environment	

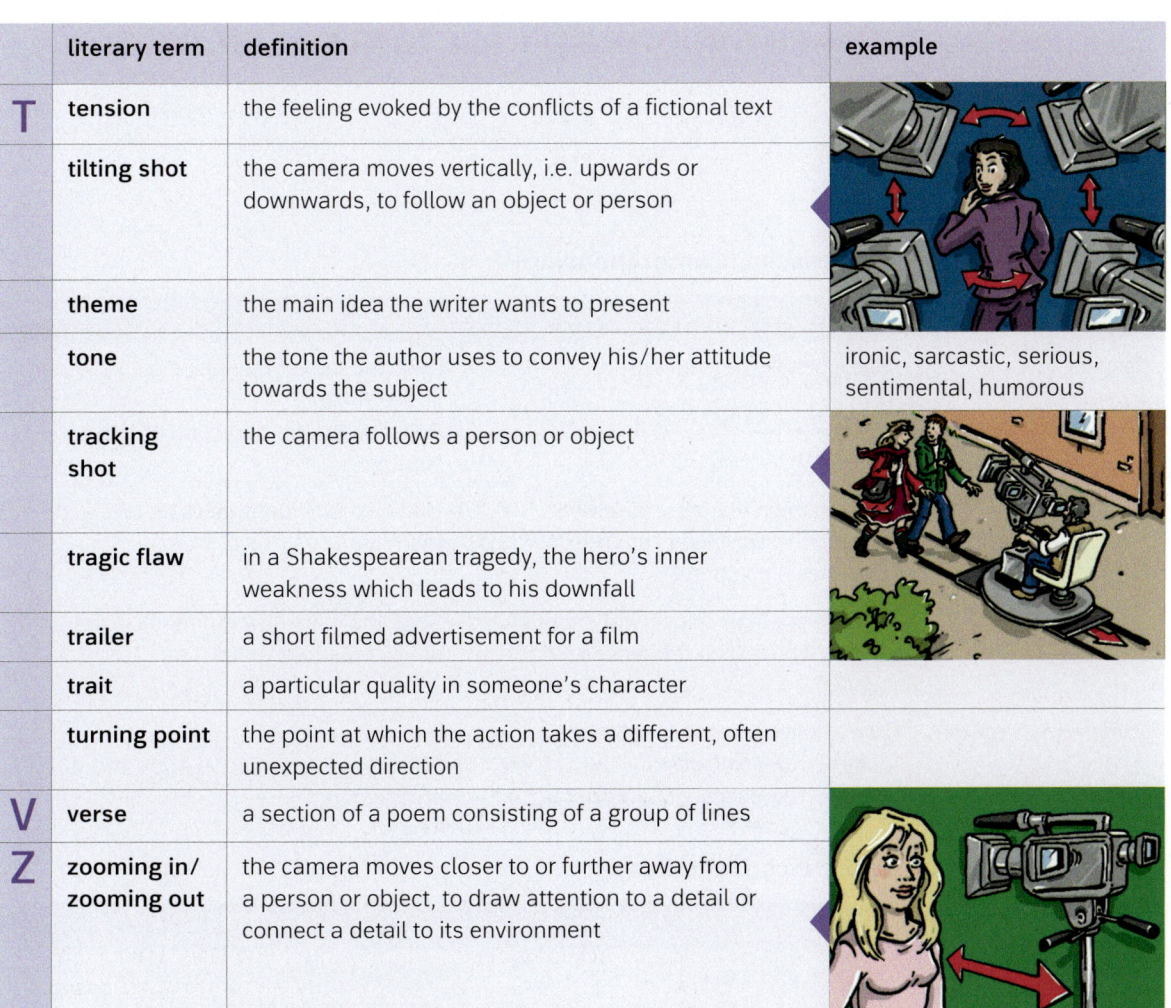

Standardized language for tasks *(Operatoren)*

In *Camden Town Oberstufe*, the same standardized language for tasks *(Operatoren)* is used as in the *Abitur* and in tests. Always make sure you understand what is expected of you before you start working on a task.

Anforderungsbereich I (Comprehension)

describe	give a detailed account of	Describe the protagonist's outward appearance. Describe the situation presented in the excerpt.
outline	give the main features, structure or general principles of sth (no line references, no quotes)	Outline the writer's views on love and marriage.
state	present the main aspects of sth briefly and clearly (no line references, no quotes)	State the main developments in the family presented in the text.
summarize, sum up	give a concise account of the main points or ideas of a text, issue or topic (no line references, no quotes)	Summarize the text. Sum up the information given about green energy.

Anforderungsbereich II (Analysis)

analyse, examine	describe and explain in detail	Analyse the way(s) in which the atmosphere is created in … Examine the opposing views on social class held by the two protagonists. Examine how the author characterizes …
compare	show similarities and differences	Compare the opinions on education held by the experts presented in the text.
contrast	emphasize the differences between two or more things	Contrast the authors' ideas of globalization.
explain	make something clear; show causes and effects in a given context	Explain the protagonist's obsession with money.
illustrate	use examples to explain or make sth clear	Illustrate the way in which school life in Britain differs from that in Germany.

Based on the list published in *Kerncurriculum für das Unterrichtsfach Englisch in der gymnasialen Oberstufe* (Niedersächsisches Kultusministerium 2017)

Operatoren

Anforderungsbereich III (Discussion/evaluation/text production)

assess, evaluate	consider in a balanced way points for and against sth and come to a well-founded conclusion	Assess the importance of learning languages for the natives' future. Evaluate the effect of the measures taken to reduce pollution.
comment (on)	give your opinion and support your view with evidence or reasons	Comment on the writer's view on gender roles.
discuss	give arguments or reasons for and against, especially to come to a well-founded conclusion	Discuss whether social status determines somebody's future options. Discuss to what extent modern media shape an individual's identity.
justify	present reasons for decisions, positions or conclusions	Justify whether the excerpt should be included in the text collection.
write (+ text type)	produce a text with specific features	Write the ending of the story. Write an interior monologue which reflects the character's view of the situation and his/her feelings. Write your letter to the editor in which you discuss Packer's statement that "the American dream quietly dies".

Special *Operatoren* for speaking tasks

talk about	produce a text referring to certain aspects	Talk about the pictures. What do the pictures suggest about our attitude towards the environment?
(try to) agree on, (try to) come to an agreement	come to one opinion or an understanding; (try to) reach a compromise	Talk about the images. Discuss which images best illustrate … Try to agree on two images that best fit the …

Special *Operatoren* for listening and watching tasks

answer	Answer the questions in 1 to 5 words.
complete	Complete the sentences below using 1 to 5 words. Complete the notes on the points listed below. Complete the table below.
fill in	Fill in the missing information using 1 to 5 words.
list/name	List/Name the most important aspects mentioned in the discussion.
match	Match each speaker with one of the statements.
state	State the ideas supported by speaker A.
tick	Tick the correct answer.

Acknowledgements

BILDQUELLEN

|akg-images GmbH, Berlin: 272; Russell Lee 215. |alamy images, Abingdon/Oxfordshire: 128, 214, 234; Action Plus Sports Images 21; AF Fotografie 273; ATHENA PICTURE AGENCY LTD 248; Atlaspix/NERVE, a film directed by Henry Joost and Ariel Schulman, written by Jessica Sharzer, and based on the 2012 novel of the same name by Jeanne Ryan 87; Baker Street Scans 21; Cal Sport Media 206; Contraband Collection 318; Cultura Creative (RF) 109; david pearson 132; Davies, Miles 264; Delimont, Danita 218; deWitt, Kathy 176; dominic dibbs 269; Doyle, Paul 269; Education & Exploration 2 144; ES Tech Archive 57; Ferrari, Nicola 264; Gado Images 218; Gibson, Andy 33; Granger Historical Picture Archive 201; Hasenkopf, Juergen 133; Heritage Image Partnership Ltd 254; IanDagnall Computing 272; Janine Wiedel Photolibrary 150; Joerg Boethling 240; Johnny Greig Int 242; keith morris 125, 184, 184; Latimer, Anna 264; LEDPIX 202; Lewis, Geraint 268; Matthews, Jenny 69; Oleksy, Walter 216; PF-(bygone1) 217; Photo 12 288; Photo 12/My Son the Fanatic Year: 1997 - uk Director: Udayan Prasad 259; PictureLux/The Hollywood Archive/Dave Franco stars as ‚Ian' in NERVE. Photo: Niko Tavernise 87; PictureLux/The Hollywood Archive/Emma Roberts stars as ‚Vee' in NERVE. Photo: Niko Tavernise 86; PictureLux/The Hollywood Archive/Ian (Dave Franco) and Vee (Emma Roberts) in NERVE. Photo: Niko Tavernise 86; RosaIreneBetancourt 14 143; RosaIreneBetancourt 9 143; Schuelke, Olaf 143; Sessions, Helen 163; Singh, Raj 237; Slater, Duncan 217; Storms Media Group 116; Sullivan, Jack 164; SuperStock 152; T. Byhre, Rey 240; The Granger Collection 226; Tuson, Pat 155; WENN Ltd 220; WENN Rights Ltd 160, 165; ZUMA Press, Inc. 51. |Asian Development Bank (ADB), Mandaluyong City: 122. |BBC Worldwide ltd.: „My son the fanatic", Directed by: Udayan Prasad; BBC Films in association with UGC DA International and the Arts Council of Great Britain presents A Zephyr Films Production 259. |bildagentur-online GmbH, Burgkunstadt: 177. |Butler, Clay, Soquel: ©1998 Clay Butler 147. |BuzzFeed, London: BuzzFeed News 81, 81. |Cagle Cartoons, Santa Barbara, CA: Cardow, Cameron 195; Paresh Nath 157. |Cartoonist Group, Seattle: Joel Pett Editorial Cartoon is used with the permission of Joel Pett and the Cartoonist Group. All rights reserved. 195; Joel Pett Editorial Cartoon used with the permission of Joel Pett and the Cartoonist Group. All rights reserved. 147. |CartoonStock.com, Bath: Allan Plenderleith 361; cgon383 262; Goddard, Clive 262; Greenberg, Steve 193; Schley, Karsten 195; Weyant, Christopher 314. |Children's Hope International: 142. |Colourbox.com, Odense: 188. |Das Bundesarchiv, Koblenz: Ballin und Rabe 99. |ddp images GmbH, Hamburg: CAMERA PRESS/Norrington, Nigel 268. |Fnoxx, Stuttgart: Arnulf Hettrich 189. |Fotofinder GmbH, Berlin: XinHua 196. |fotolia.com, New York: 167; Calek 46; Ioca4motion 76; magann 282; PDU 17; Picture-Factoy 206; Sepia100 107; Thaut Images 274; theaphotography 139; yalapeak 309. |Fuchs, Oliver, Berlin: 381, 382, 383, 384, 385, 387, 387, 387. |Future of Life Institute, Cambridge: 59. |Getty Images, München: AFP/Stringer 135; Bettmann/CORBIS 214; Bill Pugliano 138; Cremaschi, Emanuele 142; Daniel Koebe 251; Kamoshida, Koichi 60; McQuillan, Charles 26; Philip Ojisua 241; Tribune News Service 206. |Houghton Mifflin Harcourt, New York: Cover image from FOR TODAY I AM A BOY by Kim Fu. Copyright © 2014 by Kim Fu. Jacket design by Patrick Barry. Reprinted by permission of Houghton Mifflin Harcourt Publishing Company. All rights reserved. 42. |Imago, Berlin: ZUMA Press 60. |Inpho Photography, Dublin: Crombie, James 29. |Interfoto, München: Granger, NYC 192; Mary Evans/Library of Congress 227. |iStockphoto.com, Calgary: 172, 240; 3000ad 49; AdrianHancu 151; Allkindza 202; andresr 75; Baxter, Kacey 295; Bayley, Don 140; benjaminec 70; BlackJack3D 47; Bombaert 108; ClaudineVM 297; Dangubic 143; DaveBolton 317; Django 305; draco-zlat 110; drmakkoy 16; ferlistockphoto 19; franckreporter Titel; georgeclerk 152; hadynyah 230; JohnArehart 18; Keating, Courtney 305; len-pri 24; Leontura 310; Liu, Jessica 111; MACIEJ NOSKOWSKI 279; mazzzur 228; metamorworks 96; Mlenny 74; MStudioImages 144; Nikada 134; oatawa 143; Peeter Viisimaa 246; Raisbeck, Brian 108; Ramos Lopez, Enrique 18; Sasha_Litt 46; skodonell 122; toddtaulman 216; traveler1116 226; trekandshoot 198; Veronica Bogaerts 34; verve231 111; Viisimaa, Peeter 240; Wenjie Dong 304. |KAL/Kevin Kallaugher, Glyndon, MD: 195. |Kalch, Franziska, Gornau: 144, 144, 144, 144, 145, 145, 145, 145, 145. |Marckwort, Ulf, Kassel: 329, 329. |mauritius images GmbH, Mittenwald: 167; United Archives 218; W. G. Murray 202. |PantherMedia GmbH (panthermedia.net), München: Leitner, Bernd 291. |Penguin Random House, New York: Ernest Cline: Ready Player One, Broadway Books, an imprint of the Crown Publishing Group, a division of Penguin Random House LLC, New York, 2018 68. |Penguin Random House Canada Limited, Toronto, ON: „As Long as the Rivers Flow" by James Bartleman. Copyright © 2011 James Bartleman. Reprinted by permission of Vintage Canada/Alfred A. Knopf Canada, a division of Penguin Random House Canada Limited. 35. |Penguin Random House UK, London: Artwork Stuart Daly, Design Suzanne Dean, From Homo Deus: A Brief History of Tomorrow by Yuval Noah Harari, published by Harvill Secker, reprinted by permission of The Random House Group Limited. ©2016 50, 50; The Green Road by Anne Enright; Cover Photograph © Ron McBride, published by arrangement with Jonathan Cape, a division of The Random House Group Limited. © 2015 22. |Picture-Alliance GmbH, Frankfurt/M.: 41, 126, 130, 280; 91050/United_Archives/TopFoto 254; Advertising Archives 358; Anthony Quintano 210; AP Photo 215; AP Photo/Jin Liwang 66; AP Photo/Sohn, Michael 207; Bouthors/Leemage 239; Bundeswehr 130; empics/Gowthorpe, Anna 158; empics/Stevens, Ben 154; EPA 249; epa afp 144; Eventpress Hoensch 286; landov/Xiaolei, Niu 114; Lohr-Jones, Albin/ZUMAPRESS.com 212; Photoshot 175; Photoshot/Lightroom Photos/NASA 189; Reuters/AKINTUNDE AKINLEYE 252; Zakir Hossain Chowdhury/Anadolu Agenc 123; ZUMA Press/Rassol, Jim 129; ZUMAPRESS.com/India Today 142; ZUMAPRESS.com/Marshall, Peter 163. |Provincial Archives of Saskatchewan, Regina: 38, 38. |REUTERS, Berlin: Alex Coppel/Pool 168; Peter Morgan 189. |Revision Military: 60. |Sharp, Bronwen, London: 149. |Shutterstock.com, New York: 40, 45; a katz 109, 215; AJR_photo 77; Andrey VP 77; AnjelikaGr 150; arindambanerjee 108; Art work 52; AsiaTravel 75; Aysezgicmeli 104; Bachlakov, Sergei 34; BLUR LIFE 1975 93; blvdone 188; Bottino, Gerard 143; Breeze, Ceri 36; charnsitr 152, 172; Chess Ocampo 189; Chris Loneragan 130; ChrisVanLennepPhoto 151; Csak, Istvan 108; Dharmasena, Janaka 302; DNetromphotos 205; eldar nurkovic 77; FloridaStock 109; Frederic Legrand - COMEO 146; Gigowska, Aleksandra 103; Gil C 172; Grinvalds, Kaspars 74; Gusa, Cristian 150; Hajakely 77; hspimages 247; Hutchins, Kathy 278; Igor Grochev 240; Karin Hildebrand Lau 202; Keep Smiling Photography 188; Kosmider, Patryk 23; ktsdesign 92; LDWYTN 75; Lenscap Photography 150; lev radin 216; lifefoto 77; Lukassek 151; Mego studio 74; Michailidis, Alexandros 32; mikecphoto 264; MOdAMO 321; Monteil, Fabien 118; Nagaiets, Oleksandr 245; Nevesely, Tomas 181; Orighomisan Ogbebor 251; PFlemingWeb 150; PR Image Factory 126; Rawpixel.com 78, 90; reddees 319; REDPIXEL.PL 75; Reinch. Nataly 243; Rena Schild 210; Ruben Martinez Barricarte 222; Samborskyi, Roman 95; Slaven 322; Smit, Erica 46; spass 74; Stock_Good 144; Taner, Kemal 19; Thinglass 139; thomas m spindle 202; Trejo, Anibal 266; Truman, Lina 324; valeriiaarnaud 151; Vesalainen, Tero 91; xujun 111; ymgerman 77; Yongyut Kumsri 188; Yuriy Boyko 209; Zovadelli, Federico 21. |Shutterstock.com (RM), New York: Geraint Lewis/REX 268, 269; Paramount/Kobal/REX/Shutterstock (5885757ao), Leonard Whiting, Olivia Hussey, Romeo and Juliet - 1968, Director: Franco Zeffirelli, Paramount, UK/ITALY, Scene Still, Shakespeare, Roméo et Juliette (1968) 269; Rolf Konow/Castle Rock/Dakota/Kobal/REX/Shutterstock (5879407h), Irene Jacob, Laurence Fishburne, Othello - 1995, Director: Oliver Parker, Castle Rock/Dakota Films, UK, Scene Still, Shakespeare, Drama 268. |stock.adobe.com, Dublin: aleutie 145; Alexander Image 131; Anatoliy 16, 17; Antonov, Nikolay N. 282; Atkins, Peter 289; atlantic_advert 191; biker3 189; Cotton, Alistair 109; D'Cruz, Sam 270; doomu 281; Kosmider, Patryk 24; kristina rütten 263; lawcain 195; mast3r 145; matgo 25; metamorworks 96; Myvisuals 130; Nolte Lourens 219; pathdoc 285; Savina, Nata 17; seanlockephotography 191; sellingpix 136; spiritofamerica 121; stokkete 53; styf 73; takranik 280; VRD 30; WavebreakMediaMicro 293; zapp2photo 49. |Telegraph Media Group Ltd., London: 173. |Tierney, Jim, Brooklyn: 120. |ullstein bild, Berlin: AP 241; Archiv Gerstenberg 228; Granger Collection 272, 273. |Verlag Der Tagesspiegel GmbH, Berlin: Spiekermann-Klaas, Doris 60. |wikimedia.commons: 173, 173, 173, 173. |www.reportlinker.com: 80. |© Allegrofilm, Wien: We feed the world 142. |© Wilhelm-Busch-Gesellschaft e. V., Hannover: 161.

Wir arbeiten sehr sorgfältig daran, für alle verwendeten Abbildungen die Rechteinhaberinnen und Rechteinhaber zu ermitteln. Sollte uns dies im Einzelfall nicht vollständig gelungen sein, werden berechtigte Ansprüche selbstverständlich im Rahmen der üblichen Vereinbarungen abgegolten.

Acknowledgements

TEXTQUELLEN

20	Galway Girl. © BDI Music Ltd/Cold Coffee Music Ltd./Bucks Music Group Ltd./Platz Musikverlage GmbH, Hamburg; Foy Vance Songs/Primary Wave Vance Music/BMG Rights Management GmbH, Berlin; Sony/ATV Music Publishing (UK) Ltd./Sony/ATV Music Publishing (Germany) GmbH, Berlin.
20	Sunday Bloody Sunday. © Polygram Int. Music Publ. B.V. Für D/A/CH: Universal Music Publ. GmbH, Berlin.
20	The Fields of Athenry. © Celtic Songs.
22	"The End of Catholic Ireland" by Mary Kenny, in *The Guardian*, 8 August 2012. Copyright Guardian News & Media Ltd 2018.
22-23	The Green Road. From *The Gathering* by Anne Enright published by Jonathan Cape. Reproduced by permission of The Random House Group Ltd. ©2007.
27	*Love my enemy* by Kate MacLachlan, Andersen Press, 2004.
28-29	"Land of drunks, poets, friendly fans. How true are Irish cliches?" by Darragh Murphy, in *Irish Times*, 29 October 2016.
30	"Warum ‚Heimat' plötzlich wieder in ist" by Gregor Tholl, n-tv.de, 08 February 2018.
31-32	"Leo Varadkar is Ireland's new prime minister. He's also openly gay and an immigrant's son" by Lindsay Maizland, Vox.com, 14 June 2017, Vox Media, Inc., https://www.vox.com/world/2017/6/14/15801044/leo-varadkar-ireland-prime-minister-gay-elected.
33	"Abortion in Ireland: The fight for choice" by Joel Gunter, bbc.com, 08 March 2017.
35-36	As long as the rivers flow by James Bartleman, Vintage Canada, 2011.
40-41	"Canada 150: What does it mean to be Canadian today?" by Gavin Hewitt, bbc.com, 30 June 2017.
42-44	*For today I am a boy* by Kim Fu, Harper Collins, 2014.
45	*Referendum* by Sonnet L'Abbé. Excerpted from *A Strange Relief* by Sonnet L' Abbé. Copyright © 2001 by Sonnet L' Abbé. Reprinted by permission of McClelland & Stewart, a division of Penguin Random House Canada Limited.
50	Two poems from the programme *Human or machine: Can you tell who wrote these poems?*, npr.org, 27 June 2016.
52-53, 136-137	Homo Deus by Yuval Noah Harari, Vintage 2017.
55-56	"Why self-driving cars must be programmed to kill", republished with permission of Massachusetts Institute of Technology, Cambridge, from *MIT Technology Review* 2015; permission conveyed through Copyright Clearance Center, Inc.
57	"Speculations Concerning the First Ultraintelligent Machine" by Irving John Good, *Advances in computers*, Volume 6, 1966, Pages 31-88.
57-59	*Life 3.0* by Max Tegmark, Penguin 2017.
61	"The age of cyborgs has arrived" by Vanessa Bates Ramirez, singularityhub.com, 4 August 2017. CC BY-ND 4.0 (https://creativecommons.org/licenses/by-nd/4.0/legalcode).
62-64, 66-67	Never let me go by Kazuo Ishiguro, Faber & Faber 2005.
66	"How afraid of human cloning should we be?" by Philip Ball, in *The Guardian*, 25 January 2018.
68-69	*Ready player one* by Ernest Cline, Broadway Books 2011.
70-73	*Harrison Bergeron* by Kurt Vonnegut, Jr. in *The Magazine of Fantasy and Science Fiction*, 1961. (Republished in *Welcome to the monkey house* by Kurt Vonnegut, 1968.)
74	"media", businessdictionary.com.
79	"Public Opinion", in *Encyclopaedia Britannica*.
82-84	"The myth of the online echo chamber" by David Robson, bbc.com, 17 April 2018.
84-85	"Why the invention of the fridge could be responsible for our love of fake news" by Ian Leslie, in *The New Statesman*, 10 October 2018.
90-91	"Teens Explain Their Obsession With Sarahah, Summer's Hottest Anonymous-Gossip App" by Madison Malone Kircher, nymag.com, 27 July 2017.
92-94	*Cell 7* by Kerry Drewery, Hot Key Books, 2016.
96-97	"Future of news" by James Harding, bbc.co.uk, 28 January 2015.
98-99	"Lustig? Nicht auf Deutsch!" by Klaus Ungerer, in *Frankfurter Allgemeine Zeitung*, 4 March 2017.
100	"Warum Englisch nicht als Weltsprache taugt", wiesoso.com, 19 January 2018.
102-104	Pearl, Mike, "Are Duolingo Users Actually Learning Anything Useful?" *VICE*, January 12, 2017.
105-106	"Have we reached peak English in the world?" by Nicholas Ostler, in *The Guardian*, 27 February 2018. Copyright Guardian News & Media Ltd 2018.
107	"What will the English language be like in 100 years?" by Simon Horobin, theconversation.com, 10 November 2015.
113-114	Speech given by Leonardo DiCaprio, High-level Signature Ceremony for the Paris Agreement, United Nations, New York.
118-119	"The oceans are drowning in plastic — and no one's paying attention" by Dominique Mosbergen. From Huff Post, 27 April 2017 © 2017 Oath Inc. All rights reserved. Used by permission and protected by the Copyright Laws of the United States. The printing, copying, redistribution, or retransmission of this Content without express written permission is prohibited.
120-121	*The Terranauts* by T.C. Boyle, HarperCollins 2016.
123-124	"The Zara workers' protest shows why fast fashion should worry all of us" by Daisy Buchanan, in *The Guardian*, 8 November 2017. Copyright Guardian News & Media Ltd 2018.
124-125	„Wozu Mode kaufen, wenn man sie mieten kann?" by Anne Kohlick, rbb24.de, 19 January 2018.
126	*The lexus and the olive tree* by Thomas L. Friedman, Macmillan 2012.
126-127, 138-139	*Thank you for being late* by Thomas L. Friedman, Farrar Straus & Giroux 2016.
127-129	"Column: Why there's a backlash against globalization and what needs to change" by John Rennie Short, pbs.org, 30 November 2016.
131-132	*Transmission* by Hari Kunzru, Penguin UK 3 June 2004.
134-135	*The emperor of shoes* by Spencer Wise, Hanover Square Press 2018.
148-149	*Bodies* by Vivienne Franzmann, Nick Hern Books 2017.
151	"What does being British mean to you? – interactive" by Stephen Moss/Garry Blight/Nadia Hussain, in *The Guardian*, 5 February 2012. Copyright Guardian News & Media Ltd 2018.
154-155	"Brexit is entrenching some dangerous myths about 'British' culture" by Afue Hirsch, in *The Guardian*, 25 May 2017. Copyright Guardian News & Media Ltd 2018.
158-159	"The Observer view on Britain becoming mean and narrow-minded", in *The Guardian*, 23 October 2016. Copyright Guardian News & Media Ltd 2018.
160-161	"Wir sollten Ernst und Humor häufiger mischen", focus.de, 23 March 2014.
163-164	Harrison, Angus, "What It Means to Be English in 2017", *VICE*, 27 June 2017.
168-169	"Should Britain abolish the monarchy?", *The Economist*, 08 September 2015. Republished with permission of *The Economist* from "Should Britain abolish the monarchy?", *The Economist*, 2015; permission conveyed through Copyright Clearance Center, Inc.
175	"Britain's unwritten constitution" by Robert Blackburn, bl.uk, 13 March 2015.
176	"So what exactly is multiculturalism?", news.bbc.co.uk.
177	*The British (serves 60 million)* by Benjamin Zephaniah
180	"Listen Mr Oxford don" by John Agard, in John Agard, *Alternative Anthem: Selected Poems* (Bloodaxe Books, 2009), www.bloodaxebooks.com.
182	"The business of being Scottish: Are you one of 50 million?" by Lennox Morrison, www.bbc.com, BBC, 25 May 2017.
184-185	"Social class in the 21st century", spiked-online.com, 02 February 2018.

Acknowledgements

187 "The North-South divide is getting worse – because London is sucking all opportunity from the rest of the UK" by Juliette Bretan, in *The Independent*, 11 August 2017.

196-197 Speech given by Michelle Obama in Charlotte, N.C., 4 September 2012.

198-199 "Is the American Dream killing us?" by Robert L. Samuelson, in *The Washington Post*, 02 April 2017.

199-200 "Trump is killing the American Dream" by Kashana Cauley, in *The New York Times*, 22 January 2018.

201 "Let America be America again" by Langston Hughes, in *The collected poems of Langston Hughes*, edited by Arnold Rampersad and David Roessel, Arnold A. Knopf 1994.

209-210 "Confederate flag is a symbol of America's culture wars" by Matt K. Lewis, telegraph.co.uk, 2 December 2018.

211 "Ex-Schützenfunktionär: Waffenrecht in Deutschland und den USA vergleichbar", deutschlandfunk.de, 19 December 2012.

212-213 "How America's culture wars have evolved into a class war" by James Davison Hunter in *The Washington Post*, 12 September 2017.

217 "I, Too" by Langston Hughes, in *Collected Poems*, The Estate of Langston Hughes 1994.

217 *We own the night* by Amiri Baraka, 1961.

217 "Harlem" by Langston Hughes, in *Collected Poems*, The Estate of Langston Hughes 1994.

218 "Feeding the lions" by Norman Jordan, in *The New Black Poetry*, edited by Clarence Mayor, International Publishers Co., Inc. 1969.

218 "Nikki Rosa" by Nikki Giovanni, in *Black Feeling, Black Talk, Black Judgment*, HarperCollins, 1968, 1970.

219-220 "Sonny's Blues" by James Baldwin, in *Going to Meet the Man. A collection of short stories by James Baldwin*. Corgi edition 1970. pp. 100-103.

221 *Das deutsche Krokodil* by Ijoma Mangold, Rowohlt 2017.

222-225 *The Mountaintop* by Katori Hall, Bloomsbury publishing 2015.

230-231, 233-234 "Death on Facebook" by Claude Forthomme, in *Death on Facebook. Short stories for the digital age*, Amazon Digital Services LLC 2012.

235-236 "Full steam ahead: India's first women-run train station blazes a trail" by Annie Banerji. From reuters.com, 15 October 2018, © 2018 reuters.com. All rights reserved. Used by permission and protected by the Copyright Laws of the United States. The printing, copying, redistribution, or retransmission of this Content without express written permission is prohibited.

237-238 "India's caste system is alive and kicking – and maiming and killing" by Mari Marcel Thekaekara, in *The Guardian*, 15 August 2016. Copyright Guardian News & Media Ltd 2018.

242-243, 245-246 *Americanah* by Chimamanda Ngozi Adichie, 4th Estate 2013.

247 "Let our voices ring" by Efe Paul Azino, in *For Broken Men Who Cross Often*, Farafina Books 2015.

248 *Becoming* by Titilope Sonuga, lyrikline.org.

249-251 *Oil on Water* by Helon Habila, Penguin 2011.

251-253 *Nollywood – the making of a film empire* by Emily Witt, Columbia Global Reports 2017.

255-257, 259-261 *My son the fanatic: A screenplay* by Hanif Kureishi, Reclam 2007.

263 "Why Multicultural Communities Are What Makes London (and Britain) Great – and Why We Must Protect Them" by Jermain Jackman, huffingtonpost.co.uk, 27 January 2016.

278 We Are Never Ever Getting Back Together. © Sony/ATV Music Publishing (Germany) GmbH, Berlin.

278 Pop sonnet by Erik Didriksen, based on "We Are Never Ever Getting Back Together" by Taylor Swift, in *Pop Sonnets: Shakespearean Spins on Your Favourite Songs*, HarperCollins/Fourth Estate 2015.

291 *Vinegar Girl* by Anne Tyler, Hogarth, 2016.

293 *Inspirational Leadership* by Robert Olivier, Nicholas Brealey Publishing, 2013.

294-295 "Sister Imelda" by Edna O'Brien, in *A fanatic heart*, Phoenix 2003.

295 *The Gathering* by Anne Enright, Jonathan Cape, 2007.

295 *Music at Annahullion* by Eugene McCabe, in *Heaven lies about us*, Bloomsbury Publishing PLC 2004.

347 "Fire and ice" by Robert Frost, in *The poetry of Robert Frost*, edited by Edward Connery Lathem, Henry Holt and Company 1951.

356 *I have a dream*. Speech given by Martin Luther King, Jr., Washington, 28 August 1963.

AUDIO-CD:

Track 1 Ed Sheeran: *Galway Girl* (LC 02648 Asylum Records).
Track 2 U2: *Sunday bloody Sunday* (LC 00407 Island Records)
Track 3 The High Kings: *The Fields of Athenry* (LC 12799 Celtic Collection)
Track 4 *Adopted out, coming home* by Kim Wheeler, CBC/Radio-Canada, 17 June 2016.
Track 5 ©2016 National Public Radio, Inc. Excerpt from NPR news report titled "Human Or Machine: Can You Tell Who Wrote These Poems?" as originally broadcast on NPR's All Things Considered on June 27, 2016 and is used with the permission of NPR. Any unauthorized duplication is strictly prohibited.
Track 6 *Will English always be the global language?* by David Crystal, British Council, 9 November 2013.
Track 7 Speech given by Leonardo DiCaprio, High-level Signature Ceremony for the Paris Agreement, United Nations, New York.
Track 8 produced by John Green TEFL AUDIO, recorded by Tim Woolf, London. Speakers: Nigel Pilkington, Sophie Aldred, DeNica Fairman, John Green, Roger May, Brian Bowles.
Track 9 produced by John Green TEFL AUDIO, recorded by Tim Woolf, London. Speakers: Nigel Pilkington, Sophie Aldred, DeNica Fairman, John Green, Roger May, Brian Bowles.
Track 10 produced by John Green TEFL AUDIO, recorded by Tim Woolf, London. Speakers: Nigel Pilkington, Sophie Aldred, DeNica Fairman, John Green, Roger May, Brian Bowles.
Track 11 "What does being British mean to you? – interactive", in *The Guardian*, 5 February 2012. Copyright Guardian News & Media Ltd 2018. Produced by John Green TEFL AUDIO, recorded by Tim Woolf, London. Speakers: Nigel Pilkington, Sophie Aldred, DeNica Fairman, John Green, Roger May, Brian Bowles.
Track 12 *What is Britishness?* by Rebecca Devaraj, youtube.com, 28 March 2011.
Track 13 *Who's British now?* bbc.co.uk, 14 July 2014.
Track 14 *Who's British now?* bbc.co.uk, 14 July 2014.
Track 15 ©2006 National Public Radio, Inc. NPR news report titled "Could Shakespeare Survive in Hollywood?" was originally broadcast on NPR's All Things Considered on November 20, 2006 and is used with the permission of NPR. Any unauthorized duplication is strictly prohibited.

Solutions:

P. 50, 1b): The first poem was created by a computer, the second one by a human being.

P. 183, 2c): Elite, Established middle class, Technical middle class, New affluent workers, Traditional working class, Emergent service workers, Precariat

P. 216, 3 b): Thou land of blood, and crime, and wrong.

P. 268, 1 a):
1. Shakespeare: Macbeth
2. Tupac: Dear Mama
3. Tupac: Unconditional Love
4. Shakespeare: Macbeth
5. Shakespeare: Twelfth Night
6. Tupac: Fickle Minds
7. Shakespeare: Julius Caesar
8. Tupac: If I Die 2Nite
9. Tupac: Words of Wisdom
10. Shakespeare: Julius Caesar